Also by Gary Fishgall

Against Type:
The Biography of Burt Lancaster

PIECES OF TIME

· *The Life of James Stewart* ·

GARY FISHGALL

A LISA DREW BOOK

SCRIBNER

A LISA DREW BOOK/SCRIBNER
1230 Avenue of the Americas
New York, NY 10020

SCRIBNER and design are
trademarks of Simon & Schuster Inc.

A LISA DREW BOOK is a trademark of Simon & Schuster Inc.

Set in Caledonia
Designed by Colin Joh

Manufactured in the United States of America

1 3 5 7 9 10 8 6 4 2

Library of Congress Cataloging-in-Publication Data
Fishgall, Gary.
Pieces of time : the life of James Stewart / Gary Fishgall.
p.   cm.
Filmography: p.
Includes bibliographical references and index.
1. Stewart, James, 1908–1997. 2. Motion picture actors and actresses—United
States—Biography.   I. Title.
PN2287.S68F57   1997
791.43'028'092—dc21
[B]   97-10639
CIP
ISBN 0-684-82454-X

I've had many people tell me that they remember certain little things I did in pictures. I think it's wonderful to have been able to give people little pieces of time they can remember.

—*James Stewart*

CONTENTS

Genealogy   9
Acknowledgments   11
Introduction   15

PART ONE: JIM
1 Indiana, Pa.   19
2 A Gentleman's Education   34
3 A Change of Direction   49
4 Learning a Craft   61

PART TWO: JEFFERSON SMITH
5 Contract Player   75
6 Hollywood Bachelor   87
7 Rising Star   103
8 Mr. Smith and Marlene   123
9 "One of the Finest Actors Alive Today"   135

PART THREE: COLONEL STEWART
10 Fighting the Good Fight   157
11 Coming Home   174

PART FOUR: GEORGE BAILEY
12 Back to Work   185
13 Getting Tough and Getting Married   203

PART FIVE: PAUL BIEGLER
14 From Elwood P. Dowd to Glenn Miller   219
15 Number One   241
16 The End of a Decade   262
17 Westerns with Ford, Comedies with Koster   280
18 Andrew McLaglen and James Lee Barrett   301

Contents

PART SIX: BILLY JIM HAWKINS
19 Mr. Stewart Goes to Television   327
20 "I Just Keep Rollin' Along"   339

PART SEVEN: A NATIONAL TREASURE
21 The 1980s   353
22 "It's Over"   368

Filmography   374
Notes   384
Bibliography   398
Index   406

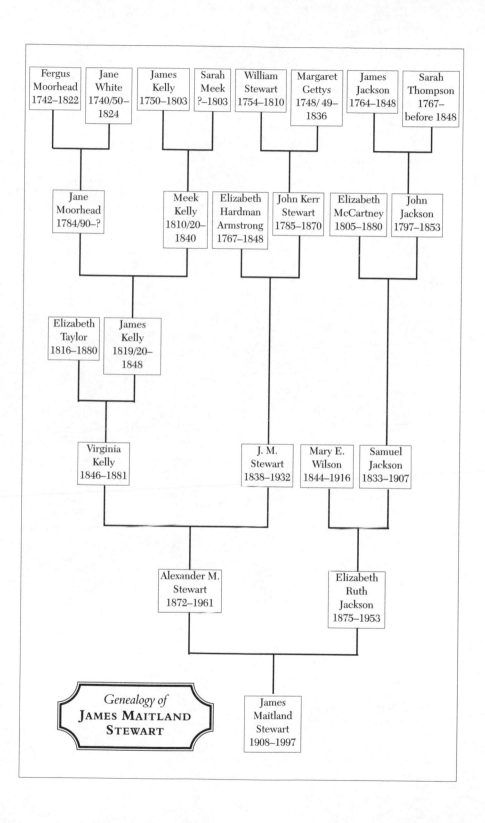

Fergus Moorhead 1742–1822 — Jane White 1740/50–1824

James Kelly 1750–1803 — Sarah Meek ?–1803

William Stewart 1754–1810 — Margaret Gettys 1748/49–1836

James Jackson 1764–1848 — Sarah Thompson 1767–before 1848

Jane Moorhead 1784/90–?

Meek Kelly 1810/20–1840

Elizabeth Hardman Armstrong 1767–1848

John Kerr Stewart 1785–1870

Elizabeth McCartney 1805–1880

John Jackson 1797–1853

Elizabeth Taylor 1816–1880 — James Kelly 1819/20–1848

Virginia Kelly 1846–1881

J. M. Stewart 1838–1932

Mary E. Wilson 1844–1916

Samuel Jackson 1833–1907

Alexander M. Stewart 1872–1961

Elizabeth Ruth Jackson 1875–1953

Genealogy of
JAMES MAITLAND STEWART

James Maitland Stewart 1908–1997

Acknowledgments

As every biographer knows, chronicling someone else's life is a very personal endeavor—lonely, intimidating, and all-consuming.

But *researching* a biography is something else again. At that stage, the author is seeking help from virtually every quarter. In the case of this book, I was incredibly lucky, for early on I won the support of those closest to James Stewart: his three children—Kelly Harcourt, Michael McLean, and Judy Merrill—and his friend and publicist of more than forty years, John Strauss. These are four wonderful individuals whom I came to like and respect enormously. Not only did they answer every question I put to them, without asking anything in return, but also their stamp of approval on this project opened many doors that I suspect would have been closed to me otherwise—especially since another biographer had begun researching his book on Stewart shortly before I did (I was unaware of this project until I had been at work for several months).

Accordingly, I am deeply indebted to those who willingly went over the same ground with me that they had traversed relatively recently with someone else. By the same token, I am very grateful to those who made me the first biographer with whom they discussed their association with Mr. Stewart. Alphabetically, those who shared their time and memories with me are Clarence J. Adams, Julia Adams, Philip Alford, Elizabeth Allen, Milton Arnold, Orson Bean, Arthur S. Beavers, Pamela Bellwood, Ed Bernds, Elinor Blair, Harold Jack Bloom, Dr. Jack Burton, Corrine Calvet, Harry Carey Jr., Wilbur L. Clingan, Jackie Cooper, Linda Cristal, Doris Day, Fred De Cordova, Sandra Dee, Woody Duke, Jack Elam, Julius Epstein, Norman Felton, Peter Fonda, Joan Fontaine, Rosemary Forsyth, Gene Fowler Jr., Marjorie Fowler, William Frye, John Gardner, Ben Gazzara, Farley Granger, Marshall Green, Barbara Hale, Kelly Harcourt, Ric Hardman, Jimmy Hawkins, Brooke Hayward, William Hayward, David Healey, Charlton Heston, Richard Peter Hoffman, Edward Hotschuh, Norris Houghton, Ruth Hussey, Jerry Jameson,

Maria Cooper Janis, Doris Johnson, Shirley Jones, Hal Kanter, David Karp, Richard Kobritz, Howard W. Koch, Howard W. Koch Jr., Joan Kramer, Howard E. Kreidler, Hardy Kruger, Hedy Lamarr, David Lavender, Janet Leigh, Jack Lemmon, Sheldon Leonard, Andrew Low, Ted Lucas, Michael Margulies, O. G. Martin, Vincent McEveety, Andrew McLaglen, Michael McLean, Audrey Meadows, Judy Merrill, Ann Miller, Robert Mitchum, Bill Moorhead, Harry Morgan, Bill Mumy, Kevin O'Connor, Maureen O'Hara, Debra Paget, Greg Paul, Stephen Porter, Ramsay Potts, T. Owen Potts, Betty Prashker, Jay Quinn, Irving Rattner, Ron Reagan Jr., John Saxon, George Schaefer, Murray Schwartz, Jacqueline Scott, Tom Shaw, William F. Sheehan, Michael Sherritt, Simone Simon, Elizabeth Simpson, John Simpson, Bernard Smith, Robert Stack, Clarence Stephenson, Peter Stewart, Harry Stradling Jr., Daniel Taradash, Jud Taylor, Lew Wasserman, Paul Wendkos, Henry A. Wentland, James Wharton, Jesse White, Richard Widmark, Billy Wilder, Michael Winner, Charles P. Wofford, Virginia Zambone, and Stephanie Zimbalist.

As for Stewart himself, he was alive until shortly before the publication of this book. But those who read this book to its end will find that he was a virtual recluse during his final years. Naturally, I would have relished the opportunity to meet with him, but, even if I had done so, I am certain that he could have contributed little to this project. Age, a rather severe hearing loss, and depression would have precluded his ability to entertain in-depth questions about long-ago events. Fortunately, he was extremely open to journalistic inquiries throughout his public life, so there is an abundant public record to draw on if one delves as I have. Accordingly, readers of this book will find Stewart's a frequent voice, telling us what he thought and felt about people, projects, and events as we journey through the milestones of his life. When quoting him, and other sources drawn from existing records, I have used the past tense. When quoting people who spoke to me directly, I have used the present tense. Occasionally, some of these individuals refer to Stewart in the present tense. He was, of course, alive at the time. Accurate reporting mandated that I keep their remarks intact.

In addition to the people I interviewed in a solid year of research, I also perused thousands of documents in the archives of the performing arts–related libraries in New York and Los Angeles. These documents included primary materials bequeathed to the libraries by film studios, producers, directors, and other related individuals. Of particular value for this project were the extensive files from Universal Pictures—where Stewart made a dozen films, including many of the memorable movies from his heyday in the 1950s. These are on file at the University of

Southern California's Doheny Library. There, too, is the Warner Bros. Collection, which is administered separately. For their generous assistance with these materials, I must thank Ned Comstock, whose purview at the Doheny Library includes the Universal Collection, and Stuart Ng, the archivist for the Warner Bros. Collection. Valuable primary material, as well as useful secondary material, was also available at the University Research Library of the University of California, Los Angeles; the Louis B. Mayer Library of the American Film Institute; the Margaret Herrick Library of the Academy of Motion Picture Arts and Sciences; and the Billy Rose Theatre Collection at the Lincoln Center Library for the Performing Arts in New York. The staffs of these institutions are extremely knowledgeable and helpful, and I thank them all, especially Sam Gill, Alan Braun, and Bergitta Kiueppers, respectively of the Motion Picture Academy, the AFI, and UCLA.

My research also took me to the places that were pivotal to Stewart's maturation: his birthplace, Indiana, Pennsylvania; Mercersburg, Pennsylvania; and Princeton, New Jersey. Naturally, there are people to thank in all three towns, notably C. Anthony Broh, Registrar, Princeton University; Karen P. Gresh, Director of Publications/University Editor, Indiana University of Pennsylvania; Ann Halliday, Assistant Secretary, Princeton University; Mary Ann Jensen, Curator, the William Seymour Theatre Collection, Princeton University; Ellen von Karajan, Museum Director, the Jimmy Stewart Museum, Indiana, Pennsylvania; John G. Kellogg, Princeton, New Jersey; Patricia H. Marks, Princeton University Libraries; Jay Quinn, Assistant Director, Alumni Affairs, Mercersburg Academy; Monica Ruscil, Special Collections Assistant, Princeton University Libraries; Daniel N. White, Director, the Alumni Council of Princeton University; Nanci A. Young, Assistant Archivist, Mudd Manuscript Library, Princeton University; and Phillip J. Zorich, Special Collections Librarian, Indiana University of Pennsylvania.

During my work on this project, I managed to view every feature film that Jimmy Stewart ever made. This was no easy feat. For helping me in this endeavor, I am beholden to Kent Jones; Lou Ellen Kramer, Reference and Outreach Coordinator, UCLA Film and Television Archive; Eddie Brandt's Saturday Matinee in North Hollywood, California; and Madeline F. Matz, Reference Librarian for the Motion Picture and Recorded Sound Division of the Library of Congress.

For other types of assistance and research support, thanks go to Laurie Andrews, Race Director, Jimmy Stewart Relay Marathon, Santa Monica, California; Mary Beth Barnard, Archivist, Mighty 8AF Museum, Savannah, Georgia; Jeanine Basinger, Wesleyan University; Rudy Behlmer; Ben Brewster, Assistant Director, Wisconsin Center for Film and Theater

Acknowledgments

Research, Madison, Wisconsin; Prof. Richard Brown; Carrie Byron, Santa Monica Airport; Bob Cozenza, the Kobal Collection; Adele Field, Oral Histories/Directory Editor, Directors Guild of America; Dr. Margaret Maxwell; Joseph McBride; Gideon Phillips; Ray Pytel, Editor, *Second Air Division Association Journal*; John J. Slonaker, Chief, Historical Reference Branch, Department of the Army, U.S. Army History Institute, Carlisle, Pennsylvania; Sara Timby, Manuscripts Specialist, Department of Special Collections, Stanford University Libraries, Stanford, California; Julian Wilson, 453rd Bomb Group Assistant Group Chairman.

Finally, I want to extend my appreciation to my editor, Lisa Drew; her assistant, Marysue Rucci, and Marysue's successor, Blythe Grossberg; and to my agent, Alexander Hoyt.

Introduction

There's no getting around it, he was an admirable guy. In a profession dominated by the neurotic, the aggressive, and the egocentric, Jimmy Stewart was self-possessed, a gentleman, and remarkably humble. In a community where the divorce rate exceeds even the national 50 percent average, he forged a loving and enduring marriage that gave him four decent, well-adjusted children. In an industry where people merely play heroes, he was the real thing, having risked his life time and again in defense of his country during wartime.

Most of this he owed to his upbringing. Far from the tightly clustered urban breeding grounds that nurtured a nation of immigrants and people on the move, his first world was a quiet, remarkably homogenous small town where his family had lived for generations. From his earliest days, he knew exactly who he was and what he was supposed to value. This sense of self initially came from his mother and father. Then from his neighbors, his school, and his church. And finally, from a prep school for middle-income youngsters and an Ivy League university.

If there was a chink in the making of James Maitland Stewart, it arguably lay in his relationship with the person whom he loved at least as much as any other in his life, his father. Boisterous, demanding, strong-willed, and opinionated, Alexander Stewart set well-defined standards of conduct for his son, and Jim willingly adhered to them. He was a good boy. But, perhaps in being so obedient, he became more submissive in adulthood than was advantageous. He was a hard worker, but affability, raw talent, and a pleasing appearance—plus a fair amount of very good luck—took him further in the theater and later in films than ambition ever did. Moreover, even at the peak of stardom, when he could have done virtually anything that he wished, he remained content to work within a rather narrow confine of roles, and except for one half-hour TV show, he evidenced no desire to expand into other arenas, such as directing and producing.

Still, within the limits that he set for himself, he forged an impressive body of work, starring in a string of movies that rank with Hollywood's best—*Mr. Smith Goes to Washington, The Philadelphia Story, It's a Wonderful Life, The Naked Spur, Rear Window, Vertigo, Anatomy of a Murder,* and *The Man Who Shot Liberty Valance,* to name the most obvious. Along the way, he became for moviegoers the world over the quintessential American—affable but a man who could be pushed only so far; attractive but not awesomely handsome; and a true believer in the old cherished values: God, country, and family. While never abandoning his screen persona, he certainly stretched it in as many directions as he could—in characters ranging from gawky, innocent idealists to grizzled cynics. That such diverse directors as Frank Capra, Alfred Hitchcock, and John Ford could utilize his essence—brilliantly—to their own particular ends speaks for itself.

Different though they are, the glue that binds Jefferson Smith and Charlie Anderson, Macaulay Connor and Paul Biegler, Elwood P. Dowd and Charles A. Lindbergh, is the humanness that Stewart invested in them. These characters are not larger than life. They are folks like us—or our fathers, brothers, boyfriends, neighbors, and husbands. Indeed, that is the legacy of Jimmy Stewart above all else: in his connection to his own roots, he connects us to ours. He is our mirror. And we like what we see.

PART ONE

· Jim ·

ONE

Indiana, Pa.

The town sits about fifty miles east of Pittsburgh on what is called the Appalachian plateau, a series of gently rolling hills and valleys that lie at the foot of the great mountain chain. By the dawn of the twentieth century, the community was bustling, thanks to its burgeoning coal industry, then about ten years old. The population had topped six thousand, and a string of shops, a railroad station, and a courthouse dotted Philadelphia Street, the main thoroughfare. The courthouse, built in 1870, had an impressive clock tower, which served to remind everyone—as if they needed reminding—that their town, Indiana, Pennsylvania, was the county seat. Here, lawyers argued cases and judges rendered verdicts on a wide variety of matters, civil and criminal, for only the most minor of infractions were considered at the municipal level.

Intermixed with the legal wheeler-dealers, the local merchants, and the executives of the local coal companies, of which there were several, were the instructors from the homegrown teachers college, which was then about a quarter century old. Collectively, these groups endowed Indiana with an aura of sophistication beyond that of most towns of equivalent size.

As for the miners, they lived in coal towns near their workplaces. Indiana did have some light industry—a glassworks, a foundry, and a brewery—and the employees of these establishments tended to live locally, but fundamentally this was a white-collar community. Although the residents were always a bit edgy about those miners up in the hills—rough men from far-off places such as Italy and the Balkans, who spoke broken English and had a penchant for violence—Indiana was basically a place of relatively little strife. It was neat and well ordered with stately Victorian homes and a solid middle-class population, mostly God-fearing Presbyterians of Scotch-Irish descent.

It was here on May 20, 1908, that the local hardware store owner, Alexander M. Stewart, and his wife, Bessie, gave birth to their first child, an eight-pound son whom they named James Maitland after his paternal grandfather. Anyone seeking to understand the man this lad would become—his quiet self-confidence, his abiding love of God, family, and country—need look no further than the town and the people from whom he sprang. No one could have had a more centered beginning.

* * *

Decades before Indiana was established, Jimmy Stewart's ancestors were putting down local roots. They were part of the wave of Scotch-Irish immigrants who sought refuge from oppression in their native Northern Ireland during the first half of the eighteenth century. They mostly settled in the south-central region of the Cumberland Valley in the colony of Pennsylvania, the region known as Franklin County.

It was Jimmy Stewart's paternal great-great-great-grandfather, Fergus Moorhead, who first came to what would become Indiana County. It was then an untamed frontier, occupied by unfriendly Indians of the Delaware and Shawnee tribes. Fergus was a first-generation American, born in Franklin County in 1742, to Samuel and Ephemia Moorhead, who had arrived from Northern Ireland some four years earlier. It was in May of 1772 that Fergus brought his wife, three children, two brothers, and several others, including another Stewart ancestor, James Kelly, to settle on the fertile green lands of the Appalachian plateau. The rigorous 130-mile journey took four weeks.

Eking out new lives in the wilderness was exceedingly difficult, and Indian attacks were a constant threat. Kelly narrowly escaped a run-in with a band of hostiles, but Moorhead was not so lucky. He was captured in July of 1776—the same month in which the Continental Congress issued the Declaration of Independence in Philadelphia. Taken by forced march to Canada, Fergus was sold by the Indians to the British, who finally returned him in a general prisoner exchange after eleven months in captivity. By that point, his wife, alone with her children in hostile, untamed country, had taken the youngsters back to Franklin County.

The Moorheads would return to the Appalachian plateau, but not before Fergus served as a private in the Cumberland County Militia during the Revolutionary War. James Kelly fought in the war as well, specifically in the battles of Monmouth and Brandywine. Thus, he and Fergus, along with two ancestors on Jimmy's mother's side, became the first in the chain of family members to serve their country. With the exception of the War of 1812 and the Korean War, someone from the clan participated in every major conflict in American history up to and including Vietnam.

In 1785, three years after the Moorheads and Kellys had made their way back to western Pennsylvania, the first of the Stewarts—William Stewart, his wife, Margaret, and their two sons, Archibald and infant John Kerr—landed in America from County Antrim, Ireland. A decade later, they, too, settled on the Appalachian plateau, and in 1794 William opened a small crossroads store in what would become Georgeville, about twenty miles north of Indiana. He was the first in a line of family merchants.

During the next few decades, the area increasingly took on the trappings of civilization, as more stores and schools opened. The first newspaper, the *American*, commenced publication in 1814. Two years later, the borough of Indiana was incorporated. The town had been created as the county seat twelve years earlier, on land acquired from a Philadelphian named George Clymer.

As the town grew, so did the Moorheads, the Kellys, and the Stewarts—with James Kelly's first child, Meek, marrying Fergus' daughter, Jane, in 1809. Mostly farmers, they tended to be industrious, hardworking people, well respected by their neighbors. Meek Kelly served in the state legislature, and his son, James, soldiered in the Mexican War (he died in a Mexico City hospital in August of 1847, some six months before the conflict ended). James Kelly left behind a daughter, Virginia, about a year old. She would become Jimmy's grandmother, marrying the actor's namesake, James Maitland Stewart, in 1868.

J.M., as Jimmy's grandfather was called, was the tenth and youngest son of that same John Kerr Stewart who had landed in America as an infant in 1784. Born in 1839, J.M. was an educated man, having attended Dayton Academy and Westminster College. He even taught school for several years after his graduation. Although he would live well into the twentieth century—he died in 1932, when his grandson was at Princeton University—he was very much a product of frontier America. His first schooling had come in a traditional one-room, log cabin house. And as he later recalled, a "man worth one or two thousand dollars was counted rich, and a girl with that sum in her own right [was] an heiress."

In January of 1864, at the age of twenty-four, J.M. enlisted in the Signal Corps to serve the Union in the Civil War. He was one of about six hundred Indiana County men who joined the Army of the Potomac. J.M. saw action at the battles of Winchester, Cedar Creek, and Fisher's Hill, as well as in the operations around Richmond, Virginia, and was promoted to sergeant before the war's end. His military service brought him into impressive company, including Generals Grant, Sherman, and Meade. He even managed to catch a glimpse of Abraham Lincoln during the president's stay with the army during the final days of the war. J.M.'s stint with the Signal Corps made a lasting impression. As the *Indiana Gazette* would note at the time of his death, "He was a good soldier and in later life maintained a deep interest in military affairs and in the various patriotic organizations that followed the War of the Rebellion, the Spanish-American and the World War."

Once the Union was restored, Stewart returned home and became a clerk in the general store owned by one of his brothers, Archibald, who was ten years his senior. The firm had been established around 1848 by John and Peter Sutton, with Archibald joining the brothers in the early 1850s, and a fourth partner, W. B. Marshall, coming on board shortly thereafter.

Although the place was called Sutton, Marshall and Stewart, everyone knew it as the Big Warehouse, and after 1853, when the outfit moved from N. Sixth Avenue, it stood as one of the principal establishments along Philadelphia Street. In 1865, the year in which J.M. joined the firm, the partners split up, with Marshall forming his own company around the dry goods and notions departments, and Archibald retaining the lines of hardware, groceries, lumber, and grain.

Three years later, J.M. married Virginia Kelly, whom everyone called Jennie. Thus, the old, distinguished Moorhead-Kelly and Stewart clans were at last united. J.M. and Jennie made a striking couple. He was a handsome man with brows low over deeply set eyes, a dashing mustache, and dark hair parted on the left. Jennie was pretty with a sweet face. A local paper recalled her "genial, sunny, light-hearted disposition" and "kindly wit and brilliant repartee." But she was frail, passing away in 1881 when she was only thirty-four years old.

J.M. and Jennie had four sons, but two of them—the oldest and the youngest—died in early childhood. In between came two lads who survived: Alexander Maitland, born in 1872, and Ernest, who arrived slightly more than two years later. By the time Alex (pronounced "Alec" for some unknown reason) was born, J.M. had acquired a one-third ownership in his brother's business. In 1883, he purchased the remaining shares and, in turn, sold a third to his cousin, A. W. Mabon. At that point the firm became J. M. Stewart and Co.

J.M. had to oversee his business and, at the same time, serve as single parent to two rapidly growing boys, but he was a man of strong character and determination. He even found time to participate in a variety of community activities, notably the Cosmopolitan Club and one of Indiana's two major literary societies, the Ingleside. He was well liked and highly respected but was reserved and apt to keep his emotions in check, qualities that his grandson Jim would inherit. He was also deeply religious. Even today, the town's senior citizens can recall his opposition to the introduction of organ music into the services of the First United Presbyterian Church, where he was a member. When he failed to stop the purchase of the instrument, he and his followers formed their own congregation, the Second United Presbyterian Church.

Eventually, J.M. remarried three times. After he was widowed twice more, his fourth wife, Marion C. Ferguson, managed to survive him, but not until he had lived a very full life. When he died, he was just shy of his ninety-third birthday. The local paper observed, "His life was an inspiration for good and the pleasantries that he exchanged with his fellow men, in his daily greetings with them, will remain cherished memories."

* * *

J.M.'s oldest surviving son, Alex, was a wild kid; even being sent away to Princeton University failed to settle him down. Years later, Jimmy would recall his dad's school pranks with barely disguised glee: "He and his friends had been the first of many generations to take a cow to the top of Nassau Hall [the oldest building on campus]"; and, "When he had a dispute with a Chinese laundryman about the quality of the ironing, he and his friends ironed the laundryman. The Chinese Ambassador demanded and received an apology from the president of the University."

Alex was a chemistry major in his senior year at Princeton when the Spanish-American War broke out. As had his father thirty-four years earlier, he enlisted in the army, taking two classmates with him. Family legend has it that he was so eager to go he forgot to turn off the Bunsen burner in the lab before he left the university. According to Jimmy, "They went to Cuba with a cavalry outfit, but they didn't see much action. When it was over, all three of them came home and were graduated in their uniforms. After that, dad forgot about chemistry and went to work in the family store."

In 1905, Alex purchased a third of the business from his father, but J.M. would remain with the firm until 1923 (at which point Alex would buy out his brother Ernest, an attorney, and assume sole ownership). Apparently, neither the war nor the merchant trade had entirely tamed Alex, who was thirty-two when he became a minor partner in the venture. He was a formidable fellow, about six foot three with less refined features than his father but still handsome. Jimmy described him as "a square and muscular Irishman, whose talk was as blunt as his face," an accurate portrait. He was capable of raising hell with a few drinks inside him. After accepting his proposal of marriage, Elizabeth Ruth Jackson, known to all as Bessie, broke off their engagement because she thought he was too wild. That finally did the trick. Alex gave up drinking and devoted his energies to the store. Bessie, in turn, relented.

She was from Apollo, a small town about twenty-five miles west of Indiana, where her lineage was every bit as distinguished as Alex's. Indeed, the Jacksons could trace their ancestry back to Bessie's great-great-grandparents, who came to the United States in 1773, eleven years before the Stewarts. She, too, had a relative who fought in the Revolutionary War, and her father, Col. Samuel Jackson, had led a pivotal charge during the Battle of Gettysburg in 1863. Later, after the battle of Spotsylvania Court House, he was brevetted to brigadier general. In the years after the Civil War, Jackson helped establish the Apollo Trust Company and served as its president. He was also an organizer of the P. H. Laufman Steel Company and held several federal and state offices. Jimmy never knew his maternal grandfather, who died the year before he was born.

Bessie was the third of five children born to Colonel Jackson and his wife, the former Mary E. Wilson. A graduate of Wilson College in Franklin County's Chambersburg, Bessie was thirty-one at the time of her wedding—relatively old for a bride at the turn of the century—but a local paper described her as "one of Apollo's most popular young ladies." She was a physically striking woman, three years Alex's junior, but it was her piano playing even more than her beauty that stirred young Stewart's heart.

The wedding took place at the Presbyterian Church in Apollo on December 19, 1906. Alex's best man was his brother Ernest. After a long honeymoon in Jamaica, the newlyweds established themselves in Indiana. Their home was at 975 Philadelphia Street, not far from the Stewart store. It was there, one year, five months, and one day after the wedding, that their son, Jim, was born.

"My earliest memories of childhood," Jimmy would recall, "are flavored by the delicious smells given off by my dad's hardware store. There were many odors, but I wasn't particular. I liked them all—the dry smell of coiled rope, the sweet smells of linseed oil and baseball gloves, the faintly acid tang of open nail kegs." It was a large, jam-packed enterprise "full to the rafters with everything needed to build a house, hunt a deer, plant a garden and harvest it, repair a car, or make a scrapbook. I could conceive of no human need that could not be satisfied in this store." Once, when he was about three or four, he ran away from home and ended up at J. M. Stewart and Co. It was the most exciting place he could think of to go.

Until he began to grow tall, Jim was slightly plump. Early on he was prescribed eyeglasses for astigmatism, which prompted the other children to call him Specks. One day he simply decided that he didn't need the glasses, so, as he put it in 1947, "I threw them away and have never worn them since," a situation that old age would eventually reverse. Sans eyeglasses, he looked slightly cherubic, with his hair parted in the middle, his dancing eyes, and his full, frequently smiling lips. It is not hard to see in the boy the young movie star he would become.

In January of 1912, when Jim was about three and a half, Alex and Bessie gave birth to a girl, Mary Wilson. She was named for her maternal grandmother, but everyone called her Doddie. A little more than two years later, in October of 1914, a second girl, Virginia Kelly, named for Alex's mother and known as Ginny, arrived. To keep up with his growing family, Alex built a Dutch Colonial house on Vinegar Hill, a steep rise two blocks north of Philadelphia Street on Seventh Street. The red-brick facade is flanked in the center by a white pillar-and-arch portico. Three windows punctuate the gambrel roof, giving the rooms on the second floor front a nice, airy feeling.

Alex and Bessie furnished the house with a combination of antiques from the Jackson family and pieces they acquired as newlyweds. "Very comfortable furniture," says a childhood friend of Ginny's, Elinor Blair. Hall Blair, her husband (now deceased) and one of Jim's boyhood pals, remembered, "They always had the *New York Times* and magazines like *Atlantic Monthly* and *Scribner's*. . . . They had good taste, a high cultural level." Another acquaintance, John Simpson, says simply, "It was a house you liked to go to."

Perhaps the Stewarts' most treasured possession—no doubt the most beloved—was in the living room. It was a Steinway grand piano, which Bessie played beautifully. Later, when the children were a bit older, the family would gather around the instrument. Doddie played the violin, Jim the accordion, and Ginny the piano. "During those sessions," the actor later remembered, "Dad sang very softly, so as not to cover up Mother's clear, sweet voice." Mealtimes were also family occasions. They would begin by joining hands atop the round dinner table to say grace.

As these vignettes suggest, they were a warm, loving quintet. At the family's center was Bessie, whom the local newspaper once described as "a lady of regal bearing, dignified and quite proper." Her love of music led her to the Music Club, where she played two-piano duets and sang in a reduced version of *Madama Butterfly*, and to the choir of the Presbyterian church to which the family belonged, but otherwise she mostly concentrated on her husband and her children. "She was so close to her family," Jim said, "that we took the place of friends. As far as I know, she had only two or three close women friends." He also remembered her as "the most tolerant and understanding of women," with a forgiving nature. From her (and Grandfather Stewart) came Jim's reserved, dignified mien, as well as that distinctive, deliberate way of thinking and speaking. People later in life would find him—like Bessie—unusually private without being guarded or defensive. Director John Ford would later say of him, "You don't get to know Jimmy Stewart. Jimmy Stewart gets to know you." Even his daughter Kelly would note, "In terms of what he's really thinking and feeling, he is very private," to which his stepson, Mike McLean, would add in an understated fashion, "He doesn't wear his emotions on his sleeve."

Bessie's tolerant nature does not mean that the Stewart kids were left to do as they pleased. On the contrary. As Jim later said, "I came from a very disciplined household." It was Alex who meted out the punishment, and he could be a demanding taskmaster, possessed of firm convictions and determined that his children act as he deemed fit. "He was pretty strict," says Elinor Blair, "and they didn't want to cross him." In this, as in so many other things, Bessie would keep Alex in check. "She stopped Dad from being—well, overboisterous," Jim once explained.

"She was the only person he would listen to about anything. And there were times when we kids sure appreciated that. He would raise his voice about pretty nearly anything—but never to her." Later, in his own more understated fashion, Jim would practice child rearing much in the manner of his father. As Mike McLean puts it, "In spite of the fact that he had a very good sense of humor and was open in many ways, he was very strict in his beliefs on how things should be done. He had a very strong Presbyterian background."

Although Alex was tough, he was also theatrical and flamboyant. His surviving friends and acquaintances invariably refer to him today as "a character." He was either incredibly absentminded—as was his son—or possessed of uncommonly fleeting whims. "He'd always have ideas in mind, about this, that, or the other thing," recalls Jim's lifelong friend Bill Moorhead (also descended from Fergus). "And he'd change his mind just as fast as he made it up." Once Alex called up James Blair—Hall's father—and said, "Jim, we're gonna go to Atlantic City. Get Carrie. I'll be around to pick you up." Several hours later, the Blairs, all packed and waiting, phoned the Stewart house to discover that Alex had gone somewhere else without them. Perhaps most outrageous was the evening when he gathered up Bessie to go out to dinner. Arriving at the restaurant, he told her to wait in the car while he checked out the menu. Then he went in and ate, forgetting all about her.

Alex was stubborn, too. In 1923, he decided that a bronze likeness of a World War I doughboy should stand as a memorial in what was then an old German Lutheran cemetery. He got a marble pillar left over from the renovation of a local bank, with the idea of placing the statue atop it. The only problem was that the Lutherans didn't want the land directed to such a purpose. Undeterred, Alex brought several of the hardware store employees over one night, and they dug a hole for the pillar. The Lutherans got a court order to stop him, but he refused to give in. Eventually, the land was deemed county property, the monument was erected, and the former cemetery became Memorial Park.

Despite his willful ways, Alex was likable. His store's vast array of goods drew folks initially, but they often stayed to swap news, share opinions, and gossip with the big, tall merchant—who held forth on a wide range of topics, including his customers' needs.

He was also kind. Jim got his accordion when Alex took it in trade from a passing carnival that couldn't pay its bill. The instrument was originally given to Ginny, but she was too small to handle it, so it went to her brother; a local Italian barber taught him to play. On another occasion, Alex traded a passing, down-on-its-luck circus for a fourteen-foot python, which he put in one of his store windows as an attention-getter. Pretty soon everyone in town was stopping by to watch the snake. This was fine, until an elderly lady fainted after the reptile struck the plate-glass window in front of her. Thereafter, Alex was ordered to remove the python. He had no idea how to do so, however. Finally, he persuaded his friend Doc Torrence to help him. Late one night, they climbed in the window, chloroformed the snake, and dislodged it from its resting place. As Jim later recalled, "they almost chloroformed themselves in the process."

Like his father J.M., Alex was a deeply religious man. "Nobody [in the Stewart family] did anything on Sunday but go to church," says Elinor Blair. "They read on Sunday afternoon, and in the evening, they sang hymns. Alex didn't preach and he didn't proselytize, but he observed the Sabbath, and he saw that his family did." He also sang in the choir of the First United Presbyterian Church, where the family worshiped.[1] "My father loved to sing," said Jim, "but he got so wrapped up in it sometimes that by the end of the song he wasn't singing the words anymore."

He was also a member of the volunteer fire department, and Jim became the company's mascot. The sight of his dad galloping down the Vinegar Hill stairs to the station at the sound of an alarm would leave a lasting impression. But Jim's parents' religious teachings would have an even greater impact. As he later put it, "They did their best to raise me to shun pomposity and glibness, to be modest, because a decent, gentlemanly man is modest. They tried to teach me faith in God."

Indeed, it is fair to say that no one would have a more profound impact on Jimmy Stewart than his dad. Said Jim years later, "I tried to take after my father in what he believed in. I was very close to him, and I don't think I've ever made an important decision in my life without thinking about how he made his decisions. Decisions about school, decisions about work, about the importance of church and values, even a decision about going into the Army."

No doubt, it was difficult at times loving, and trying to follow the wishes of, this strong-willed man, but Jim and Alex enjoyed many warm moments when the actor was growing up. As long as his activities fell within the zone that Alex deemed acceptable, he was an indulgent father—as in the time when Jim, somewhere around nine, decided he wanted to hunt big game in Africa. Or rather, capture the wildlife and bring it back home. "My father helped me plan the trip to Africa," Jimmy recalled. "We were really going to bring 'em back alive. He had even gone into the back of his hardware store with me and picked out wire for cages." Alex probably thought the boy would soon abandon the idea, but for weeks Jimmy

1. Independent-minded Alex stayed with the First United Presbyterian Church even after his father formed a rival congregation.

pestered him about the trip. Finally, Alex gave in. They boarded a train bound for Atlantic City with young Stewart fully convinced that he would soon be in the heart of the jungle. En route, they passed a train wreck, and, as Jim put it, "dad somehow convinced me that the wreck made it impossible for us to go to Africa 'at this time.' To console me, he said that going to Atlantic City was an adventure in itself. 'You may not have trapped any lions,' he told me, 'but you've never seen the ocean either.'"

A few years later, in August of 1923, another train played a role in their relationship. This one was carrying the body of deceased president Warren G. Harding. It was scheduled to pass about twenty miles from Indiana, and Jim was eager to see it go by. His mother firmly refused to indulge his wish because the train would arrive in the wee hours of the morning. But when the appointed time neared, he was awakened by his father, who drove him to the site, the two of them "bound together," in Jim's words, "by the comradeship of disobedience." As the train approached, Alex gave his son two pennies and told him to put them on the rails. Jimmy later said, "I did as he directed and jumped back to hold his hand as the monstrous engine thundered past us, pulling a glass-windowed observation car, in which we saw a flag-draped casket, guarded by two Marines, their glistening bayonets at attention. I could hardly breathe, so overwhelming were the sight and sound." After the train had roared by, he retrieved the pennies, now totally flat. He gave one to his father and kept the other for himself. Each carried his keepsake for years, and, as Jim put it, "the knowledge that what was in my pocket was also in his made me feel very close to him."

Animals played a part in the father-son adventures, too. Alex, who liked to ride, kept a horse in a barn behind the Stewart house. He taught Jimmy to groom the animal and clean out its stall, which stood the actor in good stead when he worked in Westerns many years later. A photo of him at around six or eight shows him with his friends in an open horse-drawn rig looking completely at ease.

When the circus came to town, Alex would always take Jim off to see the troupers arrive, a big event in a small community such as Indiana. "Sometimes they'd hire us kids to help 'em unload," Jimmy said later. "Before they knew it, they couldn't keep me away from the elephants." Pachyderms would remain a lifelong favorite.

Like most boys, Jimmy had a dog, a part-Airedale mutt he called Bounce, and they were inseparable. Jim was devastated when Bounce was killed by the next-door neighbor's English bulldog. Determined to avenge the murder, he climbed a backyard tree that overlooked the neighbor's property and waited for the bulldog with his Remington .22. When his mother realized his intent, she phoned her husband, who arrived a few minutes later and gently coaxed Jim down. The following morning, Alex summoned his son to the store. There, he found the bulldog waiting for him. Alex handed him a rifle and told him to use it if he wanted to. Of course, Jim couldn't pull the trigger, as his father well knew. "The three of us walked home together," Jimmy recalled, "the dog gamboling in front. No word was ever said about what had happened. None was needed. Dad had taught me I wasn't really a killer. . . . It was a great relief."

When America entered World War I, Alex volunteered for duty, and on October 9, 1917, he was commissioned a captain in the Ordnance Department. Ten days later, he left Indiana. Bessie and his son accompanied him to Blairsville on the southern border of the county, the terminus for the Indiana rail line. Then they returned home while he continued on to Washington, D.C. At the time, a local newspaper wrote, "Mr. Stewart is one of the best known and most popular young men in Indiana and will give a good account of himself in his new work."

Some months later, Bessie and Jim visited Alex in Washington and then joined him in New York the day before he was to ship out for France. "We did a lot that day," Jimmy remembered. "Mother and dad took me to the top of the Woolworth Building, so I could look up and down Manhattan, and I made them walk me into the head of the Statue of Liberty. . . . That night we found a shooting gallery on Broadway, and dad held me up so I could shoot. Woodrow Wilson was speaking at Carnegie Hall, and we walked right in. The place was jammed, and dad held me up there, too, so I could see Wilson speaking."

Assigned to an ordnance repair shop in Mehun, France, Alex served ten months overseas before being discharged from the service on May 1, 1919. When he returned home, Jim asked him if he'd been afraid. He never forgot his father's reply: "Every man is, son. Just remember that you can't handle fear all by yourself, son. Give it to God; He'll carry you."

The various artifacts of war that Alex shipped to young Jim from France—German helmets, gas masks, and swords—inspired two homespun dramas that the boy wrote and presented in his parents' basement. One of the plays, *The Slacker,* culminated with the hero, naturally played by the author, being decorated by no less than the commander of the American Expeditionary Force himself, General Pershing. The other, *To Hell with the Kaiser,* featured a rousing finale in which the villain—played by a dummy—was electrocuted by means of a dry cell battery borrowed from the hardware store.

But the best of the Stewart home dramas centered around that other object of fascination, the train. Years later, Jimmy recalled, "I had spent a week composing my masterpiece, a one-act thriller called *Death Rides the Rails.* I had written the role of Tim, a cripple boy, for myself and given the characters in the rest of my stage family to the neighborhood kids." At the climax of the drama, he was supposed to warn a railroad engineer of an impending avalanche by dragging himself down to the tracks. The problem came when Jim tried to open a door to make his exit. The school bully, whom he'd cast as his brother, was holding it shut from the backstage side. "There was no time to lose," he recalled. "I rose, walked across the stage, pushed my fist through the window painted on wrapping paper hanging on the backdrop, returned to my belly, and pulled myself through the curtain to save the day." The audience gave him a hearty ovation, which remained one of the great thrills of his life—even after stardom had accustomed him to applause.

Certainly, *Death Rides the Rails* was more fulfilling than *The Frog Prince*, the play that marked Jim's graduation from junior high school in the spring of 1923. He was a supernumerary while his friend Joe Davis had the title role.

Jim attended the Wilson Model School, a training facility for the Indiana Normal School, a teachers college founded in 1876. The Model School got its name from Wilson Hall, its home on the Normal School's campus.[2]

The Model School "was a wonderful school," says Elinor Blair, because the students had supervising teachers who were members of the college faculty. These instructors were, in turn, assisted by student teachers. Thus, the ratio of youngsters to faculty was unusually low.

Upon completion of the sixth grade, the students moved on to junior high school, which was housed in Leonard Hall, another building on the Normal School campus. There, in addition to the basics—reading, writing, arithmetic, geography, and history—the girls took home economics and the boys learned woodcrafts and other manual arts.

Stewart, by his own admission, was not a gifted student. A record book from his ninth-grade class indicates that in the fall of 1922 he earned a B in civics, Cs in Latin and English, an E in algebra (just a slight step above failing), and surprisingly, a D in phys ed. In May of 1923, he had an A in civics, a B in math, Cs in English and phys ed, and a D in Latin.

Elinor Blair says that it wasn't lack of intelligence that prevented Jim from excelling. As she puts it, he was "kind of an original thinker. And when you're an original thinker, you may be daydreaming when something else is going on." Indeed, the history of Jimmy's childhood reflects a curious, imaginative, creative mind at work. He was "mischievous, too," to quote his father. One account suggests that, at a very early age, the boy tied

---

[2] In April of 1920, when Stewart was in the sixth grade, the Commonwealth of Pennsylvania acquired the Normal School and changed its name to the Indiana State Teacher's College. Many years later, in 1965, it became Indiana University of Pennsylvania.

a kite to a wagon and launched it from the roof of the house with himself aboard; he landed unharmed on his father, who happened to be passing by. Thereafter, he was encouraged to stick to model airplanes. His first such effort was, he recalled, "a honey. I broke up mother's alarm clock to make the motor, the wheels, and the tail." Of course, he wanted to see if it would fly, so he set it aloft from the sloping gambrel roof of his home. It immediately crashed to the ground, but Jim remained undaunted.

His lifelong love of flying was aroused after World War I, when a barnstorming pilot began offering rides to the locals in his Curtiss biplane. Jim eagerly saved up for the ten-dollar adventure. Once he had the money, he convinced his father to let him go. But Alex insisted upon bringing along the family physician, Doc Torrence of the python affair, just in case.

When he wasn't building model airplanes, Jim was earning Boy Scout merit badges, camping out at Two Lick Creek with his friend Hall Blair, or creating crystal sets from oatmeal boxes and vacuum tubes. The idea of these homemade radios—invented in 1910—was to see how well and how far away one could pick up the signals from stations then just coming to the fore. Jim recalled that his homemade set enabled him to hear "the first radio broadcast to reach our corner of Pennsylvania. It came from station KDKA in Pittsburgh and it described the [March 1921] inauguration of President Harding." Then the equipment got more elaborate. One time Jim wanted an expensive radio tube called an Audion. The nearest supply outlet was a radio shop in Pittsburgh. Alex not only paid for the piece of equipment, he drove the fifty-plus miles each way to get it. "Later, when earphones became old stuff," Jim added, "dad bought me my first loudspeaker. With that loudspeaker hooked up, I could rattle all the windows in the house."

Jim and Hall became so adept at building crystal sets that they developed a flourishing business, selling their creations to the other folks in town. One day, a farmer burst into the hardware store to announce that he'd picked up KHJ in San Francisco on his Blair-Stewart contraption. "It made a big splash," said Hall. "We had our pictures taken, and there was a story in the paper. We were swamped with orders. We must have made 30 or more and sold them at $20 apiece."

Their other inventions were less profitable, but no less imaginative. "The basement of my husband's house was where they had 'trips to Mars,'" explains Elinor Blair. "They would put wax boards on the steps, and their 'trip to Mars' was to open the door and slide down." They also built an electric chair—perhaps a follow-up to the prop in *Death Rides the Rails*—and a backyard thrill ride that consisted of a chair attached to a set of cables running from a big, tall tree to the ground.

In addition to his work at the hardware store, which he had started at the age of eight, Jim's father got him a projectionist's job at the Strand, one of the town's three nickelodeons. This was just before America's entry into World War I. Jim was thrilled, for he had been an ardent fan of the era's popular serials in which dashing heroes and damsels in distress battled seemingly insurmountable perils before "Continued in our next episode" left them at the height of danger. Sam Gallo, the manager of the Strand, showed Jim how to operate the hand-cranked projector, how to set the carbon in the carbon arc lamps, and how to place tinted shades over the projector's lens when the movie called for a change of color. Later Jim said, "I concentrated on the stories so much that, once in a while, I'd forget and miss a tint mark. Once, in *20,000 Leagues Under the Sea,* I missed it for an awful long time. People saw the underwater part in blank inkiness; then, suddenly, when I remembered, it was all deep-sea green." Eventually, hand-cranked projectors gave way to electronically operated models, and Gallo kindly gave the outmoded machine to Jim along with some pieces of film. Thereafter, the Stewart basement became a movie house for the neighborhood kids.

Jim wasn't overly generous with the money he earned at the Strand and the hardware store. Hall Blair remembered, "We would go to the movies and then afterward go for a soda. He would make a big show of digging a dime out of his pocket, and he would put it right in the middle of the table and announce to his date, 'Now, this is for you *and* for me.' Nobody else could do that and get away with it and have people laughing about it." Likewise, when a carnival would come to town, Jim would tell his friends that he couldn't afford one attraction or another, prompting someone in the group to pay his way. "But then he'd see something he really wanted to do," Blair recalled, "and suddenly he'd find a quarter in some mysterious pocket somewhere. I'll bet he still has the first dollar he ever made." Indeed, Jim's reputation for being tight with a buck would follow him to Hollywood.

But, as Blair pointed out, people liked him nonetheless. He was—and is—funny, with a wry, often self-deprecating sense of humor. He's also modest, with an even disposition. And people smart. Elinor Blair recalls the time Hall's sister had a party, to which Jim, Hall, and a few other older boys were invited. After dinner, the youngsters settled in the living room, but they simply stared at one another. "There was no conversation," says Mrs. Blair. "And suddenly Jim Stewart went over to the piano. He had a way with him; he'd sit down and go like this with his fingers [she extends her hands], and he played a ditty and sang, 'Cigarettes will spoil your life / Ruin your health and kill your baby. / Poor little innocent child.' That broke the ice, and after that everyone was singing and talking, and it was wonderful. He just knew how to work a crowd. Always did."

Jim would have been content to spend his days with his family and friends in the town of his birth, but his father wanted him to go to his alma mater, Princeton, and he knew that Jim was not likely to be admitted if he attended the local public high school. So, upon his graduation from the Model School, which ended in the ninth grade, Jim was enrolled in Mercersburg Academy, a prep school roughly 100 miles southeast of Indiana, in Franklin County. As usual, once Alex's mind was made up, he was unshakable, for as Jimmy later said, "Mercersburg was full; there wasn't a chance I could enter, but dad talked me in somehow."

Jim would, of course, return to Indiana for holidays and summer vacations, but from the fall of 1923 on, the majority of his time would be spent elsewhere. Nevertheless, his happy childhood left a lasting impression. For, in his chosen profession where many of the members are insecure and angst-ridden, where portraying others means a chance to escape, if briefly, one's own unhappy life, James Stewart was an anomaly. He was a remarkably self-possessed, self-confident man with comparatively few complications and minimal ego. He valued hard work, but wasn't driven to achieve, a direct result of his loving but demanding home life and an incredibly homogenous community. Surrounded by people of like mind and background, he knew exactly who he was and the nature of his place in the world from his earliest days. In 1983, when he returned to Indiana for a gala seventy-fifth birthday celebration, he summed up the importance of his hometown, saying, "The things I've learned here have stayed with me all my life. This is where I made my decisions that certain things were good—hard work, community spirit, God, church, and family."

TWO

A Gentleman's Education

Mercersburg Academy was in its fourth decade by the time Jim Stewart arrived in the fall of 1923. Founded in 1893 in the small town of Mercersburg, Pennsylvania, near the Maryland border, the Academy occupied land that had housed a succession of educational institutions, including a seminary of the German Reformed Church and a private college.

The regents hired Dr. William Mann Irvine as first headmaster of the boys' preparatory school.[1] Irvine had both the vision needed for a new institution and the will to make that vision a reality. Jay Quinn, the Academy's current assistant director of alumni affairs, says, "He was omnipresent. His word was law. When he decided things, there was no going back, no interceding." In other words, a man in the mold of Alexander Stewart, without the latter's eccentricities.

Irvine was born in 1865 in Bedford, Pennsylvania. Like Stewart, he was the son of a merchant. He attended Phillips Exeter, one of New England's old, established prep schools, and then Princeton, where he had been a football star as well as an honors student. In part because of Irvine's strong ties with his alma mater, a sizable percentage of Mercersburg's graduates went on to Princeton each year.

The Academy began with an enrollment of fifty and a faculty of six, but by 1928, the year in which Stewart graduated, the population had grown to five hundred young men and a staff of fifty, and the campus ranged over 120 picturesque acres—making it one of the largest prep schools in the country. Jim's class, which numbered 109 at graduation, included boys from Florida, Illinois, Ohio, Wisconsin, Texas, California, and many of the other states, as well as Cuba, Korea, the Canal Zone, and Ireland. But the vast majority came from Pennsylvania, particularly the outlying areas. "Our main clientele has always been sons of small-town, middle-class families," explains Quinn. "We have never been a school for rich kids." Most of the boys in Stewart's day were white Anglo-Saxon Protestants, more a reflection of the populace in the Pennsylvania hinterlands at that time than the school's admissions policy. Jim was surrounded by people mostly like himself—and with Irvine at the helm, he was again under the auspices of a benevolent despot.

[1] Mercersburg is coeducational today.

All of the masters were men, and most were bachelors. They came from highly regarded private colleges such as Brown, Cornell, Yale, Harvard, William and Mary, and, of course, Princeton, as well as a few state universities. Some had been out of college only briefly, but the department heads, who tended to remain at Mercersburg for years, were primarily in their thirties and forties. "They were confirmed teachers," says Jay Quinn. "I mean, they really were masters." As in Indiana, the classroom routine consisted of lecture and drill. And since the ratio of students to teachers was even smaller than it had been at the Model School, each boy received considerable individual attention. The regimen was, in the words of one of Jimmy's classmates, L. Owen Potts, "disciplined and pointed. They'd pass out assignments and you'd better have your assignment ready." Students who didn't got demerits. Boys also received demerits for skipping class, going into town during the school week, and other minor infractions. "And with those demerits," says Potts, "came a thing called guard." That is, boys worked off demerits by walking a proscribed path around the campus on Saturday, the one day when they were otherwise permitted to visit the town. "Major infractions," explains Quinn, "drinking, gambling, being out of the dormitory late at night, would go much more harshly and [punishment was usually meted out] by the headmaster directly."

Stewart was basically a polite, obedient young man. As John Fentress Gardner, who roomed with him for part of his senior year, puts it, "He wasn't wild or wanton or random or rebellious. He seemed to be even tempered and earnest and somewhat pious, I suppose." Classmate Edward Hotschuh remembers Stewart as "a rather shy fellow at Mercersburg," and another Academy grad, Ted Lucas, describes him as "a private person who seemed confident and composed but not a mingler."

Although reserved, Jim was popular with the other boys—in part because of his self-deprecating wit. "He had a very dry sense of humor," says Potts. "He was a pleasure to be around." Potts also remembers him as "a calm individual who just took things as they came." Another of his classmates, Richard Hoffman, ascribes some of Jim's popularity to his musicianship: "He played the accordion, and on Sunday afternoons there was always a crowd around his room. I went a few times. The guys would sing and clown around with him."

The Academy's curriculum in the 1920s was firmly rooted in the fundamentals. Each semester, a student typically took English, mathematics (algebra, geometry, or trigonometry), a foreign language (German, French, Greek, Latin, or Spanish), a science, and history. The few electives ranged from oratory to mechanical drawing, with Bible history added in Stewart's senior year. There was no class in freehand drawing, but after Jim and Hoffman showed artistic promise, they were given time each week to explore their talent. "So we sat next to each other and drew for a whole year," Hoffman recalls. "He didn't talk much and I didn't either." In his last three years at Mercersburg, Jim was the art editor for the yearbook, the *Karux,* and in his senior year, several of his pen-and-ink renderings served as chapter headings in the publication. They tended to be in the art deco tradition, featuring multiple images in broken spatial planes. One of Stewart's drawings brought the book to a close. Appropriately, given his love of flying, he inked a pilot in an open biplane waving farewell while approaching the steeple of a building. "The End" in skywriting extends from the tail of his aircraft, making a visual pun in light of the pilot's apparent destination.

Irvine, having been a football star, believed that sports could further Mercersburg's enrollment, so he placed a heavy emphasis on athletics, specifically football, track, and baseball. Stewart's credits in the 1928 yearbook indicate that he was on the track squad in 1926, and he would later tell journalists that he was an Academy hurdler and high jumper, but he is not listed or pictured with the team in the *Karux* covering the designated season. He can, however, be found on the Third Football Team for his first three years. He progressed from third-string center as a sophomore to first string and captain as a senior.

Stewart was also a member of the John Marshall Literary Society, which had been founded in 1866, when the campus housed one of the Academy's predecessors. Marshall and its archrival, the Washington Irving Literary Society, founded a year earlier, had been debating since 1900. By the 1920s, the annual contest was the high point of Mid-Winter, the annual series of activities that fell around Washington's birthday. Every student at Mercersburg joined one society or the other, though by Jim's day there wasn't much difference between the two. "And some people rebelled at this," says Owen Potts. "They didn't like to be forced to do anything. Mercersburg was great at that. You were intimidated into doing some things that you didn't want to do." But the debating societies were part of the Mercersburg tradition, and at prep schools tradition is just about everything.

During the fall semester, Marshall and Irving held meetings every Saturday night, and members were expected to attend. In part, these events took the form of mini-debates, out of which would come the teams for the climactic intersociety face-off. Stewart never made the ultimate squad— not a surprise given his slowness of speech and deliberate manner.

As these Saturday-night meetings would indicate, dating was not a major Mercersburg activity. Indeed, relations between the sexes were primarily restricted to a few school dances during the academic year. "The girls would come in from girls' schools," says Jay Quinn. Mercersburg had a particularly close association in Stewart's day with the now defunct Penn Hall, located in nearby Chambersburg. Boys planning on attending a dance would fill out cards bearing their name, age, height, and hometown, and a member of the girls' school faculty would use this data to assign them dance partners.

Beyond the scheduled dances, the daughters of local families approved by Dr. Irvine might receive permission to invite a few boys over for light refreshments on a Saturday afternoon, and perhaps some dancing on the front porch, but the headmaster was not above telling the parents of unsuitable young ladies to keep their daughters off campus. This attitude was symptomatic of the relations between the Academy and the town. "There was quite a bit of stratification," explains Quinn. Mercersburg's principal shopping area sat at the foot of a hill with the campus at the crest; physically as well as psychologically, the students and faculty looked down on the locals. The citizenry—only about fifteen hundred people, then and now—was none too sophisticated. "A good many of the middle-aged people, I'd say most, never graduated from high school," says Quinn. Consequently, the locals were unduly deferential to both the masters and the students.

Stewart visited the town in the manner of most of his peers: through the weekly Saturday-afternoon outings allowed by the school. "Everybody went to the movie theater," recalls Owen Potts. "It was the only thing to do. And then there were two or three hamburger joints. And then we'd get really risqué—this was back in Prohibition times—and we'd buy near-beer. It was half of one percent. It tasted like beer, but that's about the end of it." Potts suspects that Stewart did not partake of the near-beer, and he's probably right—although, in time, Jim would come to enjoy a nightly cocktail or two.

Because of the boys' minimal and highly regimented relationships with girls, most of them did not become sexually active—or even comfortable around the opposite sex—until after they graduated from Mercersburg. A friend from Indiana recalls that the only girl back home who attracted Jim was "a painted-up doll. She was a good bit older than he. He liked the flashy type." Even into his late twenties and early thirties, when Stewart was dating a wide variety of Hollywood stars and starlets—and enjoying himself enormously—there was something boyish about his approach. Joan Fontaine, who went out with him during this time, says he took her to his church on their date. He took a friend of hers to an ice cream parlor. Fontaine concluded, "He was very appealing, a charming man, but he was the country boy on a date as well."

* * *

Of course, during the summer months, Stewart would return to Indiana. His father insisted that he get real-world experience by applying for jobs rather than working in the store. The teenager spent one summer as a bricklayer and another with the Highway Department, painting white lines down refurbished roads. More to his liking was assisting his friend Bill Neff, who was a magician. "We had a real magic show with all the trimmings," Stewart recalled. "It was complete with floating women, disappearing acts, guinea pigs and rabbits and all that stuff." Neff, about three years older than Stewart and a student at Penn State, was also tall and lanky. He was the star of the act, the one who delivered the diversionary patter and performed the tricks. Jim was the helpmate, the fellow who was expected to have the next piece of equipment ready when needed. "But," says Elinor Blair, who saw Bill and Jim perform, "somebody that tall couldn't be unobtrusive. He always managed to make a mistake and capitalize on it." Sometimes, when the crowd seemed restive, Jim would also enliven the proceedings with his accordion.

Indiana was too small to support such an enterprise, so Bill and Jim took to the road, sometimes on their own and sometimes in concert with an itinerant carnival or chautauqua outfit. Typically, when they arrived in a new town, Bill would tie a rope around his ankle and hang down the side of a building. Then Stewart would draw the locals' attention with his accordion. After a crowd had formed, he'd announce the location of that night's performance.

During the winter of 1927, Jim contracted scarlet fever and went home to recuperate. The illness led to a kidney infection, which forced him to miss the remainder of the school year and forestalled his graduation. Thus, he was in Indiana on May 20, 1927, when Charles Lindbergh made his historic solo flight from New York to Paris. By that point, Jim was well enough to handle light chores, so his father put him in charge of decorating the store windows. Combining business with pleasure, the aviation enthusiast created cutouts of the Eiffel Tower and New York's Woolworth Building and placed them at opposite ends of the window. In between, he located Newfoundland and Ireland. Then, shuttling back and forth between the store and the newspaper Teletype machine across the street, he tracked the aviator's progress, inching his model of Lindbergh's plane, the *Spirit of St. Louis*, ever closer to the hardware store version of France. Finally, Lindbergh landed. "It was like New Year's Eve in our town," Stewart recalled. "Church bells rang. Everybody quit work. The town busted loose. It gave the whole country an emotional lift when it needed one." Spurred on by that boyhood memory, he unabashedly campaigned for the chance to play Lindbergh on film in the 1950s.

Fully recovered in July, Jim applied for readmission to Mercersburg. Although the Academy's fall enrollment was full, a place was ultimately found for him. Perhaps because he was repeating the first semester of his senior year, he found more time for extracurricular activities. Not only did he join the Glee Club, which Dr. Irvine himself had founded and led for many years, he also played the accordion in the orchestra. The ensemble included an odd assortment of musicians: a pianist, two violinists, three trumpeters, four saxophone players, three clarinetists, two banjo players, and two drummers—but, according to Owen Potts, they had to make do with what they had: "Anybody who could read a note."

The high-water mark of Stewart's Mercersburg career came with that year's Mid-Winter play, produced by the Academy's drama society, known as the Stony Batter Club (after the birthplace of President James Buchanan, situated on the outskirts of Mercersburg). That year, oratory teacher Carl Cass, the club's faculty adviser, chose *The Wolves,* an obscure French play by Romain Rolland and translated into English by Barrett H. Clark. Modeled on the Dreyfus case but set a few years after the French Revolution, the drama had the advantages of a single set, an inn, and an all-male cast, thereby marking a change of pace from the usual Academy productions in which boys—in the well-trod prep school, male university tradition—assayed girls' roles. Stewart, decked out in a long, full mustache and a thick, black wig, played Buquet, a member of the proletariat raised to a position of power in the wake of the French monarchy's collapse. He was not yet the polished performer he would become, for, Cass recalled, "Jimmy Stewart was about as clumsy a young adolescent as a play coach ever had to work with. . . . He was a long-legged kid who looked funny in any kind of clothes he wore. I had to find a role in which he wouldn't have to wear neat-fitting clothes. And he had to be coached so that he wouldn't fall when he walked onstage."

Stewart remembered the show's opening as a near disaster, but the fault was not his. "A big sophomore named Angus Gordon was the narrator," he said. "His job was to tell the audience that there was going to be a fierce battle at midnight. He got so enthusiastic with the announcement that he took out his sword and brandished it around violently. Most of the props had been borrowed from local residents. As he swung it over an eighteenth-century table, a lady in the audience screamed, 'Stop! That belongs to me.' But it was too late. Gordon had sliced the table in half. After that catastrophe, it was tough getting the audience back in the proper frame of mind."

Despite Gordon's faux pas and the "ineffectiveness" of the play—to quote the reviewer for the school paper—Stewart's performance was rated "excellent" by the local critic, who added, "He swaggered around the stage in the accepted manner for the revolutionary citizen and spoke his lines in the most confident manner of a polished star." However, Jim's roommate Jack Fentress Gardner says, "I didn't sense the makings of an actor and a movie star." "He was just one of the fellas," adds Richard Hoffman.

The Wolves debuted on Monday, February 20, 1928, in the Academy's gymnasium. The following night, the Mid-Winter Formal Dance was held. And on Wednesday, the Mid-Winter Festivities climaxed with the 25th Annual Inter-Society debate, centering around the benefits and detriments of Prohibition. Jim's society, Marshall, won unanimously for its ringing defense of the Volstead Act.

A little more than three months later, Stewart bid Mercersburg farewell. Since the graduates' families journeyed from all over the country, commencement extended over a three-day period. Jim was appointed to the Class Day Committee, the small group of seniors who helped plan and manage the events and served as guides for the visitors. It was an honor, reflecting both his popularity and his maturity. Like all graduating seniors, he also had to give a commencement oration. Speaking in alphabetical order, the students addressed such issues as "The Winning of the West," "Choosing a School," "A Third Term for President Coolidge," and "Ambition." Stewart, near the end of the program, turned his attention to a more aesthetic issue: "Futuristic Art in Design."

That year, a pall fell over the commencement exercises. On the evening of June 5, as the students gathered for Steps Songs, the twilight singing of traditional tunes, Dr. Irvine collapsed from a stroke. Consequently, Col. James G. Barnes, president of the Academy's board of regents, awarded the diplomas to the graduates. Irvine died on June 11.

Stewart would later say, "I didn't shine at anything during my school years," but that doesn't mean that Mercersburg had no impact upon him. At a time when the majority of Americans did not even complete high school, he attended one of the leading college preparatory schools in the country—and Mercersburg's students were repeatedly reminded of their good fortune. The Academy left no doubt that it was in the business of preparing young men for leadership positions in their chosen fields. "You are the elite," they were often told. Consequently, says Jay Quinn, "a person who had a successful career here at Mercersburg would have had a great deal of self-confidence," and that was true of Stewart. The school also reinforced Jim's patriotism and faith in God and added a bit of polish to his already refined demeanor. When a boy left Mercersburg Academy, he was expected to be a gentleman.

*   *   *

Jim had initially hoped to go to the Naval Academy after high school. Alex, of course, wanted him to go to Princeton. He decided to change his son's mind subtly, by volunteering to drive him to Annapolis, Maryland, so that he could look over his first choice. Jim was impressed with the stately old campus. Then Alex suggested they continue their exploration, so they went north to Connecticut, Massachusetts, and New Hampshire, where they visited Yale, Harvard, and Dartmouth, respectively. On the way back to Pennsylvania, Alex suggested they also stop at his New Jersey alma mater. They arrived at night, so they waited until the following morning to view the campus. As Jim recalled, they proceeded "right through the front gate, with Nassau Hall rising up ahead. I'll never forget it." Indeed, the massive stone and wrought-iron FitzRandolph Gateway, designed by McKim, Mead and White and built in 1905, is impressive. So is the grand colonial building behind it, once the largest edifice in the United States and home to the Congress and President Washington in 1783. Nassau Hall, it will be recalled, was also the site of Alex's undergraduate prank with the cow. Clearly, Stewart senior had learned from his hardware customers that last seen is first sold. With stately Princeton the freshest school in his memory, Jim forgot all about the Naval Academy.

In the fall of 1928, young Stewart returned to the campus, this time as a freshman. As underclassmen (Princeton was an all-male college at the time) were required to live on campus, Jim was assigned a room in Reunion Hall, built in 1870. His roommate was Stephens Porter Brown, of Brookville, Pennsylvania. Brown, whose father was in the insurance business, had also gone to Mercersburg. Neither young man was thrilled with the living conditions. "The draft was terrible," Jim recalled, "and one night we burned our furniture because it was so cold."

While Brown laid the foundations for a geology major, Jim entered the School of Engineering with an eye toward becoming an electrical engineer. His ultimate goal was to do research for General Electric.

The engineering curriculum for freshmen included two semesters each of math, English, a modern foreign language, chemistry, and engineering drawing. In addition, a course in hygiene in the fall gave way to courses in industrial development and surveying in the spring. Moreover, all freshmen had to take physical education three hours a week throughout the year, a regimen that Stewart supplemented by going out for track. He made the squad, but he was so thin that his coach ordered him to drink several glasses of milk each day. That didn't help; whatever he gained, he burned up on the field.

The freshmen had a terrific season that year, going undefeated against Lawrenceville, Rutgers, Yale, and Penn, but Stewart had to quit before the season ended in order to concentrate on his studies. Not only was he having difficulty with his foreign-language requirement—he chose Spanish—he was also, as he later put it, "fighting a losing battle with math, a subject that would-be engineers must conquer." At one point, a professor even said to him, "Look here, old man, let's not fool ourselves. Frankly, do you think you have the slightest aptitude for mathematics?" Stewart tried grappling with the subject during Princeton's summer session— gamely staying in New Jersey rather than going home to be with his family and friends—but, in his words, "that got me nowhere." So, in his sophomore year, he became a political science major.

As a sophomore, he again roomed with Steve Brown, but this time they stayed in Brown Hall, which was twenty years newer and somewhat larger than Reunion. Jim did not return to the track team, but he did join the Glee Club as a second tenor, and he auditioned for an original musical called *The Golden Dog*.

Set in Quebec during the British siege of 1759, *The Golden Dog* centered around a dashing English major who manages to infiltrate a French military unit, only to fall in love with several local maidens. The book and lyrics were coauthored by Joshua Logan, a large, extroverted junior from Louisiana, and the show was produced by Princeton's illustrious Triangle Club. Triangle could trace its musical-comedy roots back thirty-seven years, to 1893, when its then president, Booth Tarkington, wrote *The Honorable Julius Caesar*, a parody of Shakespeare's drama. Moreover, F. Scott Fitzgerald contributed to the books and lyrics of two of the club's shows during *his* tenure at Princeton. Given Triangle's long and distinguished history, it was well endowed by 1930. Its productions were lavish, its playbills were as extensive as those for today's Broadway shows, and its scores were published; some of the more memorable tunes were even recorded. Not only was each year's show traditionally staged on campus in late December, where it was a highlight of the fall semester, but the production also toured during the ensuing Christmas break.

Stewart was one of about two hundred undergraduates who auditioned for *The Golden Dog* (freshmen were not eligible). As he later asserted, "All sophomores with any talent at all, no matter how microscopic, were urged to try out for Triangle." He remembered auditioning with classmate Robert Perry, whom he knew from Mercersburg and who also played the accordion (Perry would later marry Stewart's sister Doddie). "We plied our squeeze boxes lustily," Jim said, "hoping no one would notice the lack of tremolo effects or flash. If we weren't expert, we were loud. Those who ran the Triangle show that year must have been hard up for talent; somehow we made it." The club's faculty adviser, Dr. Donald Clive Stuart, remembered the sophomore's audition somewhat differently. He said Stewart was given lines to read, but he spoke so softly he couldn't be heard. Stuart was against casting him, but the club's president, a senior named Alfred Wade, pointed out that both Jim and Perry played the accordion and a duet could make for a good specialty number. Dr. Stuart withdrew his opposition to the casting, but cautioned Wade, "No lines, please, no lines."

The number that Stewart and Perry performed in the show was called "Blue Hell," music by R. W. Hedges and lyrics by B. Van D. Hedges. Accompanied by specialty dancer L. R. Barrett, the boys belted out such pungent sentiments as "Floating over red-hot coals you rise, / Toothless witches punching holes in your side. / Your eyes drop out, / You fry with a broomstick smell, / Old Satan yells, 'Steak today.' / Oh Lordy, Blue Hell. Hell." The Hedges brothers were not George and Ira Gershwin, but "Blue Hell" was one of the evening's showstoppers. Indeed, according to the Princeton yearbook, the *Bric a Brac*, the audience "repeatedly called for encores." The whole production was deemed a "huge success," not only locally but also during the tour by critics from papers such as the *Cleveland Plain Dealer* and the *St. Louis Post-Dispatch*.

In a departure from the norm, the production toured first—to take advantage of the Christmas break—and then played Princeton in February of 1930. The reason for the reversal was the club's move to the new McCarter Theater, which was not completed until early in the new year. As usual, the boys reached their destinations by train and were lavishly entertained by Princeton alumni at each stop. For Stewart the trip was a revelation and an incredible thrill: "You were thrown into close activity with a large group of boys from different classes and different parts of the country. You traveled for three weeks with them. You met their sisters, their mothers and fathers, and you returned after the holidays with a host of names in your book, friends whom you didn't remember and who didn't remember you. To a former stay-at-home like myself, traveling was a romantic adventure. Silly though it may seem, names like Memphis, Nashville, St. Louis, Louisville, and all the others had each its special glamour in my mind, and as we pulled into each town, I would be standing on the platform, wide-eyed and thrilled, getting my first smell of touring and beginning to taste the transcontinental tang of this sprawling, muscular country."

While they were on the road, Logan asked Stewart if he had ever considered becoming an actor. Absolutely not, the sophomore replied. "He walked away as if I had slandered him," Logan recalled. Nevertheless, Jim liked the jovial, talented Southerner. "Josh was a year ahead of me," he said later. "I had such great respect for him. He wrote all the words, the jokes, the music, and the songs to just about everything [Triangle] did."[2]

The Frog Prince and *The Wolves* had not prepared Stewart for anything like *The Golden Dog*. "That show changed my life," he said years later, "because I felt what it was like to be applauded."

He was having nowhere near the same degree of success with his studies. The Department of Politics offered only one sophomore-level course, American Government and Politics. Otherwise, the curriculum consisted of the same kind of survey courses—in English, history, modern language, science, and so forth—that had marked Jim's freshman year. He had been able to cut down on math, but he was still struggling. A slow reader, he usually found himself several books behind his classmates. Moreover, his spelling was atrocious. Shakespeare also proved elusive, but in this case the cause was sloth. The instructor, Frank MacDonald, had been one of Alex's Princeton roommates, and Jim thought the family connection would earn him a good grade with no effort. "So I didn't bother to read Shakespeare," he recalled, "and naturally I wasn't prepared for the final exam. I'll never forget MacDonald's judgment—'I've done everything for you I can in good conscience, but it's no use.'"

The Shakespeare class notwithstanding, Stewart tried to do well most of the time, recognizing his father's sacrifice in sending him to an expensive private university. Plodding through coursework left Jim little time for dating. When he did go out with girls, he rarely met with success. To get past the awkward moments at a dance or a party, he would take along his accordion, and while he was playing, his date would invariably grow bored and find other company. "Take a girl and she'd likely be whisked away from you," he concluded, so he often went stag.

In the end, what saved Stewart from flunking out of Princeton was the realization that his talent for drawing—which he lent to the university's literary magazine, the *Princeton Tiger*—might give him a viable start as an architect. Once again, he switched his major.

Because architecture was taught at the graduate level, like law and medicine, undergrads intending to pursue such a course of study enrolled in the Department of Art and Archeology but were under the purview of the School of Architecture. According to the Princeton catalog for 1929–30, the school's curriculum was "based on the belief that an architect should have a well rounded education in liberal studies, that he should approach his profession primarily as an art, that he should under-

---

[2] Logan would go on to enormous success on Broadway, as the director of *Annie Get Your Gun*, *Mister Roberts*, and *South Pacific* (he coauthored the last two as well), and in film, where his credits included *Picnic*, *Bus Stop*, *Sayonara*, and *Camelot*.

stand and appreciate the other arts in relation to architecture, and that he should be taught the science of building construction as a part of his training in design rather than as an end in itself." Thus, sophomores, juniors, and seniors took such courses as Ancient Architecture, Elements of Drafting, Introduction to Design, Principles of Drawing and Painting, Ancient Art, Renaissance Sculpture, Oriental Art, and Modern Architecture. Stewart loved it all. "Once I became interested in my courses," he concluded, "I suddenly discovered that I could study." He even made the honor roll for the first semester of the 1930–31 academic year.

Jim spent his last two years at Princeton living in Foulke Hall, which was almost brand-new, having been erected in 1923. He had also joined an eating club at the end of his sophomore year. As Princeton had no fraternities, eating clubs were the university's principal social outlet for upperclassmen, a tradition dating back to the 1870s. In the spring of 1930, when Stewart was eligible to join, Princeton had eighteen eating clubs, which averaged forty-some members each. In place of rushing, the clubs had bicker parties, occasions that enabled them to meet the new crop of sophomores and extend membership invitations to the candidates of their choice. In Stewart's case, the invitation came from the Charter Club, founded in 1909. "My father wanted me to go to Cottage," he said, referring to the university's second-oldest club, established in 1886, "because he had been in Cottage. But Cottage didn't ask me—Charter asked me."

Eating clubs in Stewart's day were not rowdy or boisterous like fraternities. "Ties and jackets were the custom at most meals," reported William K. Selden in his recent study of this Princeton tradition. "In many clubs one was personally greeted by name by a doorman at the front door. Meals were served in some clubs by waitresses, but more generally by waiters in white coats, most of whom were black, many of long time employment." Selden adds, "By eight o'clock on week nights the club houses were usually deserted," as students studied in the dorms or the library or attended school functions. As might be expected, life at Princeton was far less regimented than at Mercersburg. One of Stewart's classmates, Ted Lucas, notes that students could even ignore with relative impunity the university's prohibitions against alcohol and car ownership, but adds, "I suspect that Jimmy Stewart was far too self-disciplined to break any of these rules. He was an exemplary person then as later."

As a junior, Stewart became a recruiter for the Triangle Club. Prior to auditions in the late fall of 1930, Logan, then president of the club, tried to whip up support for the hallowed institution by addressing a group of lower classmen. He brought Stewart and Robert Perry with him, and their accordion duets drew an enthusiastic ovation from the crowd.

That year the show was called *The Tiger Smiles*. Again it was written by Logan in collaboration with several others. In a departure from the norm, it was set on campus—Princeton teams are called the Tigers, hence the title. Logan, writing the best part for himself, played Wilber Wilkins, a lazy Princeton student in 1890. After a blow to the head, he dreams that he is on campus a hundred years later. Stewart was cast as the heroic straight man of the piece, Bruce Pelham, a role that Logan conceived with the lanky junior in mind. Bruce's girlfriend was the dean's daughter, Jeanette, played, of course, by a boy, Harry Dunham.

Although Logan's campus ne'er-do-well was the flashier role, Stewart had plenty to do, including five musical numbers. Two of them, "On a Sunday Evening" and "Something in the Air," were particularly memorable. The former was even recorded by Guy Lombardo and his orchestra.

The show played the McCarter Theater on December 17 and 18, 1930, where it met with considerable success. *Time* even reviewed it, noting that its "excellence easily equals anything the club has done since it was founded." The article was accompanied by a photo of Stewart, sporting fake sideburns, a boater, a white suit with a dark vest, and his hands in his vest pockets. That year the tour took the company to thirteen cities in sixteen days, including Philadelphia; Columbus, Ohio; Chicago; Milwaukee; Cleveland; and Baltimore.

Looking back on his last Triangle Club show many years later, Logan still delighted in Jim's performance, writing, "Stewart was gangling and hilarious singing and dancing 'On a Sunday Evening,' which I had written for him. He winced as he sang my corny rhymes." But he added that Stewart's first love was still architecture. "This stage 'monkey business' was just fun. But he was so good. I knew deep down he loved acting but was too embarrassed to admit it."

In the spring of his junior year, Stewart again took to the stage, this time in a drama, *The Play's the Thing*, by Ferenc Molnár. It was produced by Princeton's other drama society, Intime, founded in 1919. Like the Triangle Club, Intime's offerings were directed, designed, and produced by students. But unlike the musical group's original material, Intime's half-dozen annual productions tended to be a mix of classics and recent New York shows. The 1929–30 season, for instance, included plays by Shaw and Shakespeare, and earlier in 1931, Intime had staged *The Hairy Ape* by Eugene O'Neill. Moreover, the women's roles were usually played by young, visiting professionals. For example, *Three Artists and a Lady* by Archibald MacLeish and Basil Bayea, the production just before *The Play's the Thing*, featured a newcomer named Margaret Sullavan. Stewart, who saw *Three Artists and a Lady*, was impressed by the perky Virginia girl. "She had this tremendous arresting talent," he recalled later. He invited Sullavan to a reception at the Charter Club and she accepted. It was the start of one of the most significant relationships in Jim Stewart's life.

In *The Play's the Thing*, Jim played a butler by the name of Dwornitschek. It was a small but juicy role. The male lead was taken by senior Myron McCormick, who would later create the wheeler-dealer Luther Billis in Broadway's *South Pacific* under the direction of his old Princeton friend Josh Logan. Casting Stewart in the play had been the idea of director-designer Norris Houghton, also a senior and that year's Intime president. Houghton had seen Stewart in *The Tiger Smiles*. "So I thought it would be interesting to see what he could do [in a drama]," he recalls. "I don't think he had done a straight play." Except for *The Wolves* at Mercersburg, this was so.

Again, Stewart enjoyed the experience. "Nobody gave us any theatrical training in the Intime," he later said. "We just walked on cold and acted our brains out until the final curtain." Apparently, that approach worked for the Molnár drama, because Prof. Donald A. Stauffer, reviewing *The Play's the Thing* for the *Daily Princetonian*, called it "smooth and coherent, even in small details." The lion's share of the acting honors went to McCormick and leading lady Florence Hastings, a New York import like Maggie Sullavan, but Stauffer noted, "Among the minor characters James M. Stewart . . . should be singled out." Houghton had also been impressed by Jim's performance, saying years later, "He instinctively knew about timing and things that were important for the butler in the play. I didn't teach him how to do those things, he just did them."

A year later, Stewart, then a senior, appeared in another Intime production, the world premiere of *Nerissa*, a sophisticated comedy by Jeanette Druce, directed by William H. Reynolds, that year's club president. Again, the production drew applause from the *Daily Princetonian*, although Stewart was not mentioned individually.

That year, Jim also served as a football cheerleader, but the honor proved to be a mixed blessing when the Tigers lost game after game. "I took the rap for the lack of enthusiasm in the cheering sections," Stewart recalled, "and finally the committee imported a guest conductor, as it were—a scintillating fellow from New York who was going to teach us some new yells. It was my job to introduce him the night of the big rally, and doggone if I didn't forget his name."

He had better luck with his lines in his final Triangle Club show, *Spanish Blades*. Donning a black pageboy wig and pencil-thin mustache, he played the hapless lover Alphonso, a strolling troubadour. The musical had the distinction of bringing together in one evening Don Juan, Carmen, and Don Quixote and Sancho Panza, but by common consent the lush score contributed more to the show's success than its book. Jim had two songs, "Day after Day" in Act 1 and "Mother Madrid" in Act 2. The *Daily Princetonian* praised his sweet tenor and predicted that the audience would be humming "Day after Day" long past the final curtain.

Given Triangle history, New York talent scouts frequently caught club productions. Thus, *Spanish Blades* served to introduce Stewart to a pivotal figure in his life and career, Billy Grady. Formerly a talent agent, Grady, then on the staff of Metro-Goldwyn-Mayer in New York, just happened to be passing through Princeton during the show's two-day run when he learned that the play he was to see in Atlantic City had been postponed. He could have driven back to Manhattan, but instead elected to see the Triangle Club offering. "Princeton shows were always interesting," he wrote in his autobiography. Impressed by what he called Stewart's "ingratiating personality," he went backstage after the final curtain to meet the young man and found himself talking with the entire Stewart clan—who had come down from Indiana to see the show. Grady liked Jim, but the following day, in his office, he made a notation for the MGM files: "James S, Princeton student, a type of no particular interest."

Max Arnow, a Warner Bros. casting director, also caught *Spanish Blades*. He, too, went backstage and introduced himself to Stewart—and invited the young man to visit him in his Manhattan office. Some months later, Jim took him up on his offer, but by then Arnow had forgotten all about him.

Jimmy graduated from Princeton in the spring of 1932. Looking back, he would later say the value of his four years of college lay in "getting my brain to work. The whole idea of education is not the question of learning so much, it's the question of getting your mind to work, getting your whole mental system going, getting it to operate." He also considered a Princeton education "a tremendous asset. . . . More is expected of you if you are a graduate of Princeton and that is right and the way it should be."

In the end, he had not only turned his grades around, he had managed to win a scholarship to study architecture at the graduate level. He had every intention of doing so in the fall. But first he would spend the summer having a bit of fun, playing the accordion and maybe doing a bit of acting with Josh Logan's summer stock company on Cape Cod. They called themselves the University Players.

THREE

A Change of Direction

The University Players operated on the same principle that guided Intime and the Triangle Club: namely that students could learn stagecraft—acting, directing, set design, and so forth—through trial and error, without significant adult involvement. "It was a very exciting way to be introduced to acting in the theatre," Stewart said years later. "There were no hang-ups, it was all just new and everybody just sort of learned their lines and made mistakes."

It was no coincidence that the company resembled Princeton's dramatic societies or that graduates such as Josh Logan were members, for the Players had been formed in 1928 by Intime's then president, Bretaigne "Windy" Windust, and his opposite number in the Harvard Dramatic Society, Charles Crane Leatherbee. The two young men had met at a Manhattan party during the previous year's Christmas vacation and were mutually electrified by the idea of translating their school experiences into a summer stock company. It was a daring concept, for at the time there were only about half a dozen such theaters in the entire country.

In large measure, the boys' vision stemmed from the need to find a launching pad for their own careers. Since neither Harvard nor Princeton offered formal training in the theater, they were well behind those of their peers who had come to New York directly from high school and had found walk-ons or apprenticeships on Broadway and in other professional venues. Moreover, pros looked on veterans of the Triangle Club and Hasty Pudding as dilettantes, and Charlie and Windy were determined to prove otherwise.

Both young men came from well-to-do families—Paris-born Windust's father was a violinist and his mother a concert soprano, while Leatherbee's grandfather owned the Crane Plumbing Company and his mother's second husband was Jan Masaryk, the Czechoslovakian minister to the Court of St. James. Therefore, they had the financial means, as well as the élan, to support their venture. They decided to set up shop—with themselves as co-decisionmakers or directors—on the Cape; specifically in Falmouth, Massachusetts, where Leatherbee's mother owned a home. After recruiting a company from their own universities—including Josh Logan—as well as Yale, Vassar, Smith, and Radcliffe, they commenced operations, having persuaded the owner of a movie house in downtown Falmouth to let them perform on Mondays and Tuesdays in July and August, traditionally slow nights, in exchange for 50 percent of their gross profits. Their premiere attraction was *The Dover Road* by A. A. Milne, which Windust directed. But the fare throughout the company's history consisted primarily of recent Broadway successes, including a healthy dose of mysteries and suspense dramas. The wealthy summer residents— people from Boston, New York, Chicago, Cleveland, and other metropolitan areas—embraced the new diversion, and the Players ended the season with a gross of about $20,000, and a net of $1,200 after expenses and the theater owner's cut.

The following year, the company moved to Silver Beach on the outskirts of town. There, in West Falmouth, the Players built their own five-hundred-seat theater, adjacent to an existing bathing pavilion and tearoom. They turned the latter into a place for after-theater refreshments, with company members serving as waiters and cooks.

That summer, Maggie Sullavan, known to the Players from her Intime role in *Three Artists and a Lady* and a subsequent guest appearance with the Harvard Dramatic Society, joined the company. Other members included Princeton's Myron McCormick, Harvard's Kent Smith and John Swope, and an Omaha boy who had been hired by another summer stock company, the Cape Playhouse in Dennis, Massachusetts, during UP's first season. He joined the newcomers after a fellow Omahan from Harvard brought him over to Falmouth to see a show. His name was Henry Fonda. Of course, Sullavan, McCormick, Smith, and Fonda would go on to major careers as professionals, as would Logan and Windust, and subsequent recruits Stewart and Mildred Natwick (Windust would direct the Broadway productions of *Life with Father*, *Arsenic and Old Lace*, and *State of the Union* as well as several films for Warner Bros.). "The knowledge that this company would produce some of the greatest talents in the American theatre would not have surprised Charlie and Windy at all," Logan noted in his autobiography. "They knew what they were after."

By the summer of 1932, when Stewart was invited to join the company, the Players had gone through their share of upheavals. Two years earlier, in the third season, Windust, with Fonda's support, had sought to limit membership to college students while Leatherbee had argued for open recruitment. It took funny, exuberant Josh Logan to effect a reconciliation between the founders. To avoid such impasses in the future, Logan was named a third company director. Then, some sixteen months later, in November of 1931, the Players attempted to become a year-round operation by performing a series of plays in repertory at a theater in Baltimore. But the venture never really caught fire—Maryland was in the throes of the Great Depression—and the company was forced to abandon the effort in March of 1932. Charlie, Windy, and their colleagues returned to West Falmouth dispirited and in debt. Moreover, they had begun losing their leading players, including Fonda, Kent Smith, and Maggie Sullavan, to the professional theater in New York. Sullavan had even made her Broadway debut—in *A Modern Virgin*—before the Players opened in Baltimore, but the play ran only a short while, so she was able to rejoin the company for several of the winter productions.[1]

On the one hand, Sullavan's Broadway debut and the lesser successes of Fonda and Smith validated Windust and Leatherbee's original objective, to give university students experience so that they might gain acceptance in the professional theater community. On the other hand, replacing these veterans with fresh college kids—now quite a few years younger than the Players' founders—and, in turn, replacing those youngsters with fresh recruits when *they* found equivalent success elsewhere meant that the company would always remain at a certain level of amateurism. After four summer seasons and a taste of year-round repertory, such a goal seemed somewhat limiting. That Leatherbee, Windust, and Logan hoped to take the company in a more professional direction could be seen in that summer's change of name. As UP member Norris Houghton recalled, they "decided to abandon the word 'University' altogether as not professional-sounding enough. The directors decided on the unglamorous but precise title of 'The Theatre Unit, Inc.'" Among members, however, the old name was still used.

At first glance, it might seem that engaging Jimmy Stewart was a logical move in recruiting. And, indeed, Logan would later write that he hoped the young Princetonian would fill the void left by Fonda, which he described as "a tremendous loss. He was the heart of the company." But the fact was that Jim, with only one high school and two small college roles to his credit, plus the lighthearted Triangle Club musicals, was nowhere near experienced enough to take on the kind of assignments that Fonda could execute after four seasons with the company (plus three years' prior experience with the Omaha Community Playhouse). At the time, Logan had much more modest goals in mind for young Jim: he wanted him to play his accordion in the tearoom as after-theater entertainment. Any acting he did in the plays would be a sideline.

According to Logan, he had to pitch the idea to Stewart for three hours. Then, when the young man was persuaded, Josh had to convince Alex. Finally, Jim's dad said okay. For his labors, the new college grad would be paid a paltry $10 a week plus board. Still, there were worse ways to

---

[1] Sullavan and Fonda were married while they were in Baltimore, but their union was brief—from Christmas Day, 1931 until May 1932. They divorced the following year.

spend July and August. Said Stewart, "The chance to summer in Falmouth appealed to me because it was on the sea. Even more appealing was the thought of earning a living by playing an accordion."

Unfortunately, he was not a hit. The tea shop's customers chatted during his sets. Some even asked him to stop playing. "Even people who had lived on tea for years refused to come back," he later told columnist Ed Sullivan.

Jim may not have been cabaret material, but he was not sent packing. He used his architectural training to design sets. On some productions, he served as assistant prop man. He even swept the stage on more than one occasion. And, yes, occasionally he acted. These roles, he later explained, were "carefully selected so they would be easy for me." Perhaps best of all, he was introduced to a company of energetic young men and women who were passionate about what they were doing. In his autobiography, Josh Logan described the environment in West Falmouth: "Anyone could try out for a part, suggest a play or criticize anyone else. Only the strong could live through this criticism because it was as hot as a baptism of fire. You didn't play the part badly—you *stank*. Your idea wasn't interesting—it was great or stupid. Physical fights were non-existent, but belligerent stand-offs could last for days. But always we were totally involved, ecstatically alive. So, from this torment and apparently continuous disagreement, came beautiful even masterful theatre." No doubt, Stewart was inspired by the passions of those around him in West Falmouth.

One of Jim's roles was in *It's a Wise Child* by Laurence E. Johnston, which had debuted on Broadway three years earlier with Humphrey Bogart. "Cool Kelly was the name of the character that he played," says Norris Houghton, "and it was the low comic. We thought he was funny." The production, Houghton recalls, "was a great success."

But Stewart's best role that summer was in a comedy called *Goodbye Again* by Allan Scott and George Haight. Years later, the star described the action: "The male lead in *Good-by Again* [*sic*] played an author touring the country, autographing his novel in bookstores. Mrs. Belle Irving, a dragon dowager, sends her chauffeur—me—to the author's hotel room with a copy of his book. The author is in the bathroom; a secretary tells me to wait—her boss 'is cleaning up.' I had two important lines. One was 'Couldn't you just take the book in to him?' The secretary refuses indignantly. I put the book under my arm, head for the door, and utter my last line, 'Mrs. Belle Irving is going to be sore as hell.' Exit. That was all I did during the entire show."

Goodbye Again marked a genuine departure for the Players in that it was done as a Broadway tryout, one of a series of such offerings undertaken by the company in association with producer Arthur Beckhard.

Beckhard, about ten years older than Leatherbee and Windust, was then enjoying tremendous success with *Another Language* by Rose Franken, which had opened on Broadway that spring. "Previous to hitting the jackpot with this play," wrote Norris Houghton, "he had been a concert manager and summer theatre entrepreneur at Woodstock, New York and Greenwich, Connecticut. He was an unromantic-looking, roly-poly Teddy bear with round eyes behind owllike spectacles, a Molotov mustache, and an incongruously infectious giggle."

Most, if not all, of the UP members saw their association with the Broadway impresario as a mixed blessing. The company would participate financially in any subsequent successes that emerged from their joint ventures, and after the losses incurred in Baltimore, they needed the income. Moreover, a relationship with a successful Broadway producer could open doors that were otherwise closed to them. Their hopes in that regard were confirmed with the first Beckhard tryout of the season, a psychological drama called *Peep Show* by Elsie Schauffler. As Houghton noted in his book, the play's opening night "was a sort of Cinderella ball for us. Boston sent down three first-string critics and the Shuberts sent up their scouts."

But with Beckhard's involvement, the Players lost some of the ingredients that made them unique. In prior productions, the company's college-age actors had played whatever older character roles the productions demanded. Now, when warranted, Beckhard imported experienced hands from New York. Moreover, the Players lost their autonomy. Logan put it bluntly in his autobiography: "Before we knew it he was swallowing our company."

Another Beckhard tryout production, *Carry Nation*, by first-time playwright Frank McGrath, followed *Goodbye Again*, and Stewart was once again in the cast. A dramatization of the life of the ax-wielding prohibitionist, *Carry Nation* was cinematic in scope, with an enormous cast and many, many set changes. Beckhard's principal interest in the piece lay in the title role, which was ideal for his wife, concert singer Esther Dale. Because he thought that his constant presence during rehearsals would make her self-conscious, he decided not to direct the play himself. Instead, he engaged actress Blanche Yurka, a close friend of Esther's.

"The tryout in Falmouth was an incredible undertaking for a summer stock company," Yurka wrote in her memoirs, "involving as it did sixteen scene changes and a cast of fifty-two players." It required, in her opinion, "an extraordinary coordination of effort." Indeed, lesser actors such as Jim had to take on multiple roles. As he later remembered it, he played a vigilante, a sheriff, a black gardener, and a crowd member. Many of the Players were unhappy about the production, including the casting of Dale,

whom they considered inexperienced, and the hiring of an outside director. Logan later wrote, "We delivered a formal protest against the entire
venture. . . . He [Beckhard] read our protest and cackled."

Carry Nation was less than a resounding triumph. In their respective
memoirs, Josh Logan called it a "groaning bore," and Norris Houghton
found it "one of the dullest . . . plays we ever attempted."

The 1932 season ground to a halt on September 10, 1932. Thereafter,
the Players rather halfheartedly returned to Baltimore to start a second
season. Even though the previous winter's experiment had failed, the
association with Beckhard had given them a new approach to play production. Now, the idea was to use their Baltimore engagement to launch
projects that could go on to tryout in other cities and, if successful, come
into New York. Their first offering, a four-character play called *There's
Always Juliet*, opened at the Maryland Theatre on October 10. None of
the actors were UP members. It was followed by *Carry Nation*, which
Beckhard—much to the consternation of the Players' guiding lights—
had decided to ready for Broadway.

Beckhard's decision put Stewart into a genuine quandary: Should he stay
with the show or return to Princeton to take up his graduate studies in
architecture as planned? "Since I didn't have to decide right away," he
recalled, "I went home to Indiana, Pennsylvania, to think about it." But he
knew that, somewhere during that strange season in West Falmouth,
he'd gotten hooked. As he put it, "Quite suddenly I didn't care if there was
never another house designed or built, just so long as I could get somewhere on the stage."

One evening he told his father and mother about the career change he
was considering. They were stunned. They "couldn't help thinking that the
practice of architecture was more respectable than becoming an 'actor fellow,' " Jim explained later. However, they rallied. " 'If that's the way you
want it, Jim,' said dad. My mother didn't approve heartily, but she went
along, bless her heart. My mind was made up." A visiting uncle told him,
"None of the Stewarts has ever had anything to do with the theater.
Except one—he was with the circus for a while. Then he went to jail."

After the West Falmouth tryout of *Carry Nation*, Yurka and Josh Logan
tried to convince Frank McGrath to rewrite portions of the play, but
McGrath, an instructor at a private school in Newark, resisted their suggestions. "Like so many first-time authors," Yurka wrote in her memoirs,
"this writer seemed unable to change any of his lines—nor would he let
anyone else touch them. There was little to be done."

Thus, on October 18, 1932, the flawed epic followed *There's Always
Juliet* into the Maryland Theatre for a week of previews. Although Stew-

art was only listed as Constable Gano in the playbill, he continued to perform all of the parts that he'd done in stock (Beckhard felt that the tripling and quadrupling of roles made the production look chintzy, so each cast member was listed only once). For his work, Stewart was paid a mere $30 a week. Still that was triple his summer stock earnings. Ten dollars from his paycheck went toward his enrollment fee in Actors Equity.

Carry Nation was not particularly well received in Baltimore, but Beckhard brought it into New York anyway. When it opened at the Biltmore Theatre on W. Forty-seventh Street on October 29, 1932, the critics were surprisingly kind. Stark Young of the *New Republic* called Esther Dale's performance "extraordinary" and the production "by all odds the most important event so far in the theatre this season." In addition to Dale, many of the critics singled out newcomer Leslie Adams, who played Carry's understanding husband, David Nation. But, despite these positive elements, the story's dramatic tension got lost as McGrath followed the title character from youth to old age. As John Chapman of the *New York Daily News* put it, the play seemed "more of a newsreel of the big moments in an intensely dramatic life rather than a drama built around that life."

In the face of high running costs, Beckhard tried to keep the show alive, but he was forced to close it after seventeen performances. Then he almost immediately reopened it—at the request of the intelligentsia, he told the press, prompting the *Post* to quip, "The Biltmore Theatre, presumably, will therefore be an excellent place to visit if you wish to find out what the intelligentsia looks like." Jim's sister Ginny, then a freshman at Vassar, came down to Manhattan for the Thanksgiving break and caught a matinee. Years later, she remembered sitting "alone in the half-empty theatre straining to distinguish Jim . . . in the role of a bearded sheriff." Later, she and her brother went to an actors' hangout called Ralph's for, in her words, "a mournful Thanksgiving dinner." Shortly thereafter, Beckhard threw in the towel, and after thirty-one performances, *Carry Nation* was history.

So, too, were the University Players. "We could not go on with the Baltimore season," Houghton explained, "for there had been a five-week break while we moved *Carry Nation* to Broadway and played it there, and now we had nothing to return with. We could not go back . . . to the Cape, for it was the beginning of December." Moreover, without the continuing income from Broadway ticket sales, the company was broke.

The demise was swift and painful and rather ignoble, in light of the virtually unprecedented accomplishments of this independent group of talented young people. But the experience would have its effect. As Houghton pointed out, company members could now come to the professional theater "with a confidence in themselves. . . . They commanded attention because they knew what they were talking about, knew what they were doing. They started in a long jump ahead of their contemporaries." After only one season with the company in small roles, Stewart had not enjoyed the success of Fonda, Logan, Sullavan, Kent Smith, and Houghton, but he was still far ahead of most aspiring actors. At twenty-four years old and less than five months out of college, he had already made his Broadway debut.

If he had endured a long period of unemployment after *Carry Nation*, Stewart might well have decided to return to Princeton or Indiana where a job in his dad's hardware store was waiting for him. He had no major stake in forging a theater career at that point. But no sooner had *Carry Nation* closed than Beckhard decided to make *Goodbye Again* his next Broadway venture—with Jim repeating his role as the rich lady's chauffeur.

Goodbye Again opened at the Masque Theatre on W. Forty-fifth Street on December 28, 1932, about a month after the final curtain of *Carry Nation*. Unlike the mixed reviews that greeted Stewart's first Broadway show, *Goodbye Again* was a smash, variously described as a "sly and ingratiating play," a "happy and mischievous farce," and "a smooth and pleasantly flowing comedy" by the *New York World-Telegram*, the *New York Daily News*, and the *New York Times*, respectively. The *New Yorker* even singled out Jim, noting "Mr. James Stewart's chauffeur . . . comes on for three minutes and walks off to a round of spontaneous applause." In his memoirs, Burgess Meredith also remembered the impression the young actor made: "I saw a tall, lanky guy, bemused and bewildered-looking, make his entrance wearing a chauffeur's uniform and bring down the house with one line: 'Mrs. Vanderlip's [*sic*] going to be sore as hell.' "

For any Broadway newcomer, such attention would represent a major step forward. In Stewart's case, it was all the more remarkable because he was a novice with no formal training. In fact, he never took an acting lesson in his life. Still, the boyish charm that endeared him to friends carried across the footlights, while that devilish sense of humor enabled him to make the most of an otherwise forgettable role. Moreover, he had exceptionally good instincts and was sincere. "He was a strange sort of a person," Norris Houghton recalls, "because he persuaded you to believe him without doing anything much about it, without any particular effort." The fact that Jim had not seriously committed to acting as a career, that performing was still just a lark, contributed to the performance, too. For he was content to just have a good time—and his pleasure pleased the audience. As Houghton puts it, "He assumed somehow that everything was going to be alright. And, as a result, everything was alright." Stewart made such an impression in this very brief role that a major New York paper, the *Sun,* even devoted a column to him after the show had been running about five months.

For his work, Jim earned the same salary he'd received for *Carry Nation,* $30 a week. "The money wasn't any better," he said later, "but the work was easier." Fortunately, an important legacy of the University Players was a circle of friends and acquaintances who could pool their resources for lodging and food. Thus, Jim roomed with Logan, Myron McCormick, who was also in *Goodbye Again,* and his UP predecessor, Henry Fonda.

At this point, a friendship between Jim and Hank blossomed. They had much in common. Fonda, three years older than Stewart, was also from the hinterlands; he was born in Grand Island, Nebraska, and raised in Omaha. Like Alex Stewart, William Fonda was a small tradesman, the owner of a printing plant. Jim and Hank even had grandfathers who had fought for the Union at Gettysburg. Each was the oldest child in his family with two younger sisters, and both were devoted to their parents, especially their fathers. Where the Stewarts were ardent Presbyterians, the Fondas followed Mary Baker Eddy and Christian Science. Both Hank and Jim had been reserved boys who loved Scouting and had a talent for drawing. Their temperaments as well as their interests meshed: Each was comfortable with silence but had an infectious sense of humor with a penchant for practical jokes. Of Fonda, Stewart would later say, "He was one of the great guys I've ever known. . . . He was such fun company to be with—life was just too *much*—laughing all the time." Watching the two of them together some years later, Hank's son, Peter, would feel that the roommates "felt more comfortable with each other than they did with many of their other friends. It was a very mystical thing that went on between these two guys."

The only area where they disagreed was politics. Fonda was a fervent liberal Democrat, and Stewart, like his father and the majority of the folks in Indiana, was a die-hard conservative Republican. The difference nearly cost them their friendship, for one night, after dinner at a restaurant, they passed a political rally, which prompted a discussion between them. Soon, their voices were raised, their tempers were up, and they were swinging at one another. Said Stewart years later, "Thank God it was snowin'—I went down on my face more than he did. We got to the hotel and he said, 'Listen carefully; if you go along with this, I will: I want us never to mention anything to do with politics again from this minute on.' And we never mentioned it."

The apartment that Stewart, Fonda, Logan, and McCormick shared was a grimy, run-down walk-up across from the YMCA on W. Sixty-third

Street near Central Park West. The place—dubbed Casa Gangrene by Fonda—consisted of two rooms, which Logan described as "a soot-colored bedroom with twin beds, a living room with two sprung studio couches, a bathroom with a mildewed shower, and a huge kitchen stove out in the hall."

Stewart would later say that their building was owned by Legs Diamond, but the notorious gangster had been murdered in December of 1931, nearly a year before they moved in. Still, there were plenty of shady characters around. Stewart and Fonda remembered strange men even busting into their apartment from time to time by mistake. Fonda guessed they were looking for the prostitutes who also lived in the building. The neighborhood was no better, with warring gangsters and inexpensive hookers plying their trades on the surrounding streets.

The boys took turns cooking, but only Fonda had any culinary skill. When his turn came, he prepared Swedish meatballs, Mexican rice, and other dishes that he'd learned from his mother. Stewart, who had always been a big eater, often packed away far more than his share, thereby putting the foursome's food budget in jeopardy. There was no money for Scotch or bourbon so the roommates mixed rubbing alcohol with gelatin. "We'd test it by pouring just a little bit on the metal running board of a car," Fonda recalled. "Then we'd light it. If the flame was blue, we'd drink it. If it was red, we'd throw it away."

In time, the roommates began hosting weekly steak-and-beer parties in the basement of a pub on W. Forty-first Street. For a dollar, all comers—typically young performers like themselves—got all the beer they could drink and hobo steaks, which Fonda described as "huge thick slabs of beef with sides of salt on top of them" (after cooking, the salt was removed and the meat was buttered and put on rolls). The room featured an upright piano, and although some of the keys were missing, the youngsters would play and sing. Burgess Meredith recalled just such an occasion in his autobiography: "One night I wandered in to find a weird concert in progress. Jimmy Stewart was behind an accordion, with Dick Foran providing harmony. As an ex–boy tenor, I was invited to join them—it didn't require much prodding—and that was the beginning of the Stewart-Meredith partnership."[2] The two young actors became good friends.

From time to time, participants in the Thursday Night Beer Club, as the weekly parties were called, included actresses Helen Hayes, Katharine Cornell, and Maggie Sullavan, and clarinetist Benny Goodman. "When he came around," Stewart recalled, "I tossed my accordion into a corner and

---

[2] Dick Foran later became a film actor, at one point playing a singing cowboy in a series of B Westerns produced by Warner Bros.

listened with the rest. He was really an artist and the club's biggest attraction. We kept him tooting night after night until he couldn't pucker. It was generally agreed that of all of us he was the most likely to succeed."

The Thursday Night Beer Club proved to be Stewart's principal social outlet. He didn't date much. "When there was work," he recalled, "I worked hard and at all hours. When I had no engagements I worked harder than ever to find new ones."

America was still in the grip of the Great Depression at the time, but the Broadway theater was bursting with creativity nonetheless. There were comedies by Philip Barry, Noël Coward, and Kaufman and Hart, and musicals by George Gershwin, Cole Porter, and Rodgers and Hart. In addition, the sobering urban dramas of Clifford Odets, produced by the Group Theater, were introducing a new realism into playwriting, acting, and directing. To be young and unencumbered at such a moment was thrilling, and Stewart, despite his impoverished living conditions, had a grand time. Every night, he would go to the Masque Theatre, where *Goodbye Again* had settled into a long run, don his chauffeur's uniform, and render his brief dialogue. Then, while waiting for the curtain call, he would often watch the star, Osgood Perkins, from the wings. "He was the kind of actor you can learn from," Stewart said later, "always the same every night, polishing up his performance, never varying or letting down. He was such a fine actor." He thought the star was particularly adept at handling props. "When he lighted a cigarette," Stewart explained, "or picked up a cup of coffee or took a drink, he did it with convincing aplomb." In time, Stewart became a master of props himself. It didn't come easily. Jacqueline Scott, who costarred with him in a Western called *Firecreek* in the late 1960s, remembers that, at one point, the script called for him to place a towel on a nail on a cabin wall. "And he would go over and over and over that," she says. "Go in and back and in and back and throw that towel up and throw that towel up until it was like a sixth sense to him, until it was like he had done it every day of his life." Consequently, when seen on film, the action looks effortless.

Above all, Stewart learned from Perkins that acting was a craft, a discipline. This notion came as something of a revelation, for he had previously considered acting—like singing or playing the accordion—light recreation, something to do for fun. Getting laughs and applause was a kick, but it wasn't to be taken seriously. Suddenly, he began to realize that creating a character and performing it night after night was like building a model airplane or designing a bridge. It was, as he put it, "a skill to be learned until it becomes a part of you." That appealed to the technician in him.

Still, he couldn't spend all of his considerable offstage hours watching

Osgood Perkins. So he and McCormick, with whom he shared a dressing room on the top floor of the theater, rented a Ping-Pong table and played for milk shakes. "Milk shakes are mighty costly," Stewart pointed out later, "and we played with desperation. Once I owed Mac over three hundred shakes; later on he owed me eighty-two."

On May 1, 1933, *Goodbye Again* moved to the Plymouth Theatre, where it ran until late June. After 216 Broadway performances, the show then traveled to Boston, where the engagement finally came to an end.

When it was over, Jim faced unemployment for the first time. But he was starting to make a name for himself in the theater. Not with the public yet, but with the small group of Broadway insiders who could give him work. "As a result," he said, "when the play closed, I got calls from other producers. If someone asked me, 'Do you have a stage credit?' I could say yes. I was identified with a hit."

FOUR

Learning a Craft

It didn't take Jim long to get work. The summer of 1933 found him back in Boston, stage-managing a production of *Camille*, starring Jane Cowl.

Once a show is on the boards, the stage manager's principal job is to cue the light changes and sound effects at each performance. The task requires a cool head and intense concentration. Otherwise cues can come late or be missed entirely. Unfortunately, Stewart was not up to the standards of the play's demanding star, especially in her death scene, for which she had devised a special lighting effect. As the tubercular courtesan faded away, Cowl had arranged for a baby spotlight with a series of increasingly pale gelatin filters to focus on her face, thereby making her appear weaker and weaker. Stewart tried to call the cues to please the star, but rarely met her exacting standards. Then, one night, a noise from the alley beside the theater distracted him at the crucial moment. He went outside to investigate and not only missed the death scene, but also let in a gust of wind that blew down one of the set's chandeliers. "The electrician working the gelatins," Stewart recalled, "had figured that what with the gale blowing into the theater and the chandelier falling on stage and my struggling with the door, it would be best to ring down the curtain and call the whole thing off." That ended Stewart's stint in Boston.

Once again, Arthur Beckhard came to the rescue. The producer's new comedy, *Spring in Autumn,* adapted by Nina Belmonte from the original Spanish play by Gregoria Martinez-Sierra, had a small role for the young actor. As *Carry Nation* director Blanche Yurka, cast as the lead in the new comedy, noted in her memoirs, Beckhard "was very loyal to those in whom he believed." Apparently, Jim fell into that select category. "He thought Stewart was very good and gave him jobs when he had them," recalls Norris Houghton.

Spring in Autumn was about a temperamental opera singer who returns home after a long separation from her husband to help arrange the marriage of their daughter. Stewart was not only to assay a small role, he was also to serve as an assistant stage manager. He also got to play the accordion onstage.

Spring in Autumn tried out at the West Falmouth theater in August. Then, after Labor Day, the comedy moved on to the Tremont Theatre in Boston. As often happens with plays on the road, *Spring in Autumn* went through extensive rewrites at these venues, but sometimes those closest to a production lose perspective and the changes are not for the better. In this instance, Yurka felt the rewrites destroyed the charm of the original comedy.

At the conclusion of the Boston run, the production shut down while Beckhard weighed the show's prospects. Finally, he decided to proceed with it, but he engaged a new set designer, replaced several members of the cast, and brought in UP founder Bretaigne Windust to take over as director (from Beckhard himself). The revamped production tried out at the Walnut Theatre in Philadelphia on October 16 and opened eight days later at the Henry Miller in New York. The opening night audience was astounded and delighted by one memorable bit of stage business—at the end of the second act, Yurka stood on her head while singing Puccini. But that prodigious feat was not enough to save the fragile comedy. Judging by the reviews, the actress' assessment of the Boston rewrites were correct. Robert Garland of the *New York World Telegram* argued that somewhere in the adaptation "the brightest dialogue [of the original] seems to have been dulled and a good deal of the comedy lost." *Spring in Autumn* closed after twenty-six performances.

By that point, Stewart was rooming with Fonda at the Madison Square Hotel on E. Twenty-seventh Street, the summer of 1933 having scattered the W. Sixty-third Street foursome to the vagaries of their profession. The new digs including a sitting room and a bedroom furnished, according to Fonda, "in early East Lynne, faded ruby and permanent gray."

About three weeks after *Spring in Autumn* closed, Jim was back on Broadway again, playing Johnny Chadwick, one of a group of American expatriates living in Paris, in *All Good Americans*. The comedy, written by Laura and S. J. Perelman and directed by Arthur Sircom, starred Hope Williams, a veteran of such hits as *Holiday* by Philip Barry and *Strike Me Pink* with Jimmy Durante.

This time, Stewart's role not only required him to play the accordion, but to throw it out of a window. Unable to bring himself to destroy an instrument he loved—even though the prop would not be his own accordion—he learned to play the banjo and convinced Sircom and the Perelmans to let him toss that instead. *New York Times* critic Brooks Atkinson, while failing to mention Stewart by name, noted in his review of the play, "Throwing a $250 banjo out of the window at the concierge is constructive abuse and should be virtuously applauded."

Unfortunately, when *All Good Americans* opened at Henry Miller's Theatre on December 5, the critics found little else to cheer. The consensus was that the show offered plenty of laughs but to no particular purpose. After only thirty-nine performances, *All Good Americans* folded.

Gentleman that he was, producer Courtney Burr threw a closing-night party for the company, and Stewart brought Fonda.[1] At around three o'clock in the morning, the merrymaking wound down, and the friends headed home. When they reached Times Square, which was, of course, deserted at that hour, an inebriated Fonda suggested that Stewart take out the accordion he'd brought to the party and strike up a tune, just to see if they could raise an audience. An equally inebriated Stewart agreed to do so and started to play. Soon, a couple of people emerged from the shadows, then a few more, and finally, they were surrounded and taking requests. "Then the next thing," said Stewart, "I saw Fonda passing the hat." Jim would recall that they earned thirty-six cents while Fonda placed the total at around half that amount, leading Stewart to quip, "So we disagree on the box-office receipts for that night." Finally, the concert was interrupted by an irate policeman, who told the actors that he'd spent hours getting the street people off the street and now he'd have to start all over again. Sheepishly, the thespians moved on to the subway—their earnings in hand.

Such escapades were not unusual when Fonda, Stewart, and a bit of booze got together. There was the snowy night when they overindulged at one of their steak-and-beer parties, which had resumed in the winter of 1934. Before they reached the Madison Square Hotel, their bladders were aching, so they decided to urinate in the street. "Let's have a contest," Fonda suggested. "We'll see who can piss the longest in a continual line in the snowdrift." Then he had a better idea: "Say, let's write our names in the snow." Stewart agreed. "Now I walked two blocks going real slow," Fonda recalled, "and Stewart walked about three blocks. He complained later that my name was shorter than his, but I had broken the rules anyhow, I only printed my initials. He wrote his whole name in those drifts. Come to think of it, Stewart must have had a helluva lot more to drink that night than I did!"

More often than not, food was on Stewart's mind, not liquor. He had long since reached his mature height—six foot three inches—but he weighed only 135 pounds. Lack of money was part of his problem, but as he later explained, "I wasn't exactly hungry, because I had found a cafeteria on Eighth Avenue where I could fill up on beef stew, rice pudding, and milk for forty cents." Still, he just couldn't seem to fill out. During his days on the Princeton track team, he'd plied himself with milk in an effort to gain weight. Now, in New York, he tried something similar—cream mixed with soda water, which he bought in large quantities at a

---

[1] Inexplicably, in Fonda's autobiography, cowriter Howard Teichmann claimed that Hank was also in *All Good Americans*, but the actor is not listed in the Broadway playbill.

drugstore. "It was a horrible mixture," he recalled, "but somebody said it would add pounds to a bony frame. A glass of the stuff cost only five cents, and in the early 1930s five cents was important to me. Later, when I had more money, I promoted my stomach to half milk and half cream." He also had a tailor pad the shoulders of the suit he wore to auditions. "The camouflage didn't fool anybody," he later conceded, "but it made me feel bulkier and gave me confidence."

All Good Americans closed in early January of 1934. Amazingly, Stewart landed another show, *Yellow Jack* by Sidney Howard, in little more than a month. "He had had the least experience [in our circle]," Josh Logan noted, "but the shortest wait for success. Day after day he would come home with a new script and a new offer."

But *Yellow Jack* was different from the run-of-the-mill fare that came Stewart's way. It represented a major leap forward, for *Yellow Jack* was a drama of genuine substance, written by Sidney Howard, the Pulitzer Prize–winning author of *They Knew What They Wanted* (and the future principal screenwriter of *Gone With the Wind*). Based on a chapter in the book *Microbe Hunters* by Paul de Kruif, the play recounted Walter Reed's investigation of the outbreak of yellow fever at the U.S. army base in Cuba in 1900. It took Howard six years, off and on, to write the drama. Not only was medical research an unusual subject for Broadway, the production was presented in a daring fashion: without intermission on a simple, skeletal platform set created by one of the theater's most gifted designers, Jo Melziner. The director was another significant talent, Guthrie McClintic, husband of actress Katharine Cornell. He replaced the legendary Jed Harris, who had cast the production but departed shortly thereafter over creative differences with Howard.

Stewart played Pvt. Johnny O'Hara, one of the soldiers who voluntarily inoculated themselves with yellow fever germs to trace the progress of the disease. It was a gem of a role, but the young actor nearly missed the opportunity to play it, because he failed to render a convincing Irish brogue at his audition. Thereafter, he worked on the accent with Frank Cullinan, a former member of Dublin's Abbey Theater. "When the actor who got the part fell ill," Stewart said later, "I was able to step into it." Two of the other soldiers were played by Stewart's former roommate and Ping-Pong opponent, Myron McCormick, and Sam (then called Samuel) Levene.

For Jim, associating with major talents such as Howard and McClintic was eye-opening. "For the first time," he recalled, "I could see these men, good mature men, out there working and concentrating and this really meant something to them—creating something on the stage. I think that's when I sort of got serious about it."

The play opened at the Martin Beck Theatre on March 6, 1934, and the critics were ecstatic in their praise. Brooks Atkinson of the *New York Times* summed up the sentiments when he wrote, "To put it simply, Sidney Howard has accomplished something of tremendous importance to the stage. . . . For *Yellow Jack* is not only a profoundly moving piece of work, but a play of extraordinary significance." Stewart's best review came from Robert Garland of the *New York World Telegram*, who asserted, "Especially do I admire the Private O'Hara of James Stewart. . . . Here is a performance that is simple, sensitive and true. And replete with poetic underbeat." Billy Grady, the MGM casting director who had caught one of Stewart's Princeton Triangle Club shows, was also impressed by the young man's progress. He noted years later that "though I couldn't give him much for his brogue, he did a very creditable job."

Stewart was invigorated by the run of *Yellow Jack.* He would later say, "The cast was wonderful. . . . There was a great spirit backstage. Those who were off stage lingered in the wings to greet the next one off, instead of going back to the dressing rooms. It was like a baseball team talking it up for another run." Among those who caught the show was John Moran, the prototype for Stewart's character, who traveled from Cuba just to see a performance. Shy and reserved, Moran was so shaken by the attention he received from the press that he could merely nod and grin at Jim and the other cast members after the curtain fell.

It was probably while Stewart was in *Yellow Jack* that he made his first foray into motion pictures. *Art Trouble* was a two-reeler from Vitaphone, a division of Warner Bros. that produced inexpensive, comic shorts in New York. Stewart was offered a small, uncredited role as one of two rich brothers who hire a couple of housepainters to take their places in a Paris art school. Slapstick comics Harry Gribbon and Shemp Howard (later of the Three Stooges) played the hapless substitutes. "I wasn't really interested in doing the picture," Stewart recalled a few years later, "but the offer of $50 a day was unbelievable, and I had to find out whether or not I was being kidded. It was true."

He appeared in only two scenes. In the first, he and his brother, played by another young, unknown actor, learn that their parents, whom they call Mater and Pater, plan to send them abroad. In the second, which immediately follows, they hire the painters. As the actor playing the other brother was short, Stewart's height may have had as much to do with his casting as his talent; they made a Mutt and Jeff combination.

Watching *Art Trouble* today, one can't help but realize how inexperienced Stewart was in 1934. Sporting a three-piece suit and a cigarette, which he never smokes, he speaks his few lines in a too loud, unappealing whine, no doubt an attempt to appear the spoiled rich kid. With his free hand often in his pocket, he appears at ease, but he obviously has no idea where to look, so he gazes down much of the time. Clearly, the director, Ralph Staub, was of no help to him nor was the camera itself, which remained stationary in both scenes, directly in front of the actors for standard two-shot exchanges. For the record, Stewart's first line on film was "No, we don't want to go to Paris," an echo of the sentiment just expressed by his brother. As for the rest of the short, it's primitive with low humor and double entendres, but Gribbon and Howard are occasionally funny.

Unfortunately, *Yellow Jack* proved to be what is known as a critic's darling. The public simply wasn't interested in a drama about a killer virus with minimalist production values and an unknown cast. As a result, the play closed after only seventy-nine performances. In 1938, it was adapted for the screen, with Robert Montgomery in Stewart's role.

Once again, Jim was at liberty for about a month. Then, on June 18, he started rehearsing a play called *We Die Exquisitely* at the Red Barn Theater in Locust Valley, Long Island. It was his first summer stock experience since the University Players. The theater's new management—Stage Associates, Inc.—had decided to go the route of the Players by trying out new comedies and dramas rather than offering proven fare. "But they're tryouts carefully selected, worthily presented and intelligently directed," observed New York drama critic Robert Garland. The company's playhouse was literally an old red barn with a back porch that served as an after-theater café. Nearby was the Long Island Rail Road station, used by commuters traveling to and from Manhattan.

We Die Exquisitely was the second play of the season. Written by John Stewart Twist and Catherine Henry, it was set entirely in the cabin of an airplane, where, the audience comes to learn, the pilot, copilot, and most of the passengers have formed a suicide pact. The dramatic tension arises from the presence of a few travelers with no death wish; they are on board by mistake. Stewart played the copilot, who wanted to die as retribution for having caused a previous plane crash.

The director, Anton Bundsmann, lacked a firm grip on the proceedings, and as a result, the actors began embellishing their characters during the short rehearsal period. Said Stewart, "Somehow I got the idea that I should be a dope fiend as well as a pilot with a load of guilt. So I adopted a nervous tic, but I got so carried away that my tic became a massive twitch."

The production sounds awful, but critic John Whitney, who traveled to Long Island to review the play for the *Newark Evening News,* argued that, while it needed rewriting and cutting, "it still emerges as a good basis for a stirring melodrama." Unfortunately, it not only needed editing, it needed another theater. For starters, the Red Barn's stage was so tiny that after Stewart's character was killed ten minutes before the final curtain, he had to stagger about rather than fall as his lanky frame lying prone on the floor would have presented a serious traffic hazard. Of course, the actor loved it. "It was the ham's dream of a great scene," he said a few years later, "and I was proud of it."

The tiny stage wasn't the only problem. Every time a Long Island Rail Road train passed, the fragile old barn shook and the whistle that the conductor inevitably blew could be heard throughout the house. Said Stewart, "If anything would destroy the illusion of a group of suicidal people riding an airplane to eternity—and it didn't need much—it would be the rattle and shriek of an earthbound train." So, by carefully orchestrating each act, the director ensured that the 9:12 would roar by at intermission. He didn't reckon on the Fourth of July, however, which fell two days after the play's opening. "To carry all the holiday traffic," Stewart recalled, "the Long Island Rail Road scheduled an extra section. Nobody warned us. The usual train came by, we called everybody back into the theater, and we started flying our airplane again. At a crucial moment, a much longer train rumbled by, and this time the whistle blast seemed endless. My death in the pilot's compartment wasn't the only one that took place that night. The play died too."

The Red Barn invited Jim to act in the show that followed *We Die Exquisitely* as well. It was *All Paris Knows* by Alfred Savoir, as adapted by John Van Druten. A backstage saga based on the relationship between Sasha Guitry and Yvonne Printemps, it starred Moffat Johnson as an impresario who tries to turn a music hall entertainer into a legitimate singer. Munich actress Greta Maren made her English-language debut as the singer, and Stewart played the understanding electrician who falls for her.

Maren's involvement turned July 23, the play's opening night, into an event far beyond that of most summer stock premieres. Paul D. Cravath, chairman of the Metropolitan Opera's Board of Directors, gave a preshow dinner at his weekend retreat in her honor, after which, as the *New York Times* noted the following day, a "capacity audience of 500 members of society who have country homes on the North Shore greeted Miss Greta Maren on her first appearance in an English-speaking play."

Of course, the Long Island Rail Road was still running, and Stewart had a love scene timed to start just after the 9:12 rumbled through. Billy Grady recalled that on the night he saw *All Paris Knows*, the train was late, and as a result, the whistling and rattling started just as Jim and Maren went into an embrace. Undaunted, Stewart simply continued kissing the star of the show until the train passed. "It was the longest kiss in the history of the American Theater," noted Grady.

That Stewart was rapidly becoming a young actor to reckon with became even more evident with his next job. He was cast as the third principal in a drama called *Divided by Three*, which started rehearsals in New York in early September 1934. It reunited him with his *Yellow Jack* director, Guthrie McClintic.

Divided by Three was written by two first-time playwrights, but they were well connected. Margaret Leech was Mrs. Ralph Pulitzer and Beatrice Kaufman was the wife of playwright-director George S. Kaufman. Together, they had concocted a soap opera–like tale centering around a wife and mother carrying on an illicit affair. Jim was to play her son, Teddy Parrish, whose world crumbles when he discovers the indiscretion. Judith Anderson starred as his mother. Also in the cast was Hedda Hopper, still a few years away from fame as a Hollywood gossip columnist.

As with Osgood Perkins in *Goodbye Again*, Stewart was inspired by Anderson. "She was a star of enormous popularity," he said years later, "and I'd never had the experience of working like that. This tremendous admiration I got for this woman who was able to project things to the audience, the effect she had on the audience—that was what convinced me that I wanted to get good in this acting thing, that it was worth trying."

After a brief stint in New Haven starting on September 27, *Divided by Three* opened at New York's Ethel Barrymore Theatre on October 2. Given the show's playwrights and director, the opening-night audience was packed with luminaries, including Lillian Gish, Edna Ferber, Ira Gershwin, Joseph P. Kennedy, Irving Berlin, Moss Hart, Bernard Baruch, Bennett Cerf, and, of course, George S. Kaufman.

The production received a glowing review from the *Times'* Bosley Crowther, who called the play "a tenderly moving drama," but most of the critics found *Divided by Three* talky and dull. "It is, I fear," wrote Gilbert W. Gabriel of the *New York American*, "another of those plays in which the scenery wins out. And maybe mercifully."

But the critics were unanimous in their praise of Stewart, who got the kind of notices a young actor dreams of. "There is a splendid performance by James Stewart as the son," wrote Burns Mantle of the *New York Daily News*. "Mr. Stewart is . . . a quietly forceful actor completely free of affectations of the cheaper tricks of his profession." Percy Hammond of the *Herald-Tribune* echoed the sentiment, while Crowther called the performance "a minor masterpiece of characterization."

Unfortunately, stage performances, no matter how memorable, are lost to time, so today there is no way of assessing specifically what Stewart did to inspire such praise. But one must remember that in the 1930s, the Method had not yet impacted stage technique. Consequently, grippingly realistic performances such as Lee J. Cobb's in *Death of a Salesman* and Marlon Brando's in *A Streetcar Named Desire* were more than a decade away. True, John Garfield and other members of the Group Theater had begun to take some of the declamatory staginess out of the craft through the dramas of Clifford Odets, but that playwright's stark, urban dramas virtually forced a modified approach. What seems to have been striking about Stewart in *Divided by Three* was that he achieved a semblance of unaffected realism in material far more melodramatic and "stagy."

Even his friends and acquaintances were impressed. It was *Divided by Three* that led Fonda to realize how good his roommate actually was. More importantly, Billy Grady, by then MGM's casting director and based in California, was at last convinced that the young actor he'd been quietly tracking since *Spanish Blades* was Metro material. "This man has finally arrived," Grady told his bosses. "Unaffected and sincere in everything he does. We should send for him and talk contract."

According to Hollywood columnist Ezra Goodman, MGM in its heyday auditioned approximately five thousand people a year. Of these, fewer than fifty were given screen tests, and only two were signed to contracts. Thus, Stewart was already among the select few when Grady's recommendation resulted in a test. It took place while *Divided by Three* was still on the boards, under the purview of Al Altman, who was the studio's man in charge of such operations on the East Coast. Altman simply asked Jimmy to sit on a stool and look in various directions while the camera rolled without sound. A second test followed some weeks later. On that occasion, Stewart was asked a series of inconsequential questions. His answers gave the MGM executives a chance to see how his voice and personality registered on film. He had felt a little foolish simply looking in various directions at the first test, but he was pleased with his conduct the second time around.

As with all of Jim's other plays except *Goodbye Again*, *Divided by Three* couldn't find an audience and closed before the end of October, after less than a month's run. Amazingly, Stewart went right into another show, *Page Miss Glory*, a comedy by Joseph Schrank and Philip Dunning and directed by George Abbott, who was already on his way to becoming a Broadway legend.

Page Miss Glory was about a promoter and a photographer who create a composite photo to represent the most beautiful girl in America and enter it in a contest. When it wins, they convince a hotel chambermaid to impersonate the striking young lady. Dorothy Hall, whom critic Percy

Hammond called "pre-eminent in the impersonation of stupid dumb-belles," was to star as the girl.

As *The Path of Glory,* the show had tried out in October, but a less than stellar reaction in Baltimore and Wilmington, Delaware, had led Dunning and coproducer Laurence Schwab to shut it down. They brought in Abbott to replace then director Phillip Loeb and engaged Stewart and Charles D. Brown to take over as the photographer and the promoter, respectively.[2] During a frantic two weeks of rehearsal—half the norm for a Broadway show at the time—scenes were extensively rewritten and the play's title was finalized. "Additions and deletions were made as late as the morning of the opening," noted the *New York Herald-Tribune.*

The hard work paid off, for when *Page Miss Glory* opened at the Mansfield Theatre on November 27, the all-important critics had a wonderful evening. Robert Garland of the *New York World-Telegram* summed up the general reaction, writing, "There are more laughs than you can shake your sides at in *Page Miss Glory. . . .* Last night at the Mansfield, the customers were in stitches most of the time." Stewart, in the somewhat thankless role of the "best friend," didn't receive the kind of personal notices that he'd garnered for *Divided by Three,* but Richard Lockridge of the *Sun* found him "engagingly wistful" and Brooks Atkinson of the *Times* listed him first among the cast's "generous assembly of good-natured clowns and actors."

Thus, 1934—Stewart's second full year in New York—ended on a high note. Fonda was also in a Broadway show, *The Farmer's Daughter,* for which he'd received glowing reviews, so the roommates had two steady paychecks and were feeling justifiably good about their careers. So much so that they took on a hobby—building model airplanes. Like two eager young boys, they would rush back to the Madison Square Hotel each night after their respective performances and relax by fitting together fragile pieces of balsa wood.

Meanwhile, despite the good reviews, *Page Miss Glory* was struggling. It closed on January 9, 1935, after about six weeks. Warner Bros., which had paid a then record $72,500 for the screen rights, released a film version of the play in August of that year. Frank McHugh had Stewart's role, with Pat O'Brien as the promoter and Marion Davies as the chambermaid.

Stewart was at liberty yet again. This time, he remained unemployed for more than two months. Fonda would later maintain that Stewart never worried between engagements, but that seems unlikely. Even as a major film

---

[2] In *Winchester '73,* shot sixteen years later, Stewart would costar with the actor he'd replaced, Millard Mitchell.

star, Jim would say, "If I'm not making a movie or just about to make one, I feel that I'm all washed up." He just knew how to mask his feelings.

Finally, around March 15, he went back to work—this time in *Journey By Night.*

Journey By Night was based on a German play by Leo Perutz, which had debuted in Vienna in early 1931 under the direction of the celebrated Max Reinhardt. American producers had tried several times to bring the show to Broadway, and twice tryout productions were launched—each with a different adaptation; one of them featured silent-film siren Pola Negri. The version in which Stewart was cast derived from yet a third adaptation, by Arthur Goodrich, and this time the star was Greta Maren, with whom Stewart had worked at the Red Barn Theater the previous summer. She was to play the estranged wife of an Austrian bar manager. Stewart, as the publican's younger brother, robs a bank in the hopes of fleeing to Paris with the woman, whom he thinks is a countess. After he learns that she is his sister-in-law, he kills her and then himself.

Private O'Hara's brogue in *Yellow Jack* caused Stewart problems, but the Viennese accent he needed for *Journey By Night* was far more demanding. "I went to a voice coach named Frances Robinson Duff to take some voice lessons," he recalled. "I asked her if it was possible to give me a slight Austrian accent. Nothing too much, you understand, just enough to get me by. She charged five bucks an hour. Three hours later, she said she was gonna have to let me go. I remember her final words: 'I can't give you an accent, but come back if you ever want to learn to speak English.'"

After a less than enthusiastic tryout in Boston, the show opened at the Shubert Theatre in New York on April 16. That evening Stewart endured the kind of performance that gives every actor nightmares. In the second act, his character has to open the door to his flat to admit a travel agent. The plot hinges on this piece of business since the agent has his tickets to Paris. But—in a throwback to his childhood experience in *Death Rides the Rails*—Stewart couldn't get the door to open. "Every time I yanked on the knob," he recalled, "chandeliers jangled and the audience snickered." He didn't know what to do. Finally, he tugged so hard that the wall—just muslin stretched over a frame of light wood—fell in on him, giving the audience an unexpected view of the backstage area, including other actors waiting for their cues. Feebly Jim muttered, "Come in" while lifting the flat back into position. After which, the door creaked slowly open, thereby drawing an enormous belly laugh from the audience. "A man in the front row had nonstop hysterics, laughing and weeping the rest of the play," said Stewart. Meanwhile, Jim's sisters, also seated in the house, squirmed in agony.

Suspiciously, none of the drama critics referred to the incident in their reviews. Perhaps they simply saw it as a onetime technical glitch, having no bearing on the production's ultimate merits. Although it is tempting to write the story off as a yarn that Jimmy enjoyed spinning when recounting the adventures of his youth—for he told it often—his sister Virginia also recalled the mishap in a short article that she wrote for *Coronet* in 1940.

Much as Stewart in later life enjoyed telling the story of his debacle in *Journey By Night,* he was equally fond of quoting the negative reviews of his performance. Specifically, he recalled one critic claiming that he "wandered through the play like a befuddled tourist on the banks of the Danube." It's a good line, but an examination of the New York dailies failed to turn up a sentiment that bald. The closest remark came from Percy Hammond of the *New York Herald-Tribune,* who wrote, "Mr. Stewart, one of the best actors that Princeton has produced, is in *Journey By Night* intensely a gaunt and square-jawed New Englander, out of place in a mess of trans-Atlantic behavior." Most of Hammond's colleagues blamed any deficiencies in the performance on the part itself, while Burns Mantle of the *Daily News* went so far as to claim that Stewart played "this misguided boy with far more earnestness and enthusiasm than the role should reasonably inspire."

All agreed, however, that the play was poorly written and staged. As Brooks Atkinson concluded, "When a play has defied adaptation for two years, there must be something fundamentally wrong with it. *Journey By Night* is hackneyed to the core."

Given such a savaging, it is not surprising that the play closed four days later. Stewart was free from an unsuitable role that he disliked, but he was still reeling from the disaster of opening night. And Fonda wasn't around to cheer him up. The previous month, Hank had gotten his big break: he was summoned to Hollywood to repeat his leading role in *The Farmer's Daughter.* So, with the Broadway season virtually at an end and little to hold him in New York, Stewart decided to go home to Indiana and, as he later put it, "lick my wounds."

While he was there, he finally heard from Billy Grady regarding his MGM screen tests. The casting director wanted to put him in a film.

It would be thirty-five years before James Stewart opened in another Broadway play.

PART TWO

·*Jefferson Smith*·

FIVE

Contract Player

MGM was far from the oldest film studio in Hollywood. In fact, of the Big Eight (Paramount, Fox, Universal, United Artists, Warner Bros., Columbia, RKO, and Metro) only RKO was younger.

But MGM had something better than maturity: the powerful financial resources of Marcus Loew, the New York movie theater magnate who had forged the new giant in 1924 by merging his studio, Metro Pictures, with the failing Goldwyn Picture Corporation and Louis B. Mayer Pictures. The head office remained in New York—initially under Loew and then, upon his death in 1927, Nicholas Schenck—but the principal power broker in Hollywood was Mayer, a thirty-nine-year-old Russian-Jewish immigrant and former scrap-metal dealer. As first vice president, L.B. ran the studio. Irving Thalberg, the twenty-five-year-old wunderkind he'd brought with him from his former film company, was vice president in charge of production.

Rotund, bespectacled, and balding, Mayer ruled Metro as Dr. Irvine had run Mercersburg and Alex Stewart had fathered his kids—like a benevolent despot. In a departure from his competitors at Paramount and Warners, L.B. placed MGM on a rigid hierarchical system whereby departments—costuming, set decoration, and so forth—reported to line producers for specific projects, the line producers reported to Thalberg, and Thalberg reported to him. It was an efficient way of doing business.

But MGM was more than just streamlined; it was the ultimate dream factory, the biggest and most important studio in the world. Designers such as Cedric Gibbons (art direction) and Gilbert Adrian (costumes) created sumptuous worlds populated by elegant people—all of whom were photographed in shimmering, high-contrast black and white by such cameramen as William Daniels and Karl Freund. As film historian Ethan Mordden put it, MGM "stood for 'production values' generally and splendid pictures specifically." And the public responded. In 1934, the year before Stewart came on board, the studio earned a profit of $7.5 million, more than the rest of the Big Eight combined.

The studio was located in Culver City to the southwest of Hollywood. It was vast, with twenty-three soundstages and an extensive backlot composed of blocks of fully decorated false-fronted buildings representing different times and places. Virtually all feature filming took place here, on the studio's 117 acres; location shooting for any but the rare exception lay far in the future. MGM's payroll in 1934 included some four thousand employees, from publicists to carpenters, electricians to editors, dance coaches to research librarians, and security guards to makeup artists—the entire spectrum of people needed to produce moving pictures. There were also sixty-one stars and featured players.

If the producers were Metro's backbone, the stars were its heart, for, more than any other studio, MGM centered its features around its high-powered talent. By the time of Stewart's arrival, the roster included Greta Garbo, Norma Shearer, Jean Harlow, Joan Crawford, Marie Dressler, Myrna Loy, Clark Gable, Wallace Beery, William Powell, Robert Montgomery, Lionel Barrymore, Laurel and Hardy, the Marx Brothers, Johnny Weissmuller, and juveniles Jackie Cooper and Mickey Rooney. To Mayer, these men and women were family. He was the paterfamilias and they his slightly backward children.

One of the newest members of the clan would become one of its most important and enduring. In June of 1935, Spencer Tracy, after several unhappy years as a Fox contract player, was making his first feature as a Metro star. Called *The Murder Man,* this modest film cast him as a crackerjack homicide reporter driven by personal demons.

Billy Grady had Stewart in mind for the role of an eager second-stringer who works for the same newspaper. As Jim remembered it, Grady took him to meet the film's producer, Harry Rapf, but Rapf rejected him because the character's name was Shorty, and he wanted to cast the role with an actor of appropriate physical stature. Only after the producer considered the irony of a tall string bean playing a fellow with such a nickname did he change his mind. According to Grady—whose recollection was probably more accurate than Stewart's—Jimmy was still in Pennsylvania when the idea of casting him in *The Murder Man* was raised. Rapf's negative reaction was the same in both accounts, only in this version, he didn't change his mind. Rather, Grady took his case to the picture's director and coscreenwriter, Tim Whelan. "Whelan and I always did see eye to eye on talent," Grady asserted, so the director approved the casting and promised to pacify Rapf. Billy then phoned Jim in Indiana—where he found the young man mowing the lawn—and told him the good news. "He let out a whoop," the casting director recalled, "and dropped the mower and two days later was at the studio."

Two days seems unlikely, for Stewart took a train to the coast. Fonda, alerted to the good news, insisted that Jim bring the model airplane they'd been working on the previous winter. In the interim, Jim had finished the craft and painted it. To protect it from mishap en route, he folded back the wings and transported it in a wooden case built especially for the occasion by one of his dad's employees. "The only trouble was the case looked exactly like a machine gun," said Stewart. "It was quite a trick, sleeping with it in the upper berth of a Pullman. The conductors kept saying, 'What do you have in that thing?' Everyone was trying to figure it out." When Jim arrived in Pasadena on June 8, 1935, Fonda was at the station. According to Jimmy, "Where's the airplane?" was all that Hank wanted to know.

MGM signed Stewart to a standard seven-year contract. That did not mean, however, that he was guaranteed employment for the life of the agreement. Annual option renewals allowed the studio to keep him or drop him as it wished. But the first review came after only three months. If Stewart did not impress Mayer, Thalberg, and the other Metro executives in very short order, he would be out.

By this point, Jim had appeared in eight Broadway shows in less than three years. He had worked with such skilled directors as George Abbott and Guthrie McClintic and such seasoned actors as Judith Anderson, Blanche Yurka, and Osgood Perkins. With their help and inspiration, he'd managed to refine his raw talent to an impressive degree, although he was still far from the polished pro he would become. But no matter how much stage experience one has, film acting demands an enormous adjustment. In the theater, everything is larger than life, so that the actor can be seen and heard at the back of the house. The movie screen, by contrast, projects an image so enormous that the actor must pare everything down to its essence, for even the blink of an eye or the slightest grin can convey considerable emotion when seen at such outsize dimensions. Moreover, in the theater, the principal technical demand is the ability to re-create the character's onstage experience eight times a week for as long as a show runs and behave as though each time were the first. In movies, that skill gives way to the ability to find one's designated camera positions—"marks" in industry parlance—without appearing to do so, and to reach the emotional state of a character out of context, for economics dictate that the vast majority of pictures be shot in a nonsequential fashion. One might enter a building on one day and come through the other side of the door three weeks later, but the audience must see the transition as seamless. Even veterans with years of stage experience need time to adjust to the medium's demands, especially with dozens of technicians working as they try to emote. Stewart was lucky. In his first time at bat, he had Spencer Tracy, one of the most gifted actors in cinema history, to ease the transition. One day, the veteran, eight years older than Stewart and with twenty-three features already to his credit, took the novice aside and said, "Take it easy, Jim. You're not onstage. Don't let the acting show." He specifically mentioned

Stewart's gait, observing, "Your legs seem to be too stiff as you walk around. See what you can do about it."

"The kindness he showed me was unbelievable," Jimmy would recall. He added, "I could see that he was making a great effort to help me, yet never did he make me feel uncomfortable about it. He tried to get me to feel at ease in doing it my way, to give me the idea that I should not get worried about how I would do the lines or how I would act, since I had been signed by MGM to do it naturally, as myself. This was wonderful guidance from a man everyone respected as among the greatest actors in Hollywood."

For his part, Spencer liked the kid and respected his desire to do well. In typical fashion, he minimized his contributions to Stewart's screen debut, saying, "I told him to forget the camera was there. That was all he needed; in his very first scene he showed he had all the good things."

Thinking back to Osgood Perkins' mastery of props, Stewart used the hat that he was given in *The Murder Man* to help define Shorty. As he said later, the snap-brim fedora "didn't fit my personality, but did fit the character I portrayed." By pushing it back off the top of his head and wearing it at all times, he fostered the impression of a jaunty, perhaps even cocky, young reporter, one who was always ready to dash off in pursuit of a fast-breaking story.

The Murder Man was shot in a mere three weeks and released to theaters by the end of July 1935. Most of the critics recognized it for what it was, a routine programmer, no better or worse than most such pictures, except for the presence of its star. As Thornton Delehanty of the *New York Post* put it, "It is the outstanding work of Spencer Tracy . . . that makes *Murder Man* worth seeing."

Stewart was largely ignored. He appeared in only half a dozen scenes and had fourteen lines. The *New York Herald-Tribune*, remembering his performance onstage in *Yellow Jack*, argued that he was "wasted in a bit" but added that he handled it "with characteristically engaging skill." Indeed, he appears far more comfortable before the camera in this feature than he did in *Art Trouble*. But Stewart hated the way he looked in the picture. "I was all hands and feet and didn't know what to do with either," he said later. Still, he kept the hat. Many actors are superstitious, and Stewart was no exception. He considered the fedora a good luck charm.

Picking up where they had left off in New York, Stewart and Fonda rented a house in Brentwood. Certainly, they could have afforded places of their own, but, as Jim explained at the time, "It's fun living like this and much cheaper. . . . We never bother to budget expenses, nor fuss over phone or laundry bills, we merely total all debts at the end of the month and divide it equally."

They were joined by Kent Smith and another original member of the University Players, Johnny Swope, who, at Fonda's suggestion, was trying his hand at assistant directing. Jim credited handsome, debonair Smith with their busy social life, saying in 1937, "That guy—he either knew everybody already or fixed it for himself within a day or two. Marvelous technique he's got, believe me. . . . Kent was appointed committee-of-one to get the girls we wanted over to the house, and that was all there was to it."

But Smith soon departed. If that didn't crimp Stewart's social life, the flea-infested bevy of wild cats in their backyard certainly did. The felines' "favorite meeting place was our rooftop," Jimmy recalled, "where they stalked back and forth, snarling at us." Fonda estimated that there were at least thirty of them. "Now I ask you," Hank later told Howard Teichmann. "Can you picture three grown men sitting around at home trying to tackle the problem of thirty to thirty-five cats? We'd be relaxing after work, drinking beer, and trying to think of the various ways of getting rid of 'em." They didn't want to kill the animals, just be free of them. But they couldn't get the ASPCA to remove them unless they were boxed, and the felines were too wild to be caught. Eventually, their neighbor, Greta Garbo, became so disgusted with the cats' yowling and mating rituals that she sold her house and moved away.

Garbo's departure badly disappointed the young actors, because they had been determined to meet her. The fence that she had previously erected to separate her property from theirs had proved only a minor obstacle. According to Stewart, they actually started tunneling under the fence but quit when they hit a water main. "It ain't true," Fonda asserted in 1980. "It's Jimmy's story, and he likes to tell it. We really just sat around and . . . talked a lot about it, but we never did it." Later, in his autobiography, Fonda amended the denial, saying that, although he didn't recall the incident, it "might have happened," but quickly added, "Of course, what Stewart doesn't remember he invents."

With his three months nearly up, Jim began to fret about his contract. He hadn't really done much to impress anybody, he wrote his folks, so the studio might drop him. His sister Ginny wrote back, "If they take up your option, Jim, please send me a record for my new Victrola." Several weeks later, she received a package in the mail. "I tore it open," she recalled, "discovering not one but dozens of records—Bing Crosby and Ray Noble, Richard Wagner and Bach! Coming home that evening, Dad heard blocks away the *Ride of the Valkyrie* booming triumphantly."

Slightly more pedestrian music resounded in her brother's ears—for, as his second picture, Metro had assigned him a small role in its big new musical, *Rose Marie*.

The operetta, which had opened in New York on September 2, 1924, had been an enormous stage success, racking up 577 performances to become the longest-running musical in Broadway history to that point (a record eclipsed by *Show Boat* several years later). With music by Rudolf Friml and book and lyrics by Oscar Hammerstein II and Otto Harbach, *Rose Marie* was lush and colorful and, for its time, well crafted. The plot centered around a stalwart young woman—the title character—who falls in love with a dashing Mountie in the rugged Canadian Rockies around the turn of the century.

MGM developed a completely new story line for its lavish production, retaining only the original setting, several of the best-loved songs—including the title tune and the oft-parodied "Indian Love Call"—and the fact that a young woman named Rose Marie falls in love with a handsome Mountie. The new story was set in the present, with the heroine a talented but temperamental opera diva. When she learns that her beloved brother, Jack, has escaped from prison after his incarceration for armed robbery and has subsequently killed a policeman, she determines to help him leave the country. En route to his remote hideout, she falls in love with a charming Mountie, not knowing that he's been assigned to capture her brother.

To play the willful diva and the resolute policeman, producer Hunt Stromberg cast Jeanette MacDonald and Nelson Eddy, the stars of the recently released, surprisingly successful Victor Herbert operetta *Naughty Marietta*. *Rose Marie* thus became the second in the couple's long collaboration. Stewart was to play the brother, the escaped convict. All but unnoticed in a bit—as one of the opera star's rich, young suitors—was future Oscar winner David Niven.

In a departure from the norm, much of *Rose Marie* was filmed on location, around Lake Tahoe in northern California, starting on September 6, 1935. At the helm was the director of *Naughty Marietta*, W. S. Van Dyke.

By 1935, Van Dyke was Metro's highest-paid director. And no wonder. He saved the studio a fortune with his no-nonsense manner and efficient way of working. His nickname, One Take Woody, would suggest a man of little style or vision, but Van Dyke was no hack. "The reckless pace at which I work," he once explained, "has a little more behind it than mere desire to get through and save money." He believed that shooting swiftly, with minimal rehearsals and few retakes, gave a crispness to the final product and preserved the spontaneity of the actors' initial impulses. Working on a Van Dyke picture was far from boring. The director possessed a lively sense of humor and enjoyed the occasional practical joke.

Van Dyke took a liking to Stewart. He thought, after viewing *The Murder Man*, that the newcomer had genuine star potential. Moreover, Jim's easy, unpretentious manner and self-deprecating sense of humor complemented Woody's own style. He may not have been as enthusiastic about the youngster's musicianship. One day, while still on location, the company was watching dailies at the local movie house in nearby Truckee, and the director was disturbed by the sound of Stewart playing rinky-tink piano music behind the screen.

According to MacDonald and Eddy's dual biographer, Sharon Rich, Van Dyke was so fond of Jimmy that he kept him on the picture for three weeks instead of the designated three days. It is hard to imagine what he would have had the actor do in that time, since the role was minor. In the final cut, Stewart is seen for the first time after the picture has been running for nearly ninety minutes (not counting his headshot on wanted posters). He appears outside his hideout, frantic over the unexpected arrival of his sister and her guide. The siblings then go into the cabin for a brief reunion, which is interrupted by Eddy, who places Stewart in handcuffs and leads him away. As they depart on horseback, MacDonald, realizing that her relationship with Eddy is over, reprises "Indian Love Call," but receives no reply. Sympathizing with the Mountie's torment, Stewart tries to mask his fears about his own future. On that note, seven minutes after his first appearance, he is gone from the screen.

Not a very well drawn character, Jack is at once a hardened criminal— a murderer as well as an armed robber—and a beloved younger brother, but the audience learns nothing about him except these bare facts and certainly never sees his dangerous side. According to Eddy, the script originally called for the Mountie to fight with the fugitive before putting the cuffs on him, but in the final version, Jack goes meekly when taken by surprise. Perhaps Van Dyke realized that Stewart would be hard to accept as a die-hard tough guy. Within a few years, casting him as a villain would be unthinkable, but in this, his second film role, no one, including Stewart himself, had yet discovered the strengths—and limits—of his screen persona.

Viewing the film today, one can see his inexperience as a screen actor, particularly in a key moment just before Eddy arrives. Seated on the edge of a bed, with MacDonald kneeling beside him, the camera over her shoulder, he talks about going to China to build a new life. But instead of looking at the actress—and by extension, the camera—he looks down to examine the pouch of money she'd given him a moment earlier. He thereby blows an important close-up, his first in the picture.

He is more effective in the final moment of the sequence, as he rides beside Eddy, trying to appear brave. "Wal, this isn't going to be so bad," he says. "At least it'll be something new. I always did like something new." In that moment, one grasps the vulnerability of the man, thanks to the ability of the actor to delve beneath the surface level of the dialogue.

It didn't hurt Stewart to be associated with a hit—which *Rose Marie* became upon its release at the end of January 1936. William Boehnel of the *New York World-Telegram* summed up the critical response, writing, "Handsome, lavishly staged, imaginative, *Rose Marie* is a gaily romantic and rhapsodically tuneful piece of work." And moviegoers agreed, making it the eighth top moneymaker of the year.

For Stewart, the best thing about *Rose Marie* was that it helped him win his first major film role, as Christopher Tyler, the dedicated foreign correspondent married to an actress in Universal's *Next Time We Love*. Based on the story "Say Goodbye Again" by Ursula Parrott, the melodrama traced the relationship of a married couple—Chris being the husband—over nearly a decade. As their careers drive them apart, they must repeatedly choose between divorce or staying together but living alone.

Stewart's sequence in the operetta gave him decent footage to show, but with the picture's release some months away, it would have gone unseen by *Next Time*'s producer Paul Kohner and director Edward H. Griffith had it not been for Margaret Sullavan, who was to play Cicely Tyler, the journalist's wife. In the four years since Stewart had met her at Princeton, Maggie had become a highly successful movie star, with four pictures to her credit.

A chance encounter between the two on Hollywood Boulevard had made Sullavan—or Peggy, as Stewart and his friends called her—think of Jimmy for the picture. Thereafter, she sprang into action, singing his praises to the Universal executives—who had never heard of him. She described him as a highly talented actor with years of Broadway experience whom MGM was carefully nurturing in small roles. She cited his contribution to *Rose Marie* as an example.

She also introduced Jim to Edward Griffith. Without question, Stewart fit the director's concept of the role, which he later described as a "young all-American Princeton type with no Delsarte overtones." However, studio head Carl Laemmle "envisioned the film in the middle-European manner," to quote Griffith, "and had already signed Francis Lederer, a handsome Czechoslovakian, with his charming accent, for the lead." Eventually, Laemmle relented, allowing Griffith to make the picture as he wished—which included casting Stewart. Of course, MGM had to approve the loanout, but that proved to be no problem.

By the time the decision had been made, Jimmy was back at Lake Tahoe, this time on vacation. When Griffith sent him a telegram with the good news, Jim scoffed, thinking Fonda, Logan, or one of his other friends was pulling his leg. It took two more, increasingly urgent, telegrams to convince him to report to Universal City for work.

He started filming on October 21, 1935. Nervous in his first major movie role and still adjusting to the new medium, he was awkward and ineffective in the early stages of production, prompting Griffith, a former actor who'd been directing pictures since 1917, to lose patience with him. Behind the scenes, the director told Sullavan that he thought the novice was going to ruin the movie, but Maggie expressed complete confidence in her friend. Meanwhile, she doggedly coached Jim in the evenings, helping him to work economically and encouraging him to ignore the director's gibes. As the shooting progressed, the after-hours sessions began to pay off, and finally, when Stewart nailed a particularly difficult scene, even Griffith was impressed.

Beyond her efforts as coach, Sullavan contributed to Jim's growth through her own performance. "When you'd play a scene with her," Stewart later told her daughter, Brooke Hayward, "you were never quite sure, although she was always letter-perfect in her words, exactly what was going to happen. She just had you off guard a little bit and she also had the director a little off guard, and later I found that this is one of the most valuable things that pictures could have because it takes away the clamp, the technical aspect of movies, and it gives a spontaneity. I've always called what your mother would do planned improvisation. . . . It's a very rare thing."

In succeeding years, Griffith was fond of saying, "It was Maggie Sullavan who made Jimmy a star!" Even Billy Grady, the man who had brought Stewart to Hollywood, acknowledged her contribution, telling Sullavan's biographer Lawrence Quirk, "That boy came back from Universal so changed I hardly recognized him. In his next few pictures at MGM he showed a confidence, a command of film technique that was startling. Sullavan had taught him to march to his own drummer, to be himself, completely—and in doing that she had released the unique and distinctive qualities that made James Stewart one of the greatest of film stars."

Many of those who knew Stewart and Sullavan—including her children—believe that he was deeply in love with her. His former roommate Kent Smith, who, of course, knew Maggie well from the University Players, said, "He never fooled me, from the beginning. He was totally in love with her. He basked in the attention she gave him in her anxiety to see him succeed in films. And the role gave him a chance to articulate emotions toward her that had not been possible up to then in real life."

There was, indeed, much to like and admire about Virginia-born Margaret Sullavan. She was not classically beautiful, but she was tiny with pixielike features, great charm, and undeniable sensuality. She also had a quick wit, a sharp mind, and an equally sharp tongue—a classic Southern belle who knew how to flirt and keep men interested. "Peggy was Scarlett O'Hara before Margaret Mitchell even dreamed of her," Henry Fonda, her first husband, said years later.

At the time of the making of *Next Time We Love*, Sullavan was the wife of director William Wyler, and Stewart was not the kind to play around with a married woman. But even if she had been free—as, in fact, she soon was, for she and Wyler divorced in March of 1936—it is highly doubtful that she and Stewart would have become romantically involved. As her daughter Brooke Hayward observes, "It could not have worked. I don't think my mother could have conceivably been in love with Jimmy. So maybe that was part of the attraction for him." In other words, he could enjoy the romantic illusion without any risk. Consequently, he would hold her up as a prototype for years, telling fan-magazine reporter Edith Driscoll, "I'll never marry until I find a girl exactly like Margaret Sullavan." Even decades later, he was still talking about her. According to David Karp, the creator of *Hawkins*, Stewart's 1973–74 television series, "We never discussed an actress where he didn't say, 'Oh, Maggie could do this so beautifully.' I would take a guess that that was the love of his life."

As for Sullavan, she enjoyed Jim's obvious affection. Again to quote Brooke Hayward, "She liked having him around. And she kind of owned him. And that's the way she felt about things; she was a very possessive woman." But Myron McCormick, another University Players alum, distinguished between Sullavan's relationship with Jimmy and her associations with other fellows. "Oddly, her attitude toward him was never predatory," he told Lawrence Quirk. "She was protective, loving, maternal. She wasn't usually like this with men."

Thanks to Maggie, Stewart had found his way through the melodramatic hurdles of *Next Time We Love*'s plot. He was particularly effective in the later scenes when, as a dying older man, he delivered his lines with a simple honesty, showing none of the gestures or verbal tics that later circumscribed his screen persona. The makeup department, however, could not disguise his very young facial features.

But Jim faced one more obstacle before the picture wrapped. One day during filming, he went home for lunch, taking with him the old brown hat that he wore in the picture. Without thinking, he tossed it on the living-room sofa—where it quickly became lunch for Fonda's new German shepherd puppy, Son. "Naturally I was scared to death," Stewart said a few months later. "I had visions of countless retakes that would cost the studio thousands of dollars, and I was sure they'd fire me. Anyway, I got another hat and cut some of the brim off—it didn't look a bit like the old one, but I kept fingering the brim and fussing with it and they never found out."

Next Time We Love wrapped on December 21, only two days behind schedule. It was released about six weeks later, virtually concurrently with *Rose Marie*. A few of the critics found it weak and overly melodramatic, but most agreed with Eileen Creelman of the *New York Sun*, who called it "a grand picture for women to cry over and generally enjoy themselves. . . . Also one of those pictures [that] doesn't bear too much thinking about afterward. . . . The harsh breath of reality does not belong here." All except *Variety* found the acting first-rate, with Regina Crewe of the *New York American* calling Stewart "convincingly earnest and genuine," and Bland Johaneson of the *New York Daily Mirror* naming him "the most convincing newspaperman the screen has yet presented." Thornton Delehanty of the *New York Evening Post* went so far as to claim the picture's "chief value is that it affords Mr. Stewart, in his first important screen role, a chance to show a temper and ability which matches him with the best of the juveniles." But the picture really belonged to Sullavan, who was billed alone above the title.

MGM managed to squeeze a performance out of its contract player while he was making *Next Time We Love* at Universal. Jim took three days off to play the boyfriend of Jean Harlow in *Wife v. Secretary*, a frothy melodrama that starred Clark Gable as a rich but unpretentious magazine publisher and Myrna Loy as the wife who comes to think he's having an affair with his secretary, Helen "Whitey" White, the role played by Harlow.

As Stewart's shooting schedule would suggest, his screen appearance was brief, consisting of a total of five scenes—none involving Gable or Loy. Moreover, his was rather a thankless role, placing him as the secretary's earnest young alternative to her charismatic, ebullient boss. But he had one well-orchestrated scene. Having broken a date with him to take some papers to her boss' penthouse, Harlow returns home early in the morning to find him outside her apartment building, asleep in his car. After listening to her talk about her boss' party, he tells her how he managed to win a salary increase out of his own employer and then tries to convince her to quit her job and settle down with him.

Those familiar with Stewart's later patented drawl and stutter would be surprised to find him handling two lengthy speeches in the scene with nary a hesitation. Most importantly, he strikes just the right note to suggest an amiable young man who is mystified by his girlfriend's all-consuming passion for her job—an approach far more effective than resorting to petulance or anger, the more obvious choices. He also appears quite comfortable with Harlow, then one of Hollywood's hottest sex symbols.

The blond bombshell's role represented a major departure from her usual screen sirens. Whitey is every bit as smart and personable as her boss, and Harlow brought a striking air of dignity to the part. Stewart was impressed. "She was just wonderful," he recalled. "I don't know what 'glamour' means, but she had it." As one who would always have to struggle with lines, he was awed by her memory, saying, "She could look at a page of dialogue and just *do* it, with every word exactly as written." Their big scene ended with a kiss, and he duly noted his partner's skill on that front as well. When they rehearsed the scene, he recalled, "she took charge of the kissing. It was then I knew that I'd never really been kissed before. There were six rehearsals, thank you, and the kissing gained each time in interest and enthusiasm. By the time we shot the scene, my psychology was all wrinkled. I'll always remember Jean Harlow as being warm, lively, and wonderfully constructed. . . . All of Jean's dresses were tight, and she wore nothing under them."

Wife v. Secretary also introduced Stewart to another of MGM's most dependable directors, Clarence Brown, "a roly-poly little fellow," as one columnist called him, who had been at the helm of three of Garbo's most celebrated pictures, *The Flesh and the Devil, Anna Christie*, and *Anna Karenina.* Looking back many decades later on his work with Brown in *Wife v. Secretary*, Stewart said, "It was a wonderful beginning and groundwork for me. He showed me the importance of a look, the importance of a movement—a visual saying of a line. I learned from watching Clarence, and I watched him all day long."

Wife v. Secretary opened in New York at the end of February, just a few weeks after *Rose Marie* and *Next Time We Love.* The critics found the sappy story far less electrifying than Stewart's previous two films—or, for that matter, the earlier pairings of Gable and Harlow, especially *Red Dust.* But many applauded the acting, especially the sexy siren for her startling departure from type. Moreover, the production was given MGM's usual glossy sheen, Brown's direction was crisp as usual, and as Eileen Creelman of the *New York Sun* put it, in "its own expensive and trivial way, the picture is often funny and usually fun"—all of which helped make *Wife v. Secretary* the eleventh-biggest hit of the year.

SIX

Hollywood Bachelor

By early 1936, the cats had finally won the battle of Brentwood, forcing Jimmy, Hank, and Johnny Swope to move. They and Josh Logan rented another house in the same community—on Carmelina Street—and decided to throw a housewarming party. Logan was then working for producer Walter Wanger, who was testing a group of stunning models for a picture called *Vogues*. Wanger saw the party as a chance to give the young ladies a respite, so he offered to provide the refreshments as long as the boys agreed to restrict the female guests to his models, to invite two handsome, single guys for every girl, and to keep the press away. Logan consulted Jim, Hank, and Johnny, who, in Josh's words, "fell over themselves approving" Wanger's terms. As one of the eligible bachelors, they invited Warners tough guy Humphrey Bogart, still several years away from superstardom.

On the night of the party, escorts in white tie and tails picked up the models and brought them to the house. The young ladies were indeed lovely, but, according to Logan, so prim and proper that they would only drink lemonade and play games like charades and musical chairs. Stewart, in a throwback to his days as a magician's assistant, performed a few card tricks—all of which prompted Logan to later assert, "It was perhaps the most innocent evening any of us had spent since we were adolescents." Bogart, who had been hoping to get at least one of the ladies into bed, was more direct. After the models went home, he told his hosts, "Anybody that would stick a cock into one of those girls would throw a rock through a Rembrandt."

Although he didn't get lucky with any of Wanger's charges, Jimmy was thoroughly enjoying himself as a young, single man in Hollywood. For the first time in his life, he had the money and freedom to date as he wished. Moreover, the town was full of women who were not averse to being squired around by a polite, attractive, amiable, if somewhat quiet, movie actor. Fonda shared Jim's enthusiasm. "I guess you could say we were swingers then—but most young unmarried guys are," Stewart later said with a hint of embarrassment, adding, "Hollywood was a great place for a bachelor in the early thirties. This was a swingin' place." Their favorite nightspots were the Trocadero and the Coconut Grove. According to Stewart, the clubs "stayed open all night, and the most famous people just got up and performed. Mary and Jack Benny, George Burns and Gracie Allen, Red Skelton, and I remember one night Judy Garland's mother brought her. Judy wore pigtails and bobby sox and she sang for an hour. Absolutely terrific!" Indeed, the movie industry in the heyday of the studio system was like a club, and outsiders were, to quote Carole Lombard, "civilians." Stewart basked in what he called the "camaraderie."

Ginger Rogers was among the first women that Jimmy dated in Los Angeles. In 1936, she was a far bigger star than he, having already made thirty features, including several in her celebrated partnership with Fred Astaire (*The Gay Divorcee* and *Top Hat* among them). But like Jim, who was three years older, she hailed from a small town, Independence, Missouri, and had launched her career on the New York stage.

On one of their dates, Rogers fixed up Fonda with her friend and fellow RKO actress Lucille Ball. After dinner at the Brentwood house—with Fonda doing the cooking—the foursome went dancing at the Coconut Grove. Jim and Hank must have been good company, because years later Ball remembered the occasion as "a hilarious, wonderful evening." It came to an end at a small place on Sunset Boulevard called Barney's Beanery.

In her autobiography, Rogers recalled another date with Stewart, this one in the spring of 1936. She and a group of friends decided to have a progressive dinner party; that is, each course would be served at a different participant's home with a rented bus carrying the group from venue to venue. Rogers was assigned the soup course. But her house in Coldwater Canyon was then only half finished. Thus, when the guests arrived, she and Jimmy handed out flashlights—there was no electricity yet—and led the way past the carpenters' work areas to the rented dining tables arranged on a makeshift floor. "There were no walls," Rogers concluded, "but who cared; the food was good, the company was good, and the view was splendid."

It is doubtful that Stewart and Rogers were more than amiable companions. Jim was having too good a time to fall hard for anyone. Unlike many in Hollywood, where divorce was uncommonly common, he considered marriage a serious commitment and didn't intend to rush into anything. In one of his first major Hollywood interviews—for *Photoplay* in August 1936—he told reporter Warren Reeve, "When I'm crazy enough about any girl to ask her to marry me, then she's going to be more important to me than anyone else in the world. It won't matter if she wants to live in a penthouse and throw parties all night, or if she wants to have a house in the country and raise ten kids—it will be alright with me. Anything she says will be law." Besides, Jim was ambivalent in his choice of female companions: he was attracted to flashy women, but he wanted to marry someone refined and dignified like his mother. In show business, it was easier to find the former.

Then, too, there was his crush on Maggie Sullavan. Wrote her biographer Lawrence Quirk, "Both [Billy] Grady and [MGM executive Eddie] Mannix told me in later years that they always felt the true reason Stewart began dating all over town, and with the loveliest unattached screen ladies, was because he was trying to get Sullavan out of his system and of course he hoped to find someone whose appeal equaled hers."

He wasn't short of willing candidates. As Fonda later said, "He was always totally hooked. Women wanted to—I don't know how to say this—mother him. They were the aggressors. They showered *him* with flowers."

Another of Jimmy's companions from this period was Barbara Stanwyck—who was struck by the actor's fun-loving nature. On one of their dates, they attended a late-afternoon soiree. At six o'clock, the affair's designated conclusion, she prepared to depart, but Jimmy protested, saying, "I'm having a swell time." When she reminded him that they were expected to leave at that point, he implored, "Aw, come on, let's stay and be a problem." After that, Stanwyck called him "the problem child." Shortly thereafter she told a fan-magazine reporter, "Gee, he's crazy."

Stewart also had fun at home. After Fonda was given a sixteen-millimeter motion-picture camera as a gift, he, Jim, Logan, and Swope became the stars, writers, and directors of their own productions. Stewart recalled that, in one of these home movies, he was cast as the villain. For his death scene, Fonda insisted upon covering him in something that looked like blood. They eventually settled on beet juice—which worked fine for the film, but infected Jim's sinuses. The next day, when he visited his doctor, he had a difficult time explaining how such an incongruous liquid ended up in his nasal passages.

Hank's home movies are still owned by the Fonda family. His son, Peter, says that some of them capture the roommates enjoying one of their favorite games—"killing babies." The macabre idea was for each participant to act out a zany, inventive way of committing infanticide. Peter cites one instance in which someone pantomimes driving a car with an imaginary crying baby on his lap. The driver "puts" the infant's head out the open window, presumably to soothe the child. Then he cranks the window up. "It's really sick," says Fonda, laughing, "but it's extraordinarily funny." Peter also remembers a mini-comedy in which Stewart played a Fuller Brush salesman, and another in which Jim was an overly enthusiastic aviator. For the latter, the roommates were on the roof of their house, with Stewart sporting a helmet and goggles. As he starts to flap his arms in anticipation of flight, Hank and Johnny Swope gesture him away from the edge of the roof, but Stewart pays no attention. "And, of course, the next shot," says Peter, "is him falling to the ground."

Such adventures didn't cease entirely after September of 1936, but they became less frequent—for, in that month, Fonda remarried. Jim, Johnny, and Josh let Hank and his new wife, Frances, keep the house on Carmelina Street, and they moved into a place nearby on Evanston. One of their neighbors was Margaret Sullavan, who married Leland Hayward in November of that year. A onetime reporter and publicist for United Artists, Hayward was among the most powerful agents in the business, with a client list that ranged from Greta Garbo to Fred Astaire to Boris Karloff, as well as writers Ernest Hemingway, Lillian Hellman, and Dashiell Hammett. After Stewart's original agent, Leah Salisbury, sold her firm to Hayward, Leland represented Jim, too—along with Fonda, Logan, and of course Sullavan. Stewart would later tell Leland's daughter Brooke, "I think he was probably one of the best agents that's ever been. . . . I think he had a great feeling for the theater and acting, great taste and judgment, nobody like that now."

The Hayward place, more sumptuous than the one rented by Stewart, Swope, and Logan, became the weekend hangout. As Brooke Hayward wrote in her best-selling family memoir, *Haywire*, "Our house was the perpetual headquarters for activity of any kind, riotous badminton matches or card games—hearts was a house favorite, since Mother always won—diving exhibitions in the swimming pool or roller-skating down the middle of San Vincente Boulevard, and the central participants were usually the same: Johnny Swope, Jimmy Stewart, Martha and Roger Edens, the Herman Mankiewiczs, the Wrights, and sometimes the Hank Fonda and Eddie Knopf clans from down the street."[1] Logan joined in, too, until he returned to the New York stage in 1938.

Jimmy relished the chance to be around Sullavan; she liked being with him as well—although in a more platonic fashion. When Hayward was away on business, which was often, she could enjoy Jim's sweet adoration and not feel lonely. Moreover, as actor Walter Pidgeon put it, Stewart's love for her "enhanced her feelings about herself as a woman, and gave her a feeling of—well, power is the best word I can come up with."

Jim was fond of Maggie's handsome, literate, and witty husband as well. They had much in common. Like Stewart, Hayward was a Princeton graduate, a gentleman, and passionate about aviation.

By 1936, Stewart had already learned to fly, having earned his pilot's license and purchased a small plane almost as soon as time and his MGM

---

[1] The Wrights were screenwriter Bill and his wife, Greta. Knopf was the head of MGM's scenario department and later became a producer.

salary permitted him to do so. Flying gave him a feeling that he found nowhere else. As he explained many years later, "There's no other place I feel as relaxed and at the same time exhilarated. You're like a bird up there. It's almost as if you're not a part of society any more. All you can think about is what you're doing, and you have a complete escape from all your worldly problems." Flying also gave him, in his words, "a feeling of real power . . . that we can completely be in command of an amazing machine, that we do have some control over our destiny."

In Leland, Stewart found a fellow air show devotee and even a racing partner. Jim fondly remembered the time he served as Hayward's copilot in the annual race between Los Angeles and Cleveland sponsored by Ruth Chatterton. That year, 1937, Leland's Waco was one of about twelve aircraft entered in the event. Because all of the planes were small, with limited ranges, the contestants took three days to make the journey, stopping in the evenings at hotels along the way. For most of the race, Hayward and Stewart led the field. Then, about 150 miles outside of Cleveland, the Waco developed engine trouble, and they were forced to land. After making the necessary adjustments, they took to the air again, but left the plane's door open. Going back for the resultant debris caused their defeat. Still, as Jimmy later told Brooke Hayward, "it was a great trip."

By the time Stewart was winging over Ohio, he had several more films to his credit. In the studio era, journeymen actors quickly went from movie to movie to movie; appearing in a half dozen or more a year was not uncommon. This system served both the players, who were able to amass considerable experience quickly and who only drew salaries when working, and their employers, who needed them for the more than three hundred features that they collectively pumped into the marketplace each year.

Small Town Girl, Stewart's first film after *Next Time We Love*, went into production at MGM on December 26, 1935, only five days after the Universal picture wrapped. Once again Jim was cast as the earnest romantic alternative to a dashing leading man. This time he was Elmer, the awkward but sincere boyfriend of a shop assistant played by the picture's wistful star, Janet Gaynor. Bored by her small-town life, she runs off with and, in a thoughtless moment, marries a dashing doctor—thereby setting off a sudsy romantic triangle with her husband's former fiancée, a big-city socialite, as the third party. Paired with Gaynor was handsome Robert Taylor, who had been signed by Metro at roughly the same time as Stewart.

Released in April of 1936, *Small Town Girl* was predictable but slickly produced and entertaining, with solid direction from William Wellman and good chemistry between the two stars. Despite his thankless role, Stewart was singled out by *Daily Variety*, which noted that he had "a small but well played part" and by Richard Watts Jr. of the *New York Herald-Tribune*. Although Watts confused Jim with Taylor, thereby dubbing him Robert Stewart, he nevertheless found him "excellent."

After *Small Town Girl*, Stewart was loaned to Metro's short-subject unit for *Important News*, in which he was the bespectacled apprentice of a crusading small-town newspaper editor played by Chic Sales, the star of a series of shorts for the studio. These mini-features, established in the mid-1930s, helped fill the bill in the Loew's theater chain and, at the same time, gave newcomers such as Stewart and Taylor additional experience when not otherwise engaged.

Finally, the studio tapped Jim for a major part, although in decidedly minor fare. *Speed* was designed quite simply to take advantage of the public fascination with automobile racing in the wake of the new speed record set by Malcolm Campbell on September 3, 1935. After arranging to use Chrysler's cars, testing facilities, and equipment, Metro assigned one of its contract directors, Edwin L. Marin, to the project, and by November, only two months after Campbell's feat, a crew was in Detroit, shooting background footage. The project then languished for some months while Marin worked on another picture. When he was free, in March of 1936, principal photography for *Speed* began, with Stewart in the leading role.

Stewart played Terry Martin, a daredevil mechanic for Emery Motors. Poor but bright and ambitious, Martin invents a new stream-lined carburetor but is too proud to ask the company for help in ironing out the kinks. Thanks to the firm's pretty new publicist (Wendy Barrie)— who turns out to be the company owner's niece—he gets the needed help, with his car setting a new world speed record along the way.

As if the plot weren't flimsy enough, Marin's directing was sluggish— the picture seems slow even at a mere seventy-two minutes—and the supporting cast was decidedly third-rate. Considerable use was made of the Detroit footage, giving car buffs an inside look at a major automobile manufacturing plant, but its insertion into the plot seemed contrived and its effect more like a documentary than part of a drama. Metro also used stock footage of the Indianapolis 500, with Stewart's car and that of another competitor shot in process photography against footage of an actual race.[2] Even by the standards of the times, the result lacked credibility.

If anything redeemed *Speed*, it was Stewart's performance as a first-time

---

[2] Process photography is the filming of people, objects, or other elements against previously shot footage, which is concurrently projected behind them through a transparent screen.

top-billed actor. One can see more clearly than in any of his previous films the early stirrings of his screen persona. There are the technical facets: the drawl is more pronounced, and he begins to slur the ends of some sentences, all of which contribute to the naturalism of his speech; the overemphasis on operative words, as in "You've *got* to give me another chance" and "You'll be carrying your teeth around in a *matchbox*"; and his dialogue is punctuated with all-American boy-next-door expressions such as "Gee" and "That's swell."

Moreover *Speed* gave Jim his first real chance to explore the dimensions of an effective character: the eager beaver, the guy with the dream, the common man who's willing to fight the establishment to prove he's right, and also the somewhat boyish, easily hurt ladies' man whom women want to protect as well as love. But Terry Martin also had a dark side: as a result of his impoverished origins, he was overly suspicious of just about everyone, and most of the time his misgivings were misplaced. The only person he trusts in the whole picture is his daffy sidekick, broadly played by vaudevillian Ted Healy, formerly of Ted Healy and His Stooges (precursor of the Three Stooges). In the hands of another actor, the mechanic might have appeared a good deal more antiheroic.

Speed debuted at the Capitol Theatre in New York in mid-May, less than two months after shooting began and about a month after the release of *Small Town Girl.* Rose Pelswick of the *New York Evening Journal* called it a "neat little program offering," but the majority of her colleagues sided with Harold Barnes of the *New York Herald-Tribune*, who found *Speed* "a very ordinary Hollywood stencil."

Despite the picture's considerable flaws, Stewart's new star status didn't go unnoticed. Wrote Kate Cameron of the *New York Daily News,* "James Stewart has jumped to top billing in his fourth picture, which is *Speed* [actually, it was his sixth film, not counting *Art Trouble* and *Important News*]." She added, "That's pretty speedy work for young Mr. Stewart." The *New York Evening Post* called it "one of the swiftest rises to the top ranks in all film history."

Today, *Speed* is rightly forgotten. For Stewart, however, the picture remained memorable because of something Ted Healy said to him during shooting. Like many comics, Healy was always "on," but one day, in all seriousness, he told his young costar, "You may get along all right out here, but one thing you should always remember: Never treat the audience as customers, always treat them as partners. Always keep the audience in mind so they'll always keep you in mind." Stewart never forget that bit of advice, remaining remarkably open to fans and autograph seekers throughout his long career.

* * *

After giving Stewart top billing in a B picture, MGM wasted him in a class act, *The Gorgeous Hussy,* a lavish historical drama starring one of the queens of the lot, Joan Crawford, who wanted to try a departure from her usual modern-working-girl sagas.

Based on the novel by Samuel Hopkins Adams, *The Gorgeous Hussy* followed Peggy O'Neal, the daughter of a Washington, D.C., innkeeper, from spunky young lady to the worldly confidante of Andrew Jackson—and her subsequent exile from the corridors of power thanks to unfounded gossip about her relationship with the president and other important male friends.

The film's producer, Joseph L. Mankiewicz, surrounded Crawford with a handful of talented actors as her beaus, including Melvyn Douglas; Franchot Tone, then Crawford's real-life spouse; Robert Taylor; and Lionel Barrymore as Old Hickory himself. Stewart's part, Roderick "Rowdy" Dow, was pathetically pale by comparison to those of the others, especially Barrymore's. In an early scene, his proposal to Peggy is rejected, after which he becomes a supportive friend, appearing from time to time as a smiling figure in the background but having no real purpose in the story. It was Stewart's most insignificant role since Shorty in *The Murder Man.* Worse, the extended sideburns he had to wear in the costume drama were unflattering to his long, thin face.

Many actors would have railed at Metro for such poor casting, but not Jim. He was, in truth, the ideal studio contract player, perfectly content to go where Mayer and company sent him and do what he was told. In part, this attitude stemmed from his background and training: he made his Hollywood bosses extensions of Alex Stewart and Dr. Irvine, and he accorded them equivalent respect. As he said time and again throughout his life, "The movie moguls were some of the brightest, the most inventive and exhilarating people in the history of the business . . . the Warner brothers, Mayer, Zanuck . . . I thought they were tremendous leaders who loved the business and had an almost uncanny knowledge of what would be right for the audience."

Moreover, Stewart was never an overly ambitious person. He believed in hard work, but in the Calvinistic sense: labor was its own reward, and conversely, idle hands were the devil's playground. By that definition, he felt no need to stretch himself as an actor; doing his best with what he was given was enough. Indeed, that is what he thought he was being paid to do. "In the studio system," he said years later, "you came to work every day, whether you were doing a picture or not, and when a script was given to you, you played it. You didn't say: 'I don't care for that.'" But many actors, including Spencer Tracy, James Cagney, Bette Davis, and even occasionally genial Clark Gable, complained mightily when they were assigned a role or project they didn't like. Sometimes they even went on suspension until their employers found properties they deemed more suitable.

Given his belief in work for its own sake, Stewart thrived within the Metro system because there was always something to do, even when he wasn't assigned to a picture. He appeared in screen tests, for example, saying years later, "I must have done five hundred of them—always with only the back of my head showing." He studied with the studio's voice coach and met with the studio publicists—who had a tough time with someone so noncommunicative. Whenever they asked if anything had happened to him that would make a good story, he invariably replied, "Nope." As Burgess Meredith put it, "He was a press agent's nightmare."

Stewart also followed the regimen prescribed by the studio in an effort to add weight to his almost emaciated frame. He worked out three times a week with a private trainer and drank as many milk shakes as his stomach would hold. He also swallowed such unappetizing fare as whale blubber and shark oil, but none of it seemed to do much good.

Aside from the work ethic, he thrived at Metro because he believed that the studio was nurturing him, helping him secure his future. "There was no such thing as 'instant' fame in those days," he explained years later, "and we accepted the fact it took a lot of time and work to create a specific image and style and the qualities the studio regarded as star material." He credited MGM and its competitors with teaching him and his contemporaries "how to act, how to dress, how to behave, in general. By the time we had achieved stardom, we had been well prepared to carry out the responsibilities." He was also certain that the system offered the best way to make motion pictures. He loved the idea that on one soundstage a musical might be in production, next door young Mickey Rooney would be making one of his Andy Hardy pictures, and elsewhere on the lot the Marx Brothers were creating slapstick mayhem, two gunfighters were preparing for a Main Street showdown, and a melodrama was wending its way toward the villain's inevitable comeuppance.

But, for a small-town preppy such as Stewart, the very best thing about MGM was, in his words, "a sense of belonging." As in Indiana, Mercersburg, the Triangle Club, and the University Players, he felt as if he were part of a tight-knit family—and his "brothers" and "sisters" included the likes of Wallace Beery, the Barrymore brothers, young Judy Garland, and his favorite, Greta Garbo. Having missed his chance to meet the reclusive star when she lived next door, he hoped he would bump into her at the studio. And one day, he did—literally. It happened that Garbo was making a picture on the soundstage adjacent to the one on which Stewart was working. Typically, she arranged for her limousine to wait for her by the stage door, so no one outside of her cast and crew saw her. "But," as Stewart recalled, "I got to know the sound man on her set. And he told me he knew just how much time it took her to get from her dressing room on the set to the stage door. 'So I'll give you a call one of these days when we finish,' he told me, 'and maybe you'll be able to run out your door and get to see her before she gets into the limousine.' And, sure enough, a couple days later he called me. He said, 'Now hurry and hang up and go out your door because she's leaving.' And so I did. I had to go on the dead run to get to the end of the stage. And as I went around the corner to the door, I ran smack into somebody. But I wasn't going to let that stop me. I just kept running right out to the door, and as I was about to open it, I stopped and looked back. And there was Greta Garbo all right—flat on her ass."

He had better luck with Joan Crawford. "She was a very considerate and professional actress," Stewart said years later, "and a lady. I had only a very small part in that film, but she was extremely pleasant to me, and to everyone else, as far as I could see." She even contributed to his weight-gain program, feeding him hot Ovaltine twice a day in her portable dressing room. Apparently, that was all she did, for although Crawford had a penchant for bedding her leading men, there were no rumors of a relationship between her and Stewart. Of course, her husband's presence in the same picture might have been a persuasive deterrent to an extramarital romance.

Despite Mankiewicz's steady hand and Clarence Brown's experienced direction, *The Gorgeous Hussy* was a troubled production. Barrymore was cranky as a result of poor health, Tone hated his role, one only slightly more significant than Stewart's, and Crawford came to believe that she had made a mistake in opting for a historical drama. When released in September of 1936, the picture garnered respectable reviews and performed reasonably well at the box office, but thereafter the actress stuck to contemporary subjects.

As for Stewart, Metro took him from a small role in a period piece to a major one in a musical. No one could say that the studio was pigeonholing him. Of course, *Rose Marie* had been a musical, too, but in that film Stewart's role called for straight acting. In *Born to Dance*, he not only had to sing, he had to tap alongside such pros as his leading lady, Eleanor Powell, and former vaudevillian Buddy Ebsen.

Cole Porter, who wrote the score for the picture—his first directly for the screen—thought of casting Stewart in *Born to Dance* after a prior choice, singer Allan Jones, fell through. As noted in the extensive diary that he kept during the project, the composer suggested Jim to the film's executive producer, Sam Katz, who considered the idea "most interesting, if Stewart could sing." The next day Stewart went to Porter's house and auditioned. "He sings far from well," the composer noted, "although he has nice notes in his voice, but he could play the part perfectly."

The screenplay of *Born to Dance* was by Jack McGowan, Sid Silvers, and B. G. De Sylva, from an incomplete stage musical they had written four years earlier. It centered around three sailors (Stewart, Ebsen, and Silvers) and the girls they meet in port (Powell, Frances Langford, and Una Merkel). In Stewart's case, the young lady wants to be a dancer, and he helps her get her big break thanks to his involvement with a Broadway star (played by Virginia Bruce of *The Murder Man*) and her producer (Alan Dinehart). There are the usual misunderstandings and breakups along the way, but, of course, Powell becomes a success and winds up with Stewart before the final fade-out. Many of those associated with the production had been involved in Metro's 1935 smash *Broadway Melody of 1936*, which had marked Powell's screen debut. The alumni included Merkel, Silvers, Langford, Ebsen, and director Roy Del Ruth.

Porter was right about Stewart's suitability. The amiable, slightly naive sailor Ted Barker provided Jim with the ideal chance to refine the persona he'd begun developing in *Speed*, without any of Terry Martin's darker qualities. The tricky part of *Born to Dance* was the singing and the dancing, for he had a share of three numbers, including the lovely ballad "Easy to Love," one of two Porter classics introduced in the film (the other, "I've Got You Under My Skin," was sung to Stewart by Bruce in a slinky, art deco peignoir).

Jimmy worked hard to meet the production's musical demands. According to his cousin, John Stewart, who was visiting him at the time, "He'd get up about a quarter 'til six to take dancing lessons, go to the set for a day of shooting, then afterward take singing lessons. He'd come home about 7:30 every night totally exhausted and go straight to bed."

But, according to fan-magazine reporter Frank Small, Jim still found time for romance. Small asserted that Powell developed a crush on her leading man almost immediately. "And I have never seen a girl so completely in love," Small wrote in *Photoplay*, "as Eleanor on the day when she first told me about him—about the little tricks they played on each other on the set, about the way they went dancing together, about the way they had grown to know each other." Stewart was fond of Powell, Small maintained, but he was even more interested in Bruce, the former wife of silent-screen idol John Gilbert, and far more sophisticated than small-town Eleanor. Bruce, in turn, liked Stewart but "adored" Cesar Romero, whom she was also dating at the time. In the way of such things, the entanglements quickly faded away once the production wrapped.

Stewart was surprised at a preview of *Born to Dance* to hear someone else's voice coming out of his mouth during the musical numbers. "It was a fella who had a little bit of an English accent," he recalled. Afterward, his friend Roger Edens, who had arranged the songs for the picture, suggested to producer Jack Cummings that they replace the dubbed versions with the original tracks, and Cummings agreed. That proved a wise decision.

"Easy to Love" is not a simple song to sing. Indeed, it was initially written for Porter's Broadway musical *Anything Goes,* but was dropped when it proved ill-suited to the range of the show's star, William Gaxton. The difficulty stems from the melody's occasional jumps from midrange to high on the scale. For a nonprofessional, Stewart acquitted himself quite well, displaying a rather small but sweet tenor.

As for the rest of *Born to Dance,* it is creaky by modern standards, with corny jokes, overblown characters, such as the boys' captain, played by Raymond Walburn, and touches that have nothing to do with the plot or the main characters, including Reginald Gardiner's turn as a cop leading an imaginary symphony, a nightclub dance number by the team of George and Jalna, and Helen Troy's monologue as a switchboard operator (a precursor of Lily Tomlin's comic turns decades later). But, by the standards of the mid-1930s, the musical was, to quote *Variety,* "corking entertainment." And the critics were pleasantly surprised by Stewart's performance. As Kate Cameron of the *New York Daily News* put it, "Girls, he dances and sings as cleverly as he simulates a shy U.S. gob."

From its opening at the Capitol in New York on December 4, *Born to Dance* went on to become one of the big hits of 1936, ranking twenty-second in box-office receipts.

While Cole Porter instinctively knew a Jimmy Stewart role when he encountered one, Metro was not so adept at identifying the principal attributes of its contract player. "Two years after Stewart had been with the studio," recalled MGM portrait photographer Ted Allan, "we still didn't know what the hell to do with him. Was he a comedian, or a romantic leading man? We tried photographing him outside, leaning over fences, working with a shovel, with a tennis racket—but while that worked with Robert Taylor in helping to make him more athletic, it didn't work with Stewart. There was no problem in making him look handsome—he had great eyes and a generous mouth—but in the time I worked with him, I wouldn't have guessed he'd become a star." Even Stewart acknowledged the difficulty. As late as November of 1939, he was telling reporters, "In Hollywood, they seem to have a hard time deciding what I am. Sometimes they call me a 'character juvenile,' sometimes it's 'character lead,' sometimes it's just 'character.'"

It's easy to see the source of the confusion. On the one hand, Jim, who was twenty-eight when *Born to Dance* was in production, photographed far younger than his actual age. On film, he could easily pass for eighteen or twenty. His soft, high-pitched voice enhanced the impression, as did the puppy-dog enthusiasm that he frequently displayed on camera. At the same time, he was credible opposite the likes of Margaret Sullavan, Eleanor Powell, Wendy Barrie, and even Jean Harlow, and they were definitely women, not girls. He genuinely looked at and listened to his leading ladies and responded with such a quiet intimacy that his love scenes were moving, involving. Moreover, in films such as *Next Time We Love, Speed, Born to Dance,* and even *Wife v. Secretary,* he demonstrated the kind of screen chemistry that separated leading men from serviceable juveniles and character players. Admittedly, he was not matinee-idol handsome like Robert Taylor or a rugged, take-charge type like Spencer Tracy or a dashing, irrepressible ladies' man like Gable or Flynn, but he had something. And the public was beginning to recognize that. As gossip columnist Sheilah Graham noted in July of 1937, "There has never been a film star like him before. The nearest to approach him for figure and temperament is Gary Cooper. They are both too tall by screen acting standards. They are both real gentlemen. And they are both unbelievably simple and modest."

But MGM, with its substantial roster of leading men, was not overly concerned about identifying what made Stewart unique. For the time being, it was enough that he was a useful utility player, someone who could act the bumpkin in one picture, a genial, rich college boy in another, and an everyday guy with grit in a third. Sometimes the role was major, sometimes not. Perhaps MGM was too close to appreciate what it had. The studios that borrowed Stewart—Universal, Fox, and soon RKO and Columbia—used him in leading roles where Metro kept him in support. Indeed, it is fair to say that other studios made Stewart a star, not MGM.

The most extreme test of Stewart's malleability came with *The Good Earth,* based on the novel by Pearl Buck. "It seems this part of Chang they wanted me for," Stewart quipped years later, "was a Chinese who had survived a famine—I was the only actor in Hollywood who looked like he'd been through a famine." So Metro decided to test him for the part. He was given a bald cap to cover his long, dark hair. His eyelashes were trimmed, and his eyelids were recessed with spirit gum. To hide his height—few Chinese men are six foot three—he had to play a scene with the picture's star, Paul Muni, while standing in a ditch. Ultimately, Mayer realized the absurdity of this idea and hired a Chinese actor by the name of Ching wah-Lee for the role. But over the succeeding decades Stewart kept a framed photograph of himself in his *Good Earth* makeup.

His next two pictures, *After the Thin Man* and *Seventh Heaven,* truly tested his flexibility.

After the Thin Man reunited Jim with his *Rose Marie* director, W. S. Van Dyke. The picture, the second in an extremely popular series that ran through 1947, starred William Powell as a debonair detective, Nick Charles, and Myrna Loy as his wealthy, unflappable wife, Nora. The initial offering, *The Thin Man*, based on a novel by Dashiell Hammett and also directed by Van Dyke, had been one of the big hits of 1934. Although it was a genuine whodunit, the mystery took second place to the relationship between Nick and Nora. Audiences delighted in the couple's sumptuous lifestyle, their complete ease in every situation, and the clever banter between them. Indeed, the playing between Powell and Loy was so natural that many fans thought they were married in real life.

The Thin Man had not been conceived as the kickoff for a series, but the same screenwriters, Frances Goodrich and Albert Hackett, were assigned to the sequel. As Van Dyke explained, "It was not an easy task for them to grope back through three years of time to catch the same characteristic idioms, voiced by Bill and Myrna in the first story. Too, Bill and Myrna had grown three years older than the original Nick and Nora and had alienated themselves from those characterizations by many successive screen roles of varied interpretation, so it was necessary for them also to step back three years."

Although the opening credits placed Stewart just behind Powell and Loy, his role was not substantial. Periodically, as Nick and Nora go their urbane way, mixing detection with repartee, he pops up as wealthy David Graham. His scenes, which are quite brief, typically show him trying to aid his former fiancée, Selma (Elissa Landi), the chief suspect in the murder of her husband. Then, when the Charleses finally gather all of the people involved in the case in one room, he is revealed as the murderer. Cornered, he confesses that he committed the killing and framed Selma as revenge because she dumped him. Pulling out a pistol, he commands everyone to stay still, adding, "I've got six bullets in this gun, one for her, one for myself—yeah, one for myself—and the rest of them for anybody that tries to stop me." But he is quickly subdued.

The role of David Graham was the closest that Stewart ever came to genuine villainy, and he later said, "To be honest, I loved the part I played in *After the Thin Man*." His elation showed during principal photography, for as Myrna Loy remembered it, "He was very excited and enthusiastic about it all, rushing around with his camera taking pictures of everybody on the set, declaring, 'I'm going to marry Myrna Loy!'"

Later, he would look back on his performance in the climactic scene and say, "The audience laughed me off the screen." But that was not so. He was entirely credible as the disturbed young man. The fact is that confessional scenes—a stock device in mysteries and courtroom dramas—typically require such abrupt shifts in character that only the most skilled actors can truly make them work. Stewart was not yet in that league, but he was more than adequate—as the critics noted when the picture was released on Christmas Day, 1936. "James Stewart is calm and possessed until the blow-off when he does his best work," asserted *Variety*, to which Kate Cameron of the *New York Daily News* added, "The co-stars of the picture are ably assisted in the working out of the mystery by James Stewart, who has one grand scene in which he demonstrates most effectively that he is something more than a musical comedy juvenile."

After the Thin Man was an enormous hit—the sixth highest grossing film of the year. Clearly the public agreed with the *New York World-Telegram*, which proclaimed the picture "a sheer delight—an amusing, exciting, entertaining amalgamation of humor and melodrama that is nearly as good as its illustrious predecessor."

The same could not be said of 20th Century–Fox's *Seventh Heaven*, which opened at Radio City Music Hall exactly three months later.

Based on a 1922 play by Arnold Strong, *Seventh Heaven* told the tender story of Chico, an engaging, philosophical sewer worker in Paris shortly before the outbreak of World War I, and Diane, the mistreated prostitute whom he rescues and eventually comes to love. A 1927 film version of the drama had starred Janet Gaynor and Charles Farrell with Frank Borzage directing.

The remake was primarily a vehicle for Simone Simon, a twenty-five-year-old French actress then under contract to Fox (her first American pictures, *Girls' Dormitory* and *Ladies in Love*, had been released just a few months before *Seventh Heaven* went into production). Looking back, Simon says, "I think [studio chief Darryl F.] Zanuck had to give me that part because he couldn't find any other part of a French girl." She, in turn, asked for Stewart as her leading man, after the studio's own star, Tyrone Power, turned down the role. Zanuck assigned his favorite in-house director, Henry King, to the project.

For this loanout, the second of Stewart's career, Metro was paid $1,000 a week plus a bonus of $3,000 at the time of the actor's signing, double the amount the studio had garnered for Jim's services in *Next Time We Love* only fourteen months earlier.

Filming took place on the Fox lot between December 2, 1936, and January 26, 1937—and the finished product certainly looks as if it was shot on sets and before false-fronted buildings. King, who had started in Hollywood as an actor in 1912 and began directing three years later, seemed well suited to the project in theory, for he had a way with chivalrous romances. But somehow the relationship between Stewart and Simon never jelled. It wasn't for lack of work on Jim's part. As Simon recalls, "He was a very conscientious actor. He spent the whole day long rehearsing his lines, going up and down the stairs [to Chico and Diane's seventh-floor garret]. He had a lot of lines to say." But, as the actress added, "there was no contact between him and me. There was no contact between anybody during that picture. The only thing was when Jimmy spoke to Henry [King] together, they spoke about airplanes. They had one common love."

When *Seventh Heaven* opened on March 25, 1937, Bland Johaneson of the *New York Daily Mirror* called it "a moving romance" and the *New York Post* preferred it to the highly regarded original, but Frank S. Nugent of the *New York Times* more accurately found that most of the story's "charm and tenderness has been lost" and the production was as "static as can be." William Boehnel of the *New York World-Telegram* blamed Stewart for the film's lack of emotion, adding, "Fine actor that he is, he somehow fails almost entirely to suggest the gentleness that is inherently present beneath the character's gruff, charmingly conceited surface. He seldom manages to penetrate the obvious surfaces. Possibly Tyrone Power might have played the part as it should have been played." Boehnel's criticism is excessive. More accurate were *Newsweek*, which noted, "As Chico, James Stewart acts naturally enough—but always as James Stewart," and Eileen Creelman of the *New York Sun*, who pointed out, "Mr. Stewart neither looks nor sounds Parisian." The actor made so little an attempt at being French he even says "mamselle."

If anything, Simon's reviews were even more scathing than Stewart's, and one must wonder why. She brings a simple, striking beauty to the role and, at the same time, manages to evoke ample sympathy for the waif who finds strength through a decent man's love.

Looking back on the project, the actress says, "We were both as miscast as you can be. The girl should have been a poor little thing who is beaten every day by her sister. Janet Gaynor was perfect. She was small, she was tiny, she was fragile, like a little imp. Well, I am anything but an imp. I felt big and strong. . . . And the boy should have been a very strong, very handsome, very silly boy. And Jimmy is tall, not strong, not very athletic, and everything but silly."

SEVEN

Rising Star

If Shorty in *The Murder Man* had moved to San Francisco and gotten his own beat, he might well have become Paul North, the character Stewart played in his next film, *The Last Gangster.* Like Jim's first journalist, Paul is a dedicated newshound, but his interest in crime czar Joe Krozak, imprisoned for tax evasion à la Al Capone, soon gives way to his love for Krozak's immigrant wife, Talya (played by Viennese actress Rose Stradner in her American film debut), and her son (Douglas Scott).

Paul eventually marries the woman and adopts the boy. But the focus of *The Last Gangster* isn't on him, it's on the title character, played by Warners veteran tough guy Edward G. Robinson. Most contract players had little say about their loanouts to other studios, but Robinson was an exception. Unhappy with the scripts he was getting at Warners, he agreed to do the picture for MGM, a decision he later regretted. "Money was the overriding consideration, not art," he wrote in his autobiography. No doubt, the cultured star figured he'd played enough gangsters since his unforgettable portrayal of Enrico Bandello in 1930's *Little Caesar.* What distinguished Krozak from most such roles was his love for his boy, and Robinson's extended sequence with Scott late in the picture set *The Last Gangster* apart from many of the genre's offerings.

If anyone had reason for complaint it was second-billed Stewart, who didn't appear until halfway into the film. Worse, his character was essentially a stock nice guy with scenes of little consequence. For him, the biggest challenge was to age ten years during the final third of the picture. To help him look older, the studio makeup men gave him a pencil-thin mustache, something of a throwback to his look in *Spanish Blades* at Princeton. "It was the darnedest thing," Stewart recalled. "One day the mustache would be slanted down, sort of like Fu Manchu. The next day it would point upward. I don't know why, but it never seemed to look the same."

When *The Last Gangster* was released at the end of 1937, Robinson garnered well-earned praise for his sensitive, controlled performance. His costars were less fortunate. As Archer Winsten put it in the *New York Post,* "James Stewart and Rose Stradner do as well as could be expected in colorless roles." Moreover, the picture seemed a throwback to an outmoded genre. By the late 1930s, with Prohibition over and most big-time racketeers either dead or in prison, gangster stories were simply no longer relevant.

Stewart made three more movies in 1937. In the next two, *Navy Blue and Gold* and *Of Human Hearts*, he played college boys—his first such roles on film—and in the third, *Vivacious Lady*, he graduated to professor.

As with *The Last Gangster, Of Human Hearts*, the second of the two projects, found Jim billed behind an older, highly experienced actor—in this case, Walter Huston. Huston was Ethan Wilkins, an admirable, morally upright, but rigid preacher on the Ohio frontier in the 1840s and 1850s. Stewart played his son, Jason, who is driven to pursue a financially rewarding career as a doctor after a youth of poverty and self-denial. As in *The Last Gangster*, Jim didn't appear until the second half of the picture. Before that, a talented child actor named Gene Reynolds played Jason.

The project was a labor of love for MGM's dependable director Clarence Brown. Brown had acquired the rights to the original story "Benefits Forgot" by Honore Morrow, then waited until he could convince the studio to let him do it. His success with Eugene O'Neill's slice of Americana *Ah, Wilderness*, released in 1935, did the trick.

Benefits Forgot, as the picture was initially called, was shot primarily at Lake Arrowhead, a popular resort area northeast of San Bernardino, California, starting on October 18, 1937. There, Cedric Gibbons' wizards erected a frontier town with about fifty buildings, cornfields and cabbage patches, a wharf, and even a steamboat. Stewart, Huston, and the other members of the company stayed at the local lodge. Early each morning, they were ferried across the lake to the production area, where they worked until sunset. They then returned to the lodge to eat and watch the previous day's rushes—which were brought up from Los Angeles. By nine o'clock, they were in bed. As one studio publicist quipped, "The return to the studio seemed like a vacation after the trip."

Stewart's best scenes took place late in the picture. Having graduated from medical school and distinguished himself as a battlefield surgeon during the Civil War, he is called to the White House. There, John Carradine, playing Abraham Lincoln, chastises him for neglecting his mother (she had written to the president thinking her son is dead). Filled with remorse, the thoughtless young man purchases the horse he forced her to sell to pay for his uniform and takes the beloved animal back to her meager home.

Curiously, in light of Stewart's already growing reputation as the all-American boy, *Of Human Hearts* was his first family drama. But it would not be his last. Nor would it be his final pairing with Beulah Bondi, who played his mother in the picture (she had previously appeared as Rachel

Jackson in *The Gorgeous Hussy,* but she and Stewart had had no scenes together in that project). She would portray Stewart's mother again in *Vivacious Lady, Mr. Smith Goes to Washington,* and *It's a Wonderful Life.* In 1970, Stewart would even pull her out of retirement to play his mother in an episode of his TV sitcom, *The Jimmy Stewart Show.* But she was never better than she was in *Of Human Hearts.* Her simple, good-hearted woman, torn between a stubborn husband and a callow son, provided the picture's solid core.

Of Human Hearts premiered in February 1938 in Greenville, South Carolina, the hometown of seventeen-year-old Roy Harris. It was Harris who had come up with the title for the picture—in a contest sponsored for that purpose by the studio. Clarence Brown was highly pleased with his film, considering it one of his best. Most of the critics agreed, praising the picture's accomplished performances, elaborate production values, and many rich vignettes of frontier life. Probably the best notice came from William Boehnel of the *New York World-Telegram,* who wrote, "What might have been in less experienced hands than those of Director Clarence Brown a sloppily sentimental story of wayward youth turns out to be under his knowing and imaginative direction a film full of warming satisfaction and deep, tender charm. It is easily the most genuinely moving, tender and pathetic photoplay of the season." But, beyond its many redeeming qualities, *Of Human Hearts* was somber and slow moving, and it never caught on with the public.

By a strange coincidence, Stewart's other college-boy picture of 1937, *Navy Blue and Gold,* shot just before *Of Human Hearts,* also featured him as a young man living with the consequences of his father's career. In this case, Jim was a cadet at Annapolis—once his own college of choice. His dad, a naval commander, had been court-martialed years earlier for dereliction of duty. At a climactic moment in the film, the young man, known to his classmates as "Truck" Cross, reveals his true identity, John Carter, and offers a ringing defense of his father. It is by far the best scene in the picture and arguably Stewart's strongest work on film to date.

Otherwise, *Navy Blue and Gold,* directed by Sam Wood, is a pleasant, undemanding picture, one in a long line of college films that mix hazing from upperclassmen, gridiron showdowns, and romances between handsome, cocky guys and pretty, spunky gals. Costarring with Stewart were Robert Young and Tom Brown as his roommates and Florence Rice as the young lady who ultimately captures his warm, shy heart.

Navy Blue and Gold opened at the Capitol in New York on December 23, 1937, where it was properly perceived as "welcome holiday fare" by

Kate Cameron of the *New York Daily News,* "a heart-warming picture" by Archer Winsten of the *New York Post,* and "entertaining, fresh and imaginative" by William Boehnel of the *New York World-Telegram.*

Six days before the premiere of *Navy Blue and Gold,* Stewart reported to RKO for *Vivacious Lady,* costarring Ginger Rogers, his final picture of 1937. Actually, the film had gone into production months earlier, on April 17, but had had to shut down ten days later because Stewart fell ill. The malady was never specified, but it must have been serious because Jim later told Hollywood reporter Gloria Hall that he had had to be hospitalized and had lost quite a lot of weight before he recovered. RKO first announced that it would replace its leading man, but abandoned the project instead. Then, after Rogers' success in another nonmusical, *Stage Door, Vivacious Lady* was resurrected. Stewart, in good health once more, was again on tap.

Stewart's casting in this romantic comedy proved a stroke of good fortune, because he was ideal for his role as Peter Morgan, a sheltered botany professor who falls in love with Francey Brent, a New York nightclub singer, then pretends they're not married until he can break the news to his stuffy father and sickly mother—a daunting task. Indeed, in *Vivacious Lady* Jim gave the clearest delineation yet of the persona that he would make his own: the shy boy-man who, for all his fumbling, knows exactly who he is without being brash or overly confident, and who can be counted on to do the right thing at the crucial moment.

Moreover, he shared top billing with Rogers, who was proving to be a gifted comic actress as well as a glamorous dance partner for Fred Astaire. And his director was George Stevens, the best craftsman that he had worked with to that point in his career. A former child actor and cinematographer, Stevens was already on his way to becoming one of the titans of the industry—his credits would ultimately include *Gunga Din, Shane, A Place in the Sun,* and *Giant* (he received Oscars for the last two). Stevens had already directed Rogers in one of her pairings with Astaire, *Swing Time.*

Many years later, Stewart recalled how prepared Stevens was before each day's shooting. "But," the star added, "he would draw us together on a scene and say, 'Now go ahead and go through the lines, or plan, and feel how you [want to do it]—or where you want to move.'" He also found the director picking up on little things that he and Ginger did unconsciously in rehearsal, making sure that the fruitful discoveries didn't get lost when shooting began.

Stevens believed that pictures were more important than dialogue. Stewart explained, "The fewer words to get the humor, the fewer words to tell the story, the fewer words necessary to get what effect he wanted on the screen, the better." Under such tutelage, Stewart furthered his ability to convey attitudes, emotions, and thoughts with a look or a change in body language. As a result, he argued, the exchanges between Ginger and him came across as "believable conversation between two people."

Stevens, in turn, credited Stewart with much of the character's credibility, telling writer-director Peter Bogdanovich, "No-ow to overcome disbelief is the most *diff*icult thing to do in films. And Jimmy with this extra*ooor*dinary earnestness he had, just walked in and *extinguished* disbelief." Of course, it didn't hurt that Jim and Ginger were simpatico, onscreen and off. As she later put it, the two of them shared "the same ridiculous sense of humor."

Because of Stevens' methodology, Stewart's developing skill as an actor, and the social relationship between the leads, the scenes between Jim and Ginger in *Vivacious Lady* are marvelously free and humorous, and at the same time, fraught with sexual tension. Particularly memorable is the couple's tryst in Francey's girls-only apartment room. There, both husband and wife—their relationship still unconsummated—try to make the willful Murphy bed fall to the floor, without seeming to do so, by banging doors and slamming drawers. Years later Rogers remembered the Murphy bed sequence, saying, "Well, this was a darling idea, and this was George['s]. Subtle, sweet, and it told much more than torrid love scenes would tell, I think." She added that she and Stewart had "a field day" with the bit.

There was also an absolutely wonderful fight scene between Rogers and Frances Mercer as Stewart's fiancée, with Francey repeatedly slapping the stuffy young woman and then shushing her before she can scream. Before the eyes of the dumbfounded Stewart and his parents (Charles Coburn and Beulah Bondi), the battle escalates into something of a wrestling match that ends when Rogers tosses Mercer to the floor.

But, for all Stevens' planned spontaneity, the camaraderie on the set, and the picture's ultimately charming episodes, *Vivacious Lady* had a troubled production period, with extensive rewriting causing delays in filming. When the picture finally wrapped, on March 5, 1938, the production was a month behind schedule—a considerable amount of time in the late 1930s, when entire movies were shot in four or five weeks.

The picture opened three months later, on June 2, 1938, following *The Adventures of Robin Hood* with Errol Flynn and Olivia de Havilland into Radio City Music Hall. The flimsiness of the plot was not lost on the critics, but they raved about the comedy anyway. Rose Pelswick caught the sense of her colleagues' views when she wrote in the *New York Journal American* that *Vivacious Lady* was "not only elegant entertainment, but also a welcome departure from the crack-brained concoctions that have been passing for comedy of late. For this one, instead of depending upon wild-eyed gags, gets its laughs from genuinely funny situations that arise from the action and become a part of it." She added, "Mr. Stewart checks in with a grand performance."

As mentioned earlier, columnist Sheilah Graham noted in 1937 that Stewart was reminiscent of a young Gary Cooper. Both actors were tall, shy, and could play rural types as well as reserved members of the upper class. The two actors even became close friends. "They saw each other often," recalls Cooper's daughter, Maria Janis. "He and Jimmy enjoyed the out-doors, hunting and fishing and that sort of thing." But, as she points out, "They weren't social-butterfly kind of people." Cooper, like Stewart, was a man of few words. That never seemed to bother Jim, who was amazingly comfortable in companionable silence—evidenced not only by his rela-tionship with Cooper but by his friendships with several other introverts, including Henry Fonda. That doesn't mean that he and Hank or he and Coop had no fun. Says Janis, "I think that the context in which they were together became the focal point. If they were off hunting and fishing, there was a lot of guy camaraderie based upon all the stuff that goes along with that. I'm sure there was a lot of horsing around and jokes." Ultimately, she says, Jim and her dad were friends because "something in their natures resonated with each other. What that was I think was a sense of dig-nity, class, taste, simplicity. You know, non-ego-consumed people."

By mid-1937, the comparison between Stewart and Cooper, then a far bigger star, finally dawned on MGM. The New York Times reported on July 1 of that year, "Believing that in James Stewart they have a property comparable to Gary Cooper, Metro is to launch him on a new career as one of the screen's strong and silent men." The first project in this makeover was to be Western, Bad Man of Brimstone, in which he would play Wallace Beery's son. But ultimately Dennis O'Keefe was cast, and Stewart's new persona never got off the ground—at least not at Metro in the 1930s. Instead, Stewart took on a role that Coop himself had played in a partial talkie released in 1929, costarring Nancy Carroll and Paul Lukas. Called The Shopworn Angel, it was based on Dana Burnett's story "Private Pettigrew's Girl," which was published in the Saturday Evening Post in 1918. A silent version of the melodrama, bearing the title of the story, had been released in 1919 with Ethel Clayton and Monte Blue.

Stewart played a young man caught up in the turmoil of World War I. Pvt. Bill Pettigrew is a total rube, a Texas cowboy who falls in love with a jaded showgirl when his outfit is stationed outside New York City on its way to France in the spring of 1917. His simple ways inspire the girl,

Daisy Heath, and her business manager to fall in love, but they sacrifice their happiness for the sake of the young man bound for war.

The remake, which began filming on March 28, 1938, was produced by *The Gorgeous Hussy*'s Joseph Mankiewicz, who saw it as a vehicle for his favorite leading lady, Joan Crawford. When she turned down the role of Daisy, Mankiewicz cast Margaret Sullavan, who had distinguished herself in his previous film, *Three Comrades,* the first project in her new multi-picture deal with Metro (she earned an Academy Award nomination for her performance). Unlike Crawford, Sullavan had no singing voice, so her number in the picture, "Pack Up Your Troubles," was dubbed—by a then unknown named Mary Martin. The role of the business manager went to Walter Pidgeon.

To direct, Mankiewicz chose H. C. Potter, who had, in fact, just directed Gary Cooper in *The Cowboy and the Lady,* another story about people of contrasting social and geographical backgrounds. But, where *The Cowboy and the Lady* was a comedy, *The Shopworn Angel* was a melodrama—and a rather heavy-handed one at that. Metro, with its preference for wholesome family entertainment, made the original material more sappy by turning a sexual triangle into a case of youthful adoration on the part of the young man and awakening love on the part of the other two.[1] The characters were also softened. As *Variety* noted upon the picture's release, "Instead of the cool schemer played by Nancy Carroll, the chorine is now generous and warm-hearted. Her shadiness is merely implied, and instead of falling for the blundering soldier, she feels a sort of motherly affection for him. The girl's lover is no longer the menace of the earlier version, but is now the typical Walter Pidgeon man-who-doesn't-get-the-girl." As a result, the reviewer concluded, "the present version seems a softer one, without the stark edges of the original." It took skilled acting from the principals to make the material work, and Stewart, Sullavan, and Pidgeon were up to the task.

Of course, Stewart could draw on his real feelings for Sullavan, a fact that didn't escape Pidgeon's notice. "It was so obvious he was in love with her," the distinguished actor later said. "He came absolutely alive in his scenes with her, playing with a conviction and a deep sincerity I never knew him to summon away from her."

But Stewart also had his own evolving technique as a guide. What he had learned from George Stevens about the value of actions over words could be seen repeatedly in his performance as Bill Pettigrew. There is, for example, an early scene in which the doughboy watches another soldier

---

[1] The Cooper-Carroll version had been produced by Paramount, then Coop's home studio.

say good-bye to a soda-fountain waitress. Stewart enviously gazes at the couple while sucking on his soda straws without realizing that they're no longer in his drinking glass. It's a nice bit, funny and wistful. Later, when Daisy drags him away from the same counter, he repeatedly glances back at his unconsumed beverage, suggesting the cowboy's agony over the waste. Then, too, there is Stewart's comically rigid body language when his army pals drag him to the stage door so they can meet Daisy, whom he's been trying to pass off as his girlfriend even though he barely knows her at the time.

Arguably Stewart's most adept piece of acting in the picture comes in his first scene with Sullavan, when the actress sarcastically tries to convince him that there are cows roaming around Manhattan. He conveys Bill's uncertainty over this story; he thinks she's pulling his leg, but he's not entirely sure. The performance is slightly exaggerated, as he carries his emerging bag of tricks—the hangdog look, the gangling height, the deliberate way of speaking—just a little beyond the norm. The result is a stereotypical yet believably ingenuous country boy. He also lets his own slight drawl substitute for a genuine Texas accent. Having learned as far back as *Journey By Night* in New York that he was not very skilled with dialects, he avoided them whenever possible throughout his career.

Of considerable help to both Jim and Maggie was Hank Potter, a former Broadway director with four prior pictures to his credit (he would go on to direct *The Story of Irene and Vernon Castle*, *Mr. Lucky*, *The Farmer's Daughter*, and *Mr. Blandings Builds His Dream House*). Like his stars, Potter was a veteran of the burgeoning summer stock movement. Said Stewart in 1973, "We were old friends from the summer theater days . . . and we had a lovely time [making the picture]."

Stewart and Sullavan continued to socialize during their off-hours. By the time *The Shopworn Angel* was in production, she and Leland had already had their first child, Brooke, with another daughter, Bridget, arriving in 1939 (their son, William, would be born in 1941). Far from detracting from the allure of the Hayward household, the presence of the children—to whom Jim was godfather, along with Johnny Swope and Roger Edens—only enhanced the appeal. "See, Jimmy didn't have any responsibilities for us," Brooke Hayward explains. "So he could have a very carefree relationship with us as children. We were around, and we were adorable, I suppose, but we weren't his problem." For Swope, who had developed an interest in photography (he would soon turn professional), the Hayward kids became favorite pictorial subjects as well. Jim was more inclined to read to them or tell them stories. "Both had a sense of humor," Hayward recalls, "and we adored them. We considered them to be older children. That's the way they treated us. They were children."

Stewart was also godfather—along with Swope and Josh Logan—to Hank Fonda's kids. Jane, like Brooke, was born in 1937, and Peter, like Bridget, was born in 1939. As with the Haywards, the Fonda youngsters were important figures in Stewart's life. "Jane and I were surrogate children," Peter Fonda recalls. "When Jimmy was at our house and Dad wasn't, it was like having Dad there, because the two of them [were so much alike]."

Every so often, Stewart would feel a pang of regret at being single. Once, at a dinner party at the Fondas', he cast his eye over Hank's brood and said, "That's just what I want in life, a family like that." Late in 1937, he even confessed to a Hollywood reporter, Gloria Hall, that bachelorhood was full of drawbacks, adding, "Some of 'em give you a kind of an ache of missing things, of time passing and cheating as it passes. For instance, I want a home. I want a home of my own and want it badly. I want to build me a house, design it, be my own architect. . . . I want to have my own furniture. I want to hang my hat on my own hatrack. I want to have my own garden and books and things. I'd like the feeling of walking on solid earth and being able to say, 'This is mine.' I'm a possessive cuss at heart. But as a bachelor, I don't dare to strike roots. I might build me a Georgian mansion and then turn around and marry a girl who wouldn't be happy in anything but a Mediterranean type villa. The result is, I don't build. I don't settle down. I don't have anything permanent or satisfying or mine own."

After Logan returned to New York in 1938, only Stewart and Swope were left in the house on Evanston Street. Swope was, to quote Peter Fonda, "more outgoing" than Stewart, and, for that matter, Hank. Says Peter, "He would be like a spokesman when they didn't want to speak." Born in New Brunswick, New Jersey, Swope was a year younger than Jimmy and came from wealth. His father was Gerard Swope, president of General Electric, and his uncle was John Bayard Swope, a celebrated reporter and editor.

Although Stewart occasionally regretted his single status, he mostly enjoyed himself. While *The Shopworn Angel* was in production, he was dating Norma Shearer, the widow of Irving Thalberg, Metro's youthful production chief who had died of pneumonia in 1936. She and Jim met in April, at the annual costume party thrown by newspaper magnate William Randolph Hearst and actress Marion Davies. Shearer came as Marie Antoinette, who she was then playing on film at MGM, and Stewart, perhaps in memory of *Bad Man of Brimstone,* was sporting cowboy gear. "In a moment of alcoholic gallantry," Logan recalled in his autobiography, Jim told Norma that she was "the most gorgeous creature he had ever seen."

The actress was bowled over. After all, Stewart was seven years younger than she and a rising star. Shearer had never been conventionally pretty. Moreover, by 1938, her career was in decline. After *Marie Antoinette*, she would make only four more pictures.

In the wake of the Davies costume party, Stewart and Shearer became an item. According to Mickey Rooney, who had an affair with the actress a couple of years later, "Jimmy gave Norma what she wanted: proof that she was still young, beautiful, and desirable. But that wasn't enough for her. She also wanted Jimmy to play a more public role, as her beau." That made Stewart highly uncomfortable, and he fought to maintain his independence. Once, for example, she gave him a lavish gold cigarette case, sprinkled with diamonds, and then asked for cigarettes when they were in public to call attention to the gift—and by extension, her intimacy with its owner. He would invariably respond by producing a package of Lucky Strikes—"his badge as a free man," to quote Logan.

She also gave Stewart a more enduring gift, an English setter puppy named Boy. Jim's longtime housekeeper, a formidable woman named Daisy Dooley, claimed that she was allergic to dogs and refused to allow the puppy in the house. "There was a shouting argument, which I won," Stewart recalled. "The dog stayed, and so did Daisy." Eventually, the housekeeper and Boy became the best of friends. Said Jim, "I was given to understand that I mustn't bother my dog. He sat in the kitchen with Daisy. As a favor to me, Daisy would let Boy into the dining room for a few minutes. I was allowed to pat his head. Then she'd say, 'Come, Boy,' and he'd run back to her."

By that point, Norma Shearer was but a memory; the affair lasted a mere six weeks.

The Shopworn Angel opened in July of 1938 to good reviews. While a few of the critics found the material dated, most agreed with William Boehnel of the *New York World-Telegram* that the picture was "definitely superior entertainment." There was universal acclaim for Sullavan, who convincingly managed the difficult transition from selfish, opinionated bitch at the outset of the film to warm, self-sacrificing woman by the end. Not everyone was as impressed with Stewart. Bland Johaneson of the *New York Daily Mirror* likened him to the skinny slapstick comic Stan Laurel, and *Variety* found his performance unfocused, an extension of his professor in *Vivacious Lady*. By contrast, Irene Thier argued in the *New York Post* that Pettigrew was "just another proof that this young man is one of the finest actors of the screen's younger roster," and Kate Cameron of the *New York Daily News* found him "ideal as the naive and charming boy from Texas."

L. B. Mayer himself was thrilled with the chemistry between the two stars. "Why, they're red-hot when they get in front of a camera," he told his associates after a screening of *The Shopworn Angel*. "I don't know what the hell it is, but it sure jumps off the screen." He ordered more pictures pairing Stewart and Sullavan. It would take sixteen months from the release of *The Shopworn Angel* for Mayer's dictum to be executed. By then, Jim was among the hottest stars in Hollywood.

The climb to superstardom started with the picture right after *The Shopworn Angel*. It was called *You Can't Take It With You*.

The Pulitzer Prize–winning comedy by George S. Kaufman and Moss Hart—their third collaboration after *Once in a Lifetime* and *Merrily We Roll Along*—was Harry Cohn's gift to Frank Capra. Columbia's mogul and his star director had been feuding since Capra's previous picture, *Lost Horizon*, had nearly bankrupted the studio. It was only when Capra, the biggest moneymaker on the lot despite the extravagance of *Lost Horizon*, brought suit to get out of his contract that peace was restored. Cohn agreed to double Frank's salary, then quickly sought a new property for his breadwinner.

Capra had caught *You Can't Take It With You* when he was in New York for the opening of *Lost Horizon* and had fallen in love. The problem was that the play's producer, Sam Harris, wanted $200,000 for the screen rights. In 1938, no studio had paid even close to that amount for a stage play. Cohn, hardly one of Hollywood's big spenders, was outraged. "I wouldn't shell out two hundred G's for the second coming!" he told Capra. In the end, however, the mogul acceded to Harris' terms just hours before Mayer could buy the property for the far richer MGM. At least Cohn had the satisfaction of besting L.B.

The acquisition was announced on January 18, 1938. By that point, *You Can't Take It With You* had been running on Broadway for more than a year, having opened to rave reviews on December 14, 1936. The comedy centered around the Vanderhof-Sycamore family, whose eccentric members are bent on following their own zany whims. The mother writes unproduced plays. Her husband makes fireworks in the basement. And one of her daughters perpetually practices ballet on point. Although the idea for a family-oriented play had been Hart's, the characters in *You Can't Take It With You* were primarily inspired by Kaufman's relatives. His father, Joe, was the prototype for the leader of the clan, Grandpa Vanderhof, portrayed onstage by Henry Travers (who would later play the angel Clarence in *It's a Wonderful Life*).

While Capra didn't intend to slight Grandpa, he was particularly attracted to a relatively minor character in the play, Wall Street tycoon Anthony Kirby Sr., whose likable young son, Tony, falls in love with the only normal member of the Vanderhof-Sycamore clan, Alice. The impact of the couple's disparate families on their romance provides what passes for a plot in the play.

Capra decided to dramatically enlarge Kirby's role for the film, creating a story line in which the tycoon seeks to acquire the Vanderhof home as part of a plan to control the nation's munitions industry. His all-consuming ambition and greed stand in marked contrast to Grandpa's laissez-faire approach to life, and their dialogues serve as the spine of the film. Thus, Capra turned a family comedy, in which a middle-class girl seeks the approval of her upper-class in-laws-to-be, into a celebration of the wisdom of the common man over the dictates of big business. Along the way, Capra reminds his filmgoers to cherish one another. He had already preached this gospel in the likes of *It Happened One Night* and *Mr. Deeds Goes to Town*—which had earned him Best Directing Oscars in 1934 and 1936, respectively. A native of Palermo, Sicily, who grew up in California, where his father worked as an orange picker, Capra was a true believer in the American dream. The old-fashioned values that he honored in his popular modern-day fables came to be known as Capra-corn.

To make the Kaufman and Hart comedy his own, the director worked closely with his alter ego, screenwriter Robert Riskin, who had also written *It Happened One Night, Mr. Deeds, Lost Horizon,* and several other Capra pictures. By the time they finished, they had fashioned something almost entirely new, with only about 25 percent of the original comedy remaining.

To play Kirby senior—the most important role in the film, in Capra's opinion—the director chose Edward Arnold, a rotund character actor who had portrayed another tycoon, Diamond Jim Brady, in *Diamond Jim* in 1935. "Arnold had the power and presence of a J. P. Morgan," Capra wrote in his autobiography. "He could be as unctuous as a funeral director, or as cold and ruthless as a Cosa Nostra chief. Furthermore, he had a laugh as unique and phony as a three-dollar bill." Thereafter, Arnold would become the director's favorite villain.

For Grandpa, the director needed an actor of considerable power, someone who could hold his own against Arnold. He found his man in Lionel Barrymore, even though the fifty-nine-year-old star was so crippled by arthritis that he had to do the role on crutches (a cast was put on his foot and he explained in an early scene that he had tripped over something and fallen down some stairs). For Alice, the female love interest, Capra reached out to the leading lady of *Mr. Deeds*, Columbia contract player Jean Arthur, but she nearly lost the part because she was feuding with Cohn at the time.

Finally, for her leading man, he went to Metro. "I had seen Jimmy Stewart play a sensitive, heart-grabbing role in MGM's *Navy Blue and Gold*," Capra wrote in his autobiography. "I sensed the character and rock-ribbed honesty of a Gary Cooper [who had starred in Capra's *Mr. Deeds*], plus the breeding and intelligence of an ivy league idealist. One might believe that young Stewart could reject his father's patrimony—a kingdom in Wall Street." The chance to work with one of the preeminent directors of the day, a two-time Oscar winner, on a picture of such importance was a tremendous opportunity for Jimmy.

They started filming on the Columbia lot on April 26, 1938. There, five hundred workmen had labored for two months to create the folksy neighborhood jeopardized by Kirby's ambitions.

In contrast to Metro, where filming tended to take place under rather cold, austere conditions, Capra ran a loose, informal set. Many of his technicians traveled with him from picture to picture, bringing a family-like aura to the process. With no one peering over his shoulder—Cohn gave Capra free rein—the director approached each day's work in relaxed good humor. "One of the things I loved about Capra," says Ann Miller, who played the aspiring ballerina, Essie, "was that he never screamed at people. When he wanted to correct something or somebody did something wrong, he'd always call them over to the corner and talked to them very quietly. He was such a gentleman." Capra's diplomacy was particularly useful when dealing with Jean Arthur, who was somewhat neurotic and high-strung, and whose face, far more attractive from some angles than others, was not the easiest to shoot.

Stewart was impressed by Capra's preproduction preparation and commitment to the picture's themes. Still, the director's vision allowed actors ample room to define their characters. Soundman Ed Bernds, one of Capra's longtime associates, explains, "He had a great way of working by indirection, by talking about the thing, joking. There would be a lot of laughs in rehearsals. He would seldom tell an actor what not to do. And he had a favorite saying, 'Every speech is the last one.' What he meant by that was that in real life the guy talking to you [says his piece and figures he's done]. What it did was cause actors to listen to what was being said, which is part of a good acting job. You'd see them formulating their reply; it wasn't just a line in a script. And maybe be a little impatient to jump in [when someone else was talking]." Because of Frank's style and manner, Stewart told the director's biographer Joseph McBride, "I just had complete confidence in Frank Capra. I always had, from the very first day I worked with him. . . . I just hung on every word Frank Capra said."

Not that Stewart's role in *You Can't Take It With You* was particularly demanding. Tony is basically a sweet, uncomplicated fellow who simply doesn't want to be a big shot like his father—an attitude made manifest in the first scene of the picture when Tony tries to stifle a yawn as Kirby Senior unveils his latest scheme to his minions. In many respects, the character was akin to Ted Barker in *Born to Dance* and especially Peter Morgan in *Vivacious Lady*. But the Capra comedy gave Jim some wonderful bits of business, which he executed most effectively. Particularly memorable were his first sequence with Arthur, in which he holds her hands at her desk so that she can't answer the phone; their date together, in which all six foot three of him dances the Big Apple in Central Park with a tiny preteen; their subsequent stop at a swanky nightclub, when he traces the progress of an impending scream from his toes to his mouth, prompting Arthur to do the shouting at the penultimate moment; and finally, his confrontation with his doting father, when he confesses that Wall Street is not for him. The latter, a more serious scene, suggests what Jim may have experienced in real life five and a half years earlier when he had to tell Alex Stewart that he wanted to be an actor.

Capra was as impressed with Stewart as Stewart was with Capra. "He's the easiest man to direct I've ever seen," said the director years later. "A man who gets what you're talking about in just a few words. You wonder if you've told him enough about the scene, and yet when he does it, there it is. . . . I think he's probably the best actor who's ever hit the screen." No longer the novice, Stewart was perceptibly gaining control over his craft. Ed Bernds, who watched him on the set every day, recalls that by this point, Jim "was self-assured, he was a veteran. Not arrogant at all, but confident."

Between takes, he continued to combat his ongoing weight problem by munching on candy bars. Ann Miller, nineteen at the time, recalls the moments when he would call her over and say, "C'mon, Annie, would you like to have a Butterfinger with me?" She would eagerly respond yes. "So," as she recalls, "we'd sit in the corner and have a couple of Butterfingers. Well, I blew up like a balloon, and he stayed skinny."

When *You Can't Take It With You* wrapped on June 29—only four days behind schedule, something of a triumph for the methodical Capra—Stewart was sorry. He'd had a wonderful time. So did audiences when the picture opened at Radio City Music Hall on September 1, just over two months later. "One of the most utterly irresistible, delightful, human and entertaining films I have ever seen," cheered William Boehnel of the *New York Telegram*. "Not only the year's best film, it is one of the finest on record," echoed Eileen Creelman of the *New York Sun*. Several of their colleagues, including Howard Barnes of the *New York Herald-Tribune* and Archer Winsten of the *New York Post*, even found the film superior to the Pulitzer Prize–winning play. *Variety* credited the romance between Stewart and Arthur for "much of the laughs," although, not surprisingly, the best acting notices went to Barrymore and Arnold in the flashier roles.

The film, which proved to be Capra's biggest box-office hit yet for Columbia, went on to win the Academy Award for Best Picture and to earn the director his third Oscar in five years. The triumph was marred only by the loss of Frank's young son, who died just before the picture's release.

Prior to *You Can't Take It With You,* Stewart had never been in a film that merited Oscar consideration, let alone a picture that won. For this reason alone, *You Can't Take It With You* served as a benchmark in his career. More importantly, however, it marked the start of his association with Frank Capra, a relationship that would soon play an even more significant role in his emergence as a major star.

By the time *You Can't Take It With You* debuted, Stewart was hard at work on his next picture, *Made for Each Other,* which had commenced filming in late August. The screenplay by Jo Swerling focused on a young husband and wife as they cope with the trials of everyday life— his demanding employer, her eccentric domestics, their cramped apartment, a new baby, and other such traumas. The project was produced by David O. Selznick, L. B. Mayer's son-in-law and a former Metro producer, who had formed his own independent production company in 1936. To star opposite Stewart, Selznick cast his stylish blond contract player Carole Lombard, best known for her screwball comedies, including *Twentieth Century* and *Our Man Godfrey.* Lombard, who often bridled at Selznick's control over her career, welcomed the change of pace that the melodramatic *Made for Each Other* represented.

To direct, the producer turned to John Cromwell, with whom he had previously worked on *Street of Chance, Little Lord Fauntleroy,* and *The Prisoner of Zenda.* Cromwell, a tall, handsome former stage actor, was particularly adept at character interpretation. When it came to the technical demands of the craft, however, he was forced to rely on his cameramen. "If I had any style," he conceded, "it was simply the wish for my work to be honest."

Such a desire was of paramount importance in *Made for Each Other,* for, as the *New York Sun* noted on the picture's release, Jo Swerling's screenplay included "practically every stock dramatic situation that has proved, over the years, its power to nudge sentimental ladies in the audience into muffled sobbing or soft laughter." The story took a particularly sharp turn when, in the climactic episode, the young couple's son needs a rare serum to avert a life-threatening illness, and a pilot braves a blizzard in a monoplane to provide the relief. The sequence, not in the original screenplay, was inspired by Selznick's brother Myron, who fell deathly ill in Santa Monica until a new miracle drug was flown to his bedside from New York. Neither Lombard nor Cromwell cared for the interpolated sequence, which they quite correctly saw as taking the domestic comedy-drama into a totally different realm.

As for Stewart, the sequence provided a challenge he had not previously encountered: he had to cry on camera at the prospect of losing his son. "I couldn't work up the tears," he told Hedda Hopper years later, "and didn't have the nerve to ask for that stuff that makes you cry when put in your eyes." After he ruined a couple of takes, Cromwell called for a break. "I walked outside," Stewart continued, "and held a lighted cigarette near my face so the smoke could pour into my eyes. When I was called into the scene, I was nearly blind. My bloodshot eyes looked as if I'd been on a week's binge. Somebody poured Murine into them, but that ended my work for the day. We finally got the scene next morning."

Other than learning to cry on cue, Stewart found *Made for Each Other* remarkably familiar territory. His scenes were well crafted, but his character, attorney Johnny Mason, was much like Tony Kirby in *You Can't Take It With You* and even more like Peter Morgan in *Vivacious Lady*. Like the latter, while out of town he falls in love with and marries a young woman he hardly knows, then has to awkwardly present her to the people in his life, including, in this case, his overprotective mother and his hearing-impaired boss. The latter was played by Charles Coburn, who had been Stewart's equally stern father in *Vivacious Lady*. Coburn's casting only reinforced the similarity between Jim's two roles.

At least, he had the gifted Carole Lombard as a partner. Stewart liked the brassy, no-nonsense actress. "She was truly beautiful," he said years later, "and was the only girl I've ever known who could let out with a stream of four-letter words and not embarrass you. It was ladylike, the way she did it. I found her rough language funny, and I would give her the laugh she wanted." Lombard was taken with her costar as well. Having played opposite such skilled professionals as Charles Laughton, John Barrymore, and Fredric March, she went into the production thinking Stewart was a lightweight, but found him, in her words, "more sincere than any of them, and just as talented . . . his timing is perfection itself."

When *Made for Each Other* opened in February of 1939, Bland Johaneson of the *New York Daily Mirror* accurately identified the picture's structural flaws, noting that "it appears to have been made in three parts. Part one is light domestic comedy. Part two is heavy death-bed drama. Part three is aviation thriller." But most of the critics gave the film high marks. While acknowledging that it was "hokum," William Boehnel of the *New York World-Telegram* asserted that it was executed "so brilliantly by everybody concerned that you can easily forgive it its deliberate and unabashed tuggings at the heartstrings. Actually, it is so human, so tender, so real that if you don't tingle with joy, melt with sorrow over its people and events, you must be made of stone."

Despite the preponderance of glowing critical notices, *Made for Each Other* was not a hit. The slight comedy-drama simply got lost in a year— often considered the best in Hollywood history—that produced such classics as *Stagecoach, Wuthering Heights, Dark Victory, Juarez, The Women, Ninotchka,* and another offering from David O. Selznick called *Gone With the Wind.*

If nothing else, *The Ice Follies of 1939,* Stewart's next picture, gave him a chance to depart ever so slightly from the *Vivacious Lady–Made for Each Other* mold. The picture was still a modern romance, but in it, Jim played one-third of an ice-skating act with visions of mounting lavish ice spectacles à la the Ziegfeld Follies. Thus, he got to try his hand at lines like "We're going to be the sensation of the country. . . . I'm gonna do things on ice that have never been done before." That sort of material was usually reserved for Mickey Rooney and Judy Garland in their backyard "Hey, kids, let's put on a show" musicals.

On the skater's way to the big time, his wife, also with the act, becomes a major movie star, and their careers pull them in different directions. The third member of the team was played in traditional "best friend" fashion by Lew Ayres. It was not a very original plot device. That MGM treated the film lightly could be seen early on, when a valet calls out the names of those waiting for limos after an ice show performance: "Mr. Gable, Mr. Tracy, Miss Loy," all Metro stars.

According to hoofer George Murphy, the film's producer, Harry Rapf (of *The Murder Man*), had initially promised *him* the role of the impresario, Larry Hall. Only after spending weeks practicing on the ice did Murphy learn that he had been replaced. But casting Stewart meant that Hall couldn't be a figure skater, as written. Said Jim in typically self-deprecating fashion, "When the producer saw me in tights he shook his head sadly and said, 'Maybe not a figure skater, maybe a comedy skater with big baggy pants.'"

To play his wife, the reluctant screen siren, MGM cast far from type with Joan Crawford, perhaps the most ambitious actress in Hollywood. Of course, she and Stewart had worked together before—in *The Gorgeous Hussy*—but this time they met as costars. She would later write in her autobiography, "I adored working with Jimmy. I wish I could again. He's such an endearing character, a perfectionist at his job, but with a droll sense of humor and a shy way of watching to see if you react to that humor."

Crawford, whose career was then in a terrible slump, was primarily interested in *Ice Follies* because her character had half a dozen songs. She hoped that her performance in the picture would open the door to other musical roles. During principal photography, a Metro publicist even told Hedda Hopper, "Crawford's singing is going to be as sensational as Garbo talking."[2] In the end, however, only two of the numbers remained, and they were dubbed. Crawford blamed Jeanette MacDonald for the changes, saying, "She had no idea I was so good. She told Mr. Mayer that there wasn't room for both of us at the same studio. Mayer could not afford to lose Jeanette. Her movies were still very popular." Later, Joan would write in her autobiography that several of the songs "hit the cutting-room floor because they slowed up the skating numbers."

She was right about one thing—the film's two ice extravaganzas, representing the fruits of Larry Hall's vision, were the driving force behind *Ice Follies of 1939*. They spotlighted real International Ice Follies stars, including Bess Ehrhardt, Roy Shipstad, Eddie Shipstad, and Oscar Johnson, and the second production number, which served as the film's finale, featured a then rare use of color photography. Both sequences were shot on a rink, 80 by 140 feet, constructed on an MGM soundstage. One would think all that ice would cause the company to freeze, but the lights needed for the Technicolor sequence were so intense that an air-cooling system—a rarity in 1938—had to be used to keep everyone comfortable.

Exactly one month after the debut of *Made for Each Other*, *Ice Follies of 1939* was released. The picture is hopelessly dated by contemporary standards and was hardly original even in 1939, but to *Variety* it was "an attractive package of entertainment," and to Kate Cameron of the *New York Daily News* it served as "a pleasant and colorful spectacle." It may not have given Crawford the career boost she needed, but it didn't do her, Stewart, or anyone else any harm either.

On October 23, while *Ice Follies* was in production, Stewart costarred with Rosalind Russell in *Up from Darkness*, a two-part original radio drama on the *Silver Theatre*, CBS's weekly Sunday-afternoon anthology series, sponsored by the International Silver company. Russell played the daughter of a mine owner who had lost a loved one in an explosion.

---

[2] When silent-film star Greta Garbo made her first talkie, *Anna Christie*, in 1930, an MGM advertising copywriter hit pay dirt with the tag line "Garbo talks!"

Together, she and her boyfriend, played by Stewart, wage a battle to make the mines safe. The drama concluded the following week.

Up from Darkness was hardly Stewart's first foray into radio. In May of 1934, while he was living in New York, he did a scene from *Yellow Jack* on the *Fleischmann Hour.* In 1936, he starred in two segments of *Hollywood Hotel* hosted by Dick Powell, repeating his role in *Next Time We Love* in the first and his role in *Born to Dance* in the second. On June 14, 1937, between work on *Vivacious Lady* and *The Last Gangster,* he did his first *Lux Radio Theatre,* perhaps the most prestigious of the anthology series emanating from Hollywood. He played the lawyer in *Madame X,* a young man, adopted as a child, who unknowingly defends his birth mother for murder. Jim also played the accordion on several episodes of the *Kraft Music Hall* and had costarred with Russell in another *Silver Theatre* multipart story called *First Love,* which had aired over four weeks in November of 1937. In *First Love* he was a talent agent who tries to get even with a tyrannical studio head by foisting a waitress (Russell) on him. But, of course, she turns out to be great.

After *Up from Darkness,* Stewart did a third *Silver Theatre* production. Called *Misty Mountain,* it aired on January 22 and 29, 1939, with Jim as a pilot torn between two women, the daughter of an airline executive and a ham operator he has never met in a town he regularly flies over. According to Stewart, the *Silver Theatre* never paid its performers in cash, but in the products of its sponsors—which was apparently all right with him. "I collected silver for myself and my relatives and enough for gifts for eight Christmases," he quipped years later.

Three weeks after the last episode of *Misty Mountain* aired, he was once again before the cameras. In another departure, he played a private detective by the name of Guy Johnson. The picture was *It's a Wonderful World,* MGM's latest entry in the screwball-comedy sweepstakes. Like Capra's *It Happened One Night,* to which it bore more than a little resemblance, the plot centered around a mismatched guy and gal—in this case, the detective and a lady poet—who share a series of adventures on the road. But a mystery overlay the fun in the Metro offering, with the detective on the lam from the cops for conspiracy to commit murder. Of course, with the poet's help, he finds the real killers just before the final fade-out. To play opposite Stewart, MGM borrowed the Oscar-winning star of *It Happened One Night,* Claudette Colbert, who was under contract to Paramount.

In a role clearly written with Gable in mind, Stewart makes his first entrance hungover and in poor humor and spouting such sentiments as "For a hundred dollars a week, nothin's undignified." For those accustomed to the idealist from *Born to Dance* and *The Shopworn Angel,* this attitude takes a bit of getting used to. In fact, he never becomes totally convincing as a would-be cynic. Lines like "Now get a smile on that kisser of yours or I'll plug you" and "I never met a dame yet that wasn't a nitwit or a lunkhead" just don't flow naturally from his lips.

Not surprisingly, the dialogue caused Stewart some difficulty during filming. In one scene, after he blew take after take, his director, Woody Van Dyke, teased him, saying, "I'm certainly disappointed in you, Jimmy. Of all the scenes I've directed with Johnny Weissmuller, he never once forgot a line." Van Dyke's comment troubled Stewart until he realized that Hollywood's Tarzan usually spoke only in monosyllables.

As the comedy gathers steam—under Van Dyke's brisk direction and the crackling script by Ben Hecht and Herman Mankiewicz—the detective hasn't time to be dour, and Stewart becomes much more palatable. There is a delightful bit when, to elude a group of reporters, he dons a Boy Scout's hat, jacket, and bottle-thick glasses and affects a lofty British accent. Later, he impersonates a Southern thespian when he discovers that his quarry is doing a play in stock. His honeyed Alabama drawl is very funny. (He couldn't do dialects for real, but his overblown attempts were just right for a farce.) Throughout, he and Colbert, a master of the screwball comedy as well as a fine dramatic actress, work well together—but then, in his previous collaborations with Margaret Sullavan, Ginger Rogers, Jean Arthur, Carole Lombard, and Joan Crawford, Stewart had proven that he could hold his own with the best of Hollywood's leading ladies.

The critics liked what they saw when the picture opened in New York on May 18, 1939. "Mr. Stewart, heretofore, an agog and stupefied young hero, surprises with the vigorous animation he puts [in] his role," asserted Bland Johaneson of the *New York Daily Mirror,* to which Eileen Creelman of the *New York Sun* added, "James Stewart, usually serious to the point of glumness, brightens up considerably in his new picture. He is, in fact, an excellent foil for Miss Colbert, playing comedy as though he were really enjoying himself." Serious to the point of glumness? She was quick to forget *Born to Dance* and *You Can't Take It With You.* Colbert, Van Dyke, and the picture itself were warmly received as well, although comparisons with *It Happened One Night* were inevitable.

It's a Wonderful World forced Stewart to work more broadly than he had in prior comedies and to tackle a role for which others, such as Gable or Tracy, were more immediately qualified. His next picture, by contrast, couldn't have been better suited to his talents. Indeed, it would come to represent the quintessence of the young Jimmy Stewart on film. It was *Mr. Smith Goes to Washington.*

EIGHT

Mr. Smith and Marlene

In 1937, Harry Cohn decided to make a film of Lewis R. Foster's screen story "The Gentleman from Montana," the tale of a naive young man—the story's title character—who is appointed to fill a vacant U.S. Senate seat. Framed by a political machine trying to hide its latest crooked scheme, he filibusters on the floor of the Senate to save his good name.[1]

The project was shelved. But a year or so later, one of Frank Capra's associates, Joe Sistrom, came across the story and showed it to the director. Capra, who had just abandoned his plans for a biography of Chopin, grabbed it.

Since Robert Riskin was then working for independent film producer Samuel Goldwyn, Sidney Buchman was chosen to write the screenplay. A former playwright, Buchman had worked without credit on two of Capra's previous pictures, *Broadway Bill* and *Lost Horizon*. He was assisted by Myles Connolly, who worked without credit on *Mr. Smith*. By the time they finished, the freshman senator, Jefferson Smith, had become a plum of a role, rich in both comedic and dramatic potential. Almost as well crafted was the role of Smith's secretary, Clarissa Saunders, a pretty young woman wise in the ways of Washington but fed up with the wheeling and dealing.

Capra knew from the outset that he wanted Jean Arthur for Saunders. He had Gary Cooper, her leading man in *Mr. Deeds Goes to Town*, in mind for the senator. But Coop was under contract to Goldwyn, and the producer wouldn't agree to the loanout. "I then thought of Jimmy Stewart," Capra recalled, "and felt I had hit upon the logical man—he was a perfect character to portray a garden variety of citizen." In time, Capra felt fortunate that his first choice was unavailable, saying, "Gary Cooper . . . had a native

---

[1] In his 1971 autobiography, *The Name Above the Title*, Capra referred to Foster's story as an out-of-print novel, but an extensive search through the New York Public Library failed to reveal any such book. Moreover, the credits for the film simply refer to the source as "A Story by Lewis R. Foster." Unknown to Columbia at the time, Foster's story bore a marked resemblance to a Pulitzer Prize–winning drama by Maxwell Anderson called *Both Your Houses*. To play safe, the studio bought the rights to the play shortly before the Capra picture's release.

honesty and decency about him, but it was on a lower level than Jimmy Stewart. Jimmy could deal with an idea."

Capra surrounded his stars with a group of talented supporting players: Claude Rains as Joseph Paine, the distinguished senior senator whom Smith reveres until he learns that the man is corrupt; Edward Arnold as Jim Taylor, the head of the political machine that controls Paine and frames Smith; Thomas Mitchell as Diz Moore, the drunken but influential reporter who's in love with Saunders; and in an unusual bit of casting, silent-movie cowboy star Harry Carey as the vice president of the United States. As technical adviser, the director engaged Jim Preston, who had been the superintendent of the Senate press gallery for forty years. Preston proved to be of enormous help in ensuring the accuracy of the proceedings.

On April 3, 1939, principal photography began on what came to be called *Mr. Smith Goes to Washington.* Most of the scenes were shot on the Columbia lot, where the Senate chamber was faithfully re-created at the then substantial cost of $100,000. But the cast and crew also traveled to Washington, D.C. It was Stewart's first time in the nation's capital since World War I, when he and his mother had visited his father there. They filmed at the National Press Club, aboard a streetcar, on the steps of the Capitol, and in the Senate Office Building. More difficult was getting the important footage of Stewart looking up at the Lincoln Memorial, a source of particular inspiration for Smith. When the crew started setting up before the giant statue, a guard informed Capra that he couldn't film his star and the likeness of Lincoln at the same time. Capra's only recourse was to return with Stewart at sunrise. Then, with no one else present, he got his shot.

Back at the studio, Harry Carey was having a difficult time grappling with his character, a politician far removed from the saddle tramps he usually played. During the shooting of his first scene, which called for him to swear in the new senator, he was visibly nervous, with sweat beading his forehead. After several takes, Capra called a lunch break. When the company returned to the soundstage, he told the actor, "I don't want Harry Carey the cowboy actor; when you swear in that young punk senator, I want you to remember that you're a heartbeat away from being president—you're swearing him in as the vice president of the United States." Those were the words Carey needed to hear. Thereafter, the character was his. In the final film, Capra made liberal use of Carey's craggy face, frequently cutting to show him relishing Smith's refreshing candor and enthusiasm without appearing to do so. The performance earned Carey an Academy Award nomination.

Stewart was also nervous during principal photography, not when filming but when he was away from the set. As Jean Arthur later told Capra biographer Joseph McBride, Jim "used to get up at five o'clock in the morning and drive five miles an hour to get himself to the studio. He was so terrified that something was going to happen to him, he wouldn't go any faster."

The chemistry between Arthur and Stewart—so delightful in *You Can't Take It With You*—was even more effective in *Mr. Smith*, perhaps because their characters in this second pairing were such opposites. He was wide-eyed, clumsy, and slow, full of optimism and passionate about the American system of government. She was smart, quick, and self-confident, but cynical and disillusioned with the whole political arena. Watching her hard shell melt as she falls for him is one of the joys of the picture.

Offstage, the costars had a cordial, professional relationship, but not a particularly warm one. "Arthur was a troubled little lady," explained a colleague. Of her two Capra costars, Stewart and Gary Cooper, she expressed a preference for the latter, saying, "Stewart is almost too much when he acts; I get tired of his 'uh, uh . . .'—his cute quality. With Cooper it just seems to *happen*. I can't remember Cooper saying much of anything. But it's very comfortable working with him."

Stewart was hardly hesitant or cute with the extended sequence that climaxes the picture. Smith's filibuster on the floor of the Senate took roughly two weeks to shoot and dominates the last half hour of the film. By the end of the sequence, the young man has to be terribly hoarse from hours of orating. After one take, Capra told Jimmy that his attempt at a sore throat was unconvincing. That night, Stewart asked a doctor if he had any medicine that could help him out. The physician thought he was crazy, but obliged by placing a couple of drops of bichloride of mercury on his vocal cords. It was perfect. Stewart could hardly even swallow! Jim wanted to take the medication with him, but the physician refused. "No, a doctor has to apply this," he insisted. "But you've got me so fascinated with this that I'll see you tomorrow morning at nine o'clock on the set." He showed up the next day and got the actor through the scene.

The picture wrapped on July 7, a staggering seven weeks behind schedule and hundreds of thousands of dollars over budget. Three months later, on October 17, it previewed in Washington, an occasion that attracted many of the government's principal power brokers, including the Senate majority leader Alben W. Barkley; Speaker of the House William Bankhead (Tallulah's father); Cabinet members Cordell Hull, Frank Murphy, and Jim Farley; and several justices of the U.S. Supreme Court. Stewart, at work on his next picture, *Destry Rides Again*, was unable to attend.

The Washingtonians were not pleased by what they saw. Sen. Jimmy

Byrnes, a powerful Democrat from South Carolina, told the press that he thought *Mr. Smith* was "outrageous, exactly the kind of picture that dictators of totalitarian governments would like to have their subjects believe exists in a democracy." Columnist Frederic William Wile expressed the same sentiment in the *Washington Star*, while John M. Cummings, editor and publisher of the *Philadelphia Inquirer*, called the film "a gross libel" of the Washington press corps as well as the Senate. According to Capra, Joseph P. Kennedy, then ambassador to the Court of St. James, even offered to buy the negative from Columbia to prevent the picture's release, but Cohn refused to sell.

By contrast, the film critics and the public loved *Mr. Smith*. When it opened at Radio City Music Hall on October 19, 1939, Bland Johaneson of the *New York Daily Mirror* called it "inspiring" and "grand entertainment." Howard Barnes of the *New York Herald-Tribune* proclaimed it "a moving and memorable motion picture." And Kate Cameron of the *New York Daily News* dubbed it "Capra's masterpiece."

All agreed that it was Jim's finest performance to date, and indeed, *Mr. Smith* marked the apotheosis of the screen persona that he'd been developing since 1936. It wasn't that he forged new territory with the character. He had done the rube who is awed by the big city in *The Shopworn Angel*. He'd played the defender of a beloved cause in *Navy Blue and Gold*. He'd even acted the guy who's ready to give up before finding the strength to go on in *Made for Each Other*. But never had he been given a role that combined all of these elements in one complete human being, nor had he grappled with a character so special, so admirable, and so likable. Never as a leading player had he been associated with so much talent in front of and behind the cameras (in *You Can't Take It With You*, he was in support of Barrymore and Arnold). Never before had he worked with a script so well polished or one that so seamlessly combined comedy and drama.

The filibuster sequence alone was star-making material, with Smith alternating between earnest, ringing statements about American liberty and comic nonchalance ("How'm I doin'?" he asks another senator at one point). The climax, often shown in outtakes, finds him exhausted but rallying to tell Paine, "You think I'm licked. You all think I'm licked. Well, I'm not licked. And I'm going to stay right here and fight for this lost cause even if this room gets filled with lies like these. . . . Somebody will listen to me." In this poignant moment, Stewart manages to make audiences weep for him and cheer for him at the same time.

But, beyond the filibuster, three scenes in *Mr. Smith* stand out for what they reveal of Stewart's maturing talent. The first is his initial appearance ten minutes into the feature. By then, Smith's virtues have been extolled by the children of his state, his courage headlined in a local newspaper, and his idealism made the object of the smug politicians' mirth. Finally, he is spotlighted in a banquet scene celebrating the Senate appointment. Looking about eighteen years old and sporting an ill-fitting suit and unfashionably long hair, he rises and sputters his first words: "I-I-I can't help feeling there's been a big mistake somehow." Clearly, this is not going to be a conventional hero. But it will be one whom the audience can relate to. If most average men and women suddenly found themselves appointed to the U.S. Senate, that's how they'd react.

The second scene finds him in the presence of the senator's daughter, Susan, on whom he has a crush. As he and actress Astrid Allwyn converse in voice-over, the camera dollies in on his torso, and he is seen repeatedly fiddling with and dropping his hat. Nothing in the Buchman screenplay suggests shooting the exchange this way, but it is an extremely inventive approach, and Stewart's ability to master the tricky handwork reflects well on his days as a magician's assistant.

The third is the scene in which Smith and Saunders set out to draft a piece of legislation. At the outset Stewart is a steamroller, his energy unchecked by the secretary's litany of obstacles to a bill's passage. Then, as he segues into his reasons for proposing the bill, he becomes the impassioned champion of liberty and the ardent lover of nature. His simple eloquence even arouses Saunders' dormant idealism. Finally, he turns quiet and attentive, asking the young woman about herself. Stewart brilliantly negotiates these shifts in attitude, thereby setting the stage for his character's transition from rube to rustic hero.

Stewart's work in *Mr. Smith* took him to a new level in Hollywood: major stardom. He went on to win the New York Film Critics Award for Best Actor at the end of the year, beating Henry Fonda for *Young Mr. Lincoln* and Robert Donat for *Goodbye, Mr. Chips*. He also earned his first Academy Award nomination, but lost to Donat. The comedy-drama was nominated in ten other categories, including Picture, Supporting Actor (Rains, Carey), Directing, and Writing (Original Story and Screenplay). Foster won for his story, but *Gone With the Wind* swept most of the awards that year. Rains and Carey, however, lost to their *Mr. Smith* costar, Thomas Mitchell, not for his role as Scarlett O'Hara's father, but as the drunken doctor in his third picture of the year, *Stagecoach*.

After *Mr. Smith* wrapped, Stewart had a short break between pictures and decided to use the time to do something he'd always wanted to do: travel around France by car. Because this was a last-minute decision, he was unable to book a flight to New York or even a sleeping berth on a train. Instead, he sat up in a regular coach car, watching the country go by. In Manhattan, he managed to arrange for passage aboard a ship that would give him nine days in France before he had to return to Hollywood. When he landed in Cannes, he had one suitcase and a movie camera—with lots of film.

That war in Europe was imminent seemed to have escaped his notice. "Everyone seemed so calm and business-like about it in France and England," he said a few years later, "that I felt that way, too." If anything, he was thinking more about the previous war, spending an entire day in Bourges, trying to locate the ordnance shops that his father had helped build in 1918. "I found them," he recalled, "huge, empty steel buildings hidden away in the woods outside the city."

Near the end of August—only weeks before the outbreak of World War II—he boarded the *Normandie* and headed for home. On the ship the impending conflict became more real. "We weren't allowed lights in our cabins," he said, "and the steamer ran with no lights on deck." In retrospect, the trip seemed ill-advised to say the least. By August 28, he was en route back to Los Angeles, having no idea that the war would soon touch him directly.

In the meantime, a peaceable deputy sheriff's conflict with a town full of bad guys was of far greater concern. On September 7, Stewart reported to Universal for the first Western of his career.

Based on a novel by Max Brand, *Destry Rides Again* had been cowboy star Tom Mix's first talkie in 1932. The remake was the inspiration of Hungarian-born producer Joe Pasternak, who needed a change of pace from his popular musicals starring young Deanna Durbin. Although B Westerns were a staple at Universal, Pasternak wanted to do something different with the genre. Borrowing Stewart from MGM gave him a starting point. So did hiring a German refugee, Felix Jackson, to write the screenplay.

Both the producer and the writer agreed that Jimmy could not be presented in the rough-and-tumble mold of a Tom Mix. So Jackson told Pasternak, "Let's do a story about a man who doesn't believe in guns." They also decided to add a major female character to the plot. "In the original movie," said Pasternak, "the girl was a frail, silly little child waiting for her man to come home." He wanted a character that was, in his words, "the equal of Destry in looks, drive, and personality."

What emerged was a screenplay that bore little resemblance to either the novel or the original picture. In the new version, Thomas Jefferson Destry Jr. is imported to lawless Bottleneck by the town's new sheriff, the former sidekick of Destry's famous father. Tom is an expert marksman, but instead of gunplay, he prefers whittling napkin rings and telling parables that invariably start with "I had a friend once." In time, he wins

Jimmy Stewart's family has lived in Indiana County, Pennsylvania, since 1772. Pictured here are his grandfathers, Samuel McCartney Jackson *(left)* and James Maitland Stewart, the actor's namesake *(below)*. Both men fought for the Union during the Civil War, and these photos date to that era. *(The Jimmy Stewart Museum)*

(Below) Jim's birthplace, Indiana, Pennsylvania, was a tidy middle-class community populated mostly by God-fearing Republicans of Scotch-Irish descent. Here young Stewart developed many of his strongly held ideas about family, religion, and community. *(The Jimmy Stewart Museum)*

Philadelphia Street, looking East, Indiana, Pa.

The Stewarts were a close-knit family, with boisterous Alex, a demanding but loving father, and quiet, dignified Bessie, an understanding mother. Jimmy's sister Mary has her arms around her parents. The baby of the family, Virginia, is standing at center. *(The Jimmy Stewart Museum)*

Jim's father, Alex, owned the local hardware store, a place the young boy found magical. "I could conceive of no human need," he later recalled, "that could not be satisfied in this store." Out front are Jim, his grandfather J.M., and his father. *(The Jimmy Stewart Museum)*

At Princeton, Jim joined the Triangle Club, which produced original musicals, marking the start of his acting career. He is seen here as the hapless lover Alphonso in his senior-year production, *Spanish Blades*. *(Triangle Archives, William Seymour Theater Collection, Dept. of Rare Books and Special Collections, Princeton University Library)*

Stewart's first real acclaim as an actor came with his fifth Broadway show, *Yellow Jack* by Sidney Howard, which opened in New York on March 6, 1934. He played an army sergeant who served as a guinea pig for a yellow fever experiment. His friend Myron McCormick *(right)* was a fellow soldier. *(Corbis-Bettmann)*

Signed to a movie contract with MGM in 1935, Jim played the n'er-do-well brother of Jeanette MacDonald in his second feature, *Rose Marie*. Nelson Eddy was the
valiant mountie who brought him to justice. *(MGM/The Kobal Collection)*

Stewart's first leading role came with his third picture, Universal's *Next Time We Love*. He
owed being cast to his friend—the star of the film—Margaret Sullavan. Mutual friends claim
that Jim was madly in love with "Peggy." *(Universal/The Kobal Collection)*

Back at MGM, Stewart played a variety of supporting characters. An exception was in 1936's *Speed*, a B picture in which he took the lead as a daredevil mechanic named Terry Martin. Wendy Barrie was his leading lady and Weldon Heyburne his rival for her affections. *(MGM/The Kobal Collection)*

After four years in Hollywood, Stewart was cast as a gauche, idealistic senator in Frank Capra's *Mr. Smith Goes to Washington*. The role made him a major star and cemented his boyish all-American image. *(Columbia/The Kobal Collection)*

A bachelor, young Stewart dated a variety of beautiful, well-known actresses in Hollywood, including Ginger Rogers, Rosalind Russell, and Marlene Dietrich. But he fell the hardest for Olivia de Havilland, whom he started dating in late 1939. (*Archive Photos*)

(*Above*) Katharine Hepburn initially wanted Clark Gable and Spencer Tracy as her costars in *The Philadelphia Story*, but she happily accepted Stewart and Cary Grant (*second from left*). At the far left is John Howard as her stuffy fiancé.
(*MGM/The Kobal Collection*)

(*Left*) On February 27, 1941, Stewart was named Best Supporting Actor by the Academy of Motion Picture Arts and Sciences for his role in *The Philadelphia Story*. Backstage he posed with the winner for Best Actress, his sometime date and former costar, Ginger Rogers. (*Archive Photos*)

Drafted in March 1941, Stewart became an officer in
the Army Air Corps and a bombardier pilot with
twenty missions to his credit. Among his numerous
decorations was the Distinguished Flying Cross,
presented to him in May 1944 by his friend and
commanding officer, Col. Ramsay Potts.
(The Jimmy Stewart Museum)

(Below) After more than four years in the military,
Stewart returned to Hollywood uncertain of his
career and his talent. His first postwar role was
George Bailey, the beloved family man of *It's a
Wonderful Life*. *(RKO/The Kobal Collection)*

Of all the directors with whom he
worked, Stewart most admired
Frank Capra. Their mutual admiration is evident in this shot,
taken during a break in the filming of *It's a Wonderful Life*, their
last film together.
(The Jimmy Stewart Museum)

At the age of forty-one, Hollywood's most eligible bachelor finally said "I do." His wife was the beautiful, vivacious Gloria Hatrick McLean, ten years his junior. The wedding took place at the Brentwood Presbyterian Church on August 10, 1949.
(The Jimmy Stewart Museum)

After the failure of several sentimental postwar pictures, Stewart decided to toughen up his image. He got an opportunity to do so in the third Western of his career, 1950's *Winchester '73*. His profit participation in this and subsequent films also made him wealthy. *(Universal/The Kobal Collection)*

Stewart was so eager to play Elwood P. Dowd in Mary Chase's comedy *Harvey*, he even did two brief stints in the Broadway production. Here, in the film adaptation, he and the invisible rabbit share a moment with Elwood's sister, played by Josephine Hull. *(Universal/The Kobal Collection)*

On May 7, 1951, Gloria gave birth to twin girls, Kelly and Judy. She had two sons from a previous marriage, Ronald and Michael. *(Archive Photos)*

A few months after the birth of twins, the Stewarts moved into a lovely Tudor-style home in Beverly Hills. Jim lived there for the rest of his life. *(The Jimmy Stewart Museum)*

One of the biggest hits of Stewart's career was *The Glenn Miller Story*, the third most popular picture of 1954. June Allyson played the bandleader's devoted wife. It was the second of her three films with Jimmy. *(Universal/The Kobal Collection)*

Rear Window, also released in 1954, teamed Stewart with the future princess of Monaco. The star confessed, "I was just absolutely smitten by Grace Kelly, a wonderful, wonderful girl." *(Paramount/The Kobal Collection)*

During the 1950s, Jimmy and Gloria guest-starred virtually once a year on the popular TV show hosted by Jack Benny, their friend and neighbor. Stewart liked coming into people's homes this way, to subtly entice his audience into seeing his films. *(Archive Photos)*

Perhaps the most significant relationship of Stewart's career was his association with director Anthony Mann. The two men made nine films together in only five years. They are seen here on the set of their last picture, 1955's *The Man from Laramie*. *(Archive Photos)*

In *Vertigo*, his fourth and final film with Alfred Hitchcock, Stewart played a man racked with guilt and fear and obsessed with a lost love—hardly a typical role for him. What's most remarkable about his performance is how much emotion he conveys through facial expression. *(Paramount/The Kobal Collection)*

Stewart delivered one of his finest performances in 1959's *Anatomy of a Murder*, in which he portrayed a rural defense attorney whose country ways belie a canny legal mind. His client, played by Ben Gazzara, is on the right. *(Archive Photos)*

In *The Man Who Shot Liberty Valance*, released in 1962, Stewart is once again an attorney, this time in the Old West. His faith in law and order puts him at odds with a local outlaw played by Lee Marvin *(left)* and sometimes with John Wayne's character, a rugged, independent rancher. *(Paramount/The Kobal Collection)*

During the 1960s, Stewart made three domestic comedies with director Henry Koster and screen-writer Nunnally Johnson. In each, the star played a hapless dad coping with the complexities of modern family life. The first, 1962's *Mr. Hobbs Takes a Vacation,* was the best of the three. *(20th Century–Fox/The Kobal Collection)*

The real Stewart family circa 1961. From left to right, the children are Judy, Rob, Kelly, and Mike. *(The Jimmy Stewart Museum)*

The screen lit up whenever mild-mannered Stewart lost his temper. Such was the case in 1965's *Shenandoah*, as the star, playing a Virginia farmer, lashes out after the death of his son during the Civil War. *(Universal/The Kobal Collection)*

As the 1960s progressed, Jim segued into character roles, an example of which was his grizzled, old-fashioned pilot in *The Flight of the Phoenix*. He is seen here with costars Richard Attenborough *(left)* and Hardy Kruger. *(20th Century–Fox/The Kobal Collection)*

When work in features became scarce, Stewart turned to television. The second of his two series, *Hawkins,* aired in 1973–74. The ninety-minute dramas found him playing a character akin to the shrewd country lawyer in *Anatomy of a Murder. (Archive Photos)*

(Right) Having roomed together as journeymen actors in New York and later as rising stars in Hollywood, Jim and Henry Fonda were devoted friends. In 1975, when this photo was taken in London, each actor was starring in a West End play. Stewart's was *Harvey. (Archive Photos)*

In 1983's *Right of Way,* made for Home Box Office, Stewart and Bette Davis played a husband and wife who decide to commit suicide. After the production wrapped, Davis told the press that "working with Jimmy was just heaven." *(Corbis-Bettmann)*

over the tough saloon singer whose employer/boyfriend, Kent, has the town in the palm of his crooked hand.

Universal wanted Paulette Goddard for the role of the saloon girl, then called Angel. But she was under contract to her then husband, Charles Chaplin, who planned to use her in *The Great Dictator*, and it was scheduled to film at the same time. Pasternak then decided to tailor the part for his friend Marlene Dietrich. "I called the character Frenchie," Jackson explained, "because Marlene had been living in France."

Casting Dietrich was a bold move. Not only because envisioning the European sophisticate in the rugged Old West took some doing, but also because a series of unsuccessful films had made her "box-office poison" according to America's motion-picture exhibitors. Still, Pasternak wanted her. He felt that Dietrich had been ill served by her recent directors and that the role in *Destry* could revive her career. His success with the Durbin pictures gave him the clout to persuade the studio to hire her, but the actress had to be convinced as well. According to Julie Gilbert, author of a dual biography of Goddard and Goddard's husband, writer Erich Maria Remarque, that task fell to Remarque, then Dietrich's lover.

Casting Stewart met with resistance at Universal as well. The studio executives couldn't imagine how the skinny actor, usually seen in modern comedies and romances, could be the big strapping hero of a Western. Once again, the studio let Pasternak have his way. But, if the picture flopped, he was told, he would be held responsible. To protect himself, he hired George Marshall to direct; Marshall had been at the helm of the original *Destry* seven years earlier.

The screenplay was still being written when principal photography began—and those scenes that were scripted were revised just before they were shot. Consequently, filming proceeded slowly. Matters weren't helped by a record heat wave that made the Universal soundstages extremely uncomfortable. Six weeks into a scheduled six-week shoot, the script was still unfinished. "We are without definite knowledge of what the remaining requirements may be," studio executive M. F. Murphy noted in the studio's weekly status report dated October 21, 1939, "although we know nothing will be demanded in the way of new sets." Finally, two units worked simultaneously—George Marshall with the principals and a second unit filming atmosphere and extras—to wrap the picture at 4:40 on the morning of November 1, roughly ten days behind schedule.

While in production, Dietrich told her daughter, Maria Riva, "The film is difficult. This little studio is not Paramount," where Marlene had been under contract during the first half of the decade. She added that "Stewart has something. I don't know exactly what it is, but there is something so sweet about him."

In fact the costars had fallen in love. According to Pasternak, Dietrich was attracted to Stewart immediately, but the actor was more interested in Flash Gordon comic books than his leading lady. "So," the producer said, "she did something incredible—the most incredible thing I ever saw. She locked him in his dressing room and promised him a surprise. The surprise was that she presented him with a doll, which she had had the whole studio art department come in over a weekend and make for him—a life-size doll of Flash Gordon, correct in every detail! It started a romance!"

It's a good story, but given Stewart's active romantic life at the time, it is difficult to imagine him preferring science-fiction comic books to Marlene Dietrich. More likely, he was lavishing all his attention on actress Loretta Young, whom he was dating at roughly the same time. The beautiful brunette was also in love with him, but she wanted to get married, and Jimmy was not ready to settle down. When Young was asked by another of her concurrent boyfriends, radio producer Tom Lewis, she accepted.

"I liked taking Marlene out to dinner and to dance back in the days of *Destry*," Stewart would later recall, adding that they "dated quite a few times, which was fairly romantic." Jim put an innocent spin on the affair, but it was, in fact, intense. Remarque, who followed Dietrich to Hollywood, noted in his diary that the actress confessed she had slept with her costar from the outset of their relationship. Quoting her, Remarque wrote, "It was a dream: it had been magical. For him [Stewart], too."

But Marlene was far more involved than Jimmy. According to Remarque, "She never knew from one week to the next [where she stood with him]. He had never talked about love, but told her he was not in love, couldn't afford it." Then, she told the writer, she became pregnant with Stewart's child. Remarque noted in his diary that she wanted to have the baby, but that Jim insisted she have an abortion. She acceded to his wishes, traveling to New York for the then illegal operation. Stewart, the writer noted, neither went East with Marlene nor monitored her condition by phone. "She was not even angry with him," he added. "She blamed herself for getting pregnant."

Beyond Remarque's diary, Steven Bach wrote in his 1992 biography of Dietrich that "Maria [Riva] told people who would listen that Stewart had made Marlene pregnant during the making of *Destry*, that Marlene confronted him with the fact on a dance floor in Hollywood, that Stewart (unmarried) walked away without a word, and that Marlene (married) did what women do who don't want unexpected souvenirs of romance." Curiously, in her own book about her mother, hardly a flattering portrait, Riva wrote virtually nothing about Dietrich's relationship with Stewart and avoided the pregnancy issue entirely.

Given Stewart's squeaky-clean image and conservative values, some might find such a story difficult to accept, but it is credible. If there was a flaw in Jim's character, it was that he was not a stand-up guy. Yes, he believed in the sanctity of the family, and certainly, in later years, he was antiabortion, but he clung to notions without reflection; he simply accepted them. But fight for them? Take risks for them? Not likely. The fact is that, aside from his military service during World War II, Stewart never fought hard for anything. Career, money, women, friends, they all came pretty easily. As a rather affable, unassertive person, he preferred to sit back and let good things come his way. When something untoward did happen, such as Dietrich's pregnancy, he would have been inclined to ignore the whole matter, to drive it from his mind. If one doesn't think about something, doesn't do anything about it, it arguably didn't happen.

In later years, Dietrich remembered Stewart as something of a vacuous character. In her 1987 autobiography, she chose to ignore their personal relationship entirely—it is a very sanitized book—but she observed, "Obviously, his sense of humor was poorly developed. He performed his way throughout his life and became very rich and very famous." She also noted, "The only really admirable actor with whom I worked was Spencer Tracy."

Regardless of what did or did not happen on a personal level, Stewart and Dietrich made great costars. Jim remembered one piece of advice that Marlene gave him while making the picture: "'If you've got an over-the-shoulder shot and you're talking to the person, never try to look at the person in both eyes, because you really can't do that. You've got to look at the woman or the man in one eye or the other, without switching your focus back and forth between eyes."

She didn't help him with his gunmanship, however. Even though *Destry* goes without pistols for most of the picture, Stewart had one scene in which he had to shoot the knobs off a saloon sign. He also had to twirl the revolver. "I rehearsed it over my bed at home," the actor recalled, "so I wouldn't break that handle when I dropped it. And really, really rehearsed the fan-shooting, loosened the thing up, so I could really do him shooting the knobs off the thing." He loved that scene.

On November 29, less than a month after *Destry* wrapped, it opened at the Rivoli Theatre in New York. Once again the critics raved about a Stewart picture.[2]

---

[2] Such was the appeal of the 1939 version of *Destry Rides Again* that the picture, itself a remake, gave rise to two subsequent films: *Frenchie* (1950) with Shelley Winters as the dance hall queen and *Destry* (1954) with Audie Murphy. A musical version, bearing the title of the 1939 version and starring Andy Griffith and Dolores Grey, opened on Broadway in 1959. It featured a score by Harold Rome.

For Dietrich, the film was a triumph. Giving the role her all in an effort to revive her career, she sang three songs, including "The Boys in the Back Room," which thereafter became one of her trademark numbers. She also rolled her own cigarettes, engaged in an amazing catfight with a townswoman played by Una Merkel, threw everything imaginable at Stewart after he dumped a bucket of water on her, and radiated sex even when soaking wet. It was, to quote William Boehnel of the *New York World-Telegram,* "a rousing comeback."

Destry, released only six weeks after *Mr. Smith,* was a triumph for Stewart as well. Many of the critics saw the similarity between his two quiet, principled, idealistic characters, and the combination, like one-two punches, did much to cement his image and popularity. As Boehnel wrote, "Here is a performance, coming as it does right on the heels of his work in *Mr. Smith Goes to Washington,* which should prove once and for all how fine an actor as well as how attractive a personality Mr. Stewart really is."

Thus, as the 1930s came to an end, Stewart had, at last, developed a fully formed screen persona. Asked to define its essence, fellow actor Robert Stack said, "He is the prototypical American. If America is ever going to work, this is it." Bernard Smith, who produced two of Stewart's later films, *How the West Was Won* and *Cheyenne Autumn,* put it similarly, saying, "He is the ideal American hero."

But Stewart was not, and never would be, heroic in the classic movie-star tradition. He would never be a swashbuckler like Douglas Fairbanks or a tough guy like Jimmy Cagney or suave like Ronald Colman. He would not be the one to take over the ship from the tyrannical captain, as Clark Gable did in *Mutiny on the Bounty,* or single-handedly capture a group of German soldiers, as Gary Cooper would in *Sergeant York.* His heroism would be that of the average guy, the fellow who's just like the folks in the audience. He'd do what they would like to think they'd do in similar circumstances. And like them, he could be hurt. Stewart once said that he favored characters who were vulnerable, so that, as he put it, "the audience would say, 'Jeez, maybe he's not gonna make it. Maybe he's in real trouble.' I think I tended toward that."

On another occasion, Stewart described his type of role thus: "I suppose I have specialized in playing the boob during my career. I play a fellow who gets pulled into something he really can't handle, a guy who gets pushed on and put upon by other people, but finally manages to muddle through." Ric Hardman, who wrote the 1966 Stewart Western *The Rare Breed,* pinpointed that very quality in seeking to define the actor's early popularity. "You loved his confusion," the screenwriter said, "you loved his eagerness. His wish to do right. You kind of walked with him and talked with him."

And one *could* walk and talk with James Stewart, because he looked and sounded so ordinary. He was also attractive. He had long, thick hair, warm, soft eyes, and sensuous lips, and an almost angelic quality about him when he looked up. But his were regular features, not those of a matinee idol. You could find someone like Jim in any city or town in the country. When the situation called for it, he could render dialogue as quickly and cleanly as any other polished professional, but his use of a slow, hesitant delivery, when it suited his character, as it did in *Mr. Smith* and *Destry*, gave him a naturalism that few of his peers could match. Actor John Saxon, who came of age twenty years after Stewart, when the Actors Studio was introducing a new style of realism into film performances, acknowledged Stewart's pioneering achievement, saying, "He was one of the first to have that kind of halting delivery that was so natural. Searching for words and 'um, um, um, well, you know' kind of thing."

Of course, the style was exaggerated. In real life, Stewart could talk like anyone else when he wished. He had what they used to call breeding: after all, he was the product of a fine prep school and an Ivy League college. But he came from the hinterlands and was a true believer in traditional American values. He was also absentminded and reserved, like Mr. Smith, and even-tempered like Destry. And he was a genuinely nice person, one unaffected by his stardom. "He was just exactly the way you see him on the screen," says Philip Alford, who played his son in the 1965 film *Shenandoah*. "The same warm personality." His friend Burgess Meredith put it this way: "Jimmy's screen roles reflect his real-life personality: a boyish, shy, rather inarticulate individual. But he capitalizes on these weaknesses, if that's what they are. Instead of trying to be someone else, he plays himself under various circumstances." Even Stewart said, "I couldn't mess around doing great characterizations. I play versions of myself. Audiences have come to expect certain things from me and are disappointed if they don't get them."

He had become, in the parlance of the trade, a personality actor. Where others, such as Alec Guinness or Rod Steiger or Dustin Hoffman, disappear into their roles, the personality actor imbues everything he or she does with a certain essence. Humphrey Bogart, for example, was invariably the fast-talking, cynical tough guy with a tender heart. John Wayne was the cowboy—or marshal or cavalry officer or marine—with a quick temper and a penchant for speaking his mind. Cary Grant was the unflappable, debonair fellow with a quick retort for any occasion.

It's harder for personality actors to gain critical recognition because what they do seems to come so easily to them. They're just being themselves, is the theory. Critics would raise that specter with Stewart from time to time, but they did so far more often with Wayne and Grant and in more recent decades, Clint Eastwood. That Stewart's talent didn't go unappreciated was due largely to the fact that it took several years and nearly twenty pictures before his image began to coalesce into something coherent and definable. By that point, his military service was imminent, which, in a way, was fortunate, because the majority of his remaining prewar pictures—with a few notable exceptions—were so mundane that his star might have faded rather quickly if he'd stayed in Hollywood. In 1940 and 1941, there are definite hints pointing to the limits of that boy-next-door image. Rose Pelswick of the *New York Journal American* argued, for example, that he went "overboard on the head-hanging, shuffling, boyish awkwardness routine" in *Come Live with Me,* released in February of 1941. Likewise, in *Pot o' Gold,* which premiered about a month later, *Variety* reduced his performance to "James Stewart plays James Stewart."

Fortunately, Jim returned from Europe a free agent, and his work thereafter, especially in the 1950s, allowed him to stretch his persona far beyond its prewar limits—indeed, beyond the norm of most personality actors. Even so, in 1963 he would say, "I take a lot of criticism because my personality always comes through."

But that lay far in the future. As 1939 came to a close, it was enough that James Stewart had brought something new and fresh to Hollywood. He was, at last, a major star.

NINE

"One of the Finest Actors Alive Today"

L. B. Mayer finally got his wish. Stewart and Margaret Sullavan were reteamed in two pictures, back to back. The first, *The Shop Around the Corner*, went into production on November 2, 1939, the day after *Destry* wrapped. It found the twosome as bickering clerks in a Budapest store. Without realizing it, they've fallen in love with each other through their unsigned correspondence. Each knows his amour only as "Dear Friend."

This charming romance was adapted by Samson Raphaelson from Nikolaus Laszlo's Hungarian play *Parfumerie*, which had opened in Budapest on March 21, 1937. Thereafter, the screen rights were acquired by director Ernst Lubitsch, who had just formed his own independent production company. But Lubitsch was unable to interest any of the major studios in the property. Then, he was hired by MGM to direct Greta Garbo in *Ninotchka*, and as part of the deal, Mayer agreed to produce *The Shop Around the Corner* as well.

Lubitsch sought Stewart for the role of the salesclerk, Alfred Kralik, because the actor was, in the director's words, "the antithesis of the old-time matinee idol; he holds his public by his very lack of a handsome face or suave manner." European actress Dolly Haas was originally targeted for the salesgirl, Klara, and Raphaelson maintained that she was perfect for the part, but Lubitsch got nervous about casting an unknown. He considered the unconventional story gamble enough.

Best known for his frothy comedies about the upper classes, the German-born director was once described as a "little man, strongly built, with a great deal of coal black hair crowning his massive head." He was famous for his attention to detail. And, indeed, the celebrated Lubitsch "touch" pervaded *The Shop Around the Corner*. The leather goods store, Matuschck and Company, in which much of the film is set, was meticulously researched. And Sullavan was dressed in the kind of simple frocks a salesgirl would actually wear. In fact, when the actress purchased a likely dress for $1.98, Lubitsch told her that even it was too stylish. He had it altered so that it fit her poorly and hung it in the sunlight so that its color would fade. For the winter scenes, he insisted on using real snow, so Metro had to import thirty tons of ice and shave the blocks into flakes. The result justified the effort. The picture, shot entirely on soundstages and MGM's backlot, had a verisimilitude totally lacking in *Seventh Heaven.*

Lubitsch also brought a keen understanding to the film's characters and milieu. "I have known just such a little shop in Budapest," he explained at the film's premiere. "The feeling between the boss and those who work for him is pretty much the same the world over, it seems to me. Everyone is afraid of losing his job and everyone knows how little human worries can affect his job. If the boss has a touch of dyspepsia, better be careful not to step on his toes; when things have gone well with him, the whole staff reflects his good humor." Given his familiarity with the material, the director worked with his screenwriter to bring little touches to the film that were not in Laszlo's play. Lubitsch was justifiably proud of the authenticity. "Never did I make a picture in which the atmosphere and the characters were truer than in this picture," he later said.

"It was wonderful to work with him," Stewart recalled. "He had such great style and an inspiring sort of comic touch. You could see it every place in the movie. He was a very talented man." The respect was mutual. "Lubitsch told me after the picture's completion," said Raphaelson, "that he thought Jimmy Stewart was a very fine artist indeed, with an unusually pliable and cooperative approach to suggestions." Under the director's guidance, Stewart worked more simply and cleanly than he had in either *Mr. Smith* or *Destry.* In place of the hemming and hawing, the drawl, and the dropping of *g*'s from the end of words, he spoke softly but distinctly. And his gestures and facial expressions were tightly controlled. As a consequence, he imbued Kralik with a European middle-class sensibility without affecting an accent or any specific mannerisms. He slipped once or twice, notably in the scene in which he loses his temper at, and fires, another clerk (played by Joseph Schildkraut), but by and large, he was far more acceptable as a Hungarian than he had been as a Parisian in *Seventh Heaven.*

Of course, he relished the chance to work with Sullavan again. But he drove her nuts during the shooting of the final scene. Earlier in the picture, Klara accuses Kralik of being bowlegged, and in this moment of reconciliation and revelation, he offers to roll up his pants to prove that he's not—and then does so. "For some reason I couldn't say the line," Stewart recalled, which infuriated the actress. He was, he admitted, embarrassed about displaying his skinny legs. Finally, he said in a moment of self-disgust, "I don't want to act today; get a fellow with decent legs and just show them." But Sullavan refused to work with a body double, so they kept filming. Stewart estimated that the scene took forty-eight takes—the most he ever had to do in a movie—before he got the moment right.

The climax aside, the filming of *The Shop Around the Corner* went swiftly, with principal photography completed in a mere twenty-seven days, half the time that it took Lubitsch to shoot *Ninotchka.* Moreover the director managed to film in sequence, a rarity in pictures.

The Shop Around the Corner opened at Radio City Music Hall on January 25, 1940. Lee Mortimer captured the sense of the critics, writing in the *New York Daily Mirror,* "*The Shop Around the Corner* is the best picture in town. It is gay and light and beautiful and as sparkling as the foam atop a glass of Pilsner." Praise went to the stars and the director, but the warmest notices were reserved for Frank Morgan—best remembered as the title character in *The Wizard of Oz*—who was utterly convincing and moving as the aging merchant, Matuschek.[1]

After *The Shop Around the Corner* wrapped, Stewart went East to visit his family for the Christmas holidays. He started by meeting his sisters in New York, a visit that made them fully aware of his celebrity for the first time. As Ginny put it the following year in an article for *Coronet* magazine, "Going about with Jim introduced Doddie and me to a type of person we never knew existed—the strange young man who raced down the street to shake his hand; the eager little girl who jumped on the running-board of the taxi and begged for an autograph 'for Geraldine'; the aristocratic little lady who wished him a Merry Christmas on the Avenue. They seemed to be marvelous people—natural and spontaneous and charming."

While Stewart was in Manhattan, Leland Hayward asked if he would escort Olivia de Havilland to the New York premiere of her latest film, *Gone With the Wind.* The fix-up had been the brainstorm of Irene Mayer Selznick, wife of the film's producer, David O. Selznick. Stewart didn't know the actress, but he had read in a gossip column that she wanted to meet him, so he eagerly complied with his agent's request. "Jimmy met me at La Guardia airport," de Havilland recalled, "even had the limousine drive out to the airfield—we were both quite shy and ventured one word at a time in our conversation." Still, a definite spark passed between them. Over the next few days, Stewart took her to the theater several times and to the "21" Club. She recalled that one of the plays they saw was *Mornings at Seven,* directed by Jim's old friend Josh Logan, whom she met for the first time backstage.

---

[1] In 1949, MGM would remake the picture as a musical, *In the Good Old Summertime,* starring Judy Garland and Van Johnson, with turn-of-the-century Chicago substituting for the original setting. Composer Jerry Bock and lyricist Sheldon Harnick would return the story to its European milieu for the 1963 Broadway musical *She Loves Me.*

Jim and Olivia continued to see each other after they returned to Los Angeles. On one occasion, Stewart arrived at her Spanish-colonial house in the Hollywood hills driving his brand-new La Salle convertible. She was impressed until the automobile began making a weird groaning sound and then started rolling down the hill. The brakes had failed! Jim took off in pursuit, but the La Salle picked up speed down the incline, denting other cars and ruining curbside shrubbery along the way. Finally, it crashed into a telephone pole. Naturally, Stewart, who had been trying to impress his date, was terribly embarrassed, but she laughed and thanked him for the entertainment. They then continued their evening as planned—in her car.

Around the same time, actress Maureen O'Hara remembered having dinner one night at de Havilland's house. A fish that Stewart had caught was the main course. It was fine, but they decided to play a prank on him by telling him that it had made them sick. "But he didn't pay the slightest bit of attention," O'Hara recalled, laughing. "He knew."

One tends to think of de Havilland as ladylike and kind because she played such characters on the screen. But Joan Fontaine painted a different picture in her book, *No Bed of Roses*. She remembered inviting her sister and Stewart to dinner to mark de Havilland's birthday. "Two hours after the time they were asked for," Fontaine wrote, "Olivia and Jimmy rang our bell. When I remonstrated that the dinner was hardly palatable any longer, Olivia answered, 'It's my birthday. I can arrive whenever I like!'"

Livvy came from a background radically different from Stewart's. Eight years younger than he, she had been born in Tokyo to a British patent attorney and a former actress. Her parents divorced when she was quite young, and she and her sister grew up in California. Her film debut came in the same year as Jim's, 1935, when she played Hermia in the Max Reinhardt production of *A Midsummer Night's Dream*. Since then, her frequent pairings with Errol Flynn—including *Captain Blood*, *The Charge of the Light Brigade*, and *The Adventures of Robin Hood*—had made her a popular favorite.

De Havilland was in all probability the first woman that Stewart ever seriously considered marrying. After all, she was well-bred, college educated, and refined—all qualities that he desired in a wife. He did, in fact, propose, although de Havilland would later say, "I think his offer of marriage was just a frivolous thing on his part. Jimmy wasn't ready for a wife. I guess he still had a few more wild oats to sow." The exact nature of their relationship never became public, but the Hollywood press used plenty of ink speculating on what was transpiring between the two stars, including the possibility that they might elope in the spring of 1940. Columnist Gloria Hall also reported that Warner Bros., which had de Havilland under contract, wanted to team the actress and her new boyfriend in a picture, but the stars refused. According to the reporter, they gave as their reason that "they would be embarrassed to make love—in *public.*" Thus, de Havilland spent the spring of 1940 making *My Love Came Back* and Stewart did *The Mortal Storm* and *No Time for Comedy.*

The Mortal Storm was the second of Jimmy's back-to-back features with Margaret Sullavan, and the last of their four pictures together. Once again, they were cast as Europeans, this time as Germans. She was Freya Roth, the daughter of a distinguished Jewish science professor and an Aryan mother. He was Martin Breitner, an old family friend and a farmer studying veterinary medicine at the university where Roth teaches. As the film opens, the professor is happily celebrating his sixtieth birthday with his family, colleagues, and students. That same evening, Adolf Hitler is appointed chancellor of Germany. From that moment forward, the harmony within the family is broken. Freya's half brothers—from her mother's first marriage—and her fiancé, Fritz Marberg, become fervent Nazis while she and Martin, with whom she eventually falls in love, abhor the new regime.

Stewart's character was not in the 1938 novel by Phyllis Bottome, on which the film was based. The closest equivalent was Freya's Communist lover, Hans, who is forced to flee the country after the German parliament, the Reichstag, is burned. Crossing the border, he is shot by Marberg.

Much of the rest of the screenplay by Claudine West, Anderson Ellis, and George Froeschel differed from the novel as well. In the book, for example, Freya is left pregnant with Hans' child and, at the end, manages to leave Germany to raise the infant in America, where her dead boyfriend's family lives. In the film, she and Martin never consummate their relationship—such a thing would have been unthinkable in the Hollywood of the 1940s—and she is killed while trying to escape into Austria. Bottome defended the changes, writing in the *New York Times* upon the picture's release, "The new incidents invented by the scriptwriter[s] are not alien incidents. They could have happened in the book itself without violating its contents. In the one or two radical changes in the film, I think that the greater success sometimes lies with the script." Her only disappointment, she added, was the watering down of the moment in which the professor tells his young son, Rudi, what it means to be a Jew. Indeed, the words *Jew* and *Jewish* are not even used in the film; the professor is called a "non-Aryan."

The picture's director, Frank Borzage, believed that the essence of the story lay in what he called "a family's disintegration" in the face of a dictatorship. "It just happens to have Nazi Germany as its background," he added. This sentiment would explain why Stewart, Sullavan, and Frank Morgan, cast as the professor, evidenced almost none of the sensibilities that made all three of them so subtly credible as Europeans in the Lubitsch picture. The same could be said of virtually everyone in *The Mortal Storm*, although Robert Young does a fair amount of bowing and heel-clicking as Fritz. To attempt such a topical subject without trying to place the characters in their proper milieu was, in retrospect, an ill-advised choice.

Likewise, Borzage asserted, "Our picture won't have any 'heavies' and it's not an attack on Germany." But the Nazis are presented throughout as one-dimensional stereotypes. In an instant, Fritz and Freya's half brothers, played by Robert Stack and William T. Orr, go from typically jovial college students to fanatics, intolerant of anyone who doesn't share their fervor for the new Germany. And their leaders, especially Dan Dailey in his film debut, are simply thugs.

Moreover, Utah-born Borzage had a tendency to overlay his films—which included the silent version of *Seventh Heaven*—with a religious-romanticist veneer, and *The Mortal Storm* was no exception. The story was prefaced by a long prologue, in which a stentorian voice traces Man's inhumanity back to the caveman days while a cloudy sky appears on the screen. "The tale we are about to tell," the narrator concludes, "is of the mortal storm in which Man finds himself today. Again, he is crying, 'I must kill my fellow man.' Our story asks, 'How soon will Man find wisdom in his heart and build a lasting shelter against his ignorant fears?' " Even for 1940, this was a bit thick.

In his 1993 biography of Louis B. Mayer, Charles Higham asserted that Sidney Franklin was the original director of *The Mortal Storm*, and he was replaced by Victor Saville. Others have credited Saville with some of the direction as well. But, an examination of the project's records at USC indicates that Borzage was at the helm from day one. Furthermore, Robert Stack remembers Borzage as *The Mortal Storm*'s sole director. Franklin was, in fact, the picture's producer, and he was replaced in *that* capacity during filming by Saville.

Stewart did not remember the making of *The Mortal Storm* with fondness. "I'd read the papers, the horrifying headlines," he said shortly after the picture wrapped, "go on the set, and walk right into the headlines. Same thing. The emotional and nervous strain was terrific." Moreover, in February, March, and April of 1940, while the company was filming, Hitler was enjoying victory after victory on the battlefields of Europe. According to Stack, the Nazis were fully aware of *The Mortal Storm*. When the war was won, a Swiss diplomat informed Victor Saville, everyone involved with the film and *Confessions of a Nazi Spy*, another unflattering picture, would be "taken care of." The atmosphere on the set was, to quote Stack, "tense."

On a lighthearted note, Jim had two scenes in the picture that called for his character to ski. One of them was the final sequence, in which he and Freya try to cross the border into Austria. Of course, the actors had doubles. "Wal, after the picture came out," Stewart liked to joke, "and people said they didn't know I could ski, I told them I couldn't—that Metro had used a *real* skier in the sequence. A year later, I was saying, 'Wal, I only did *part* of the skiing.' A year after that I was saying, 'Wal, you know how it was when I did all that skiing in that scene. It's like swimming. When you learn it as a child, it always comes back to you.' "

He didn't have to ski, but he did have to carry Sullavan in his arms for the close-ups in the second of those sequences. And he couldn't do it—which, of course, made tiny Maggie furious. To help him out, the crew finally rigged up a pulley system, but even then he did a take in which the skis slid out from under him, causing him to drop his costar on her ass. He later told her daughter Brooke Hayward that that outtake became a favorite at MGM parties.

The Mortal Storm opened at the Capitol Theatre in New York on June 20, 1940. "It is quite a cast and, as directed by Frank Borzage, an effective one," argued Eileen Creelman of the *New York Sun,* and few of her colleagues disagreed. Stewart's performance even inspired Howard Barnes of the *New York Herald-Tribune* to call Jim "one of the finest actors alive today" and his portrayal of the freethinking German "superbly good." He *is,* in fact, effective, just not Germanic. As Archer Winsten put it in the *New York Post,* he was reminiscent of "a very American Mr. Smith."

Although *The Mortal Storm* was well produced, events had overtaken the project, and it was not a major success. With much of Europe under Hitler's domination and France and England battling to stop the seemingly invincible German army, the topic of the film—Hitler's rise to power—seemed long ago and of little consequence. Indeed, France fell to Germany five days after *The Mortal Storm* premiered.

Ten days after *The Mortal Storm* wrapped, Stewart got back to lighter fare. The picture was *No Time for Comedy,* in which he played Gaylord Esterbrook, the author of a series of hit comedies and the husband of actress Linda Paige. When he falls under the spell of a bored socialite who likes to play muse to handsome, talented men, his wife has to fight to keep their marriage from falling apart.

The project began as a sophisticated drawing-room comedy by S. N. Behrman, which opened on Broadway in April 1939 starring Katharine

Cornell and Laurence Olivier. Warner Bros. acquired the movie rights for a then considerable $55,000 as a vehicle for its most important actress, Bette Davis. Eventually, however, the role went to Rosalind Russell, Stewart's former radio costar and sometime date. The shapely brunette usually played sarcastic, fast-talking dames who could more than hold their own with the men they encountered—as in *His Girl Friday*, released earlier in 1940—but as the elegant actress in *No Time for Comedy* she would be asked to work on a more subdued level.

Warners had acquired Stewart in a trade with David O. Selznick, who held a one-picture option from Metro for the actor's services. In return for borrowing Olivia de Havilland for *Gone With the Wind*, Selznick relinquished his option to Warners. Initially, the studio had planned to feature Jim in a comedy called *Honeymoon for Three*, so he took that script home to read. "Funniest thing, I kept thinking how familiar it all was," he said shortly thereafter. "Right from the first I had the strangest feeling that I knew all this. Even the lines were familiar. Then all of a sudden it hit me." It was an adaptation of *Goodbye Again*, his first Broadway comedy.

Prior commitments for Stewart's services—to Columbia for *Mr. Smith* and to Universal for *Destry*—forced the studio to give the part in *Honeymoon for Three* to George Brent. Jim was then assigned to a property called *It All Came True*. But, as *Mr. Smith* fell further and further behind schedule, Warners was again forced to use another actor, this time Jeffrey Lynn (thus, Stewart lost his only opportunity to work with Humphrey Bogart, who costarred in *It All Came True*). At the time, Jack Warner was furious at having to wait so long for his turn with the Metro contract player, but he calmed down after *Mr. Smith* was released: it made Stewart a much more valuable property. Consequently, four days after the Capra picture opened in New York, Warner exhorted his production chief, Hal Wallis, to find an "important vehicle" for the star. Testament to Stewart's new status was his billing for *No Time for Comedy*—he was in the premier spot for the first time since *Speed;* even in *Mr. Smith* and *Destry* he had taken second place to his better-established female costars.

Once the studio decided to cast him in *No Time for Comedy*, a major rewrite was required. After all, the character in the play was a Broadway sophisticate played by Laurence Olivier—not exactly Jimmy's territory. Screenwriters Julius and Philip Epstein devised an entirely new first act, in which the playwright is summoned from his home, a small Minnesota town, to doctor his debut Broadway comedy. Gay thus becomes Jefferson Smith with a typewriter. Outside the theater, he gazes with wonder at the play's framed poster with his name on it. The leading lady, Russell, mistakes him for a gofer and asks him to buy her a pack of cigarettes. He insists on riding the subway at rush hour and shouts, "Boy, this is great," as he is jostled by the crowd. At the end of the sequence, his play opens, it's a smash, and he and Linda decide to marry. Then Behrman's plotline takes over, and the vitality of the picture drops considerably. Arguably, the studio, known for its fast-moving, urban melodramas about ordinary folks, didn't know what to do with the posh drawing-room comedy. As Julius Epstein says in retrospect, "It wasn't a Warners type of picture really. It was more a Metro type of picture."

Under the studio's contract director, William Keighley, a former stage actor and director, filming proceeded in an orderly fashion. The company commenced work on April 29, 1940 (Stewart's first day was the thirtieth), and the picture wrapped on June 12, one day behind schedule. Says Epstein, "The making of it was something that wasn't too common then and isn't too common now, freedom from stress or disagreements. Everybody did their job and went home."

Billed as starring "That Guy from Washington . . . That Woman from *The Women*," the latter a reference to Russell's performance in the catty Clare Boothe Luce film of 1939, *No Time for Comedy* opened at the Strand Theatre in New York on September 6. The critics found it amusing and raved about Stewart and Russell. Archer Winsten of the *New York Post* called her performance "one of her best," while his counterpart on the *New York Times*, Bosley Crowther, argued that Stewart was "the best thing in the show." But Howard Barnes of the *New York Herald-Tribune* quite rightly noted that the film "isn't Behrman. . . . Where the play brooded humorously and wisely about creative inspiration, the contemporary conditioning of artists and human relationships," the film was more simplistic, focusing on the romance between Gay and Linda.

Less than a month after *No Time for Comedy* wrapped, Stewart was before the cameras again in another sophisticated comedy based on a Broadway play. This time his costar was Katharine Hepburn. Like Marlene Dietrich, the Oscar-winning actress had been labeled "box-office poison" by America's motion-picture exhibitors in 1938. And, as had been the case with her German colleague, the film that she shared with Jimmy Stewart would revitalize her career.

The comeback started on the stage. Hepburn's friend Philip Barry had written a delicious role especially for her in a sophisticated drawing-room comedy called *The Philadelphia Story*. The character, Tracy Lord, was a beautiful but cold, unforgiving young woman who was about to be married for the second time without really understanding what love is. She finally learns with the help of two other suitors, C. K. Dexter Haven, her first husband, and Macaulay "Mike" Connor, a writer covering her wedding for a shady magazine. Barry based Tracy on a real Main Line debutante, Hope Montgomery, who had married one of his college class-mates, Edgar Scott.

The play opened on Broadway on March 28, 1939, with Joseph Cotten as Dexter Haven, Van Heflin as Mike Connor, and Shirley Booth as Mike's colleague, magazine photographer Elizabeth Imbrie. Of Hepburn, drama critic Richard Watts Jr. wrote, "Few actresses of the modern theater have been mocked and criticized so cruelly and unjustly, and now she turns upon the skeptics and offers one of the most enchanting performances of the season." Watts also found the comedy "a lively and entertaining play, written with all of Mr. Barry's graceful wit"—an opinion shared by the rest of the press as well.

Not surprisingly, Hollywood clamored for the film rights to the new hit. Warner Bros. saw it as a vehicle for Ann Sheridan. MGM hoped to snare it for Joan Crawford or Norma Shearer. Zanuck at 20th Century–Fox wanted it for . . . well, he didn't have anyone special in mind, he just wanted it. No one, however, expressed an interest in taking Hepburn as part of the package. But Kate was prepared for that: with the help of then amour Howard Hughes, she had acquired the screen rights to *The Philadelphia Story* prior to the play's debut. And no one was going to get them unless she played the lead—and got to choose her costars and director.

That caused some of the studios to give up, but not Samuel Goldwyn, who offered to pair Hepburn with Gary Cooper and give her William Wyler as her director. It was a tempting package, but ultimately Hepburn turned to Metro. Not only was L. B. Mayer offering $175,000 for the film rights (she had paid somewhere between $25,000 and $30,000), he threw in another $75,000 for her to star in the picture. He also agreed to her choice of director, George Cukor, who had previously directed her in her screen debut, *A Bill of Divorcement,* as well as in *Sylvia Scarlett, Little Women,* and the film version of another Barry play, *Holiday.*

As for her costars, Hepburn asked for MGM contract players Spencer Tracy and Clark Gable. Mayer said he would speak to his stars but made no promises. When they turned him down, he suggested Jim, and Kate liked the idea; she had been delighted by his performance in *Mr. Smith Goes to Washington.* For the other star, Mayer gave her $150,000 and told her to hire whom she wished. She chose Cary Grant, her leading man in *Sylvia Scarlett, Bringing Up Baby,* and *Holiday.* To get him, she even agreed to let him have first billing in what was clearly her vehicle. She also let Grant decide which of the two roles—Dexter Haven or Macaulay Connor—he would play; he opted for the ex-husband. The role had been expanded by combining it with another of the play's characters, Tracy's brother, Sandy (onstage, it is the brother, not the ex-husband, who is responsible for the magazine's coverage of Tracy's wedding).

Jim was delighted to be involved in the production. "When I first read the script," he recalled, "I thought I was being considered for the part of the fellow who was engaged to her. As I read, I thought to myself, 'Oooh, that part of the reporter is a good one, but I'll be happy to play the other one.' " When he finished, he went to the film's producer, Joseph Mankiewicz, with whom he'd last worked on *The Shopworn Angel,* and asked who was going to play Connor. He was shocked to find out he was!

Filming began on July 5. By that time, Hepburn had been away from pictures for two years. Still, she knew her role intimately, having played Tracy 416 times on Broadway. To keep her fresh during filming, Cukor purposely offered suggestions and interpretations that forced her to look at scenes anew. And, of course, she had to adjust to Grant and Stewart, who brought their own slants to the roles created onstage by Cotten and Heflin.

Given his successful collaborations with numerous actresses, particularly Hepburn, Cukor has come to be known as a woman's director. But, as his biographer Emanuel Levy argued, "he also worked extremely well with men." As Cukor himself once said, "I'm an interpretive director, really. I get a text of a play and I *think* that's what determines the way I will do it; that influences me a great deal." In *The Philadelphia Story,* for example, the material determined the picture's pace. "You couldn't take it too quickly," the director explained, "because these are people for whom conversation is a kind of art, they say witty things and they're witty about serious things." In an era dominated by breakneck screwball comedies, such as Hepburn and Grant's *Bringing Up Baby,* one of the great charms of *The Philadelphia Story* is the leisurely, but far from plodding, way in which it moves.

Coming originally from the theater, Cukor had an appreciation for the craft of acting, which many film directors do not—especially those who start as editors, cinematographers, and in other technical disciplines. Like Capra, Cukor worked gently, taking his players aside and talking to them about their characters. "He wasn't overbearing," says Ruth Hussey, who played Liz Imbrie in *The Philadelphia Story.* "He made suggestions rather than saying, 'It should be this way, it should be that way.' "

Stewart, cast as someone far more cynical and worldly than the likes of Jeff Smith, Tom Destry, or even Gay Esterbrook, benefited from Cukor's guidance. Hepburn remembered the director telling Jim to stand still when he spoke, not to paw the ground with his foot like a circus animal. Watching his performance, one is struck by the absence of the vocal and physical affectations that were becoming his trademark.

His greatest difficulty stemmed from his principal love scene with Hepburn. It takes place on the grounds of the Lord estate, late on the evening before Tracy's wedding, after both she and Connor have had quite a bit to drink. At one point, Mike says to her, "You're lit from within, Tracy. You've got hearth fires banked down in you, hearth fires and holocausts," not easy material for anyone. On the day the scene was shot, Stewart was struggling. Then, Noël Coward, a friend of Cukor's, stopped by the set. The celebrated British author/actor took a moment to tell Stewart how well he was doing. Seeing his star perk up, Cukor quickly called for another take, and Jim nailed the scene.

In the end, the director thought the relationship between the stars worked because Stewart and Hepburn, in his words, "played it in their own styles. That's what makes it comic and adorable." Indeed, Jim's quiet, smooth voice and soft features contrast nicely with Kate's clipped, sharp tones and angular countenance.

Stewart enjoyed working with Hepburn. Even though she knew the material intimately and had been responsible for the film's casting, he felt that "once the picture started, she was just like a regular hardworking actress. No semblance of any 'I want this and I want that. I've done this on the stage for three years, so I know, so don't do it that way.' "

Hepburn liked Stewart as well. "He's a helluva nice guy," she said a few years later, "and wonderful to work with." She also recalled a delightful moment they shared off camera: "We were about to shoot the love scene on a chaise lounge and didn't especially want any onlookers. Jimmie [sic] was sitting on the foot of the sofa when Hedda Hopper burst in and sat herself down on the back of the chaise lounge. I beckoned to Jimmie, and as he got up, Miss Hopper [sitting on what was effectively a seesaw] went crashing to the floor."

As usual, between setups, Stewart was fun to be around. One time, the principals were waiting for the cameras to roll on a set decorated with artificial flowers for Tracy's wedding. "So he took a rose," Ruth Hussey recalls. "It was an imitation rose—it had a wire stem, you know. Turned the wire around to make a base and put it on his head. There he stands with this rose supposedly growing out of the top of his head and said, 'What did I want to see Ripley about?' Everybody had a chuckle. He had a pixie sense of humor."

One Friday, as the company prepared to break for the weekend, Hepburn asked if he would take her up in his private airplane, so they met the following morning at Clover Field. "From the time I started the engine," Stewart recalled, "she asked about everything." Thanks to her relationship with Howard Hughes, she knew enough about flying to offer suggestions. He tried to explain his decisions patiently, but after a while the nonstop inquiries began to pall. At one point, he prepared to make a turn, and she told him not to. "Kate," he replied with exasperation, "if we don't turn, we'll be in China." Finally, she asked him to return to the field, and he gladly complied. But she peppered him with so much advice on the way that he could barely set the plane down. "In fact," he said, "the landing wasn't really a landing, but more like a controlled crash." Back at work on Monday, he noted that "she was just as delightful as ever, and she never brought up that episode again."

Stewart enjoyed working with Grant as well. Their biggest scene together required Stewart, inebriated from Tracy's engagement party, to seek a showdown at Dexter Haven's home. "I'd decided I would have the hiccups," said Jim, "but I wouldn't tell anyone about it, just sort of try it out, we could always do a retake." When he hiccuped, Grant, taken by surprise, ad-libbed, "Excuse me," which led to a wonderful, knowing glance between the two. Later, Cary would tell writer-director Peter Bogdanovich that he was "absolutely *fascinated* with" Stewart when they worked on that scene, adding, "You can see it in the film—he was so *good!*"

And, indeed, he was, showing a gift for sophisticated comedy that he'd never had a chance to display before. In the final analysis, Jim was convinced that playing with two such skilled professionals helped make his own performance memorable. "When you work with Grant and Hepburn," he explained, "you *work!* You let up for a second and they'll steal the movie from under your nose! They're the best sort of competition an actor can have. Talent like that keeps you on your toes."

The Philadelphia Story wrapped on August 14, five days under schedule. But MGM waited until the day after Christmas to unveil the finished product at Radio City Music Hall. Bosley Crowther of the *New York Times* wrote that it had "just about everything that a blue-chip comedy should have," and the *Christian Science Monitor* said, "There are times when *The Philadelphia Story* flashes across the Music Hall screen more brilliantly than any other filmed comedy of its genre that we can recall offhand."

It was not just a critical success, it was enormously popular as well. In fact, after twenty-five days, *The Philadelphia Story* broke the Music Hall's all-time attendance record held by Walt Disney's *Snow White and the Seven Dwarfs*. Only a commitment to exhibit Alfred Hitchcock's *Rebecca* forced an end to the engagement after six weeks. The film would go on to earn a profit of $1.3 million.[2]

Shortly after *The Philadelphia Story* wrapped, Stewart helped organize a benefit in Houston, Texas, to support Great Britain, then standing alone

---

[2] In 1956, MGM would remake *The Philadelphia Story* as a musical called *High Society*. Featuring an original score by Cole Porter, it costarred Frank Sinatra in Stewart's role, Bing Crosby as Dexter Haven, and Grace Kelly as Tracy.

against the forces of Nazi Germany. The event, which took place in August at the Houston Coliseum, also featured Henry Fonda, Tyrone Power, and character actor Mischa Auer, who had costarred with Stewart in *You Can't Take It With You* and *Destry Rides Again.* Hearkening back to his youth, Jim did magic tricks with Hank as his assistant. As a bonus, the friends rendered a duet, with Stewart playing the accordion and Fonda the cornet.

Also on the bill was Olivia de Havilland, who had recently returned to Hollywood from location filming for her latest picture, *Santa Fe Trail.* She had been bored and lonely away from home. According to biographer Charles Higham, "Her only consolation was the chance of returning to Stewart on an occasional weekend for flying lessons and romance." Nevertheless, the relationship between the stars had cooled. De Havilland increasingly felt that Stewart's marriage proposal was pro forma, that he didn't really want to settle down. Still, they continued to date for nearly another year. Then Livvy fell in love with John Huston, the director of her then current film, *In This Our Life,* and the relationship with Stewart came to an end. By that point, Jim was in the service.

After the Houston benefit, he joined his parents and sisters for a fishing trip in Canada. "Everywhere they had a sign telling us to stop," Stewart quipped when he returned to Hollywood. "If the sign said Joe's Lunch Wagon, we stopped. Or Hot Dogs Ahead, we stopped. Or See The Rattlesnake Farm, we stopped." It may have been dull, but it was far safer than his excursion to France a year earlier.

Finally, on October 7, after a two-month break, he reported back to work. *Come Live With Me* put him behind a typewriter yet again. This time, he was Bill Smith, a writer in the same vein as Macaulay Connor: talented but undiscovered—and proud. Unlike his *Philadelphia Story* counterpart, however, Smith doesn't have a job with a disreputable magazine or any other form of employment. He's literally down to his last dime when he agrees to a pro forma wedding to a beautiful young Austrian, Johanna Janns, in order to meet his living expenses. Janns, who answers to the more colloquial Johnny Jones, has to marry an American to avoid deportation back to Vienna—and the Nazis, who killed her father. The luminous Hedy Lamarr, herself a refugee from Hitler's fascism, was cast as Johnny.

Beyond its touch of topicality—handled delicately—*Come Live With Me* was made on the assembly line, with dashes of *It Happened One Night* and dozens of other comedies thrown in. Not only did it lack originality, it had no zest, no energy. Even director Clarence Brown, working with Stewart for the fourth and final time, couldn't give it the kind of vigor that he'd found for *Wife v. Secretary.*

Part of the problem may have rested with Stewart's physical condition during filming: he had a terrible cold. "I'd come on the set every morning," he recalled, "with a gallon of orange juice under one arm and a box of tissues under the other, and Clarence Brown, the director, would say, 'When are you going to get over that cold?' That was something I wanted to know myself. I also wanted to know how. My doctor gave me everything—which I took, to keep my conscience clear. But how I got over it, finally, was that I just outlived the germs."

Moreover, Lamarr was busy with another film, *Comrade X*, when *Come Live With Me* commenced production, and she had to shuttle back and forth between the assignments. Then, before the picture wrapped, she and Stewart were both cast in *Ziegfeld Girl*, which started shooting on November 4. At least, Stewart didn't have to juggle the two projects for long: he started *Ziegfeld* on November 26, and *Come Live With Me* was in the can four days later.

The picture opened at the Capitol on February 27, 1941—to surprisingly favorable reviews. But the *New York Times* more accurately noted that "for all the superior craft in it, *Come Live with Me* lacks sparkle and spontaneity. It is too stiff in the joints for a madcap antic; its sentiment is oversoft." And while Jim and Hedy had their champions, the *New York World-Telegram* was right when it asserted that Stewart was "pretty unconvincing for him, going through the role not only as if he hated it but also everyone else concerned with the production."

By the fall of 1940, as Stewart lightly confronted on film the impact of Nazi oppression, American involvement in the European conflict seemed increasingly likely. As a measure of preparedness, Congress passed the Selective Training and Service Act, and on September 16, 1940, President Roosevelt signed it into law. Thereafter men between the ages of twenty-one and thirty-six were required to register with their draft boards, and those selected were to undergo a year of training and military service. The first nine hundred thousand inductees were chosen by a lottery held on October 29, an event carried live over radio.

Stewart, age thirty-two, was among those selected. Later, the Hollywood press would report that he voluntarily joined the army, and over the years, that has become the accepted version of his induction. But the fact is, he was drafted. Stewart himself said in 1961, "The only lottery I've ever come close to winning was the drawing for the first draft before Pearl Harbor. My number was the 310th pulled out of the fishbowl."

The manner of Stewart's initial call to service takes nothing away from his patriotism, for on November 26, the day he started work on *Ziegfeld Girl*, he was given a deferment: he had failed to meet the requisite weight for his height. Thus, if he had wanted to, he could have stayed in

Hollywood, making movies and earning a sizable income. Instead, he appealed his classification. Since his hearing wasn't scheduled until February, he continued to report to Metro during the interim.

Ziegfeld Girl was MGM's lavish follow-up to its Oscar-winning hit of 1936, *The Great Ziegfeld.* This time, instead of dramatizing the career and marriages of the celebrated showman, screenwriters Marguerite Roberts and Sonya Levien focused on three girls from different walks of life who become mannequins in his Follies. Like the characters in Jacqueline Susann's *Valley of the Dolls* two decades later, the musical's heroines lead troubled lives: one is an earnest, talented performer unwittingly held back by her father, an old-fashioned vaudevillian; another is a worldly beauty torn between a Follies star and her husband, an unemployed concert violinist; and the third is a brassy elevator operator from Brooklyn who loses herself to rich men and liquor. When the screenplay was completed in mid-1938, the stars were to be Joan Crawford, Margaret Sullavan, and Eleanor Powell, and their men Walter Pidgeon, George Murphy, and Frank Morgan. But, by the time the cameras finally rolled—with Robert Z. Leonard, director of *The Great Ziegfeld,* again at the helm—Judy Garland had become the singer, Hedy Lamarr the worldly beauty, and Lana Turner the ill-fated Brooklynite. Stewart was cast as Turner's boyfriend, Gilbert Young, a truck driver who becomes a bootlegger.

It is likely that Jim's assignment was inspired by the draft. No doubt, Mayer wanted to get another movie in the can in case he lost his popular contract player to the army for a year. Otherwise, the casting made no sense, for although Stewart received top billing in *Ziegfeld Girl,* his role was hardly central to the story, and by the end of 1940, his days as a supporting player were well behind him. Moreover, he wasn't exactly the logical choice for a truck driver. Sporting a leather jacket and a cloth cap, he tried his best to suggest a blue-collar worker, but his skinny physique, refined features, and soft voice were not ideal building blocks for credibility. Even the film's producer, Pandro Berman, later acknowledged that Stewart "deserved a much better part than he got."

In December, with *Ziegfeld Girl* making only intermittent demands on his time, Stewart reported to United Artists. There President Roosevelt's son, James, was producing his first and only feature, a musical called *Pot o' Gold.* The picture was primarily designed to showcase Horace Heidt and his Musical Knights, a big band that appeared on an NBC radio giveaway show of the same name as the film. But Heidt was no actor, so he and his musicians took center stage during the production numbers and left the romantic comedy to Stewart and his costar, Paulette Goddard.

Playing close to his roots, Jim was small-town merchant Jimmy Haskell. When his music store fails, he reluctantly goes to the big city to work for his uncle, a misanthropic food manufacturer. There, he falls in love with Molly McCorkle (Goddard). She and her mother own the boardinghouse in which Heidt and his struggling band members live. Molly also sings with the outfit.

If one wants to see what a Capraesque comedy is like without Capra, *Pot o' Gold* is the picture to catch. Under the direction of *Destry*'s George Marshall, the film has almost no charm whatsoever. The character actors are irritatingly over the top, especially Mary Gordon as Ma McCorkle and Charles Winninger as Stewart's uncle. The seven musical numbers, including "When Johnny Toots His Horn," with Stewart as the featured vocalist, were totally forgettable, and the chemistry between Stewart and Goddard was virtually nonexistent.[3] Observers noted that, behind the scenes, the costars were cool and distant with one another, and that Paulette didn't think much of Jim's acting. "Anyone can gulp," she reportedly said.

Shuttling back and forth between *Pot o' Gold* and *Ziegfeld Girl* didn't help either of Stewart's performances. His involvement with the former was so tangential that, about a decade later, he turned on the television one night and caught a scene from the picture, in which Goddard squirts him with a seltzer bottle, and thought it was a sitcom until he took a close look at the screen. As for *Ziegfeld Girl*, he later told Hedda Hopper that he knew Turner had a death scene, but the day it was shot, he returned from UA and asked, "How did she die— did I have anything to do with it?"

Pot o' Gold opened first—on April 3, 1941—at the Capitol Theatre in New York. Surprisingly, a few voices were raised in its defense. Wanda Hale of the *New York Daily News* called it "lively, tuneful and moderately amusing," and the *New York Journal American* found it "an entertaining little comedy." But the more discerning critics were dismissive of the film, and *Variety* noted, "Stewart's lines and characterization all consciously play up the familiar items in this young actor's bag of tricks. He contrives to infuse some sincerity and to look better than most leading men would probably look in such surroundings."

---

[3] For a nonsinger, Stewart warbled more tunes on camera than most actors in Hollywood. *Born to Dance* immediately comes to mind, but in addition, in *The Philadelphia Story* he rendered part of "Over the Rainbow" while carrying Hepburn to her house after their moonlight swim. In the 1957 Western *Night Passage,* he not only sang, he accompanied himself on the accordion. In 1970's *Cheyenne Social Club,* he warbled an a cappella duet with Henry Fonda. And, in 1978's *The Magic of Lassie,* released when he was seventy, he croaked out part of the opening musical number "Hometown Feeling."

Ziegfeld Girl also played the Capitol later in the month, opening on April 24. It wasn't as bad as *Pot o' Gold*, but it wasn't up to the standards of *The Great Ziegfeld* either. As the *New York Times* put it, it was basically "another conventional musical show, only bigger." Garland and Turner, in the flashiest parts, received the best acting notices, while first-billed Stewart was all but overlooked in what *Newsweek* accurately called "a thankless role."

By the time *Pot o' Gold* and *Ziegfeld Girl* opened, Jim belonged to Uncle Sam. Two months earlier, in February, he was reclassified 1-A. The press reported at the time that he had assiduously gained weight after failing to pass his physical exam the previous November, and the story has been repeated ever since. But, in fact, Stewart weighed only 138 pounds in February of 1941, five pounds below the minimum. He had simply convinced his draft board—No. 245 in West Los Angeles—to list him at the acceptable level. Thus, while others in Hollywood were looking to avoid military service, he had actually cheated to get in. "I had to," he said shortly thereafter. "My father fought in World War I and the Spanish-American War, and in this one it's my turn—Dad's too old now, although he doesn't think so."

Over the next few weeks, Stewart focused on winding up his affairs. He sold his airplane, a Stinson, shipped his dog, the English setter Norma Shearer had given him, back to his folks, and rented his house for a year to Burgess Meredith (by then, Johnny Swope had moved out). "The whole thing was very formal," Meredith told Louella Parsons. "We signed a contract, which, after we both had handled it and read it, looked like an old, tired movie script."

Metro decided not to suspend his contract while he was away. Of course, he was expected to be gone for only a year—the United States had not yet entered the war—but still it was a generous gesture. The studio also threw a farewell cocktail party for him on the top floor of the administration building. "Roz Russell kissed me," he recalled, "Lana Turner kissed me, Judy Garland kissed me, Joan Crawford kissed me, and wiping off their lipstick left my handkerchief covered with red splotches. I wrote each girl's name under her splotch. Call me sentimental, but I still have that handkerchief."

On February 27, he took time out to attend the annual rites of the Academy of Motion Picture Arts and Sciences at the Biltmore Hotel. For the second year in a row he was nominated for Best Actor, this time for *The Philadelphia Story*. The film had garnered five other nominations: Best Picture, Best Actress, Best Supporting Actress (Ruth Hussey), Best Directing, and Best Writing.

Stewart's competition was every bit as formidable as the year before: Charles Chaplin for *The Great Dictator,* Henry Fonda for *The Grapes of Wrath,* Raymond Massey for *Abe Lincoln in Illinois,* and Laurence Olivier for *Rebecca.* With all of the preparations for his induction, Jim had just about decided not to go to the banquet; he was certain he wasn't going to win. He had cast his own vote for Fonda. Then someone from the Academy phoned to find out his plans. "I know it isn't my place to say so," the caller told him, "but I really think you would find it in your best interests to attend."

No single picture dominated the ceremonies for 1940, as *Gone With the Wind* had the year before. John Ford, nominated for *The Grapes of Wrath,* beat Cukor, and Jane Darwell's Ma Joad won out over Ruth Hussey's Liz Imbrie. Ginger Rogers was chosen over Hepburn, for her shopgirl in *Kitty Foyle,* and *Rebecca* took the top honor as Best Picture. But the two Stewarts saved the night for *The Philadelphia Story:* Donald Ogden Stewart won for his screenplay and Jim was named Best Actor.

"I want to assure you that this is a very, very important moment in my life," the star told the assemblage. "As I look around the room, a warm feeling comes over me—a feeling of satisfaction, pride, and, most of all, gratefulness for the encouragement, instruction, and advantage of your experience that has been offered me since I came to Hollywood. With all my heart I thank you."

Privately, he thought the award represented belated recognition for his performance in *Mr. Smith,* and this may be so. Certainly, his role in the Capra picture is the one that best delineates his prewar years. It is arguably the definitive performance of his career. Still, it is tough to find a better example of skilled drawing-room comedy than Stewart's Mike Connor in *The Philadelphia Story.*

Back in Indiana, his father heard the news on the radio. "What'd they give you, a plaque?" he asked his son on the phone. "No, a statue," Jim replied. Alex suggested that he send it home for safekeeping, and Jim dutifully complied. For the next twenty years, the statue stood on proud display in A. M. Stewart's hardware store.

The day before his induction, Jim told Louella Parsons, "I am glad to go to training camp, and I have never been so excited over anything in my life. It will be an entirely new experience for me, and I know the discipline, the regular hours, and the outdoor life will do me good." But he had one more fling in him before he went: that night, his pals Henry Fonda, Buzz Meredith, and MGM casting director Billy Grady threw him a farewell bash at Franchot Tone's house. Hank Potter, Spencer Tracy, Jimmy Cagney, and a host of other pals were there—all dressed as knights of the Round Table. As Stewart's dinner companion, Grady called upon a well-endowed movie extra known as the Belle of the Ozarks. He had her decked out in a gown once worn in a picture by Greta Garbo. "Man and boy, did she fill it," Grady wrote in his autobiography, "leaving nothing to the imagination." Just to be sure, he had the studio wardrobe department cut a hole in the backside of the gown, so that "the hills," as he called them, would be fully visible. Arranging for the rest of the girls was Meredith's job. Grady wrote that they "looked like parolees from a detention prison. I had misgivings when I saw several of them finish their drinks and place the empty glasses in their purses." All in all, it was, to quote Meredith, who also recalled the affair in his autobiography, "a crazy celebration."

At seven-fifteen the next morning, March 22, 1941, Billy and Buzz drove Jim to the draft board office on Santa Monica Boulevard. Wearing a brown suit, blue shirt, and brown slouch hat and carrying a single brown suitcase, he presented himself to the chief clerk, P. H. Brown, who gave him his draft papers. Then he said good-bye to his friends, and with the press watching and newsreel cameras rolling, he boarded a trolley with sixteen other draftees. They got off at the Hill Street terminal in downtown Los Angeles and proceeded to induction station No. 2 at 106 W. Third Street. There they were given physicals and identification numbers; Stewart's was 0-433210. The final stop was Fort MacArthur, the processing center in San Pedro, where Jim and the others were formally inducted. As he raised his right hand and swore allegiance to the armed forces of the United States of America, his salary dropped from roughly $1,500 a week to $21 a month.[4]

Five years and nine months had elapsed since Henry Fonda went to the Pasadena train station to meet the young Pennsylvanian carrying a model airplane in a suspicious-looking container. During that interval, Jimmy had made twenty-eight features, an average of five pictures a year. He had gone from virtually a bit player to a top-billed star and had received the highest award his industry could bestow on one of its members. If his career had ended that day in March of 1941, his reputation would have rested securely with this body of work.

---

[4] Stewart's weekly paycheck from MGM in March of 1941 has been variously reported over the years. The figures range from $1,500 to $3,000. The lower figure, used here, was cited in newspaper accounts at the time of his induction.

PART THREE

· Colonel Stewart ·

TEN

Fighting the Good Fight

Stewart spent his first morning as a private on KP—peeling potatoes. During the afternoon, he and the other inductees drilled. One of them, Gene Stout, turned out to be a projectionist from MGM. "Let's team up," Jim suggested, and that evening they went into San Pedro and caught a movie.

Army life requires a difficult adjustment of anyone, certainly a movie star. Stewart later recalled that he had butterflies during the first few days, a sensation that he likened to a "pigeon with a wing off, flapping around in your stomach." Given his early calls at Metro, getting up at 5:45 in the morning wasn't so difficult, but now he had to accomplish in fifteen minutes everything—shaving, showering, and so forth—that he used to do in an hour. That he was about ten years older than most of the other inductees made the transition even more difficult.

Fort MacArthur was a way station, a place where recruits were evaluated and assigned to various branches of the service. Stewart had 325 hours of civilian flying time—which qualified him for classification as a commercial pilot—so he hoped to win assignment to the Air Corps, the precursor of the Air Force (which did not become a separate branch of the military until after World War II). The age ceiling for a cadet pilot was twenty-six, and Stewart was thirty-two, but the requirement was waived. At that stage of the military buildup, the Air Corps was in need of skilled personnel.

Thus, on March 27, five days after he arrived at Fort MacArthur, Jim transferred to the Air Corps school at Moffet Field in Sunnyvale, California, southeast of San Francisco. At a brief layover in Los Angeles, he was met by Leland Hayward, who took him to Cedars of Lebanon to see Maggie Sullavan; she had just given birth to a son, William. Two hours later Stewart was back at Union Station, ready to continue the journey north. The next time Hayward heard from his friend and client, it was by mail: when Stewart received his first paycheck—$21—he forwarded the agent his usual 10 percent commission, $2.10. In the accompanying note, he jokingly complained, "I have only one change of costume. The dressing room isn't so good, but it will do. There are a lot of other fellows here playing bit parts who have better costumes with brass buttons and lots of gold braid. It's a pretty good script, though."

Indeed, the "dressing room" wasn't much—even by army standards.

Because base facilities couldn't keep pace with the buildup of the Air Corps, Stewart wasn't housed in a barracks. He and four other fellows lived in a tent with a wooden floor.

"I thought he was a very nice person," recalls Arthur S. Beavers, who was in the tent next door. "Very polite. He didn't act like a movie star. He just acted like a regular fella. He was very popular."

Beavers arrived after Stewart had been on the base for some months. In his early days at Moffet, Jim was treated as a freak. Decades later, he remembered the time when "five of us were sitting in our tent in the rain one day, and suddenly someone swung open the entrance and shouted out, 'There he is, guys,' and eight fellows stood looking at me as if I had sixteen heads." His isolation made him feel, in his words, "really lonely." His solution was to return to Los Angeles as often as possible. Indeed, he flew home almost every weekend.

On his first leave, he brought one of his instructors with him. Burgess Meredith invited them to stay at the home he had rented from Stewart. As Jim and the instructor neared Evanston Street, they saw a sign that read Diphtheria, Keep Out. Nearby, what appeared to be a body was hanging by a rope from a tree. When Jim reached his house, he saw a stuffed gorilla emerging from the chimney. Then he knocked on the door, and a woman answered, followed by twenty dogs. Finally, in his bed, he discovered two men in thick beards who greeted him nonchalantly. The prank had been rigged by Meredith and Maggie Sullavan. Stewart later told her daughter Brooke, "The poor man that I brought with me never really got over it."

In June, Stewart attended Judy Garland's party to celebrate her engagement to David Rose. At Christmastime, he played Santa Claus for the Fonda children. And the following February, he did what was expected of the previous year's Oscar winner—he presented the award to his successor, who turned out to be his friend Gary Cooper, who won for his performance in *Sergeant York*.

Of course, Jim continued to date the lovely ladies of Hollywood on his outings, including a blonde from Earl Carroll's revue and actress Yvonne DeCarlo. In her autobiography, DeCarlo recalled their evening together: "We had a lovely candlelight dinner, and he was such a perfect gentleman. It was like a scene from one of his movies." She added that, although she was a virgin, she would not have been averse to something more than dancing. But, when he took her home, he simply kissed her on the cheek and said good night. She never heard from him again.

The trips to Hollywood served as diversions, but they were distractions as well. Once, when he was home, his parents came to visit. Alex, ashamed of his son's behavior, berated Jim for being so irresponsible. Jim said,

"Suddenly I was ashamed too—and sore, because I knew dad was right to rebuke me." That marked a turning point in his army career. Thereafter, he began to work hard at becoming an officer. In July, he was promoted to corporal and made a weapons instructor. Five months later, on December 7, the Japanese bombed Pearl Harbor, and America entered the war. That intensified Stewart's resolve; he was in the service for the duration.

Even before the bombing of Pearl Harbor, he had logged the flying time required of a commissioned officer. After meeting the requisite academic requirements, he was commissioned a second lieutenant on January 19, 1942. He wanted to be assigned to flight duty but was ordered to report instead to Stockton Field for a guest appearance on a special episode of the popular Edgar Bergen–Charlie McCarthy radio program. Trading barbs with the dummy—who was dressed in a pint-size uniform for the occasion—Stewart said, "In our efforts to make the Army Air Corps the finest in the world, we've enlisted men from the backwoods. We've enlisted men from the front woods. But this is the first time we've ever enlisted the woods themselves."

The Bergen-McCarthy program was not Jim's only public appearance in uniform. Recognizing the unique asset it had in Lieutenant Stewart, the Air Corps pressed its advantage at every turn. He joined Walter Huston, Edward G. Robinson, Edward Arnold, and Walter Brennan for a reading of the Bill of Rights on a radio show commemorating the 150th anniversary of this cornerstone of American democracy. "At the close of his long dramatic part," one newspaper noted, "he pulled off his earphones and let down his emotions, excusing himself from the studio and reportedly breaking into tears in private." On March 15, 1942, he starred in an episode of *Plays for Americans* on NBC, in which he played a soldier writing to his folks back home, describing his reasons for fighting in the war. Three weeks later, on April 4, he narrated *This Is War*, a half-hour NBC documentary covering the Army Air Corps' involvement in the early months of the worldwide conflict. In July, he even repeated his role in *The Philadelphia Story*, joining his movie costars Katharine Hepburn, Cary Grant, and Ruth Hussey on CBS's *Lux Radio Theatre*. It was a special edition of the popular anthology series, produced for the U.S. government.

Articles also appeared under Stewart's byline in various newspapers and magazines (it is unlikely that he actually wrote them himself), including one that ran in the *Los Angeles Times* on July 13, 1941. "I'll tell you," he noted on that occasion, "it's a kick to see how this Army training works and gets results. Just as it's a kick to see the pride that a master airplane mechanic and his crew have in the airplane they maintain on the ground. That airplane is their baby."

But his most effective public relations turn came with an eighteen-minute short called *Winning Your Wings*, produced by Warner Bros. in cooperation with the War Activities Board of the Motion Picture Industry. In this recruiting film, Stewart talked directly to the young men of America, informing them of the need for thousands of officers, noncoms, airmen, and support personnel and outlining the steps that a recruit follows. It was a hard sell, but he made an attractive pitchman, appearing relaxed with a sense of humor and talking plain talk. He was also credible, speaking from direct experience. Later, the Air Corps chief of staff, Gen. Henry "Hap" Arnold, would credit *Winning Your Wings* with the recruitment of more than one hundred thousand men.

Stewart did a second film for the army called *Fellow Americans*, which examined the implications of Pearl Harbor, but by then he had grown weary of the public relations gestures; he wanted to be a regular lieutenant like anyone else. Finally, he appealed to his commanding officer, Col. George L. Usher. Usher agreed to protect him from interviews, publicity photographs, and radio appearances—and he kept his word. Thereafter, Jim somewhat disappeared from public view.

In April of 1942, he was transferred to Mather Field, also in California, for a four-week course in flight training. By then, cadets were no longer in short supply, but experienced hands were badly needed to instruct them. That became Stewart's job. "In two months I was instructing in advanced trainers, AT-9s," he said, adding, "Now, at last, I began to feel like an officer and a pilot."[1] But, because he was a movie star, he still had to prove himself, and he did. "He never scratched an airplane," asserted his friend Col. Beirne Lay Jr., who wrote a two-part article about Stewart's World War II experiences for the *Saturday Evening Post* in late 1945. For his diligence, Jim was promoted to first lieutenant in early July of 1942.

But he didn't want to stay an instructor forever. Eager to prove himself in combat, he spoke to Leland Hayward, who was friendly with a number of senior Air Corps officers. Hayward, in turn, took the matter up with Gen. Kenneth McNaughton, then scouting locations for pilot training schools. In August of 1942, McNaughton helped Stewart transfer out of Mather.

His first stop was the Bombardier Training School at Kirkland Field in Albuquerque, New Mexico. There, he flew the bombardier students on their training runs, using twin-engine planes. It was a far cry from combat, but the experience gave him considerable exposure to bombing techniques—useful information if he ever did get overseas. Then, several months later, he got a big break: he was assigned to Hobbs Field in New

[1] The AT-9 was a twin-engine airplane made by Curtiss.

Mexico, to learn to fly four-engine bombers: the B-17, the Flying Fortress, and the B-24, the Liberator. "When I was transferred to heavy bombers," he recalled, "I had to work pretty hard at subjects I'd forgotten and was never any good at anyway. Math, for instance. Most of the fellows were ten years younger than I, and they'd work out in a few minutes the navigational problems that I'd have to mull over for an hour or more."

Given the haste with which men were being trained for air combat during America's first year of war, fatalities at training schools such as Hobbs were all too common. "It was a bad period," said Stewart. "Many men I flew with were being killed in training." He sought solace in the Protestant church, although he had given up Sunday-morning services in Hollywood out of what he called "laziness." "Religion meant a lot to me for the rest of the war," he said.

When he completed his training at Hobbs Field, Stewart hoped to be assigned to a unit headed overseas. That was the next logical step. Instead, he was posted to the 52nd Squadron of the 29th Bombardment Group at Gowen Field in Boise, Idaho. Once again he was to be an instructor. "There must be some hitch about your going into combat," his new commanding officer, Col. "Pop" Arnold, told him shortly after he arrived. "I've got instructions to classify you as 'static personnel.'" In other words, Jim wasn't going anywhere. Clearly, the brass didn't relish the idea of a movie star flying over enemy territory and possibly becoming a prisoner of war.

Like Hobbs Field, Gowen represented the last stage of training before pilots and their crews shipped out for combat. Stewart's job was to make sure that his students were ready for the hazards that awaited them. Conversely, he was expected to weed out those who, in his opinion, were potential risks to themselves and their mates. To hold such a position, one had to be a capable pilot. Stewart was also his squadron's operations officer. As such, he supervised the other instructors in his unit.

Given its geographical location, Gowen was even more hazardous than Hobbs. Says Jack Burton, who, like Stewart, was an instructor in the 29th Bombardment Group, "If you made a left turn, you went right into the mountains. We had several guys try it, but it killed them all." Wilbur Clingan, who trained there, recalls, "At one time, we had butchered up so many airplanes that we were down to about two." On one unlucky day, Stewart's roommate, also an instructor, was killed. On another occasion, a plane crashed on the runway, which led to the wreckage of about a half dozen of the planes assigned to Jim.

There were mishaps, but the pressure to train the young men quickly remained intense. It was, to quote Beirne Lay, "physically exhausting work, and with students, dangerous work."

Jack Burton, who was a bombardier instructor, flew on several occasions when Stewart was the check pilot (that is, Burton was instructing or checking the bombardier while Stewart was doing likewise in the cockpit). He considered Stewart "an excellent pilot. He was a very intelligent guy, and . . . he knew how to instruct." Burton also thought Jim was "a terrific guy. We knew him, of course, as a celebrity, but he was just one of us."

While in Boise, Stewart was promoted to captain. He actually heard the news aboard a plane, traveling to San Francisco for a ten-day leave. Clarence Adams, his counterpart in another squadron at Gowen, was piloting the craft, and when word of Stewart's promotion came through, the young Texan, already a captain, took the bars off his tunic and loaned them to his friend.

From San Francisco, the new captain traveled to Los Angeles for the wedding of his pal and fellow longtime bachelor Johnny Swope to actress Dorothy McGuire. The ceremony took place on July 18, 1943, at the Hayward home, with Jim doing double duty, playing "The Wedding March" on the piano as the bride came down the aisle and acting as best man.

Finally, in August of 1943, Stewart got the break he had been seeking. His CO, Colonel Arnold, knew that Lt. Col. Robert Terrill, the commanding officer of the 445th Bombardment Group, based in Sioux City, Iowa, was looking for a good squadron operations officer in anticipation of a posting overseas. Arnold told Terrill about Stewart, and Terrill agreed to take the captain on. The danger of losing a movie star over enemy territory hadn't changed, but at last Jimmy had found an officer willing to assume the risk.

The 445th was a new outfit, having been activated in April. In early July, a month before Stewart came on board, it had been dispatched to Sioux City—after training in Wendover, Utah. "We still did not have a great many planes," noted Rudolph J. Birsic in his history of the 445th, "but those we did have were getting lots of flying time and giving our maintenance men plenty of experience."

From his vantage point as operations officer of the 703rd Bomb Squadron, Stewart developed enormous respect for Terrill. A graduate of West Point, the colonel was efficient, dedicated, and a natural leader. Stewart's subsequent commander, Ramsay Potts, remembered that Jim and Terrill had "a very friendly, natural, easygoing relationship." Indeed, a few weeks after Stewart arrived in Sioux City, the colonel placed him in command of the 703rd.

Suddenly, Jim was in charge of a dozen or more B-24 bombers and roughly 350 people. Most of the men were in their early to mid twenties, and although they had all gone through specialized training, they were still fairly raw. Jim's first task was to complete their training and to get them to function as a unit. He soon demonstrated that he was a hardworking, conscientious taskmaster, not aloof from his men. When, for example, the squadron prepared to leave Sioux City for combat duty, he ordered everyone to clean up the area—and then picked up a broom himself.

That was in early October. Just before he shipped out, Alex and Bessie traveled to Sioux City for a farewell visit. Jim remembered that he and his dad were "very self-conscious with each other. . . . At the time of the greatest crisis in my entire life, he would have to stand aside. We were both afraid." Despite the awkwardness of the occasion, Alex managed to communicate his feelings in a letter that he gave to his son as he said good-bye. Jim read it in his bunk that evening. "My dear Jim boy," Alex wrote. "Soon after you read this letter, you will be on your way to the worst sort of danger. I have had this in mind for a long time and I am very much concerned . . . but Jim, I am banking on the enclosed copy of the 91st Psalm. The thing that takes the place of fear and worry is the promise of these words. I feel sure that God will lead you through this mad experience. . . . I can say no more. I only continue to pray. Good-by, my dear. God bless you and keep you. I love you more than I can tell you. Dad." It was the first time that Alex had ever actually told his son he loved him, and the words caused Jim to weep. Then he looked at the little booklet containing the psalm. He found the sentiment: "I will say of the Lord, He is my refuge and my fortress. . . . His truth shall be thy shield and buckler. Thou shalt not be afraid for the terror by night; nor for the arrow that flieth by day. . . . For he shall give his angels charge over thee, to keep thee in all ways. They shall bear thee up in their hands, lest thou dash thy foot against a stone." Jim drew comfort from the ancient words and the man who had given them to him.

Finally, on October 20, the 445th's ground personnel left Iowa for New York and a ship bound for Great Britain. Stewart, however, traversed the Atlantic like the other pilots in the group—by flying his plane down through South America and across the Atlantic to the coast of Africa, then north to England. "We flew one leg every day," recalls fellow squadron commander Howard Kriedler, who estimates that the entire journey required about a week. Because they started later than the ground personnel, they began arriving in England at the end of November 1943.

By then, the tiny island had become the staging area for an enormous concentration of Allied personnel—more than 350,000 men and women in total. The 445th Bombardment Group was assigned to the 2nd Combat Wing of the 2nd Air Division of the Eighth Air Force. Under the command of Gen. Edward "Ted" Timberlake, the wing included two other groups—the 453rd and the 379th. All three were based in Norfolk County, about a hundred miles northeast of London. General Timberlake was headquartered near the village of Hethel, along with the 379th. The 445th and the 453rd were assigned to the bases at Tibenham and Old Buckenham ("Old Buc"), respectively. Each base was about seven miles from the other, and all three were similar in appearance—with wooden Quonset huts serving as barracks, hospitals, and administration offices. The presence of cows and fields of crops reminded the Americans that they were in the midst of farm country.

Jimmy's arrival on November 25 didn't go unnoticed. Four days later, the *Los Angeles Examiner* reported, "Captain James Stewart . . . has just arrived in England as commander of an American Liberator bomber squadron." The paper also noted that he was "the first actor to be assigned to actual combat flying, his Hollywood predecessor overseas, Captain Clark Gable, having had primarily a movie-making assignment, although participating in five bombing raids." In mid-December Jim held a formal press conference at the headquarters of the Eighth Air Force in London.

But he was too busy to spend much time with the press. He and the rest of his outfit had to learn the latest in aerial maneuvers from the hardened veterans. They also needed to familiarize themselves with the crowded airspace over England and the Channel and make last-minute adjustments to their planes. Shortly after they arrived, the rains came, turning the pastureland on which their base was situated to mud. Spirits plummeted as the newcomers tried to keep dry and warm. "It was decidedly commonplace," recalled Rudolph Birsic in his unit history, "to see bedding rolls, pup tents, overcoats, and up to eight blankets piled on many beds, until it seemed that the weight of so many items would crush the humans buried in its depth." Stewart, who'd grown accustomed to the warmth of southern California, never did adjust to England's damp chill. Howard Kriedler, who served with him at the wing headquarters late in the war, remembered Jim walking around the office in a sweater with his leather jacket zipped up to his neck. Moreover, his complaints about the weather in letters to his parents prompted all sorts of remedies from the folks back home, including a collection of crystal bowls. One evening Kriedler came into Stewart's room and found Jim in bed surrounded by the bowls, which he was filling with hot water. "I just about died," Kriedler recalls.

Morale in the 445th wasn't helped by the nightly blackouts, which were necessary to guard against the continuing threat of German bombing. But Stewart and his comrades did enjoy the enemy's "propaganda radio broadcasts." As Birsic noted, they "were always good for a laugh," not to mention popular music.

* * *

By the time Stewart arrived in Tibenham, the war was entering its fifth year, but finally, the tide had turned against the Axis powers. The previous July, the last of the German troops had been driven from northern Africa, and since September, the Fifth Army under Gen. Mark Clark had been moving steadily up the Italian peninsula. In the Pacific, the Japanese advance had been halted, and the initiative now lay with the Allies.

For the bomber crews in England, the principal goal was to impede the ability of the Germans and Italians to wage war. That meant striking at munitions factories, airplane-manufacturing plants, and other heavy industry, railway stations, communications facilities, and so forth. Each B-24 was a powerful force of destruction, capable of carrying up to 12,800 pounds of bombs. The specific targets were determined on a daily basis by the Supreme Allied Command in London, with the details worked out, in turn, by the commands of the Eighth Air Force, the 2nd Air Division, the 2nd Combat Wing, and finally, the 445th, 453rd, and 379th Bomb Groups. The items to be determined included reconnaissance information about the target of the day, the number of bombers required, the type of bombs to be used, and the best route to the site. Because the B-17s and B-24s were heavy aircraft, difficult to maneuver, they were escorted by faster, lighter fighter planes, P-38s, P-47s, and P-51s. The fighters were to engage enemy aircraft and protect the bombers during their missions.

Bomb crews flew in rotation. When Stewart arrived in England, crewmen had to complete twenty-five missions before they could transfer out of combat. In the spring of 1944, the number was raised to thirty. Squadron leaders such as Stewart, group officers, and even wing commanders directed the missions in turn. To do so was considered an essential component of leadership. "You had to be out there with your troops," asserts Howard Kriedler, "flying the same combat missions they had, or you were useless." These officers did not have permanent crews. Rather, the best of each bombardment group were designated lead crews, and these, like the mission commanders, flew on a rotating basis. Control of the lead plane was left to the crew's pilot. Stewart or whoever else was directing the mission on a given day had too much to do to fly the plane as well.

Initially, the missions tended to be over France and other parts of occupied Western Europe. Some were, according to Wilbur Clingan, "what we called milk runs, which were just a little hop just barely across the Channel into the coastal defenses or something with no opposition and decent weather." But, as they approached the more strategically important targets, they would tend to encounter enemy aircraft and flak, firepower from the ground. "Most of the time you wondered how you got through it," says Clingan. "It could be miserable." Even under attack, the bombers had to try to stay close together and maintain a steady course and altitude. "You could not take any evasive action," Clingan explains, "because then you'd throw your bomb accuracy off. So once you were committed to this thing, you sat there just like a duck, and of course, the longer you sat there, the more accurate the flak became."

Finally, the 445th joined the action. "So great was the speed with which our Group completed its preparations for combat missions," noted Birsic, "that it probably set a record for a newly arrived group." In its maiden outing on December 13, the unit contributed fifteen planes toward a mission over Kiel, Germany—with Stewart in command. Jim quickly discovered that practice runs were not the same as the real thing. As he later put it, "*Every*thing's different from the way you'd planned—everything's wrong. And you're nawt supposed to—but everybody gets on the radio and starts yelling!" Despite the chaos, twelve of his crews managed to drop their bombs over the designated target that day, and although they encountered heavy flak, they suffered no losses. It was an auspicious beginning.

But Stewart knew that such good fortune couldn't last. "There were, oh, lots and lots of times when I must have wondered whether I was going to get back after a mission," he said years later, "but I didn't think of it at the time. There just wasn't the time." Once, however, he did indulge in morbid speculation. That day, the group returned from a mission devastated by casualties, and he knew that he was scheduled to lead the attack the following morning. Panic set in. He said, "I knew my own fear, if not checked, could infect my crew members, and I could feel it growing in me." So he read the little pamphlet containing the Ninety-first Psalm that his father had given him, and he felt better. On that occasion, as on numerous others, he also prayed—not for his own safety or the lives of his men. He prayed that he wouldn't make a mistake. For luck, he carried a rabbit's foot into combat. Like the pamphlet, it was a gift from his father.

Luck was with Stewart again on his second mission, which came six days after the first. This time the target was the German port of Bremen. Beirne Lay described his performance on this and the Kiel run as "workmanlike. He made no mistakes, but neither was he faced with any difficult decisions by which Colonel Terrill and General Timberlake could assess the judgment of the green commander."

Stewart's third mission, which came on January 7, 1944, was a different matter. The run to Ludwigshafen, Germany, went as planned, but on the return flight, the group leader diverted from the prescribed flight path. Stewart, following in support, broke radio silence to inform the commander of his error, but the man insisted that he was on target. At that point, Jim had two choices: he could keep the formation together, even though they were flying blind with regard to the flak and enemy aircraft ahead; or he could break away and lead his planes back to Tibenham by the prescribed route, the safer route. If he chose the latter, he would leave his comrades understrength in the event of attack. According to Beirne Lay, he chose to stay with the main body. As it turned out, Lay continued, they *were* attacked—by about sixty Messerschmitts and Focke-Wulfs— and their leader was shot down and killed. The presence of Stewart's planes kept the formation from being annihilated. Later, Terrill commended Jim on his good judgment.

Curiously, Stewart's subsequent commander, Ramsay Potts, recalls a similar incident. In his version, Stewart made the opposite decision—he broke the formation and followed the prescribed route to the base—and had to account for his actions at an inquiry at division headquarters. "He stood up to that very well and was completely exonerated of any faulty judgment," Potts concludes, adding that, in his opinion, Stewart had made the right decision. "There were enough planes in the formation," he asserts, "so that they could protect themselves [without the 445th's involvement]."

Is it possible that Jim was involved in two missions in which the commander lost his way and made a different decision each time? "It's possible but not likely," Potts concedes. Lay's account, written close to the end of the war, would seem the more probable version—assuming that he and Potts were remembering the same incident. But, in fairness to Potts, Lay's articles carried a number of mistakes. Moreover, Stewart's former CO and friend has a clear impression of the incident and its aftermath. Lay is deceased, and Stewart's other Air Corps colleagues consulted for this book had no knowledge of such incidents.

Whatever the specifics of the January 7 mission, it clearly had no negative impact on Stewart's record for he was promoted to major at the end of the month. He also flew two more missions in January, one over France, the other over Frankfurt, Germany. The following month he participated in raids on Nuremberg and Galze Rigen, Holland. And on February 20, he led the attack on Brunswick, Germany.

"Brunswick was heavily defended," recalled Rudolph Birsic, "and on that particular day, although major damage was done to German fighter-plane production facilities, the Eighth Air Force suffered heavy losses also. Our own losses totaled three planes, with twenty-seven crewmen missing in action and four others injured. However, our gunners were credited with the destruction of six German planes, plus two probably destroyed and two damaged." For his participation in this hazardous raid, Stewart was awarded the Distinguished Flying Cross. In the accompanying citation, the commander of the Eighth Air Force, Gen. James

Doolittle, wrote, "In spite of aggressive fighter attacks and later heavy, accurate antiaircraft fire, he was able to hold the formation together and direct a bombing run over the target in such a manner that the planes following his were able to release their bombs with great accuracy." As with his Oscar, Stewart sent his DFC back home to his father. Jim was, in his words, "mighty proud of it."

In March, Jim tried twice to return to Brunswick. On the first occasion, he led an enormous armada of some fifteen hundred bombers. Once they were airborne, he found the weather so soupy that maintaining even a semblance of a formation was impossible. Finally, he decided to abort the mission. Putting that many men and machines in the air was no simple feat, so one did not blithely send them home empty-handed. Stewart called it the "hardest decision" he ever made. He tried again on March 15. This time, the weather over England was better, but low clouds over Brunswick forced him to divert his planes to their secondary target.

A week later, on March 22, 1944, he finally reached the big B—Berlin, capital of the Third Reich. That turned out to be his last mission with the 445th.

Four days earlier, Col. Joseph A. Miller, commander of the 453rd Bombardment Group—also part of the 2nd Combat Wing—was shot down over Fredrickshafen, Germany. His replacement was Col. Ramsay Potts. Unlike Terrill, Potts was not a professional soldier. He'd been commissioned while a cadet pilot a few days after the Japanese attack on Pearl Harbor. But, like Terrill, he was a superb CO, highly respected and liked by his men.

"When I got to the 453rd," Potts recalls, "I was told that I could ask for any officers I wanted to, to fill key slots, and I asked for a new group operations officer, because the fellow who was doing the job wasn't up to it. And, lo and behold, much to my surprise, they sent Jimmy Stewart to me. And that's when I first met him. We met and talked, and I could see right away that he would be a very good man."

As the 453rd's group operations officer, Stewart had a hand in planning each mission as it came down from the wing. "The group operations officer really runs the war," says Gen. Andrew Low (Ret.), then Stewart's assistant and later his successor. "He runs the missions each day. He calls on the squadrons to give him people, he tells them how many airplanes he wants, what the mission is going to be, that sort of stuff."

He also conducts the briefings before each day's takeoff. "Since Stewart was a natural actor," says Potts, "it was clear that he would be able to do that very well." And, indeed, Jim became adept at transmitting the dry technical information clearly and concisely. His briefings were also enlivened by his droll sense of humor. Actor Walter Matthau, then a staff sergeant in one of the group's squadrons, later said that he liked to sit in on Stewart's briefings simply because they were entertaining.

Low, who was a graduate of West Point and nine years younger than his boss, soon discovered that he was working for "a real professional" who was not above yelling and slamming his hand on his desk if matters were overlooked or done improperly. Indeed, by the time Stewart joined the 453rd, his days of clowning around on the soundstages of MGM and his nights of dancing at the Coconut Grove and Trocadero were far behind him. He had been in the Air Corps for three years and had more than half a dozen combat missions to his credit.

Still, he wasn't all business. Low recalled one afternoon when Jim pulled an outrageous practical joke. Having finished his reports for the division on that morning's missions, he asked his assistant to book a plane for them. Once they were airborne, he said with a wry smile, "My former group commander always has his nap about now. Let's go wake him up!" With that, he headed for Tibenham—where he buzzed the field in a series of low-level maneuvers. After several passes, the controllers in the tower were on the radio, ordering him to stop his reckless behavior. Instead, Stewart buzzed the tower, flying so close to the elevated platform that the men inside evacuated it by scrambling down an external ladder. Satisfied, Jim and Andy then flew back to Old Buc.

But the incident didn't end there. At the office, Stewart received a serious dressing-down from Potts, who had been chastised, in turn, by *his* superiors. Jim tried to explain that he'd done nothing dangerous, but the CO was in no mood for explanations. Years later, the star recalled, "The more I struggled for words (the Colonel did not give me much opportunity to speak), the more I realized that what we had thought was a grand idea some three hours earlier now seemed pretty dumb." As if Potts' tirade weren't enough, Stewart was also chewed out by Gen. Milton Arnold, who had replaced Timberlake as wing commander at the end of March, and by the object of the exercise, Colonel Terrill. Jim was apologetic but never totally cowed. "As I look back on that training mission," he wrote years later, "I remember it as a really fun flight."

He had few opportunities for such levity, however; being group operations officer was an extremely demanding job. On many occasions, he and Low worked so late that they simply slept in their clothes at the office. When they could get away, they shared quarters with Potts. Unlike most of the base structures, theirs was not a Quonset hut but a building made of concrete bricks, plastered on the outside and painted a dull color. Stewart and Low bunked in the room at one end, and Potts had the bedroom at the other. In between was a sitting area, where they could read, chat, or have tea—prepared for them by their British orderly. There were nights, Low recalls, when Jim would ask him about his wife and young child before they drifted off to sleep. "I know lots of women in Hollywood," Stewart said with wonder, "but that commitment. Gosh, I never knew anyone that I wanted to say for better or for worse with. That commitment must be a very serious thing." Sometimes he would read Low the letters that he'd received from his father, missives that typically contained prayers for his continued good fortune.

Occasionally, the officers would hold base dances. On those evenings, Stewart would mingle with the women from the neighboring towns and villages—who were naturally thrilled to find themselves in the company of a movie star. But he didn't really date. "While he was at the group with me," says Potts, "we had an extremely intense period of combat flying, so we all stuck pretty close to the base during our duty."

Stewart and Potts enjoyed a close relationship. "I was delighted with him [as an officer]," the CO recalls, "and our friendship began to flourish." Work permitting, they would spend the occasional evening in Norwich, and once or twice they even managed to get to London. But their main social outlet was the base officers' club. "He was wonderful at tinkling the piano," Potts recalls, "and he had a great touch with the men." Wilbur Clingan, then a squadron commander in the group, shared the colonel's appraisal, describing Jim as "unassuming" and "easily approached" and adding, "He was really a good guy."

Of course, Stewart continued to fly missions in rotation with Potts, Low, and the group's squadron commanders. Although the Allies had crimped the Luftwaffe's power by the spring of 1944, bombing raids over France and Germany were still perilous.

In Potts' opinion, Stewart's careful nature served him well in combat. Moreover, the colonel considered him "a very good leader" and "a good pilot." Low also respected Stewart's skill, saying, "When he stepped on board an airplane, no one was going to argue about who was in charge of the airplane." As testimony of his prowess, Stewart was awarded the Air Medal on April 8. Five days later, he flew his first mission with the 453rd, leading eighteen bombers against an airplane parts factory and repair station in Oberfallenhafen, Germany, near Munich. The mission was a success, but one officer, a lieutenant named Dooley, had to bail out.

Stewart was less fortunate in a subsequent raid on the railway marshaling yard at Troyes, France. As his plane neared the target, he became convinced that he was ten degrees off his flight path, but his navigator and bombardier insisted they were on course. While they compared notes, Low, flying as deputy leader in another plane, tried to notify Jim that he was correct—his plane was headed for a marshaling yard, but not the right one. Stewart, busy on the phone with his crewmen, failed to get Low's message before his plane discharged its bombs. By that point, the situation in the cockpit was bordering on chaos. Wisely, Stewart radioed Low, saying, "Andy, we've got trouble in this airplane. Take over." At that point, the deputy assumed command of the formation and opted for the secondary target, which was Paris.

Low praises Stewart's decision, explaining that "he had to do something and he wasn't sure what to do. So he asked me if I knew where I was and if I knew what we were doing and I said, 'Yes, sir.' " Later, back at the base, Stewart was, in Low's words, "very upset about his crew, who literally were lost, disoriented, and dropped on the wrong target. And bothering him was the Frenchmen who were probably down there in that little railroad yard shouting, '*Victoire, victoire,*' and the next thing you know the bombs dropped down on them."

On June 3, Stewart was promoted to lieutenant colonel. Three days later, he conducted the group's briefing for the largest air-sea-land offensive in history, D day, the Allied invasion of occupied France. Then, on July 2, Low took over as operations officer. Stewart had been transferred to the wing headquarters at Hethel.

For the next ten months, first as wing operations officer and then as chief of staff, Jim reported to Gen. Milton Arnold. Like Ted Timberlake, the wing's second commander was an experienced combat veteran, having previously led the 389th Bombardment Group—at a time when the Luftwaffe was at its deadliest. Arnold, like most Air Corps men, ran an informal operation. He expected his officers to, as he puts it, "use their own judgment." In addition to planning missions at the wing level, Stewart was expected to evaluate lead crews—the keys to the success of their air operations—as well as participate in postmission debriefings. He also supervised the training of replacement personnel.

Arnold was pleased with Stewart's performance, calling him "a superior leader," "a good administrator," and "very conscientious about carrying out his duties." In time, the general promoted his chief of staff to full colonel.

As at the 453rd, Jim continued to fly. Then he drew another hairy assignment. He and his planes reached their target but encountered heavy enemy firepower, which left the formation widely scattered. Stewart managed to gather a group of planes and head them toward home, but en route, they passed over Abbeville, France. Unfortunately, Abbeville was home to a legendary cadre of old Luftwaffe officers. There weren't many left by then, and their replacements, basically raw recruits, were nowhere near as wily. "Anyway," says Arnold, "they picked up the group. I don't know how many planes he had with him, maybe twelve or fifteen, something like that. They shot him up pretty badly." Thereafter, Arnold sensed that Stewart's nerves were beginning to fray and took him off combat duty. "It wasn't ever official," the general recalls, "but I just told him I didn't want him to fly any more combat. He didn't argue about it."

Finally, on May 7, 1945, the war in Europe came to an end. Three days after that, General Arnold became chief of staff of the 2nd Air Division, and Stewart took command of the wing. Technically the position should have gone to a brigadier general, but with the hostilities against the Axis powers at an end and no plans to send the wing to the Pacific, the commanding officer's only real responsibility was to get his men back to the States.

Thus, Stewart joined his outfit on the *Queen Elizabeth* several months after the fighting ended. The ship was packed with roughly twenty-eight thousand combat-weary veterans. "They lined up [for meals] from the time we got on the ship until we got off," recalls Clarence Adams, Stewart's friend from Gowen Field who was also on board. "There were meals round the clock. They were sleeping on floors and in hammocks and in every bunk there was to sleep in."

At last Jimmy Stewart, Colonel, U.S. Army Air Corps, was home. For four years and nearly two months, he had served his country. Among the first in Hollywood to answer the call to arms, he sustained a record of achievement that few of his peers had equaled and none could better. While colleagues such as John Wayne, Spencer Tracy, and Errol Flynn played heroes on the silver screen, Stewart had risked his life on twenty real missions. He was a hero.

But real heroes often a pay a price for their laudable deeds, and Jim was no exception. Clarence Adams, who hadn't seen him since 1943, noticed the change aboard the *Queen Elizabeth*, saying, "He was more nervous and a little bit shaky."

For years thereafter, Stewart would suffer from nightmares. Even his digestion was affected. He told Elinor Gordon Blair, his friend from Indiana, that soft foods such as ice cream and peanut butter had gotten him through the war. "He just couldn't eat he was so upset by everything," she says. "And when he came back, that wonderful robust appetite we remembered was gone." Peanut butter would remain a staple of his diet thereafter.

The experience was so devastating that, once it was over, he assiduously refused to talk about it. Journalists were told in the flush of his return—when there was great interest in his wartime activities—that he would not answer questions about his military service. Decades later he still avoided the topic. He didn't even want to discuss it with his children. In this, he was not terribly unusual. "It was decades after the war before I felt like I wanted to talk about it," says Ramsay Potts. "I think the experience was so profound and the danger so great that you would feel when talking to people who hadn't experienced it that maybe they'll think I'm exaggerating, maybe they'll think I'm bragging, maybe they'll think that I'm trying to make this out to be more than it really was. But the fact of the matter is that it was an extremely dangerous, hazardous task every damned day you went on one of these missions. You could even say that to some extent you were exposed to danger on the ground at your base because occasionally the Germans would try to launch some kind of attack against the bases in England."

Stewart didn't even want to play military figures on film. Only once, in 1960's *The Mountain Road,* did he don a uniform to portray an officer in a war zone (in *The Glenn Miller Story* and *Strategic Air Command,* he played civilians—a bandleader and a baseball player, respectively—who joined the Air Corps, but neither saw combat).

Despite the war's terrible personal toll, Jim never regretted his service. "He was very proud that he had done what he was called upon by his country to do," says his stepson Mike McLean. "And the ramifications for him personally are the price that one accepts for fighting for freedom." Jim even felt that he'd gained something positive along the way. "I think it was maturity," he said. "I had never experienced the total responsibility I did in the war . . . never experienced the realization that it was up to me physically to make a thing work, to survive."

ELEVEN

Coming Home

Leland Hayward was waiting at the dock when the *Queen Elizabeth* landed. "How he got in, I don't know," Stewart later told his friend's daughter Brooke. "Absolutely top secret, no one was allowed, but your father could always get in anywhere." During the war, Leland had decided to become a theatrical producer, so he sold his agency to the Music Corporation of America (MCA). Thus, Stewart was now represented by Lew Wasserman, whom he had known casually before the war. That was the first of several changes that marked his return.

His parents were waiting for him at a Manhattan hotel. Bessie was shocked by his appearance, for his hair had begun to gray and he looked even thinner than usual. In an effort to fatten him up, the three Stewarts celebrated that night at an expensive restaurant where Jim ordered a steak and cherries jubilee. A day or two later they joined the Haywards at their farm in Connecticut—Leland's career change having brought Maggie and the family east.

A few days later, on September 1, Jim, still in the service, held a press conference in the office of Maj. Gen. Clarence H. Kells, commanding general of the New York Port of Embarkation. Jim told the reporters that he wasn't exactly sure when his discharge would come through, although he expected it to be soon, and that he planned on returning to acting. "It will take a while to get over camera shyness," he confessed, "and there's a lot of technique you forget—like any skill—which I'll have to learn over again." He said that he was particularly eager to do a comedy.

Thereafter, the Stewarts drove back to Indiana, so that Jim could enjoy part of his thirty-day leave in peace and quiet. When they arrived, he learned that the hometown folks were planning a hero's welcome, complete with a big barbecue at the fairgrounds. But he didn't want any fuss. "I'm just another returning serviceman," he said, "and I'm entitled to nothing extra." Nevertheless, he consented to coverage of his homecoming in *Life* magazine, and Henry Luce sent celebrity photographer Peter Stackpole to get the story. The result, which appeared in the issue of September 24, 1945, showed Jim at home with his parents and sisters (who had married during the war), chatting with friends at the hardware store, visiting some of the local hangouts, and even fishing in a rowboat with Clyde "Woody" Woodward, a longtime employee of his dad's. The cover photo showed Jim in uniform, perched on a wall (probably along the rim of Vinegar Hill) with the 1870 courthouse in the background. One can see on the courthouse tower the V for *victory* that his father had erected and a sheet below with the words *Welcome Jim* in big handwritten letters.

While in Indiana, Stewart tried to claim the English setter that he'd shipped home four years earlier. By then, his parents had placed the dog with some friends who owned a farm. When Jim went to get Boy, however, the dog snapped at him. Apparently, he preferred the open spaces of Indiana to the Hollywood fishbowl, so he remained where he was.

On September 29, Stewart traveled to Andrews Field in Washington, D.C., where he received his discharge. Before mustering out, however, he enlisted in the Officers Reserve Corp. From there it was back to Manhattan. Then, finally, on October 3, he caught the *Super Chief* to Los Angeles. Billy Grady remembered accompanying him on the train. "To pass the time en route," Grady wrote in his memoirs, "I introduced Jim to gin rummy. From Chicago to Pasadena, he didn't win a game. I wound up with 8 million matches."

Henry Fonda was on hand to greet Jim when the train arrived in Pasadena. So was his new agent, Lew Wasserman, and the press. The reporters asked Jim about his graying hair, and he replied in his typically understated fashion, "It got pretty rough overseas at times." And of course, someone asked about his love life, saying, "This is a bad question, Jimmy, but is there any sweet little thing you're coming home to?" To which Stewart answered, "No. That is, not yet. But you're right—it's a bad question."

With the house on Evanston still rented out—no longer to Burgess Meredith, who had gone into the army in 1942, but to an advertising man, his wife, and their two children—Stewart was temporarily without lodgings. Said Fonda in his autobiography, "Well, hell! You can't leave a full colonel who's a genuine hero, who's also been your roommate in New York and California, who double-dated with you and made the sacrifice of getting beet juice up his nose, you just can't leave that kind of guy out on the street. In Brentwood the police take a dim view of that. Especially if they see him wandering around after dark." So Fonda and his wife, Frances, invited Jim to stay with them at Tiger Tail, the two-story Pennsylvania Dutch Colonial that they'd built in the hills above Sunset Boulevard. Specifically, Jim lived in what they called the Playhouse. "It was really lovely," recalls Peter Fonda, "with a huge old walk-in fireplace and a bedroom and two baths. It was fully stocked, with a refrigerator and a bar. And Dad's record collection, old 78s. I remember them putting them on so carefully and listening to great music, boogie-woogie stuff."

*   *   *

Stewart had been back in California only a few days when he received a call from his old colleague Frank Capra. Like Jim, the director had been away from Hollywood for a long time, having spent the war in the Army Signal Corps as a documentary filmmaker. "I have this idea for a picture," he told Stewart on the phone. "Why don't you come down to the house and I'll tell it to you." As Jim recalled, "Frank lived quite a ways away, but I think I was there in three minutes."

Actually, Capra had previously contacted Wasserman about the project, and the agent had told him that Stewart would do it without even reading the script. But the director insisted on a meeting. "If Jimmy was as scared as I was about making another film," Capra wrote in his autobiography, "I'd like to know it."

The reunion took place on October 10, 1945. Capra and Stewart were joined by Wasserman and Sam Briskin, Harry Cohn's former right-hand man, now a partner with Capra, George Stevens, and William Wyler in a new independent production company called Liberty Films. Liberty would produce the new Capra picture as one of two initial ventures, the other being Wyler's *The Best Years of Our Lives*.

Capra found Stewart "older, shyer, ill at ease." He was nervous himself; it had been years since he had tried to sell a project to an actor. And, indeed, Lew Wasserman remembers that Capra told the story poorly. "Jim," Frank said, "you're in a small town and things aren't going very well. You begin to wish you'd never been born. And you decide to commit suicide by jumping off a bridge into the river, but an angel named Clarence comes down from heaven, and, uh, Clarence hasn't won his wings yet. He comes down to save you when you jump into the river, but Clarence can't swim, so you save him."

As he talked, Capra felt sure that he was losing his audience. Stewart, in particular, looked bored. Finally, the director stopped before coming to the end. "Goddamn, Jim. I haven't got a story," he exclaimed. "This is the lousiest piece of cheese I ever heard of. Forget it, Jimmy. Goddamn, forget it! Forget it!" But Stewart replied, "Frank, if you want to do a movie about me committing suicide, with an angel with no wings named Clarence, I'm your boy." Two weeks later, he signed to play George Bailey in *It's a Wonderful Life*.

Five months would pass while Capra readied the film for production. Meanwhile, Jim lived at Tiger Tail and hung out with Fonda. Both men were having a hard time readjusting to civilian life. The quiet, the leisurely pace, and too much free time created a kind of lassitude after the regimentation of the military and the rigors of combat (Fonda had served as an assistant operations and Air Combat Intelligence officer in the Pacific). Then there was the fear of trying to jump-start careers that had been in mothballs for, in Stewart's case, more than four years. Other stars had come along during that long interval. Van Johnson, for example, had made his film debut in 1942, picking up the wholesome-boy-next-door niche abandoned by Stewart. On another front, Gregory Peck, whose first film was released in 1944, was staking a claim on the Mr. Smith, man-of-integrity roles, the principled fighters. Hank and Jim wondered if they could reclaim their places in the Hollywood pantheon. Moreover, could they still work the magic? As Stewart had said at his New York press conference, acting was a skill like any other. Without practice, the muscles atrophy.

Beyond that, Jim wondered if acting made sense in light of what he'd been through. After one has led a thousand men in planes over hostile enemy territory, can one still put on makeup and costumes and engage in make-believe for a living? Can one rejoin the social scene—the parties, the nightclubs, the premieres—so vacuous yet so integral to membership at the top of the motion picture fraternity?

Stewart and Fonda pondered these questions during the fall and winter of 1945, but given their private natures, they didn't ruminate out loud very often. As Jim recalled, Hank "never sat down and talked about acting, but every now and then he'd say something about its importance and your ability and your chance to make it a fine profession. He'd put this in very simple ways, but it impressed me and got me to feeling that I was capable of continuing on after the war."

Mostly, they readjusted through quiet companionship. Peter Fonda remembers that they started constructing gas-engine model airplanes again. "I would watch them build," he says, "but I was not allowed to help. Which I understood totally. I would mess up one piece of balsa wood, and they would have to find a new one or make a new one. I just watched and listened. And I would be there for quite a while, and I can tell you that ten minutes, then twenty minutes, would pass, no words, and then, 'Hank?' 'Yeah.' 'I got A-23.' And Dad would look over at some piece of paper. 'Oh, A-23 goes in B-7.' 'Okay.' And then there'd be another ten or fifteen minutes of silence." Once the planes were completed, there were test flights. "I mean, these two men were perfectionists," says Peter, laughing. "Maiden voyages were done in the field to see how much lift was needed, if there was more clay needed in the nose, a bend here or there, whatever was needed, the tuning." Then, when the models had proven themselves, they'd be launched from a boat or a high precipice.

Flying kites became another hobby. Peter explains, "Dad, having been in the navy, got these old target kites and would rig them up to a marlin rod, and he and Jimmy would be out playing. Of course, all of this was under the idea that we were going to take Peter kite-flying. Actually, I was the excuse for these two men to be children themselves."

Slowly, the former stars made their way back into the Hollywood scene. Peter remembers a party at Tiger Tail for which Jim donned a white dinner jacket. Hank insisted upon showing him a new pen he'd bought. When he did so, ink squirted all over the front of Stewart's pristine jacket. "Now I ran and hid," says Peter, "because I was accused of doing everything, and even though there were witnesses to the fact that I had nothing to do with this, I ducked behind the couch. And within a few minutes the ink disappeared. It was disappearing ink. And these two men just cracked up, and I rarely saw either of them crack up."

Then there was the annual William Randolph Hearst–Marion Davies costume party, the same event that had triggered Stewart's romance with Norma Shearer in 1938. In 1946, the theme was the American Revolution. Fonda suggested that he, Johnny Swope, and Stewart go as the Spirit of '76, after the famous painting in which one veteran limps and plays the fife, another bangs the drums, and the third carries the American flag. But Fonda added a wrinkle—they would be the Spirit of '76 as played by the Marx Brothers. Stewart was Chico the fifer, Swope was Harpo the flag bearer, and Fonda was Groucho the drummer. They were the hit of the party and winners of the second-place prize for best costume. "God knows who won the first prize," said Fonda, "probably Mr. Hearst. Seems he had some influence with the judge—Miss Davies."

On the dating front, Jim saw starlets Myrna Dell and Martha Vickers. He was also among the many captivated by beautiful blond-haired, green-eyed Anita Colby (aka Anita Counihan). Nicknamed The Face, Colby had been a model. In fact, she was once the highest-paid model in the United States, whose lovely countenance graced fifteen magazine covers in a single month. The daughter of cartoonist Bud Counihan, she was pals with Ernest Hemingway, Damon Runyon, John O'Hara, the Averell Harrimans, and composer Deems Taylor. She had come to Hollywood as an actress, but had found her niche as an executive, setting the style for the female stars under contract to David O. Selznick. In January of 1945, some months before Stewart met her, *Time* made her its cover story—under the heading "Hollywood's Anita Colby: 'The Face' has a brain to match." She was thirty at the time. Inside the magazine, *Redbook* editor Voldemar Vetluguin called her "the most beautiful face this side of Paradise" with "the sharpest tongue this side of hell." And her love life was described as a long line of "eligible and often famous men" who, if laid end to end, "might reach from the Stork Club to the Mocambo."

According to one columnist, who caught Stewart and Colby at the Los

Angeles premiere of Alfred Hitchcock's *Spellbound* in 1945, "They are constantly together these days." Anita said many years later that Stewart even proposed marriage—which she declined (she turned down a proposal from Clark Gable as well). But she also claimed to have introduced Jim to the woman he married, which is not true. So her assertions must be considered somewhat suspect.

Whether he proposed to Colby or not, Stewart was warming to the idea of marriage. After all, by the fall of 1945, he was thirty-seven years old. But he wasn't merely aging; his personality was changing. As he told Louella Parsons some years later, in the 1930s he "couldn't stand having anybody around me all the time. I had to be alone most of the time—or I thought I had to. Then I went into the Army, and like every soldier I was mixed up with other fellows every second." Thereafter he found himself growing edgy if left alone too long. As he told Susan Peters of *Photoplay*, "When you get home from work tired—too tired to go out or to have people over—you get kinda lonesome. Loneliness can be an awful thing." Still, he recognized the precarious nature of his position, saying, "I don't want to marry one of these actresses and have it last a month, and if I find some nice girl and bring her out here, what would Hollywood do to her? I'm not so conceited that I think I can buck what a lot of other guys haven't been able to buck."

Leland Hayward thought he had a solution. As Jim later told Brooke, "When I got back from the service, he came to me and said, 'Now, look, you've been away for five years and the movie business is all changed and God knows what, you don't know what you're gonna do—what you ought to do is marry a rich girl and take it easy. And I know exactly the one.'" The next time Stewart was in New York, he escorted the woman to dinner and the theater, but the evening was less than spectacular. In fact, both parties had a rotten time. The next day, when Hayward learned that Jim hadn't sent the lady flowers as a thank-you for the night before, he took it upon himself to have something delivered in Stewart's name—naturally, forwarding the bill to Jim. The lady called to thank him, saying, "I've never had so many flowers, the flowers absolutely cover the whole room. I don't know where to put any more flowers. There are more flowers than I've ever seen in my life. Thank you very much." Stewart never saw her again.

Finally, after several months, Jim was able to leave the Fondas and return to his own home. He furnished the modest, white stucco structure with Early American pieces, enlivened sporadically with prints by van Gogh and Utrillo. "You'd never have guessed it was a movie star's home," reported Hedda Hopper in May of 1946. "The house, utterly devoid of ornamentation, was as plain as Jimmy and a great deal more severe. I found no scripts; no volumes of plays; no busts of the great; no autographed pictures; no photographs of girls. Even his Oscar was missing." She added, "For pin-ups, Jimmy had sketches of airplanes. His books dealt with aviation and history. In his den were a clock (not running), a model plane and a gadget for practicing piloting." Once again, the manse became the domain of Daisy Dooley, Jim's formidable housekeeper. In the words of one reporter, she was "not in the least dazzled by her daily proximity to a movie star and regards Stewart as a great big helpless male on whose bony frame she would like to pile a few extra pounds."

As life gradually returned to normal, Stewart focused on rebuilding his career. Metro wanted him back and could have had him because his seven-year contract had not expired when he was inducted—were it not for Stewart's former girlfriend Olivia de Havilland. Until the actress brought suit against Warner Bros. in 1944, the studios could suspend a personal service contract any time an employee was not working—when he or she was ill, between pictures, on jury duty, or serving in the military—or for that matter, when he or she refused an assignment. Given such discretion, a studio could retain the services of popular stars, directors, or writers long past the expiration date of their contracts. That, in the wake of de Havilland's suit, was deemed a form of servitude and hence illegal. Thus, Stewart returned to Hollywood as a free agent.

Of course, he had been happy at Metro before the war and could have re-signed with the studio. But he feared that if he did so, Mayer wouldn't let him make *It's a Wonderful Life* with Capra's fledgling Liberty Films. Moreover, his agent advised him to remain free. "He'd been at MGM a long time," says Lew Wasserman, "and it was a different business by then. There were much greater opportunities on the outside than there were at MGM." Among other factors, independent production companies, such as Capra's, were becoming increasingly prevalent. Within a few years, some eighty-five such units would be producing roughly half of all Hollywood pictures. An actor who could work from picture to picture with an array of independents and studios could earn far more money than a contract player who received a fixed weekly salary, especially since the studios never shared any overages they made from loanouts for a star's services (which were often tens of thousands of dollars). Stewart might even want to consider forming a production company of his own, as other actors were starting to do (he never did). Jim, who tended to heed his advisers throughout his career, was easily convinced, especially since most of his friends, including Fonda and Gary Cooper, had already chosen to freelance.

As a way of getting his feet wet, he agreed to do a radio version of

Destry Rides Again on *Lux Theatre* with Joan Blondell as Frenchie. The show's host, William Keighley, who had directed Stewart in *No Time for Comedy,* reintroduced the star to American audiences by saying, "We welcome back to the airwaves and to *Lux Radio Theatre*—a gentleman we've missed for almost five years: Jimmy Stewart! He appears in one of his favorite roles—as the soft-spoken, gentlemanly guardian of the law in Universal's western melodrama." As the show began, Stewart was clearly nervous. In fact, reporter Joseph Wechsburg noted that his "hand holding the script was shaking so hard they could see it from the control room."

He'd broken the ice, but *It's a Wonderful Life* still wasn't ready to go into production and offers from other quarters weren't exactly pouring in. So Stewart decided to buy a used car—which one journalist called "a medium-priced machine of interesting eccentricity"—and tour parts of California that he'd never seen before, including Carmel and Palm Springs, and Mexico's Baja California. It was a good old-fashioned vacation, with plenty of swimming, fishing, golfing, and sailing.

Then, finally, on April 8, 1946, nearly a year after V-E Day, Stewart was ready to face the motion picture cameras again. *It's a Wonderful Life* was ready to roll.

PART FOUR

· *George Bailey* ·

TWELVE

Back to Work

It began as a short story called "The Greatest Gift." The author, Philip Van Doren Stern, had written biographies of Lincoln, Lee, and John Wilkes Booth, as well as several novels, but no one wanted to acquire his fable when it made the rounds of magazine publishers in 1943. So Stern printed two hundred copies himself, which he sent to friends as a Christmas greeting. One of the recipients, his Hollywood agent, Shirley Collier, then sold the story to RKO for $10,000. Thereafter, it appeared in *Good Housekeeping* as "The Man Who Never Was" and, in 1945, became a small book under its original name.

RKO assigned the adaptation to Dalton Trumbo and later Clifford Odets and Marc Connelly, but none of these gifted writers could produce a satisfactory screenplay. In Trumbo's version, for example, the protagonist started out as an idealistic politician and became a cynical power broker who contemplates suicide after losing his race for governor—a concept far removed from the setting and characters of the original story. Finally, Charles Koerner, RKO's studio chief, brought the project to Capra. When the director read Stern's fable, he was thrilled. "It was the story I had been looking for all my life!" he wrote in his autobiography.

On September 1, 1945, slightly more than a month before he met with Stewart, Capra purchased "The Greatest Gift" from RKO for $50,000. He then commissioned a new screenplay. As Robert Riskin (screenwriter for *You Can't Take It With You*) had just formed his own independent production company and Sidney Buchman (screenwriter for *Mr. Smith Goes to Washington*) had become a producer at Columbia, Capra hired Frances Goodrich and Albert Hackett, the husband-and-wife team who had written *Rose Marie* and *After the Thin Man* (the final screenplay would also bear the director's name and that of Jo Swerling, who rewrote some scenes). According to Capra's biographer Joseph McBride, two other writers, Michael Wilson and Dorothy Parker, also made contributions without credit.

What emerged from their labors was a rich tapestry of small-town life centering around an admirable young man, George Bailey, whose hunger for travel and adventure is constantly thwarted—from the day of his intended departure for a dream vacation until the moment he faces a serious shortfall in his firm's cash flow. These events ultimately contribute to his contemplated suicide. Almost none of the screenplay's Americana flavor or, for that matter, the key plot points were in Stern's story, although his character, bank clerk George Pratt, does express ennui over his mundane job and uneventful life. Moreover, the screenplay extended Stern's theme—that life is a precious gift—to embrace one of Capra's cardinal precepts: the goodness and wisdom of the common man. This notion plays out in George's running battle with a character created for the film, Mr. Potter, the town's richest man.

There were many other additions and alterations as well. Among them: the bank became not just the place of George's employment but a small savings and loan with a great deal more impact on town life than the enterprise in the story; and, as Capra told Stewart when they first discussed the project, the angel was given a name, Clarence Oddbody, and handed a personal stake in his assignment—to earn his wings.

With Stewart on board, Capra sought to engage Jean Arthur, Jim's costar in *You Can't Take It With You* and *Mr. Smith,* as George's wife, Mary. But Arthur was rehearsing a Broadway comedy, *Born Yesterday,* and was unavailable (she would eventually leave the play during an out-of-town tryout, paving the way for Judy Holliday's star-making performance). Even if she had been free, it is difficult to picture her in the role. Mary Bailey is far less interesting than George or, for that matter, the characters that the comedienne had played in Capra's previous films. The director also considered Ginger Rogers, Olivia de Havilland, Martha Scott, and Ann Dvorak. Then he saw twenty-four-year-old Donna Reed in a film and knew that he'd found the right actress. An MGM contract player since 1941, Reed had appeared mostly in the studio's light fare, including a *Thin Man* sequel, an Andy Hardy picture, and a Dr. Kildare film. Her most challenging role thus far had come when she played a wartime nurse in John Ford's 1945 saga *They Were Expendable,* opposite John Wayne. For the miserly Potter and George's befuddled uncle, Capra turned to two of Stewart's former costars, Lionel Barrymore, Grandpa Vanderhof in *You Can't Take It With You,* and Thomas Mitchell, Diz Moore in *Mr. Smith.* And, for Clarence, he chose Henry Travers, Broadway's Grandpa Vanderhof.

Much of the filming took place at RKO's ranch in Encino. There, in the then rural San Fernando Valley, art director Jack Okey created the fictional town of Bedford Falls, a massive set that extended over four acres and whose main street included seventy-five stores and buildings and twenty-four full-grown oak trees transplanted especially for the film. But the celebrated scene in which young George Charlestons with Mary in the school gym and then inadvertently falls into the swimming pool below was shot at Beverly Hills High School. The swim-gym, built in 1939 by employees of one of the New Deal's alphabet agencies, was still in use in the 1990s.

Capra was extremely nervous when filming began. Not only was he making his first feature since the war, but also the financial future of his production company rested on his success. His distress did not go unnoticed. As Joe Walker, who photographed part of the picture, put it, "He wasn't the careful, happy director on *Wonderful Life* that he had been before the war."[1]

Stewart was in wobbly shape himself, trying to compensate for his time away from Hollywood. In his words, he "had lost all sense of judgment. I couldn't tell if I was good or bad. I mean, in a given scene. Usually you can tell what is the right thing to do when you're acting. But I couldn't. I was uncertain." Sheldon Leonard, in the small role of Nick the bartender, noticed Stewart's discomfort. "He was not as smoothly professional as I would have expected him to be with all his background," Leonard recalled.

Fortunately, Jim was surrounded by supportive people. There was unpretentious Donna Reed. "I just fell in love with her right off the bat," he said. "She just seemed to be everything . . . everything just seemed to come to her." Perhaps because she sensed that Jim would lose his edge if he overrehearsed, she encouraged him to put their scenes on film without much preparation, a technique that also suited Capra. Stewart liked to recall one instance, in which George and Mary talk on the telephone to one of their friends—his rival for her affections. As they share the earpiece, they become increasingly aware of each other sexually. "And we did that scene with one take," said Stewart. "Can you believe it? We did it in one great, unrehearsed take."

He also drew strength from Lionel Barrymore. "Forget about being away for five years," the old pro told him. "Don't you realize you're moving millions of people, shaping their lives? What other profession has that kind of power? Acting, young fella, is a noble profession. Now just do what you're doing." Looking back, Stewart said, "I think he helped me more than anybody."

Capra helped, too. Despite his own angst, he was, as Sheldon Leonard recalls, "very sympathetic and understanding, but also highly profes-

---

[1] *It's a Wonderful Life* was initially shot by Victor Milner, but he left the picture after several weeks due to creative differences with Capra. Joseph Walker, who had been the director's cinematographer before the war, then took over, and much of Milner's work was redone. But Walker, still under contract to Columbia, was only on loan to Liberty until his home studio needed him again. When Harry Cohn called him back after about five weeks, Joseph Biroc, Milner's cameraman, took over. Walker and Biroc share the credit for the film.

sional." He let Stewart explore the character and make his own choices, but he knew what he wanted, and if Jim struggled with a moment or made an ill-advised choice, he was there to point the way. "If there was any question or discussion about the approach to a scene," Leonard recalled, "he [Stewart] deferred to Capra."

Stewart confessed at the outset of principal photography that, at thirty-seven (he turned thirty-eight during filming), he was nervous about playing someone just a few years out of high school. Capra told him, "Well, leave it to me. If I think something ought to be done about your aging or getting younger, I'll let you know." As it turned out, the director never said a word to him about it. Once Jim lost his inhibitions, he was, in his words, "having so much fun on the film" that being young came naturally.

The breakthrough came about a week into principal photography. Stewart said that by then he "knew everything was gonna be all right, because I fitted in, and I hadn't forgotten the things I'd learned before the war. It [acting] still meant a lot to me. I could have sworn that I'd never been away."

The picture wrapped on July 27, only four days behind schedule. Capra, working with his own money instead of Columbia's, was far more efficient than usual, exposing only 350,000 feet of film instead of the 400,000 or more he had typically shot before the war.

Given the final Christmas sequence, RKO, Liberty Films' distributor, held up the release of *It's a Wonderful Life* until December 21, when the film opened at the Globe Theatre in New York. The critics were enthusiastic, although Bosley Crowther of the *New York Times* and John McCarten of the *New Yorker* found the picture overly sentimental. Howard Barnes answered them: "However easy it may be to pick flaws in the show," he wrote in the *New York Herald-Tribune*, "it is loaded with artistry and sincerity."

Barnes, like virtually every other member of the press, praised Jimmy, writing, "Stewart dominates every scene, as Capra unquestionably wished him to do. He does it with remarkable skill and persuasion. Here is a screen performance which ranks high among those of recent years. Whether he is fighting shy of an early romance, or attacking the tycoon who could have made Bedford Falls a feudal domain, he is extraordinarily appealing and real." To which John L. Scott of the *Los Angeles Times* added, "It is truly a magnificent characterization. Stewart has matured surprisingly, and in this, his first civilian job since becoming a civilian, he should prove a serious contender for Academy Award laurels."

With George Bailey, the melding of actor and image became complete. "Jimmy Stewart and George Bailey are basically one and the same," says Jimmy Hawkins, who played the youngest son in the picture.

Beyond a similar upbringing to his character's, the actor brought a greater emotional depth to his role than he had to any previous performance. Nowhere in his prewar career had he grappled with the kind of hopelessness that George exhibits in a bar shortly before the attempted suicide or the fury that builds in George when minor irritations at home cause him to lash out at both his loved ones and his cluttered desk.

At the same time, Stewart was able to invest the picture's early sequences with the kind of humor and zest that had marked the best of his prewar work—as in his first moment on-screen, describing the gigantic suitcase that he wants for his anticipated adventures abroad; and at the savings and loan, when Bailey thwarts the avaricious Potter's desire to close the place down. It is hard not to remember the weary Jefferson Smith on the floor of the Senate when Stewart says, "Just remember this, Mr. Potter, that the rabble you're talking about, they do most of the working and paying and living and dying in this community. Well, is it too much to have them work and pay and live and die in a couple of decent rooms and a bath?"

It has become part of Hollywood lore that *It's a Wonderful Life* was a failure upon its initial release, but this is not accurate. Ranking a respectable twenty-seventh among the most popular pictures of the year, it broke even or perhaps even realized a slight profit on its $3 million cost. Moreover, it received five Oscar nominations, including ones for Best Picture and Best Director. And Jim got a Best Actor nod—his third.[2]

But Capra's previous pictures had been blockbuster hits, and by that standard, his first postwar feature was a major disappointment. Given its reviews, its cast and director, and its Oscar nominations, it should have done much better. Years later Stewart explained the response by saying, "The country had been at war for four years, and what people wanted then was Jerry Lewis and Red Skelton and the Three Stooges—things they could just laugh at, you know." But a look at the big box-office hits of 1946 and 1947 reveals a polyglot of features—from musicals such as *Blue Skies* and *The Jolson Story* to melodramas such as *Spellbound* and *Green Dolphin Street* to wholesome stories such as *The Yearling* and *Life With Father*. Arguably, it wasn't the dramatic elements in the story or the locale, the fantasy element, or the creative talents that dampened the reception for *It's a Wonderful Life*. It was Capra's celebration of the common man and the heavy swipe at big business in the person of Scrooge-like Potter. With America enjoying an economic boom and feeling optimistic in the wake of

---

[2] Ironically, *It's a Wonderful Life* lost in all three categories to Liberty Films' other inaugural picture, *The Best Years of Our Lives*, with William Wyler and Fredric March besting Capra and Stewart, respectively.

its recent victory over fascism, concerns about the little guy in the hands of unscrupulous tycoons seemed old-fashioned, a throwback to the previous decade and the horrors of the Depression. Even the looks on the faces of the people in the crowd scenes of Capra's picture suggested images that folks in 1946 were eager to forget.

What made *It's a Wonderful Life* the timeless classic that it is today was television—and a clerical error. With Liberty Films long since defunct, no one thought to renew the picture's copyright when it expired in 1974. Thereafter, with no royalties to pay when it aired, TV stations across the country picked it up and showed it repeatedly during every Christmas holiday season. In one year alone—1991—it could be seen in the Los Angeles area on five local stations, as well as four cable channels: USA, AMC, the Family Channel, and the Disney Channel. Thus, millions of people far too young to have seen it in theaters fell under its spell, and eventually it became yuletide's most popular picture, eclipsing even *A Christmas Carol* and *Miracle on 34th Street*. It also transformed Stewart from a popular movie star of Hollywood's golden age into an American icon.[3]

Despite its disappointing initial reception, *It's a Wonderful Life* became Stewart's favorite film (and Capra's as well). Part of the reason that it was so special to Stewart was its place in his own life story: it was his first film after the war, the picture that showed him that he could still have a career in Hollywood. He also loved the people involved—among them Lionel Barrymore, Donna Reed, Beulah Bondi, who played his mother once again, and Ward Bond, who had a continuing role as the town cop. Moreover, much as he respected his other legendary directors, he had a special regard for Capra. "Without any doubt Frank Capra was the greatest director I ever knew," he once said. "I have the utmost respect and admiration for him. He was able to do things like no one else, there's no question about it." Finally, he liked the picture's theme and the way it was executed. As he put it, "It bears out my feeling of the picture business, that it's not a production line business—but magic."

* * *

[3] Finally, in 1994, the situation changed. Republic Pictures, which had acquired the rights to Philip Van Doren Stern's short story, acquired the rights to the film's music from several publishers, including Warner/Chappell Music and Edward B. Marks Music. Thereafter, as the owner of "underlying" material, it asserted its claim on the picture itself. Its right to do so, by a strange coincidence, had been determined by a case involving another Stewart picture, *Rear Window*. (See page 361–62.) Once it controlled the rights to *It's a Wonderful Life*, Republic decided to license only one airing on network television per year with the idea that that showing, like the annual airing of *The Wizard of Oz*, would become a major family event.

By the time *It's a Wonderful Life* opened, Stewart was busy with his next picture, *Magic Town*, which had commenced principal photography on October 24. The project was under the auspices of its screenwriter, Robert Riskin, whose new production company—like Liberty—was aligned with RKO.

Drawing on a story by Joseph Krumgold, Riskin sought to capture the glow of his Depression-era films with Capra by focusing on a small fictional community called Grandview, dubbed the quintessential American town. The man responsible for the appellation is Lawrence "Rip" Smith, a Manhattan pollster who discovers that the local citizens represent a microcosm of the country as a whole and uses them without their knowledge or permission as subjects for his clients' opinion surveys. Of course, he ends up falling in love with the pretty community—and its female newspaper editor, Mary Peterman.

Stewart was playing another Mr. Smith but the character's resemblance to the idealistic senator ended with his name. Until late in the film, when Rip tries to rescue Grandview from near-oblivion, he is a smooth operator, a "city slicker," as one of his friends calls him, who's not above subterfuge to save his faltering business. Stewart was totally wrong for the role. It needed someone with a much harder edge, an actor who could make a believable and emotionally compelling transition from cynical manipulator to good-hearted neighbor and friend. Jim, with his distinctive drawl, innocent look, and general affability, rendered the schemer harmless from the outset.

His pairing with Jane Wyman didn't help matters. As the dedicated editor, she bore more resemblance to the prickly character in her recent film *The Yearling*, for which she would soon win an Oscar nomination, than to the leading ladies in Stewart's Capra films. There was little chemistry between the stars, who never even kiss in the picture. Perhaps out of frustration with his role or his leading lady or the screenplay—or all three—Stewart tried to inject some life into the proceedings with exaggerated facial expressions and occasional bits of slapstick, as when he trips over a small flight of stairs while proclaiming how tough he is. But rather than being funny, he simply overacts. He was far more effective late in the picture when Rip becomes devoted to saving the town.

Beyond Stewart and Wyman, the screenplay failed to capture the whimsy of Riskin's earlier writing as well as his celebrated ability to tug at the heartstrings. Moreover, the director, William Wellman, who had last worked with Stewart on *Small Town Girl* in 1936, was ill equipped to maximize the material's minor potential. He was more skilled with rugged fare such as *The Public Enemy* with James Cagney, *Beau Geste, The Ox-Bow*

Incident, and *The Story of G.I. Joe.* Later, Wellman would sum up his opinion of *Magic Town* in two words: "It stunk!" When the picture opened at
the Palace Theatre in New York on October 7, 1947, few disagreed.

Magic Town had wrapped on January 15, 1947. The following month, on
February 22, Stewart returned to Princeton University to receive an
honorary M.A. at a convocation marking his alma mater's bicentennial.
July found him in the East once more, doing something most unusual for
a star of his caliber—taking over the lead role in a Broadway play while
the regular headliner was on vacation.

The play was *Harvey,* the Pulitzer Prize–winning comedy that had
opened in New York on November 11, 1944, while Stewart was in England
as chief of staff of the 2nd Combat Wing. Written by Denver reporter Mary
Chase, *Harvey* was a piece of gentle whimsy about a sweet, alcoholic bachelor named Elwood P. Dowd, his dotty sister, Veta Louise Simmons, and
his best friend, an invisible, six-foot rabbit called Harvey. The title character is a pooka, a large fairy spirit in animal form, the likes of which had
populated the Irish folktales Chase learned from her uncles as a child.

Universal Pictures had purchased the film rights to *Harvey* for the
enormous sum of $750,000.[4] But the studio was contractually prohibited
from releasing the picture until the Broadway production closed, and in
the summer of 1947, after a run of more than two and a half years, no end
was in sight. Thus, instead of going into production and keeping the
picture on the shelf for an indefinite period, Universal simply bided its
time. The studio had not even cast the comedy—which is why Stewart
volunteered for the replacement gig. "I did it to prove I could do the
part," he said later. "It was up for grabs and Universal couldn't see me
doing the lush."

Returning to the stage entailed several definite risks. First, there was
the loss of income. The play's producer, Brock Pemberton, could pay Jim
only a pittance of what he earned doing a film. Rather than lower his asking price, says Lew Wasserman, Stewart did the seven-week stint for free.
Pemberton just paid his hotel room and other expenses. Moreover, Stewart hadn't done a play in twelve years. Going back to the theater meant
readjusting to the technical demands of live performance—projecting

---

[4] It will be recalled that when Harry Cohn paid less than a third of that amount for *You
Can't Take It With You* in 1938, he had broken the record for such acquisitions by a wide
margin. But, as if the purchase price for *Harvey* were not spectacular enough, it was generously rounded upward to $1 million for publicity purposes. The line item in the film's
production budget carries the figure of $750,000. Chase got an additional $25,000 for
writing the screenplay.

one's voice to the back of the house, acting broadly enough to be "read" when one's facial features are discernible to only a select few, re-creating the same emotional throughline every night. Worse, he would have only a few rehearsals to get up in the part—without the guidance of the director, Antoinette Perry, who had died in 1946. And beyond all of that, he had to step into a role that had become the personal property of the man who had created it, Frank Fay (Fay would ultimately play Elwood for 1,351 of the show's 1,775 Broadway performances). A hard-drinking Irishman with a pixielike face, Fay was an ex-vaudevillian who knew how to get every laugh the role had to offer. Audiences adored him. Even if he'd wanted to, Stewart couldn't have duplicated Fay's performance. He was younger, taller, slimmer, and gentler.

Richard Watts Jr. of the *New York Post*, who rereviewed the show for Jim's opening along with the other major drama critics, noted the differences in the actors' styles, writing, "Mr. Stewart makes Elwood a shy, good-looking young man with the commendable and unusual virtue of being good-natured in his cups who really should have been going out with girls instead of spending his time with an oversized animal. Mr. Fay, on the other hand, portrayed an odd, daft, other-worldly sort of fellow, who lived in an alcoholic universe all his own and was obviously more at home with mythical creatures than with men and women." He added that Fay infused his interpretation with a "zany quality" that Stewart lacked. But Jim had his boosters, too. Mildred Gordon of the *New York Morning Telegram* called his performance "top-notch" and John Chapman of the *New York Daily News* praised his "instinct for timing and emphasis which is so important in a comedy."

Audiences clamored for the chance to see the movie star live. "A special detail was necessary to keep the youngsters and the autograph hunters from mobbing Jimmy," a Hollywood press agent noted shortly after his debut. "The crowds clustered around the stage door and along the side street leading to the stage, reminding old-time police of the days when John Barrymore, James K. Hackett, and William Faversham were the matinee idols of Broadway."

On opening night, such was the fervor that Stewart's first entrance stopped the show cold. Later that evening, at the final curtain, he made a short speech, thanking Fay for letting him "fool around with his role," and acknowledging the support of the cast and crew, and of course, Harvey himself. According to Brooklyn reporter Jane Corby, he "was stampeded by wild applause."

Jim particularly liked working with Josephine Hull, who had previously won the hearts of audiences in the stage and film versions of *Arsenic and Old Lace* and who was a sheer delight as Veta Louise. "Just to see a wonderful girl like that," said Stewart during his Broadway run, "makes you proud to be an actor. She's so skillful, so accomplished, so lovable, so wonderful—well, it just makes you proud of your business." He also got a kick out of Jesse White, the brash comic who had created the role of Wilson, the attendant at the sanitarium where Elwood is nearly committed.

Finally, on August 30, the brief stint came to an end. Stewart was glad that he'd taken the chance, calling the experience a "real hoot." But he didn't plan on returning to the theater anytime soon. "No," he told *Los Angeles Times* reporter Jack O'Brian. "Too tough. Too gosh darned tough."

Less than a month later, on September 22, he was back on firmer ground, playing a Chicago reporter named Jim McNeal in 20th Century–Fox's *Call Northside 777*. His character was based on a real journalist, James McGuire of the *Chicago Tribune*, who had won the Pulitzer Prize for his articles seeking to clear an innocent man, Joseph Majeczek, of the murder of a policeman.

Stewart had played reporters before—notably in *The Murder Man*, *Next Time We Love*, *The Last Gangster*, and *The Philadelphia Story*—but for the first time with *Call Northside 777*, his character was actively practicing his craft. In fact, McNeal's pursuit of the story is the driving force behind the picture. In the first draft of the screenplay the role was little more than a standard Hollywood journalist. But Darryl F. Zanuck, Fox's studio chief and a former screenwriter himself, kept pushing for the richest possible character development. McNeal "should be more caustic and skeptical and hardboiled at the start," Zanuck wrote in one memo. "I don't mean that he is a tough guy but he is a calloused newspaperman and this is just another story to him, therefore, following this line, we should see him won over step by step by Joe's innocence so that as the story progresses McNeal fights a battle with himself." Zanuck also insisted that the paper's editor, Brian Kelly, be well drawn, and indeed, the byplay between Stewart and Lee J. Cobb, who played his boss, is one of the distinctive features of the film.

Beyond character development, Zanuck wanted *Northside* to have a hard edge—just the opposite of Stewart's postwar projects so far, but in keeping with *The Lost Weekend*, *The Best Years of Our Lives*, *Gentleman's Agreement*, and other uncompromising hits of the late 1940s. Thus, Zanuck chose Henry Hathaway to direct. The son of a stage manager and an actor, Hathaway had been around the motion picture industry since he was a child, acting in Western shorts for the American Film Company. His first directing assignment had come in 1932 with *Heritage of the Desert*, a B picture starring Randolph Scott. In more recent years, he had put his stamp on a series of harsh, realistic films at Fox—*House on 92nd Street* in

1945 and *13 Rue Madeleine* and *Kiss of Death* in 1947. These films were distinguished by their documentary-like style with extensive location filming, stark black-and-white photography, and crisp dialogue. *Call Northside 777* would follow in the tradition, with location work at the Statesville Prison near Joliet, Illinois, and at a variety of Chicago locales, including the city's Polish quarter, the 19th Precinct Station, Police Headquarters, and the Criminal Courts Building. Hathaway was even able to get Leonard Keeler, inventor of the polygraph—a device that figured prominently in the story—to play himself in the picture.

Before filming began, Henry Fonda, who had worked with Hathaway in *The Trail of the Lonesome Pine* and *Spawn of the North* in the 1930s, warned Stewart about the director. Hathaway, he said, had a terrible temper and was known to berate actors and technicians on the set. But Jim and Hathaway got along fine. In fact, after Jim was married, the Stewarts often socialized with the director and his wife. Meanwhile, on the set, Hathaway worked to keep Stewart from his usual vocal mannerisms, and as a result, *Call Northside 777* offers one of the actor's cleanest, most controlled performances. The critics duly noted this when the picture opened in February of 1948. As for the film itself, the *New York Times'* Bosley Crowther summed up the consensus, calling it "a slick piece of modern melodrama in anybody's book" and a "remarkably photogenic film."

From a well-crafted studio production, Stewart went into what could be called the movie star's version of "let's put on a play": Jim's friend Burgess Meredith had an idea for a picture that he wanted to produce, and Stewart agreed to star in it. As did Henry Fonda, Fred MacMurray, Dorothy Lamour, Victor Moore, and Meredith's then wife, Paulette Goddard.

What the actor had in mind was an anthology film, three independent stories loosely linked together by his character, an aspiring roving reporter who asks average people provocative questions and then prints the best of their responses in a daily column. The question that sparked the tales in the picture—shown in flashback—was "What influence has a little child had on you?" One reply came from a film actress (Lamour) who got her big break at the behest of a bratty kid star. Another found two grifters (Fred MacMurray and William Demarest, the future costars of MacMurray's TV sitcom, *My Three Sons*) tormented by a Dennis the Menace. The third centered around two ragtag musicians who rig a talent contest in the boondocks as a way of paying for the repairs on their broken-down touring bus. The "little child" in this case was actually a beautiful young woman, the daughter of the mechanic who fixes their vehicle.

Stewart and Fonda were the musicians. Unlike the other cast members, who were content to let Laurence Stallings and Lou Breslow write the screenplay and King Vidor and Lesley Fenton direct, Stewart and Fonda took it upon themselves to flesh out their story with a writer of their own choosing, John O'Hara. They phoned the celebrated author of *Appointment in Samarra* and *Butterfield 8* in New York, laid out the basic story line, and he produced a script for them in ten days.

Then they got John Huston, the talented director of *The Maltese Falcon*, to direct their sequence. "We'd shot about a week," Stewart recalled, "and one morning we got there and there was no John Huston. And the phone rang, and he called and he said, 'I forgot. I have this commitment that I've had for three years and I'm calling you from New York, because I have to start tomorrow and it slipped my mind.'"

After that bizarre brush-off, they asked George Stevens, who had directed Stewart in *Vivacious Lady*, to take over. He agreed to do it, with the proviso that he receive no credit for the sequence. Consequently, his name does not appear in conjunction with the finished film.

Stevens "kept everyone on the set sort of on a tightrope," Jim recalled, "not knowing exactly what was going to happen next, and for this type of comedy that we had in this, this was perfect." Looking back on his second collaboration with the director, Jim said, "It didn't last long, a couple of weeks, but the whole thing was a wonderful experience for all of us."

Jim and Hank's hands-on approach worked to their advantage, for when the picture, *A Miracle Can Happen* (but also known as *On Our Merry Way*), opened at the Warner Theatre in New York on February 3, 1948, two weeks before *Call Northside 777*, virtually all of the critics found their segment the best of the three. That wasn't saying much, however. As *Cue* put it, the Lamour story line was "pathetically unfunny" and the MacMurray-Demarest segment was a "frantic failure." Moreover, the scenes involving Meredith, the glue that holds the anthology together, were, in the words of Bosley Crowther of the *New York Times*, the "most painful business in the melange." In retrospect, the chief virtue of *A Miracle Can Happen* is that it afforded audiences their only opportunity to see Stewart and Fonda together when the actors were at the top of their form. It would be twenty years before the old friends would costar in a movie again.

On January 12, 1948, just a few weeks after his segment in *A Miracle Can Happen* wrapped, Stewart started work on a very different picture. Not only did it mark a departure from the type of role that he usually played and the genres in which he had starred, it was to be shot in a unique way. It was called *Rope*, and the director was Alfred Hitchcock.

By 1948, the rotund master of suspense had already forged a considerable international reputation, first with a series of thrillers in his native England, including *The Man Who Knew Too Much* and *The 39 Steps*, and then with his American films produced by David O. Selznick, among them *Rebecca, Foreign Correspondent, Suspicion, Saboteur, Shadow of a Doubt, Spellbound,* and *Notorious.* He liked working in Hollywood but not for Selznick. Thus, with his contract finally at an end, he set off on his own, forming Transatlantic Pictures, an independent production company. His partner was Sidney Bernstein, the head of a major chain of British movie houses.

As he cast about for a project that could be produced inexpensively, Hitchcock hoped to find a story that would also support an experiment that he'd been wanting to undertake for some time: to shoot a movie without any cuts for close-ups or shifts in camera angles, thereby giving the appearance of nonstop action. He felt that such a technique would offer the best way to, in his words, "sustain the mood of the actors, especially in a suspense story." In *Rope's End,* he found a vehicle that would satisfy both needs. The play was by Patrick Hamilton, author of the acclaimed thriller *Angel Street,* known to moviegoers as the 1944 Ingrid Bergman–Charles Boyer film *Gaslight.*

Although Hamilton denied the influence, the two antagonists in *Rope's End,* Wynham Brandon and Charles Cranillo (called Shaw Brandon and Phillip in the film), bore a marked similarity to Nathan Leopold Jr. and Richard Loeb, two young, rich Chicagoans who had murdered a fourteen-year-old boy, Bobby Franks, in 1924. Like Leopold and Loeb, Brandon and Cranillo were brilliant college graduates, believers in the superman theory of Friedrich Nietzsche, who had taken a life just to prove that they could get away with the crime. But unlike the real killers, Brandon and Cranillo's downfall came at the hands of their former mentor and schoolmaster, Rupert Cadell, who attends a dinner party at their home on the night of the murder (with the corpse stashed in a trunk that's in plain view of all the guests).

After its London debut, *Rope's End* opened at the Theatre Masque in New York on September 19, 1929, with British actors Sebastian Shaw as Brandon and Ivan Brandt as Charles, and an American, Ernest Milton, as Rupert. "Those who can stomach it must be prepared to relish an evening of pure morbidity," cautioned Brooks Atkinson of the *New York Times.* Apparently, quite a few theatergoers had iron constitutions, because *Rope's End* ran a full one hundred performances, a respectable engagement in the immediate aftermath of the stock market crash.

For Hitchcock's purposes, the mystery was perfect: it took place entirely in the killers' apartment and spanned exactly the running time of the play. Moreover, the cast was relatively small: just a few other dinner guests beside the three principals.

Given his tight budget, Hitchcock could afford only one star. The character most likely to attract someone of the requisite stature was Rupert, the dogged intellectual who deduces his former students' dastardly deed from virtually no clues. Milton had played him as, to quote Robert Littell of the *New York World,* "a warped orchid of an effeminate Oxford decadent with florid but sure and sudden strokes of something very much like genius." Hitchcock's first choice was Cary Grant, with whom he had worked quite successfully in *Suspicion* and *Notorious.* But Grant was unavailable, so Hitch approached Stewart. Even though the screenplay by Arthur Laurents, from an adaptation by actor Hume Cronyn, toned down all three of the principal characters (onstage, the killers, like Leopold and Loeb, are gay) and made them Americans (with the action set in New York), Jim was still an unlikely prospect to play a glib, somewhat arch sophisticate. Given the myriad alternatives in Hollywood, why Hitchcock chose him remains puzzling. In all likelihood, Lew Wasserman, who represented both men, brought them together.

With Stewart on board, Hitch proceeded to cast the rest of the roles with actors largely unknown to American filmgoers: Farley Granger and John Dall as the killers, Edith Evanson as their housekeeper, and Joan Chandler, Sir Cedric Harwicke, and Constance Collier as the other dinner guests.

In point of fact, extensive experience—stage as well as film—was of greater importance to the project than the actors' marquee values, for Hitchcock's plan of attack would place enormous demands on his players' technical skills. As it would on the crew.

The plan was this: A reel of film was 950 feet, representing ten minutes' shooting time. The estimated length of the picture was eighty minutes. Therefore, it would be shot in eight ten-minute intervals. Hitchcock planned to end each reel by focusing on a solid object, like the trunk or the back of a chair, and start the succeeding reel with the same element. Thus the finished product would appear seamless.

Most films are shot in small snippets of two or three minutes. By contrast, once the camera started rolling during a ten-minute segment of *Rope,* there would be no breaks in the action whatsoever. When actors moved from room to room in Perry Ferguson's elaborate version of a Manhattan penthouse or from one part of a room to another, the camera would simply travel with them. If Hitchcock wanted to focus on a face or some other element and then move back to a larger subject, he would not shoot one and then the other in the customary fashion and then splice the footage together in the cutting room. Instead, the camera would pan from whatever it was pointed at to the desired subject. To effect these movements, the camera was placed on a specially constructed, rolling hardwood platform that sat about four inches off the floor. Operating it took four technicians. Other crew members were engaged to move walls and furniture out of the camera's path at designated moments and then return the objects to their regular positions after the boom had passed.

As if all this weren't complicated enough, behind the set was an elaborate miniature representing the skyline of New York. It included eight thousand incandescent bulbs with each building wired separately, the idea being that, as the action of the film moved from late afternoon to night, the cyclorama behind the skyline would turn yellow, then crimson, and finally black and the lights would begin to come on in the tiny individual apartments, just as they would in real life. To most effectively plot the passage of time for the audience, Hitchcock decided to shoot the picture in color, which he'd never done before.

Rehearsals began on January 12, 1948, on a soundstage that Transatlantic rented from Warner Bros. For ten days, the company wrestled with the material, primarily its technical demands. Little time was spent on character development, but then Hitchcock was hardly known as an actor's director. Having entered the industry as an artist, initially designing silent-film titles, his primary strength lay in imagery and composition. Acting was largely a mystery, best left to those who practiced it; he became involved only if someone diverged from the desired path.

In the case of Stewart's performance, Hitchcock's principal contribution was to give the character a limp. It wasn't in the script, but he told the star, "We must change you. I want people to be reminded that this is a different kind of characterization." Jim had a hard time mastering the slight infirmity. During one rehearsal, he nearly tripped. At another point, he got caught up in the dialogue and began favoring the wrong foot. Finally, the wardrobe mistress removed about a quarter inch of leather from the heel of the appropriate shoe, and the problem was solved. Beyond the limp, Hitch told the actor early in production, "Jimmy, never do anything you don't feel like doing. If it doesn't feel natural, then we'll work on it till it does." Otherwise, he left the star to his own devices.

The lack of directorial input didn't bother Stewart, who had matured into a self-sufficient actor. Not only was he adept at dissecting a script in terms of his character and then working out the playing of each scene, he was well aware of how a movie got made and what a star needed to do to maximize a performance on film. What did have him spooked as *Rope* went into production was the new way of filming. "By the time it came to the actual shooting of a full reel," he recalled, "I was practically in a state of nervous collapse. I was having nightmares, the kind I had not known since my first days in the theater. The kind in which you see yourself go totally blank standing in front of an audience of a thousand grimacing people all waiting for you to get your mind back." He particularly feared screwing up a minute or two from the end of a ten-minute segment, thereby ruining the entire reel and forcing everyone to start again. But, after the first reel was in the can, he began to relax. In fact, he found the rest of filming, in his words, "pure joy because it was like returning to the stage where action is continuous for a full act and you either do or die." Making *Rope* was invigorating, but it was also, as Farley Granger recalls, "pretty crazy," as the actors tried to emote with technicians frequently moving walls and furniture around them.

As it turned out, every reel had to be shot at least three times, and one required fifteen takes. Says Granger, "There were endless, endless technical things that were problems." The biggest mishap occurred when a wall wasn't shifted quickly enough, and the camera dolly crashed into it, suspending filming for the day. Getting the color right also caused time-consuming retakes. Still, *Rope* was shot in less than a month. On February 20, Stewart was done, and the picture wrapped the following day.

Released six months later, it was a hit at the box office and with critics—who called it "a magnificent psychological study in murder and detection" *(Cue)*, "the work of a master" (Howard Barnes, the *New York Herald-Tribune*), and a "real thriller" (Kate Cameron, the *New York Daily News*). But a few dissenting voices were raised. Leo Mishkin of the *New York Morning-Telegraph* found it "more of a stunt, a tour-de-force for its great director's ingenuity and imagination, than it is a compelling absorbing motion picture," and Bosley Crowther of the *New York Times* asserted, "In certain respects, it is possibly one of the dullest pictures ever made, for it is a deliberately circumscribed experiment in a camera technique which does not come off."

Today, the minority views prevail. The problem starts with the screenplay, which is far more talky than Hitchcock's other thrillers, with dialogue that is often mundane. Moreover, as critic Andrew Sarris has pointed out, the plot had "nowhere to go after its ghoulish premise is established except in the direction of hollow moralizing. The suspense is misplaced in that we do not care enough for the two murderers and their victim to have any feelings about their fate." Above all, the way in which the picture was filmed ultimately robbed it of Hitchcock's greatest gift: the ability to use little snippets of film to build incredible tension (a gift that arguably reached its zenith with the shower sequence in his 1960 masterpiece, *Psycho*). Hitchcock himself would say years later, "When I look back, I realize that it was quite nonsensical because I was breaking with my own theories on the importance of cutting and montage for the visual narration of a story."

Stewart recognized the technique's shortcomings as well, noting, "So much of film acting is reacting. And this is done very effectively by the

cut. . . . Well, the very fact that the camera had to move off the person saying the line to the person reacting did something to the tempo and the
effectiveness of the reaction." He also conceded that he "just didn't come
to grips with" his character. And, indeed, while he should be credited for
departing from his usual screen persona to try something new, he is not
credible or even interesting as the arch teacher. No doubt Grant or Laurence Olivier or James Mason would have served the material more
effectively.

Fortunately, Stewart and the master of suspense would do better by
each other during the next decade.

A month after he finished with *Rope,* Stewart returned to New York for a
second stint in *Harvey.* This time, Frank Fay was in Philadelphia, launching a national touring company. Jim took his final bow on April 24 and was
on location at Newark Airport two days later for his next movie, a comedy
called *You Gotta Stay Happy.*

Like every film he had done since the war except *Call Northside 777,*
You Gotta Stay Happy was an independent production. In this case, it was
the second offering from Rampart Productions, a company formed by
actress Joan Fontaine and her then husband, William Dozier.

Based on a story by Robert Carson, which was being serialized in the
Saturday Evening Post as the picture went before the cameras (Dozier
had purchased it from advance galleys), *You Gotta Stay Happy* was a
throwback to the screwball comedies of the 1930s, with Fontaine as a rich
heiress, Dee Dee Dillworth, who flees from her stuffy husband on the
night of their wedding and winds up in the nearby hotel room of Marvin
Payne, the co-owner of a struggling air-freight service. That, of course,
was Stewart. In the fashion of such romances, the twosome are thrown
together on a long journey—in this case, on Payne's beat-up plane—
before winding up together at the fade-out.

Directing was Stewart and Fontaine's mutual friend, Hank Potter,
who had last worked with Jim on *The Shopworn Angel.* Since then, Potter had directed *The Farmer's Daughter* and *Mr. Blandings Builds His
Dream House,* two delightful comedies. But he was not involved in the
location filming. That was under the purview of the second-unit director,
Jack Hively, who also shot Stewart and Eddie Albert, cast as Jim's pal
and co-owner of the air-freight company, in Chicago. Fontaine was not
present in either city. In the early stages of pregnancy and not feeling
well, she remained in Los Angeles while her stand-in, Norma Holm,
took her place.

Fontaine, who was thirty-one at the time, was sick throughout the
filming. "Quite frankly, I was so concerned with my physical condition,"

she says, "and getting through it before I had another miscarriage, that that's all I could think of." In fact, she injured herself when Potter ordered her to jump off a hay wagon. "Half an hour later, I was rushed to the emergency ward of St. John's Hospital [in Santa Monica]," she noted in her autobiography, but the baby was not lost. She was touched that her costar visited her there while she recuperated. "I'll never forget that," she says. "It was the dearest thing. My mother didn't come. My sister didn't come. But Jimmy came." She returned the favor by baking a cake for Stewart's fortieth birthday, which took place while they were filming. Shortly after the picture wrapped, Stewart expressed his admiration for Fontaine, telling Louella Parsons, "There were times when we thought maybe she wouldn't finish the picture, but you never heard a complaint out of her."

THIRTEEN

Getting Tough and Getting Married

You Gotta Stay Happy wrapped on July 14, 1948. Shortly thereafter, Stewart attended a small dinner party at the home of Gary and Rocky Cooper—and met the woman with whom he would share the next forty-five years.

Back in 1936, when he was still new to Hollywood, Jim had described his ideal mate to *Photoplay*. He said that he wanted someone who was "the product of breeding and good taste," someone "beautiful" and "easygoing," and with "poise and a fund of humor." He couldn't have offered a better description of Gloria McLean.

Born in 1919 in Larchmont, New York, a Manhattan suburb, Gloria was the daughter of Edgar B. Hatrick, a onetime publicist and later vice president and general manager of the Hearst Metrotone News. At Hearst, he helped pioneer the movie-house newsreels that were so popular before the advent of television. One of three children, Gloria attended two-year Finch College in New York City, but found time for myriad social activities at home. She participated in bridge tournaments, entered beauty contests, and enjoyed the local country club, frequently making the newspaper society columns. "But she wasn't a socialite in the conventional sense of the word," explains her daughter, Kelly Harcourt. "She had a lot of class and a lot of style, but she wasn't fancy and formal. It wasn't a top priority of her life to be seen." In fact, she was an outdoorswoman, enjoying golf and camping. Joan Fontaine likened her to the heiress she had played in *You Gotta Stay Happy*, a "kind of gun-toting, social, no-airs woman, very brusque, very direct," while to Robert Stack she "was like Bogie, in the sense that she would take a pin and stick it in all the blowhards. If anybody was pompous, they wouldn't be pompous around her very long."

While she didn't hold a steady job, Gloria eschewed an unproductive life. After college, she studied acting in New York, with an eye toward a stage career. Instead, she married—in 1941. Her husband, Edward Beale "Ned" McLean II, was a member of a wealthy newspaper family, whose mother, Evelyn Walsh McLean, had owned the Hope diamond.

Ned and Gloria moved to a ranch in Colorado, where she gave birth to two boys, Ronald in 1943 and Michael in 1946. A few years later, she left Ned and moved to Los Angeles with her young sons.

Her meeting with Jim at the Cooper home was no accident. "That was set up in the hopes that maybe the introduction would take," says Gary and Rocky's daughter, Maria. "You see, my mother was an old friend of Gloria's. She'd seen her through her first marriage and the divorce and all that." Gloria didn't need a lot of persuading; Stewart was her favorite actor.

Also present that evening were several other couples, including the Ronald Reagans, Maggie and Leland, and actress Ann Sothern. After dinner, they went to a nightclub, Ciro's. "Nat King Cole was playing," Gloria recalled, "and we danced. I saw Jimmy making hand signals to Leland, not to cut in. But I pretended not to notice."

Afterward, Stewart took her home. "As I opened her door for her," he said years later, "a German shepherd about like that"—waist high—"came at me with all his teeth bared. I drew back and Gloria talked to him sort of almost baby talk, and the dog kind of cringed and walked away." Notwithstanding the canine, Bello, Jim was intrigued. "I wanted to see her again," he said, "but I knew I would have to win that dog over, because Gloria was obviously devoted to it." For their first real date, he took her golfing, a sport that he'd taken up after the war, with Billy Grady his usual partner. Gloria beat him. "But he didn't mind," she recalled, adding that his attitude showed her "right away what kind of man he was."

As they continued to date, Stewart wooed not only the girl but also the dog. Said Jim, "I brought him steaks from Chasen's. I talked baby talk to him, patted him, praised him. It was terrible, humiliating, but I finally got to be friends with him and was free to court Gloria." He also came to know her children. Usually, when he visited her house, he would make time to chat with the boys, but she was pleased that he never, in her words, "knocked himself out to win them over. He liked the boys—he treated them as friends."

On one of their first dates, he took her to a preview of *You Gotta Stay Happy*. When the comedy officially opened at Radio City Music Hall on November 4, it drew enthusiastic notices from the critics. Virtually everyone liked Fontaine and Stewart as well, but the era of screwball comedy was over, and *You Gotta Stay Happy* lost money.

As for Jim, *Time* magazine noted in its review of the picture, "This is the kind of role that Jimmy Stewart could play blindfolded, hog-tied and in the bottom of a well." Which was not necessarily a good thing. Despite *Rope* and *Call Northside 777*, he was still trapped in the nice-guy, boy-next-door mode of his late prewar films, and as he passed his fourth decade, the trick was becoming increasingly harder to turn. Moreover, newer stars, such as Kirk Douglas, Burt Lancaster, and Robert Mitchum, were introducing a more rugged, less polished type of hero to the screen, and audiences, toughened by the bitter experience of the war, liked what they saw. Stewart began to realize that, without greater shadings to his persona, he was in danger of becoming passé. He needed to get tough.

He made something of a transition with his next picture, *The Stratton Story,* which started filming the very day that *You Gotta Stay Happy* debuted. The story of baseball pitcher Monty Stratton left plenty of room for Jim to mix naïveté with inner determination, to display a shy but winning way with his leading lady, June Allyson, and to offer slightly amused but respectful devotion to his widowed mother, played by Agnes Moorehead. But the biopic—Stewart's first—had a few distinguishing elements. For starters, Stratton's profession took Jim out of his customary suit and snap-brim hat and put him in a baseball uniform, a refreshing change of pace. Moreover, he had numerous scenes in which he was doing something physical, pitching primarily, and Stewart, having worked extremely hard at mastering Stratton's craft, looked very natural on the mound. To that point, he had rarely appeared on-screen doing anything more exhausting than dancing the Charleston or bounding up seven flights of stairs. But, most importantly, he got to examine the dark side of an otherwise genial country boy. For, at the height of his career, Stratton shot himself in a hunting accident, forcing the amputation of his leg. The loss, not only of his extremity but seemingly of his profession as well, sent him into a profound depression. He turned sarcastic and hostile. Stewart's effectiveness in those scenes, like the scenes leading up to the suicide attempt in *It's a Wonderful Life,* set the stage for the best of his work in the 1950s.

The Stratton Story was Douglas Morrow's idea, and he spent weeks developing it in Greenville, Texas, Stratton's home. The writer was surprised to find that the lanky former White Sox great had actually returned to his sport and was pitching quite successfully with the Sherman Baseball Club, a team in the minor leagues. Monty's attitude was, "Shucks, a person'd be surprised at what he can do if he sets his mind to it. About the only thing that can really lick a fellow is himself. And what would a fellow want to lick himself for?" That philosophy became the core of the picture.

The film's director was Sam Wood, Stewart's personal choice. Not so much because of their previous collaboration, *Navy Blue and Gold,* but because he admired the tall, rugged, somewhat puritanical director's success with the Lou Gehrig story, *The Pride of the Yankees,* starring Gary Cooper. Wood's studio, MGM, produced *The Stratton Story,* thereby bringing Stewart back to his former home for the first time since the war. Initially, however, L. B. Mayer hadn't liked the script. According to Jim, the mogul asked, "How do you think people will feel when this man with one leg goes to bat and hits a single and can't run to first base? How will all the pregnant women in the audience feel watching such a disgusting thing?" After it was released, however, the picture became one of L.B.'s favorites.

Stewart was asked to play Stratton after Van Johnson and Gregory Peck had proven unavailable, but he had always been Monty's personal choice, and the men worked closely together before and during filming. The baseball player expected that Stewart would ply him with questions, but that was not Jim's way. Said Monty, "He just kept watching me and studying me. Once he thought he knew me and what I was like, that was all he needed. He went right from there and became more like me than I am myself."

The two men also worked out every day for three weeks before the cameras started to roll. "When he'd throw the ball," Stratton recalled, "he'd always ask me if that had been right. Once in a while I'd give him a suggestion, such as following through more, but he got the hang of it in two days." Tougher was learning to walk as if he had a prosthetic leg. To simulate the gait, Stewart was fitted with a brace above and below his knee.

Filming took place between November 4 and December 23. As he had with *The Pride of the Yankees,* Wood imported an impressive roster of real-life baseball players to portray themselves, including pitcher Gene Bearden and slugger Bill Dickey, two of Stratton's toughest opponents. Jimmy Dykes, who managed the White Sox when Stratton was on the team, also played himself.

Stewart remembered the scene in which he had to pitch to Dickey: "All of a sudden, I had buck fever. I never had imagined what it must be like to stand out there on the mound and look at Dickey standing at the plate. And, mind you, this was only for fun. Bill just laughed and said: 'Get it somewhere near the plate and I'll hit it.' I knew he wouldn't because it wasn't in the script, but I was so nervous I kept missing the plate. Seemed like by fifteen feet, sometimes. I got so bad we had to call a halt. But when we went back to it after a while, I managed to get the ball over and Bill struck out."

Stewart's labors were amply rewarded at the box office. Opening at Radio City Music Hall on May 12, 1949—an ideal time for a baseball movie—*The Stratton Story* was an enormous hit, the sixth-biggest box-office draw of the year and the most successful picture of Stewart's postwar career thus far. It was a critical triumph as well, with *Newsweek* capturing the consensus in calling it "that rare achievement, a baseball movie that makes its point on a ball field without sacrificing its validity as personal drama." Howard Barnes of the *New York Herald-Tribune* dubbed it "a great personal triumph for Stewart," but his colleague Thomas M. Pryor of the *Times* got even closer to the heart of the matter, noting, "Call it luck or what you will but the circumstance which took Van Johnson off the mound and brought James Stewart in as the star of *The Stratton Story* was the best thing that has yet happened to Mr. Stewart in his postwar film career." In other words, Jim needed a hit, and he got it.

Meanwhile, Stewart continued to see Gloria McLean. In early February of 1949, a little more than a month after *The Stratton Story* wrapped, he took her on a trip to Mexico. They were joined by Jack Bolton, who represented Jim (under Lew Wasserman) at MCA, and Bolton's wife, Peggy. The Hollywood press, learning of the vacation, suspected that the star and his girl were going to tie the knot in Mexico, but that was not the case. "When and if I do get married," Stewart reassured them, "I'm going to tell you all about it. I don't want anybody to be left out."

A few weeks later, on the twenty-third of the month, he returned to MGM for *Malaya,* his second picture in a row with the studio. In keeping with his search for tougher roles, he played John Royer, an American journalist who volunteers to smuggle badly needed rubber out of Japanese-held Malaya during the early days of World War II. The screenplay by Frank Fenton was based on events set in motion in January of 1942 by Manchester Boddy, publisher and editor in chief of the *Los Angeles Daily News,* in his capacity as chairman of the California Committee for Rubber Supply and Use. In the film, Lionel Barrymore played a fictionalized version of Boddy.

For Stewart, the principal attraction of the project was the chance to work again with Spencer Tracy, cast as Royer's friend Carnahan, an Alcatraz convict with extensive connections in Malaya. Indeed, it was Tracy's casting that inspired Jim to ask to see the script. Nearly fourteen years had passed since they last worked together in *The Murder Man.* Since then, Tracy's fortunes in Hollywood had risen as high as they could get, with two Oscars to his credit (he won back-to-back for *Captains Courageous* in 1937 and *Boys Town* in 1938). But the gifted actor was a troubled man. He was alcoholic, had a deaf son, and was in love with Katharine Hepburn—but, as a staunch Roman Catholic, could not divorce his wife. Working with him on *Malaya* was not easy. As Stewart recalled, "It was a constantly edgy situation. Spence was more cantankerous than usual because the film was a real potboiler."

In an effort to keep his friend engaged, Jim proposed that they take a trip to Europe and Asia when the picture wrapped. "Every day we'd talk about what countries we were going to visit," he said, "and I kept collecting brochures to show him. He'd pore over the brochures and talk with great excitement about Greece and Rome and the Taj Mahal. Wal, anyway, the strategy seemed to work, and Spence showed up every day and did his usual fine job." But, no doubt, Tracy realized that he was in no shape to become a globe-trotter, and when filming ended, so did plans for the trip.

Stewart may have considered it a "potboiler," but *Malaya* turned out to be a good adventure story, "first-rate melodramatic entertainment," as *Cue* noted upon the picture's premiere on December 27. Stewart couldn't compete with Tracy, who had the flashier role, but he was fine as the journalist who starts out pragmatic, even cynical, and winds up dying in a patriotic gesture.

On May 20, Stewart turned forty-one. That evening, as he and Gloria celebrated at a private dinner party, he asked her to marry him, and she accepted. The reign of Hollywood's most eligible bachelor had come to an end.

The wedding was set for August. In the meantime, on June 6, Stewart reported to 20th Century–Fox for his next picture, his first Western since 1939's *Destry Rides Again*.

Broken Arrow, the story of the friendship between an Apache chief, Cochise, and a white man, Tom Jeffords, was the fulfillment of a dream for Julian Blaustein. An executive with David O. Selznick, Blaustein wanted to be a producer. So he acquired a property—the novel on which the film was based, *Blood Brother* by Elliott Arnold—and engaged Albert Maltz to write the screenplay.[1] Instead of the usual shoot-'em-up, Blaustein wanted his picture to portray Native Americans as real human beings with their own culture and dignity—the first talkie to do so. Considerable research and preparation went into capturing the Apache lifestyle, from the tribe's music and dances to its jewelry to its tepees. Even the war paint was authentically reproduced. Moreover, the Native Americans were to speak in grammatical English, rather than the usual film pidgin—an issue addressed by Stewart in voice-over at the beginning of the picture. Cochise, in particular, was treated in a dignified manner. As played by a relative newcomer, Brooklyn-born Jeff Chandler (who received an Oscar nomination for his performance), he emerged as a genuine leader and visionary with a lively sense of humor.

Stewart would play Jeffords. According to Lew Wasserman, *"Broken Arrow* was a package deal. We represented the producer and the script

---

[1] In 1947, Maltz and nine other producers, writers, and directors were cited for contempt by the House Un-American Activities Committee for refusing to divulge information about Communists in the motion picture industry. Known as the Hollywood Ten, they were blacklisted, and therefore, Maltz could not be hired directly to write *Broken Arrow*. Michael Blankfort, his friend, fronted for him and received sole screen credit for the picture. In 1991, after both men were dead, the Writers Guild voted to change the credit.

and Jimmy. When Jimmy agreed to do it, we went to Fox and sold them the whole package." In keeping with the spirit of the picture, Blaustein chose Delmer Daves to direct. Known for his humanistic approach to material, Daves had spent three months wandering among the Indians of the Southwest upon his graduation from Stanford Law School in the 1920s. Since then, the onetime propman, actor, and screenwriter, who had directed his first film, *Destination Tokyo,* in 1943, had strongly disliked the way Native Americans had been portrayed by Hollywood.

The relationship between the Apache chief and Jeffords was drawn from history, but novelist Arnold invented the romance between the white man and Sonseeahray, the Apache maiden whom he eventually marries. However, the author explained in a note to *Blood Brother* that Jeffords had told American friends he was "intimate with a lovely Indian girl." Since the Apaches frowned on sex outside of marriage—indeed, they cut the noses off of such offenders—the author conjured up a likely scenario. To play the lovely innocent, Daves chose Fox contract player Debra Paget, who had appeared in only two previous films, *Cry of the City* with Victor Mature and Richard Conte, and *House of Strangers* with Edward G. Robinson and Susan Hayward. At sixteen, she was twenty-five years younger than Stewart. "And, of course, he didn't know my age," Paget recalls, laughing. "Delmer Daves and the producer had told me under no circumstances to let him know how old I was." When Jim finally figured it out, he exclaimed, "Oh my God, they'll think I'm a dirty old man."

Paget remembers her costar with fondness, saying, "He had a great sense of humor. And he was so kind." She cites as an example the way he helped her and Chandler improve their performances by sharing his camera savvy with them—showing them how to find their light, suggesting where to look for the camera. He also fluffed lines on purpose if he thought they could do better in another take. "Actors don't usually do that," she adds.

They spent two-thirds of the nine-week production schedule on location in northern Arizona, with Sedona, just south of Flagstaff, as their headquarters. There, the 200 cast and crew members from Hollywood were joined by 375 extras—men, women, and children of the Apache tribe, most of whom came from the nearby White River Reservation. Today, Sedona, with its glorious mountain formations, is a major tourist center, but at the end of the forties, it was barren: just a lodge used primarily by Western-film crews.

Back at Fox, the company filmed pickups and close-ups and used the backlot's Western street for Tucson, the nearest white community to Cochise's mountain stronghold. Then, on August 2, Jim was released. He finished up just in time for his prenuptial activities. Indeed, on his last day of shooting, he went with Gloria to get their wedding license with his makeup still on.

With postproduction still a relatively simple process, pictures in the late 1940s were typically released a few months after they were shot. But moviegoers had to wait almost a year—until July 2, 1950—for *Broken Arrow*. Then, the Western enjoyed a warm reception. Although Bosley Crowther of the *New York Times* found the attempt to accurately portray Native Americans more laudable in concept than execution, Robert Gessner of the *Saturday Review* called the picture "a first-rate entertainment with moments of artistic sincerity," and *Cue* found it "an intelligent, literate, spectacular and superbly photographed Western drama." Indeed, the majestic Arizona countryside looked breathtaking in full Technicolor glory, and as Jeffords, Stewart displayed an appealing combination of integrity, passion, and tenderness.

By the time *Broken Arrow* premiered, Jim was an old married man. The wedding took place on the afternoon of August 9, 1949, at the Brentwood Presbyterian Church. The rites, performed by Rev. Dean Osterberg, lasted a brief twelve minutes. Among the fifty guests were Jim's and Gloria's parents; the matchmakers, Gary and Rocky Cooper; Spencer Tracy; David Niven; Johnny Swope and Dorothy McGuire; Ann Sothern; Frank Morgan; and future U.S. senator George Murphy.[2] Billy Grady was Stewart's best man, and Gloria's brother-in-law, Gregg Draddy, gave her away, with her sister, Ruth Draddy, serving as her attendant. After the ceremony, a reception was held at the Beverly Hills home of Jack Bolton.

Eventually, Jim and Gloria honeymooned in Hawaii, but several prior commitments came first. A few days after the wedding, the newlyweds flew to Akron, Ohio, where Stewart served as parade marshal for the National Soap Box Derby. Then, they went to Indiana, Pennsylvania, to spend a few days with Jim's parents. Finally, on September 2, they flew to Cleveland, Ohio, to catch the conclusion of the Bendix Air Race two days later. Stewart had a major stake in the contest, for one of the entrants, a Beverly Hills real estate agent named Joe De Bona, was flying his plane, a blue Mustang P-51 that he had purchased at a surplus dump in Arizona and lovingly restored, using a twelve-cylinder Rolls-Royce engine. De Bona won the race, which started in the Mojave Desert, setting a new record, four hours and sixteen minutes. As with his Oscar and Distinguished Flying medal, Stewart sent the Bendix trophy to his father. He kept the Mustang until around 1951, when he sold it to record-breaking pilot Jacqueline Cochrane. By then, he owned a state-of-the-art Beechcraft Bonanza.

[2] Gloria's sons, Ronald and Michael, were with their father in the East.

On September 7, Jim and Gloria left for Honolulu. There, they encountered actress Helen Hayes and her husband, writer Charles MacArthur, who had just lost their daughter to polio. The Stewarts generously invited the bereaved parents to join them for several days of marlin fishing, a gesture that Hayes never forgot. "I credit Gloria and Jimmy for helping me back to life," she wrote in her 1990 autobiography.

When they returned to Los Angeles on October 21, the newlyweds took up residence in Gloria's house at 1262 Coldwater Canyon. For several more months, Jim continued to concentrate on being a new husband—and a new father. Although he and the boys had gotten along well before the wedding, Gloria worried that now, when they were thrown together all the time, tensions would arise. She realized that Jim was not a young man and that he'd been a bachelor a long time. Maybe he wouldn't want a couple of typically rowdy boys underfoot. As for Ron and Mike, they had a father. Could they accept Jim as an authority figure? As her husband? After all, broken homes followed by second marriages were not common as the fifties dawned. But Gloria's fears proved groundless. In those early months of family life, Jim turned out to be a tolerant and playful parent, and the boys came to view him as their father. In fact, everything about his new life seemed to turn him on. "I have never, in all the years I have known Jim, seen him as full of plans, as animated, and as happy," wrote Louella Parsons that fall. She concluded, "Yes, I think Mr. and Mrs. Stewart are going to be happy. Jim always said when he married it would be for keeps and I have known Gloria since she was a little girl, and I can't help but say I think they are so right for each other."

As the forties gave way to a new decade, it was time for Jim to pick up his career. On February 13, Jim and Gloria attended the annual Gold Medal Awards at the Beverly Hills Hotel. Readers of *Photoplay* magazine had voted him the most popular actor of 1949, thanks to *The Stratton Story*. His *Magic Town* costar, Jane Wyman, was named most popular actress for *Johnny Belinda*. The next day, he went back to work on his second Western in a row, *Winchester '73*.

Winchester '73 turned out to be one of the pivotal films in Jimmy Stewart's career, not only because he finally found in Lin McAdam the breakout tough-guy role that he'd been seeking since shortly after *It's a Wonderful Life* and *Magic Town*, but also because the payment plan that Lew Wasserman structured for him with the film's producer, Universal Pictures, would become the benchmark for his future projects and make him rich.

Ironically, the film was an afterthought. With the Broadway run of *Harvey* finally coming to an end, Universal had agreed to let Stewart do the movie version, but the studio wanted a two-picture deal. The second project was to be the Western. The scenario by Robert L. Richards, depicting the passage of an exquisitely made rifle from owner to owner, had been languishing for some time; no one wanted to make it. In Stewart's intense desire to play Elwood P. Dowd, William Goetz, Universal's production chief, saw a way of getting *Winchester '73* off the shelf.

The only problem was that the impoverished studio couldn't meet the star's asking price—around $200,000—for either picture. "So," said Goetz, "I asked Jimmy's agent if he might be interested in doing the picture as a partner, taking no salary but splitting the profits." Other versions credit Lew Wasserman, Stewart's agent, with the brainstorm. Wasserman himself remembers offering Universal a choice, saying, "We met with them and told them he would do both pictures in a twenty-six-week period back-to-back, and they would have the right to pay him his salary—which I think was either $200,000 or $250,000 then—for both pictures, or he would take fifty percent of the profits of both pictures." Universal opted for the percentage deal.

Regardless of who conceived the idea, it was a bold stroke. A cornerstone of the studio system had long held that stars, like directors, writers, and other creative people, were part of an assembly-line process, employees who were expected to do what they were told. By giving an actor a percentage of the profits instead of a salary, Goetz opened the door to star involvement in casting, location shooting, and other such issues. After all, if one is gambling that a picture is going to make money, it's reasonable to want a say in how much it's going to cost and where the money's going to be spent. Because of Stewart's success with this form of payment, other studios began striking similar arrangements with his peers, consequently weakening the studio system. Conversely, the deal helped launch the star producer, a major factor in contemporary motion picture making. L. B. Mayer, Goetz's father-in-law, never forgave the treachery.

Stewart, however, did not set out to be a pioneer. He didn't even know if the deal was a good one or not. "I pretty much left the financial things up to my agents," he said years later. But Wasserman knew what he was doing. The agent believed *Harvey* would fail to turn a profit because of the high price Universal had paid for the screen rights, but he thought "the Western could make him a minimum of his salary for both pictures, and it did far better than that."

In *Winchester '73*, Stewart was to play a man with a sober mission, to track down and kill the outlaw who had murdered his father—his own brother. Although he was the protagonist of the story, he was cut from a different, darker cloth than the typical Western hero. He was no idealist like Tom Jeffords and certainly not a pacifist like Tom Destry. But, by the outset of the 1950s, the genre was coming of age. *Winchester '73*, along with Henry King's *The Gunfighter*, released that same year, with Gregory Peck as an aging, increasingly reluctant quick-draw artist, would pave the way for psychologically infused "adult" Westerns such as Fred Zinnemann's *High Noon* and George Stevens' *Shane*, released in 1952 and 1953, respectively.

Winchester '73's original director was Viennese-born Fritz Lang. Lang had helmed two effective Westerns in the 1940s, *The Return of Frank James* and *Western Union*, but had made his reputation with such expressionist films as *Metropolis* and *M*. When Lang withdrew, the assignment went to Anthony Mann. The native Californian, two years Jim's senior, had also launched his career with dark material, in his case film noir. But it was Mann's first Western, *Devil's Doorway* starring Robert Taylor, that got him *Winchester '73*.

Once on board, Mann called for a redraft of Robert Richards' scenario and worked closely with the new screenwriter, Borden Chase, whose credits included 1948's highly regarded Western *Red River*. Mann also put together a group of character actors who would appear in many of his and Jim's subsequent pictures, including J. C. Flippen, John McIntire, and Dan Duryea, plus Universal contract players Stephen McNally as McAdam's brother, Shelley Winters as an ex–dance hall girl, and newcomers Rock Hudson and Tony Curtis in small roles. Winters was not thrilled with the assignment. She had wanted to do a stage production of Bertolt Brecht's *Galileo* with Charles Laughton. Moreover, she thought that, in her words, "the real star of that film was the goddamn Winchester rifle." But she had to do the picture or go on suspension, which would have kept her from doing the play anyway. Millard Mitchell, the actor Stewart had replaced in the 1934 Broadway comedy *Page Miss Glory*, costarred as Lin's sidekick.

The picture, budgeted at a mere $850,000, had an extremely tight thirty-three-day production schedule. Much of the time was spent on location around Tucson, Arizona, with the balance of filming taking place on the soundstages and backlot at Universal. It was on the studio's Western Street that Mann shot the opening sequence in which Stewart wins the Winchester in a contest. The competition took four days to film, with a world champion trick shot, Herb Parsons, serving as technical adviser. Mann was impressed by Stewart's hard work, mastering the rifle under the guidance of a Winchester Arms Company representative, saying, "His knuckles were raw with practicing."

Principal photography concluded on March 24, with the film roughly $50,000 over budget. A little more than two months later, on June 1, the result was previewed for the press in the Winchester company's home base, New Haven, Connecticut. On June 7, nearly a month before *Broken Arrow*, the picture debuted at the Paramount Theatre in New York.

Time magazine caught the essence of the critics' enthusiasm, writing, "Strikingly photographed in black and white, the film is directed with an eye toward realistic detail, an ear for the script's frequently natural dialogue and a knack for building suspense."

Except for *Variety,* which called Stewart's portrayal "lean" and "concentrated," most critics failed to notice how far the actor had moved from the genial, doe-eyed characters of his prewar career. The *New York Times*' Bosley Crowther, who must have been watching another movie entirely, noted that, in *Winchester,* Stewart "drawls and fumbles comically, recalling his previous appearance as a diffident cowpoke in *Destry Rides Again.*"

Nothing could have been further from the case. For, in Lin McAdam, Stewart's genial persona was twisted just enough to make him driven without losing the sympathy of the audience. Near the end of the picture, for example, he questions an outlaw (Duryea) in a bar, and as the killer goes for his gun, he pulls the man's hand behind his back and pushes his head forward. The look on his face as he does so, his eyes wide, his mouth turned down in a grimace, his body shaking from the exertion, is chilling. As the collaboration with Mann progressed through five more Westerns, Jim would push the limits of his characters' neuroses even further. These efforts, plus the director's gift for action and symbolic use of the rugged Western terrain, were the highlights of the partnership, the longest and arguably most fertile of Stewart's career.

Ironically, the star and the director had little in common. Mann, who became an actor and stage manager fresh out of high school, was not college educated. He was rather crude and tough, fond of peppering his conversation with four-letter words. Still, Lew Wasserman maintains, Stewart and Mann formed an instant bond. But actors who worked on their pictures saw little evidence of a deep rapport. "I never detected any great warmth or affection between the two of them," says Harry Morgan, who appeared in five of the eight Stewart-Mann projects. Nor did Julia Adams, who costarred in *Bend of the River,* the second film in the collaboration. Further, Adams asserts, "I never really saw him give Jimmy Stewart much direction. Maybe they talked in some way that I didn't see, but I never saw him give many directions." Her viewpoint was shared by Morgan, Marshall Green (assistant director on several Mann-Stewart pictures), Janet Leigh (who costarred in *The Naked Spur*), and others who were witness to their interaction on the set.

More likely, the intense emotionality of Stewart's characters in these Westerns derived not from buttons that Mann pushed in his star's psyche but from Jim's ability to mine those qualities on his own. Given the scripts, he would have found his way to roughly the same place with any director. That doesn't mean that he didn't appreciate Mann's technical prowess or that Mann took his talent for granted. Quite the contrary. Each man clearly respected the other. Beyond that, both recognized that their collaboration worked—they produced hit movies—which was the most important reason for them to stay together.

In fact, successful collaborations were particularly important to Stewart. Once he left MGM and took charge of his career, he assiduously sought to build new projects around individuals with whom he'd previously enjoyed hits. Director Andrew McLaglen says, for example, that after their 1965 picture *Shenandoah*, "there wasn't one movie that he made that he didn't want me to do." Likewise, after 1962's *Mr. Hobbs Takes a Vacation* introduced Jim to Nunnally Johnson, he sought the screenwriter for any comedy that he undertook. The converse applied as well. A friend of Donna Reed's maintains that when Stewart's *It's a Wonderful Life* costar was up for another role opposite him, he asked for another actress. He liked working with Reed, but the Capra comedy hadn't been the hit it should have been, so he considered the relationship jinxed.

Stewart's superstitious nature extended to props as well as people. After *Winchester '73*, he wore the same basic outfit in virtually all of his succeeding Westerns. His gray, sweat-stained hat became one of his trademarks. He considered it a good luck charm. Of course, with his thin, lean face, finding the right kind of headgear took some doing. As Mann recalled, on *Winchester '73*, "It took us something like two months to get the right one for Jimmy." He added, "Some of the tests we made were hysterical."

It was also *Winchester '73* that introduced Stewart to the costar of all of his succeeding Westerns through 1970's *The Cheyenne Social Club*—Pie. He discovered the horse, whom he described as "this beautiful sorrel, sort of half quarter horse and half Arabian," at a ranch owned by Stevie Myers, a former stunt girl who specialized in providing livestock for the movies. "When I was looking for a horse," the star recalled, "she brought about four of them over. I looked them over and they were great big, fat, ugly nags and just didn't seem right." Then he saw Pie looking around the corner of a building, and it was, as he later put it, "love at first sight from my point of view." Myers told him that she didn't rent the horse out because he was frisky, but Stewart could be stubborn when he made up his mind about something, and eventually Myers relented.

As a result of Jim's childhood exposure to horses—the animals that his father had kept in the backyard stable—he sat a saddle well. In addition, his tall, thin frame was perfect for cowboy gear, and his drawl seemed to go with the great outdoors. As Mann put it, audiences "never got the feeling that, oh, this was an actor playing at westerns. They felt he belonged there." It just took thirty-seven features before that became apparent. Once it did, the genre became a cornerstone of Stewart's career. "You know, Jimmy loved making Westerns," recalls Shirley Jones, who costarred with him in *The Cheyenne Social Club*. "He loved the Western format of the movies. He was very comfortable in that. He believed in that, how the West was won." He also liked dressing up in the regalia and being outdoors. As he once said, "Getting out on the open plains with a rifle and a western hat sort of restores an actor's sense of balance between the everyday world of modern movies and the world of the sagebrush and the open spaces." Moreover, he saw the Western as pure cinema. "It is the best example of how to use the medium," he explained, "because it uses it visually. It does not depend on the spoken words, a catastrophe, or an enormous number of stars. It treats a complicated subject in an uncomplicated way, and it is truly an original. There is no other country like ours, and no other type of film depicts our uniqueness better. We are recognized for the western all over the world."

He would ultimately make eighteen contributions to the genre, roughly 20 percent of his entire oeuvre, including *Destry* and *Broken Arrow*. But the first picture with Anthony Mann remained something special, because it was the one that finally allowed him to part from the romances that had dominated his previous work. As he put it, "Gosh, *Winchester '73* was a lifesaver."

PART FIVE

· *Paul Biegler* ·

FOURTEEN

From Elwood P. Dowd
to Glenn Miller

"*Harvey* is a warm, simple story and we're not going to gum it up with any gimmicks," Stewart said shortly before filming began. Although he'd only done eighty-eight performances of the comedy onstage, he felt protective of the material and of the role that he'd wanted so badly. This delighted his Broadway costar, Josephine Hull. "I was truly alarmed about one or two of the candidates who were mentioned for the starring role," the actress noted shortly before the picture's release. While she didn't mention names, others under consideration had included Bing Crosby, Cary Grant, Rudy Vallee, Joe E. Brown (who had also substituted for Frank Fay on Broadway), Gary Cooper, Jack Benny, Jack Haley, and James Cagney—and indeed, some of the possibilities for the middle-aged, alcoholic bachelor were either dangerously precious or lacked the requisite whimsy.

But Hull needn't have worried. After paying a fortune for the rights to the comedy, Universal wasn't about to tinker too dramatically with its winning ways. Its author, Mary Chase, was even engaged to write the screenplay, and for the most part, she and her collaborator, Oscar Brodney, simply did what virtually all writers do when translating a piece of theater to film—they opened it up to a wider range of settings than the confines of the stage had permitted.

Also, in keeping with the spirit of the original, Hull and another of Stewart's Broadway costars, Jesse White, were hired to re-create their performances. They were joined by Cecil Kellaway, Charles Drake, Peggy Dow, and Victoria Horne as, respectively, the head of the sanitarium, his assistant, the facility's comely nurse, and Elwood's niece. To direct, Universal engaged Henry Koster. The forty-four-year-old, Berlin-born director, once under contract to the studio but then at Fox, had demonstrated a knack for comedy in such films as *It Started With Eve,* one of several pictures that he did with Deanna Durbin; *The Bishop's Wife* starring Cary Grant, David Niven, and Loretta Young; and *The Inspector General* with Danny Kaye. He considered *Harvey,* in his words, "right up my alley." Stocky, balding, and jovial with large horn-rimmed glasses and a thick accent, Koster, like Tony Mann, would become a major presence in Stewart's career. They would do five pictures together.

Filming began on April 18, 1950, roughly three weeks after *Winchester* '73 wrapped. Although the production was faithful to the stage hit, certain concessions had to be paid to the demands of the medium. For starters, since Elwood's peculiar viewpoint is that which the audience should adopt, Stewart frequently played directly to the camera, offering a sly glance here and a knowing smile there, actions that could never have been read past the first few rows of a stage audience. To some extent this behavior took the place of Elwood's drinking, which would have been inappropriate for the mass moviegoing public in 1950. His tippling couldn't be dodged entirely, so a compromise was reached: Stewart wouldn't imbibe on camera, but a martini glass would be shown by his elbow in the bar scenes. As Jim put it during filming, the "implication is there."

A trickier problem was how to make the invisible rabbit's presence felt. For Stewart the task was easy. "When I'm talking to Harvey," he explained, "I get a mental picture of him in my mind as clear as a bell. All I have to do is say, 'Hello, Harvey,' and I'm looking at another actor who is perhaps distinguished from the other players in the picture by the unusual length of his ears. If I didn't see him, I would be as dead as a dodo as far as playing my part."

But the filmmakers couldn't simply rely on Stewart, for as audiences come to realize by the comedy's end, the rabbit is not just a figment of Elwood's inebriated imagination. Stewart credited cinematographer William Daniels with the idea of leaving room for Harvey anytime he was supposed to be in a scene, even though the result left the composition unbalanced. "Without that space," the actor asserted, "I don't think the picture would have worked." Daniels added, "We also had to be careful that chairs and tables weren't placed in spots the rabbit might bump into during his impatient pacing of the floor in certain sequences with Stewart." To complete the effect, nearly invisible piano wire was used to open and close doors as the rabbit passed through a room, and a fan introduced a little breeze to stir the curtains and thereby suggest the pooka's rather imposing presence. Chase wanted Harvey to actually appear at the end of the picture. Indeed, she had given him a brief moment in the original version of the play, but audience reaction to his entrance on the first night of tryouts in Boston forced a revision. Stewart was adamant that the pooka be left to the filmgoer's imagination, and he won. It was probably a wise decision, for even the painting of Elwood and Harvey in the Dowd mansion makes the rabbit look silly rather than magical.

Taking place entirely on the Universal lot, principal photography went so smoothly that, when the picture wrapped on June 3, the company was six days ahead of schedule. But Bill Goetz and his associates saved the comedy for the Christmas holiday season, opening it at the

Astor Theatre in New York on December 21. Although Otis L. Guernsey Jr. of the *New York Herald-Tribune* thought it lacked the charm of the stage production, John McCarten of the *New Yorker* spoke for the majority of his colleagues in calling *Harvey* "a movie that only a case-hardened wowser would fail to find beguiling. Even if you saw the play, I don't think your familiarity with the hallucinations of Elwood P. Dowd, the hero, will diminish your enjoyment of the film, and though James Stewart, who plays Dowd in the picture, doesn't bring to his part all the battered authority of Frank Fay, the originator of the role, he nevertheless succeeds in making plausible the notion that Harvey, the rabbit, would accept him as a pal."

The film would enjoy popular as well as critical success and go on to earn Oscar nominations for Stewart, his first since *It's a Wonderful Life*, and for Josephine Hull. Jim would lose to Jose Ferrer as Cyrano de Bergerac, but the inimitable Hull won. Despite the picture's reception, Lew Wasserman was right. Because of the huge payment for the screen rights to the play, *Harvey* failed to turn a profit, at least for many, many years, so, as Stewart put it, "I acted in that movie for free." Moreover, he wasn't terribly satisfied with his performance. Looking back two decades later, he said, "I played him a little too dreamily, a little too cute-cute."

Over the years, however, *Harvey* has become one of the defining pictures of Stewart's career. In part it is because Elwood is a wonderful character: gentle, kind, a fellow who thinks the best of everyone and makes the most of every moment and is completely unflappable as chaos and confusion swirl around him—qualities that played right into the best of Stewart's folksy manner. Today, when film buffs think of the hemming and hawing, the slow delivery, and the other elements in Jimmy's bag of tricks, it is often his performance in *Harvey* that comes to mind.

And then, of course, there's the rabbit. People simply love Harvey. And that affection endears them to Stewart as well. "People will stop me and ask me how he is," the actor once explained. Of course, Stewart being Stewart, he invariably played along, explaining that Harvey was somewhere else at the time, but promising to pass along the well-wishers' sentiments the next time he and the rabbit met.

After making only two pictures in 1949, no doubt a concession to his brand-new marriage, Stewart doubled his output in 1950. Just as he went into *Harvey* a few weeks after finishing *Winchester '73*, he began work on *The Jackpot* a mere thirteen days after the Mary Chase comedy wrapped. The 20th Century–Fox production cast Stewart to type, as Bill Lawrence, an ordinary department store executive in a typical Midwestern suburb whose life and marriage are thrown into turmoil after he correctly identifies the "voice" on a fictional radio program called *Name the Mystery Husband.*

The screenplay by Phoebe and Henry Ephron was based on an article in the February 19, 1949, issue of the *New Yorker,* in which author John McNulty detailed the mishaps of an actual Rhode Island man, Jimmy Caffrey, who won $24,000 worth of prizes on the giveaway show *Sing It Again.* As Caffrey discovered, most of the prizes were, in McNulty's words, "just so many albatrosses around the neck." They included dozens of wristwatches, $2,000 worth of fruit trees, 7,500 cans of soup, and gallons and gallons of paint and varnish. Not only did Caffrey lack the storage space for all these goods, he had to pay income tax on them.

At first glance, the winner's situation seems funny, but it "wasn't all laughs," McNulty explained. "It was tough on Jimmy." In the Ephrons' hands, however, the tale became a genial comedy that managed to have fun, not only with the quiz-show programming then in vogue, but with the newly emerging suburbs, postwar marriage and parenthood, and the business world in the age of the Organization Man. Playing Stewart's wife was Barbara Hale, a shapely brunette under contract to Columbia Pictures. Her film career began with *Gildersleeve's Bad Day* in 1943, but she is best remembered today as Della Street on TV's *Perry Mason.* Natalie Wood, who turned twelve during filming but was already a veteran of a dozen features, played the Lawrences' daughter, and Tommy Rettig, who would become Lassie's first TV master in a few years, was their son. Behind the camera loomed Fox contract director Walter Lang. Described by one columnist as "a rugged man of massive build," Lang was particularly adept at family entertainments. His previous film had been *Cheaper by the Dozen,* and he would go on to direct *Call Me Madam* and *The King and I.*

Opening at the Roxy Theatre in New York in November, a month before *Harvey, The Jackpot* drew applause from the critics. Darr Smith of the *Los Angeles Daily News* even called it "one of the funniest comedies ever made into a film." But, because it was sandwiched in between *Winchester '73* and *Harvey,* this genial comedy has become a minor footnote in Stewart's career. It is not even available on videotape, which is unfortunate, because it illustrates how well his all-American ordinary-Joe persona could be used in a postwar setting when the material was well crafted. It also offers textbook illustrations of the actor's deft comedic touch, not only with dialogue but also in reaction shots. Moreover, in Stewart's portrayal of the befuddled family man, *The Jackpot* points the way toward his comedies of the next decade, *Mr. Hobbs Takes a Vacation; Take Her, She's Mine;* and *Dear Brigitte.* But the Walter Lang film takes a more effectively satiric look at the fifties than its successors do at the sixties.

* * *

Stewart's final project for 1950 took him to Great Britain. There, on September 25, he reported to Denham Studios in Denham Bucks, home of Fox's British affiliate, for the start of *No Highway in the Sky*. Based on the popular 1948 novel *No Highway* by Nevil Shute, the plot centered around a mild research scientist, Theodore Honey, who is convinced that a particular type of aircraft called the Reindeer has a structural defect that will cause its tail to crack after 1,440 hours of flying time. The plot thickens when Honey finds himself on that very model airplane en route to investigate a crash and then discovers the plane is close to the requisite number of hours.

Shute described the character as short, unkempt, and ugly: "He had a sallow face with the features of a frog, and rather a tired and discontented frog at that. He wore steel-rimmed spectacles with very thick glasses, and he was as blind as a bat without them." Not exactly the spitting image of Jimmy Stewart, but Darryl F. Zanuck, who adored the character, thought the star of three of his recent productions, *Call Northside 777, Broken Arrow,* and *The Jackpot,* might be right for it. It was an inspired bit of casting, for Stewart approached the role like a character actor. He walked with his shoulders stooped to suggest a man who spends most of his time bent over experiments, and he used little chipmunklike gestures to give the impression of a mousy introvert. He didn't have to affect an accent: the character was changed from British to American. But his usual speech pattern furthered the character's distracted air, which Stewart embellished with expressions of discomfort when confronted with strangers. The combination added up to the quintessence of an absentminded professor, without the usual bottle-thick glasses or Albert Einstein hairdo. At the same time, the character was endearing enough to attract two very different women: the stewardess on the imperiled plane and one of the passengers, an aging movie star. Lovely, throaty-voiced Glynis Johns and Stewart's former lover and costar Marlene Dietrich played the leading ladies, and *Harvey*'s Henry Koster directed.

For Stewart, the making of *No Highway* was not the most pleasant of experiences. To begin with, the weather in England in late fall and early winter is penetrating, especially to someone from Los Angeles. In addition, Marlene Dietrich, who basically did the picture for the money, was frequently unpleasant on the set, snapping at Koster and jealous of the younger Johns. Worst of all, on November 15, Stewart's appendix burst and had to be removed at a London hospital.

But all of the difficulties paled beside the joyous news that Stewart received in England—Gloria was pregnant. Not only that, but she was carrying twins! Jim was unable to celebrate with his wife and sons at

Christmas, but four days later, on December 29, the picture wrapped, and he was able to get home for the New Year's festivities.

No Highway premiered in London at a command performance attended by then Princess Elizabeth and other members of the royal family, after which it opened on September 21, 1951, at the Roxy in New York. The picture garnered respectable notices, as did the stars and director, but the public failed to respond to what was little more than a mildly amusing, mildly suspenseful entertainment. As Lew Wasserman puts it, "It's very tough to sell metal fatigue to an American audience." The picture's most significant element was—and is—Stewart's deft performance. Anyone who considers him a limited actor should watch it and *Winchester '73*—shot the same year—back-to-back.

Between the time that *No Highway* wrapped and its premiere some nine months later, Stewart was a busy man. Not only did he make two more pictures, *The Greatest Show on Earth* and *Bend of the River*, he found a new home and became the father of two baby girls.

First came the home. Since his wedding, he and Gloria had stayed in the house that she had lived in before their marriage. They had wanted to find a new place, one they could furnish together. In fact, Jim had been hoping to construct a house of his own design on a hillside in Pacific Palisades, an affluent community abutting the ocean, but Gloria considered such a location too dangerous for small children. While they debated the issue, they simply stayed where they were. Finally, however, the impending additions to the family spurred them to action. One afternoon they passed a two-story, ivy-covered Tudor-style house on Roxbury Drive in Beverly Hills. Gloria thought it looked like a dormitory, but Jim said, "Well, that's what we need, isn't it?" Gloria grinned and replied, "I guess it is," and they bought it. It became Jim's home for the rest of his life.

"It's not imposing when you walk in," says daughter Kelly. "There's not a chip of marble anywhere. So there's not a big, open grand hallway. It's a carpeted, sort of a cozy hallway." The foyer gave entrance to the living room, which was decorated in muted tones, beige and green, with two large sofas and an imposing coffee table facing a fireplace. A featured attraction here was Jim's baby grand, which he used to entertain guests, accompanying himself on "Ragtime Cowboy Joe" and other selections from his repertoire. The paintings in this room included an Utrillo, which Gloria gave Jim as a Christmas gift before their wedding; a portrait of the lady of the house by her husband's *It's a Wonderful World* costar Claudette Colbert; a few Rouaults; and several oils painted by disabled veterans, Jim's contribution to the decor. There was also a large library and TV room—the family's favorite gathering place—as well as a formal dining room, a kitchen, and a breakfast room, site of the family's meals.

Upstairs there were five bedrooms. The children's rooms were to the left of a central staircase—which they called the Great Divide—and the master bedroom was to the right. "I used to think," Stewart said when the children were little, "that maybe our room was too far away from the kids, but when the four of them get up at six in the morning, I'm real glad that they're in one half of the house and Gloria and I are in the other." The house, in short, was like its owner—comfortable and pleasant but far from ostentatious.

The girls were born on May 7 at Cedars of Lebanon. One was named Kelly, for Jim's paternal grandmother, Virginia Kelly, who died long before he was born. The other was called Judy, after one of his favorite songs by Hoagy Carmichael. The delivery was difficult, and Gloria's condition quickly turned serious. Over the next week, she endured four operations and hovered near death several times. Jim remained at his wife's bedside throughout the ordeal. As the Hollywood press kept movie fans apprised of her condition, letters, religious medallions, and flowers flooded the hospital from all over the world. Finally, on May 14, her physician, Dr. Mark Rabin, told Jim that she was out of danger.

Ironically, when it came time to take his wife home, Stewart proved that playing the absentminded scientist in *No Highway in the Sky* was closer to type than appearances would indicate. When he arrived at Cedars, he first carried her bags and gifts to the car. After the vehicle was loaded up, he remembered a camera that he wanted to investigate and set out for a camera store, where the clerk began demonstrating several models. "Here's one that even your wife could work," he said. "My wife!" Jim repeated. "Why, I've left her at the hospital." He then dashed back to Cedars. The episode seems apocryphal until one recalls the similar antics of his father. Moreover, his daughters swear it's true.

With Gloria's health crisis over, Jim was able to turn his attention once more to his current film project, *The Greatest Show on Earth*, which had gone into production on January 31.

"There had been several good, and some not so good, pictures with a circus background," wrote the film's producer-director, Cecil B. DeMille, in his autobiography, "but there had never been what I would call a circus picture, one in which the circus itself was the star." That's what he wanted to make, an epic that would capture on film the vast panorama of the traveling American circus.

The idea had, in fact, originated with David O. Selznick. In May of

1948, the producer announced that he had signed an agreement with John Ringling North for a picture about North's outfit, the giant Ringling Bros. & Barnum and Bailey Circus. It was expected to feature Gregory Peck, Joseph Cotten, Jennifer Jones, Louis Jordan, Dorothy McGuire, Shirley Temple, and Robert Mitchum. With a budget of $6 million, it was also to be the most expensive movie ever made to that point. But Selznick couldn't raise the financing, and the project languished until mid-1949, when he finally abandoned it entirely. DeMille, having seen a small notice to that effect in the *Hollywood Reporter,* quickly stepped in and made a new deal with North. On June 20, DeMille's home studio, Paramount, paid a very considerable $250,000 for the rights to make the picture and to shoot the circus at the Ringling Bros. headquarters in Sarasota, Florida, and on the road.

That summer, DeMille and his secretary traveled with the troupe, soaking up the atmosphere. When they returned to Hollywood, they had notebooks full of anecdotes, definitions of circus slang, and what DeMille called "vignettes of life in the 'backyard,' " that is, moments when the performers were doing laundry, cooking, chatting, and going about the general business of life, as in any other community. From this rich vein, he, Fredric M. Frank, Theodore St. John, and Frank Cavett fashioned a story, which Frank, St. John, and Barre Lyndon then turned into a screenplay. Basically, the plot followed the troupe from the opening day in Sarasota through an imperiled railroad tour. The principal focus lay with a handful of stock characters: the tough ramrod of the outfit (played by Charlton Heston in his second feature film); the beautiful, daring lady trapeze artist (Betty Hutton); her handsome, dashing rival (Cornel Wilde); the elephant girl who vies with the aerialist for the affections of the ramrod (Gloria Grahame); and the most original character in the piece, a clown called Koko (later changed to Buttons), who's actually a doctor hiding from the police for the mercy killing of his wife. That was Stewart.

According to Henry Koster, Jim landed the job when they were making *No Highway* in England. Said the director, "He heard that Cecil B. DeMille was planning a circus picture in which there was a clown part. He called DeMille up and asked for the role. 'It's a very small part,' DeMille told him, 'and the clown never takes off his makeup.' 'Is the role essential to the plot?' Jim asked. When DeMille said, 'Yes,' Jim said, 'It's a deal.' " He was so eager, he even took a 75 percent reduction in his usual asking price. But $50,000 was what the other stars—Hutton, Wilde, and so forth—were getting as well. He also agreed, for the first time, to last billing: "And James Stewart as Buttons, a Clown." He made these concessions because, as he put it, "Wal, it's a good part, even if it is short. And I've wanted to work for this man."

"This man" was indeed a legend. Born in Massachusetts in 1881, Cecil B. DeMille helped to pioneer the motion picture industry, forming a company (the precursor of Paramount) with Jesse Lasky and Samuel Goldwyn in 1913 and producing one of the first great Hollywood features, *The Squaw Man,* a year later. Long before directors were well known to the average moviegoer, DeMille was a household name. He was particularly known for silent epics such as *The Ten Commandments* and *The King of Kings,* sweeping but rather vulgar entertainments that were wildly popular but lacking in subtlety. He continued the tradition with talkies such as *Cleopatra, The Plainsman,* and the film just before *Greatest Show, Samson and Delilah.* By the time the circus picture went into production, the showman was sixty-nine and in his thirty-seventh year of filmmaking.

The cast and crew—all three hundred of them, not counting the circus folk—assembled in Sarasota where they filmed for six weeks. A highlight of the Florida interval was the troupers' parade through the heart of town, with a crowd of nearly one hundred thousand cheering them on—a sequence staged solely for the picture as Ringling Bros. had stopped doing preshow parades years earlier.

Stewart did not go to Sarasota. He had little to do in the picture's early sequences, and since his character was never seen without his makeup, a double simply covered for him. His work began at Paramount when the company returned. In keeping with circus tradition, he had designed his own makeup—in conjunction with makeup man Wally Westmore. It consisted of a bald pate with a fringe of hair around the ears, a tiny derby perched on the top of his head, a typical red ball nose, and a huge upturned mouth. He also sported a large polka-dot bow tie, an oversize striped coat, baggy checked pants, and large, floppy shoes. And he carried a little white mutt called Squeaky, which Paramount found at a local pound. To get into character, he worked with the legendary Emmett Kelly and studied several other Ringling buffoons—Lou Jacobs, Paul Jerome, and Buzzy Potts. "I never got a bigger kick out of anything in my life," Stewart said, adding, "I know I looked like a fool, but the thing is, I didn't *feel* like one." He also enjoyed working with DeMille. The director was widely regarded as a stern taskmaster, but Stewart said, "He never shows you how to play a scene. He just talks about the mood and what it should mean to the audience, and boom—you have the feel of it." Jim was also impressed by the director's showmanship, saying years later, "Old DeMille was always conscious of the set as a place of magic. He played it to the hilt and for the benefit of everybody, not just the visitors. He even got the extras excited. He made you feel that something was going to happen, but you didn't know just what or when."

After filming in Los Angeles, the company joined the Ringlings in

Washington and Philadelphia. There, DeMille spent much of the time capturing actual acts in performance as well as the crowds' reactions to the mayhem and derring-do. One of the biggest challenges lay in finding a way to light the big top for the Technicolor cameras. Most pictures were illuminated from the top down, but the giant tent made that approach impossible. Finally, after a year of experimentation, Technicolor came up with a three-pronged solution, utilizing incandescent lights, highly sensitized film, and a new camera shutter that could quickly capture the action.

In Philadelphia, Hutton astounded the audiences by actually performing her feats on the high bar, tricks that she'd spent months perfecting. "It was not a question of spurring her on," wrote Henry Ringling North in his family history, *The Circus Kings*, "but of holding her back, keeping her from taking unnecessary risks." Gloria Grahame also demonstrated considerable bravery, lying on her back and allowing an elephant to place a giant foot on the tip of her nose. According to Thomas M. Pryor of the *New York Times*, she was nearly stomped as she rolled clear.

Gloria Stewart's hospitalization had forced Jim to remain behind when the company went East, but her recovery allowed him to fly to Philadelphia in time to be part of the action. "When I arrived," he recalled, "nobody had time to work with me in what I was supposed to do—I just jumped into my costume and makeup and somebody tossed me into the arena." Nevertheless, he had a ball, camping it up for the crowds. As he put it, "All of my old inhibitions took a vacation. I was a clown—and a clown can tear the roof off if he wants to."

Returning to the studio, the company shot five days of close-ups, and then, on June 7, after eighty-three days of filming, they were done. Seven months later, on January 10, 1952, the picture premiered at Radio City Music Hall. "As has come to be expected from DeMille," wrote *Variety*, "the story line is not what could be termed subtle," but no matter. *The Greatest Show on Earth* was, to quote *Cue*, "lavish, sentimental, eye-filling, and a lot of fun." Moviegoers certainly agreed, for the picture earned $12 million in its initial release, becoming the top grosser of the year and Paramount's biggest moneymaker to date.

It also earned five Oscar nominations—including one for DeMille and one for the editing—and won for Writing (Motion Picture Story) and for Best Picture, beating out *High Noon, Ivanhoe, Moulin Rouge*, and *The Quiet Man*. Looking at the film today, the top award is a little difficult to fathom, for the characters are trite, the plot simplistic and melodramatic, and DeMille's voice-over narration pretentiously laughable. But the circus atmosphere—the crowds, the parade, the real troupers performing their acts—is thrilling. In this, DeMille fulfilled his goal: he brought the circus to life on the screen.

For Stewart, hidden behind makeup the entire time, Buttons was more a lark than a serious acting challenge. A month after *The Greatest Show*'s premiere, he called it "the most comfortable role" he had ever played, explaining, "With that clown make-up, you can just relax and forget all about facial expression. No matter what you do with your face, it won't show. You're shut off from the world behind that mask and can just take it easy."

A more formidable challenge lay with *Bend of the River*, a Universal production that Jim started filming on July 25. The Western marked his second collaboration with Anthony Mann and with the producer of *Winchester '73*, Aaron Rosenberg. As before, he worked for 50 percent of the profits.

This time, Stewart was Glyn McLyntock, a wagon-train guide whose easy manner masks a dark past: he was once an outlaw, a raider along the Missouri border. Jay C. Flippen, who had played a grizzled cavalry sergeant in *Winchester '73*, was back, as the leader of the settlers that McLyntock takes West. And Harry Morgan, best known today as Colonel Potter on TV's *M*A*S*H*, made his first appearance in one of Jim's pictures, playing a minor bad guy. Like Flippen, he would become part of the Stewart-Mann stock company. "I liked him enormously," Morgan says. "You couldn't be any more professional than Jimmy as an actor. Even though these pictures were rough, the atmosphere on the set was always—not tranquil, but there were never any blowups or anything." He credited Stewart with setting the pleasant tone.

Bend of the River's leading lady was Julie Adams, a relatively new Universal contract player, with four pictures to her credit. At twenty-five, she was stunned to be playing opposite someone she'd seen on the screen as a kid. But, when she and Jim were introduced, he quickly put her at ease. "He was so gentle and charming," she recalls. "He said how happy he was I was doing the picture and this and that. He was just as wonderful as I thought he should be."

Playing the principal bad guy was Arthur Kennedy, a veteran of the New York stage who had recently earned a Tony Award as Biff in Arthur Miller's *Death of a Salesman*. In *Bend of the River*, he was Cole Garrett, an outlaw whom Stewart saves from hanging at the outset of the picture. The two become friends until Cole finally turns on Glyn, leaving him stranded in the mountains, presumably to die. The scout vows vengeance. "You'll be seein' me," he promises. "Every time you bed down for the night, you'll look back in the darkness and wonder if I'm there. And one night I will be. You'll be seein' me." Stewart's intensity as he delivers these lines is riveting. Even a little bit frightening. Moreover, until this climactic moment, the audience isn't entirely sure who is the hero and who is the villain; Kennedy's character is much more affable than Stewart's.

Offscreen, the actors liked each other. Adams says that Arthur, younger by six years, held his costar in near awe. A few times the three of them had dinner together. Adams recalled that Kennedy once asked Stewart if he was interested in directing. He replied, "Well, no. I don't think I'm smart enough to direct"—a rather telling remark. To which Adams adds, "There are different kinds of smart. And one great kind is to know what you do the best and to do that." For Stewart that was acting. He loved it, and it's all he wanted to do.

But, in the case of *Bend of the River,* that was no easy task. To capture the wagon train's frontier journey, the cast and crew assembled on July 25 in the Mt. Hood National Forest located in the north-central part of Oregon. For two weeks, they worked in extremely rugged terrain, climbing to eight thousand feet on Mt. Hood, the highest peak in the state. Stewart and his costars were carried to the locations by ski lift, but getting the wagons to the site required bulldozing a road up the side of the mountain. Steel cables, out of camera range, kept the vehicles—and the actors perched on them—from crashing onto the crags below. A few weeks later, when the company moved to the Sandy River, a bulldozer was again needed, this time to clear away perilously large rocks in the water and to create a path beneath the surface so that the horses and their vehicles could ford the rapids. Said Stewart at the time, "It was the roughest, most rugged picture I've ever made. I don't see how the early-day pioneers ever made the trip. We had every known type of modern equipment to aid us during four weeks of filming along their trails in Oregon. And it was still the worst physical beating I'd ever encountered."

Finally, the company got a respite, filming in Portland for about a week, before winding up the picture on the Universal backlot. When they wrapped on September 14, Mann was thirteen days behind schedule.

But there was no question of where the money went, for the northwestern countryside looked magnificent when the Technicolor production—shot by Irving Glassberg—opened in Portland on January 23, 1952, an event that commemorated the centennial of the first wagon train to reach the Oregon territory. Stewart, Adams, Flippen, Rock Hudson (who played a gambler in the picture, a big step up from his Indian in *Winchester '73*), and others were on hand for the two days of festivities, which included a parade through the city, a square dance, and a formal ball.

Aside from the scenery, which drew praise from every quarter, *Cue* caught the essence of the critics' response when the picture opened in

New York the following April, noting, "This big, splashy, forthright Western . . . has lots more substance, truth, reality and conviction than the usual pat and patterned Western. It also packs more entertainment. . . . [I]ts characters are full-bodied people, neither all good nor all bad, but a fair human mixture of both." To which Otis L. Guernsey Jr. of the *New York Herald-Tribune* added, "Stewart is every inch the Western hero capable of winning out over multitudinous enemies." He'd come a long way since *The Shopworn Angel* and *Pot o' Gold.*

The repeating rifle at the heart of *Winchester '73* was state of the art in 1876, the year in which that Western had been set. Jump ahead seven decades and the New Haven company's mainstay was the M1 rifle, a lightweight carbine. For his final project of 1952, Stewart played the man who invented the weapon, David Marshall Williams, a convict sent to prison in the 1920s for murder.

A March 1951 profile in *Reader's Digest*'s popular feature "The Most Unforgettable Character I Ever Met" had inspired Dore Schary to acquire the rights to the ex-con's story. Schary, by then MGM's studio chief, having replaced L. B. Mayer the previous year, also hired Williams to serve as the film's technical adviser. Schary then assigned the project to contract director Richard Thorpe. Since working with Stewart on *Malaya,* Thorpe had directed two biographies, both musicals: *Three Little Words,* the story of songwriters Burt Kalmar (Fred Astaire) and Harry Ruby (Red Skelton), and *The Great Caruso,* with tenor Mario Lanza. Producer Pandro Berman said of him, "At that time he was the most efficient, fast-moving, competent, physical director that we had at Metro."

Given Thorpe's experience with action films and biopics, Stewart's success with his previous true-life character, Monty Stratton, and Williams' inspiring story—which took him from an independent-minded miner/moonshiner to an embittered convict to the owner of some seventy arms patents—*Carbine Williams* should have been a lively, engrossing picture. Instead, it was rather flat. It presented only a halfhearted indictment of the penal system in Williams' day, although clearly the filmmakers found his incarceration brutal. In addition, the central character, as written by Art Cohn and played by Stewart, was simply not unsavory enough to give his reformation significant dramatic impact. Finally, Williams' rehabilitation through his skill as an inventor was not explored in enough depth to imbue his triumphant return to society with the requisite emotional payoff. As *Time* magazine noted when the picture opened at the Capitol Theatre in New York on May 7, 1952, it was more "factual than inspired." It would take the story of another true-life convict, Robert Stroud, in John Frankenheimer's *Birdman of Alcatraz,* released a decade after *Carbine Williams,* to demonstrate how compelling drama could be forged from a man's prison redemption through scientific study.

A second project with MGM—the back half of a two-picture deal—followed about three months after Stewart finished *Carbine Williams. The Naked Spur* was a psychologically charged Western written by Sam Rolfe and Harold Jack Bloom. Instead of using the usual sprawling Western canvas, the novices focused on just five people: Howard Kemp, an embittered rancher turned bounty hunter; Ben Vandergroat, an affable outlaw with a sizable reward on his head; Lina Patch, a young woman traveling with Vandergroat; and two men Kemp meets on the trail, a grizzled prospector and a cashiered army officer. Driven alternately by greed and the threat of death, the quintet traverse the harsh wilderness, with the alliances shifting among them as they go. In a sense, the story was a product of the early fifties, when the rise of the Cold War and McCarthyism were dealing severe blows to the national psyche. As film historian Louis Black noted, "It was the perfect time for a capitalist Western, with no heroes, only winners; no ideals, only financial rewards; no friendships, only business relationships; no stability, homestead or nuclear family, only motion across the land."

Ironically, Stewart originally thought he was going to play the engaging outlaw, but his agents at MCA told him that audiences wouldn't accept him as a villain. At first, he refused to consider the role of the bounty hunter, but finally he relented. Thereafter, versatile Robert Ryan was signed for Vandergroat. For the other two men, Anthony Mann—brought in to direct at Stewart's request—cast Millard Mitchell, a veteran of *Winchester '73,* and newcomer Ralph Meeker.

That left Lina, Vandergroat's companion. Bloom wanted his then girlfriend, Anne Italiano, later known as Anne Bancroft. But she was under contract to Fox, and MGM insisted on giving the only female role in the picture to one of its own contract players, Janet Leigh. Before the casting could be finalized, however, Leigh had to make a test with Stewart. "They wanted to see if it was believable that we would fall in love," she explains, because the star was nearly twenty years her senior. Actually, he was older than her father. At the time, such casting was not uncommon. Indeed, before the teenage market revolutionized the motion picture industry in the late 1960s, aging stars such as Clark Gable, Gary Cooper, and Cary Grant were often seen in romantic roles opposite much younger women. As far as Leigh was concerned, the age difference was of little consequence. As she put it, "He put me so at ease right away, I never thought about it."

Filming took place between May 21 and July 10 in the majestic San

Juan Mountains of southern Colorado, with the company headquartered at the rustic El Rancho Encantado, fifteen miles outside of Durango. "Physically it was hard," recalls Leigh. "You're up there, and you're looking down at this rushing, raging river and huge rocks and waterfalls and gushing rapids and everything. It's scary."

Not even in *Winchester '73* and *Bend of the River* had Stewart played someone as driven as Howard Kemp, arguably the darkest character of his career. Nothing—not Indians nor an injury incurred on the journey nor the machinations of his fellow travelers—could deter him from doing what he set out to do. Cold and mean, scarred by an old love's betrayal, he stands in marked contrast to the conniving but jovial Vandergroat. "I don't know of any other actor who could have gotten away with that part and been acceptable at all," says Leigh.

The picture climaxed with a scene as physically and emotionally demanding as anything in Stewart's career. Amid furious river rapids, Kemp struggles to secure Vandergroat's dead body so that he can bring it in for the reward. Lina tries to dissuade him, but he's near psychotic in his determination. Finally, she says she'll marry him if he abandons his mission. At that point, he starts to cry, his fury finally spent. As Leigh recalls, "It was extremely emotional, and I'd never seen Jimmy in anything like that. So when we rehearsed it, I was really moved by his performance." She adds, "It could have been maudlin, but he did it with anger, which was so wonderful."

Stewart's fine work was not lost on the critics when the picture opened at the Loew's State in New York City on March 25, 1953. Joe Pihodna of the *New York Herald-Tribune* even labeled Kemp "one of the best roles of his career." The screenplay, Mann's direction, and the other performances earned praise as well. So did Joe Mellor's color cinematography, for Mann used the breathtaking Colorado landscape to such a powerful effect in *The Naked Spur* that it virtually became a sixth character: not only are Kemp, Vandergroat, and the others fighting one another, they're battling the elements as well. As for the picture itself, *Cue* noted, "This is not merely a fine western. It is an absorbing drama, a penetrating psychological study of five diverse characters, and a first-rate show." Rolfe and Bloom's screenplay would go on to earn an Academy Award nomination.

In August of 1952, a month after *The Naked Spur* wrapped, Stewart fell victim to a bizarre extortion plot. A fifty-five-year-old truck driver by the name of Sidney C. Davis threatened to harm him and his family unless he was paid $1,000. The threat was mailed to MGM on a postcard enclosed in an envelope. Before the studio discovered the demand, however,

Davis surrendered to the police in Carthage, Missouri, his hometown. Later, he confessed that he had made the threat in the hope of landing a "home" in a federal penitentiary. As a final twist to the story, Stewart thanked Davis for, in his words, sparing him and his family "anxious moments by giving himself up."

Four days after Davis' arrest, Stewart was at the Pentagon in Washington, D.C. As an officer in the Air Force Reserve, he was required to annually serve a month on active duty. Some years he was assigned to the newly formed Strategic Air Command in Omaha, Nebraska, which marked the start of his friendship with SAC's commander, Curtis E. LeMay, later the Air Force chief of staff. When he was at the Pentagon, Stewart typically reported to Andy Low, his assistant during World War II and a career officer. Their CO, Ramsay Potts, had an office nearby. Stewart took his military role seriously. "I work hard to stay abreast of what our Air Force is doing," he once told Hollywood reporter Vernon Scott, "and when and if I'm called to active duty I'm going to be as ready as is humanly possible to contribute everything I can."

On September 23, his commitment to Uncle Sam over for the year, Stewart started work on his next film, *Thunder Bay*.

His fourth picture with Anthony Mann—and third with producer Aaron Rosenberg—was a contemporary melodrama, their first. Set in 1946, *Bonanza*, as the project was originally called, focused on the conflict between fishermen and oil wildcatters, as the latter searched for riches in the offshore waters of the Gulf of Mexico. Rosenberg likened the conflict to the range wars between cattlemen and sheepherders in the Old West.

Stewart was cast as the kind of character he played so well, the man with a vision, driven to prove his theory and willing to drive everyone around him in the process. To prepare for the role of Steve Martin, he spent a month studying oilmen in the Gulf. Costarring with him were Dan Duryea, this time as Stewart's sidekick, a rare good-guy role; Jay C. Flippen; Harry Morgan; and Gilbert Roland, who had taken a supporting role in *Malaya*. Joanne Dru and Marcia Henderson were cast as Stewart and Duryea's respective love interests.

Filming began in Morgan City, a fishing community in southern Louisiana. "It was very small and very Cajun," recalls the film's assistant director, Marshall Green. "You couldn't understand anybody. It was certainly different." The locals were well aware of the large cast and crew in their midst, for housing the visitors required every spare room in town—from hotel to motor court to boardinghouse—and feeding them so overtaxed the few restaurants that the townsfolk took to inviting guests home for meals. About one hundred members of the community also worked on the picture as extras. Conversely, Stewart involved himself in local affairs, using his off-hours to support a regional recruiting drive for the Boy Scouts; he was on the organization's National Council at the time.

Much of the company's time was spent in the Gulf, working on what was supposed to be Steve Martin's offshore oil rig—for which they used an old World War II LST. Getting to the location took an hour's flight on a PBY, a plane so small that only a third of the cast and crew could be transported at a time. A seventy-five-foot yacht rented from a local sportsman served as a floating dressing room.

Adding to the production challenge was Universal's decision to film the picture in a new wide-screen format that would allow for the projection of images at 23 ½ feet by 43 ½ feet on a slightly convex screen (three feet deep at its deepest point). The process was even bolder than Fox's CinemaScope and, like it, was invented to combat the advent of television. Given the small, black-and-white living-room screen of the early 1950s, making pictures bigger was supposed to draw audiences back to their neighborhood movie houses. Said Mann after the picture's release, "I'll admit I was apprehensive at first when producer Aaron Rosenberg told me that the studio had selected the film as the first motion picture to be exhibited on its new panoramic screen. I didn't know what supermagnification would do to personal formulas of direction and photography which have been an integral part of my life ever since I've been directing. The results, though, have been gratifying." Critics, however, would give the process widely divergent marks, with *Variety* calling it "tremendously impressive" and its images "sharp and clear," and Philip Scheuer of the *Los Angeles Times* arguing that the actors' heads and bodies were sometimes cut off.

After four weeks in southern Louisiana, the cast and crew returned to Hollywood, where filming resumed at Universal Studios on October 30. The picture wrapped on November 10, four days behind schedule.

Stewart was present when *Thunder Bay* premiered at the Loew's State Theatre in New York on May 19, 1953—as was a contingent from Morgan City, which had organized a junket for the event. Given the introduction of the new wide-screen process, coupled with the use of a three-speaker stereophonic sound system, the premiere was particularly well covered by the press. But, as Andrew Weiler of the *New York Times* noted in his review, "Sadly enough, *Thunder Bay* does not appear to be the most impressive vehicle to launch sight and sound systems." Indeed, the picture was rich in local color, nicely photographed by

William Daniels, and boasted an exciting hurricane sequence, but it was the weakest offering in the Stewart-Mann collaboration. The director himself recognized this, later saying, "Some of the things we showed were effective and beautiful . . . but I don't think it was a very good script."

After finishing *Thunder Bay*, Stewart took an unusually long hiatus, with only two TV guest appearances to occupy him over the next six months. The first, a spot on *The Jack Benny Show* on December 28, 1952, marked his television debut. The plot found Jim and Gloria hoping for a quiet New Year's Eve only to have their plans ruined by Benny—who was a neighbor and friend in real life—and Jack's date, played by Bea Benaderet. Fred de Cordova, who produced the series, was particularly impressed by Mrs. Stewart. "She was completely at ease," he recalls. "Gloria was a very bright woman, with a very, very solid sense of humor, slightly deprecating on purpose."

The Stewarts enjoyed working on the Benny show so much that they frequently visited the program thereafter. Unlike the loners in Jim's concurrent Westerns, the characters in these TV appearances publicly underscored the solidity of his marriage. Even though he and Gloria played exaggerated versions of themselves in the sketches with Jack, Jim came across as a happily married man—which he was. He was also a loving father, a regular churchgoer, and a gentleman, qualities that made him something of an anomaly in Hollywood. Ironically, before the war, when he was playing sweet, bumbling idealists such as Bill Pettigrew and Jefferson Smith, he was considerably less straitlaced offscreen. Now, when many of his characters were far more psychologically skewed, he was a font of middle-class morality.

Stewart's second TV outing between features came on Ed Sullivan's *Talk of the Town* on May 17, 1953. The popular CBS variety show included a tribute to Joshua Logan, with Stewart in a filmed re-creation of a number from *The Tiger Smiles*, the Triangle Club production cowritten by the director in 1930. Stewart performed for free. To return the favor, Sullivan aired clips from *Thunder Bay*. Finally, on June 4, 1953, it was time to go back to the big screen.

"Every studio in Hollywood wanted to make *The Glenn Miller Story*," said Anthony Mann during filming, "and they were all but besieging Miller's widow, who lives in Pasadena." Universal had the edge because it had Jimmy Stewart, the only actor that Helen Miller wanted to play her husband.

Born in Clarinda, Iowa, in 1904, trombonist Alton Glenn Miller became the most popular orchestra leader of the Big Band era. He was such a dominant figure that by the early 1940s, a third of all records played on American jukeboxes featured his distinctively sweet sound. Then, in October of 1943, at the height of his career, he disbanded his orchestra and joined the Air Force. His new band, made up of servicemen, performed throughout the European theater of World War II—until, on December 15, 1944, he was killed in a plane crash over the English Channel. "He wasn't a simple person," Helen Miller told Hedda Hopper. "He was deep, tense, and honest as the day is long. . . . At heart he was a farm boy, who loved music and America." Comparing Stewart with her husband, she said, "They don't look alike. But basically they're the same kind of men. I've seen all his films. They're heart-warming, wonderful movies."

Although the Big Band era was over by the early 1950s, Miller's music was still popular, having sold an estimated 16 million records by 1953. Moreover, for millions of moviegoers who grew up in the years before World War II, "Moonlight Serenade," "String of Pearls," and his other standards evoked warm, youthful memories. Wisely, Rosenberg and screenwriters Valentine Davies and Oscar Brodney decided to feature a solid array of Miller hits on the sound track, including "Little Brown Jug," "In the Mood," "Pennsylvania 6-5000," and "Tuxedo Junction," and engaged seven members of the actual band to participate in the recordings. For added verisimilitude, bandleader Ben Pollack, Miller's first employer, was hired to play himself in the picture, as were Louis Armstrong, Gene Krupa, Frances Langford, and the Modernaires.

Originally called *Moonlight Serenade*, the screenplay followed Miller from 1925, when he was a struggling musician, to his death. At the heart of the story were two principal threads: his search for a distinctive musical sound; and his relationship with his wife, played by Stewart's *Stratton Story* costar June Allyson. "The movie of Glenn's life . . . may have presented some inaccuracies and some exaggerations," wrote Miller's biographer George T. Simon, "but nothing in it could have been more true to life than the warmth and love and understanding that June Allyson and Jimmy Stewart portrayed in their roles as Helen and Glenn Miller." Slightly less accurate, Simon asserted, was the relationship between Miller and pianist Chummy MacGregor, well played in the picture by Harry Morgan. According to Simon, the men met in real life later than they do in the film, and MacGregor was, in the biographer's words, "super-dependent upon Glenn"; in the movie, he is a rock of support. But, then, MacGregor was a technical consultant on the picture.

Calling Miller "sort of one of my heroes," Stewart prepared diligently for the role, talking with Glenn's widow, MacGregor, other members of the band, and Miller's manager, Don Hayes. He also read the bandleader's diaries and letters and watched him on film. "By that time," he said, "I knew everything about Glenn Miller—except how to play his trombone."

For that, he secured the services of slide man Joe Yukl—then lost him. "My music teacher quit," Stewart joked, "because he said the sounds I made were so terrible he went home and yelled at his wife." The only way he could convince Yukl to reconsider was by plugging up the bell of the trombone so that it wouldn't make any sounds. Thereafter, he became quite comfortable with the lip and slide positions for the numbers featured in the film. Even Yukl was impressed when he saw Stewart on the set. "He blew out his lip on the mouthpiece," said the trombonist, "crossed his legs musician-style, fiddled around with the spit-valve, then picked up his chorus right on the beat. Suddenly I felt like I was looking in a mirror. Jimmy had been studying my mannerisms while I taught him how to handle the trombone, and when the cameras turned, he put them to use. He's the most thorough guy I've ever known." Jim even used one of Glenn's own instruments, loaned to the production by Helen Miller, along with a pair of her husband's eyeglasses.

Filming began at the ballroom on the Santa Monica pier, which served as the site of one of the band's engagements. After shooting at several other locations around Los Angeles and on the Universal lot, the cast and crew traveled to Denver on July 13, thereby becoming the first movie company to shoot a feature in the Mile High City. A variety of Colorado backdrops were used: Lowry Air Force Base, which served as Miller's British posting during the war; the University of Colorado at Boulder, where Glenn met Helen when they were undergraduates; and the Elitch Gardens Ballroom, which substituted for the Glen Island Casino, site of one of Miller's greatest triumphs. It was at Elitch's that Stewart met Miller's eighty-two-year-old mother. She told him, "You're a good actor, Mr. Stewart, but you're not as handsome as my son."

To fill the cavernous ballroom, the production company placed an advertisement in the Denver newspaper, inviting the local citizens to be extras. "My God, they turned out," recalls Marshall Green, the picture's AD; there were three thousand, according to a Universal press agent. But, after filming began, the novelty quickly wore off, and people wanted to go home long before the required footage was in the can. The production assistants were frantic, trying to keep them from deserting. "And Jimmy noticed that," says Green. "So after a take he got up on the stand—he didn't go sit down—and they all came over and he thanked them for being there." He also explained what the cinematographer was doing, and why there were delays between takes. When the crew was ready, he sent the people back to their places but invited them to return at the next break. Which they did. "He stayed up there all afternoon," says Green with admiration, "and kept those people there. He knew we were in trouble, and he saved our lives. And it was a magnificent performance. I found myself listening to him after a while."

When they finished in Denver on July 19, the picture wrapped. Stewart was supposed to do one day of postproduction work at Universal on August 6, but it had to be postponed: his mother, Bessie, had passed away four days earlier. Her death came after several heart attacks during the previous week. After the first one, on July 26, Jim's father phoned him and he flew home. Thus, he was with his mother when she died. "We buried her in the family plot in Indiana, Pennsylvania," Jim recalled, "and afterward Dad took me on a brief tour of the headstones. He pointed out Uncle Archie, who died at ninety-two; and another uncle, who died at ninety-three; and my grandfather, James, who died at ninety-one. He was making the point that he had a long time to live yet, and I shouldn't worry about him."[1]

Alex was with Jim and Gloria in Miami Beach on January 19, 1954, when *The Glenn Miller Story* had its world premiere. In fact, the senior Stewart took the stage to tell the audience, "We lost a perfectly good hardware store man to get one more movie star." Gloria then informed the audience that *The Glenn Miller Story* was not only the greatest movie she had ever seen but would be one of the greatest of all time. Her remarks prompted the event's emcee to say, "That's a lovely speech, Gloria, from someone who's not in show business. Did you write it yourself or did someone help you?" She then pointed to Jim and said, "He did," which drew a big laugh.

No one was laughing harder than Jim—for he was entitled to 50 percent of the picture's profits. And, as Lew Wasserman says, *The Glenn Miller Story* "was a huge success. Jimmy took more money out of that picture than any picture he ever made."

The film was a triumph as well for him as an actor. Not since *Harvey*, released more than three years earlier, had he played such a genial character, and the return to form made a refreshing change after the obsessed individuals that he'd been portraying in the intervening years. At the same time, one sensed that this was not a case of Stewart being Stewart, but an attempt to capture the essence of a figure celebrated in his own right. As *Time* magazine put it, "Actor Stewart has managed all along the line—in walk, talk and conducting—to effect a graceful compromise of gesture that should please both Miller's public and his own." Moreover, the picture marked the second in a trio of successful pairings with June Allyson. Although the actress had an image every bit as wholesome as Stewart's, they offered a study in contrasts: she matched his shyness with a perky self-

[1] J. M. Stewart was, in fact, nearly ninety-three when he died.

confidence, his slow rhythm with snap. Where he is tall and soft-spoken, she is a mere five feet one inch and husky voiced. Beyond the pleasing contrasts, they played off each other beautifully and were entirely credible as husband and wife.

As for the picture, Bosley Crowther of the *New York Times* wrote, "Not since *Yankee Doodle Dandy,* the film about George M. Cohan, have we seen as appealing and melodic a musical biography as this charmer." To which he added, "And not since Jimmy Cagney's spirited playing of Mr. Cohan have we seen as likable and respectable a portrait of a show-world personage as James Stewart's genial performance in this picture's title role."

FIFTEEN

Number One

After only a month's break, Stewart reteamed with Mann and Rosenberg for a third picture in a row. *The Far Country* took them back to the Old West, actually to the last American frontier, Alaska, site of the 1890s gold rush.

By this point, certain commonalities were becoming evident in the team's Westerns. For starters, the hero was always a flawed and often unsympathetic individual, a man propelled by an unfortunate past. The supporting characters usually included his sole companion, often an old man; a villain who was the most likable figure in the piece; and a woman, who was typically involved with someone else and got together with the hero only at the end, a resolution that offered the hope that he would find inner peace at last. Finally, the nature of the protagonist—restless, driven, isolated—mandated that the pictures play out far from civilization's door, in hostile country, where the elements were as unforgiving as the men and women who traversed them.

Borden Chase's screenplay for *The Far Country,* from a short story called "Alder Gulch" by Ernest Haycox, stayed well within the tradition. As rancher Jeff Webster, Stewart espoused a simple philosophy, which he explained at one point to his elderly sidekick, played with the usual gusto by Walter Brennan: "I don't need other people. I don't need help. I can take care of me." This time, two women vie for his affections, a worldly saloon keeper, portrayed by Ruth Roman, and a lively, optimistic young tomboy, played by Corinne Calvet. Calvet, a beautiful Parisian, typically cast as a slinky modern-day siren, seemed an absurd choice when her agent first suggested her to Rosenberg. But she auditioned for the producer wearing a simple white dress, her brunette tresses in pigtails, and using another name. He wasn't fooled by the disguise, but he was convinced that she could play the role. Rounding out the cast were Jay C. Flippen and Harry Morgan. Jack Elam started his string of five Stewart Westerns playing one of the bad guys, while the principal villain, a crooked judge, brought back John McIntire of *Winchester '73.*

The action centered around a hazardous cattle drive across the tundra—with Stewart ramrodding the herd. That and the other outdoor sequences took the company to Jasper National Park in Alberta, Canada, where filming began on August 19, 1953. As with *Bend of the River* and

The Naked Spur, Mann led his players into hazardous territory, namely the Columbia Icefield at the south end of the enormous, 4,200-square-mile park. The company spent two weeks shooting there, including four days on the Athabasca Glacier, a mass of ice eight hundred feet thick. To reach the location, Stewart and his colleagues had to trek two and a half miles on foot, wearing spiked rubber boots. Getting the cameras, lights, and other equipment up meant reducing them to their smallest parts so that they could be carried on the backs of the crew. Although filming took place in late summer, daytime temperatures in the ice fields averaged between thirty and forty-five degrees.

To maximize the opportunity, Mann frequently used three cameras simultaneously, a highly unusual move. "The cameras were so positioned," explained a Universal publicist, "that when the action passed from the view of one lens it was immediately picked up by the other further on. Simultaneously the sound boom was pulled along a path improvised just behind the camera positions so that there would be no break in the dialogue."

If the treacherous terrain weren't bad enough, heavy rains forced serious delays in the schedule and caused the budget to rise by nearly $100,000. Stewart was so miserable that he told Gloria to cancel her planned visit. But nature cooperated in one respect: an avalanche plays a significant role in the plot. Mann had been planning on using dynamite to force the event, but a real avalanche saved him the trouble. Hoping for that eventuality, the company had maintained an avalanche watch and thus was ready when the massive pileup occurred. Although the actors were at a safe remove, Stewart recalled that it was "a very awesome sight to see tons of ice start down off a mountain. A very terrifying sight."

Calvet was one of the few cast members having fun in Canada. "I loved every minute of it," she says. "The air was very clean and fresh and invigorating. And we had horses and all the snow. It was like going camping. It was like being a Girl Scout again." She also enjoyed working with Stewart. "Well, I was a little bit in a dream," she recalls. "First of all, I was—what?—twenty-five, twenty-six maybe [she was twenty-eight], and I was playing a virgin. And he was Jimmy Stewart, the guy I had always admired and wanted to meet when I was in France, you know, before I came here." At first, she found him polite, but cool. She says, "In France, we kiss people hello and good-bye on the cheek, you know," but she felt that she could not indulge in that informality with her costar. As filming progressed, however, she says, "He warmed up to me a lot."

The location shooting gave rise to one of Stewart's favorite stories. One day he was sitting around in Jasper, waiting for a setup, when an old man approached him. As Stewart told it, the fellow said, " 'Just thought

I'd come and see you. I've seen a couple of your picture shows'—that's what he called them, 'picture shows'—'and I remember you in this room and your lady friend in the next one. There was fireflies and you said a piece of poetry to her. I thought it was nice. Glad to see ya.' " With that, the man disappeared. The picture that he'd recalled was *Come Live With Me*, released more than a decade earlier. "Yet he remembered," said Stewart with a tinge of wonder. "What greater tribute can you receive?" That incident served to prove his favorite theory, that movies are ultimately popular because they give people moments they remember and treasure. He called them "little pieces of time."

After leaving Canada on September 14, the company spent a month filming indoor sequences and town shots at Universal. Jim's proudest moment came with the climactic scene of the picture, shot on the backlot. Webster, knowing that the bad guys are waiting for him in town, creates a diversion by sending his horse in alone. The tinkling of a little bell atop his saddle distracts the killers while he sneaks in on foot. The plan was to use a stunt horse, but Jim convinced Mann to give Pie a try. First, however, he wanted a short break so that he could talk to the horse. "I went over to Pie," he recalled, "and explained the scene to him and told him I wouldn't be there and he'd have to do it alone." He added that there would be guns going off, but Pie was to pay no attention to the noise. The crew thought he was nuts. "But," said Stewart proudly, "the minute the sound board clacked, Pie did it all just perfectly—and he didn't turn a hair when the shooting began." The picture wrapped on October 14.

In an effort to recapture the box-office success of *The Glenn Miller Story, The Far Country* premiered on February 1, 1955, at the same theaters in Miami. As with Mann's previous Westerns, the scenery again looked spectacular. As Jesse Zunser wrote in *Cue,* "It's a mighty pretty Western." Moreover, Stewart was fine, Calvet was engaging, McIntire made a suitable villain, and in the best Anthony Mann tradition, there was plenty of action. But, to quote Andrew Weiler of the *New York Times, The Far Country* was "a fairly standard adventure of man against ill-natured men and raw nature." As film historian Jeanine Basinger correctly noted in her study of the director's oeuvre, the picture followed "the pattern of the three other core [Mann-Stewart] films, [but] it has a self-conscious, artificial quality. It is as if Mann, understanding his own game, decided to abstract it, treat it almost as a joke."

On September 20, shortly after Stewart returned home from Canada and while *The Far Country* was still in production, he began playing another Western hero, Britt Ponset, on a weekly radio program entitled *The Six Shooter.* The thirty-minute drama, which aired Sunday evenings on NBC, was something of an anthology series in that Stewart's character, described by *Variety* as "fast on the draw but slow on the drawl," was a drifter. Each week he'd land in a different place and help the locals— played by guest actors—out of some crisis or another. Thus, the show's writers, Frank Burt and Lee Williams, could concoct a wide variety of tales. Most of the episodes, which were directed by Jack Johnstone, who also produced the series, were taut and aimed at adult listeners. But, well executed though it was, *The Six Shooter* never gained a wide following, as the advent of TV was rapidly bringing the era of radio dramas to an end. NBC tried the Western at several Sunday time slots, then moved it to Thursday evenings on April 1, 1954. But to no avail; on June 24, the last original episode aired, after which *The Six Shooter* was canceled. By then, *The Far Country* had not only wrapped, but Stewart had also completed two other features, *Rear Window* and *Strategic Air Command*.

In the six years since the making of *Rope*, Alfred Hitchcock had directed five films, with mixed success. His independent production company, Transatlantic Pictures, was history, but in 1953 he signed a nine-picture deal with Paramount.[1] His first project was *Rear Window*, adapted by John Michael Hayes, coauthor of *Thunder Bay*, from a 1942 short story by Cornell Woolrich. Such was the success of Hayes' first collaboration with Hitchcock that he would go on to write the director's next three pictures—*To Catch a Thief, The Trouble With Harry,* and *The Man Who Knew Too Much.*

Lew Wasserman, who represented Hayes and Hitchcock, arranged for Stewart and two of his other clients, Leland Hayward and Joshua Logan, to coproduce the picture. But Jim and his friends would be silent partners; Hitch had sole control over the property (the dialogue would include a passing reference to Hayward, an inside joke).

Stewart also agreed to play the leading role, one that better suited his talents than had Rupert Cadell in *Rope*. L. B. Jeffries is an award-winning photojournalist who is laid up in a wheelchair with a broken leg. To pass the time, he observes the tenants in the Greenwich Village apartment buildings across the courtyard from his. The plot escalates when he becomes convinced that one of them has committed murder.

To Woolrich's story, Hayes added two important women characters: Jeffries' wisecracking nurse, played by Thelma Ritter in her usual crisp manner, and the photographer's girlfriend, a fashion model named Lisa Fremont. Hitch had one actress in mind for the role: cool, blond Grace Kelly, the leading lady of his previous film, *Dial M for Murder*. With only

---

[1] He would, in fact, make only six of the nine pictures.

three other pictures to her credit—*Fourteen Hours,* which marked her film debut in 1951; *Mogambo* with Clark Gable; and *High Noon* with Gary Cooper—Kelly was in the enviable position of having to choose between a second Hitchcock picture or playing opposite Marlon Brando in *On the Waterfront* with the hot director of the moment, Elia Kazan. She chose *Rear Window.* Stewart was delighted, for he had seen her previous films and wanted to work with her.

His respect for his leading lady deepened once filming began on November 23, 1953. "A lot of things impressed me about her," Stewart recalled. "She seemed to have a complete understanding of the way motion picture acting is carried out. And she was so pleasant on the set; she was completely cooperative. She was really in a class by herself as far as cooperation and friendliness are concerned." He also praised her ability to concentrate, and the naturalism of her delivery. "In filming that movie with her," he said, "I got the feeling that they were real scenes. She was very, very special."

The fact is that he fell in love with her. He himself confessed years later, "I was just absolutely smitten by Grace Kelly, a wonderful, wonderful girl." But in all likelihood he never acted on his feelings. Although she had a history of romantic attachments with her leading men, he took his marriage vows seriously and had an iron will. Still, of all the stars with whom he worked, he never spoke about anyone else the way he spoke about her. In fact, he was so disappointed when her impending marriage to Prince Rainier of Monaco forced her withdrawal from their second pairing, the comedy *Designing Woman,* that he left the film as well, a decision he later regretted.

Hitchcock was also in love—or, perhaps more accurately, obsessed—with Kelly, a condition which has been amply covered by the director's and princess' biographers, Stewart told Hitchcock authority Donald Spoto, "I think it's all ridiculous. Why anybody would have thought that, I have no idea." But, in his superb *The Dark Side of Genius: The Life of Alfred Hitchcock,* Spoto makes a persuasive case for the director's unrequited passion, starting with his insistence on shooting twenty-seven takes of her kissing Stewart's forehead and continuing with the attention that he lavished on her wardrobe.

In addition to his leading lady, Stewart enjoyed making *Rear Window* because, after the rigors of filming in Canada, Louisiana, and Colorado, he was able to do an entire picture on a studio soundstage sitting down. His biggest challenge lay in reacting to the normal—and not so normal—events in his neighbors' lives. "First, Hitchcock would show what I was seeing through my binoculars," he explained. "Then he'd show my face, and I'd reflect what I saw. I spent an astonishing amount of time looking into the camera and being amused, afraid, worried, curious, embarrassed, bored, the works." But he considered the ability to react one of his strengths as an actor, and he was right.

For Hitchcock, showing the neighbors going about their daily lives was a major undertaking, one that made *Rope*'s New York skyline pale by comparison. In total, the set was 98 feet wide, 185 feet long, and 40 feet high and included elements of thirty-one apartments. Since the shots into the homes across the courtyard had to appear to come from Stewart's perspective, some tricky camera angles were required. Moreover, audiences had to believe that the apartments were forty to eighty feet away from his window. Adding to the complexity were the many areas that had to be lit separately, for both day and night. Accomplishing this feat took almost every light fixture at Paramount's command and required ten days to rig (instead of lighting each setup as the shooting schedule demanded—which is the way movies are normally shot—all of the fixtures were placed in advance; otherwise the picture would have taken more than one hundred days to film). The heat generated by all of this equipment was so intense that, in the early days of principal photography, the soundstage's sprinkler system was inadvertently activated. It had to be disconnected before shooting could continue. Finally, the actors who occupied these spaces had to go about their pantomimed activities on cue. Directions were given by means of shortwave radios and hidden microphones.

Hitchcock introduced the entire milieu at the outset of the film in a sequence that included one amazing take, lasting nearly ninety seconds. He started by focusing on an awakening couple who had chosen to sleep on their fire escape because of the indoor heat. He then panned into another apartment, where a dancer is getting dressed, then down to the alley, and then back up until he reached Stewart's apartment. Carrying the viewer through the window, he came to rest on the star, asleep in his wheelchair. The camera then continued moving back to reveal elements in Jeffries' apartment, including the photo of the motor-speedway crash that landed him in his present predicament. Filming the sequence took Robert Burks ten takes and half a day. The cinematographer, who had worked on three previous Hitchcock films, *I Confess, Strangers on a Train,* and *Dial M for Murder,* called *Rear Window* the most difficult picture he'd ever done. But little effort was wasted. According to a Paramount publicist, Hitchcock planned every scene in the production so carefully that only one hundred feet of exposed film went unused, a remarkable accomplishment. Stewart himself marveled at the smoothness of the process. "The set and every part of the film were so well designed," he told Donald Spoto, "and he [Hitch] felt so comfortable with everyone associated with it, that we all felt confident about its success."

That confidence was well placed. For, upon the picture's release in August of 1954, *Rear Window* was dubbed "absorbing and entertaining" by Bosley Crowther of the *New York Times,* "a masterpiece" by *Newsweek,* and "an unusually good piece of murder mystery entertainment" by *Variety.* It was also a smash hit, becoming the fifth highest grossing picture of 1954, two notches below *The Glenn Miller Story.* Given the nature of the melodrama, a minimum of critical attention was devoted to the acting, but Stewart delivered a well-modulated performance as an ordinary guy caught up in an extraordinary situation. The highlights included Jeffries' conflicted relationship with his "perfect" girlfriend, his mounting terror as he watches her trapped in the suspected murderer's apartment, and on a lighter note, his enormous relief when he manages to scratch an itch under his cast, a feeling understood by anyone who's ever broken a limb.

With two pictures in the top ten, Stewart was riding high. In fact, 1954 represented the zenith of his popularity, the peak moment in the decade of his greatest success. And the diversity of the movies—a heartwarming biography and a nail-biting thriller—pointed to the reason for this accomplishment. His persona had at last developed an elasticity that lent itself to a variety of intriguing possibilities: with equal credibility, he could be a genial musician, a misanthropic cowboy, or the average American who stumbles upon the dark side of daily life. The following year, he would even be named box-office king—Hollywood's most popular star—leading a list that included Grace Kelly, John Wayne (who had held the title for the previous three years), William Holden, Gary Cooper, Marlon Brando, the comedy duo Dean Martin and Jerry Lewis, Humphrey Bogart, June Allyson, and Clark Gable.

Ironically, Stewart didn't see himself as the king of anything. He told Hedda Hopper in 1954, "I don't think actually that in the sense you get the name Gable, I've ever gotten to be a star. Or Gary Cooper. There's a real, real movie star." Being at the top of the heap wasn't very important to him anyway. He just wanted to continue working at the craft, doing the best job that he could.

Meanwhile, his part ownership of *Rear Window* and his percentage deals with Universal were making him wealthy by the movie-star standards of the day. In fact, according to *Look* magazine, his profits from his two 1954 hits made him the highest-paid actor in Hollywood history to that point. And his pictures would continue to generate income through the years. By 1966, Hollywood columnist James Bacon reported that Stewart had earned $530,000 for *Winchester '73*, $750,000 for *Bend of the River*, $300,000 for *Thunder Bay*, and $2 million for *The Glenn Miller Story*. Of course, when VCRs came along, a whole new profit center opened up, and Stewart quickly seized the opportunity, promoting the release of the pictures in which he had a financial stake and providing voice-over introductions for several, including *Harvey*.

But he was not particularly savvy about financial matters. When it came to investing, he relied on Guy Gadbois, his close friend and long-time business manager. In time Gadbois put him in real estate, primarily in Los Angeles; oil and gas; several ranches, including one in Hawaii that not only bred cattle but also grew macadamia nuts; and a portfolio of stocks and bonds. Upon Gadbois' death in the mid-1970s, the job fell to Greg Paul, then a lawyer with the Los Angeles firm O'Melveny and Meyers. By 1995, Paul had become chief operating officer for Castle Rock Entertainment, but he continued to manage Stewart's finances.

Some of Jim's holdings, namely his ranches, became vacation spots as well as investments. One in Nevada encompassed some 365,000 acres. Jim and Gloria's oldest son, Ron, would actually join the ranch's cowboys on their cattle drives, which were, according to brother Mike, "serious business." But all four children would spend several months in Nevada each summer. "We looked forward to it," says Mike, "from the day we left until the day we got back." To which daughter Kelly adds, "I think that's where the love of the outdoors began, for all of us." By the 1960s, the Stewarts had acquired a more modest spread of about 1,200 acres in California's Santa Ynez Valley. It included a house with four bedrooms plus a dwelling for the ranch manager and another for guests. "That was even better [than Nevada]," says Mike, "because we could go there at Christmas, Easter, midterm break." Stewart sold the property in 1975 for $1.25 million.

Of course, Jim used his earnings to enhance his lifestyle. When the house next door on Roxbury Drive became available, he bought it, razing the structure and using the land for a garden. "Best thing they ever did," says daughter Judy, because the garden provided a place of solace, especially for Gloria. He also sent the kids to private schools and provided them with a French governess, Irene Des Lierres. Mademoiselle, as they called her, was really their closest adult contact—more so even than their mother, who was busy with her own avocations and who often accompanied her husband on location shootings and promotional junkets.

But, by movie-star standards, Stewart lived rather modestly. Some have said he was cheap, and the star himself once admitted, "Sure, I like money," but his earnings, like his stardom, didn't impress him. He didn't, for example, own a Mercedes or a Jaguar; he owned a Volvo and kept it for years. He liked it because its high ceiling gave him ample headroom, important for a man of his height. "And once he likes something," says Kelly, "he sees no reason to get anything else. And that pertains to clothes, shoes, hats, anything. I mean, he will wear a pair of shoes until there's a hole in it. I can't tell you the number of Christmas presents Mom gave him that he returned. He saw no reason why he should have this other sweater when he had one that he loved, that was perfectly good."

One aspect of major stardom that he did relish was the occasional chance to indulge in a project close to his heart. Such an opportunity came with Stewart's picture after *Rear Window, Strategic Air Command.*

Founded in 1946, the Strategic Air Command (SAC) was a major element in America's Cold War military preparedness, for it gave the United States the capability of launching bombers—propeller-driven B-36s and subsequently jet-propelled B-47s—within minutes of an attack. After 1948, when in-flight refueling became possible, SAC could strike anywhere in the world. Initially, the bombers carried conventional weapons, but in 1958, three years after the film's release, nuclear ICBMs were introduced. As a colonel in the Air Force Reserve, Stewart fully believed in this defensive system, which he called "the biggest single factor in the security of the world." He thought it important that the American people think so, too, for with more than 120,000 military and civilian personnel in SAC and 300 very expensive bombers, taxpayer support was vital. Thus, he persuaded Paramount to make the movie.

In December of 1952, he and his friend writer Beirne Lay Jr., who was also a colonel in the Reserve, spent two days familiarizing themselves with operations at SAC headquarters at Offutt Air Base near Omaha, Nebraska. From these briefings, Lay forged a screen story, which he then scripted with Valentine Davies, coauthor of *Glenn Miller.* Their central character, Robert "Dutch" Holland, was—like Stewart—a celebrity, in this case, a major league baseball player, who had served as a bomber pilot in World War II and then returned home to resume his career. An officer in the Reserve, he finds his life completely uprooted when he is called back to active duty, to serve in the Strategic Air Command.

To direct the picture, Stewart called on Anthony Mann, who agreed to do it more as a favor to the star than out of fondness for the material. Stewart also turned to another former colleague, June Allyson, to play Holland's devoted wife. As with *The Glenn Miller Story,* she agreed to do the role without even reading the screenplay.

When filming commenced in March of 1954 at the St. Louis Cardinals' spring training camp in Tampa, Florida, the scene was reminiscent of *The Stratton Story:* Stewart was back in a baseball uniform and Allyson was again rooting in the stands. But *Strategic Air Command* took on a different aspect once the cast and crew moved on to SAC's Carswell Air Force Base near Fort Worth, Texas. There, through Holland's training, movie-goers would get a detailed look at the Strategic Air Command—its mission, personnel, and equipment.

To give the picture the ring of authenticity, Mann and producer Sam Briskin were obviously dependent upon the Air Force. As the director said, he was "held within the bounds of what they wanted. The story itself was restricted and the whole concept of shooting it was confined to what they would let me show, which is perfectly all right." He realized that the plot was minimal and that Dutch and his wife were, in his words, "papier-mâché," so he worked to make the B-36 and B-47 his "two great characters."

In this he was eminently successful. As Bosley Crowther noted in the *New York Times* when *Strategic Air Command* opened at Manhattan's Paramount Theatre on May 20, 1955 (following the picture's world pre-miere in Omaha at the end of March), it was "far and away the most elab-orate and impressive pictorial show of the beauty and organizational power of the United States air arm that has yet been put upon the screen." Adding to the excitement was yet another studio's wide-screen process, VistaVision. Although Paramount had initially introduced the format in its Bing Crosby–Danny Kaye musical *White Christmas* some months earlier, the studio's technicians had since improved its clarity. Paramount then spent $100,000 to outfit the New York theater with a gigantic screen sixty-four feet wide by thirty-five feet high. Critics raved about the process, which was generally considered superior to Fox's CinemaScope and to the three-camera, three-screen format, Cinerama (introduced in 1952 with the travelogue *This Is Cinerama*). Two months before *Strategic Air Command*'s New York premiere, VistaVision earned Paramount an Academy Award for technical achievement.

The aerial footage was stunning, but Mann was right about the picture's plot and characters. As the *New Yorker* put it, "The story that is supposed to hold the business together is limp and tired at best." It took all of Stew-art's charisma, Allyson's charm, and the special chemistry between them to keep *Strategic Air Command* afloat between Holland's training missions.

By 1954, Bill Goetz, the man who had given Stewart his first profit-participation deal, had left Universal to form an independent production company in association with Columbia Pictures. His inaugural project, a Western called *The Man From Laramie*, brought Jim back to Harry Cohn's fiefdom for the first time since *Mr. Smith Goes to Washington*. Naturally, Stewart brought Anthony Mann with him.

Based on a novel by Thomas T. Flynn, *The Man From Laramie* shared some of the trappings of the other Stewart-Mann Westerns. The star was once again a loner, he had an elderly sidekick (played by Wallace Ford), and the principal female character was an attractive young shopkeeper (Cathy O'Donnell) who was involved with another man until he turned out to be a ruthless killer (Arthur Kennedy). The main difference lay in Stewart's character, Will Lockhart, who was neither as antisocial as *The Far Country*'s Jeff Webster nor as cold as *The Naked Spur*'s Howard Kemp. Like them, however, he was a man with a mission: to find and gun down the individual who sold rifles to the Apaches and thereby fostered a massacre in which his younger brother was killed. Given Lockhart's social skills, the plot plays out in a setting more civilized than in Stewart's prior Westerns with Mann—in the New Mexico town of Coronado and at the nearby ranch of a powerful cattle baron (Donald Crisp).

To capture the texture and beauty of the Southwest, Mann filmed much of the picture on location, including lands owned by the Pueblo Indian nation, with Santa Fe as the company's base. He also used CinemaScope to enhance the film's visual sweep, the first of his Westerns to feature a wide-screen format. After his work on *Thunder Bay* and *Strategic Air Command,* he was accustomed to working on an expanded canvas, and as film historian Jeanine Basinger noted in her study of his oeuvre, one can see "the complexity of his compositions" in *The Man From Laramie.* Principal photography commenced in late September, four months after *Strategic Air Command* wrapped, and ended November 16.

If there was a flaw in *The Man From Laramie,* it lay in the watering down of Stewart's character and the use of the genre's traditional town-ranch milieu. As Bosley Crowther noted in the *New York Times* when the picture opened at Manhattan's Capitol Theatre on August 31, 1955, Lockhart was "an easily recognizable western hero—the type that finds himself lonesomely aligned against the elements of tyranny and injustice in a frightened frontier town." By contrast, characters such as Webster and Kemp brought fresh psychological twists to the genre. Nevertheless, *The Man From Laramie* was distinguished by solid acting, Charles Lang's impressive color cinematography, and Mann's usual swift pace and lively action. Particularly memorable were a couple of brutal sequences, one in which Stewart is roped and dragged through a campfire and the other in which he is shot in the hand at close range.

On December 11, nearly a month after *The Man From Laramie* wrapped, Stewart was back home in Indiana. His father, then eighty-two, had decided to remarry, and Jim had been selected best man. The bride was a seventy-six-year-old Canadian widow. "Dad sure picked a good one," he told the press. "It sure is wonderful. You know, to see them you'd never get the impression that they are old."

The following month he and Gloria went to Tokyo for the opening of *Rear Window,* with subsequent stops in Macao, Hong Kong, and the Philippines. While in Macao, they decided to take a look at the Chinese border. As Jim later told the AP's man in Hollywood, Bob Thomas, they "drove along a little road next to a canal that separated China from Macao. As we passed a Red sentinel, he held a huge tommy gun at the ready, and he kept his eye on us, moving so he faced us as we drove by. Boy, were we glad to get out of there." Surprised to discover how well known he was so far from home, he called the trip "a shot in the arm for me. It made me realize all over again the power of the film industry. I want to make more trips to other parts of the world now."

In March, he embarked on another adventure, one less dangerous and closer to home: he appeared in his first TV drama. Then, as now, major movie stars did not do television, except for an occasional personal appearance on a variety show such as Ed Sullivan's *Talk of the Town* to promote a favorite project. But Stewart considered the exposure, in his words, "a sort of reminder to people that I'm still around, still in business." He added, "An occasional appearance on television like this is a kind of teaser for my movies. It's like taking an ad out in 150 newspapers."

He chose as his forum *G.E. Theater,* a half-hour anthology series on CBS hosted by his friend Ronald Reagan. The drama was a Western called "The Windmill." As with his features, his character, Joe Newman, was a man with a past: he was a former gunfighter. But, as the drama opened, Newman had become a law-abiding family man who wants to build a windmill on a creek but lacks the money to do so. Playing his wife was Barbara Hale, his costar from *The Jackpot,* with James Neilson directing.

Born in Shreveport, Louisiana, Neilson had been a longtime stage manager for Guthrie McClintic. In fact, he had served in that capacity on *Yellow Jack,* Stewart's Broadway triumph in 1934. Both Stewart and Hale were impressed by Neilson, who had started directing for television in 1952. "Oh, this man was so prepared, so prepared," Hale recalls. "I mean, he knew exactly what he was going to shoot." The result, which aired on April 26, 1955, was well received. According to *Variety,* "James Stewart contributed a sure, even, slow-footed pace, and Director James Neilson let the story have its head, and it rolled like a tumbleweed."

Finally, after six months away from a motion picture set, Stewart returned to Paramount to resume his collaboration—financial and artistic—with

Alfred Hitchcock. This time he was the title character in *The Man Who Knew Too Much*, a Midwestern American surgeon by the name of Ben McKenna who is vacationing abroad with his wife and son. Along the way, they stumble onto a plot to assassinate a major European political figure. The conspirators then kidnap the boy in an effort to keep the doctor quiet. Twenty-one years earlier a seventy-five-minute, black-and-white version of the story starring Leslie Banks and Edna Best had established Hitchcock as a master of film suspense.

The director had wanted to redo the picture as far back as the early 1940s. Then the plan had been to Americanize the original British characters and to shift the action from Switzerland and London to Sun Valley, Idaho, and New York City, with the Metropolitan Opera substituting for Albert Hall, the site of the assassination attempt in the original. But, by the time Stewart came on board, Hitchcock and screenwriter John Michael Hayes had chosen a much more exotic, dangerous setting than either Switzerland or Idaho—Morocco. As in the original, the action would climax at London's celebrated concert hall, but this time, instead of filming on a studio re-creation, as Hitch had done in the 1930s, the cast and crew would shoot in the actual setting.

The remake would also devote considerably more attention to character development and to the steps in McKenna and his wife's attempt to rescue their son. As a consequence, the new version would run one and a half times as long as its predecessor.

To play Jo McKenna, Hitch selected Doris Day, a former band singer far more at home with musicals than thrillers. But the perky blonde had hidden depths as an actress, as she had revealed in her picture just before *The Man Who Knew Too Much, Love Me or Leave Me,* in which she had played singer Ruth Etting. Moreover, Day, like Stewart, could be convincing as an average American caught up in international intrigue—although Jo, a famous Broadway musical star, was not exactly the girl next door.

Initially the actress was elated by the prospect of working with Hitchcock and costarring with Stewart. Then she learned that the picture would be filmed in Marrakech and London, and she nearly withdrew. "I had never been out of the United States," she explained in her autobiography, "and with my uneasiness about air travel being what it was and is, I thought maybe I'd pass up this Hitchcock for the next one." But her then husband, Marty Melcher, insisted that she honor the commitment.

Filming commenced in Marrakech on May 13, 1955. Stewart, having embraced the joys of international travel with his trip to the Far East earlier in the year, was delighted to find himself in northern Africa. He later told Hedda Hopper, "Marrakech was one place I'd longed to visit after I'd read about Churchill and other people being there. So I was working in a picture there—it was business, but enjoyable at the same time." *Life* magazine captured the tourist in a delightful spread called "Innocent Abroad." As published in the September 5 issue, Stewart could be seen buying a cup of water from a native; sporting a baseball cap, short-sleeve shirt, and penny loafers while watching a wood-carver make a table; accompanying Day on the hotel's piano, a snap-brim hat resting at a raffish angle on his head; enjoying a film break in a café with Gloria and a cigar-smoking Hitchcock; and visiting a Romanian baron's palace, with his wife decked out in a beautiful native dress.

Day, by contrast, wasn't having any fun at all. To her Marrakech was a place where, as she put, a "few rich people . . . had everything, and the rest of the people, and the animals, had nothing." She was so disturbed that she once again considered withdrawing from the picture. Matters worsened when she found Hitchcock unresponsive to her performance. "He didn't direct," she recalled. "He didn't say a word. He just sat next to the cameras, with an interpreter on either side of him (French and Arabic), and all he did was start and stop the camera." Day took the silence personally, becoming, as she put it, "convinced that I must have been the worst actress he'd ever had." She shared her feelings with Stewart, who simply told her, "Well, that's the way he is." After *Rope* and *Rear Window,* he knew what to expect and was content to find his own way through the material. But Day remained dissatisfied. Finally, she confronted the director. Amazed by her attitude, he told her that he interfered only when an actor did something wrong, and since her performance had been perfect, he'd kept quiet. Thereafter, she said, "we got along famously and I adored him."

Adding to the difficulty of shooting in northern Africa was the lack of a completed script. "I continued to write eight or ten pages a day from Hollywood," said John Michael Hayes, "and they were flown over by courier to the set." He still hadn't finished when the company moved from Morocco to London on May 24, so he went to England and proceeded to feed pages to Hitch and the cast on the spot. Work had been scheduled to resume with outdoor locations on the twenty-eighth, but several days of rain kept the company idle. Finally, they picked up on the thirtieth at Albert Hall. Although they had an extremely long and complicated sequence to shoot there, they had to work swiftly as the concert house was scheduled to shut down after June 4 for cleaning and repairs. According to Stewart, while they were filming there, Hitchcock made a bold decision: to eliminate much of the dialogue that Hayes had written and shoot the action in pantomime under a vibrant Bernard Herrmann orchestral composition. "Doris thought he had suddenly gone bananas," the star recalled, "but we did the scene as he suggested, with the result that the scene was twice as effective as it had been with all that dialogue."

With the climactic sequence in the can, they filmed at a variety of locations, including a Park Lane home, St. Savior's Church, a taxidermy shop, and Heathrow Airport. The working conditions stood in marked contrast to those in Morocco. Says Day, "It was extremely, and I mean extremely, hot in Marrakech and we were just about fainting every day. And it was extremely cold in London and we were just about freezing every day." By the time the cast and crew left the British capital on June 21, they were thirteen days behind schedule. They fell even further behind when they picked up at Paramount on the twenty-seventh. In fact, by the time the picture finally wrapped on August 24, they had gone over schedule by thirty-four days, a significant amount of time in the midfifties.

The Man Who Knew Too Much opened at the Paramount Theatre in New York in May of 1956, a long nine months after principal photography had come to an end. "While the current product . . . is unquestionably much bigger and shinier than the original," opined the *New Yorker*, "it doesn't move along with anything like the agility of its predecessor." Other critics agreed. But Hitchcock liked the remake. He considered the first attempt "the work of a talented amateur," while the second version "was made by a professional."

The original picture aside, critical opinion held that *The Man Who Knew Too Much* was a lesser effort than Hitchcock's other recent offerings, including *Rear Window*. Nevertheless, it was, to quote Bosley Crowther of the *New York Times*, "a fast, lively, sharp, suspenseful show." Still, despite the picture's sterling qualities, it failed to approach the box-office success of the previous Stewart-Hitchcock collaboration, winding up only eighteenth among the top-grossing films of 1956.

After its reissue in 1984, critical opinion of *The Man Who Knew Too Much* turned far more favorable. David Denby of *New York* took the occasion to note that, while the picture had been "invariably dismissed as a minor work in the master's canon," it was "so much better than any new movie that one feels both elated and dismayed." Perhaps its biggest champion, Andrew Sarris of the *Village Voice*, described it as "a thrilling piece of cinema for anyone who can appreciate the working out of formal problems as a means of stirring the murky depths of the unconscious." He also found the resolution far from rosy, writing, "If you come out of the movie relieved that Stewart and Day are back together and happy again with their surprisingly sissyish little boy, then you have missed the whole point of Stewart's implacability and Day's delirium. This is no ordinary nuclear family."

While there is clearly something off-kilter in the surgeon's relationship with his wife, Sarris' conclusion is debatable. In any event, the most distinguishing element of Stewart's performance is the way in which he exaggerates his own all-American manner by playing to McKenna's discomfort with foreign customs and his refusal to be cowed by foreign authority without making the character the slightest bit haughty. He thereby turns the Indianapolis doctor into a Midwestern everyman thinking his way through the kind of events that he might have read about back in his suburban home but never expected to touch him. It was Hitchcock's most effective use of the conventional Stewart persona.

Fatigued by *The Man Who Knew Too Much*'s difficult and overlong production schedule, Stewart arrived in Paris on August 30, six days after the Hitchcock picture wrapped. He was met by Billy Wilder and his old friend Leland Hayward, respectively the cowriter-director and producer of his next film.

Based on Charles A. Lindbergh's Pulitzer Prize–winning book, *The Spirit of St. Louis* would trace the Lone Eagle's historic solo flight across the Atlantic in May of 1927. The project was the second in Hayward's three-picture deal with Warner Bros., following the film version of his smash Broadway hit, *Mister Roberts*. Wilder was also coming off of several adaptations from the stage, specifically *Stalag 17* with William Holden; *Sabrina* with Holden, Humphrey Bogart, and Audrey Hepburn; and *The Seven Year Itch* with Marilyn Monroe and Tom Ewell.

The trio were in Paris to shoot the climax of the picture, Lindbergh's triumphant landing at Le Bourget airdrome, which would be re-created, from photographs, at Guyancourt, a rural community near Versailles. Stewart would also appear in a series of establishing shots, seated in a re-creation of Lindy's single-engine monoplane, called *The Spirit of St. Louis*, for which he would travel to various locales—Ireland, Spain, Gibraltar. Stewart, Hayward, and Wilder would then return to Los Angeles and commence principal photography. Had they taken the traditional approach and shot in the opposite order, they would have ended up in Paris in winter, and the look of the footage would have been at odds with Lindy's spring landing.

Five thousand French extras were on hand when the cameras started to roll at Guyancourt on Friday, September 2. Although rain threatened to spoil the evening, luck held and Hayward told Steve Trilling, Jack Warner's executive assistant, they "got some terrific shots." They resumed the following Monday and finished on Tuesday.

The establishing shots were to come next. But then Stewart dropped a bombshell: he told Hayward and Wilder that he was exhausted from the Hitchcock picture and wanted to go home to rest up for principal photography. Weighing on his mind was that Lindbergh had been nearly half his age at the time of the historic flight and credibility demanded that he look his best. The establishing shots, he argued, could be done at the studio using process photography. Wilder and Hayward were adamant that he stay and film the sequences as planned. Over the next several days, the trio met repeatedly to find a resolution, but got nowhere. Finally, in the middle of a working lunch, Stewart jumped up from the restaurant table, said, "I've got to go," returned to his hotel, packed his bags, and caught a flight home.

Wilder and Hayward were stunned. As Leland, Stewart's former agent and longtime friend, told Steve Trilling, "I've never seen him behave in the irrational, ridiculous, kind of crazy fashion he did in Paris." They thought maybe he had walked off the picture entirely.

On that score, they needn't have worried, for Jim considered playing Charles A. Lindbergh the role of a lifetime. He had lobbied hard for the part, remembering how he had lovingly tracked the aviator's flight in the window of his father's hardware store when he was a boy. At first, Hayward thought Stewart was nuts; he was simply too old. So the producer offered the role to John Kerr, a newcomer who had recently triumphed on Broadway in *Tea and Sympathy* and was slated to re-create his role on film. But Kerr, Stewart's junior by twenty-three years, was disdainful of Lindbergh's political conservatism and turned the producer down. Since Jack Warner wanted a star, and Hayward and Wilder could find no other viable alternatives, Stewart won by default.

Elated, Jim spent hours during the making of *The Man Who Knew Too Much* studying newsreel footage of the aviator. "I wanted to catch his mannerisms," he explained. "For instance, I noticed he has a very distinctive walk. He has a habit of swinging his left arm in front of him, even when he only takes three steps; I tried to imitate that." He also practiced flying in one of the three replicas of the plane created for the film so that, as he put it, he'd "know exactly how it reacted and so that close-ups showing my hands on the controls would reveal the muscles working correctly." He realized that the average moviegoer wouldn't know the difference—or care—but, as a pilot himself, he wanted to get the details correct. Finally, before filming began, he had his hair and eyebrows dyed reddish blond to match the young Lindbergh's coloration.

Ironically, he derived little from direct encounters with Slim, as the aviator was called, although they met several times before filming began, invariably with Leland and Wilder present. As Stewart later told Brooke Hayward, "I didn't know what to ask Lindbergh." Finally, on one occasion, he told the Lone Eagle, "I hope I can do a good job for you," and Lindy replied, "I hope so too."

But first the relationship with Wilder and Hayward had to be mended. After Stewart left Paris on September 13, Lew Wasserman flew over to meet with the producer and the director. When they asked if Jim still wanted to do their film, the agent told them that it was the *only* picture that he had wanted to make in years. That settled the issue, and thus the star was still on board when principal photography started on October 14. The company began in Santa Maria, California, where an airplane hangar substituted for the equivalent facility at Roosevelt Field, the Long Island airstrip from which Lindbergh had launched his 3,610-mile journey. Thereafter, filming would continue on various Warners soundstages, on the backlot, and at the Platt Ranch. Sixteen days were devoted solely to shooting Stewart in the cockpit, with six cameras recording his actions and facial expressions from various angles. Ironically, he ended up spending many more hours on board the re-created *Spirit of St. Louis* than Lindbergh did during his epic flight.

It was, in fact, the nature of the flight that made the picture so difficult. For during his thirty-three-hour-and-thirty-minute journey, Lindbergh had been all by himself—with no one to talk to. Without dialogue, how were Wilder and coscreenwriter Wendell Mayes supposed to create drama? Worse, the outcome was a foregone conclusion; there was no suspense. And Lindbergh, who had approval over the screenplay, refused to accept any significant deviations from the historical record.

"I found out that I was beating my head against a cement wall," Wilder recalls, "because I could not write a single personal scene with him, only what was in the book." The Austrian-born director, noted for his arch point of view, urbane repartee, and sophisticated characters, was trapped. He had initially hoped to inject a bit of romance into the story involving Lindy and a Long Island waitress shortly before takeoff, an incident that may have had some basis in fact, but Lindbergh refused to go along. So he had to settle for Stewart doing voice-over narration and periodic flashbacks from the flight to moments in Lindbergh's past.

Wilder was also allowed to introduce a fly into the cockpit to give Stewart something animate to relate to. "I recall getting a little annoyed with the fly," the star said. He told Wilder that they should get rid of it as soon as possible, as the cockpit sequences were, in his words, "difficult enough to do without this bug buzzing around in my face." Wilder disagreed, and they got into what Stewart called "a bit of an argument." As this incident might suggest, the star and the celebrated director did not enjoy the smoothest of relationships. As Wilder recalls, "Once in a while we did have a dispute about the meaning of a scene or a line that seemed awkward to him." But he adds, "We thrashed it all out between ourselves, and there was no animosity, no nothing." Indeed, Stewart looked back on the picture as "wonderful fun to shoot."

Fun perhaps, but time-consuming and expensive, with principal photography requiring nearly five months not counting the European filming. When the picture finally wrapped on March 2, 1956, it was twenty-eight days behind schedule, and the original budget of $2 million had tripled.

Nearly another year was spent in postproduction. But, finally, on February 21, 1957, *The Spirit of St. Louis* opened at Radio City Music Hall in New York. The critics raved, with *Cue* calling it a "thrilling documentary drama," and *Newsweek* finding it "as entertaining as it is instructive, as gripping as it is nostalgic." Stewart also drew cheers, with John Beaufort of the *Christian Science Monitor* hailing his performance as "remarkable." He was particularly effective in the cockpit sequences, deftly acting out the thoughts and attitudes he expresses in voice-over narration. But ultimately there was no escaping his age. He never found the boyish enthusiasm that the twenty-five-year-old Lindy must have experienced as he organized and executed the flight.

Moreover, despite its good intentions, *The Spirit of St. Louis* lacked zest, and with a running time of 138 minutes, it often dragged. In short, it was, to quote *Variety*, "Class A picture-making" but without "entertainment wallop." As a consequence, it earned back only about a third of its production costs (not counting negative and advertising costs) by the end of the year, at which point Jack Warner called it a "disastrous failure. Every studio has them from time to time, but this was one of the worst. We should never have put it in production."

Still, Stewart never lost faith in the picture. "It was a good film," he said many years later, "and when the moment is right I think someone ought to revive it." He also considered Lindbergh "one of the two best parts I've ever had in films" and was proud of his performance, asserting, "I think I got right into Slim's character."

Jim took a badly needed six months off after *The Spirit of St. Louis* wrapped. After four months of leisure, he met his obligation to the Air Force Reserve in July, serving part of his annual interval of active duty at SAC headquarters, flying to Offutt Air Base in the very B-47 he used in *Strategic Air Command*. He spent the rest of the time at the Castle Air Base in California, training in the B-52 Stratofortress program. The following month, he and Gloria took a vacation in Italy. Accompanying them were Fran Johnson, a businessman from Fort Worth, Texas, and his wife, Bess. The Stewarts had initially met the Johnsons through pilot Joe

De Bona, and thereafter the two couples had become extremely close. Not only did they share business ventures, including the ranch in Nevada, they frequently vacationed together, with the Johnsons introducing the Stewarts to a variety of exotic locales, including Africa, which became Jim and Gloria's abiding love thereafter.

When Stewart did return to work—on September 14, 1956—it was in a Western. Not counting "The Windmill" for television, *Night Passage* marked his first foray in the genre since *The Man From Laramie* nearly two years earlier. But this time he was in the saddle without Anthony Mann behind the camera.

That hadn't been the case when the Universal production began. According to film historian Jeanine Basinger, Mann cast the picture and even directed the first sequence. Then he withdrew because he felt that Borden Chase's script from a novel by Norman A. Fox was, in his words, "of such incoherence" that audiences wouldn't understand it. Moreover, he had come to believe that Chase "worked too much in the same way" from screenplay to screenplay. Neither argument was valid. Judging by the final film, the plot of *Night Passage*, which focused on two brothers, one law-abiding (Stewart), the other an outlaw (Audie Murphy), wasn't hard to follow. It wasn't very original or compelling, but it was clear. As for Chase's methodology, his scripts for Mann and Stewart—*Winchester '73*, which he coauthored, and *Bend of the River* and *The Far Country*, on which he soloed—had common elements, but *Vera Cruz*, the 1954 Gary Cooper–Burt Lancaster picture for which he wrote the story, and 1955's *The Man Without a Star*, starring Kirk Douglas, were quite different.

In any event, Chase was a gifted Western writer who could probably have handled any changes that Mann demanded. Instead, the director chose to leave the picture. Worse, in its place, he opted to do another Western, *The Tin Star*, with Henry Fonda and Tony Perkins. Stewart felt betrayed, and relations with Mann remained strained for years thereafter. The fruitful six-year collaboration was at an end, and the two men never worked together again.

At the time, Universal attributed Mann's withdrawal to "a prior commitment" while concurrently announcing his replacement, James Neilson, who had directed Stewart in "The Windmill" for *G.E. Theater*. Neilson had won this, his feature-film debut, on the star's recommendation.

Roughly 70 percent of *Night Passage* was shot in the mining country of Colorado. As with *The Naked Spur*, Durango served as the company headquarters, but the principal locations were several hours away. Nearly three weeks were spent in Animas Canyon, a place of "solid rock gorges and chasms," to quote one studio press release. To get there each day, the cast and crew traveled on the famous narrow-gauge line operated by the Denver and Rio Grande Western Railroad. It served not only as transportation, but also as a setting in the picture.

Periodically, nature reminded Stewart and his colleagues of their raw surroundings. One day while they shot in an isolated mountain area near Durango, a violent snowstorm erupted without warning, trapping the star and other members of the company in an abandoned mine shaft for three hours. Some of the locations were at such an altitude—two miles up—that cast members were hard pressed to breathe. Particularly difficult to execute was an exuberant outdoor dance sequence that comes early in the picture. For Stewart, however, that scene was one of the highlights of the film—because it featured him singing and accompanying himself on the accordion. Tony Mann later said that it was the opportunity to crack out the old instrument that blinded Stewart to the deficiencies of the script.

Departing Durango on October 23, the company continued working at Universal, where *Night Passage* wrapped on November 28, twenty-one days behind schedule. The following summer, Stewart was back in Colorado for the film's world premiere on July 17, 1957. When it opened a week later at the Mayfair Theatre in Manhattan, William K. Zinsser stated in the *New York Herald-Tribune* that it was "no better or worse than its hundreds of predecessors," not exactly a rave. But he and his colleagues liked the performances of Stewart and Audie Murphy and the beautiful photography of William Daniels—by then one of Stewart's favorite cinematographers. But clearly the edge of the Anthony Mann Westerns was missing. According to Marshall Green, the picture's assistant director, James Neilson had come to the set extremely well prepared and was a far gentler fellow than his predecessor, but no one took him seriously. "He was probably the quietest and least vociferous director that I've ever worked with," says the AD. "He was almost bashful. I felt that he knew what he was doing, but he had trouble expressing that to people." As a consequence, Daniels and producer Aaron Rosenberg had much more input into the film's direction than they normally had on a Tony Mann picture—and the lack of a single strong hand showed in the final cut. It is, of course, impossible to know if *Night Passage* could have been better had the veteran not departed, but there is little question that the picture remains the least memorable of Stewart's 1950s Westerns. He would avoid the genre—at least as far as features were concerned—for four years.

SIXTEEN

The End of a Decade

After *Night Passage* wrapped, Stewart again enjoyed a long break, ten months. But he wasn't completely idle. On January 15, 1957, he and Gloria embarked on a six-week tour of South America, one that took them to seven countries. On February 10, while he was away, his second TV drama, "The Town With a Past," aired on the *G.E. Theater.* Like "The Windmill," it was a Western, but this time the script was based on one of the radio plays, "Silver Annie," for the defunct *Six Shooter* series; Stewart had purchased three of the best Britt Ponset tales when the program was canceled. Playing Annie, an old woman who refuses to sell her silver mine to a railroad company, was Beulah Bondi, Jim's "mother" in four features, including *Mr. Smith* and *It's a Wonderful Life.* As with "The Windmill," James Neilson directed. But this project was in the can before the release of *Night Passage.* After the feature's lukewarm reception, the collaboration between the director and the star was over.

Two weeks after the *G.E. Theater* presentation, President Dwight D. Eisenhower nominated Stewart to a brigadier generalship in the Air Force Reserve. Given Jim's war record, Senate confirmation seemed likely. Then Republican senator Margaret Chase Smith raised her voice in opposition, charging that Stewart had failed to serve the requisite hours of active duty since his discharge from the Army Air Corps in the fall of 1945.

Stewart's former CO Ramsay Potts maintains that the senator's motives were not entirely selfless. "Margaret Chase Smith," he recalls, "had a very simple objective: she wanted her administrative assistant, who was in the Reserve, to be made a brigadier general. She wasn't about to release the list until the Air Force did that." Indeed, *Newsweek* reported on September 2, 1957, that she had campaigned on behalf of the fellow, Reservist William C. Lewis Jr., who had been passed over for promotion. But Smith denied a personal motive. Her only interest, she told the press, was "the morale of the Air Force."

As if to prove his fitness, Stewart started his temporary duty that year in Limestone, Maine—Smith's home state—piloting a B-52 jet bomber on an extended flight over the northeastern United States. The mission included two simulated bombing runs and one in-flight refueling. He then finished his tour at Castle Air Force Base in California, where he had trained the previous year.

On August 22, the Senate Armed Services Committee rejected his nomination and that of one other candidate, J. B. Montgomery. Eisenhower's eleven other nominees, including Ramsay Potts, were approved. Disappointed, Lt. Gen. Emmett O'Donnell, the Air Force's assistant chief of staff for personnel, said, "Stewart has made a great contribution to the Air Force. We don't think we should promote people to general officer [merely] on the basis of a good attendance record."

The actor was greatly embarrassed by the incident. But he ultimately got his star. Eisenhower nominated him again on February 12, 1959, and this time the Senate voted in favor of the appointment. One crucial difference between the two attempts lay in Stewart's designated duty in the event of mobilization: in 1957, he would have been deputy operations chief of the Strategic Air Command, an important position. In 1959, he was made a public information officer at the Pentagon, a role of far less consequence. "That was more like it," said Smith, who this time voted in favor of the promotion.

"I didn't realize," Stewart told Alfred Hitchcock's biographer Donald Spoto, "when I was preparing the role what an impact it would have, but it's an extraordinary achievement by Hitch." He was referring to his fourth and final collaboration with the master of suspense, *Vertigo*, arguably their most profound picture together.

Based on a French novel, *D'entre les Morts (From Among the Dead)* by Pierre Boileau and Thomas Narcejac, *Vertigo* centered on Stewart's character, John "Scottie" Ferguson, an ex-police officer in San Francisco with a debilitating fear of heights. A man of independent means, he is hired to follow Madeline Elster, the beautiful but disturbed wife of an old college friend, and they fall in love. Then she plunges to her death in an apparent suicide from the bell tower of an old Spanish mission; because of his vertigo, he is unable to save her. After a nervous breakdown, he discovers a shopgirl named Judy Barton, who resembles the deceased, and sets out to remake her into Madeline's exact replica—with dire consequences.

The original novel had been something of a potboiler, but Hitchcock was looking to turn the material into more sophisticated fare. Instead of a murder mystery like *Rope* or *Rear Window* or a spin on a spy thriller like *The Man Who Knew Too Much*, he wanted a psychological study, an exploration of human fear and obsession as rooted in Stewart's character. Donald Spoto has maintained that the director also wanted something more personal, writing, "This film was his ultimate disclosure of his romantic impulses and of the attraction-repulsion he felt about the object of those impulses: the idealized blonde he thought he desired [embodied in previous films by Grace Kelly and Doris Day] but really believed to be a fraud." Given his motivations, Hitchcock was even willing to give away the novel's twist ending well before the picture's denouement. But it took three screenwriters— playwright Maxwell Anderson (who had written Hitchcock's previous film, *The Wrong Man*), Britisher Alec Coppel, and playwright Samuel Taylor— to plumb the depths Hitch was seeking. Only Coppel and Taylor would receive credit for the screenplay.

After Vera Miles appeared in an episode of Hitch's television series, *Alfred Hitchcock Presents,* he became convinced that she was the right actress for the dual role of Madeline and Judy. He even put her under a personal contract. But the former Miss Oklahoma, who had also starred in Hitch's *The Wrong Man* opposite Henry Fonda, became pregnant shortly before *Vertigo* went into production. Hitch was willing to wait until the birth of the child, but Paramount insisted that he recast.

He chose Kim Novak. At twenty-four, the sultry blonde was a hot new star with such hits as *The Man With the Golden Arm, Picnic,* and *Pal Joey* to her credit. But she was under contract to Columbia, and Harry Cohn was not going to loan her out without a major concession. What he got was Stewart's agreement to do two Columbia pictures in return for Kim's appearance in *Vertigo.* Since Jim was again a part owner of the Hitchcock film, he had good reason to agree to the trade.

Although she was a major star, Novak had virtually no acting training. Samuel Taylor thought her inexperience actually worked to their advantage. "If we'd had a brilliant actress who really created two distinctly different people," he argued, "it would not have been as good. . . . There was no 'art' about it, and that's why it worked so very well." Still, after the picture wrapped, Hitchcock told Hedda Hopper, "It was very, very hard for me to get her to do what I wanted. Her head was too full of weird ideas about acting." Of course, to the director, "weird ideas about acting" included the questions Novak asked him about her character's motivation. Once, when she did so, he told her, "Kim, this is only a movie. Don't take it so seriously," hardly an encouraging reply.

At first, Stewart had reservations about his costar. "I was alarmed when I first saw her," he said, "this great big busty blonde, twice the weight I was." But, after filming began on September 30, 1957, he found that they clicked on camera. And off camera as well—although they were just friends. "She was fun," he recalled, "and she was warm; she is a girl who knows what love and cuddling is all about." She liked Stewart also. In an article for *TV Guide* some three decades later, she wrote, "He was sexy, a term overused then as now; but I tell you that he was the sexiest man who played opposite me in thirty years. And if you ask me why, I'll tell you it was the boyish charm, that enchanting innocence." She also remembered him as a source of solace on the set, writing, "I still felt intimidated by nearly everything in those days, especially the big stars alongside me. But Jimmy made me feel like I belonged. He had a wonderful way of making you feel that he'd never met anybody like you before. In the weeks ahead, he looked after me. He was like the boy next door, my father, and the brother I wished I had had."

They spent much of their time together on location in San Francisco, shooting at a wide variety of sites, including Mission Dolores, the oldest building in the city; the Palace of the Legion of Honor, one of San Francisco's noteworthy art museums; Fort Point, in the shadow of the Golden Gate Bridge; and the McKitrick Hotel, where Madeline supposedly had a rented room. The chapel where the woman meets her fate, San Juan Bautista, was ninety miles to the south. In actuality, the mission had no bell tower at that point. One was built at the studio and optically superimposed on the structure. The interiors, including the dining room of Ernie's Restaurant, a real place and the site of Scottie's first glimpse of Madeline, were filmed at Paramount after the company returned from San Francisco. By far the easiest of Stewart's four pictures with Hitchcock from a technical perspective, *Vertigo* took two and a half months to shoot, wrapping on December 19.

Five months later, on May 28, 1958, the picture opened at the Capitol Theatre in New York City. Today, thanks to *Vertigo*'s rerelease in 1983, the film is widely regarded as Hitchcock's masterpiece, but in 1958 it received only a lukewarm response.[1] The *Los Angeles Times*' Philip K. Scheuer, for example, found it to be "part thriller and part panorama" and added, "Except for a few startling dramatic moments, the scenery has it." John McCarten went even further in the *New Yorker*, calling the picture "far-fetched nonsense," a sentiment shared by *Cue*. Many also complained about the length, the slow pace, and the lack of humor.

There were some rooters, however. Paul V. Beckley of the *New York Herald-Tribune* dubbed *Vertigo* "a suspense film of distinction" and "an ingenious thriller," and Bosley Crowther of the *New York Times* raved over the plot twist, which he called "so clever, even though it is devilishly far-fetched, that we wouldn't want to risk at all disturbing your inevitable enjoyment of the film."

Most of the critics also appreciated Stewart's sensitive performance, which is at the core of the film; he is on-screen almost the entire time. That this was not the man in *Rear Window*—a celebrated photographer

---

[1] The film's reputation was enhanced even further by a fully restored, 70-mm rerelease in 1996.

with a beautiful, wealthy girlfriend—or the hero from *The Man Who Knew Too Much*—a successful doctor with a famous actress wife—takes some time to become apparent. For example, in an early scene with his best friend, Midge—a character created by Samuel Taylor and nicely played by Barbara Bel Geddes—he appears in the typical Stewart mold, folksy, easy to talk with, nondemanding, and even able to joke about his vertigo. But, by the end of the film, he's become a man racked with guilt and fear, obsessed by a lost love and willing to totally dominate someone else in her name. Certainly, Jim could never have played this role without the impact of World War II. As he once said, "I had known fear like that and I'd known people who'd been paralyzed by fear. It's a very powerful thing to be almost engulfed by that kind of fear." What's most remarkable about the performance is how much Stewart conveys through facial expression—following Madeline about the city in a daring extended sequence with no dialogue; being with her in his apartment for the first time; witnessing her fall from the bell tower; awakening from a sweat-inducing nightmare; encountering Judy; and so on.

Despite the star's powerful performance, Novak's popularity, and the Hitchcock name, *Vertigo* performed relatively poorly at the box office, coming in only twenty-first among the year's highest grossers, three notches below the ranking of *The Man Who Knew Too Much* two years earlier and sixteen below *Rear Window*.

On December 15, 1957, four days before Stewart finished *Vertigo*, his third half-hour TV Western aired on the *G.E. Theater*. Like "The Town With a Past," broadcast ten months earlier, "The Trail to Christmas" was adapted from one of Frank Burt's radio scripts for *The Six Shooter*. As the original title, "Britt Ponset's Christmas Carol," suggests, the plot borrowed from the Dickens classic, with Stewart's roving cowboy using the story of Scrooge and the three ghosts to bolster a runaway child's yuletide spirit. The star directed the episode himself, his first foray behind the camera. It was a solid job; *Variety* even called it "masterful." But the experience did nothing to whet Stewart's appetite for other such assignments.

Early in the new year, a vacation took Jim and Gloria to southern Florida, where he enjoyed game fishing in the Keys. His catch included an eight-and-a-half-foot bonefish, which he proudly displayed for a photographer from the Associated Press.

In early February, he went to work on *Bell, Book and Candle*, the first of his pictures for Columbia as payback on the loan of Kim Novak. She was again his leading lady, but this time the fare was far different. "This is high comedy in a crystalline style," wrote William Hawkins of the *New York World-Telegram* when John Van Druten's play opened at Manhattan's Ethel

Barrymore Theatre on November 14, 1950. Robert Coleman of the *New York Daily Mirror* ranked it with *Blithe Spirit;* like that popular Noël Coward comedy about ghosts among the British upper crust, *Bell, Book and Candle* had supernatural underpinnings: Gillian Holroyd, played in the West End and on Broadway by Lilli Palmer, was the leader of a coven of modern-day witches who longs to feel love. But she finds out the emotion isn't what it seems after casting a spell on her neighbor, a book publisher named Shepherd Henderson, portrayed onstage by Palmer's then husband, Rex Harrison. What made *Bell, Book and Candle* so delightful was not the witchcraft, but, like *Blithe Spirit*, the sophisticated characters, Van Druten's witty dialogue, and the moving romance between the leads.

All of which doomed the film version from the outset, for Stewart, as he had demonstrated in *Rope*, was not credible as a worldly urbanite; it is difficult to imagine him and the suave, polished Harrison sharing the same role. Worse, Novak, with minimal training and an extremely narrow range, hadn't the least flair for high comedy.

According to screenwriter Daniel Taradash, who had brought the property to Columbia, Harrison had initially been asked to re-create his stage role—Palmer being considered too old to play Gillian on film—but nothing came of the effort. Which was okay with Taradash, who had been hoping to land Cary Grant and Grace Kelly. They would have been ideal, but Kelly's marriage precluded her involvement, and Grant asked for certain script changes that didn't suit Taradash and his partner, Julian Blaustein.[2]

Ironically, the film that Grant opted to do instead of *Bell, Book and Candle*, Hitchcock's *North by Northwest*, was a project that Stewart had expected to land. In fact, Jim kept putting Harry Cohn and the Van Druten comedy off while he waited for the script from Hitch. Meanwhile, the director tried to figure out how to tell him that his latest thriller had been written with Grant in mind. He was finally off the hook when Stewart informed him that he couldn't stall Columbia any longer.

In addition to the ill-advised casting, *Bell, Book and Candle* was hampered by the choice of director. Originally, Taradash and Blaustein had approached Alexander Mackendrick, the force behind several intelligent Alec Guinness comedies for Britain's Ealing Studios, but Mackendrick didn't like the script. So Richard Quine got the job.

Once described as "a tall, handsome ex-actor who could step back into leading man roles tomorrow," Quine was Novak's choice for the assignment, as he and she were romantically involved at the time. Stewart ini-

---

[2] Taradash and Blaustein produced *Bell, Book and Candle* as part of their independent production company's multipicture deal with Columbia.

tially opposed the selection, but Novak persuaded him to go along—which turned out to be a mistake. It wasn't that Quine was a poor craftsman. He'd done quite well with such solid American comedies as the 1955 remake of *My Sister Eileen* starring Betty Garrett and Janet Leigh and *The Solid Gold Cadillac* with Judy Holliday and Paul Douglas. Moreover, he had worked extremely well with Jack Lemmon and Ernie Kovacs—both of whom had been in his film just before this, *Operation Mad Ball.* The two comic actors had major supporting roles in the Van Druten–Taradash comedy, Lemmon as a warlock with a penchant for jazz and Kovacs as a writer out to expose the coven.

What made Quine wrong for the project was that he didn't understand it. Instead of focusing on the romance, he wanted to emphasize the witchcraft, urging Taradash to add more magic to the screenplay. "And we fought that," Taradash recalls. "We said, 'You do that and you'll destroy the love story and that's what it's all about.' " But Quine won.

"I don't think it was one of his better pictures, frankly," says Jack Lemmon, Quine's close friend. "I don't think Dick nailed it." Lemmon adds, "I know I didn't nail it. I never could figure out that character. I just couldn't get him." But he got closer to the mark than the principals.

As a consequence, when *Bell, Book and Candle* opened in New York on Christmas Day, 1958, what could have been an ethereal delight was simply another rather leaden comedy. As *Time* magazine observed, "Somewhere between Broadway and Hollywood the broomstick broke down," adding, with reference to Stewart's performance, "As the bewitched hero, he stumbles around most of the time with a vaguely blissful expression—rather like a comic-strip character who has just been socked by Popeye."

Stewart fared much better playing himself in an episode of *The Jack Benny Show* on March 9, while *Bell, Book and Candle* was still in production. Then, on August 11, *The FBI Story* took him back to melodrama. The picture marked his first role for Warner Bros. since the disastrous *Spirit of St. Louis.*

The FBI Story was based on a book of the same name by two-time Pulitzer Prize–winner Don Whitehead, then Washington bureau chief of the *New York Herald-Tribune.* Published by Random House in December 1956, it was an enormous success, spending thirty-eight weeks on the *New York Times* best-seller list. At the time, J. Edgar Hoover was considered one of the great Americans of the twentieth century, and what distinguished Whitehead's book was the access that he had gained to the director and his files.

Translating Whitehead's 328-page text to the screen was not easy, for it covered roughly five decades and dozens of cases. Ultimately, screenwriters

Richard L. Breen and John Twist settled on eight examples of the Bureau at work, cases dealing with the Ku Klux Klan's attempt to kill a crusading newspaper editor; the murder of two Native Americans who owned oil-rich land in Oklahoma; the FBI's war against mobsters such as Baby Face Nelson, Pretty Boy Floyd, and John Dillinger; a case of espionage in South America during World War II; the breakup of a Communist spy ring in Manhattan; and the incident that opens the film, an airline bombing that resulted in the death of forty-nine people. What linked the stories was a single fictional agent by the name of Chip Hardesty, played by Stewart. Glimpses of his family life were freely intermixed with his caseload, foreshadowing to some extent *Mr. Hobbs Takes a Vacation* and Jim's other domestic comedies of the next decade. Vera Miles, Hitchcock's original choice for the dual roles in *Vertigo*, played his wife, the first of two such pairings for Stewart and the twenty-nine-year-old actress.

Don Whitehead's initial agreement with the Bureau had given Hoover the right to approve any motion picture deal that might arise from his book. Thus, before proceeding, Jack Warner had to get the director's blessing. Hoover asked for approval over the principals, including the producer, director, and screenwriters; the screenplay; the final film; and the use of the Bureau's name in the film's advertising and exploitation. Warner agreed to all of these conditions.

As might be expected, Hoover wasn't shy about expressing his opinions. He made numerous changes in the script, mostly eliminating historical inaccuracies and scenes that showed members of the Bureau engaged in practices he considered objectionable. In one instance he deleted a scene in which an agent rifled a businessman's files, because he thought the script made him appear to be seeking information for his personal advantage. In another incident, he objected to agents giving a suspect what appeared to be the third degree. His principal concerns, he told Jack Warner, were that the picture be "on a dignified basis and properly portray the functions of the FBI."

Regarding personnel, Hoover heartily approved Mervyn LeRoy, Warner's choice for producer-director; Hoover and LeRoy were friends. The director also applauded Stewart's casting, telling Jack Warner, "I have always held Jimmy in the highest regard, both personally and professionally, and I feel certain that he can be counted on to give a splendid portrayal of a Special Agent."

While Hoover's supervision was taxing, his cooperation meant that Warners got virtually open access to the Bureau. And the studio took full advantage of the opportunity, filming for five full weeks at FBI headquarters in Washington, D.C., including the fingerprinting section, the serology lab, and the firearms collection. LeRoy even showed Hoover at work at his desk, although the director had fought against appearing on camera. They also filmed an impressive sequence at the Bureau's training facility in Quantico, Virginia. "It was all authentic," LeRoy recalled in his auto-biography, "down to the smallest detail." He added that, when they were not at FBI facilities, they still had two agents with them, assigned by Hoover to, as LeRoy put it, "make sure of the technical details."

Outside of Washington, the bulk of the work took place at Warners' Burbank studio. Given the sprawling nature of the story, 167 different sets were required. They ranged from an Oklahoma boomtown complete with a life-size working oil derrick—built on the studio backlot—to an exact replica of the Biograph Theatre in Chicago, site of John Dillinger's capture, to a South American jungle. Principal photography lasted until December 17, when the picture wrapped, ten days behind schedule. Looking back, LeRoy wrote, "The actual filming of The FBI Story went smoothly. In our two stars, Vera Miles and James Stewart, a great American in his own right, we had two extremely able and cooperative actors, and they were both excellent."

Both Hoover and Whitehead were pleased with the result. After a private screening at Bureau headquarters, the director told LeRoy, "It's a great film." And Whitehead wrote, "As the author, I'm very happy with the interpretation of the book and the picture's honesty, imagination and humor."

The critics were less fulsome when the picture opened at Radio City Music Hall on September 24, 1959. "Obviously, this long, respectful history of the FBI is crammed with exciting factual incidents," noted Hollis Alpert in the Saturday Review. "But trying to present them all through the eyes of a single agent not only strikes a false note, it has the effect of padding the picture with inessentials." Most of his colleagues agreed. They were also irked by the many scenes of Stewart's character's domestic life, although Bosley Crowther of the New York Times conceded that they resulted in a "remarkable job of equating the Federal Bureau of Investigation and the American family."

After The FBI Story wrapped, Stewart took Gloria, his four children, and their governess to Europe. The impetus was the Berlin Film Festival, where Jim was to receive an award, but in addition to Germany, the family stopped in Switzerland, Italy, Spain, and other places of note. "That was a great trip," recalls Jim's daughter Judy Merrill—in part, because the girls, at seven and a half, were no longer babies, and their parents could begin to relate to them on a mature level. Judy says that, even at the time, she could tell that "Mom and Dad were enjoying us on that trip. We would all sit in the hotel and have these jokes together."

Of course, Jim, as usual, worried about everything, but J. Edgar Hoover helped pave the way as the family moved from country to country. "Wherever the Stewarts went," wrote Mervyn LeRoy in his autobiography, "FBI men were there, to meet them at the plane and to help them."

But it was Jim who took action when they arrived at a run-down hotel in Mirvella, Spain, not at all what they expected. He and Gloria decided to go somewhere else—not a simple matter for a major movie star traveling through Europe with a party of seven. Son Mike McLean recalls, "Ronnie and I had the room right next to them, and he was up late into the night, worrying about it, making phone calls. Finally, the next morning or the next afternoon, we left for Biarritz."

As a coda to the trip, when the party landed back in New York, Stewart spotted yet another FBI agent. He went up to the man, thanked him for meeting their plane, and told him that now that they were back in America, he could handle matters himself. "Oh, I'm not here to meet you," the agent told him. "I'm just here to keep an eye on a jewel thief we've been following. I want to make sure he stays on the plane until it gets to Los Angeles, where we'll pick him up." Sure enough, two agents quietly whisked the man away at LAX.

Like *The FBI Story*, the second film of Stewart's quid pro quo deal with Columbia was based on a popular book. In fact, *Anatomy of a Murder* was an even bigger success than Whitehead's tome, appearing on the *New York Times* best-seller list for sixty-one weeks. Writing under the pseudonym Robert Traver, John D. Voelker, a judge on the Michigan Supreme Court, based his novel on an actual 1952 case. In his version, a soldier kills the owner of a local inn for raping his wife—or so he claims. Voelker set the story in Michigan's Upper Peninsula, the rugged strip of land that connects Michigan with Wisconsin. It was familiar territory, as the judge had been born there and was a prosecuting attorney there for fourteen years. What made the novel particularly gripping was its ring of authenticity. The narrator, the soldier's attorney, Paul Biegler, was patterned after Voelker himself, and the clever defense he devised—that his client had been seized by an "irresistible impulse" to kill after the alleged violation of his wife, not the usual grounds for legal insanity—had its roots in an obscure, late-nineteenth-century precedent.

The screenplay by Wendell Mayes adhered closely to the tone of the novel and encompassed many of its episodes, but Mayes introduced pivotal testimony from a defense witness, a young woman named Mary Pilant, which was not in the book. The result was one of the best scenes in the picture. He also boldly eliminated closing arguments, traditionally the set pieces in any courtroom drama. But what was particularly clever about the screenplay was that, by the end, the audience was rooting for Biegler to win while doubting the innocence of his client.

Stewart was well suited to the role of the attorney. Like Biegler, he was a fisherman and from a small town. He'd even played a lawyer twice before—in *Made for Each Other* and *The FBI Story,* although, in the earlier film, his occupation had been tangential to the plot and, in the latter, his character never got around to starting a practice. In *Anatomy of a Murder,* however, his way of organizing and presenting his case was at the heart of the story.

The project introduced Stewart to a cinema legend, its producer-director, Otto Preminger. A native of Vienna, Preminger's film credits included the mystery *Laura,* for Fox, where he had been under contract, and a string of pictures for his own production company, including *Carmen Jones, The Man With the Golden Arm, Porgy and Bess,* and *The Moon Is Blue.* The latter, released without the approval of the film industry's powerful Motion Picture Association of America, helped bring an end to decades of film censorship.

Typically, Preminger's films had sweep and big-name casts, but they lacked subtlety. By contrast, most of the leading players in *Anatomy of a Murder,* aside from Stewart, were not well known—although several would become stars as a result, at least in part, of this film. To play the plum role of the defendant's sexy wife, for example, Preminger cast Lee Remick, who had made only two previous pictures. His first choice had been Lana Turner, Stewart's *Ziegfeld Girl* costar, but she and Preminger had a falling-out after she insisted on using her own couturier, Jean-Louis, to design her wardrobe. Preminger rightly felt that such attire would be inappropriate for a second lieutenant's wife. The other newcomers included George C. Scott as Claude Dancer, the skilled prosecuting attorney, and Ben Gazzara as the defendant, Lt. Frederick Manion; the picture would be the second feature for each of them. And to play the judge who presides over the case, Preminger cast someone with no acting experience at all, Joseph Welch. The Boston attorney had endeared himself to millions of Americans by defending the U.S. Army in the televised hearings staged by Sen. Joseph McCarthy.

As *Anatomy of a Murder* was not scheduled to start production until March of 1959, Jim and Gloria joined their friends Fran and Bess Johnson on a trip to India shortly after the Stewart family returned from Europe. "I spent a lot of time sitting in a tent, pitched in the jungle," the actor recalled, "memorizing my lines for the movie. That picture demanded a lot of work and thought. . . . So I read my script each night until I fell asleep.

When I got home, I felt better prepared, physically and mentally, than I'd ever been."

Filming lasted eight weeks, from March 23 to May 16, with all of the scenes shot—in black and white—on location in Michigan. Voelker's tiny hometown, Ishpeming, served as the company's headquarters. In fact, the judge's eighty-year-old home, the place of his birth, also became Paul Biegler's domicile in the picture. The rooms were so tiny that, according to a studio press release, scenes involving three or four people forced Preminger to direct through the doorway of an adjoining room. They also filmed at the local jail, cathedral, hospital, and railroad depot, at the docks in nearby Marquette, and at the bar where the actual shooting took place. For the extensive trial sequences, the company used the Marquette County Court House. Such was the combined weight of the cast, crew, extras, and equipment that the fifty-year-old structure had to be bolstered with five thousand feet of lumber. Going to Michigan, despite its remove from California, was a wise decision, for the landscape and architecture gave the picture a look wholly different from that of most Hollywood offerings.

Given the distance from an established film production center, Preminger created virtually his own studio on the spot, including a camera-servicing department and a fully equipped film-editing room (with three film editors). He even imported the composer of the picture's score, Duke Ellington, to work on the spot (and then gave him a small on-screen role). The exposed film, however, was processed in Hollywood and flown daily to Ishpeming, where it was screened at a local movie theater.

For those used to southern California, spending two spring months in northern Michigan took some doing. "The region is so remote," Stewart recalled, "that even Detroit, Lansing, and other Michigan cities feel it is a part of the polar ice cap. I won't mention the weather, which ranged all the way from a jolly seventeen below to a sweltering thirty. It snowed as late as the middle of May."

The company—about 130 strong—stayed in scattered locations in Ishpeming and Marquette. Orson Bean, making his feature debut as a crucial defense witness, describes the actors' quarters as "kind of a funky little hotel." Eve Arden, who played Stewart's secretary, recalled in her autobiography, "At night after dinner, we gathered in the inn and told stories and played games. One evening someone brought a large canvas, paints and brushes, and we began a collective painting, each one filling a small section in any way he was inspired to."

During the day, those waiting to work tried to keep busy. "Lee Remick did needlepoint," Arden recalled, "others sketched, read, or played

Scrabble or gin. Jimmy Stewart, watching the group of busy bees, dubbed us Hobby Lobby." As he was in virtually every scene in the picture, Jim had little time for idle pursuits himself. In fact, he kept to himself in the evenings as well. "He closeted himself," Ben Gazzara explains, "because he had a great deal of dialogue. I never even saw him taking lunch, actually. I think he did that alone, totally concentrated on this character, totally immersed in it."

Gazzara, twenty-two years younger than Stewart, was a product of the Actors Studio, whose approach to character development—the Method—was very different from Jim's. Nevertheless, the newcomer was impressed by the old pro. "I watched in awe," he recalls. "I said, 'Holy shit, look at this, look at this. Actors Studio, schmactor's studio. This guy can act. How natural, how simple, what a sense of humor, tongue in cheek, how he could pause and hold it forever, hold your attention.' He had all the moves. I was really awestruck. It taught me a great deal."

He was also impressed by Jim's generosity, saying, "You never had a sense from Jimmy Stewart that he wanted to crowd you out, that he wanted his moments framed, that he wanted you to change your rhythm to help him along, which a lot of greedy actors do. He let you be yourself and work and think." George C. Scott was also impressed, particularly by Stewart's insistence on standing off camera when his costar had his close-ups and feeding him his cues—in full costume so that when Scott looked at him, he saw Biegler as he was used to seeing him. For Jim, dressing for off-camera cues was a regular practice, one that impressed many of his other costars through the years.

If working with Stewart was impressive, working with Preminger was a surprise, for the director had a major reputation for browbeating actors. But, in Michigan, he was, to quote Gazzara, "like an altar boy." Orson Bean adds, "Preminger is black-and-white from what I hear. If the movie ain't going well, he's a nightmare. . . . But on our show it was all going swimmingly. He would order a take. He would say, 'Action.' The take would finish and he would say, 'Cut. Print. Perfect. Next.' Just like that. And everybody was happy." Stewart had no complaints. In 1966, he said, "I'd like to do another picture with Preminger, he's a good picture maker."

Amazingly, the director had *Anatomy of a Murder* cut, scored, and in previews a month after the picture wrapped, "something of a record for a big budget motion picture," according to *Variety*. Thus, when the world premiere came in Detroit on July 1, 1959 (followed by the New York opening the next day), *Anatomy* beat Stewart's previous project, *The FBI Story*, to the nation's movie houses by nearly three months.

It was an enormous hit. "Not since *Witness for the Prosecution*," opined

Variety, "has there been a courtroom melodrama as beguiling, forceful and enthralling as Otto Preminger's *Anatomy of a Murder.*" To *Cue* it was "probably the best courtroom drama of our time," and Bosley Crowther of the *New York Times* called it "well nigh flawless."

Wendell Mayes' screenplay, Preminger's direction, and all of the actors won widespread praise, with the biggest cheers reserved for Stewart in what Crowther called "one of the finest performances of his career." It is a classic case of the perfect role coming along at the very moment when the actor who plays it is at the peak of his craftsmanship. What makes Stewart's performance particularly memorable is the way he uses his own unpretentious, small-town manner to belie Biegler's razor-sharp legal mind. Near the end of the picture, when he says, "I'm just a humble country lawyer trying to do the best I can against this brilliant prosecutor from the big city of Lansing," the audience—the one in the courtroom and the one in the movie theater—knows it's not true, but it's an effective guise. Stewart is also fascinating to watch outside the courtroom as he banters with Biegler's old, alcoholic friend, played by Arthur O'Connell, gently coaxes a fragile young woman (Kathryn Grant) to give him the help he needs to win the case, and deftly negotiates his way through his dealings with the rather unsavory Manion and Manion's loose wife.

Anatomy of a Murder went on to become the seventh most popular picture of 1959, earning Stewart the New York Film Critics Award and the Venice Film Festival Award for Best Actor. After being overlooked by the Motion Picture Academy for *The Spirit of St. Louis* and *Vertigo,* he was again nominated for an Oscar, marking the first time since *Harvey* in 1950. The picture was also nominated, as were Arthur O'Connell, George C. Scott, Wendell Mayes, editor Louis M. Loeffler, and cinematographer Sam Leavett.

Stewart thought he had a good chance of winning, but 1959 was *Ben-Hur*'s year, and the epic claimed most of the major categories, including Best Picture, Best Supporting Actor, Best Director, and Best Actor, Charlton Heston. The other nominees were Laurence Harvey for *Room at the Top,* Jack Lemmon for *Some Like It Hot,* and Paul Muni for *The Last Angry Man.* Coincidentally, Heston and Stewart had arrived at the ceremony at the same time, and they posed together for the media. "As the flashbulbs finally petered out," Heston recalled in his autobiography, "and we turned to go to our seats, Jimmy took my arm. 'I hope you win, Chuck,' he said. 'I really mean that.' " Heston was quite touched by his colleague's obvious sincerity, writing, "I don't know another actor alive who would've said such a thing. He's an extraordinary man." What Heston didn't know was that Stewart considered his own chances of winning pretty good—and he *wanted* to win. Thus his remarks to his colleague were even more generous.

After *The FBI Story* and *Anatomy of a Murder,* two huge, high-profile movies, Stewart ended the decade on a quieter note, with one more feature for Columbia and two TV appearances.

The feature, called *The Mountain Road,* was based on another book, this one by Theodore H. White. White, who would soon become famous as the chronicler of the quadrennial American elections in his *Making of the President* series, had been the chief of *Time* magazine's China bureau during World War II. Out of that experience, he forged his novel about a team of American GIs ordered to delay the Japanese advance into East China during one critical week in 1944. Specifically, their mission was to destroy roads, bridges, and anything else that might help the enemy traverse the main roadway, an effort that culminated in close combat at a village called Tushan, where the Japanese had a cache of armaments. The leader of the outfit, a major by the name of Baldwin, was based on Lt. Col. Frank Gleason, whom White had met when they were both stationed in China. Gleason served as a technical adviser for the film.

When principal photography started on June 8, 1959, the cast and crew were headquartered in Phoenix, Arizona, but filming took them to the rugged countryside some sixty miles to the northeast and later to the southern portion of the state—where temperatures climbed to 118 degrees by midday. Such was the heat that the cast and crew went through more than 500 gallons of water and 2,500 pounds of ice a day, and a portable six-bed hospital was standing by at all times. One of the unit's assistant directors, Irving Moore, a veteran of thirty-five years of filmmaking, called it "the toughest location I can remember."

The most dramatic moment in the shooting schedule came with the scene in which the GIs blow up a pivotal bridge. An explosives expert, Willis Cook, rigged the blast using seven tons of dynamite, one ton of TNT, three hundred pounds of C-3 (a compound used in cutting steel), four hundred pounds of phosphorous bombs, seven thousand gallons of high-test gasoline, and three thousand gallons of diesel fuel. The resultant explosion could be felt in Nogales, sixteen miles away.

The balance of the action was shot at the Columbia Ranch in the San Fernando Valley and at the Burbank Airport (which served as a U.S. Army airstrip in China for the picture's opening sequence).

At the heart of the action was Stewart's character, Major Baldwin. Hungry for his own command, the demolitions officer is decisive but not particularly likable, boldly asserting at one point in Alfred Hayes' screenplay, "On this road, I'm the only justice there is." Moreover, he has no feeling for China, which complicates his budding romance with Sue-Mei Hung (played by Lisa Lu), a cultured, American-educated widow who accompanies the team in an effort to reach a safe haven. In the end, Baldwin succeeds in his mission but recognizes his failings as a human being. "I had more power than I knew what to do with," he tells Sue-Mei.

The character was the first and only combat officer that Stewart ever played, and he attacked the role with gusto. Assisting him was the picture's director, Daniel Mann, a former actor and stage director whose film credits included *Come Back, Little Sheba* with Shirley Booth and Burt Lancaster, *The Rose Tattoo* with Lancaster and Anna Magnani, *I'll Cry Tomorrow* starring Susan Hayward, and *The Teahouse of the August Moon* with Marlon Brando and Glenn Ford. Harry Morgan, reunited with Stewart as the team's feisty sergeant, recalls the solid rapport between the star and the director. "I remember one time we were up in the mountains outside of Tucson," he says. "A bunch of us were down on one level. And Jimmy and Danny were up on another level, discussing something. . . . And after a while, Jimmy turned around and said, 'My God, I finally found a director who knows how to direct.' He meant that Danny knew how to talk to him as an actor, about the part, his characterization, and his relationships with the other people."

All of which was, of course, to the good. But *The Mountain Road* had the makings of a thrilling war-based adventure story, like *The Guns of Navarone* a few year later. However, it needed an action director. Anthony Mann (no relation to Danny) would have been the obvious choice, but Stewart was still furious with him over *Night Passage*. In Danny Mann's hands, the dialogue and character development took precedence over the derring-do, and they were simply not strong enough to keep the picture afloat. Moreover, the film was shot in black and white, which was passé by 1960 for most mainstream films. Stewart supported the decision, saying that World War II was a black-and-white war and the use of color would have made the film look like a typical Hollywood product. But color did not hurt the Academy Award–winning *Bridge on the River Kwai*, a movie with similar overtones, set in the same era and part of the world.

Howard Thompson of the *New York Times* accurately diagnosed *The Mountain Road*'s problems when the film opened at neighborhood theaters on June 29, 1960. He wrote, "Even with its final, philosophical overtones, this remains a curiously taciturn, dogged and matter-of-fact little picture—none too stimulating." To which *Variety* added, "It reveals nothing new in the way of a World War II film."

Stewart acquitted himself well in what *Newsweek* described as a "tough, generally clear-eyed performance from an old trouper," but that was not enough to save *The Mountain Road* from a quick death at the box office. The star was baffled by its failure. "I voted it one of the best scripts I'd ever read," he said, "and it was beautifully produced. You never know about this business."

He ended the year on a lighter note, appearing as himself on the November 15 episode of *The Jack Benny Show* and as an Old West peddler on the December 15 airing of NBC's anthology series *Ford Startime.* The latter, a frontier version of Cinderella called "Cindy's Fella," costarred James Best as the rancher who throws the ball (in this case, a barn dance), comic George Gobel as a troubadour-cum–fairy godmother called the Drifter, and newcomer Lois Smith as Cindy. Stewart's character was the equivalent of the fairy tale's prince.

On a personal note, Jim was sworn in on October 23 as a trustee of his alma mater, Princeton University, having been elected an alumni trustee-at-large in a nationwide vote of the university's graduates. He would serve a four-year term.

Thus, the fifties came to an end. The decade had brought great change to the motion picture industry. An increased reliance on location photography and the widespread use of color coupled with the rising power of creative artists, notably actors and directors, had sent production costs soaring. At the same time, the movie audience was shrinking dramatically due to the advent of television. The studios tried to fight back, offering pictures of sweeping proportions, featuring huge casts and massive sets and shown on giant screens in large formats such as VistaVision and Cinerama, which further escalated production costs.

By decade's end, Louis B. Mayer and Harry Cohn were dead and Darryl F. Zanuck had resigned as Fox's head of production to become an independent producer. RKO had ceased to exist, and within a couple of years, Universal would be acquired by a giant talent agency, Stewart's own, MCA. Only Jack Warner remained, still running the studio that bore his name, but Warner Bros. had survived by embracing weekly television production in a major way. By 1960, it was becoming clear that the future lay with independent production companies and freelance creative artists. Studios would still produce some pictures, but they would mostly become distribution houses for properties launched elsewhere. The day of the factory system was over.

Passing, too, were the biggest stars of the golden age. Bogart and Flynn were dead. Gable's last movie would be released in 1960 and he would pass away shortly thereafter. Cooper would go in 1961, the same year in which Cagney retired. The actors who had risen to stardom during the fifties—Montgomery Clift, Marlon Brando, James Dean—were a different breed. They acted from a highly emotional center, more needy, more neurotic, and offscreen they eschewed the glamour that had surrounded their predecessors.

The 1950s was a time of significant change for Jimmy Stewart as well, but he fared far better than most of his contemporaries or the industry as a whole. On the personal side, he started the decade as a newlywed. By 1960, his had become one of the most stable and enduring marriages in Hollywood. He was also the father of four children, including twins who had been born virtually with the decade. Once the industry's most eligible bachelor, he had become a pillar of the community—as well as a brigadier general in the Air Force Reserve.

Professionally, he had made tremendous strides between 1950 and 1960. Free at last from the shadows of MGM and World War II, he embraced a wide variety of roles. He had stretched the limits of his screen persona further than anyone could have imagined ten years earlier and, as a result, found even greater popularity. He'd also tackled television.

But he was fifty-two when the sixties dawned. He still looked fit, but after decades of looking younger than his years, his age was beginning to show. His face was fuller, and having lost the hair on the crown of his head, he had resorted to tucking a toupee under his widow's peak before the cameras turned. How long he could remain at the top of his game remained to be seen.

SEVENTEEN

Westerns with Ford,
Comedies with Koster

"He's a wonderful actor," says Richard Widmark of Jimmy Stewart. "He really talks to you. And he listens to every word you say." To which Shirley Jones adds, "To me, good acting is really good concentration. And he [Jim] was a master of that. I mean, he could redo it and come back and do it exactly the same way. Or try something new. His concentration was so wonderful."

The picture that united the three of them—Stewart, Widmark, and Jones—was *Two Rode Together*, directed by John Ford. The winner of more Academy Awards than any other director in history, Pappy, as he was known by colleagues, had taken the helm of his first film in 1917. Although he subsequently worked in many genres, his way with Westerns was unique. In classics such as *Stagecoach, My Darling Clementine, She Wore a Yellow Ribbon,* and *Rio Grande*, he established a lyrical approach to the people and the land—coupled with frequent dollops of broad humor—that struck a responsive chord. His 1956 picture *The Searchers*, about an embittered man's relentless pursuit of a niece captured by Indians, is arguably the best Western ever made. Like many of Ford's finest features, it starred John Wayne, who had risen to stardom in *Stagecoach* and was one of Pappy's close friends. Having worked with many great directors, it was only fitting that Stewart make a picture with this, the most celebrated filmmaker of them all.

Stan Shpetner brought the two men together. A young independent producer with three low-budget features to his credit, Shpetner took a novel that he'd acquired—*Comanche Captives* by Will Cook—to his agency, MCA, which also represented Stewart and Ford. Once the star and director signed up, Shpetner added Widmark to the package and sold it to Columbia, which had produced one of the go-getter's prior features, *The Legend of Tom Dooley*.

Like *The Searchers, Two Rode Together* considered the plight of the settlers who had lost loved ones to Indian war parties, in this case the Comanches. Widmark, who frequently played bad guys, was cast against type as Jim Gary, an idealistic cavalry lieutenant who attempts to win the release of Chief Quannah Parker's white prisoners. Stewart's Guthrie McCabe, a corrupt town marshal, shares Gary's mission, but his motives are less honorable: he wants to charge the settlers for the return of their kinfolk even though he believes that the psychologically scarred captives will be unable to rejoin white society. McCabe wasn't exactly the villain of the piece, but he was certainly venal, the coldest, least admirable character Stewart had played since Howard Kemp in *The Naked Spur.*

He doesn't start out that way. When the character is introduced at the outset of the film, he's snoozing quietly in the town of Tascosa, where he is the law, sporting a white suit and a large panama hat, his long legs propped up on a railing (Ford's homage to his depiction of Wyatt Earp— Henry Fonda—fourteen years earlier in *My Darling Clementine*). Widmark arrives and the two banter amiably. Clearly, McCabe is slightly crooked, but he's also debonair and charming, with a devilish sense of humor. His rapport with the impoverished lieutenant, dusty from the road, is a delight. It is only upon reaching the fort where the settlers are encamped that McCabe begins to change into a cantankerous, hot-tempered lout, a transformation that is more puzzling than intriguing. Likewise, in the final portion of the picture, he changes again. Having become involved with one of the rescued Indian captives, a beautiful Hispanic woman played by Linda Cristal, he becomes the voice of tolerance. As with the previous shifts in character, this transformation seems to come from nowhere.

That filming began with the script unfinished may explain the unfounded jumps in McCabe's personality. According to Linda Cristal, the marshal was nowhere near as unsavory initially. She says that Stewart himself, improvising some of his dialogue on the spot, gave the role what she calls its "chili pepper." Harry Carey Jr., a long-standing member of the Ford stock company, agrees with her. Over the years, several company members have asserted that Jim even took his slant from Ford himself. The director was more than a little crusty.

Ford was in particularly rare form during the making of *Two Rode Together,* for he wasn't crazy about the material. He only agreed to do the picture for the chance to work with Stewart and Widmark and to keep busy. As Widmark says, "He wasn't getting a lot of work at the time, so he took it." He was also attracted by his salary—$225,000 plus 25 percent of the profits.

Given his age—sixty-five—and his disinterest in the material, Ford was listless and uninvolved when principal photography began on October 17, 1960. Then, one of his dearest friends, actor Ward Bond, died while the picture was in production, and his attitude worsened.

Stewart and the director had a minor clash before filming began. The issue was McCabe's hat. Naturally, Jim wanted to wear the gray, sweat-stained good luck charm that had seen him through his Westerns with Tony Mann. Ford didn't like the headgear, not even after Stewart told some whopper about the hat being a family heirloom and how much it would mean to him to wear it on camera. Exasperated, Ford asked Jack Bolton, one of Jim's agents, "Does this SOB have hat approval? I don't remember it being in his contract." Nevertheless, Pappy finally relented.

Once filming began, a rapport developed between the two veterans. "Ford was one of those real macho directors," says Shirley Jones, who played Widmark's love interest, a settler hoping for the return of her captured brother. "Insults were part of the way he showed affection." Just ask John Wayne, whom Ford razzed unmercifully on every picture they did together. "But," Jones continues, "he didn't insult Stewart. He felt he had to be a little softer with him, I thought." Cristal puts the relationship in even rosier terms. "They tiptoed through the tulips with each other," she says. She contrasted the relationship with that between Ford and Wayne, which she saw on the set of *The Alamo,* filmed shortly before *Two Rode Together* (Wayne directed the epic about Texas independence, but Ford hovered in the background much of the time). "With Wayne," she says, "he could just tell him, 'Do this, don't do that,' or 'No, I don't agree. What are you talking about?' He would never talk to Stewart like that. Never. Stewart was someone to respect, to admire, to give his place."

But, like all of Ford's relationships, the one with Jim carried a hint of paranoia. "On *Two Rode Together,*" the star said, "he told me to watch out for Dick Widmark because he was a good actor and that he would start scene stealing if I didn't watch him. Later I learned he'd told Dick the same thing about me. He liked things to be tense. He liked actors to be suspicious of other actors."

Like Hitchcock, Ford wasn't an actor's director. "You never discussed a character," says Widmark, laughing. "Ever. If you asked a question, that was heresy." Perhaps nothing indicated his approach more than the famous scene in which Stewart and Widmark converse beside a riverbank as the lieutenant's men pass behind them. The dialogue is of less consequence than the way the scene was shot—with the camera positioned in the water and the actors trying to talk over nature's turbulence. Widmark recalls the filming: "Now he had to run about seventy-five cavalry and wagons across a river, and we had this six-page scene to do. . . . We sat on the bank or a log or whatever we were sitting on, and he did a two-shot. We did the six pages in one shot. That was it. Cut. Okay. And one slight reverse, where I got up and we started to walk off, and we had a couple of more pages to go there. So it was two setups. And on the second setup we just got up and started to walk away, and he said, 'Cut. That's enough.' So he did this whole damn thing in about two hours, faster than any television guy you could find." Indeed, six pages in two hours is remarkable. Normally, a feature company will shoot about two or three pages a day.

For all Ford's nonchalance during filming—or perhaps because of it—both stars found the old man amusing. Indeed, Widmark calls the making of *Two Rode Together* "a wonderful experience," adding, "I had more fun on that than anything I've done, I think. Because of Jimmy and Ford." He didn't even mind the picture's location, Brackettville, Texas, a dreary backwater whose only attraction was the standing sets created for *The Alamo,* a picture in which Widmark had also costarred. In fact, Dick liked Jim so much, he says, "There are three actors, if I could work with them all the time, I'd never quit. One was Spencer Tracy, [one was] Hank Fonda, and the other Jimmy Stewart. He was just wonderful to work with."

The rapport between the two certainly showed when the picture was released in July of 1961. In fact, the best scenes are those early sequences featuring the bantering McCabe and Jim Gary. The rest of the picture, reflecting an unfinished script and the director's disinterest in the project, was less successful. Philip K. Scheuer of the *Los Angeles Times* called it "probably John Ford's most disappointing western," while *Time* found it pointless. Stewart's crusty marshal did not go unsung, however. "Only rarely in his long career has James Stewart matched the performance now adorning neighborhood screens in *Two Rode Together,*" wrote Eugene Archer in the *New York Times.* He called the characterization "memorable" and "steeped in authenticity." Nevertheless, Jim's first collaboration with John Ford failed to resonate at the box office.

Principal photography on *Two Rode Together* had concluded on December 16, 1960. Stewart's next picture, *How the West Was Won,* didn't go into production until the end of May 1961, five months later. During this hiatus, Jim basically relaxed, serving his annual hitch with the Air Force in February. That year he was stationed at the Pentagon. And on April 17 he appeared at the Academy Awards ceremonies to accept a special Oscar for his friend Gary Cooper, who was too sick to attend. In fact, the legendary actor was dying, a closely guarded secret. In accepting, Stewart said, "We're proud of you, Coop . . . awfully proud." Then tears began to roll down his cheeks. Too choked up to continue, he simply held the statuette high in the air, turned, and left the stage. With that emotional moment, the Hollywood community and the viewers at home came to realize how ill Cooper was. Less than a month later, on May 14, he was gone. Stewart was one of the pallbearers at the funeral, held at the Roman Catholic Church of the Good Shepherd in Beverly Hills. Two weeks later, on May 28, the cameras started to roll on *How the West Was Won.*

Based on a series of articles that ran in *Life* magazine in the spring of 1959, *How the West Was Won* was a Western on an epic scale. The idea behind James R. Webb's Oscar-winning screenplay was to trace the faming of the American frontier from 1838 to 1889 through one fictional family, the Prescotts. It starts when the patriarch and matriarch of the clan, played by Karl Malden and Agnes Moorehead, take their young daughters, Eve and Lilith (Carroll Baker and Debbie Reynolds), down the Ohio River to farm what was then an untamed wilderness. Later, Lilith carries the story to the far West, joining a wagon train "bound for the Promised Land," while Eve's son, Zeb Rawlings (George Peppard), joins the Union Army to fight in the Civil War. Thereafter, he settles with a family of his own in Arizona, where the picture concludes. The story was told in five distinct segments, linked by voice-over narration. A sixth episode, centering around a cattle drive, was eliminated before filming began.

Initially budgeted at $7.5 million, the picture would ultimately cost $15 million, involve a company of twelve thousand, and take eleven months to film—with shooting ranging over nine states.

Adding to the grandeur of the project was the use of Cinerama. The biggest wide-screen process of them all, it involved the employment of three cameras to capture a single image—which was subsequently projected on three adjacent screens. Although the first Cinerama film had been released in 1952, it was a travelogue. *How the West Was Won* was to be one of the initial features to use the process in a narrative fashion, part of a four-picture deal struck in early 1960 between the Cinerama company and MGM. As it turned out, the studio released only one other picture in the format, *The World of the Brothers Grimm*—which beat the Western to the screen.

Befitting the scale of the rest of the project, the film's producer, Bernard Smith, put together an all-star cast. Stewart, one of the first to be hired, would play Carroll Baker's love interest, a trapper by the name of Linus Rawlings. He signed on, in part, because a portion of the picture's proceeds would benefit St. Johns Hospital in Santa Monica, an organization that both he and Gloria actively supported.[1] Other stars included Henry Fonda as a scout, Richard Widmark as a railroad man, Gregory Peck as a gambler, Robert Preston as a wagon master, Lee J. Cobb as a marshal, Raymond Massey as Abraham Lincoln, and John Wayne as William Tecumseh Sherman. Spencer Tracy provided the voice-over narration.

In the name of efficiency, speed, and sanity, three directors were assigned to the project, all of whom had previously worked with Stewart: John Ford would direct the Civil War segment; George Marshall the third segment, dealing with the coming of the railroad; and Henry Hathaway the other three, the river, the wagon train, and the Arizona episodes.

[1] Bing Crosby, who had initially acquired the film rights to the *Life* magazine series, sold them to Metro with the proviso that a portion of the proceeds benefit the hospital.

When the cameras started to roll in Paducah, Kentucky, Ford was at the helm, for the scene in which Zeb Rawlings leaves the family farm to join the Union Army. Stewart was on hand to lend Pappy his support. Then Ford turned the reins over to Hathaway for the river sequence, the one that featured Jim.

"Paducah was selected," Carroll Baker explained in her autobiography, "not only because it was sparsely populated and situated in a vast open countryside, but also because it marks the spot where the Kentucky River, having converged into the Tennessee River, meets in a triangular fork with the Clark and Ohio rivers. In the midst of this watery triangle lay a deserted island, perfect for our filming." The beautiful blond actress, who became a star with Tennessee Williams' *Baby Doll* in 1956, didn't know Stewart before shooting began. Consequently, their car ride from the motel to the location on their first day working together was somewhat awkward. "After the hellos and nice-to-be-working-with-yous," she recalled, "we were both at a loss for words. I racked my brain for something to say, but absolutely nothing entered my head. It was ridiculous how awkward the ride was becoming, and I was forced to say something totally banal about the weather." Finally, Stewart asked her if she knew a game called count the cows. She told him no. To play, he said dead seriously, she should count the cows on her side of the road as they drove to the location; he would do the same on his side. Whoever had counted the most cows when they reached their destination would win. Only Jimmy Stewart could have suggested something like that to a beautiful young actress at the height of major stardom. But it worked. "I know it sounds asinine," she wrote, "but I have never played a game that was more fun. We were passing grazing country and there were so many cows that often the car had zipped by a herd faster than I could count them. We played the game for over an hour and we arrived on location, breathless, giggling, slightly hoarse, and instant good friends."

Playing Linus Rawlings offered Stewart about as much of a challenge as counting cows. The somewhat naive, gentle man, interested in but shy around ladies, was simply an older, frontier version of *The Shopworn Angel*'s Bill Pettigrew. But *How the West Was Won* was about sweep not character development; all of the roles were basically Western archetypes—as the critics noted when the picture premiered in Los Angeles in February of 1963 at a theater specially outfitted for the Cinerama format (the world premiere had taken place in London the previous November).[2]

---

[2] By the time of the Western's release, one hundred theaters in the United States and Europe were equipped to show Cinerama features. After its road show engagement in this format, the picture could be seen in a standard 35-mm print.

The *New Yorker* went so far as to note, "Had the real pioneers been any-thing like as dim-witted as the figures depicted here, the United States would still live huddled well this side of the Appalachian barrier." But no matter. *How the West Was Won* was, to quote Leo Mishkin of the *New York Morning-Telegraph,* "probably the most visually spectacular Western ever put on the screen." By year's end, the picture had grossed $17 mil-lion to become the biggest hit of 1963, beating out such other block-busters as Elizabeth Taylor in *Cleopatra,* Darryl F. Zanuck's *The Longest Day,* and David Lean's *Lawrence of Arabia.*

In July of 1961, shortly after completing his scenes in *How the West Was Won,* Jim went on vacation with Gloria and the Johnsons. They had become world travelers over the last few years, but this trip was special. It was the Stewarts' first African safari. Both Jim and Gloria bagged their share of game. She brought down a leopard and a water buck, Jimmy an eland and a rhinoceros, and each of them got an elephant.

Beyond the thrill of the hunt, they fell in love with the place. "The thing about getting in the jungle that makes it so relaxing," Stewart explained around a year later, "is you have so much to think about—your own safety and the weather and the snakes and malaria. You can't think of two things at once so you can't think of whether your kid is failing to get into college or how your last picture is doing or how the Russians are doing in Berlin. When you do get back, you're really relaxed."

Thereafter, the Stewarts returned to Africa as often as they could. Sometimes, when Jim was tied up with a movie, Gloria took the children. Soon rifles gave way to cameras. "You don't want to kill the animals—you just watch them," Gloria wrote in the summer of 1962 after a return visit. Indeed, she and Jim became animal rights activists and environmental pro-tectionists. In an interview with Ron Reagan Jr. in 1983, Stewart said, "You can't disrupt an area of 500 square miles that has enormous 100 foot trees and streams and everything. You can't just wipe this out because it will affect things for thousands of miles around. It's just criminal."

Their children would share their passion. After several trips to Africa and her subsequent graduation from Lewis and Clark College in Port-land, Oregon, in 1973, Judy worked as a jack-of-all-trades—housekeeper, gardener, tour guide—at what she describes as a "coffee-farm-cum-game-lodge" in Kurachu, Tanzania. Kelly, upon graduation from Stanford in 1973, became assistant to Dian Fossey, the renowned gorilla expert.[3]

[3] Eventually, when Fossey went on sabbatical, Kelly and her future husband, Sandy Harcourt, ran Fossey's celebrated Karisoke Research Center in Rwanda. By then, Kelly had decided to make gorillas her life study as well, earning a Ph.D. from Cambridge University.

But that lay in the future. Jim and Gloria returned from their first safari around the middle of August 1961. Three weeks later, Stewart started work on his second film with John Ford. It was Jim's third Western in a row.

Unlike *Two Rode Together, The Man Who Shot Liberty Valance* was Ford's baby. He had acquired the property, a short story by Dorothy M. Johnson published by *Cosmopolitan* magazine in 1949. He had also engaged Willis Goldbeck and James Warner Bellah to write the screenplay and worked closely with them during its development. And he arranged for Stewart and John Wayne to play the leads (they were later joined by Vera Miles, as the woman torn between them). He even raised $1.6 million—half the financing—after Paramount, the studio where Wayne had recently signed a multipicture contract, agreed to put up the other 50 percent.

This was to be Pappy's elegy to the passing of the frontier, shot, because of budget constraints, in black and white. Stewart was cast as Ranse Stoddard, a principled attorney but a greenhorn, totally unequipped to deal with the likes of Liberty Valance (played by Lee Marvin), the ruthless outlaw he initially encounters on his stagecoach journey into the town of Shinbone. By contrast, Wayne as rancher Tom Doniphon is in his element in the community's free-for-all environment. Nevertheless he's an anachronism in the making—and he knows it. He can recognize and even appreciate civilization's advance, but he wants no part of it. Although he's a decent man, he's more akin to the outlaw than to Stoddard. As the film opens, Ranse has built a political career on his supposed killing of Valance while Doniphon has died alone and forgotten. But, as their story plays out in flashback, filmgoers come to realize that the passing of the strapping rancher and his kind—rugged, hearty, independent individualists—is America's loss. Stoddard, for all his success and fame, is a hollow shell, just another politician.

Although Ford used the breathtaking vistas of the American West as well as or better than any other filmmaker, *Liberty Valance* was shot at Paramount, giving the finished film a curiously claustrophobic quality. In his biography of his grandfather, Dan Ford argued that, by the time principal photography commenced, the director had lost interest in the project. As with *Two Rode Together,* the biographer maintains, Ford was curiously uninvolved while the cameras rolled, willing to cut corners wherever possible. However, Stewart said shortly after principal photography, "Now what pleases me most about this picture is that Ford, for the first time since *Stagecoach,* has worked on every phase of it, never lost interest. He kept up with the cutting, the music, and the dubbing. Every frame is all his, which has not always been the case. And it is basically picture, not talk." If, however, Dan Ford's impression is accurate, Ford's inattention didn't hurt the final product.

Stewart was also pleased to be working with John Wayne, whom he later called "the top of the pile." But, for Duke, *Liberty Valance* was a tough picture. For one thing, he didn't really understand his place in the fabric of the film. He considered Stewart the hero and Marvin the villain. The comic relief came from character actors Edmond O'Brien and Andy Devine—as the town newspaper publisher and lawman, respectively. Where did he fit in? Moreover, during filming, Ford ragged him even more than usual. Some argue that *The Alamo* was at the root of the tension, for Pappy had gone down to Brackettville expecting to take over, and instead Wayne continued shooting the picture himself. In any event, Ford was always on Duke's case. Harry Carey Jr. points out that on a previous Ford-Wayne picture, 1945's *They Were Expendable,* costar Robert Montgomery had asked the director not to belittle Wayne in his presence, and Ford honored the request. Had Stewart done likewise, Pappy might have let up, but Jim kept silent.

Then Stewart spoke up about something else and incurred Ford's wrath himself. It happened late in the shooting schedule, during the filming of a scene involving Woody Strode, who played Doniphon's sidekick, Pompey. Ford came over to Jim and asked him what he thought of Strode's costume. The star looked at the African-American, dressed in overalls and a beat-up hat, and said, "Waall, s'a little Uncle Remus, isn't it?" He knew immediately that he'd said the wrong thing. And he was right, for Ford had selected the costume himself. Stewart tried to backpedal, but Pappy, quickly working his way up to fury, asked the assistant director to gather the entire cast and crew together. He then told the assemblage they had a racist in their midst. After going on in that vein for several moments, he dismissed the company and ordered Stewart off the set. "I was silently walking back to my dressing room," the star recalled, "so humiliated I couldn't even speak, and then I felt a tap on my back. I turned around to find Duke there, and he was just beaming." Said his costar, "You thought you were going to make it right through, didn't you?" But Stewart was philosophical about the incident. As he put it, "It was all a part of the game of making movies with John Ford."

The Man Who Shot Liberty Valance opened at the Capitol Theatre in New York on May 23, 1962. Critics admired the craft behind the picture, especially the vignettes of frontier town life, but John L. Scott of the *Los Angeles Times* considered it "old hat" overall, his *New York Times* counterpart, Andrew H. Weiler, called it "creaky," and Brendan Gill of the *New Yorker* dubbed it "a parody of Mr. Ford's best work." Stewart and Wayne were effective as the contrasting protagonists, but Jim looked awfully mature to be playing a lawyer just starting out.

Today *The Man Who Shot Liberty Valance* is considered Ford's last great picture. The reevaluation reflects the changes in the national psyche over the last three decades, for in a post-Vietnam, post-Watergate environment, Ford's disdain for political image-making and his sorrow at the passing of rugged individualism resonate in a way that they could not in 1962, when a young, vigorous, handsome John F. Kennedy was in the White House.

After Stewart's variety of roles in the fifties, the sixties brought far more routine fare, with Westerns comprising 75 percent of his feature film output during the decade. Three of the four other pictures were domestic comedies written by Nunnally Johnson and directed by Henry Koster.

The first was *Mr. Hobbs Takes a Vacation,* based on the 1954 novel *Mr. Hobbs' Vacation,* by Edward Streeter, a New York banker. Streeter's forte was middle-aged businessmen who are perplexed by modern family life and the seeming decline of middle-class society. A previous novel, *Father of the Bride,* which had inspired a hit movie starring Spencer Tracy and Elizabeth Taylor, examined the contemporary American wedding. In *Mr. Hobbs,* he considered the family vacation, with his hapless hero, Roger Hobbs of Cleveland, renting a summer house in an East Coast resort community called Rock Harbor. Hobbs is joined there by his wife, Peggy, and his teenage daughter, Kate. In time, they also play host to his two married daughters, Susan and Jane, their husbands, and his grandchildren, as well as two eccentric acquaintances, the Turners (played in the film by John McGiver and Marie Wilson).

Independent producer Jerry Wald acquired the novel as the eighth and final project in his multipicture deal with Fox. He then hired Nunnally Johnson to write the screenplay—after offering the assignment to humorists S. J. Perelman and James Thurber. Johnson, a Georgia-born former journalist, had a string of notable pictures to his credit, including *The Grapes of Wrath, Tobacco Road, The Gunfighter, The Desert Fox,* and *The Three Faces of Eve.* In scripting *Hobbs,* he adhered to the tone, characters, and basic premise of Streeter's novel, but created new incidents drawn from his experiences with his own children, including a charming sequence in which Hobbs, chaperoning a local dance, helps his youngest daughter, Kate (played by newcomer Lauri Peters), overcome the embarrassment of having braces on her teeth. "The girl with braces," says Johnson's widow, Doris, "that was our second daughter. We had such experiences with her. She was always shying away from smiling or opening her mouth, she felt so self-conscious." The model for an older daughter whose husband is having a hard time landing a job was Marjorie Fowler, Johnson's child by his first marriage and a distinguished film editor.

While the novel was told in the third person and covered events as they unfolded, Johnson spun out the screenplay in flashback with Hobbs providing voice-over narration. He wrote with Stewart in mind. "Nunnally had a high regard for Jimmy," Doris Johnson recalls, "and I think Jimmy felt that way about him. He liked Jimmy's style. It seemed to fit his way of writing humor."

Originally, Leo McCarey, the Academy Award–winning director of *The Awful Truth* and *Going My Way*, was slated to direct. When he fell ill, Stewart suggested Henry Koster. In the years since *No Highway in the Sky*, the director had taken the helm on a wide range of pictures, from religious epics *(The Robe)* to war stories *(D-Day the Sixth of June)* to musicals *(Flower Drum Song)*. His hiring and the casting of Maureen O'Hara as Mrs. Hobbs were announced the same day, April 12, 1961.

Like Stewart, O'Hara was a member of the John Ford stock company, having starred in *How Green Was My Valley, The Quiet Man,* and *The Long Gray Line*. Tall with beautiful red hair and a hint of her native Ireland in her speech, she often played strong, fiery women—rather the opposite of homemaker Peggy Hobbs. Which is why—in that curious Hollywood fashion—Wald started looking to replace her almost immediately after signing her up. With Stewart and Koster's support, he worked out a deal with O'Hara whereby she would bow out of *Hobbs* in favor of another, as yet undetermined, film for Fox. Then he, Stewart, and Koster pursued just about every other mature leading lady around: Loretta Young, Polly Bergen, Lucille Ball, Olivia de Havilland, Ginger Rogers, and Rosalind Russell, to name just a few. But one by one, these actresses proved unavailable, too costly, not quite right, or not interested. After three months of looking, they decided their initial impulse hadn't been so bad after all, and Wald schmoozed O'Hara into coming back.

Since the picture went into production on November 21, shooting on the chilly East Coast was out of the question, so the setting was changed to a California locale—with the Hobbs family coming from St. Louis instead of Cleveland (presumably on the theory that Missourians would more readily trek to the West Coast than Ohioans). Filming took place on Carillo Beach, a state park, where the exterior of the Hobbses' rented Victorian house—constructed at Fox—was mounted. The company also worked briefly at the Newport Harbor Yacht Club—for a sailboat sequence involving Hobbs and his son, a character added by Johnson and played by Michael Burns. Otherwise, the rest of the picture, including the house interiors, was shot on Fox's soundstages and briefly at the studio's ranch. The work went smoothly, but Stewart suffered a major personal loss during filming: on December 28, his father, Alex, passed away at the age of eighty-nine. Jim arrived in Indiana, Pennsylvania, in time to say farewell, but the blow was incalculable. As Hedda Hopper had noted in 1954, "If any crisis arises, Jimmy is immediately on the phone to Indiana, Pa., seeking advice from his sage old father. If there is no particular problem, Jimmy calls several times a week just for conversation." After the funeral, he quickly went back to Hollywood, having missed only one day of production.

On May 11, 1962, Fox staged what it called "an almost premiere" of *Mr. Hobbs Takes a Vacation* at the Fox Wilshire Theater. Present were six of Stewart's leading ladies—Rosalind Russell, Ruth Hussey, Joanne Dru, Lee Remick, Shirley Jones, and, of course, Maureen O'Hara. On the twenty-fifth, the picture opened in Los Angeles, and on June 15, at New York's Paramount. The notices were moderately favorable, with Philip K. Scheuer calling it a "winner," *Cue* "an amiable comedy," and *Variety* a "fun picture." Given Stewart's marquee value for the older crowd and the presence of Fabian for the teen market (the rock idol played young Kate Hobbs' boyfriend, a role created for the film), *Hobbs* ended up the nineteenth highest grossing picture of the year.

But *Mr. Hobbs* is a creature of its time. It is occasionally amusing, but mostly it is broadly played, with characters who bear little resemblance to real life. In fact, with its wisecracking, mildly rebellious kids, bewildered father, and unflappable mom, the picture is more akin to a TV sitcom than to the best of Stewart's previous comedies. As a consequence, *Mr. Hobbs* is of only passing interest today.

It was only mid-January when *Mr. Hobbs* wrapped, but Stewart's output for the rest of 1962 consisted solely of two TV appearances. The second, on November 20, marked one of his and Gloria's returns to *The Jack Benny Show*. Before that, on October 4, came a sixty-minute drama called "Flashing Spikes," based on a novella by Frank O'Rourke, which kicked off the second season of ABC's anthology series *Alcoa Premiere*. The drama was directed by John Ford.

For their only TV project together, Jim and Pappy turned to the world of major league baseball. Stewart played Slim Conway, a former pro who was expelled from the league years earlier for taking a bribe to throw a game. Now he's accused of bribing his protégé, Bill Riley, a pivotal figure in the present World Series. John Wayne's son, Patrick, played the young baseball star. His father made a cameo appearance, and Los Angeles Dodgers pitcher Don Drysdale had a featured role.

*   *   *

Stewart was relatively idle in 1962 because of a major crisis at 20th Century–Fox, where his second Nunnally Johnson–Henry Koster comedy, *Take Her, She's Mine,* had been scheduled to start filming on August 15. The picture had been put on hold, along with all of the studio's other projects, because the making of *Cleopatra* starring Elizabeth Taylor had left Fox virtually bankrupt. Returning to the studio's helm after his personal triumph with *The Longest Day,* Darryl F. Zanuck shut down production entirely until he could reorganize the operation and evaluate each property in development. That took nine months.

With a pay-or-play contract in hand, Stewart could have forced Fox to remit his salary anyway. But he didn't hold the studio to the obligation. "They're having enough trouble," he told Louella Parsons, "and I want to see them get out of it. I'll make the picture for them any time they're ready." Such gestures made Stewart a beloved figure in Hollywood.

Take Her, She's Mine was virtually a direct descendant of *Mr. Hobbs Takes a Vacation.* The source this time was a Broadway comedy by Henry and Phoebe Ephron, authors of *The Jackpot.* The play had opened on Broadway on December 21, 1961, with newcomer Elizabeth Ashley as Mollie Michaelson, a pretty, free-spirited college kid, and Art Carney and Phyllis Thaxter as the parents trying to cope with her myriad personality changes as she matures. Robert Coleman of the *New York Mirror* called it a "very human study of the problems of present-day parents," and most of his colleagues agreed. Beyond the ring of truth, the Ephrons' way with dialogue, including dashes of topical humor, took precedence over the rather slight plot.

In Nunnally Johnson's hands, the characters became even more stereotypical than in his last collaboration with Stewart and the situations more farcical. But the connection between Frank Michaelson and Roger Hobbs is unmistakable. Like Hobbs, Michaelson is a professional man, in this case a lawyer, living comfortably in the suburbs with his wife and daughters. He is just as bewildered by his children and the trappings of modern life as the St. Louis businessman. Maybe more so, because Michaelson is constantly being taken for Jimmy Stewart, a running gag that the real movie star didn't care for (he thought it would take audiences out of the story by reminding them of his real identity, a valid criticism). Like Peggy Hobbs, Anne Michaelson, played by Audrey Meadows, is the stabilizing influence in the family. And Mollie is simply what Kate Hobbs would probably become, given a few years. (To play the coed, Fox borrowed Sandra Dee from Universal. As with Fabian in *Mr. Hobbs,* the goal was to capture the teen market at the box office.) Adding to the similarity between the two properties was Johnson's decision to again use the flashback motif. In this case, Stewart's character takes moviegoers through the story as he accounts for a series of embarrassing public incidents before the school board that he chairs. Moreover, his pompous nemesis on the board is played by John McGiver, who was the pompous guest in *Hobbs*.

Finally, like Stewart's previous domestic comedy, *Take Her, She's Mine* primarily plays out away from the central character's home turf. In this case, Michaelson goes to his daughter's college, where he gets arrested for participating—unintentionally—in a ban-the-bomb demonstration. He also follows her to Paris, where she has earned an art scholarship. The French sequence, which consumes roughly the last third of the film, is not in the play. Zanuck, who had been living in Paris before returning to Fox, wanted to give the picture an international flavor and insisted that Johnson carry the action to the City of Lights. The screenwriter protested, but to no avail.

Of course, with the studio's financial crisis, the company didn't film in Paris. Rather, the entire picture was shot on the Fox lot—from April 23, 1963, until June 13. It was the first project to go into production after the nine-month ban.

Sandra Dee was in awe of Stewart when filming began. She was no newcomer, having made her first feature in 1957, when she was only fifteen. Since then, she had become the popular teen star of *A Summer Place*, *Gidget*, and *Tammy Tell Me True*. But, having never worked with someone of Stewart's stature before, she was so intimidated that she was afraid to say more than good morning to him when they met on the set each day. Finally, Jim asked Henry Koster if he was doing something wrong; he couldn't figure out why Dee didn't like him. After Koster relayed Stewart's concern to the perky, blond actress, she tried to relax with her costar. "But it was really hard," she recalls. "It was really hard not to call him 'Mr. Stewart.' I mean, I was only eighteen years old. I tried to get 'Jimmy' out and it just always came out 'Mr. Stewart.' "[4]

Eventually, however, their scenes together loosened her up, and they grew rather close. "Jimmy is without a doubt the consummate actor," she recalls. "When I was working with him, he was my father, he was Audrey's husband. We clicked. He adopted me as his daughter for the production, and I adopted him as my father." She even wound up talking to him about her problems with her then husband, singer-actor Bobby Darin.

But she felt she saw the real Jimmy Stewart when they went on a ten-day junket to promote the picture starting in Abilene, Texas, on November 4, 1963. "I mean, he was like the host, the emcee, the comedian," she recalls. "He kept everybody's spirits up. On the picture, he did one

---

[4] Born on April 23, 1942, Dee was, in fact, twenty-one during filming.

thing. He was Mr. Michaelson. On this thing, he took charge like an entrepreneur would." She was particularly surprised by Stewart's sense of humor, saying, "When he wasn't on the set or in character, he was the funniest man to be around. And I've been around some clowns. I think he's funny because he never changes his intonation on things. So you never know what's coming out of his mouth. He can tell you the bird died or he can tell you something hilarious, and you have to listen, 'cause it's in the same tone."

Take Her, She's Mine was not nearly such a laugh riot. When the picture opened at Manhattan's Criterion Theatre on November 13, 1963, Leo Mishkin of the *New York Morning-Telegraph* compared it unfavorably with the play, finding the movie "drawn with broad, heavy strokes as to make it grossly and dismayingly exaggerated. The people here aren't real; they're caricatures of what they once were, and what they should be." Bosley Crowther's reaction in the *New York Times* was even more scathing: "Let's all be thankful that society is generally, if not entirely, free of such farcical types as the doting father played by James Stewart. . . . And let's hope the screen will not be burdened for too much longer with such drivel as this old-hat Hollywood picture."

Surprisingly, despite such notices, *Take Her, She's Mine* performed well at the box office, outdrawing such concurrent releases as *Becket* starring Peter O'Toole and Richard Burton, Anthony Mann's *Fall of the Roman Empire*, John Wayne in *Circus World*, and a better comedy based on another Broadway play, *Sunday in New York*, with Jane Fonda, Rod Taylor, and Cliff Robertson.

One day, John Ford told producer Bernard Smith, "I've killed a lot of Indians in my time," referring to his treatment of Native Americans in his Westerns. "I want to make amends. I've read a book called *Cheyenne Autumn* by Mari Sandoz. I'd like to make a picture of it and I'd like you to work with me." Delighted, Smith convinced Jack Warner to finance and distribute the project, then called *The Long Flight*.

Sandoz' book, published in 1957, detailed the 1878 trek of three hundred men, women, and children of the Cheyenne nation. Disgusted with conditions on their barren reservation in Oklahoma, they sought to return to their homeland in the Yellowstone area of Wyoming, some fifteen hundred miles away. Having left the settlement without authorization, they were pursued en route by ten thousand members of the U.S. cavalry.

Initially, Ford wanted to faithfully adhere to the historical record. He also wanted to cast unknown actors in the Native American roles and have them speak Cheyenne rather than English. Soon, however, the practical demands of making a big-budget Hollywood film diluted these ambitions. Ricardo Montalban, Sal Mineo, Dolores Del Rio, and Gilbert Roland were cast as the principal Indian characters, and of course, they spoke English. In addition, Carroll Baker was hired to portray a fictional Quaker teacher who accompanies the Cheyenne on their journey. Naturally, she would have something of a romance with one of the pursuing cavalry officers, played by Richard Widmark. Ford also added scenes set in Washington, D.C. These featured Edward G. Robinson as Secretary of the Interior Carl Schurz. Robinson replaced Ford's first choice, Spencer Tracy, who fell ill prior to the start of filming.

But the oddest change was the insertion of an episode having virtually nothing to do with the Cheyenne trek. The Indians passed through Kansas on their way north, and according to Bernard Smith, contemporary issues of the *Dodge City Times* reported that bands of the local citizens were roaming the plains in the hope of taking on the Indians; but they accomplished nothing. Moreover, said Smith, the research revealed the presence of Wyatt Earp and Doc Holliday in Dodge at the time. Bat Masterson was the sheriff, but he was in Hot Springs, Arkansas.

From these strands, Ford and screenwriter James R. Webb fashioned a satiric sequence they called "The Battle of Dodge City." Pappy then hired Stewart to play Earp and decked him out in a white suit and broad panama hat, à la the opening sequence in *Two Rode Together* (but bearing no resemblance to the real Earp whatsoever). "It's just a ten-minute bit," Stewart told Louella Parsons shortly after he finished the assignment, "but any time Ford says, 'I think you'll be good in this,' I'll jump." (In the director's cut, the sequence ran twenty-four minutes.) To play Doc, Ford chose Jim's *Bend of the River/Man From Laramie* costar, Arthur Kennedy. Elizabeth Allen, who had been featured in the director's previous picture, *Donovan's Reef,* was cast as a madam called Guinevere Plantagenet.

Essentially, the sequence consisted of two scenes. In the first, Wyatt, Doc, and their cronies are playing poker in a saloon—with Guinevere hovering nearby. Then comes the news that the Cheyenne are on the march, and the townsfolk, determined to attack the Indians before the Indians can attack them, run amok, forcing a reluctant Wyatt to take charge. The second scene follows Earp, Doc, Guinevere, and the townsfolk out to the prairie where one shot from an Indian who has nothing to do with the Cheyenne band sends them scattering.

These were the first scenes shot for *Cheyenne Autumn.* Beginning on September 23, 1963, the company filmed the saloon interior on a Warners soundstage, then moved to the town shots on the backlot, and finally ended up at the Conejo Ranch for the chaotic climax. "John Ford rarely told you what he had in mind," Stewart recalled, "and kept you guessing." He remembered specifically the moment when he and Arthur Kennedy were to come out of the saloon, board a buggy with the townsfolk—about two hundred extras—swirling around them, and then head out of town. "Well, he told us to go in one direction," Jim said, "but he had all his assistants tell the crowd that we were going in a different direction so that when we charged into the crowd they didn't know and there was a great confusion and people got pushed by the horses and screamed and yelled and ran and it was just a wonderful scene!"

They finished the sequence on October 4. Three days later, Ford was in his favorite location, Monument Valley, Utah, working on the rest of the picture. In the months that followed, he and his company traveled to Colorado, Wyoming, and Arizona as well.

Cheyenne Autumn was screened for 184 members of the international press in a four-day celebration in Cheyenne, Wyoming, starting on October 1, 1964. Stewart was present, as were many of his costars. So, too, were Secretary of the Interior Stuart Udall, the governor of Wyoming, the state's U.S. senators, and the governors of the states the Cheyenne crossed on their journey. The festivities included a barbecue, a trip to historic Fort Laramie, a rodeo, and a parade. The climax of the long weekend came with the showing of the picture on Saturday, October 3.

What the audience saw was a visual feast. Photographed in deep, saturated colors by William H. Clothier, *Cheyenne Autumn* featured some of the most beautiful Western landscapes ever captured on film. Moreover, Ford and screenwriter Webb courageously confronted a little known and shameful moment in America's past. But the actors playing the Indians were the exact opposite of what the director had hoped for at the outset of the project; they were simply not credible as Cheyenne men and women. Moreover, at a running time of 154 minutes, the basically downbeat picture was interminable.

The biggest flaw, however, was the Dodge City sequence. It came from nowhere and led to nothing, bore only the most tangential relationship to the rest of the story, and had a wild, comic quality that was totally at odds with the overall tone of the film. Given Stewart's marquee value, the sequence couldn't be eliminated entirely, but, before the picture's world premiere in London on October 15, Warners forced Ford to make dramatic cuts.[5] In fact, the director eliminated entirely the townsfolk's wild ride out to the plains to meet the Indians and the ironic aftermath. Without that segment, the part that remained made no sense at all.

Some of Ford's colleagues champion the merits of the sequence. Bernard Smith maintains that it was a "very important segment. It says much [about the whites' attitudes] that we were unwilling to say in direct

---

[5] The American premiere came in Denver on December 18.

dialogue." On a more pragmatic level, Elizabeth Allen explains that to Ford it was a badly needed bit of comic relief, and he purposely placed it just before the intermission that would break up the picture's initial road show engagements. Otherwise, he told her, audiences might not come back for the second half.

Harry Carey Jr. has a different take on the sequence's inclusion. "The only guess that some of us old-timers have about that," he says, "is the fact that Ford wanted to work with Jimmy again, and he just put that in there." Carey adds that Pappy "really enjoyed directing this sequence." But both Carey and Richard Widmark agree that "The Battle of Dodge City" was at odds with the rest of the picture. "Well, it was like two different movies," says the latter. (For those who would like to judge for themselves, the entire sequence has been restored for the videocassette release of the picture.)

The Dodge City sequence notwithstanding, the critics savaged *Cheyenne Autumn*. Although Bosley Crowther of the *New York Times* called it "a beautiful and powerful motion picture that stunningly combines a profound and passionate story of mistreatment of American Indians with some of the most magnificent and energetic cavalry-and-Indian lore ever put upon the screen," the *New Yorker* dubbed it "far and away the most boring picture of 1964." *Newsweek* argued that "Ford has apparently forgotten everything he ever knew about actors, about cameras, about the Indians, and about the West," and *Time* archly decided that it had "everything it takes to make a great western epic, except greatness." Ending up a disappointing twenty-eighth among the year's top-grossing films, *Cheyenne Autumn* marked the conclusion of Stewart's fruitful collaboration with John Ford. The director made only two subsequent pictures, neither of them a Western.

Dear Brigitte, which went into production seven months after the filming of "The Battle of Dodge City," brought an end to another of Stewart's long-term relationships, this one with Henry Koster.

Based on the satirical novel *Erasmus with Freckles* by John Haase, this domestic comedy, the third in the Stewart-Koster-Johnson trilogy for Fox, centered around a highly regarded poet/college professor, Robert Lake, who lives on a houseboat in San Francisco Bay with his wife and two children. His son, eight-year-old Erasmus, is a mathematical genius who writes love letters to the French film goddess Brigitte Bardot. After the boy wins a small fortune handicapping horse races, he and his father travel to France to meet BB in the flesh.

Just as *Take Her, She's Mine* was more farcical than *Mr. Hobbs Takes a Vacation*, so *Dear Brigitte* was less rooted in real life than *Take Her, She's*

Mine. Where, for example, Hobbs and Michaelson were conventional businessmen who are simply baffled by social norms, Lake is an absent-minded, sometimes ill-tempered eccentric, who lives on a boat and rails against the evils of academe.

The professor's nonconformity might have sparked some interesting comic turns, but *Dear Brigitte* settles for satire with an iron fist. Stewart's first appearance, for instance, finds him fulminating against nuclear power as he storms out of a university building, his arms loaded down with books—a moment that is neither funny nor thought-provoking. Likewise, a subsequent scene in which Lake applies for unemployment offered a chance to poke fun at governmental bureaucracy, but it is handled in a pedestrian fashion, with the clerk, a frumpy, middle-aged woman, tossing slight sexual innuendos at the professor. Even the swipes at psychiatry, an easy target, fall flat.

Beyond the lack of engaging satire, the plot gets tangled up in the horse-racing business, a scheme abetted by a couple of con men (played by John Williams and Jesse White). And Fabian, the teen idol from *Mr. Hobbs*, returns as Erasmus' sister's boyfriend, yet another attempt to exploit the youth market at the box office. Neither the young man nor the con artists are in Haase's novel, and their story lines contribute little to the picture's appeal. Nor, for that matter, does Ed Wynn as a retired sea captain who lives with the Lake family. He narrates the picture.

That Nunnally Johnson had no feel for the project is evident. "I hadn't wanted to do it," the screenwriter recalled. "I didn't think there was enough material in it, but I really allowed myself to be persuaded to do it. Jimmie [*sic*] would sign if I would write it, and Koster would get a job if Jimmie would sign. It all got around to that, one depending on another."

When Koster suggested that they add the captain, a character who would speak directly to the audience as in Tony Richardson's Oscar-winning comedy *Tom Jones,* Johnson withdrew from the project. Koster, who also produced the picture (Jerry Wald having died in 1962), replaced him with Hal Kanter, who had written several Elvis Presley pictures as well as *Move Over, Darling,* the remake of *My Favorite Wife,* starring Doris Day and James Garner. At Johnson's request, Kanter received sole credit for the screenplay, even though much of the material was Nunnally's.

During filming, which took place between May 11 and July 24, 1964, Stewart developed a warm relationship with Billy Mumy, the cute child playing his son. In fact, Jim later told Hollywood reporter Bill Davidson that his costar was the "only kid actor I knew who was worth a damn." Although he was only ten, Mumy had been performing professionally for five years. He had a handful of previous features and dozens of TV shows to his credit. By coincidence, Gloria Stewart had been his Sunday-school teacher at the Beverly Hills Presbyterian Church.

Reflecting on his relationship with Stewart, Mumy, who has since made the transition to adult actor, says, "We had a great time together for those ten weeks or so that we spent together in '64." He particularly remembers the star playing catch with him while they ran lines between takes. When they filmed the houseboat sequences in Sausalito, Jim even took Billy to a Giants game at Candlestick Park and got him a ball auto-graphed by all the players.

They also went to Paris together for the climactic scene with Bardot, which was filmed on a set designed to resemble the actress' real home. "We actually had to film the sequence with her twice," Mumy recalls. The first time she wore a short, low-cut dress. After reviewing the dailies, the executives at Fox decided that the costume was too sugges-tive and ordered a retake. "She wore the same dress," Mumy explains, "but then she ended up having this big corsage in the middle of her cleavage." Extremely well guarded with just a minimal command of English—she memorized her lines in the film phonetically—Bardot had little contact with Stewart and Mumy off camera. "Put it this way," Bill says. "When we weren't filming, Mr. Stewart and I were sitting in our chairs and talking together and tossing the ball around. And Miss Bardot was immediately herded off to her little special trailer away from every-body, and when we were ready to roll, she would be escorted back to the set." He hastens to add that "she wasn't the slightest bit snobbish, she was just kind of kept separate from everybody." Later, BB would remem-ber Stewart fondly, saying, "I thought he was absolutely extraordinary. He was so kind and considerate and had such professional integrity. I thought he was one of the greatest stars in the world."

Despite the presence of the French sex symbol and the Presley-like Fabian, *Dear Brigitte* failed to come close to the success of *Mr. Hobbs* or *Take Her, She's Mine.* If anything, when the picture opened in Manhattan on January 27, 1965, the combination of a foreign film star, a teen idol, Jimmy Stewart, Ed Wynn, the houseboat, the family's music fests (with Stewart playing the accordion, naturally), the campus scenes, the scenes between Erasmus and the psychiatrist, the horse-racing angle, and so forth, became too much. As Bosley Crowther of the *New York Times* observed, "A little something for everybody is what it appears they've tried to cram into *Dear Brigitte.*"

Moreover, the screenplay's lack of finesse was reinforced by Koster's labored direction and Stewart's forced performance. The *New York Her-ald-Tribune*'s Judith Crist attacked the "inanities of the plot and the clichés of character," while *Newsweek* simply called the film "a vulgar little comedy."

Clearly the string was played out. Sadly, Nunnally Johnson was capable of far richer material than he ever mined for his three Stewart films.

As for Koster, he and Stewart got along, but Koster did little to elicit performances from Jim or the other actors with whom they worked. "I don't remember Henry giving us much direction at all," says Audrey Meadows, Stewart's costar in *Take Her, She's Mine*. "When I think back, he must have been intimidated by Jimmy, because of all the work I've done, I never remember a director doing so little." Bill Mumy adds, "I don't recall him ever taking me aside or taking any other actor in that film aside and giving them a focus, concentrate on this, here's what we're doing, the scene is about this. No, Henry Koster was a quiet guy who made a nice, little family film. It was no big deal."

Of course, Stewart was accustomed to directors who left the performances to him. In melodramas that was fine. But his best work in comedy came under the likes of George Stevens, Frank Capra, and George Cukor, gifted craftsmen who could help him shape his delivery. Left to his own devices, he often mugged and pressed too hard. And except for *Harvey*, where he had his prior Broadway experience as a guide, this was the case in his comedies with Koster.

Moreover, in a strange sort of way, the domestic trilogy began to desex him. Although his characters were married to three maturely attractive women—played by Maureen O'Hara, Audrey Meadows, and Glynis Johns—he grew progressively less virile with each outing. He was fifty-six when *Dear Brigitte* was filmed, and his paternity of an eight-year-old boy bordered on the incongruous, despite his use of a sandy brown hairpiece.

Stewart must have known it was time to move on, for he never again attempted a big-screen role like those in the Johnson-Koster tradition. There were still other genres—and the fertile field of television—to explore, but after *Dear Brigitte*, his film career in light comedy was over.

EIGHTEEN

Andrew McLaglen and
James Lee Barrett

Relationships end, and new ones begin. In 1964, Stewart's collaborations with John Ford, Nunnally Johnson, and Henry Koster concluded, but that same year, he formed new partnerships with director Andrew V. McLaglen and screenwriter James Lee Barrett. Jim would make four pictures with each of them. The project that brought the trio together was *Shenandoah*—which also took Stewart back to Universal Pictures for the first time since *Night Passage*.[1]

A native of South Carolina and a former Marine, Barrett had previously worked in television and had written a few features, including the George Stevens epic *The Greatest Story Ever Told*. But *Fields of Honor*, as *Shenandoah* was originally called, was something special. His sweeping family saga set against the turbulence of the Civil War was a deft mixture of action, poignant drama, and comedy in the classic tradition. The patriarch of the clan, Charlie Anderson—Stewart's role—was particularly well drawn. The Virginia farmer is feisty and opinionated with a unique point of view but also capable of great tenderness. A widower, he is determined to keep his family— six sons and a daughter—out of the devastating conflict, but when his beloved youngest boy is taken prisoner by Union soldiers, he is roused to action.

"*Shenandoah* is the best yarn I've come across for years," Stewart said during filming. He considered the story a throwback to the kind of sentimental, but well-made, family pictures that Louis B. Mayer loved so much. Stewart was also pleased that the project was written directly for the screen rather than adapted from a book or a play. Except for *How the West Was Won*, which wasn't really a Jimmy Stewart picture, he hadn't worked on original material since *Strategic Air Command* a decade earlier.

It was Jim who involved Andrew McLaglen. The son of the Oscar-winning actor Victor McLaglen, Andy had been an assistant director to

---

[1] The previous year, Universal had been acquired by MCA, the giant talent agency that had represented Stewart as well as many other major creative artists in the motion picture industry. As Wasserman and company could not operate a movie studio and a talent agency at the same time, Jim had to find new representation. He went with Chasin, Park, Citron, owned by former MCA employees.

John Ford (with whom his dad made several pictures). He was, there-fore, part of that special band, like Stewart, whose mettle had been tested by the crusty but beloved director. He then moved into television, where he directed dozens of episodes of *Gunsmoke* and *Have Gun Will Travel.* His first feature, *Gun the Man Down,* was released in 1956, but it was his seriocomic 1963 Western, *McLintock!* with John Wayne and Maureen O'Hara, that really launched his big-screen career. He and Stewart knew each other casually; they even played golf occasionally at the Bel-Air Country Club, where they both were members. But they were hardly close friends. So McLaglen was surprised when Jim phoned one day and told him he had a script that the director might want to do with him. After Andy read it, *Shenandoah* became the first project in a six-picture deal that he signed with Universal.

McLaglen considered shooting the film in its original setting, the Shenandoah Valley. "But I'd heard about the lushness of Eugene, Oregon," he recalls, and after spending a week in the west-central part of the state, he decided to film there. Principal photography commenced on August 11, 1964, and when the cast and crew left Oregon about five weeks later, roughly 60 to 70 percent of the picture was in the can. The bal-ance of the scenes were shot at Universal and at the Disney studio's ranch.

Looking back on the work in Oregon, Rosemary Forsyth, who made her feature film debut as Charlie's daughter, Jennie, says, "It was won-derful, it was beautiful," adding, "We became in many ways, I feel, a lit-tle family on that movie. It was almost like not doing a film. It was almost like hanging out with your buddies. I thought, it being my first movie, that that's how all films would be. And, of course, they're not." She cred-ited Stewart with setting the tone that made such camaraderie possible.

She also loved working with him. "The naturalness he has," she says, "is like you and I sitting here talking to each other. So it was a wonderful experience." She further notes, "But there's no playing movie star with him . . . it's just working with another actor. He was there, he was avail-able, he was professional. And I forgot that he was *Jimmy Stewart.*" She was especially impressed by the scene she shared with him at the ceme-tery, when Charlie talks about her deceased mother. "I literally started to cry because he was so beautiful doing that," she recalls. "That was an experience in my life and my career that I'll never forget. On this hill with this actor, listening to him speak. I just thought, 'Whoa.' "

Philip Alford, who played the young kidnapped son, also relished working with Stewart. "I felt like I was part of his family," he says. "Warm and open and like he'd known me all his life." The young actor, fifteen when filming began and best known as Jeb in *To Kill a Mockingbird,* also found the star, in his words, "just exactly the way you see him on the screen. The same warm personality. No fear. Totally confident about himself and how he was.... And that's what impressed me most about him. Never saw him lose his cool. Never saw him get angry. Never saw him flustered. Never saw him unprepared. He was always right there the whole time."

Stewart's preparation for a role *was* awesome. During the making of *Shenandoah*, for example, McLaglen noticed that Stewart *used* gestures. They were not simply expressions of the actor's innate behavior but carefully planned bits of business. "If he is doing a scene," the director explains, "a two-page scene, for instance, and on a given word in a given speech, he scratches the back of his neck, you think, 'Oh, that's a good old Jimmy Stewartism.' But he'll do it the same way every time. In other words, he's got that figured out." Pauses and facial expressions were also carefully planned, McLaglen adds.

The director also refers to the pivotal scene when a young Confederate soldier accidentally kills one of Anderson's sons, and Charlie becomes nearly psychotic. It was reminiscent of the bar scene between Stewart and Dan Duryea in *Winchester '73* and the moment in *Bend of the River* when Arthur Kennedy's Cole Garrett betrays Stewart's Glyn McLyntock. In all three cases, the man of control finally lets go. McLaglen calls them "moments where he comes out of the escape hatch." The director says that playing that sort of rage comes easily to Stewart: "When Jimmy gets tough, he's fierce. He's a strong man. Listen, he wasn't just a play general in the Air Force. He was a real general. He's got a lot of character."

Occasionally, that toughness would be evident in real life as well. Andy Low had seen it when Stewart was the operations officer of the 453rd Bombardment Group. Billy Wilder and Leland Hayward felt it when Stewart wanted to leave Paris before the start of principal photography on *The Spirit of St. Louis*. And McLaglen glimpsed it when Universal made minor changes to *Shenandoah* after Stewart saw what he had been told was the final cut. The actor had previously waived his contractual right to billing the same size as the title, recognizing that making his name equal to the word *Shenandoah* would be unwieldy. But, says McLaglen, when Jimmy saw the re-edited film at a Directors Guild preview, he "came out of that theater, he grabbed [the film's producer, Robert] Arthur, and he said, 'Listen, don't you expect me to do anything about that goddamn billing. Forget what I said and don't ask for any favors.' " In fact, Arthur hadn't been responsible for the re-edit, and Stewart's fury gave Arthur the leverage he needed to have the changes eliminated. Says McLaglen, "They spent about forty thousand, fifty thousand dollars putting that picture back together, I tell you." More to the point, when Stewart felt betrayed, he reacted in no uncertain terms.

When *Shenandoah* opened at neighborhood theaters in New York on

July 28, 1965, there wasn't much fanfare. "For Universal, it was kind of a routine [picture]," says McLaglen. "They didn't know what they had, let me put it that way." The critical response was lukewarm as well, with the film's sentimental tone and length—105 minutes—the object of most of the carping. But Stewart's personal notices were solid. Howard Thompson of the *New York Times* found him "perfectly cast," *Newsweek* praised his "strength and simplicity," and the *Christian Science Monitor* called the film "James Stewart's movie. The whole casual-seeming length of him dominates the screen, threatening to overshadow the Civil War itself."

Indeed, the role of Charlie Anderson draws out of Stewart the best elements in his bag of tricks. Like Tom Destry, the farmer is a cracker-barrel philosopher. Like Paul Biegler, he is a persuasive advocate for his beliefs. Like Howard Kemp, he won't let anything stop him once he's chosen a course of action. And, like Elwood P. Dowd, he can be slightly befuddled, especially by the opposite sex—as is evident from his attempt to explain women to his future son-in-law, played by Doug McClure. That scene, on the porch of the Anderson homestead, is one of several memorable set pieces in Stewart's engaging performance. There is also his graveside conversation with his deceased wife, when he says, "I wish I could just know what you were thinking about it all, Martha. Then mebbe things wouldn't look so bad to me." And that terrible confrontation with the Confederate soldier that ends with Charlie gently telling the lad to remember what has happened.

It must also be noted that with *Shenandoah,* Stewart made the transition to character actor. No longer concerned about his appearance, leaving the romance to the youngsters, he looked every bit his age—fifty-six—and then some. With a few exceptions thereafter, his days as a typical leading man were over.

Moviegoers discovered *Shenandoah* despite the tepid studio support and mediocre reviews. So much so that the picture ended up sixth among the top-grossing films of 1965, making it Stewart's biggest hit (not counting *How the West Was Won*) since *Rear Window.* Moreover, like *The Shop Around the Corner* and *Destry Rides Again, Shenandoah* would eventually find new life on Broadway. Featuring music by Gary Geld, lyrics by Peter Udell, and a book by James Lee Barrett himself, the musical *Shenandoah* opened in Manhattan in January of 1975 and ran for 1,050 performances. John Cullum, who played Charlie, won a Tony Award for his performance, as did Barrett for his book.

"It was almost taken for granted that I would do *The Rare Breed,*" says McLaglen, referring to the Western that he and Stewart started filming roughly four months after *Shenandoah* wrapped. After all, the director had a multipicture commitment to Universal, which owned the property; he was an experienced hand at Westerns; and he and Stewart had just worked extremely well together.

As with *Shenandoah,* the screenplay was based on an original story, in this case, about an English widow, Martha Evans, who comes to America in 1884, with her teenage daughter and a Hereford bull named Vindicator. Her goal is to mate the bull with Texas longhorns and thereby create a hardy, new breed of stock. Stewart is Sam Burnett, an aging cowboy who catches her dream and then falls for the widow herself.

The screenplay was by Ric Hardman, the author of about thirty episodes of the TV series *Lawman* starring John Russell. In fact, one of his teleplays for the series—an episode featuring Sammy Davis Jr. as the owner of a beloved bull—prompted him to write *The Rare Breed.*

McLaglen and producer William Alland assembled a solid cast, including Stewart's *Hobbs* costar, Maureen O'Hara, as the widow; Juliet Mills, in her screen debut, as O'Hara's daughter; Don Galloway as the girl's love interest, a rancher's son; Brian Keith as his dad, Stewart's employer and rival for O'Hara's affections; and Jack Elam as one of the bad guys who tries to steal Vindicator on the bull's way to Texas.

A veteran of dozens of Westerns, the Arizona-born Elam was making his fourth appearance in a Stewart picture, having played villains in *The Far Country, The Man From Laramie,* and *Night Passage* as well. In each case, Stewart managed to kill him off. But, in *The Rare Breed,* his demise came after a spectacular sequence in which the two cowboys clash on horseback. "That wasn't in the script," says McLaglen. "I thought, 'What's something new, so we don't just have two guys shooting at each other?'" What the stuntmen devised took place on the outskirts of a rocky canyon, with Sam and his rival charging toward each other at breakneck speed. Since neither cowboy gives way, their horses collide in a resounding thud. The stunt was executed by Stewart's double, a fellow by the name of Van Horne, and Elam's double, Hal Needham (later a director), with the actors moving in, of course, for the close-ups. Although the footage looks realistic, McLaglen maintains that neither animal was injured during filming, and the assistant director, Terry Morse, agrees; Elam says otherwise. In any event, the moment, as captured on film, is impressive.

The confrontation between Stewart and Elam was shot in Indio, California, near Palm Springs. Filming also took place in the Mother Lode country around Sonora, and in the San Fernando Valley. Surprisingly, Keith's imposing home, where much of the second half of the film plays out, was constructed on a soundstage at Universal. But its location is extremely well disguised in the final cut. Looking back on principal photography, McLaglen says, "No production is easy. They're all hard work, but as pictures go, of the ones I've done, that was very smooth. Because there were no hitches. Everybody was compatible."

Certainly, there was a solid rapport between McLaglen and his star. Of the three long-standing Western directors in Stewart's career, Andy was, by far, the most even tempered, possessing neither Mann's crude manner nor Ford's crusty paranoia. Moreover, as Elam notes, "Andy took care of Jimmy in shots. He was very careful about it. In other words, when you're shooting a picture, you protect your star. . . . You make sure he looks good, you make sure the macho is there, and so forth."

That care showed when *The Rare Breed* opened at New York's neighborhood theaters on April 13, 1966. Stewart was particularly effective in the latter stages of the film when Sam is gripped by Martha's dream. As noted before, the star specialized in playing men of vision.

Although the picture lacked the edge of the best of Jim's Westerns with Anthony Mann, *The Rare Breed* was pleasant entertainment, "as winning as it is conventional," to quote Howard Thompson of the *New York Times*. But craftsmanship couldn't disguise the picture's falling into two parts—the journey to bring Vindicator to the ranch and the aftermath— and the affect of the two were quite different. Nor could one overlook the inconsistency in Sam Burnett's character. In the first half of the picture, he attempts to deceive Martha and participate in the theft of the bull, a rather despicable betrayal of the woman he's been sent to guide and protect. Only an actor with Stewart's basic integrity and decency could get away with such behavior and then make Sam's change of heart credible.

As a rule, Stewart's projects were initiated by others; he simply picked what appealed to him from the scripts that were submitted. But it was Gloria who brought *The Flight of the Phoenix* to his attention. After reading the 1964 novel by British author Elleston Trevor, she thought that he would be perfect for one of the principal characters, a cantankerous veteran pilot named Frank Towns. When Jim checked around, he discovered that the novel had already been acquired by Robert Aldrich, the director of such hits as *Vera Cruz* with Gary Cooper and Burt Lancaster, *The Angry Hills* with Robert Mitchum, and *What Ever Happened to Baby Jane?* with Bette Davis and Joan Crawford. According to Aldrich's assistant director, William Sheehan, Gloria then phoned the producer-director to suggest her husband for the role. Aldrich was delighted.

The Flight of the Phoenix was a gripping adventure story about a disparate group of men who are stranded in the North African desert when their small transport plane crashes. As adapted by screenwriter Lukas Heller, the melodrama pivots around two men: Towns and Heinrich Dorfmann, a German passenger who convinces Towns and the others that he can construct a new plane from the wreckage (the character was a quiet young Brit named Springer in the novel). Precise but mechanical, almost devoid of human feeling, Dorfmann, the technician, epitomizes the way of the future while Towns, the rugged individualist who relies on instinct and experience, is a dinosaur. Ironically, the dichotomy is somewhat akin to that between Stoddard and Doniphon in *The Man Who Shot Liberty Valance*, only this time Stewart plays the anachronism. But, unlike the Western, where the rancher's passing is absolute, Aldrich and Heller suggest that both the individualist and the technocrat are needed, for ultimately Dorfmann can't fly the plane without Towns.

To play the maddening engineer, Aldrich cast Hardy Kruger, an engaging Berliner who had made his film debut in 1944 when he was sixteen and had recently costarred with John Wayne in *Hatari!* Joining him and Stewart was a stellar international cast, including George Kennedy, Richard Attenborough, Peter Finch, Ernest Borgnine, Christian Marquand, Dan Duryea, and Ian Bannen.

"None of us had worked together at any time," Stewart said, referring to himself and the Europeans, "but for some reason there was a tremendous amount of excitement generated. I think for one reason because of the fact that we were sort of strangers, that we hadn't worked together, but we had a sort of mutual respect for one another."

At Aldrich's insistence, they rehearsed for a week at Fox, which was distributing the picture, starting on April 26, 1965. Then they traveled to Yuma, Arizona, to shoot in the sand dunes just across the border in California. The director filmed in sequence whenever possible, because the actors' beards had to grow and their costumes deteriorate as their characters wasted away in the desert.

The heat, the mundane location, the ensemble nature of the story, and Aldrich's skill with actors combined to unite the company while they were in Yuma. "In the thirty years I've been in film," Stewart said at the time, "I've never known a group of actors who have had so much enjoyment off screen and got along so well together." Hardy Kruger recalls, "We always stuck together, whether we were hanging out at a particular joint or at one of our suites at the hotel, or in the dining room. It was incredible really."

He, Attenborough, Finch, and the other Europeans adopted Stewart. Jim officially joined the "club" one evening when they returned to their hotel, a Holiday Inn, a bit worse from drink. Spotting a chandelier in the lobby—which Kruger describes as "incredibly ugly and overdone and huge"—they hoisted Finch up and began pushing him around. Then Kruger took his turn. And finally, Stewart volunteered. "It was not hard to get him up there because he's so tall," Kruger says. "Anyway we hung him from that chandelier and pushed him around and the crystals came down and the manager stood there." Suddenly, a group of reporters filled the lobby—a contingent from Hollywood that the studio had imported to report on the filming. "And all these notorious critics and writers stood there," Kruger continues, "and they saw Gen. James Stewart, movie star, hanging from the chandelier. We stopped pushing him around, but he didn't know what had happened until the chandelier somehow turned around and he saw that gang on the floor. He didn't let go. He just said, 'Hi, there.' "

Stewart was also present for the club's celebration of Queen Victoria's birthday on May 24. In fact, to mark the occasion, he fired a twenty-one-gun salute into a barrel! Looking back, Kruger concedes, "We were very disciplined during working hours but pretty wild after hours, and we painted the town red—Yuma, but also Hollywood. . . . And Jimmy thought that was fantastic. He wanted to be young again. He wanted to be as childish as we were, I guess."

Stewart had fun, but the making of *The Flight of the Phoenix* was not without its unpleasant side. By early July, when the company returned to Fox, Aldrich was weeks behind schedule. Meanwhile, Jim, having expected to finish by the twelfth of that month, had promised Gloria and the kids that he would join them on safari in Africa. In an effort to honor that commitment, he tried to negotiate for time off. Since he had already received three days' grace at the end of May to appear as the grand marshal in a parade for the Indianapolis 500 and had gotten another four days off to promote *Shenandoah* in Texas, Aldrich insisted that he stay and complete his scenes. In a replay of the situation in Paris during the making of *The Spirit of St. Louis*, the star and the producer-director met several times to try to resolve the issue, but got nowhere. Aldrich also discussed the matter with Richard Zanuck, then the head of Fox, and both of them met with Stewart's agent, Herman Citron. Finally, on July 27, with the issue still unresolved, the star simply departed—leaving word that he would return on August 2. Given the nature of air travel in the mid-1960s, he ended up spending less than two days with his family, but he made the trip anyway. Says son Mike McLean, "I think it's a good indication of how important vacations with the family were to the whole family." He also points out how strong-willed his father could be, noting, "When he decides he's going to do something, he does it. And whatever happens after that, he's willing to accept it."

In this case, the consequences were minimal. At first, Aldrich was furious that Stewart had simply walked off. The director even put his star on call for work—knowing that Jim was out of the country—so that he would be in violation of his contract. But Zanuck, who was more sanguine about the situation, refused to join in any legal action against Stewart.

Therefore, the issue more or less faded away once Jim returned. Kruger explains that the rest of the cast was not privy to the battle. Aldrich, he says, even threw a surprise party for Jim at the end of filming in August to mark the completion of this, the star's seventieth picture (including the two shorts *Art Trouble* and *Important News*). Jim was given a propeller blade from one of the airplanes created for *Flight of the Phoenix*, with the signatures of the cast and crew engraved on it.

Although it was screened in Los Angeles for a week in December 1965 to qualify for Academy Award consideration, thereby beating *The Rare Breed* to release, *The Flight of the Phoenix* had its world premiere in London on January 20, 1966—with Jim and Gloria on hand for the festivities. Bosley Crowther of the *New York Times* found the picture illogical and overly long, but his colleague on the *New York Post*, Archer Winsten, captured the critical consensus, writing, "From plot, to character clarity, to individual performance of stars, and on to the pace of the director's work, the picture is an exceptionally perfect piece of work." To which Arthur Knight of the *Saturday Review* added, "No less important, Aldrich helps remind us what a splendid actor James Stewart can be." Kate Cameron of the *New York Daily News* even called the star's performance "one of his best characterizations." And she was right. Looking grizzled and even older than he did in *Shenandoah*, Stewart captured and held the moral center of the picture, matching Kruger's cool precision with passion and fury—and fear. It is among his last great pieces of work.

Despite glowing notices, *The Flight of the Phoenix* was a major box-office disappointment. Arguably, with only one woman in the cast—dancer Barrie Chase in a short mirage sequence—the picture failed to attract large numbers of female moviegoers. In any event, the adventure picture placed no better than forty-first among the hits of 1966.

The Flight of the Phoenix wrapped on August 13, 1965. Stewart didn't act again until December of 1966, a layoff of fifteen long months. He spent part of the time honoring his obligation to the Air Force Reserve. In May of 1966, he had knee surgery, and in September, he and Gloria went to Europe to drop the twins off at school. Although Judy and Kelly regularly attended Westlake, a private school in Los Angeles, they had elected to spend this year abroad, at a fashionable school in Switzerland (Ronnie had gone to Orme, a prep school north of Prescott, Arizona, and Mike had attended Jimmy's alma mater, Mercersburg).

The month after their return from Switzerland, Jim and Gloria participated in a most unusual weekend: to mark Rosalind Russell and Frederick Brisson's twenty-fifth wedding anniversary, Frank Sinatra threw a gala weekend-long celebration for fifty in Las Vegas. In addition to the

Stewarts, the guests included the Cary Grants, the Dean Martins, the Kirk Douglases, the Mike Romanoffs, the William Goetzes, the Vincente Minnellis, Roddy McDowall, Bill Frye, Leonard Gershe, the Bennett Cerfs, Claudette Colbert, Pat Kennedy Lawford, the Alan Jay Lerners, the Leland Haywards, and the Josh Logans. The party flew by chartered plane to Vegas, where they were booked into the Sands Hotel, then Sinatra's home away from home. The highlight of the weekend came with a black-tie dinner on Saturday evening. Each guest received as a keepsake a framed photo of himself or herself (which had served as place markers) and a silver cigarette box inscribed "25th–Roz and Freddie." In addition, the women were given bags with twenty-five silver dollars apiece for gambling. "I want to freeze this night in my mind forever," said Josh Logan's wife, Nedda. "I'll never get over it. I don't think any of us ever really will."

Some six weeks later, Stewart was back at work.

"Simply put, it's a story of a town that has been slowly put together by losers," said Stewart of the Western *Firecreek*. "They were all people who didn't want to face up to life." His character was Johnny Cobb, a farmer with a wife and two kids, who is also the sheriff of the community. It's only a part-time job, for nothing much happens in the town of Firecreek. Then a gang of outlaws arrives, and Cobb has to find the courage that has been dormant since he settled in the dusty community.

The project had originated at CBS, which wanted to do a feature film using many of the people who worked on *Gunsmoke*, the network's hit series. Calvin Clements, who wrote the screenplay, was a frequent contributor to the Western drama. When the project proved too costly, the network brought it to Warner Bros., which agreed to a joint venture. Philip Leacock, *Gunsmoke*'s executive producer, became the producer of the film as well.

Naturally, Stewart wanted McLaglen to direct the picture, but Andy was unavailable (when he wasn't directing Jim, he was usually directing John Wayne). So the assignment went instead to Vincent McEveety, one of *Gunsmoke*'s principal directors. McEveety had also shot episodes of *The Fugitive* and *The Man from U.N.C.L.E.* and a Disney television movie entitled *Adventures of Hector, the Stowaway Pig.*

Henry Fonda was hired to play the picture's other male lead. More than eighteen years had passed since the two old friends had last worked together, but this time they weren't playing pals, they were enemies. Fonda was cast as Larkin, the leader of the outlaw gang, an intelligent but deadly killer. At first glance, the pairing seems curious. Why put two buddies in a picture together but not play off of their offscreen friendship? McEveety points out, however, that a reunion wasn't really the issue. "We were looking for Everyman in both characters," he explains, "two good men, so there wasn't a black heavy and a white hero." Fonda, who normally played good guys, fit the bill. Thus, the stars' friendship was merely coincidence.

Inger Stevens, best known from the television series *The Farmer's Daughter*, was chosen as Fonda's leading lady, a young woman Larkin meets at the boardinghouse where he holes up. Jacqueline Scott, not as big a name as Stevens but known to TV fans as the sister of Dr. Richard Kimble in *The Fugitive*, was cast as Stewart's wife. "I think he was disappointed there wasn't a bigger star," McEveety recalls, "because we went over the list of people who were available. Being the pro that he was, he never said anything to me, but I think in his heart of hearts he would have preferred some name." The role, however, was too small to interest the appropriate candidates.

In the end, Stewart worked extremely well with Scott, and their relationship in their two scenes together is very moving—tender and loving and quite natural. "He gives an enormous amount," says Scott. "He was very easy to work with. He was very kind and very warm and very funny. All you had to do was listen and remember the words." Looking back, she considers the picture "one of the great experiences of my life. It's a very small role, but to be able to work with somebody like that, those are the times that you treasure."

McEveety feels the same way. "I was working with two legends," he explains, "and I was virtually a novice. It was quite an experience. But they were what all real stars are. They were gentlemen and beautiful performers. For me it was an extremely memorable time."

What did he see in the relationship between Stewart and Fonda? "Very warm," he says, "friendly. Mostly loners. [Between takes] they'd go to their own corners or wherever to sit down and rest." Jack Elam, cast as one of Fonda's gang members, adds, "They were extremely close. They were very good friends. They were very comfortable with each other." While waiting to work, Hank liked to hang out with Elam, James Best, and the other heavies, who were usually playing poker. But Stewart was not a gambler. "Jimmy would just go back and sit in his chair in the shade," says McEveety. "And look at what he was doing next. He was constantly working. Not running around. Acting. Thinking."

Filming began in Sedona, Arizona—where Stewart had shot *Broken Arrow*—on December 5, 1966, but the bulk of the work took place at the Albertson Ranch in Thousand Oaks just outside of Los Angeles. There with the Santa Susana Mountains as a backdrop, the town of Firecreek was constructed.

When the picture opened in Manhattan on February 21, 1968, Howard

Thompson of the *New York Times* called it "a kind of vest-pocket *High Noon*," which was an apt comparison. Like the Oscar-nominated film by Fred Zinnemann, Stewart's seventy-first feature was a compact little drama, set in a small Western town, with a lawman reluctantly standing alone against a group of dangerous killers. Also, like *High Noon*, those who made *Firecreek* were more interested in ideas and character development than in traditional shoot-'em-up action. The only problem was that *High Noon* had been released in 1952. By 1968, the idea wasn't fresh anymore. Moreover, *Firecreek* moved at an agonizingly slow pace. Stewart, working in familiar territory, was fine as Cobb, but Fonda, in a different sort of role for him and for Western fans, was ultimately more interesting.

In sum, the picture was, as *Time* put it, "Not terribly original, but not bad of its kind." By the time of its release, however, Warners had been acquired by Seven Arts. The new owners offered the Western little support, and it quickly disappeared from view.

Another very long hiatus—roughly eleven months—followed Jim's work on *Firecreek*. The increasing frequency of these extended layoffs was not by choice. Stewart would have preferred to work steadily; a few weeks, maybe a month off, between projects would have suited him fine. As Andrew McLaglen says, "I've never seen an actor or star who loved to work like Jimmy Stewart. I mean, if he was working on a movie, he was a happy guy."

But Jim was aging fast, and in a business where one's looks are his bread and butter, nature was not his friend. "I know I've changed," he said around 1966. "I've lost a lot of hair and I'm getting new lines on my face. There's been a lot of mileage on the entire frame, but that's living. I enjoy life far too much to start worrying about age." He did, however, consider plastic surgery, a route that other stars of his generation were pursuing. But he rejected the option, a decision he regretted a few years later when the roles became even leaner. By then, however, physicians told him that such a procedure wouldn't do him much good.

He was also growing hard of hearing. His longtime friend Bill Moorhead claims that the deterioration started when Jim exposed himself to icy water for the scene in which George Bailey rescues Clarence the angel in *It's a Wonderful Life*. Perhaps that was so. Or perhaps his years as a pilot exacerbated his condition. Or both. In any event, the impairment, while not necessarily costing him work, wasn't making him more desirable.

Concurrent with Stewart's physical decline came a change in the tone and content of mainstream motion pictures. The transition started with the disappearance of the Production Code, ending decades of industry self-censorship. Then came the sexual revolution of the 1960s, coupled with the summertime riots in cities such as Detroit and Los Angeles. These events helped foster an increase in sex and violence on film. A few years later, protests against the war in Vietnam and the rise of the youth movement—with its antiestablishment bias and penchant for recreational drugs—furthered the climate for adult film fare. Stewart, a staunch conservative, wanted nothing to do with such material. As early as 1962, when the trend was in its infancy, Jim was proclaiming, "Movies used to be good wholesome family entertainment to which parents could take their kids and enjoy a couple of hours with them. Not any more. Nowadays, a kid sneaks off to the movies alone. Why? Because a majority of the Hollywood films being made now are nothing but petty peep shows . . . as lewd as some stag movies. Some half-dressed girl on a bed with a guy moving in . . . it's disgusting." A year later, he dug in even deeper, writing in the *Hollywood Reporter* that he wanted nothing to do with what he called "sensational and sordid pictures," adding, "Good stories are scarce, but I think I have some more mileage in me and I'd like to work more; but when producers advise me to do something different, something daring, I tell them thanks, but no thanks. I'd rather not work."

Some of the Hollywood fare was exploitative and forgettable and would have demeaned Stewart's stature had he appeared in it, but noteworthy, thought-provoking, well-crafted films were also emerging from the new permissiveness, pictures such as Arthur Penn's *Bonnie and Clyde*, released in 1967; Mike Nichols' *The Graduate*, the biggest box-office hit of 1968; and John Schlesinger's *Midnight Cowboy*, the Oscar-winning film of 1969. In the face of such achievements, Stewart's insistence on doing only wholesome family entertainment made him increasingly irrelevant. The industry was evolving, but he was not willing to change with it.

Thus, he spent most of 1967 away from the Hollywood fray. In May, however, he saw action of a very different kind. For his stint on active duty that year, the Air Force sent him on an inspection tour of Vietnam. America had been supporting the South Vietnamese since the Eisenhower administration, but it was in 1965 that President Lyndon Johnson dispatched the first contingent of combat troops. By the time Stewart arrived, the U.S. military presence in Vietnam had reached four hundred thousand.

Stewart was what they called "a hawk," a proponent of the war, as was his oldest son, Ron. But Mike opposed the conflict. The twins were caught in the middle. "I was confused," Judy recalls, "because Mom and Dad were saying one thing, and Mike was saying another. And everybody was right." Dinnertime, especially when Mike was present, could be mighty tense. As Kelly puts it, "When Dad feels strongly about something, it's pretty difficult." So, for the most part, everyone tried to avoid topical subjects. On the few occasions when the war did come up, the words were heated. "It wasn't conversation," Judy recalls. "There wasn't give or take."

Aside from his tour of Vietnam, Jim did a guest spot on Dean Martin's TV variety program on September 14, 1967, the first episode of the fall season, Dean's third on the air (Jim taped it in late July). Stewart and the crooner genuinely liked each other, and the host was so relaxed during taping that the show was fun to do. Thus, following the demise of *The Jack Benny Show* in 1965, Stewart found a new outlet for the guest appearance that he liked to make on TV each year.

Appropriately, when Jim went back to features on October 2, Martin was his costar. *Bandolero!* was a Western on a larger scale than *Firecreek* but with less lofty thematic ambitions. Written by James Lee Barrett and directed by Andrew McLaglen, it found Stewart playing Mace Bishop, a basically law-abiding rancher who helps his ne'er-do-well brother, Dee Bishop (Martin), and his gang escape the gallows. Joining the stars were George Kennedy and Andrew Prine as the lawmen in pursuit of the gang, and Raquel Welch as the outlaws' beautiful Mexican hostage.

For the Bishops' escape into Mexico and Kennedy's pursuit, McLaglen took his company to Page, Arizona, where the nearby Glen Canyon National Recreation Area provided ample scenic splendor. The opening sequence, set in the fictional town of Val Verde, and the climactic shoot-out between the lawmen and the gang, situated in another hamlet called Sabinas, were both filmed in Brackettville, Texas—on the refurbished sets originally built for John Wayne's *The Alamo* and later used for *Two Rode Together.* Additional outdoor footage was shot around Del Rio, about twenty-five miles west of Brackettville.

"I think Jimmy had more fun on that location than he ever had," McLaglen recalls. "Dean and Jimmy and I would take Raquel Welch to dinner, and we'd kid around with her." Stewart came to like the era's reigning sex goddess. But, when filming first began, she was full of questions about her character's psychology and motivation, inquiries for which neither he nor Martin had much patience. Jim told Dean, "I think she'll be fine, but let's loosen her up." So they invited her out to dinner, and as he told critic Rex Reed, they "got her good and drunk." Stewart added slyly, "She was OK from then on."

While in Texas, General Stewart participated in the pilot graduation ceremonies at nearby Laughlin Air Force Base. He and ten thousand other spectators were stunned when a jet exploded above the runway. According to *Variety,* "Debris from the craft impacted several hundred yards from where Stewart presented 42 graduating pilots with wings."

Bandolero! wrapped on December 7, 1967, and premiered in Fort

Worth, Texas, on June 16, 1968. Although the cinematography by William Clothier was admirable, the ease between Stewart and Martin evident— although the notion of them as brothers was incredible—and Jim had some fun in the early going when Mace impersonates a hangman, *Bandolero!* was more or less a formula Western without any of the touches that had made James Lee Barrett's previous screenplay, *Shenandoah,* so rich. "As westerns go," *Time* noted, "this one doesn't. It saddles up a big-name cast, but the giddyap! gets mired in a lot of giddy yapping! The intent was to lighten carnage with comedy; the result is heavy-handed Grand Old Horse Opry."

Shortly after *Bandolero!* wrapped, the Stewarts went to Kenya, where they celebrated Christmas. Two months later, in February of 1968, Jim spent his last months of active duty in the Air Force Reserve visiting his old unit, the 445th Bombardment Group—renamed the 445th Military Airlift Wing—at Dobbins Air Force Base in Marietta, Georgia. Back in L.A., he taped a guest spot for *The Dean Martin Show,* which aired on April 4; it featured Jim rendering his old standby "Ragtime Cowboy Joe." Then, on May 20, he turned sixty. Having reached the Air Force's mandatory retirement age, he took his final leave of the service. "It was the first time that I became aware of growing old," he said a few years later. His military career had meant a lot to him. As he noted in 1959, "The men in the Air Force are the finest group of individuals I've met anywhere. Being in the Air Force has made—a better man, and, yes, a better American out of me." The Air Force, in turn, recognized his ongoing contributions since 1941, awarding him its Distinguished Service Medal. He was only the second Reserve officer to be so honored.

Still wanting to contribute to the national welfare, Jim joined the American Red Cross' upcoming fund-raising campaign as national vice chairman for entertainment. In this capacity, he traveled to Washington, D.C., on October 15 to narrate a fifteen-minute television film, focusing on the Red Cross' efforts to evacuate wounded soldiers from Vietnam. A month later, in what would be the first of many lifetime achievement awards, he was recognized by the Screen Actors Guild for "outstanding achievement in fostering the finest ideals of the acting profession." The award was presented by SAG's then president Charlton Heston before a gathering of a thousand actors at the annual membership meeting at the Hollywood Palladium. Past honorees had included Bob Hope and Barbara Stanwyck.

Thus, 1968 passed—without Stewart's appearing once before a motion picture camera.

On January 12, 1969, he and Gloria embarked on a seventeen-day tour of Vietnam, sponsored by the USO and the Hollywood Overseas Committee. Jim didn't stage any shows; he and his wife simply traveled around the military encampments, chatting with servicemen. The highlight of the trip was their reunion with their son Ron, who had enlisted in the Marines in October of 1967, shortly after his graduation as a business major from Colorado State University. In February of 1968, the young man had received his commission as a second lieutenant, following completion of the officer training program at the Marine base in Quantico, Virginia. When Jim returned to Los Angeles at the end of January, having shaken hands with roughly twelve thousand men and women, he was elated, saying, "I've never seen such spirit in any GIs; and I've never seen such a smart crowd. And, physically, they're stronger than any doughboys ever."

Less than six months later, Ron was dead. On June 11, he was leading a patrol near the Demilitarized Zone with four other marines when they were ambushed by North Vietnamese regulars. Although attempts to rescue the unit by helicopter were unsuccessful, the other men in the outfit escaped. Ron, however, wasn't so lucky.

Only twenty-four, he is remembered by his brother as a quiet person who loved the outdoors. "Even as a young boy," says Mike, "and a young man, he was very reflective, very inward looking. He tried to be very helpful to other people. I know that when he was in high school, if anybody had a problem, they could go talk to Ronnie about it. He was a very good listener."

By a cruel coincidence, the news of Ron's death reached Mike as he was en route to Little Rock, Arkansas, home of his fiancée, Barbara Thompson. The two had met when McLean was a student at Claremont Men's College in Claremont, California, and were about to be married. "I was in Seligman, Arizona [when he heard about Ron]," he recalls, "driving with a friend, and we turned around and came back. The whole family was then together. It was a very tough time."

The funeral was held on June 17 at the Beverly Hills Presbyterian Church with Rev. Dr. James T. Mathien presiding. Among the one hundred mourners were Henry Fonda, Cesar Romero, Gene Kelly, Gregory Peck, Ann Sothern, and Rosalind Russell.

Although Jim and Gloria grieved for their loss, they didn't consider Ron's death a tragedy. "We simply think of him as a man who gave his life for his country," the star said in 1978. Gloria stopped going to church, however. To the extent that Stewart felt anger, it was directed at those who opposed the war. In 1978, he asserted, "The tragedy was that our boy and so many like him were sacrificed without having a unified country behind them." On another occasion, he spoke out against those who protested the conflict, saying, "I hate them. I absolutely hate them. Right or wrong, their country was at war and their country asked them to serve and they refused and ran away. Cowards, that's what they were." Years later, he lent support for the creation of the Vietnam Veterans Memorial in Washington, D.C. He said in 1990, "Every time I go to Washington I go there. There are fifty-seven thousand names there, but I can pick out my son's name almost with my eyes closed."

Mike's marriage took place on June 21. On July 10, his dad went back to work.

Written by James Lee Barrett, *The Cheyenne Social Club* was a lighthearted Western about a crusty old cowboy, John O'Hanlan, who inherits—to his great surprise—a whorehouse. As Stewart explained, "Although the premise could be called bawdy, there's nothing really risqué in the film. There's some innuendo, but most of the humor is in the character and the situations, not in the double entendres."

In this respect, *The Cheyenne Social Club* was unabashedly old-fashioned. That was fine with Stewart. He didn't care for the new breed of Westerns, such as *Hombre* with Paul Newman, released in 1967, and Sergio Leone's "Man with No Name" trilogy starring Clint Eastwood, pictures with considerable violence featuring cynical antiheroes. Spoofs, such as the recent *Support Your Local Sheriff* starring James Garner, didn't suit him either. "I don't see any purpose in the modern westerns," he said just before making *The Cheyenne Social Club*, "where they try to apply things today to the way they were. They're trying to excuse the violence by equating things now with things then. This really bores me."

What distinguished Jim's latest Western was the presence of Henry Fonda as Harley O'Sullivan, an easygoing saddle tramp who decides to follow O'Hanlan to Cheyenne, Wyoming, simply because hanging out with his friend is what he's used to. He talks during the entire journey.

Finally, Jim and Hank were paired in feature-length roles that allowed them to draw on their enduring friendship. "They truly almost didn't need the script," says Shirley Jones, who costarred as the bordello's madam and Stewart's love interest. "They knew the characters and they would get up and sort of improvise. I mean, they had the script and they were aware of the words, but they would sort of improvise around the words, and I thought it was truly incredible to just watch them—the way they played off of each other. It was as though they had worked together all their lives."

Barrett even inserted an inside joke into the screenplay. When the two old cowboys briefly mention politics, O'Hanlan, voicing Stewart's outlook, champions the Republicans while O'Sullivan, like Fonda, favors the Democrats. It was fun. But getting Hank to do the role in the first place—Stewart's idea—wasn't easy. Barrett had not initially fashioned the screenplay as a buddy picture, with two equal roles. Before Fonda would sign on, his part had to be enlarged.

Once again McLaglen was unavailable, so Jim offered the director's chair to another Hollywood veteran and friend, Gene Kelly. Best known for his singing and dancing, Kelly had never done a Western, but he had codirected several of his musicals at MGM, including *On the Town* and *Singin' in the Rain.* Just before *The Cheyenne Social Club,* he had taken the helm of two pictures in which he did not appear, *A Guide for the Married Man* starring Walter Matthau and Robert Morse and the big-budget musical *Hello, Dolly!* with Matthau and Barbra Streisand.

It was a blessing for Stewart to be working with two such old friends, as well as William Clothier, the cinematographer who had shot virtually all of his Westerns since *Liberty Valance.* For, when filming began in Santa Fe, New Mexico—on a townscape created just for the picture—Jim was still in mourning. "Now, I did everything I could to take his mind off it," Fonda recalled in his autobiography. "We chawed about old times at the Madison Square Hotel in New York, and our early bachelor days living together in Brentwood."

Kelly was also sensitive to Stewart's state of mind. When the director saw that Jim was too fatigued to work, he didn't press. "I knew what he was suffering," Gene said, "and whenever it happened, I'd either shoot around him or cancel work for that day, depending on the schedule. And we'd all go fishing." According to Richard Kobritz, the unit production manager, the director, Fonda, and Clothier took turns accompanying Stewart to dinner, to make sure that he wasn't alone.

Jim also took solace from Shirley Jones, a sweet, unaffected actress and his costar in *Two Rode Together.* She loved working with him. "Well, he was incredible," she says. "He gave so much as an actor. I have worked with so many actors of his era who don't do that, who have a style of their own, and they're movie stars, and they're not what I call in-depth actors. Well, Stewart was not one of those. Everything was very well thought out with Jimmy. It was not just learn the lines and say them."

And, of course, there was Pie. The horse was old and ailing, and Stewart knew in advance that he wasn't likely to do well in the high altitude around Santa Fe. But, he said, "I felt so close to Pie, I didn't want to make a western without him." As things turned out, the plucky old veteran lacked the requisite strength to work on the picture, and another horse was used. Still, he was there, and after lunch each day, Jim would pay him a visit, bearing something good to eat. "That's when I began to realize what Pie meant to him," Fonda recalled. "His boy was gone, and I couldn't do anything about that, but now seeing the expression on Jim's face when he reached for something to take to his horse—I had an idea." What Hank did was sketch Pie in his off-hours. When he returned home, he then painted a watercolor of the animal, had it framed, and gave it to Jim. Stewart loved it, saying, "You know, it's absolutely the horse. He caught the horse—the eye, the look. Absolutely caught the horse." Shortly thereafter, Pie died. Stewart arranged for him to be buried in his owner's corral and paid for a tombstone that reads simply, "Here lies Pie."

The Cheyenne Social Club opened in New York on September 16, 1970. Seen today, the picture is surprisingly entertaining, and watching Stewart and Fonda together is a delight. But in 1970, buddy movies were just coming into fashion, and the pairing of seasoned veterans—à la Burt Lancaster and Kirk Douglas in *Tough Guys* and Walter Matthau and Jack Lemmon in *Grumpy Old Men*—had yet to take root. Moreover, at the outset of the new decade, the pulse of the motion picture industry was elsewhere. Small, independent youth-oriented films such as Peter Fonda and Dennis Hopper's *Easy Rider*, released the previous year, were setting a new standard for filmmaking in general, while smart, hip fare such as *Butch Cassidy and the Sundance Kid* starring Paul Newman and Robert Redford—also released in 1969—was taking the Western far from the turf favored by Stewart. Although *Time* correctly identified his picture as "a wonderfully outdated odyssey of bawdy innocence," and *Newsweek* argued that "it's hard not to like the natural camaraderie that these seasoned easy riders show," *The Cheyenne Social Club* could place no better than eighty-third among the year's box-office hits. A year earlier, *Butch Cassidy* had been fourth.

Shortly after *The Cheyenne Social Club* wrapped, the Stewarts went to Sun Valley, Idaho, for the Christmas holidays. While Gloria and the girls relaxed, Jim buried his nose in a script. He wasn't reading James Lee Barrett's latest Western; it was Mary Chase's *Harvey*. At the age of sixty-one, he had decided to return to the stage in the whimsical comedy that he'd first played on Broadway twenty-two and a half years earlier.

"I've always sort of secretly wanted to do it again," he said a few months later, "because I didn't think I was right for it when I did it before. I was too young." He added that, with the twins in college, he and Gloria were ready for a change of pace. A final inducement was the willingness of his old friend Helen Hayes to join him as Veta Louise. Affectionately known as "the first lady of the American stage," the diminutive sixty-nine-year-old actress had recently completed a major supporting role—the wily stowaway—in Ross Hunter's blockbuster film *Airport*. The picture would be released shortly after *Harvey*'s Broadway opening.

It was Hayes who arranged for the Phoenix Theatre to produce the revival. A well-regarded nonprofit theater company in Manhattan, the Phoenix had been affiliated with the recently defunct APA Repertory Company, of which Hayes was a member.

The actress also suggested that Stephen Porter direct. Porter, who was particularly adept at reviving classic comedies and dramas with stars in the leading roles, had worked with Hayes on several APA productions. Aside from Jim and Helen, the cast included Jesse White as the sanitarium attendant, Wilson, the role that he had originated on Broadway and re-created on film; and stage veterans Henderson Forsythe as Dr. Chumley; Marian Hailey as Veta Louise's daughter, Myrtle May; and Joe Ponzecki as Dr. Sanderson.

Early in the new year, Jim traveled to New York where the rest of the cast—including Hayes—had started rehearsal some weeks earlier. His work in Sun Valley paid off. According to Porter, when Jim joined the company, he knew the role "perfectly." Says the director, "He wanted to play an older, more defeated person than he had been able to play when he was young. He was still very glamorous when he did the movie. . . . This man, who had washed out his liver, who was going kind of crazy from drinking for decades, was something he didn't get the first time, couldn't get it, and that's why he wanted to do it again."

Although Stewart knew how he wanted to play the role, he was worried about returning to the stage after an absence of more than two decades. As he put it, "I had almost forgotten . . . about how you have to project your voice. You get lazy about it in the movies." At first, Porter also worried about the movie star's ability to project. "I always thought in rehearsal," the director recalls, "that he wasn't going to be heard because he was so quiet. But on the stage he could be heard perfectly well, way up in the balcony."

As was the custom with APA productions, the University of Michigan's Professional Theater Program sponsored a tryout engagement of *Harvey* in Ann Arbor starting on February 2, 1970. Stewart worried before the first preview that the students wouldn't know who he was, but, as Helen Hayes wrote in her autobiography, "The performance went off beautifully. When we took our curtain calls, they all stood up and cheered, and Jimmy came offstage from his solo call wiping a tear from his eye." Nathan Cohen, who covered the tryout engagement for the *Toronto Daily Star,* noted the special synergy between the two veteran actors and the Ann Arbor theatergoers. "There is no other way to put it," Cohen wrote, "the audiences at the Mendelssohn Theatre are in love with Miss Hayes and Stewart. They identify with them in a very real way. To be in a theatre where such a relationship obtains and to feel it in all its sincerity has become a rare and therefore precious experience."

The engagement in Michigan was magnetic, but nothing could have prepared Jim for the reception that he received when *Harvey* opened at Manhattan's ANTA Theatre on W. Fifty-second Street on February 24. Outside, a police line was needed to restrain the throng of autograph seekers and celebrity hounds, while inside, a glittering array of luminaries, including the mayor of New York, John V. Lindsay, cheered Stewart's return to the Great White Way.

And there was much to cheer about. As Douglas Watt observed in his review for the *New York Daily News*, it was "a simply marvelous production," in which Stewart offered "a master's class in acting with each performance." Richard Watts of the *New York Post* called Jim's Elwood "one of the most endearing performances conceivable," adding, "Unless my memory deceives me, he is even better than the late Frank Fay, who created the part." And John Bartholomew Tucker told audiences on the local ABC affiliate, WABC-TV, that missing Stewart in *Harvey* would be like missing Laurence Olivier in *Oedipus Rex* or Yankee great Joe DiMaggio in center field. Then he changed his mind, arguing that no metaphor accurately suited the occasion, "and all you can say is if you miss seeing Jimmy Stewart play the role of Elwood P. Dowd in *Harvey* then you've missed something as grand as seeing Jimmy Stewart play Elwood P. Dowd in *Harvey*. He's his own metaphor. There is nothing quite so wonderful."

While the Stewarts lived at the Waldorf-Astoria Hotel, Jim held sway over the biggest party in town. As the original six-week engagement neared its end, he agreed to add seven more weeks to the run. The Phoenix subsequently asked for a second extension, but by then, Stewart was staring to tire, so he refused. As a consequence, the curtain rang down on the final performance of *Harvey* on May 2. A few months later, Jim told Wayne Warga of the *Los Angeles Times* that the grind of eight performances a week had been tough, but he added, "It was a great experience at this stage of the game to take a twenty-five-year-old play back to New York and play thirteen weeks without an empty seat." Nearly two years later, on March 22, 1972, he, Hayes, and Jesse White would reprise their roles in a ninety-minute adaptation for NBC-TV's *Hallmark Hall of Fame*.[2]

Having conquered Broadway, Stewart rewarded himself with a trip to Africa in July. He and Gloria visited the Aberdare Mountains in Kenya, where the nightly temperatures dipped to a very chilly forty degrees.

---

[2] The Stewart-Hayes version was actually the second time that *Harvey* was produced on network television. A ninety-minute version starring Art Carney and Marion Lorne had aired on the *DuPont Show of the Month* in 1958. A third version, featuring Harry Anderson, Swoosie Kurtz, and Leslie Nielsen, was scheduled for viewing in late 1997.

Stewart, who occasionally dabbled in poetry, was prompted to comment on the frigid weather in verse.

Two months later, he was again in the mountains—this time the Appalachians of West Virginia—where his latest film, *Fools' Parade*, was in production.

Stewart had brought the 1969 novel by Davis Grubb to the attention of Andrew McLaglen and James Lee Barrett. McLaglen, who agreed to direct and produce the picture (with Barrett as screenwriter and executive producer), then sold the package to Columbia. "And it was a deal very quickly," the director recalls, "for just what Jimmy wanted. They were very eager to have the picture with Jimmy."

Set in 1935 in Glory, West Virginia, *Fools' Parade* is about three men, Mattie Appleyard, Lee Cottrill, and Johnny Jesus, who have just been released from prison. They plan to open their own general store, using as their bankroll Appleyard's savings from his many years of convict labor. But Mattie's attempts to withdraw his money from the local bank are thwarted by the vicious warden, Doc Council, who wants the old man's earnings for himself.

Stewart was ideal for Mattie, described by Grubb as "craggy-browed, towering and white haired . . . a tall man toppled in somehow upon his very height yet holding, erect and proud mouthed." George Kennedy was cast as Doc Council. Strother Martin, another McLaglen favorite, best known to filmgoers as the warden in *Cool Hand Luke* ("What we have here is a failure to communicate"), played the eccentric Lee Cottrill, with Kurt Russell as Johnny Jesus. Russell, then nineteen, had been a child star for the Walt Disney Studio, appearing in *The Absent-Minded Professor* among other films.

Fool's Parade was shot in Moundsville, West Virginia, Grubb's hometown and his model for the fictional Glory. Based in Wheeling, just to the north of Moundsville, McLaglen and his company were astounded at how neatly the film's requirements dovetailed with the local landmarks. "Everything is right there," says the director, "starting with the penitentiary and the courthouse and the bank and the railway and the river." A few sets were constructed at the edge of town, including a railway stop where the three protagonists are waylaid by Doc Council's thugs, and a riverboat was created as the home of the local madam, played by Anne Baxter. Otherwise, the existing structures were simply stripped of four decades of modernization. In addition to the town itself, a number of Moundsville citizens were pressed into service as the film's minor characters.

"It was a pretty friendly atmosphere," recalls Howard Koch Jr., who served as the film's assistant director. "There was a real camaraderie between everybody, and yet there was this respect for the real star,

Jimmy Stewart. Because of who he was, there was this reverence toward him."

McLaglen recalls how delighted Stewart was to be playing crafty old Mattie Appleyard, and indeed, Barrett gave him the kind of business that any actor would relish. At one point, for example, the character bamboozles one of Doc's thugs (Morgan Paull) by turning religious revivalist, even to the point of removing his glass eye and waving it about as if it were a real eyeball.

As with *No Highway in the Sky* twenty years earlier, Stewart approached the role like a character actor, investing Mattie with a distinctive look—including a mustache and the glass eye—and a unique quality. "I don't think he was playing Jimmy Stewart in that picture," asserts Howard Koch Jr., who has since become a successful producer at Paramount. "You look at *Shenandoah,* and you look at *Rear Window,* and you look at *It's a Wonderful Life,* I don't think you see the same guy. He's not Olivier, but I think he should be accorded a better actor than a lot of people give him credit for."

The glass eye was effective, changing Jim's appearance dramatically, but it was a major nuisance. Says McLaglen, "We had eyes from Chicago. We had eyes from Miami. We had eyes from all over the States." Of course, they weren't really glass eyes. They were large contact lenses that fitted over Stewart's own cornea and iris. But to do the job, the lens had to be much larger than the average contact. Stewart worked with the lens before going to West Virginia, but on the first day of filming, the bright movie lights caused such irritation that he had to seek medical treatment in Wheeling, rendering him unavailable to the production company for several days. Thereafter, he could work in spurts of no more than twenty minutes. The picture's cinematographer, Harry Stradling Jr., recalls, "People used to ask, 'Is the eye in? Does he have the eye in?' because there couldn't be any delays once he had the eye in." The pressure and discomfort occasionally got the better of Jim. "Sometimes he'd kind of get ornery," says Koch, "and I knew the eye was bothering him."

But his pains were rewarded when *Fools' Parade* opened at neighborhood theaters on August 18, 1971. Robert Greenspun of the *New York Times* noted, "The movie belongs to Stewart, who has never been more wonderful. With white hair and mustache he looks like a taller William Faulkner, and in the flexible complexity of his character, even down to his removable, prophetic glass eye, he really seems Faulknerian." *Cue* added, "Stewart . . . stamps scene after scene with his own homey brand of comedy." They liked Jim, but the picture drew mixed notices. The *Saturday Review* dubbed it "one of the most satisfying 'actioners' in many a year," and Richard Schickel of *Life* found it "suspenseful, surprising, entertaining, and, in the most interesting sense of the word, mysterious." Conversely, *Variety* thought it "contrived," and Archer Winsten of the *New York Post* found it "silly beyond redemption."

Schickel added, "It deserves better reviews and bigger audiences than I fear it will get." And in this he was right. Given the film's offbeat story and quirky characters, it might never had appealed to a mass audience, but McLaglen maintains that it would have done better if Columbia had opened it selectively and allowed it to gain momentum through word of mouth. Instead, the studio sent hundreds of prints into the South, Midwest, and West, where Stewart's previous pictures had done extremely well. Since *Fools' Parade* was not another *Shenandoah* or *Bandolero!* the launch failed.

McLaglen would go on to make movies through the 1970s. In fact, his 1978 action-adventure melodrama *The Wild Geese,* starring Richard Burton, Richard Harris, Roger Moore, and Hardy Kruger, would become one of the biggest hits of his career. James Lee Barrett would also end the decade with a blockbuster, 1977's *Smokey and the Bandit.* But, after *Fools' Parade,* Stewart's professional associations with the director and screenwriter were over.

In fact, the picture brought Jim's career as a feature-film leading man to a close. A few cameos loomed on the horizon, but never again would a picture rest on his capable shoulders.

PART SIX

· *Billy Jim Hawkins* ·

NINETEEN

Mr. Stewart Goes to Television

The rumors started flying in March of 1970, while Stewart was on Broadway with *Harvey*. At the end of May, after several coy denials, Jim confirmed that they were true: he was coming to television in a weekly situation comedy starting in September of 1971.

The networks had been trying to land him for several years. His occasional appearances on *The Dean Martin Show* had confirmed their belief that his gift for light comedy and his easy, folksy manner made him a natural for the small screen. Only two other stars—Cary Grant and Jack Lemmon—were considered as potent.

Still, according to Bob Thomas, Stewart's acquiescence came as a surprise. "After all," one industry observer told the AP correspondent, "Jimmy's still making a couple of movies a year, at good money, plus a percentage of the take. He's had all the fame, and he's loaded. At his age, sixty-two, why would he want to take on the grind of a TV series?"

The answer was simple: Stewart wanted to work, and film offers were far less frequent than Bob Thomas' source thought. The actor himself confessed, "There are less and less movie parts—let's face it—because of my age. And I'm not the kind of feller to be satisfied with one picture a year." He added, "Besides, the money's good."

Indeed it was. "At that time," says Hal Kanter, who created and produced the series known as *The Jimmy Stewart Show*, "he was the highest-paid star in television. I think he was getting one million dollars for the season."

Kanter had replaced Nunnally Johnson on *Dear Brigitte*, but Stewart had known him far longer than that, since shortly after World War II when the Georgia-born writer was working on Bing Crosby's radio program. His other screenplays included *The Road to Bali* for Hope and Crosby; *The Rose Tattoo*, from the play by Tennessee Williams; *Artists and Models* for Dean Martin and Jerry Lewis; and *Loving You* and *Blue Hawaii* for Elvis Presley. After *Dear Brigitte*, he returned to television, having worked in the medium in its golden early days, and by 1970, he was riding high as the creator-producer of *Julia* starring Diahann Carroll; it was the first sitcom to feature an African-American woman in the leading role.

When NBC, *Julia's* network, asked Kanter to develop a project for

Stewart, the writer-producer was thrilled. He says, "Jimmy Stewart, to my mind, was the best comedy actor that we have in films. He was a cinch to write for, to establish something for."

What Kanter devised was a domestic comedy, in which Stewart would play James Howard, an absentminded professor who teaches anthropology at a fictional college in the fictional town of Easy Valley, California. The show was to have a multigenerational slant, for living with Howard and his wife would be his grown-up son, his son's wife, and their son. Adding to the fun—at least in theory—would be Howard's second child, a boy the same age as the professor's grandson. In the tradition of *The Burns and Allen Show*, Jim would address the television audience directly. Coproducing the series would be Warner Bros.

As the other networks, several film studios, and a number of independent producers were also pitching TV concepts to Stewart, including dramas, Kanter, NBC, and Warners arranged a meeting to unveil their idea. Kanter began by telling Stewart, "I think you would be making a mistake if you did a drama or you did an adventure story or you did a mystery. The airwaves are full of those with good actors. Nobody as good as you, but they're good actors. There are a lot of comedies, too, but there is nobody working in front of a camera today who handles comedy as well as you do. And I think your future in television should be in comedy. The last few pictures you've done, you've sort of avoided comedies. That's a disgrace. You have wasted that comedy ability with dramas that anybody can do." He then segued into an overview of his premise.

Stewart was noncommittal at the end of the meeting, but the following day Kanter got the word: he was in. Jim admired the writer-producer's track record. Moreover, a comedy about the generation gap suited him, as long as the writers avoided Vietnam, the war then dividing the star's own family and ripping apart college campuses around the country.

Next came casting. Stewart wanted Gloria to play his wife. After Kanter watched several *Jack Benny* shows, in which Gloria appeared with her husband, he okayed the idea. "She was not a finished actress," he says, "but she was quite good. She was very natural and very attractive, and I like Gloria very much." But NBC insisted on a test, which Mrs. Stewart agreed to make. "She was reasonably good," Kanter recalls. "She was certainly as good as several other women we had tested. But the network turned her down. They didn't think she was a good enough actress." Stewart was furious. So much so that, in Kanter's opinion, it soured Jim on the entire project. "I think in the back of his mind," the writer-producer asserts, "he said, 'I will show these people. I'll do what I'm supposed to do this first year, but at the end of the year, that's it.' And he made sure it was the end of the series." How he did that, Kanter couldn't say.

Eventually, the role of Martha Howard went to Julie Adams, Stewart's leading lady in *Bend of the River*. She was forty-four when the show went on the air, but she looked far younger than her years—too young to be the mother of a grown son, especially when seen with Stewart, who was eighteen years her senior. "I thought Julie was a little too young myself," admits Kanter, "but we sort of winked at that. And she was very good." The producer also brought in John McGiver, Stewart's *Mr. Hobbs/Take Her, She's Mine* costar, to play Dr. Luther Quince, Jim Howard's colleague and friend. Rounding out the cast were Dennis Larson as Jim's eight-year-old son, Jonathan Daly as his firstborn, Ellen Geer as his daughter-in-law, and Kirby Furlong as his grandson.

By a strange coincidence, the 1971–72 season was riddled with film stars trying to make the transition to television. In addition to Stewart, Glenn Ford, George Kennedy, Anthony Quinn, Shirley MacLaine, Rock Hudson, Tony Curtis, and Rod Taylor put new series before the public. So did James Garner, Dick Van Dyke, and David Janssen—stars who had scored first on the tube, then went to the big screen, and were returning to their roots.

Most of these actors discovered that stardom in one medium does not guarantee success in another. Jim was among the unfortunates. "We only wish that Stewart had been given a better character to play than an absent-minded professor bogged down with a family," opined Kay Gardella in the *New York Daily News*, after the show's September 19 debut.

Clearly *The Jimmy Stewart Show* derived from a long line of domestic comedies—*Father Knows Best, The Danny Thomas Show, The Adventures of Ozzie and Harriet,* and *My Three Sons,* to name a few. But, in the turbulent early 1970s, audiences wanted heartier fare. *The Dick Van Dyke Show* and *The Mary Tyler Moore Show* had paved the way for witty, urbane sitcoms, featuring ensemble companies and focusing at least as much on the workplace as the home. Shows with angry, even somewhat detestable protagonists, such as *All in the Family,* were bringing a new topicality and heightened realism to the genre. Weighed against such competition, the gentle humor and familiar family crises of *The Jimmy Stewart Show* seemed decidedly old-fashioned. As Gardella noted, "The typical situation comedy about a family is beginning to wear very thin and it doesn't matter who turns up in the cast. The format has been overworked until one show looks like every other show." The *Los Angeles Times* and the *New York Times* agreed.

To some extent, Stewart had no one to blame but himself. He had cast approval and script approval, and he exercised both. In fact, arguments with Kanter about a story line or a supporting player were not uncommon. Even before filming began, the producer and the star tussled over the hiring of the company manager. Kanter wanted to use Dave Silver, who had been the assistant director on *The FBI Story,* and Stewart wouldn't okay the decision because, according to Kanter, once during the making of the film, Silver had called Jim for makeup at seven o'clock in the morning and he didn't go before the camera for an hour and a half. On another occasion, Kanter wrote an episode depicting Professor Howard's grandfather during the Civil War (with Stewart doubling as the old man). "And in the story," the writer explains, "his grandfather turns out to be a coward, and that's how he had won a certain battle or whatever. I can't remember the details now." The star rejected the teleplay because he didn't want his grandfather to be unheroic. Kanter pointed out that the character was fictional, he wasn't *Stewart's* grandfather, but Jim remained adamant. Looking back on the relationship, Kanter says, "Somebody asked me what it was like working for him and I said, 'Just remember, you're dealing with a brigadier general in the United States fucking Air Force, and don't you forget it, 'cause he doesn't.' " The producer adds, "He could be very, very kind to people. I saw many instances where he was very kind and was the first to help someone out. And I could see other times where he could be absolutely cold as a fish. Very mercurial."

Notwithstanding Kanter's belief that Stewart doomed the series when Gloria was rejected as his leading lady, the star wanted each show to be as good as time permitted. "Oh, his attitude about working was always perfect," recalls Julie Adams. "His professional level was never less than impeccable." She also praised his comic timing, saying, "He knew if it was off by a second. He was great."

If anything, Jim felt that he hadn't allowed enough time for the concept to jell properly before the day-to-day grind began. After the show was canceled, he said, "I think I was a little impatient to get the series started. I've never been like that. I like to think things through very quietly, carefully. But here we were, all of a sudden, with a series—and on the air. TV is more important than that. It demands more care and thought—like pictures and plays. You've got to take time." He also came to feel that the show's format was untenable, saying, "It left us with not enough places to go. We had a lot of people trapped in that house doing one-liner jokes."

The last episode aired on September 3, 1972.

Stewart fared better with his second foray into weekly television.

Hawkins was created by David Karp, who was an experienced hand with legal dramas, having written several episodes of the highly acclaimed series *The Defenders.* He was also the creator of a short-lived series of his own, *The Storefront Lawyers.* He had even tried to develop *Anatomy of a Murder* into weekly fare. The concept didn't sell, but it left the writer-producer intrigued by the potential in a series built around a savvy rural lawyer. The fundamental difference between Paul Biegler and Billy Jim Hawkins, the West Virginia country boy created by Karp, is that the former was firmly rooted in the small Michigan town of his birth while Hawkins would jet around the country, taking on cases wherever people were in need. Thus, he would always be an outsider, at odds with the environment in which he found himself. At the same time, his folksy manner would be one of his greatest assets, leading his city-slicker adversaries to invariably underestimate his canny legal mind. The only other regular in the cast would be Billy Jim's sidekick, an uncle by the name of R. J. Hawkins.

After CBS expressed interest in the concept, Karp brought in Norman Felton as executive producer. Felton, in turn, involved MGM as coproducer; he had been the studio's director of TV programs from 1960 to 1966, developing *Dr. Kildare* and *The Man from U.N.C.L.E.*, among other successful series. Meanwhile, Karp fleshed out his concept in a pilot teleplay, called "Hawkins on Murder" (changed to "Death and the Maiden" for rebroadcast during the run of the series). In it, Billy Jim defends a possibly insane heiress accused of three murders.

Although Stewart had starred in *Anatomy of a Murder*, *Hawkins* had not been created with him in mind. Nor was he the first actor offered the role. Karp and Felton initially approached Andy Griffith, the folksy North Carolina–born actor who had starred in the highly successful rural sitcom bearing his name. "He loved it and wanted to do it," says Karp, but Griffith insisted on making his personal manager the show's executive producer, so the *Hawkins* team went elsewhere.[1] Karp then turned to Harris Cattleman, the head of television at Metro, to see if he could find a young Jimmy Stewart—Hawkins having initially been conceived as roughly the age of Paul Biegler when Jim made *Anatomy of a Murder*. Instead of a copy, Cattleman came back with the original. "Well, I wasn't going to argue with him," Karp says. "I thought Jimmy Stewart was wonderful." As a concession to the star's age, the sidekick went from Hawkins' uncle to his cousin. "There's no one in life old enough to be my uncle," Stewart joked. Strother Martin, the quirky character actor from *Fools' Parade*, won the role. Otherwise, the pilot went forward as written.

Filming began on January 3, 1973, with Bonnie Bedelia as the heiress and Kate Reid, David Huddleston, Dana Elcar, and Robert Webber in supporting guest roles. It was directed by Jud Taylor, a former actor who had previously worked for Felton on *Dr. Kildare* and other MGM series and who, like Stewart, was represented by Chasin, Park, Citron.

For Bedelia's mansion, the company filmed at the lavish, forty-four-room

---

[1] In time, Griffith would star in a *Hawkins*-like series called *Matlock*.

manor house built by silent-movie star Harold Lloyd in 1929. Otherwise, the show was shot at MGM. Nearly a decade had passed since the making of *How the West Was Won,* Jim's last film for the studio. Returning to the Culver City lot where he'd spent so much of his youth was a shock. "It had fallen into terrible disrepair," says Karp. "Everything was broken. The grass was brown. It looked like hell. And he could not get over it."

But then, Jim had changed since the old days, too. Karp remembers sending his son to the MGM parking lot to greet the actor on the first day of shooting, and the young man came back empty-handed. "Of course, what happened," explains Karp, "was he thought Jimmy Stewart, a star, would show up in a convertible. He didn't know Jimmy Stewart would show up without his hairpiece and a lunch pail—like a grip. That's exactly what he looked like."

But the old pro still knew how to deliver when the cameras rolled. "Stewart was very prepared," says Jud Taylor. "When it came to shooting, he was letter-perfect. And he did something I've never seen before or since. After we blocked a scene and the technicians would be lighting it, very often he would continue to do his lines and action instead of the stand-in. And I said to him, 'Jim, why don't you go and sit down.' And he said, 'I have to get all this business down so I can forget about it.'" What he meant, explains Taylor, is that he wanted to determine exactly what he would do at each moment for two reasons: first, so that he could match in subsequent shots whatever he did in the master; and second, so that his gestures and movements would seem spontaneous, not come across as acting but simply as behavior. Taylor was so impressed that he found the making of the pilot, in his words, "a wonderful, stimulating experience, working with one of the great film actors of all time."

In mid-February, after "Hawkins on Murder" wrapped, Jim and Gloria went to London, where their son was studying law at Oxford.[2] On the thirteenth, Mike's wife, Barbara, gave birth to a boy, Benjamin, the Stewarts' first grandson. In addition to attending the baby's christening, Jim appeared as a presenter on the British Academy Awards telecast.

Then, on March 13, "Hawkins on Murder" aired on CBS. Cecil Smith of the *Los Angeles Times* called it a "whopping good mystery," and Morton Moss of the *Los Angeles Herald-Examiner* argued that "unlike so many series pilots, this one is a coherent film, not a parade of sequences mainly conceived as a demonstration on how numerous episodes may be spun out of it." Moss also found Billy Jim Hawkins a character far more

---

[2] Mike received his MA in jurisprudence in 1973. He and Barbara subsequently moved to Phoenix, where he taught high school for nine years. Today he is a self-described "private investor."

suited to Stewart's talents than the absentminded professor in his defunct sitcom. *Variety* agreed, calling Hawkins' bumpkin guise "a pose the actor can pull off with great persuasion, using his familiar (but still effective) homespun delivery and sincerity for telling effect."

Given the critical response, Fred Silverman, then in charge of programming at CBS, commissioned seven ninety-minute episodes to air on Tuesday evenings, starting on October 2, 1973, in rotation with *Shaft*, starring Richard Roundtree, and a series of made-for-TV movies. Rotating shows were then in vogue, the idea being that more care could be devoted to each episode without the pressure of a weekly airing. Moreover, audiences could experience several different vehicles, and the less popular shows could be replaced without jeopardizing the entire time slot.[3]

Shooting each episode of *Hawkins* took ten days. Norman Felton explains, "We were forced to film them back-to-back, without any rest in between, for reasons of budget. If we had taken a break between each film, we would have had to pay everyone involved in the crew their full salaries."

The schedule was grueling, particularly for Stewart because Billy Jim had a great deal of dialogue, including the lengthy courtroom summations that marked the climax of each episode. "I wonder whatever possessed me to play a lawyer," the star joked during filming. "Lawyers talk all the time. You can't imagine the words I've got to learn for each one of these." But, despite his age—sixty-five—he adjusted to the pace surprisingly well. "Physically he was fine," says Jud Taylor, who continued as one of the series' principal directors. "He was no more tired than anybody else. They were long days, twelve-hour days. He was always there, always attentive. Knew his lines. He did have in his contract that he could leave at six o'clock, but that was not uncommon. If you were a star and you could command that, you got it."

Paul Wendkos, who spelled Taylor, directing three of the seven episodes, was struck by Stewart's professionalism, saying, "He cared, he cared. He had a lot of pride. And he always wanted to do his best—and always wanted everyone around him to do their best as well." He also found the star, as he put it, "a joy, an absolute joy."

Unlike the sitcom, *Hawkins* pleased Stewart. Consequently, he was fun to work with. "I never had any of the problems that Hal [Kanter] had with him on that other show," says David Karp. "I don't know if Jimmy was

---

[3] Among the most successful entries in the genre was the *NBC Mystery Movie* (later the *NBC Sunday Mystery Movie*), which consisted of Peter Falk as *Columbo*, Dennis Weaver as *McCloud*, and Rock Hudson and Susan Saint James as *McMillan and Wife*.

simpatico with Hal. Jimmy Stewart and I shared the same form of conservatism. We're both very patriotic. We're both anticommunist. We're
both straitlaced in terms of morals. We saw things eye to eye." By contrast, Kanter was a liberal. "And I think that was what Jimmy was fighting," Karp says, "and didn't know how to express it or didn't want to come
out and say so."

The *Hawkins* episodes, mostly written by Karp, covered a fairly broad
spectrum. The premiere, "Murder in Movieland," took Billy Jim to Hollywood to defend the husband (Cameron Mitchell) of a fading movie star
(Sheree North). It drew even better reviews than the pilot, with Cecil
Smith of the *Los Angeles Times* calling it "a corker," and John J. O'Connor of the *New York Times* dubbing it "the most impressively acted, written, directed and photographed of the new series so far this season."
Subsequent episodes found the attorney grappling with such issues as
homosexuality, mercy killing, suicide, the cruel realities of professional
sports, and scandal in high places in Washington, D.C.

But, despite the critical acclaim and a Golden Globe Award for Best
Actor in a Television Series, Stewart decided to bring *Hawkins* to an end
after the first season. He told Mary Murphy of the *Los Angeles Times*, "It
just got to be too much work for me. I think I've earned the right to have
more than Saturday and Sunday off." Which was true. But David Karp
maintains that there was more to the story. He says that CBS decided to
break *Hawkins* out of the rotation format, reduce the show to sixty minutes, and air it as a weekly series. Karp was thrilled. But Jim didn't like
the idea. He wanted to keep the show the way it was. "You can't believe
the inducements," says the show's creator, "the begging, the blandish-
ments that went on. But you're dealing with a two-star general who has a
lot of money. Who's stubborn. Plus he likes to do what he likes to do. And
he had the right to do what he wanted to do."[4]

Thus, the last episode of *Hawkins* aired on September 3, 1974. The
show had never been a ratings champ, failing to crack the season's top
twenty-five despite a powerful lead-in, *Hawaii Five-O*, which was the fifth
most popular show of the 1973–74 season. Nevertheless, *Hawkins*
enabled Jim to erase the stigma of *The Jimmy Stewart Show*. For its day,
it was quality television.

While he was filming *Hawkins* at MGM, Stewart managed to squeeze in
an appearance in *That's Entertainment!*—the studio's big-screen celebration of its beloved musical films. Along with other stars of Metro's
golden age, including Frank Sinatra, Fred Astaire, Gene Kelly, Debbie

---

[4] In fact, Stewart had been a brigadier general, a rank denoted by one star.

Reynolds, and Elizabeth Taylor, Stewart narrated a segment of the picture, appearing on-screen while his younger self performed in clips. Specifically, his rendition of "Easy to Love" in *Born to Dance* served to remind moviegoers that at Metro musicals weren't just the province of singers and dancers.

When *That's Entertainment!* debuted to rave reviews in April of 1974, it marked Stewart's first feature-film appearance in three years. Nine months later, movie buffs in Los Angeles could catch him on the big screen in a two-month-long retrospective called "A Tribute to James Stewart" sponsored by the Los Angeles County Museum of Art. Jim had been scheduled to introduce *It's a Wonderful Life*, which kicked off the series on January 10, 1975. However, a bout with the flu prevented his appearance. He was present instead for the screening of *Rope* on February 8.

Two months later, he and his old invisible pal, Harvey, were reunited for a sixth and final time—for a revival of Mary Chase's comedy in the West End of London. Although Stewart had wanted Helen Hayes to reprise her role as Veta Louise, the actors' union, British Equity, refused to sanction the appearance of two Americans in the cast. So the role went to a London favorite, Mona Washbourne.

Under the direction of actor Anthony Quayle, *Harvey* opened at the Prince of Wales Theatre on April 9, 1975. After six curtain calls from a celebrity-packed audience, Stewart made a brief speech, saying, "It's been my dream to play on the London stage and you've made my dream come true. Thank you very much." He received rave reviews from the British press, but the critics were less enamored of the thirty-year-old play, which Michael Billington of the *Guardian* called "a piece of sentimental nonsense."

"I was really amazed that Dad could do it," says daughter Judy, who stayed with Jim and Gloria in a house they rented in a suburb of London. At the age of sixty-six (he turned sixty-seven shortly after the opening), he put everything he had into every performance, and as Judy notes, "He got a standing ovation every single day." She adds that he was so nervous before each show he would develop a stomachache. "He's a worrywart," she explains. "You know, he's afraid he's going to forget a line, the set's going to crash down on him. And so I think this was his way of worrying."

Stewart's onstage triumph, which lasted seven months, was made richer by the presence of Henry Fonda, who was appearing in London in his one-man show, *Clarence Darrow*, at the same time. The two old friends were photographed for the September 1 issue of *People* magazine, sitting on a park bench in Grosvenor Square, dressed in coats and ties with Jimmy sporting his accordion. "Things have changed a lot, but one thing is the same," he drawled. "Henry Fonda still can't sing."

*   *   *

Performing onstage in a foreign country was exciting, but for thirty years Stewart's career had been rooted in motion pictures. Thus, it was with considerable pain that he said in 1975, "I don't think I'll be making many more movies. I just don't fit in anymore." He cited as one example a script that he'd recently received, adding, "Frankly I didn't even understand who the hell was doing what to whom—or the reason why!"

Another case in point was Peter Bogdanovich's attempt to bring Jim, Fonda, and John Wayne together in a Western called *Streets of Laredo*. The author, Larry McMurtry, had written the novel *The Last Picture Show*, which had become a breakout hit for Bogdanovich in 1971 (the director and McMurtry cowrote the screenplay). Where *The Last Picture Show* was about Texas in the 1950s, *Streets of Laredo* was set in the late nineteenth century and centered around a group of retired Texas Rangers who take a herd of cattle to Montana. "I wasn't impressed," Stewart said, "so I called the Duke and asked him what he thought of the script. He said, 'Jimmy boy, they're trying to make three old fogies out of you, me, and Fonda.' And he was right. So we all turned it down." The screenplay later became the basis for McMurtry's Pulitzer Prize–winning novel *Lonesome Dove*, which, in turn, became a hit miniseries starring Robert Duvall and Tommy Lee Jones.[5]

Stewart and Wayne passed on what became very rich material, but they did get one more chance to work together.

Glendon Swarthout's novel *The Shootist* was the winner of the Western Writers of America's prestigious Golden Spur Award. It had been optioned before publication by independent producers M. J. Frankovich and William Self, who formed a partnership to produce the project with Dino De Laurentiis. Paramount was the distributor. The screenplay by Swarthout's son, Miles, was primarily a study of the title character, John Bernard Books, an elderly gunfighter dying of cancer in Carson City, Nevada (changed from El Paso, Texas, in the novel). The story was set in 1901, which gave the picture a look quite different from most Westerns.

"It's going to be a study in vulnerability like the old films," said Stewart shortly before filming began. "Not one of these psychological westerns that try to make things relative, or blame the old West for the violence of today. I can't stand these pseudo-westerns that make fun of the old cowboys, calling Jesse James a coward and Wyatt Earp a drunk. They really hurt what we were trying to do and are unsuccessful with the public because they are unbelievable."

---

[5] McMurtry didn't forget about his original title, however. He used it for the sequel to *Lonesome Dove*. That, too, became a TV miniseries, starring James Garner.

Wayne was Books. Costarring were Lauren Bacall as the owner of the boardinghouse where the gunfighter comes to die and Ron Howard as her impressionable teenage son. Stewart played Dr. Hoestetler, one of several smaller roles taken by an impressive group of "guest stars," including Richard Boone, Hugh O'Brian, Harry Morgan, John Carradine, Sheree North, Richard Lenz, and Scatman Crothers. In fact, Jim had only two scenes plus a brief nonspeaking appearance at the film's conclusion. In the first, he examines Wayne to determine the gunman's illness, and in the second—a rather depressing sequence—he describes the agony Books will suffer as the cancer spreads, subtly suggesting the gunman consider suicide. Don Siegel, the picture's director and a veteran of seven Westerns, including two with Clint Eastwood (plus Eastwood's most famous film, *Dirty Harry*), was surprised that Stewart took the assignment. "I didn't think," he wrote in his autobiography, "Mike [Frankovich] would get him as the part was too small." Stewart didn't hide his motivation for accepting. He told Guy Flatley of the *New York Times*, "The reason I'm playing a small role in *The Shootist* is very simple. I wasn't offered a bigger role and since I still consider acting my profession, I jumped at the chance to do this."

The company worked for two weeks in Carson City, but Stewart's scenes were shot at the Burbank Studios starting in late January 1976. Wayne's health had been aggravated by the high altitude of Nevada. In addition, he and Siegel jockeyed for power during the early days of production. But Duke was in better spirits by the time Stewart arrived. Hollywood reporter Joseph McBride, who observed them together on the set, noted, "The two veteran actors used a kind of shorthand with each other, conferring mostly on timing and other technical points." In addition, Wayne evidenced a moving sensitivity to Jim's hearing impairment, quietly alerting his friend if he failed to hear Siegel call "Action." Still, Stewart muffed quite a few lines during takes. He simply couldn't catch his cues. Moreover, he'd always been private, but his impairment seemed to draw him even further into himself. While waiting to be called to the set, he tended to sit in his chair on the sidelines, quietly lost in thought.

But his performance in the final cut looked as polished as ever, and his rapport with Wayne enriched their exchanges. "It was very interesting to watch these two old pros working together in complete harmony and accord," wrote Siegel. "They knew that I knew that they knew what they were doing. Just about all I did was direct traffic." And when it was over, Stewart told Joe McBride, "It was a very pleasant experience. It was like not having been away at all."

The Shootist debuted at Manhattan's Astor Plaza Theatre on August 11, 1976—during America's bicentennial summer. *Time* magazine's Jay Cocks was among those who cheered what he called "the welcome participation of Stewart." Not counting Jim's cohosting duties in *That's Entertainment!* this was his first big-screen acting appearance in five years.

Stewart's was a reassuring presence, but without question, *The Shootist* was John Wayne's picture. It also turned out to be his last, for, ironically, the actor, playing a man dying of cancer, succumbed to the illness himself in 1979. The world mourned his passing, but John Books, a complex, introspective character, marked a fitting conclusion to his remarkable career. The picture even opened with a montage of images from his many Westerns—in order to track Books' equally remarkable career as a gunfighter. As Frank Rich noted in the *New York Post*, "The principal virtue of *The Shootist* . . . is that it allows Wayne's distinctive star qualities to emerge in all their splendor. Watching this film is like taking a tour (albeit a very slow tour) of a Hollywood legend." The critic went on to call Stewart, not Bacall or Howard, Wayne's "actual co-star," adding, "A palpable shudder crosses the screen as these two men contemplate their own mortality. Certainly the moment is larger than life, but it is not disconnected from life—and it's the grand, almost primal humanity of Wayne and Stewart rather than the fusty museum-like hush of *The Shootist* that really tells us what movie legends are about."

TWENTY

"I Just Keep Rollin' Along"

Aside from *The Shootist,* several endeavors occupied Stewart during the first months of 1976. On January 17, shortly before his work on the Western, he participated in a bicentennial concert at Los Angeles' Dorothy Chandler Pavilion, narrating Aaron Copland's "Preamble" and "Canticle of Freedom" in conjunction with the Sinfonia Orchestra and the Los Angeles Master Chorale. The concert was conducted by the composer.

A few weeks later, on February 4, he celebrated the birth of another grandson, James McLean. By then, he was on the stump for his friend Gov. Ronald Reagan, who was contesting President Gerald Ford for the presidential nomination of the Republican Party. This was a relatively new arena for Stewart. In the era of the studio system, stars were expected to be patriotic while keeping their politics to themselves. But in more recent decades the curtain had been lifted, and since the late 1960s, Stewart had freely lent his voice to conservative causes, including the war in Vietnam. He was a true believer, but he never became belligerent like John Wayne, whose hawkish posture evoked hostility among the doves. Consequently, the liberals didn't declare Jim persona non grata as they did Duke. Ron Reagan Jr. remembers Stewart's impact during the primary season of 1976, saying, "His effect on the crowd was pretty much what you'd expect. This was a big Hollywood star, and these were small towns for the most part. So it was quite an encounter with Hollywood glamour for most of those audiences: to not only have Ronald Reagan, who was an actor in his own right, but to also have Jimmy Stewart there. Wow!"

In early April, Stewart looked back to an earlier age, playing a veteran pilot in a twenty-minute educational film called *Sentimental Journey,* which marked the fortieth anniversary of the development of the DC-3 aircraft. Written, produced, and directed by Fred Grofe, Jr., it was intended for use by schools, libraries, and educational television stations.

Four months later, Stewart was before a film camera once again, taking a small role in a much bigger budget feature about aviation, *Airport '77.*

Universal Pictures had discovered the powerful box-office potential in a film that mixed lavish production values, soap-opera subplots, a bevy of stars, and an airplane disaster when it brought Arthur Hailey's bestseller *Airport* to the screen in 1970. Produced by Ross Hunter and headlined by Burt Lancaster, Dean Martin, Jean Seberg, and Jacqueline Bisset, the picture grossed nearly $50 million, making it the biggest moneymaker in Universal's history to that point. Four years later, the same formula gave rise to *Airport 1975*, starring Charlton Heston, Karen Black, and George Kennedy (in the role that he created in *Airport*). It cost 50 percent less than the original film and grossed roughly the same amount.

Going back to the well a third time, the producer and executive producer of *Airport 1975*, William Frye and Jennings Lang, conceived *Airport '77*. In this case, the screenplay by Michael Scheff and David Spector (from a screen story by H. A. L. Craig and Charles Kuenstle) placed the disaster underwater, as a hijacked private jet crashes into the Atlantic Ocean. But the original formula—stock characters played by a mix of current and veteran stars; overlapping, melodramatic subplots; a slick, glossy production; and state-of-the-art special effects—still prevailed.

Bill Frye enlisted Stewart, one of his close personal friends, to play millionaire Philip Stevens. It is Stevens' plane—carrying a group of distinguished guests to his Palm Beach, Florida, home—that plunges into the drink. Others in the all-star cast were Lee Grant, Brenda Vaccaro, Joseph Cotten, Olivia de Havilland, Darren McGavin, Christopher Lee, and, for the third time, George Kennedy. Starring as the courageous pilot of the plane was Jack Lemmon.

Stewart's role consisted primarily of an opening scene, in which he established the basic situation by means of an informal press conference at his estate. Thereafter, he appeared in snippets, looking anxious as he follows the plight of his guests, including his granddaughter, who was on the plane. Serving as his Italianate, art-laden mansion was Miami's Viscaya, the $100 million former home of International Harvester scion John Deering, which had become a museum. The company also filmed at Wakulla Springs, near Tallahassee; in and around San Diego; and for the airplane cabin and underwater sequences, the Universal lot.

Like all of the other characters in the picture, Philip Stevens was a stock figure, a millionaire reminiscent of J. Paul Getty, made only slightly remarkable by the fact that Jimmy Stewart was playing him. After all, Stewart's career had been built on and maintained by characters of modest means, men of the people. Nevertheless, he handled the role of the tycoon with ease, exuding an aura of wealth and power through his erect posture and forthright speech—without a hint of a stammer or hesitance. As Pamela Bellwood, who played his granddaughter, notes, "I think at that point in his life it would have been harder to convey *Mr. Smith Goes to Washington*. . . . It was easy to play a person of stature and wealth and dignity and power because he's enjoyed a certain amount of that."

Most striking to those who watched Jim work was the way he sparkled on camera. Although he looked distressingly old in life, the director would call "Action," and suddenly he would become two inches taller, the sagging skin in his face would grow taut, and he would look great. "I've never seen anything like it," the cameraman told producer Bill Frye in amazement. Frye adds that the next day, when they watched the rushes, no one could believe that they were looking at the same fellow who'd been sitting on the sidelines twenty-four hours earlier.

Clearly, Stewart wasn't the attractive, debonair fellow of decades past, but people were still in awe of him. "The thing that I noticed when I was working with him," says the picture's director, Jerry Jameson, "is that he represents something to the general public that I have never seen in terms of other actors that I've worked with, many of whom have been big stars. People had a reverence for him almost. People would walk up to him and say, 'Mr. Stewart, it's so good to meet you,' and he'd take a moment with them. And they really meant it sincerely. . . . It was something quite different than the way fans approach most actors."

Hoping that box-office lightning would strike twice, Frye and Jennings Lang premiered *Airport '77* in Anchorage, Alaska, on March 24, 1977. Like *Airport 1975*, which had debuted in the same city, the premiere benefited the Anchorage Fine Arts Museum. The following day, the picture opened in New York—to a critical drubbing. Summing up the response, John Simon wrote in *New York* magazine, "It's a disaster all right, but it never quite makes it to being a movie. . . . Characters and plot elements are introduced as if they were so many pickup sticks dropped on a table; we have not the faintest idea who most of these sticks are and why we should care a tinker's damn for them."

Stewart was philosophical about the response, saying, "Well, you know, you never start out to make a bad picture, but it's that kind of business." Good or bad, *Airport '77* went on to gross close to $15 million, far less than its predecessors but enough to make the picture seventeenth among the biggest hits of the year—and to inspire yet another sequel, *The Concorde—Airport '79.*

On June 28, three months after the release of *Airport '77*, Stewart was in England for the wedding of his daughter Kelly to Alexander Harcourt. The service took place at London's Queen's Chapel, a prestigious house of worship next to the Savoy Hotel (where the wedding reception was held). The bride and groom had met in Rwanda four years earlier. At that point, Sandy was a Ph.D. student from Cambridge working, like Kelly, at Dian Fossey's Karisoke Research Center. Jim and Gloria were thrilled with Kelly's choice. "They thought it was just great," she says, "that I fell in love with this person who was doing what I was doing and that we shared this interest and everything. And they hit it off with Sandy immediately."

But, until the wedding, Harcourt had never witnessed the price of celebrity firsthand. "I remember coming out of the church," says Kelly, laughing, "and there were all these photographers. It was just crazy. It was wild. And I could just imagine Sandy thinking, 'My God, what have I gotten myself into?' "

Nearly twenty years later, they are still together, living in Davis, California, where Harcourt is on the faculty of the University of California.

A little more than a month after the wedding, Jim was back in England—albeit briefly—to play Gen. Guy de Brisai Sternwood in producer-director-screenwriter Michael Winner's remake of *The Big Sleep*. The original 1946 production, based on Raymond Chandler's 1939 novel—his first Philip Marlowe mystery—had starred Humphrey Bogart and Lauren Bacall under the direction of Howard Hawks.

To remake such a well-remembered, highly regarded film was daring enough, but Winner, who was British, went a giant step further: he reset the story in the present and moved it from Los Angeles to London. "I knew the risks I was taking in doing *The Big Sleep*," he says. But then, he had never been particularly conventional. He'd made his reputation in the mid-1960s with a series of sly British comedies including *The Jokers* and *I'll Never Forget What's 'is Name* and then proceeded to produce and direct a series of Hollywood films, including 1974's *Death Wish* starring Charles Bronson as a modern vigilante.

Winner's reason for updating and relocating *The Big Sleep* was simple: he wanted to give the story a different slant. As he puts it, "Shakespeare is done in many ways in different periods, and I think that is the same for the great literature of the twentieth century. It is open to interpretation, and I don't think there's anything wrong in that."

When it came to casting, he was less adventuresome, choosing American tough guy Robert Mitchum to play Marlowe. Mitchum had, in fact, portrayed the detective once before—in 1975's *Farewell, My Lovely*, also a British production, but one steeped in the mystery's original setting and time period. Winner surrounded Mitchum with an array of celebrated British and American actors, including Sarah Miles, Candy Clark, Richard Boone, Joan Collins, Edward Fox, John Mills, and Oliver Reed.

In the fashion of *Airport '77*, Stewart had little more to do than set the stage for the melodrama—in this case by hiring Marlowe to take care of his youngest daughter's gambling debt (or blackmail scheme, as the case might be). Later, he summons Marlowe to his bedside to ask the detective to find his older daughter's missing husband—which is what he had hoped the detective would do all along.

Initially, Winner's coproducer, Elliott Kastner, wanted John Wayne to play the general. But Duke wasn't willing to take such a minor role, so the director suggested Stewart. Looking at the finished film, it is hard to imagine Wayne allowing himself to appear as such a fragile, worried old man. At one point, Marlowe, who narrates the picture in the best film noir tradition, says of the general, "He was used up. He looked more like a dead man than most dead men look." Once again, Stewart wasn't coy about his reason for accepting the assignment, telling entertainment reporter Rex Reed, "I don't believe in re-makes and it isn't much of a part, but I like to keep a finger in the pie. There isn't much work for an old codger like me back home."

The entire job took him a mere two days, one day for each scene. Once again, Jim's hearing loss caused him to miss cues and trip over his lines. "And I think that," says Winner, "like any great professional, that may have annoyed him. He may have felt that he was letting the team down. I didn't mind at all, because he was my hero." Mitchum recalls that Stewart even apologized to him after ruining several takes. The actor, who was a big fan, simply said to himself, " 'He's apologizing to me?' I couldn't get over that."

Although Jim struggled from time to time, Winner was pleased with his performance, particularly the tenderness that he brought to the role. "There was one point [in the bedroom scene]," the director recalls, "when he was making this speech, which was very heartrending, and he had me crying."

Taken as a whole, however, the picture didn't work. When it opened in New York on March 15, 1978, the reviews made the critical reaction to *Airport '77* look like raves. "Sheer artistic ineptitude is the hallmark of the new version," wrote Judith Crist in the *New York Post*, while Andrew Sarris asserted in the *Village Voice* that "every scene in this movie is lacking skill, snap, and spontaneity." Even the headlines of the reviews—playing off the picture's title—were devastating, such as the *Los Angeles Times'* "*Big Sleep* Aptly Named."

At the root of the problem was the decision to remove Chandler's story from its own time and place, thereby eliminating so many of the qualities that made the 1946 version crackle: the shadowy black-and-white photography; the snappy 1940s-style dialogue; the lush Max Steiner score; the architecture and fashions that, through an abundance of dark mysteries in the postwar period, have come to represent film noir to many moviegoers. As Molly Haskell noted in *New York*, "Marlowe, with his ironically inflated American idiom, is as out of place in the English countryside as a baseball game at Wimbledon."

Given his minor role, Stewart could hardly be blamed for *The Big Sleep*'s failings. Nevertheless, Harry Haun of the *New York Daily News* wasn't far off when he noted that "it's really sad to see James Stewart struggle so earnestly with material that just isn't there."

In a brief reminder of the old days, Jim started another film, *The Magic of Lassie*, less than two months after shooting *The Big Sleep*.

It was in 1943 that MGM introduced moviegoers to the lovable collie, the first dog star since Rin-Tin-Tin debuted at Warners in 1922. Based on the novel by Eric Knight, the picture, *Lassie, Come Home,* had also starred fifteen-year-old Roddy McDowall and eleven-year-old Elizabeth Taylor.

Over the next eight years, the collie appeared in six additional features—through 1951's *The Painted Hills.* Three years later, she debuted in a television series that ran from 1954 through 1975. Throughout this thirty-two-year reign, the collie—despite the character's name—was played by a series of males, all of which were descended from the original star, Pal (the female of the breed doesn't have as thick a coat and, therefore, isn't as photogenic).

The idea for a new feature came from another MGM veteran, Bonita Granville, who had appeared with Stewart in *The Mortal Storm.* Since then, the former child star and her husband, business tycoon Jack Wrather, had acquired the media rights to Lassie. Not only would their feature have a contemporary American setting, it would be a musical—with a score by Richard M. Sherman and Robert B. Sherman, whose delightful songs for *Mary Poppins* included the Oscar-winning "Chim-Chim-Cheree."

By 1977, Lassie was played by a frisky two-and-a-half-year-old, Pal's great-great-great-grandson. The star was supported, in turn, by two other collies: an athletic dog, for the scenes requiring the canine to run through fields, jump fences, and engage in other rigorous activity; and a trick dog, capable of turning doorknobs, taking plates off dinner tables, and other stunts. All three were trained by Rex Weatherwax. For the scenes in which Lassie was inert due to injury, the Wrathers used a stuffed dog, which the picture's cinematographer, Don Margulies, likened to "a rag dog, but with a Lassie coat."

As the picture opens, the collie is owned by Clovis Mitchell—Stewart— a crusty old winemaker living in the Sonoma Valley with his two grandchildren, Kelly (played by Stephanie Zimbalist in her feature-film debut) and Chris (twelve-year-old Michael Sharrett, who had recently costarred with Jim Dale in a Disney movie called *Hot Lead and Cold Feet*). Not only was Clovis a bigger role than any Stewart had played since *Fools' Parade*, it gave him the chance to show considerably more spunk than he had displayed in either *Airport '77* or *The Big Sleep*. Still, he was not the star of the picture. The majority of the screen time went to the dog and to Sharrett's Chris, each of whom run away from home after a wealthy neighbor, played by Pernell Roberts, claims Lassie for his own.

Filming began on September 19, 1977, at CBS's studios in Studio City, where a series of sets served as the Mitchell farmhouse interiors. For the exteriors, the cast and crew traveled to the Griffen Winery, located in Healdsburg, just north of Santa Rosa, the company's base of operations. Filming also took place in San Bernardino, California; Boomtown, Nevada; and Utah's Zion National Park.

Naturally, Stewart was delighted to be working again. "There aren't too many good grandfather parts around," he said while on location, "so when this came my way I grabbed it with both hands."

He even got to sing—or rather talk/sing—part of the opening number, "Hometown Feeling," which takes place as Clovis drives the kids into town in his Jeep. The only problem, as the company discovered when they started filming the scene, was that Stewart couldn't see to steer without his eyeglasses—but his character didn't wear spectacles. To make matters worse, the road that they had to traverse was rather narrow and windy. When the director, a good-humored Brit named Don Chaffey, called "Action," Jim, the kids, and Lassie started off in the Jeep. But, immediately thereafter, the star started shouting, "Where's the gol-darned road? Do you see a line?" Laughing, Stephanie Zimbalist adds, "And it's pretty hard to sing at this point, because we're supposed to be singing this song."

In fact, the music added another wrinkle to the situation. To help the actors lip-synch, the Jeep was outfitted with a tape recorder with the sound track. But Stewart's hearing problem mandated that they turn up the volume so high that they couldn't hear the instructions from the assistant director, who was communicating with them by walkie-talkie. The result was total chaos. "It was so funny," Zimbalist says, laughing. "He had us all in stitches."

Despite his infirmities, Stewart was, in his costar's opinion, a "total professional, knew all his lines. He didn't have a lot of patience with people who weren't professional. He expected everybody to be at his level of professionalism. And so we were." She also points out, "Everything that we know that is wonderful in Mr. Stewart is there . . . when you meet him. The integrity that the man has on film he has in spades as a person. The humor that you get from him on film is tripled when you meet him in person. The stature that he has as an actor on film is quadrupled when you spend time with him. Everything that we know that we love about Jimmy Stewart is the real thing."

Michael Sharrett, now in his thirties, also remembers Jim kindly, saying, "He didn't tell me what to do. He didn't try to tell me how to make something better," as many adult actors would have. "He left that to the director. It was so professional." He adds, with a sense of wonder, "He didn't seem to raise his voice to anyone."

When the picture wrapped, Stewart gave the boy a watch engraved, "To Chris. Love, Grandpa." He did the same with Zimbalist. "And it's a beautiful watch," she says, "which I still treasure."

Two years would pass before Stewart would work in another feature film. Sometimes he resented what was happening to him. In January of 1977, for example, he told *Newsweek*, "I'm sixty-eight years old and I feel every goddamn day of it. I don't feel young. I feel old. And I'm resigned to it."

His attitude wasn't helped by his inability to continue flying. After he retired from the Air Force Reserve, he'd acquired a Piper Cub, which he kept at the Burbank Airport. "It's very noisy," he said in 1976, "and uncomfortable and subject to turbulence; it's not a means of transportation really, and I can't even get anyone to go up with me. But I can't stay up long enough to get lonely; and besides . . . it's a way to keep my hand in."

However, as his ability to hear diminished, he became something of a hazard to himself and to others. "I knew I was in trouble," he joked, "when the guys in the control tower called me in and said, 'We have a good bit of traffic landing and taxiing, and you keep calling, "Say again." We're spending too much time repeating instructions.'" He tried using a special pair of earphones, but they didn't help. So he had to quit. He recognized the necessity, but giving up his beloved hobby was still painful.

Nevertheless, he tried, at least most of the time, to be philosophical about growing old. At the end of 1976, he said, "I've had an unbelievably wonderful life and I don't want to spoil it by becoming bitter because life can't go on as it has for these last sixty-eight years. . . . So I live day to day and I've pretty much decided now just to run the course, come what may. However, I still want to live the time I have left to the fullest."

Cases in point: On November 27, 1977, he served as the grand marshal for the forty-sixth annual Hollywood Santa Claus Lane Parade of Stars, sponsored by the Hollywood Chamber of Commerce. Eight days later, he was the narrator of a National Geographic special on PBS entitled *Yukon Passage*. The documentary followed four young men as they walked in the footsteps of Alaska's early settlers, men like Jeff Webster in *The Far*

Country. In January of 1978, Jim agreed to appear in a series of television commercials for the Firestone Tire and Rubber Company, with the first spots slated to air in September. His earnings over the three-year term of the contract were estimated at $1 million, but he would never have considered being a TV pitchman even a few years earlier when his film career was still flourishing. The following month, he and Gloria were back in Kenya, this time on a camera safari for the East African Wildlife Foundation. While he was there, the *Hollywood Reporter* announced that he would return to London's West End for another production of *Harvey.* He also wanted to take the comedy to Australia, but neither engagement materialized.

Instead, he appeared on three American television programs. First, he participated in the "American Film Institute Tribute to Henry Fonda," which aired on March 15. Then, on May 10—just two days after his seventieth birthday—he was the guest of honor on "Dean Martin's Celebrity Roast: James Stewart." As was the custom with such outings, he took his share of good-natured ribbing. Many of the jokes centered around his deliberate way of speaking. For example, Mickey Rooney quipped, "In the early days of MGM, they didn't have television and they didn't have slow motion. Then Jimmy came to Hollywood and we got slow motion. Television came later." Others made fun of his wholesome image. Said Sen. Barry Goldwater, "Everyone [during the war] had pinups of Betty Grable and Rita Hayworth. Jimmy had a pinup of John Wayne." Stewart's third TV project for the year was "The General Electric All-Star Anniversary," a sixty-minute potpourri that ABC aired on September 29 to mark the sponsor's one hundredth birthday. Blending current television actors such as Cheryl Ladd and Henry Winkler with such film greats as Elizabeth Taylor and Henry Fonda, the show found Jim impersonating Mark Twain. Interviewed by Michael Landon, he reminisced about life on the Old Mississippi.

Two months before "The General Electric All-Star Anniversary" aired, Jim returned to New York for the first time in nine years to promote *The Magic of Lassie,* which opened on August 2 at the then financially beleaguered Radio City Music Hall. In between interviews and events, he and Gloria took a horse-drawn carriage ride and caught the Tony-winning musical revue *Ain't Misbehavin'.* In characteristic fashion, he stood in line for the tickets himself. Mostly, he went about unnoticed, but, as the *New York Daily News* reported on July 30, "Leaving the Palm Restaurant one evening after a quiet dinner upstairs at his request, Jimmy, 70, was spotted and given a standing ovation by other diners. It almost moved Stewart to tears."

Unfortunately, the critical reception for *The Magic of Lassie* was nowhere near as enthusiastic. In fact, the reviews were brutal. *Variety* found the film manipulative and dishonest, while Linda Gross of the *Los Angeles Times* called the songs "syrupy." And Janet Maslin of the *New York Times* asked, "To whom is all this a worse insult—the dog lover, the music lover, the child forced to sit through the film by a well-meaning relative, or the optimist who thought the Music Hall's reprieve might amount to something? Whatever your sentiments, the point is best argued at home."

Initially, parents ignored the reviews. Children in tow, they flocked to Radio City Music Hall, where Lassie "himself" was appearing in person. In fact, the film's gross for its first week was $309,746, a new box-office record for the picture palace. Then Lassie's live engagement ended, word of mouth caught up to the musical, and its early financial promise vanished. It didn't even finish among the top one hundred movies of the year.

Travel, two personal milestones, a pair of public salutes, and a final feature film marked the end of the 1970s for Jimmy Stewart.

First, the salutes. On December 7, 1978, CBS aired "An All-Star Tribute to Jimmy Stewart." Sponsored by the Variety Clubs of America, the program, which followed previous nods to John Wayne and Elizabeth Taylor, was designed to raise money for the wing of a children's hospital. It took the form of a nightclub party, attended by a few dozen of Jim's friends, including Carol Burnett, Henry Fonda, Shirley Jones, Angie Dickinson, and Glenn Ford. Rich Little donned a rabbit suit, à la Harvey, for his patented Jimmy Stewart imitation, and the star himself took a turn at the piano, rendering his old favorite "Ragtime Cowboy Joe," with his friend Fred MacMurray accompanying him on the saxophone. As usual, Jim suffered stage fright beforehand. "Never been s'nervous about anything in my life," he said later. "But once I got *on* the thing, I had a fine time."

The second tribute came nearly a year later, on November 2, 1979. This time, the sponsor was the Friars Club, which bestowed its Life Achievement Award on Stewart at a black-tie dinner at the Beverly Hilton Hotel. The luminaries in attendance ranged from comics Don Rickles and Milton Berle, who was the emcee, to Gen. Omar Bradley and former President and Mrs. Gerald R. Ford.

In between these two public affairs came two more private celebrations. On May 19, 1979, Jim's daughter Judy married Steven Merrill, a venture capitalist from San Francisco who was ten years older than she. More rebellious than Kelly, Judy had gone through a hippie period during college, bringing home bearded, long-haired boyfriends that her mother and father had intensely disliked. After her graduation, she had traveled, sometimes with Jim and Gloria, sometimes on her own, taking odd jobs in

Nepal as well as Africa. Her choice of husband, therefore, came as a considerable surprise to her parents. Says Judy, "They thought they had died and gone to heaven when they met Steven. It was such a change. I had been dating all these hunters in Africa, so they were so thrilled that I was settling down, so to speak." The marriage has endured. The Merrills live in San Francisco with their two sons, John, born in August of 1982, and David, who followed in November of 1983.

Judy's wedding took place at the Presbyterian Church in Beverly Hills, followed by a reception in the backyard of the Stewart home. Two months later, the house on Roxbury Drive was the site of another celebration, this one to mark Jim and Gloria's thirtieth wedding anniversary. The affair was intimate, restricted to just eighty of the couple's close friends.

Sadly, one who was not present was Johnny Swope, Jim's former roommate, who had passed away that June. The photographer was the latest in a string of friends and relatives whom the star lost during the 1970s. Leland Hayward and John Ford had passed away in 1971 and 1973, respectively. Jim's sister Virginia died in 1972—followed by his other sister, Doddie, in 1977. As for Jim himself, he said at decade's end, "My heart is in good shape, knock on wood. Duke Wayne's had cancer, Hank Fonda had a heart attack, and Walter Pidgeon is recovering from a blood clot on the brain, but I just keep rollin' along like Ol' Man River."

As if to prove the point, he returned to Kenya to make one last feature film, *The Green Horizon*.

Produced by Sanrio Communications Ltd., a Japanese entertainment conglomerate, *The Green Horizon*, also known as *A Tale of Africa*, was ostensibly about an old man who lives with his granddaughter, Maya, in a house in the rain forest. Once a gold miner, he turned his back on civilization years ago, after a mine explosion killed his son. But, as the picture opens, his Eden-like existence is threatened by the arrival of a pilot whose plane has crashed nearby. The screenplay was by the film's executive producer, Shintaro Tsuji, from an original story by Shuji Terayama. The director was Susumu Hani, with an assist from the cinematographer, Simon Trevor.

Aside from wanting to work again, Stewart took the assignment because the picture offered a not-so-subtle message in support of wildlife conservation—and because it afforded him an opportunity to be in Kenya when Gloria, his daughters, and their husbands were going to be nearby on a photographic safari. Thus, the whole clan could spend Christmas together. In fact, when Jim arrived at their campsite from the film's location in west Kenya, Kelly greeted him decked out in a Santa Claus outfit, complete with a beard made of shaving cream. "After the laughs had died down," he recalled, "we all gathered around the fire, had a wonderful Christmas Eve dinner, and sang carols. Here we were, thousands of miles from home, and repeating a scene we had played so many times before in Beverly Hills." It was, in his view, a "memorable" occasion, one that he would fondly remember.

Unfortunately, *The Green Horizon* was far more prosaic. Director Susumu Hani spoke no English, which precluded conversation with his star. To make matters worse, he couldn't decide if he wanted to make a documentary or a melodrama, so he did neither. To the extent that the story existed at all, it was ridiculously simplistic, with stock characters: the unspoiled, young beauty; the handsome, gallant pilot; and the cantankerous but loving old man. Worse was Tsuji's silly, minimalistic dialogue.

The only redeeming element of *The Green Horizon* was its loving shots of lions, wildebeests, gibbons, and other African wildlife in their native habitats. Impressive though this footage was, the filmmakers' use of it undercut the flow of the picture, adding a disjointed quality to what was already undeveloped and confused. As *Variety* observed, "This may be the slowest moving picture this side of a Cezanne still life. . . . [The] obsessive fascination with wild animals . . . not only serve[s] to break the already stately pace of the story, but to stretch this paper-thin tale to an almost unbearable length."

Prior to *The Green Horizon,* Sanrio had produced animated films and documentaries for the Asian market. The company had hoped that this, its first live-action feature, would give it an international presence. Instead, producers Terry Ogisu and Yoichi Matsue failed to find an American or British distributor, and consequently, the picture went unseen on movie screens in both the United States and Great Britain.

PART SEVEN

· *A National Treasure* ·

TWENTY-ONE

The 1980s

Jimmy Stewart acted in only three projects during the 1980s, but he did not meet with the decline in popularity that most film stars experience when the major roles disappear. Rather, an unusual combination of circumstances transformed him during the decade into an American icon.

The first of these factors was the public domain status of *It's a Wonderful Life*, which led to saturation showings of the film each Christmas season during the decade. Just as annual airings of *The Wizard of Oz* have forever kept Judy Garland a teenager in a blue-checked dress, so Frank Capra's small-town fable made Jimmy Stewart an American Everyman for millions of baby boomers and their children. Unlike those who saw the film upon its release in 1946—when America was experiencing tremendous growth at home and assuming a leadership role in the world community—the postwar generations found resonance in the film's depiction of a simpler time and its espousal of clear-cut wholesome values. Like the concurrent president, Ronald Reagan, and the decade's most popular TV star, Bill Cosby, sweet, ebullient, honorable George Bailey was a hero for the 1980s, and Jimmy Stewart *was* George Bailey.

Without intending to do so, Jim reinforced the image through his occasional appearances on *The Tonight Show Starring Johnny Carson*— the second of the elements that accounted for his iconic status during the decade. Again, circumstance played a role in this development: the demise of *The Dean Martin Show* in 1974 had left Jim without an outlet for the annual appearance that he liked to make in America's living rooms. Starting in October of 1979, when he helped celebrate *Tonight*'s seventeenth anniversary, the late-night chat fest became his new TV venue.

In a significant respect, *The Tonight Show* was better than *The Dean Martin Show* or its predecessor, *The Jack Benny Show*, because it was not a variety program. Instead of acting in skits or rendering ditties, Jim simply chatted with Johnny Carson, who clearly treasured the old pro. As the star talked about his recent activities, including his trips to Africa, and occasionally recited one of his poems, millions of Americans grasped what his friends and family already knew, that he was a man with a delightful, often self-deprecating, sense of humor. Stammering and stuttering, drawing blank expressions that suggested he had no idea where he was headed in whatever yarn he was spinning, he would delight the host, the studio audience, and the viewers at home with his cornpone wit and unique point of view.

To some extent, the Jimmy on the tube was as much an act as the roles he had played on the big screen. A consummate storyteller, he was fully cognizant of the elements of the persona that made him so beloved. When he wanted to, he could talk in a brisk, straightforward manner; he could also be stubborn and willful. But he did not fabricate a personality out of whole cloth. He merely exaggerated the best of himself—as anyone might do at a party or other public setting. And the public loved what he gave them. If George Bailey was the father everyone wanted, Jimmy Stewart was the ideal grandfather: not the Jimmy Stewart who played ineffectual old men in forgettable movies such as *Airport '77, The Big Sleep,* and *The Magic of Lassie,* but the real thing, the avuncular, slightly dotty old man who sat next to Johnny and talked about his dogs, his family, and his travels. As Fred De Cordova, who produced *The Tonight Show,* put it, "He was—it's a strange word to use—but he was a darling. And you felt that a friend was in your home, not just a movie star."

Of course, the myriad honors befitting a star of nearly eighty feature films also kept Stewart in the public eye during the 1980s. One of the most important of these, the Lifetime Achievement Award from the American Film Institute, came at the dawn of the decade.

Broadcast on CBS on March 16, some two weeks after the actual banquet was held at the Beverly Hilton Hotel, the tribute was hosted by Henry Fonda and featured remarks by Princess Grace of Monaco, Frank Capra, Walter Matthau, Beulah Bondi, and other friends and colleagues. The most moving tribute came from Dustin Hoffman. Representing a younger generation of actors, he spoke eloquently about Stewart's talent and, in particular, about *It's a Wonderful Life,* which he had seen for the first time only a few days earlier. Stewart graciously accepted the award at the conclusion of the evening, saying, "I promised myself to talk fast, so you could all get home tonight. The problem is, I don't know how to talk fast." Only the eighth individual to be honored by the AFI, he added that getting the award was "like tying a wonderful ribbon around a lifetime that has allowed me to get paid for what I loved to do. I'm grateful for every wonderful day in this wonderful business."[1] The *Hollywood Reporter*'s Hank Grant called the tribute "a beautifully planned and executed affair. . . . A thrilling night for a most deserving gent."

[1] The previous honorees were John Ford, James Cagney, Orson Welles, William Wyler, Bette Davis, Henry Fonda, and Alfred Hitchcock.

* * *

Four days after the airing of the AFI tribute, Stewart was again before a TV camera, this time in an acting role.

Developed by Mike McLean of Salt Lake City's Bonneville Productions (no relation to Jim's son of the same name) and produced in association with the Church of Latter-Day Saints, *Mr. Krueger's Christmas* was about a poor, lonely widower—Stewart—whose holiday is brightened by a heavenly vision. The star had hoped that Frank Capra would direct the half-hour fable, but the director, distrustful of the Mormon Church's involvement in the project, declined. It was directed instead by Keith Merrill.

For Jim, the high point of the filming, which took place in Salt Lake City, came with a sequence in which Krueger imagines himself conducting the Mormon Tabernacle Choir. He called it "one of the damnedest experiences I've ever had. I've been a great fan of the Tabernacle Choir for years and years, and to suddenly find myself up there on the platform, facing the choir and leading them in a song—it's something I'll never forget."

Sold by syndication, *Mr. Krueger's Christmas* aired on local stations during the 1980 holiday season—it was seen on KTLA, Channel 5, in Los Angeles, on December 19. John Corry of the *New York Times* found that it offered "traces of the famous Stewart charm," but likened it to a home movie and ultimately reduced it to "a sentimental curio." Frank Torrez, his colleague on the *Los Angeles Herald-Examiner*, was more enthusiastic, calling the program "a fine opportunity to watch the artistry of James Stewart in an often-touching, well-mounted drama."

By the time *Mr. Krueger's Christmas* aired, Stewart was at home, recuperating from a painful sciatic condition that had sent him to St. John's Hospital in Santa Monica in September. Only a month earlier, he'd spent six days in the hospital's coronary unit due to an irregular heartbeat—a malady from which he made, in the words of a hospital spokesperson, "a complete recovery."

In fact, by January 1, 1981, he was well enough to serve as the grand marshal in the annual New Year's Day Tournament of Roses Parade in Pasadena, followed on the nineteenth by the gala at the Capital Centre in Landover, Maryland, to mark the inauguration of Ronald Reagan as the fortieth president of the United States. The bill for the gala included Bob Hope, Ethel Merman, Mel Tillis, Debbie Boone, Charlie Pride, and Charlton Heston with Johnny Carson as the master of ceremonies. For his bit, Stewart accompanied a wheelchair-bound Omar Bradley, representing the armed services. Dressed in a tuxedo with his pilot's wings and service medals on his jacket, Jim said to his old friend Reagan, "It is an honor for me to salute you as the new commander-in-chief. It is an honor for me to be able to call you, from now on, Mr. President." Jim then snapped off a salute, which Reagan, rising from his chair, returned with tears in his eyes. On February 6, Jim and Gloria were back in Reagan's company, this time to mark the president's seventieth birthday in a private party at the White House.

A third trip to the Beltway came on December 6, 1981—to salute Cary Grant, one of the year's Kennedy Center honorees. This event kicked off another round of activity. On February 14, 1982, Jim participated in the gala Night of 100 Stars at Radio City Music Hall. He was part of a group, representing Hollywood's golden age, that included Bette Davis, Myrna Loy, Gene Kelly, Ginger Rogers, Lillian Gish, and James Cagney.

From New York, Jim and Gloria flew to Germany, where he was honored with a retrospective and a special Golden Bear Award at the thirty-second Berlin International Film Festival. The following month, starting on March 15, he joined host David Hartman for a series of interviews on *Good Morning America.* And on March 21, he fired the starting pistol for the first annual Jimmy Stewart National Relay Marathon in Los Angeles. The event featured 512 five-person teams and raised $150,000 for one of Jim and Gloria's favorite charities, St. John's Hospital. Since then, the marathon, which still bears Stewart's name but is hosted by others, principally Robert Wagner, has raised in excess of $5 million. Finally, in May, Jim and Gloria returned to Europe. A highlight of the trip was an audience with Pope John Paul II on the twenty-first of the month.

Three months later, on August 11, Henry Fonda died. The previous March, the actor's delightful performance in *On Golden Pond* had earned him the Academy Award that had eluded him throughout his career. But he had been too ill to attend the ceremonies. Indeed, he had been bedridden for months. Stewart had faithfully visited him during this period—usually two or three times a week. When they had something to say to each other, they shouted, Fonda being nearly as hard of hearing as Jim. But they spent most of the time in companionable silence, just as they had in better days.

After Hank's death, old friends mourned with the family at his widow Shirlee's home. His son, Peter, remembers Jim sitting in the library in a big chair that Hank had used for reading. Jim didn't say anything. He just sat there staring into space as the other guests conversed around him. Then, finally, he spread his hands to indicate a span of about five feet and said quietly, "It was this big." Because he'd been silent for so long, everyone turned to look at him. "It was this big," he repeated. "The airplane model we built." For a moment, he was back in 1935. He and Hank were young, their careers full of promise, and they were coming back to the hotel on Madison Avenue after their respective Broadway shows to build their first model airplane, the same one that Jim would finish and bring with him to California that summer. Says Peter, "For me it was reliving a moment that was magical and listening to a man who knew how to tell a story magically."

Ten days after Fonda's death, Stewart returned to the coronary unit at St. John's, looking wan and complaining of chest pains. He was still profoundly depressed over Hank's death. "I still think of him," Jim told Hollywood reporter Gregory Speck, "as a very loyal and close friend with tremendous energy and a total love of theater and of acting." He added, "It was a wonderful influence on me, too, to see him apply this constant effort to his craft. I learned a great deal from watching him work. We learned from one another, I guess."

Ironically, the last major project of his career—which began filming on October 11, two months to the day of Fonda's passing—had to do with the pain of growing old and the loss of a loved one.

Right of Way by Richard Lees was about an elderly Santa Monica couple, Mini and Teddy Dwyer, who decide to take their lives after they discover that she is suffering from a terminal illness. Their adult daughter, Ruda, unable to accept their decision, enlists a local social service agency to stop them.

Lees' stage play was initially produced at the Tyrone Guthrie Theater in Minneapolis, where it was well received. But plans to move it to New York were thwarted by the presence of two somewhat related plays on Broadway, the comic drama about an elderly couple in which Fonda would star on film, *On Golden Pond*, and a drama about suicide, *Whose Life Is It Anyway?* With nowhere else to turn, Lees sent the script to Bette Davis, his ideal choice for the role of Mini.

The two-time Oscar-winning actress, one month Stewart's senior, had been more successful than he at keeping her career afloat. Indeed, since 1972, she had made thirteen well-produced films for television, including *The Dark Secret of Harvest Home*, from the best-seller by Tom Tryon; *Family Reunion;* and *Little Gloria . . . Happy at Last,* the story of the custody battle over young Gloria Vanderbilt. One of her most successful projects, 1982's *A Piano for Mrs. Cimino,* had been directed by George Schaefer, so she sent *Right of Way* to him. In turn, he acquired the property for the independent production company that he had recently formed with Merrill Karpf.

"It was not a subject networks were eager to buy," Schaefer recalled. But he managed to sell it to Home Box Office, which was then starting to produce original films for its premium cable channel. HBO bought *Right of Way* because it was, to quote the company's vice president, Jane Deknatel, "extraordinary, provocative, and interesting material." She added, "I think the issue of two people taking their own lives—and whether they have the right to do so—is fairly tough stuff."

Of course, the presence of Davis was a big plus—as was Stewart as her costar. Lees had, in fact, written the part of Teddy with Jim in mind. Given his own enduring marriage, the star had no trouble identifying with the project's theme. He told Elizabeth Mehren of *Emmy Magazine* that he could "sympathize with loneliness in old age, and the desire for two people who have been together to be together in old age." Could he commit suicide? she asked. "I've thought about it a lot," he replied, "and, yes, I think I could imagine myself in that position."

As this was the largest part he'd had in years, Stewart devoted a month to learning his lines. He wanted to have the dialogue thoroughly memorized so that, during production, he could concentrate on his blocking, building his character, and relating to Davis and Melinda Dillon, the actress cast as their daughter. "Bette said she did the same thing," he said with surprise. "She was letter-perfect the first time we rehearsed."

Given their similar ways of working and their love of acting, Stewart and Davis—who barely knew each other beforehand—got along beautifully during the five days of rehearsal and twenty days of filming, most of which took place at the Laird Studios in Culver City. "I've never had a more delightful experience," Bette told one reporter shortly thereafter. "We were both in practically every scene, and if we hadn't liked each other, we would have made it, but it wouldn't have been nearly as special an occasion. I just found him *heaven*." Returning the compliment, Stewart said, "Bette is absolutely amazing. Professional just isn't . . . it's more than that. She's just a master of craft. When she's there, she's *there*." Schaefer wasn't surprised by their rapport. "Well, they're both likable people," he says, "and both big stars who had a greater heyday than this. So they could look back on the past and the record. All the time they kept saying 'Why haven't we worked together?' and 'My goodness, we should do this again' and that sort of thing."

The director remembers that the production went smoothly, despite the menagerie of cats playing the Dwyers' pets (all named after movie stars). Moreover, he and Davis were patient when Stewart's hearing loss caused occasional problems. These were mostly minor, Schaefer says, recalling only one scene in which the star had genuine difficulty with his dialogue. It came when Mini and Teddy are in bed, and the husband is railing about the state of the world. It was, in Schaefer's words, "a very hard-hitting speech to do, and he kept fluffing on it. And there were four or five takes of it when he went up completely in the second line." After one muff, Schaefer told the cameraman to cut. But, not hearing him, Stewart did the speech again, and, unfortunately, that time he was letter-perfect. Extremely upset when he learned that the camera hadn't been rolling, he nevertheless rendered the lines once more. "I don't think he was quite as good as he had been on the take that we didn't get," says the director, "but it was imperceptible, and it was a wonderful reading of the speech. He conquered it finally."

Although filming ended before the close of 1982, HBO didn't air *Right of Way* until November of 1983—a considerable delay for television, where films are typically shown a month or two after wrapping. What kept Lees' drama on the shelf was its ending. As written, the Dwyers' suicide attempt is thwarted, and Mini and Teddy are placed in separate nursing facilities. Thereafter, a repentant Ruda tells her mother that she will help if the occasion arises again. "It was a disturbing ending," explained Schaefer, "because you wanted them to succeed."

The biggest advocate for giving the audience a cathartic conclusion was Michael Fuchs, then president of HBO. In fact, he hated the ending as it played in the director's cut. Schaefer concedes that the executive wasn't totally wrong. He recalls a screening of the film with the original ending at the Directors Guild, saying that, when the lights came up, "the audience who was there, who had been very involved in the story, were in no mood to celebrate. They were angry. It was like being at a wake practically. They were grumbling and saying like 'Why couldn't they get away with it?' and all that."

But neither the stars nor Schaefer wanted to end on a purely pat note. So the picture remained unseen for months while those involved tried to negotiate a new course. Finally, Stewart came up with the solution: let the daughter return to the house while her mother and father are killing themselves by running their car in a closed garage. Therefore, the decision to save them or not rests with her—and she decides to let them follow their wishes. "To me that was fine," says Schaefer, and Fuchs okayed it as well. Thus the interior set was rebuilt, and Melinda Dillon brought in for a reshoot. She, Schaefer, and the crew also had to film at the Santa Monica home initially rented by the company; but neither Stewart nor Davis was needed. Schaefer places the cost of the additional filming at roughly $150,000.

Unfortunately, the finished product failed to justify the effort. Although many of the TV critics, including the influential Kay Gardella of the *New York Daily News*, celebrated the first—and only—pairing of two of Hollywood's greatest stars, with the inevitable comparison to the initial teaming of Fonda and Katharine Hepburn in *On Golden Pond*, Fred Rothenberg of the *New York Post* asserted that "even these two troupers can't save HBO's boring, humorless made-for-TV movie." As for *On*

Golden Pond, he argued that the feature "was about life, revealing with warmth and great wit the devotion of its old couple. *Right of Way* has no such life to it, offering two eccentrics who mainly because of a dull script touch but never seem to feel."

He was right. Long stretches of conversation between Mini and Teddy in the 106-minute telefilm seem pointless—about whether he owns too many books and the best route for a drive. At times, the dialogue almost resembles *Waiting for Godot,* but without Samuel Beckett's humor.

Moreover, Stewart, despite several endearing moments, is unnecessarily weak and doddering. Davis is more effective in the stronger role, and Dillon is poignant as the conflicted daughter. Ultimately, the film has an important point to make—that senior citizens have the right to live their own lives—but it never comes into effective focus. Perhaps a sixty-minute version of the drama, without the padding, would have rendered the theme more clearly. Still, Stewart had no regrets about the project. Working with a star of Bette Davis' caliber and talent was, in his words, "something I'll never forget." Indeed, he considered *Right of Way* "one of the finest experiences I've had in my whole career as an actor." Aside from a brief cameo, it was also his last on-camera role.

On May 8, 1983, Jim turned seventy-five. His hometown, Indiana, Pennsylvania, marked the occasion with a lavish three-day celebration that included a parade, a Jimmy Stewart film festival, a dinner dance, and the unveiling of a nine-foot statue of the honoree, which was sculpted by a Californian, Malcolm Alexander, and set before the county courthouse on Philadelphia Street. During the festivities, roughly forty thousand people swelled the ranks, more than double the local population.

Jim and Gloria spent the weekend with his boyhood friend Hall Blair and Hall's wife, Elinor. "It was an eye-opener for me," Mrs. Blair recalls. "I had no idea what we were getting into when we asked him to stay. Because everybody we ever knew wanted a special chance to meet him. Finally, we had to get our telephone to have an unlisted number, because it would have rung every minute he was here." She adds, "He was gracious, always gracious." He was also impressed by the planning that went into the celebration. "He really thought it was wonderful," she says, "and he said that to everybody."

Later that month, Jim took Gloria to England for another glimpse into his past, his service during World War II. The occasion was the dedication ceremony of the 453rd Bombardment Group Memorial in Norwich. Rather than a plaque or statue, the former airmen had commemorated their fallen comrades by financing the construction of a new wing for the Village Hall.

Then, in October, came another reminder of the star's glory days, the rerelease of *Rear Window.*

For years, Alfred Hitchcock had refused to allow screenings of this and four other pictures that he had made during the late 1940s and 1950s, the rights to which had reverted back to him eight years after each film's release. But three years after the director's death in 1980, his estate granted Universal Pictures the right to license the vintage properties. So great was the interest in these long-unseen classics that *Rear Window,* the first to be released, set new opening day box-office records at three Manhattan theaters. In five months, it grossed $6.8 million, more than it had earned initially.

As *Vertigo, Rope,* and *The Man Who Knew Too Much* were three of the four other pictures in the package (*The Trouble With Harry* being the only non-Stewart vehicle), this series marked yet another in those unusual circumstances that kept Stewart firmly in the public consciousness during the 1980s. For each picture opened with considerable fanfare and sparked major critical attention. *Rear Window,* for example, prompted Vincent Canby of the *New York Times* to write, "At the heart of the film are the grand performances of Mr. Stewart, whose longtime star status in Hollywood has always obscured recognition of his talent, and Miss Kelly, who, after receiving star billing in three previous films, showed that she was entitled to it in *Rear Window.* After nearly 30 years, the enormous glamour of these two personalities remains as fresh and attractive as ever." When *Vertigo* was released a month later, Peter Rainer of the *Los Angeles Herald-Examiner* called Jim's work in *that* picture "perhaps his most delicate, heartbreaking performance. Stewart's acting holds the film together and gives it much of its overpowering emotional force."

Beyond the star's work, the rereleases caused major critical reappraisals of the pictures, particularly of *The Man Who Knew Too Much,* elevating what had once been considered minor Hitchcock to a much higher plateau. By the same token, the rerelease of *Vertigo* caused Andrew Sarris, who had dismissed the picture years earlier, to change his mind. "*Vertigo* looks and sounds magnificent after more than a quarter of a century," he asserted in the *Village Voice.* "Of how many contemporary films will we be able to say the same 25 years hence?"

A significant side issue came with the rerelease of *Rear Window.* During the 1970s, the 1940 short story on which the film was based had been acquired by a self-described literary speculator named Sheldon Abend. Abend sued Stewart and the other owners of the picture for a share of the film's profits by virtue of his ownership of the underlying material. Ironically, if the story's author, Cornell Woolrich, had been alive at the time, the issue would have been moot, because he had granted Hitchcock and his partners the film rights to the story in perpetuity. However, Woolrich had died in 1968, just before his copyright came up for a twenty-eight-year renewal.

In a landmark 1990 decision, the U.S. Supreme Court held that an author could not sign away a property's second twenty-eight-year earnings, because it deprived his or her heirs of the potential profits from such licensing. Moreover, without such approval, the derivative material could not remain in the public arena. This argument ran counter to the widely held interpretation of films and plays as works independent of their source material. In the decision, Justice Sandra Day O'Connor wrote that the "aspects of a derivative work added by the derivative author are that author's property but the element drawn from the preexisting work remains on grant from the owner of the preexisting work."[2]

By a strange coincidence, this decision would inspire Republic Pictures to acquire the copyrights to the underlying material in *It's a Wonderful Life* a few years later and, thereby, gain control of the picture itself.

Capping off a memorable 1983, Stewart became a Kennedy Center honoree in a December 4 ceremony held at the performing arts center in Washington, D.C. Although the awards, which honored lifetime achievement in the performing arts, were less than a decade old, they carried considerable prestige—as evidenced by those named along with Stewart: Frank Sinatra, dancer-choreographer Katherine Dunham, director Elia Kazan, and composer-critic Virgil Thompson. Previous Hollywood honorees had included Fred Astaire, Henry Fonda, James Cagney, Helen Hayes, Lillian Gish, and Gene Kelly.

Stewart, Sinatra, and the others received their medallions at a State Department dinner on December 3. The following evening, they attended a White House reception, at which President Reagan made a few remarks about each of them. When he came to Stewart, he mentioned *Mr. Smith Goes to Washington,* saying, "I wish everyone here would see that film." Then he recounted the famous story in which Jack Warner, upon learning of Reagan's decision to run for governor of California, quipped, "No. Jimmy Stewart for governor. Ronald Reagan for best friend." At the gala that followed, Jim sat next to Nancy Reagan as the portion of the program devoted to him unfolded onstage. It was narrated by Burt Lancaster, who described Stewart as "the most complete cinema personality in the American scene." Then Jim's friend and ardent admirer Carol Burnett sang "Easy to Love," the song that the star had introduced in *Born to Dance.* She

---

[2] This decision only applied to works before 1976. More recent material is governed by the Copyright Act of 1976, which became effective on January 1, 1978.

was joined by the Cadet Chorale of the United States Air Force. A few weeks later, the gala was broadcast on television.

More accolades followed in 1985. On March 25, Stewart received an honorary Oscar for lifetime achievement from the Academy of Motion Picture Arts and Sciences. Exactly two months later, on May 25, President Reagan bestowed on him the Presidential Medal of Freedom. Jim shared the moment with twelve other honorees, including bandleader Count Basie, pilot Chuck Yeager, and former U.S. ambassador to the United Nations Jeane Kirkpatrick. And finally, in June, he received a lifetime achievement award from the Cannes Film Festival and the French government. The occasion was marked by the showing of a newly restored print of *The Glenn Miller Story*, with June Allyson on hand to share the moment with her three-time costar.

During the year, Stewart also narrated a one-hour documentary called *Air Force One: The Planes and the Presidents*, which PBS aired on March 7. On that occasion, John Corry of the *New York Times* wrote, "Mr. Stewart has an all-time, all-American voice, and it's a comfort to hear it, a sign that traditional culture persists. A man who played Charles Lindbergh can lend a sense of history."

No doubt, the same thinking inspired producer David Wolper to cast Stewart in a cameo role in *North and South, Book II*. Based on the 1984 novel *Love and War* by John Jakes, the twelve-hour miniseries aired on ABC over five evenings in May of 1986. It followed the equally long *North and South*—from Jakes' novel of the same name—which had aired the previous November. Combined, the two miniseries covered the tribulations of two fictional families, the northern Hazards and the southern Mains, from the 1840s through the Civil War. In *Book II*, the principal actors— Patrick Swayze, James Read, and Lesley-Anne Down—were joined by a number of stars in cameos, including Morgan Fairchild, Linda Evans, Nancy Marchand as Dorothea Dix, Anthony Zerbe as Ulysses S. Grant, Lloyd Bridges as Jefferson Davis, and Hal Holbrook as Abraham Lincoln. Stewart, playing a southern attorney named Miles Colbert, had only one scene, which was shot at an antebellum-style mansion in Los Angeles. The critics found both miniseries ponderous and silly, but they performed extremely well in the ratings.

The following March 13, Jim made another televised appearance, this time as himself in a segment of PBS's *Great Performances* entitled "James Stewart: A Wonderful Life." Created by documentary filmmakers David Heeley and Jean Kramer and written by John L. Miller, the 110-minute program offered what *Variety* called "an affectionate and satisfying glimpse into Stewart's career and personal life." In addition to film clips, Heeley and Kramer brought together wonderful home movies from the

Stewart family's private collection and interviews with a wide range of stars—including Nancy Reagan, Richard Dreyfuss, Clint Eastwood, Katharine Hepburn, and Sally Field. As an added bonus, Johnny Carson hosted and narrated the show and appeared on camera in a series of brief chats with Stewart himself. These were filmed on the Universal backlot, where so many of Jim's hits from the 1950s had been made. "What was fun about it," says Jean Kramer, "was that they were really having a good time. Jimmy was returning to the scenes of so many of his movies, and Johnny was like a kid. . . . I knew he was a fan of Jimmy, but I didn't know he was that well versed [in Stewart's body of work]. In particular, he saw every one of his Westerns when he was a kid."

Prior to the filming at Universal, Heeley and Kramer taped Stewart at his home, eliciting comments that were inserted at various points within the narrative. Like those who worked on *Airport '77*, the filmmakers were struck by the way Stewart came to life on camera. "Jimmy lost years," says Kramer, "both in his house and certainly on the backlot with Johnny." Still, the long stretches between jobs, plus his age and hearing loss, had taken their toll. "This is conjecture," says Heeley, "but I think when we had him, he was reaching the point where he was getting a little nervous about could he do it."

No doubt, Heeley was right. Stewart was eager to continue acting. "I want to keep working," he said in 1985, adding, "When it's time for me to quit, I know I'll get the message loud and clear—from the audience." But he also limited the options available to him. At one point, he groused, "I keep looking for a script that doesn't have a part designed for me as a grouchy old grandfather. I don't see why all grandfathers have to be grouchy." Nevertheless, in 1987, he turned down something very different, the role of a lively old writer and teacher in a feature film called *Rocket Gibraltar.* He declined because the character died at the end. The part went instead to Burt Lancaster.

Even William Hayward, the son of Jim's old friends Leland and Maggie Sullavan, tried to find worthwhile projects for the star. Says Hayward, "I'd ask him, 'Jimmy, do you want to read this or that,' and he'd come up with some goofball reason [for refusing]. I'd just go, 'Oh, okay.' It's like you can't even argue with it." Perhaps it was fear or stubbornness or both, but as Hayward asserts, "He took himself out of the loop more than other actors would have, in part by only doing family fare. He may not have intended to do that, but he certainly achieved it. Movies, in his mind, kind of went down the toilet. In his mind they weren't making many of the kind of movies that he thought they ought to make."

* * *

For Jim, 1988 was much like its predecessors. On February 25, the American Museum of the Moving Image, whose facility in Astoria, Queens, would open a few months later, paid tribute to him in a benefit at the Waldorf-Astoria Hotel. Nearly a thousand celebrities attended the black-tie affair, with Nancy Reagan and eight other notables offering remarks. The highlight of the evening was the tribute by Oscar-winner Richard Dreyfuss, who said, "You have taught and trained me to be an actor. You inspired me as a storyteller. You personify for me a part of this nation. You symbolize an America that is gentle, ironic, self-deprecating, tough, and emotional."

On June 16, a "tough and emotional" Jimmy Stewart was in Washington, D.C., appearing before a Senate committee to protest the computer colorization of old movies on television. The previous fall, he'd expressed his outrage in an article in the Screen Actors Guild magazine, *Screen Actor*, writing, "Adding a layer of color to a black and white film is like painting over something that's already been painted perfectly well. It's terrible." He cited, as an example, *It's a Wonderful Life*, which had aired in a colorized format the previous year. "When I think," he wrote, "of Frank Capra's fine cinematographer, Joe Walker, and the time he spent on the delicate lighting and built-in shadow of *It's a Wonderful Life*—to have that work wiped out by computerized color which destroys the delicate shadows and depths of each scene—it makes me *mad*." He also placed before the Senate the similar views expressed in a letter by Frank Capra, who was too ill to appear in person.

On September 23, Jim and Gloria were again in the East, this time to attend a Manhattan screening of *Gorillas in the Mist* to benefit the African Wildlife Foundation, of which Mrs. Stewart was a board member. The film, starring Sigourney Weaver, was based on the book by daughter Kelly's former boss Dian Fossey. A much sadder occasion brought them back to New York in mid-November: a memorial tribute to Joshua Logan, who had died the previous July at the age of seventy-nine. Remembering how the director had talked his father into letting him join the University Players more than fifty years earlier, Stewart told the assemblage, "I'll always, always really be grateful with all my heart to Josh Logan, because he gave me my acting career."

At least the decade ended on a rosier note for Stewart, with two new ventures. The first was Crown Books' publication of *Jimmy Stewart and His Poems*. "He got my name from someone," says Betty Prashker, Crown's executive vice president and editor at large, "and he called. And, of course, I couldn't believe that he was on the phone. He said that he had these four poems that he wanted to publish in a book, and would I be interested. And I said I definitely was."

The first piece was actually written in the late 1950s. At the time, Jim and Gloria were on a fishing trip in west-central Argentina with Fran and Bess Johnson. When they stopped at a hotel in Junín de los Andes, they found themselves tripping on the top step in a flight of stairs that led to their rooms. Later Jim told Gloria, "That step in Junín was mean," inadvertently making a rhyme. Thus inspired, he fleshed out the story and the result was a twenty-line poem.

His second effort was the one inspired by that chilly night in the Aberdare Mountains of Africa (see page 321). The third, "I'm a Movie Camera," also stemmed from a safari. In this case, Stewart recounted the misfortunes of a new Instamatic eight-millimeter movie camera that was chewed up by a hyena in Nairobi. The fourth and final poem recalled a willful but beloved family pet, a golden retriever named Beau. It ended with Stewart mourning the dog's death. Says daughter Judy, "I've often felt that the poem that Dad wrote about Beau was really about Ron. That's just a personal opinion, but it was such a devastating poem. . . . I mean, he loved Beau, but it feels like it was more than that."

In the years since they were written, Jim had read the poems on *The Tonight Show,* and after fans began writing for copies, he decided to have them published. Prashker says that he had approached others before coming to her, but everyone else had asked him either to produce more poems or to create lengthy commentaries between the quartet to make the book bigger. "And he didn't want to do that," she says. "He just wanted to do the four poems. I thought the book could stand alone, because it was Jimmy Stewart, and it was so outrageous. And he was very determined. I didn't see how it could fail." With his permission, she hired Cheryl Gross to illustrate the material, adding an extra dimension to what became a very slight thirty-two-page book.

But Prashker's instincts proved correct. Published in hardcover in August of 1989 at $9.95, *Jimmy Stewart and His Poems* became a major *New York Times* best-seller with sales of several hundred thousand copies—a feat helped significantly by the promotional tour that Stewart undertook on the book's behalf. Despite his success, Jim had no illusions about the quality of his writings. "I just hope the readers see some humor in them," he said at the time. "I think it's a little too much to call it poetry. They're just sort of stories that rhyme."

Given the popularity of his first book, Prashker naturally asked for a follow-up. She knew that Stewart was out of "stories that rhyme" and that he was not willing to undertake a full-scale autobiography. His major contributions in that regard had come with his participation in

James Stewart: A Wonderful Life and, before that, with a five-part series of feature articles "as told to Pete Martin," which the *Saturday Evening Post* had published in 1961. Since then, numerous publishers had tried to interest him in telling his story in book form. But, in 1978, he said, "I'm not a journalist and I don't like the idea of hiring a 'ghost' or having a life story written by someone other than the person who lived it." According to one friend, however, he did agree to do an autobiography at one point. A writer was hired and the book contracts were signed, and then his collaborator backed out. Stewart felt so betrayed that he refused to even consider the option thereafter.

What Prashker had in mind, however, was far less ambitious. She wanted him simply to tell the stories that he loved to recount, such as the yarn about taking Kate Hepburn flying while making *The Philadelphia Story* and the one about knocking Greta Garbo down in his haste to meet her at MGM. It would have been a simple undertaking. But Jim was not interested. He'd done the book he'd wanted to do, and that was enough. Thus, his career as a best-selling author came to an end.

He concluded the 1980s as a significant presence—once again—on American television. He wasn't in a new cable movie or a sitcom or on *The Tonight Show*. In fact, his face wasn't even seen. But his voice was unmistakable in a series of commercials for a brand of soup called Campbell's Home Cookin'. This well-orchestrated campaign linked wholesome family values and the sponsor's product. In one spot, for example, Stewart offers soup to calm a teenage girl who is fuming over her boyfriend. In another, a steaming bowl helps him talk his six-year-old grandson out of running away from home.

Curiously, the campaign was not created with Jim in mind, but no one could have better suited the all-American image that Campbell's wanted to evoke. That his face was never seen simply added to the mystique. Jim didn't mind not appearing on camera. As he put it, "It sorta tickled me— the idea of doing a voice-over and having a hand come out and take the soup."

TWENTY-TWO

"It's Over"

For Stewart, the 1990s began as an extension of the 1980s. There were more honors—the Woodrow Wilson Award on February 24, 1990, from Princeton, recognizing his service to the nation; a tribute from the Film Society of Lincoln Center two months later. There were a few personal appearances, including his participation in "Night of 100 Stars III," which aired on NBC on May 21, 1990. There were family milestones: on May 7, 1991, the twins turned forty, which gave rise to a celebration at Chasen's.

There was even a bit of work, as Jim gave voice to a character in Universal's animated feature entitled *An American Tail: Fievel Goes West,* the sequel to the 1986 megahit about a family of immigrant mice, *An American Tail.* Both features were coproduced by the most popular filmmaker of the modern era, Steven Spielberg—who directed Stewart's performance for the voice-over at the actor's insistence.

Jim was nervous, being in unfamiliar territory, but his performance as a gunfighting hound dog called Wylie Burp virtually stole the picture. However, the feature, released on November 22, 1991, failed to equal the charm of its predecessor or the brilliance of the Disney studio's *Beauty and the Beast,* which debuted a few days earlier. Despite its considerable $20 million budget, *An American Tail: Fievel Goes West* was a box-office disaster. As one Universal executive put it, "It was charmless. Even the animation was fairly pedestrian."

The animated feature was Stewart's last professional job. Having finally reconciled himself to retirement, he said in 1992, "It's over. I think it's a time thing. I've run out of acting ability. And I think it's just age. I'm sorry if people don't like it that way."

At roughly the same time, his active personal schedule was curtailed by health problems. In July of 1990, he canceled a planned visit to Great Britain because his doctors felt that the transatlantic flight would be too strenuous. Moreover, that September he was unable to attend a tribute in his honor at the annual video trade show in Toronto. Then, in mid-March of 1993, he was hospitalized for an irregular heartbeat, the same malady that had plagued him a decade earlier. His stay at St. John's was brief, only about four days, but he was placed on medication and outfitted with a pacemaker. When some forty friends gathered at his home two months later, to mark his eighty-fifth birthday, he acknowledged his condition, saying, "I've been under the weather for a while, but things are getting fixed up now." Nevertheless, he was unable to participate in the public birthday gala at the Beverly Wilshire Hotel two days later. The event, attended by about eight hundred well-wishers, raised $150,000 for St. John's Hospital. Acknowledging her husband's absence, Gloria said, "There's really nothing wrong, but he just didn't feel well enough."

Given Jim's physical condition and his ten years' seniority over his wife, he, his children, and his friends—even Gloria herself—assumed that he would die first, which is what he wanted. But this was not to be.

Around the beginning of October of 1993, Gloria discovered that she had lung cancer. She underwent chemotherapy, but she needed more. "Then," explains daughter Kelly, "she had to kind of make a decision. The doctor had to come over and say, 'You're not going to be cured, but it might add six months, a year.' And Mom said basically the hell with it." Rather than endure the pain and the terrible aftereffects of more radiation, she chose to enjoy the time she had left to the best of her ability. That meant not thinking about the future, but living each day as it came. In customary fashion, she put on a brave front. "It was so convincing," says Judy, "that for a long time, before Mom started losing so much weight, it was like Mom wasn't sick." Indeed, the next few months were surreal for the Stewart family. Gloria was dying, but she and everyone else acted as though nothing were wrong.

That went for Jim as well. He denied the future as much for his own sake as for his wife's. Inside, however, he was devastated, absolutely shattered, by his impending loss. Gloria was his world. She was the one who kept him energized. Once Judy happened by the library when her parents were taking a rare moment to quietly acknowledge their situation. "Mom put her arm around Dad," she recalls, "and said, 'Things sure aren't the same, are they, Jimmy?' " Judy adds, "That's the only hint I got that they had registered Mom was dying."

As 1993 gave way to a new year, Gloria still functioned relatively normally. On Valentine's Day, the family even held, to quote Kelly, "sort of a party up in her room. We all toasted—cocktail hour—and it was as good as could be." Two days later, on February 16, Gloria passed away. She was seventy-five. At the time, former president Reagan said, "She was a very special woman with a wonderful sense of humor and not an ounce of self-pity." In addition to the African Wildlife Foundation, she had been on the boards of the Greater Los Angeles Zoo Association, the Natural History Museum, and St. John's Medical Center.

Somehow Jim found the strength to see the family through the funeral. "He was amazing," says Judy. "I mean, I really thought that Dad, when Mom died, was going to disappear. We would never see him again, that we would have to do everything for the funeral. But Dad was a pillar of strength. I mean, he held up beautifully." Indeed, he rose to the challenge as one would expect an Air Force general to do. Fred De Cordova remembers with wonder how well the star comported himself at the service, saying, "A man totally broken by her death, he stood as people left and shook hands, and he knew us. Not just 'Thanks a lot.' He remembered everybody by name."

But, according to Judy, the funeral "was kind of like a last act." She explains, "Well, he started retreating more and more and more and more and more. By retreating, I mean not communicating as much, not being interested in things, not doing things." Says Kelly, "It looks like deep depression, but from all I've read about clinical depression, that isn't exactly it. He's just withdrawn. And he's found a place where he can cope."

Of course, his physical condition furthered his isolation. "Dad's very hard of hearing," Kelly explains, "and being a perfectionist—even with close friends he wants to be outgoing and amusing—and he just feels like he can't do it. He feels like he'll let people down. He feels like he'll bore people. So there's that side of it, too. Especially without Mom there, I think he sort of lost confidence socially. His friends wouldn't be like that. But he's demanding of himself. He's a perfectionist, and he sort of doesn't want to do it if he can't do it right."

In contrast to the bustling birthday party in 1993, and of course, the public gala for St. John's, Stewart spent his eighty-seventh birthday on May 20, 1995, at home. To keep him company, his son, Mike, flew in from Phoenix, where he now lives with Barbara and the kids. Meanwhile, the twins made their first visit to Indiana, Pennsylvania, to represent the family at the opening of the Jimmy Stewart Museum, a 4,500-square-foot facility on the third floor of the Indiana Free Library building. Featured among the many framed posters from the star's films and an extensive collection of photographs are such memorabilia as the outfit Stewart wore in *Night Passage* and the propeller blade signed by the cast and crew of *The Flight of the Phoenix*.

According to Jim's friend Bill Moorhead, vice president of the James M. Stewart Museum Foundation, the original plan had been to build a freestanding structure on the outskirts of town, but Jim had refused to sanction anything so ostentatious. Thus, the museum, situated on Philadelphia Street, is modest, but it is also closely linked to the star's roots: the site of his dad's hardware store, now a bank, is across the street; his birthplace is only a block west; the statue erected in 1983 is a few doors east; and the family home on Vinegar Hill, still in private hands, is just a short walk to the north.

As with the gala birthday celebration in 1983, the creation of the museum aroused the anger of some Indiana citizens. Why lavish all this attention on Jimmy Stewart? they ask. What has he done for them aside from growing up there? Elinor Blair, who was a member of the museum committee, answers this charge by saying, "He's been so generous to this community. You don't know the things that he's done. He never wants to do the flashy thing, but behind the scenes . . ." She cites, as examples, his financial contributions to the restoration of the old court-house and to memorial services in the park, and a loan to an African-American church whose mortgage was in jeopardy. She adds, "One of the best things he's done for our town is his image as a man. It's put a stamp on our town." For his part, Stewart appreciated the efforts of the museum's organizing committee, chaired by attorney Jay Rubin. "Natu-rally," he said when the museum was in the planning stages, "I feel greatly honored that the residents of my hometown, Indiana, Pa., have decided that they want to create a museum which will bear my name. I love the town of Indiana, my birthplace, where I grew up in the happiest of families, friends, and circumstances."

Life had changed enormously since the days when Pennsylvania was home. Having turned eighty-eight in 1996, Jim continued to spend his time quietly on Roxbury Drive, with his two golden retrievers, named after the twins. The family cook and the housekeeper, Ann and Celia, who had worked for the Stewarts for many years, maintained the rou-tines that Gloria established, carrying on as if she were still the lady of the house. Jim read the newspaper. He watched television. He had a secretary who came in each day to help him answer his mail. He talked occasionally with friends, including his publicist of some forty years, John Strauss. It was "a very quiet, low-keyed routine," said Kelly at the time, "but it fills up the day."

Many of Stewart's friends and colleagues felt sorry for him. "You know," said Judy in late 1995, "I did for ages. Everybody wants every-thing to end with a little bell. He didn't fling himself on the grave and have a heart attack. That would be a neat, clean ending. This is not dra-matic. . . . This is just his way of living after the death of someone who got him up. But I really think that this is where Dad wants to be right now, so I don't feel bad anymore."

The end finally came on July 2, 1997. Jim developed a blood clot in his lung and died at his home. He was eighty-nine, the same age as Alex Stewart at the time of *his* passing.

The outpouring of sorrow from colleagues and film buffs the world over was immediate and profound. Speaking for fans everywhere, Pres-ident Clinton declared, "America lost a national treasure today. Jimmy Stewart was a great actor, a gentleman, and a patriot. We will always remember his rich career of great performances that spanned several decades and entertained generations of Americans. Like all Americans, Hillary and I will miss him greatly, but his work lives on, and for that we can all be grateful." Director Steven Spielberg called Jim "the apple of America's eye," and Tom Hanks, a much younger star in the Jimmy Stewart tradition, said, "The true gift that Jimmy Stewart shared with us will linger forever, both before our eyes and in our hearts because of his spirit. . . . We will all miss him."

With the world media camped outside his father's home, Mike McLean read a brief statement, his sisters Judy and Kelly at his side: "We would like to thank the public for the support and affection they gave to our father over many, many years. This meant a great deal to him and a great deal to the whole family. Thank you very much."

Jimmy Stewart's life, as he acknowledged in 1989, had been filled with so much good fortune." From his childhood as the beloved first-born in a wholesome, loving family, he set forth on a journey that took him further than he could ever have imagined: to the bright lights of Broadway in the 1930s and the fabled soundstages of Metro-Goldwyn-Mayer at the zenith of the studio system, to the turbulent air war over Nazi Germany, to the wilds of his beloved Africa, and to the very pinnacle of the industry that he loved so much. He garnered every award, honor, and accolade that someone in his profession could earn. He married a woman he truly loved and lived with her for nearly forty-five years. He raised four wonderful children. And he experienced, as very few ever have, the adulation of his countrymen and people the world over. That's a lot. More than most folks can even imagine.

Then, too, there is his legacy, a body of work that extends over sixty years and encompasses a treasure trove of pictures, with a score of brilliant performances. Called "the most complete actor-personality in the American cinema" by critic Andrew Sarris, he has carved a special place for himself in the Hollywood pantheon, that of the all-American boy next door, bashful, modest, good-humored, and honorable. He has also made a unique contribution to the art of film acting, effecting a naturalism on-screen that few have ever equaled. He was so good at it that it actually looked effortless, but, in fact, it was the product of considerable labor. As Stewart himself once said, "People call me a natural-born actor, and I get mad. I say there's nothing natural about a camera, lights, and forty or fifty people standing around watching you all the time. It's hard. And if I give a natural appearance on the screen, you can be damn well sure I'm working at it."

As for the man, few stars have ever been as genuinely unaffected as Jimmy Stewart. After all the honors and accolades, he remained humble to the end. That's his legacy, too. It's a panacea in a world where too many people are self-impressed by far less. To him, it was just a matter of being true to his roots. He didn't ask to be honored as an Academy Award–winning actor. Or the highest-paid star of his generation. Or even a brigadier general in the Air Force Reserve. His sights were far more modest. "I'd like to be remembered," he said in 1987, "as somebody who worked hard for what happened, and who had certain values that he believed in. Love of family, love of community, love of country, love of God."

There are far worse ways to be remembered. For to honor one's own code and to be comfortable in one's own skin—and James Maitland Stewart did and was—are to be true to oneself. And who can ask for more?

FILMOGRAPHY

Unless otherwise indicated, dates reflect the opening in New York City. An asterisk reflects the film's availability on videotape.

Feature Films

1. *The Murder Man* (MGM). July 26, 1935. Produced by Harry Rapf. Directed by Tim Whelan. Screenplay by Whelan and John C. Higgins, from the screen story by Whelan and Guy Bolton. With Spencer Tracy, Virginia Bruce, Lionel Atwill, Harvey Stephens, Robert Barrat, William Collier Sr. 70 minutes. b&w.

2. *Rose Marie* (MGM). January 1936 (Miami Beach, Fla.). Produced by Hunt Stromberg. Directed by W. S. Van Dyke II. Screenplay by Frances Goodrich, Albert Hackett, and Alice Duer Miller, from the operetta with music by Rudolf Friml and book and lyrics by Otto A. Harbach and Oscar Hammerstein II. With Jeanette MacDonald, Nelson Eddy, Reginald Owen, Allan Jones, George Regas. 113 minutes. b&w.*

3. *Next Time We Love* (Universal). January 30, 1936. Produced by Paul Kohner. Directed by Edward H. Griffith. Screenplay by Melville Baker, from the story "Say Goodbye Again" by Ursula Parrott. With Margaret Sullavan, Ray Milland, Grant Mitchell, Anna Demetrio. 87 minutes. b&w.

4. *Wife v. Secretary* (MGM). February 28, 1936. Produced by Hunt Stromberg. Directed by Clarence Brown. Screenplay by Norman Krasna, Alice Duer Miller, and John Lee Mahin, from the short story by Faith Baldwin. With Clark Gable, Jean Harlow, Myrna Loy, May Robson, Hobart Cavanaugh. 88 minutes. b&w.*

5. *Small Town Girl* (MGM). April 11, 1936. Produced by Hunt Stromberg. Directed by William Wellman. Screenplay by John Lee Mahin, Edith Fitzgerald, Frances Goodrich, and Albert Hackett, from the novel by Ben Ames Williams. With Janet Gaynor, Robert Taylor, Binnie Barnes, Lewis Stone, Elizabeth Patterson, Frank Craven, Andy Devine. 90 minutes. b&w.

6. *Speed* (MGM). May 15, 1936. Produced by Lucien Hubbard. Directed by Edwin L. Marin. Screenplay by Michael Fessier, from the screen story by Milton Krims and Larry Bachman. With Wendy Barrie, Una Merkel, Weldon Heyburn, Ted Healy, Patricia Wilder, Ralph Morgan. 72 minutes. b&w.

7. *The Gorgeous Hussy* (MGM). September 5, 1936. Produced by Joseph L. Mankiewicz. Directed by Clarence Brown. Screenplay by Ainsworth Morgan and Stephen Morehouse Avery, from the novel by Samuel Hopkins Adams. With Joan Crawford, Robert Taylor, Lionel Barrymore, Franchot Tone, Melvyn Douglas, Louis Calhern, Alison Skipworth, Beulah Bondi. 102 minutes. b&w.*

8. *Born to Dance* (MGM). December 4, 1936. Produced by Jack Cummings. Directed by Roy Del Ruth. Screenplay by Jack McGowan and Sid Silvers, from the screen story by McGowan, Silvers, and B. G. De Sylva. With Eleanor Powell, Virginia Bruce, Una Merkel, Sid Silvers, Frances Langford, Raymond Walburn, Alan Dinehart, Buddy Ebsen, Juanita Quigley, Reginald Gardiner, George and Jalna. 108 minutes. b&w.*

9. *After the Thin Man* (MGM). December 25, 1936. Produced by Hunt Stromberg. Directed by W. S. Van Dyke II. Screenplay by Frances Goodrich and Albert Hackett from a short story by Dashiell Hammett. With William Powell, Myrna Loy, Elissa Landi, Joseph Calleria, Jessie Ralph, Alan Marshall, Teddy Hart, Sam Levene, Dorothy McNulty. 112 minutes. b&w.*

10. *Seventh Heaven* (20th Century–Fox). March 25, 1937. Produced by Darryl F. Zanuck. Directed by Henry King. Screenplay by Melville Baker, from the play by Austin Strong. With Simone Simon, Jean Hersholt, Gregory Ratoff, Gale Sondergaard, J. Edward Bromberg, John Qualen, Victor Kilian, Thomas Beck, Sig Ruman, Mady Christians. 102 minutes. b&w.

11. *The Last Gangster* (MGM). December 9, 1937. Produced by J. J. Cohn. Directed by Edward Ludwig. Screenplay by John Lee Mahin, from a screen story by William A. Wellman and Robert Carson. With Edward G. Robinson, Rose Stradner, Lionel Stander, Douglas Scott, John Carradine, Sidney Blackmer. 81 minutes. b&w.

12. *Navy Blue and Gold* (MGM). December 23, 1937. Produced by Sam Zimbalist. Directed by Sam Wood. Screenplay by George Bruce, from his novel. With Robert Young, Lionel Barrymore, Florence Rice, Billie Burke, Tom Brown. 94 minutes. b&w.*

13. *Of Human Hearts* (MGM). Early February 1938 (Greenville, S.C.). Produced by John W. Considine Jr. Directed by Clarence Brown. Screenplay by Bradburty Foote from the story "Benefits Forgot" by Honore Morrow. With Walter Huston, Beulah Bondi, Guy Kibbee, Charles Coburn, John Carradine, Ann Rutherford, Charley Grapewin, Gene Reynolds. 105 minutes. b&w.*

14. *Vivacious Lady* (RKO). June 2, 1938. Produced by Pandro S. Berman. Directed by George Stevens. Screenplay by P. J. Wolfson and Ernest Pagano, from a novelette by I. A. R. Wylie. With Ginger Rogers, James Ellison, Charles Coburn, Beulah Bondi, Frances Mercer. 90 minutes. b&w.*

15. *The Shopworn Angel* (MGM). July 7, 1938. Produced by Joseph L. Mankiewicz. Directed by H. C. Potter. Screenplay by Waldo Salt, from the story "Private Pettigrew's Girl" by Dana Burnett. With Margaret Sullavan, Walter Pidgeon, Hattie McDaniel, Nat Pendleton, Alan Curtis, Sam Levene. 85 minutes. b&w.*

16. *You Can't Take It With You* (Columbia). September 1, 1938. Produced and directed by Frank Capra. Screenplay by Robert Riskin, from the play by George S. Kaufman and Moss Hart. With Jean Arthur, Lionel Barrymore, Edward Arnold, Mischa Auer, Ann Miller, Spring Byington, Samuel S. Hinds, Donald Meek, H. B. Warner, Halliwell Hobbes, Dub Taylor. 127 minutes. b&w.*

17. *Made for Each Other* (Selznick International/United Artists). February 16, 1939. Produced by David O. Selznick. Directed by John Cromwell. Screenplay by Jo Swerling, from a story idea by Rose Franken. With Carole Lombard, Charles Coburn, Lucille Watson. 90 minutes. b&w.*

18. *The Ice Follies of 1939* (MGM). March 16, 1939. Produced by Harry Rapf. Directed by Reinhold Schunzel. Screenplay by Leonard Praskins, Florence Ryerson, and Edgar Allan Woolf, from the screen story by Praskins. With Joan Crawford, Lew Ayres, Lewis Stone, Bess Ehrhardt, Lionel Stander. 82 minutes. b&w and color.*

19. *It's a Wonderful World* (MGM). May 18, 1939. Produced by Frank Davis. Directed by W. S. Van Dyke II. Screenplay by Ben Hecht, from the screen story by Hecht and Herman J. Mankiewicz. With Claudette Colbert, Guy Kibbee, Nat Pendleton, Frances Drake, Edgar Kennedy, Ernest Truex. 86 minutes. b&w.

20. *Mr. Smith Goes to Washington* (Columbia). October 19, 1939. Produced and directed by Frank Capra. Screenplay by Sidney Buchman, from the screen story "The Gentleman from Montana" by Lewis R. Foster. With Jean Arthur, Claude Rains, Edward Arnold, Guy Kibbee, Thomas Mitchell, Eugene Pallette, Beulah Bondi, H. B. Warner, Harry Carey, Astrid Allwyn. 126 minutes. b&w.*

21. *Destry Rides Again* (Universal). November 29, 1939. Produced by Joe Pasternak.

Directed by George Marshall. Screenplay by Felix Jackson, Gertrude Purcell, and Henry Myers, from the novel by Max Brand. With Marlene Dietrich, Mischa Auer, Charles Winninger, Brian Donlevy, Una Merkel, Jack Carson. 94 minutes. b&w.*

22. *The Shop Around the Corner* (MGM). January 25, 1940. Produced and directed by Ernst Lubitsch. Screenplay by Samson Raphaelson from the play *Parfumerie* by Nikolaus Laszlo. With Margaret Sullavan, Frank Morgan, Joseph Schildkraut, Sara Haden, Felix Bressart, William Tracy, Inez Courtney. 97 minutes. b&w.*

23. *The Mortal Storm* (MGM). June 20, 1940. Produced by Sidney Franklin. Directed by Frank Borzage. Screenplay by Claudine West, Anderson Ellis, and George Froeschel, from the novel by Phyllis Bottome. With Margaret Sullavan, Frank Morgan, Robert Young, Irene Rich, Maria Ouspenskaya, William Orr, Robert Stack, Bonita Granville. 100 minutes. b&w.*

24. *No Time for Comedy* (Warner Bros.). September 6, 1940. Produced by Hal B. Wallis. Directed by William Keighley. Screenplay by Julius J. and Philip G. Epstein, from the play by S. N. Behrman. With Rosalind Russell, Genevieve Tobin, Charles Ruggles, Louise Beavers, Allyn Joslyn, Clarence Kolb. 93 minutes. b&w.

25. *The Philadelphia Story* (MGM). December 26, 1940. Produced by Joseph L. Mankiewicz. Directed by George Cukor. Screenplay by Donald Ogden Stewart, from the play by Philip Barry. With Cary Grant, Katharine Hepburn, Ruth Hussey, John Howard, Roland Young, John Halliday, Virginia Weidler, Mary Nash. 112 minutes. b&w.*

26. *Come Live With Me* (MGM). February 27, 1941. Produced and directed by Clarence Brown. Screenplay by Patterson McNutt, from the screen story by Virginia Van Upp. With Hedy Lamarr, Ian Hunter, Verree Teasdale, Donald Meek, Barton MacLane. 86 minutes. b&w.

27. *Pot o' Gold* (United Artists). April 3, 1941. Produced by James Roosevelt. Directed by George Marshall. Screenplay by Walter De Leon, from the screen story by Monte Brice, Andrew Bennison, and Harry Tugend. With Paulette Goddard, Horace Heidt, Charles Winninger, Mary Gordon, Frank Melton. 86 minutes. b&w.*

28. *Ziegfeld Girl* (MGM). April 24, 1941. Produced by Pandro S. Berman. Directed by Robert Z. Leonard. Screenplay by Marguerite Roberts and Sonya Levien, from the screen story by William Anthony McGuire. With Judy Garland, Hedy Lamarr, Lana Turner, Tony Martin, Jackie Cooper, Ian Hunter, Charles Winninger, Edward Everett Horton, Philip Dorn. 131 minutes. b&w.*

29. *It's a Wonderful Life* (Liberty Films/RKO). December 21, 1946. Produced and directed by Frank Capra. Screenplay by Frances Goodrich, Albert Hackett, and Capra, from the short story "The Greatest Gift" by Philip Van Doren Stern. With Donna Reed, Lionel Barrymore, Thomas Mitchell, Henry Travers, Beulah Bondi, Ward Bond, Frank Faylen, Gloria Grahame. 129 minutes. b&w.*

30. *Magic Town* (Robert Riskin Productions/RKO). October 7, 1947. Produced by Robert Riskin. Directed by William Wellman. Screenplay by Robert Riskin, from the screen story by Riskin and Joseph Krumgold. With Jane Wyman, Kent Smith, Ned Sparks, Wallace Ford, Regis Toomey, Ann Doran, Donald Meek. 103 minutes. b&w.*

31. *A Miracle Can Happen* (*On Our Merry Way*) (Miracle Productions/United Artists). February 3, 1948. Produced by Benedict Bogeaus. Directed by King Vidor and Leslie Fenton (the Stewart episode directed without credit by John Huston and George Stevens). Screenplay by Laurence Stallings, Lou Breslow, and John O'Hara,

from the screen story by Arch Oboler. With (in the Stewart sequence) Burgess Meredith, Henry Fonda, Eduardo Ciannelli, Dorothy Ford, Harry James. Also starring Paulette Goddard, Dorothy Lamour, Victor Moore, Fred MacMurray, William Demarest. 107 minutes. b&w.

32. *Call Northside 777* (20th Century–Fox). February 18, 1948. Produced by Otto Lang. Directed by Henry Hathaway. Screenplay by Jerome Cady and Jay Dratler, adaptation by Leonard Hoffman and Quentin Reynolds, from the newspaper articles by James P. McGuire. With Richard Conte, Lee J. Cobb, Helen Walker, Betty Garde, Kasia Orzazewski, Joanne de Bergh. 111 minutes. b&w.*

33. *Rope* (Transatlantic Pictures/Warner Bros.). August 28, 1948. Produced by Sidney Bernstein. Directed by Alfred Hitchcock. Screenplay by Arthur Laurents, adaptation by Hume Cronyn, from the play *Rope's End* by Patrick Hamilton. With Farley Granger, John Dall, Joan Chandler, Sir Cedric Hardwicke, Constance Collier, Edith Evanson, Douglas Dick, Dick Hogan. 81 minutes. color.*

34. *You Gotta Stay Happy* (Rampart Productions/Universal). November 4, 1948. Produced by Karl Tunberg. Directed by H. C. Potter. Screenplay by Tunberg, from the serialized magazine story by Robert Carson. With Joan Fontaine, Eddie Albert, Roland Young, Willard Parker, Percy Kilbride, Porter Hall, Marcy McGuire. 100 minutes. b&w.

35. *The Stratton Story* (MGM). May 12, 1949. Produced by Jack Cummings. Directed by Sam Wood. Screenplay by Douglas Morrow and Guy Trosper, from the screen story by Morrow. With June Allyson, Frank Morgan, Agnes Moorehead, Bill Williams, Bruce Cowling, Cliff Clark, Mary Lawrence, Eugene Bearden, Bill Dickey, Jimmy Dykes. 106 minutes. b&w.*

36. *Malaya* (MGM). December 27, 1949 (Greensboro, N.C.). Produced by Edwin H. Knopf. Directed by Richard Thorpe. Screenplay by Frank Fenton, from the screen story by Manchester Boddy. With Spencer Tracy, Valentina Cortesa, Sydney Greenstreet, John Hodiak, Lionel Barrymore, Gilbert Roland. 98 minutes. b&w.*

37. *Winchester '73* (Universal). June 7, 1950. Produced by Aaron Rosenberg. Directed by Anthony Mann. Screenplay by Robert L. Richards and Borden Chase, from the screen story by Stuart N. Lake. With Shelley Winters, Dan Duryea, Stephen McNally, Millard Mitchell, Charles Drake, John McIntire, Will Geer, Jay C. Flippen. 92 minutes. b&w.*

38. *Broken Arrow* (20th Century–Fox). July 2, 1950. Produced by Julian Blaustein. Directed by Delmer Daves. Screenplay by Michael Blankfort (actually written by Albert Maltz), from the novel *Blood Brother* by Elliott Arnold. With Jeff Chandler, Debra Paget, Basil Ruysdael, Will Geer, Joyce MacKenzie, Arthur Hunnicutt, Raymond Bramley, Jay Silverheels. 93 minutes. color.*

39. *The Jackpot* (20th Century–Fox). November 1950. Produced by Samuel G. Engel. Directed by Walter Lang. Screenplay by Phoebe and Henry Ephron, from the magazine article by John McNulty. With Barbara Hale, James Gleason, Fred Clark, Alan Mowbray, Patricia Medina, Natalie Wood, Tommy Rettig. 87 minutes. b&w.

40. *Harvey* (Universal). December 21, 1950. Produced by John Beck. Directed by Henry Koster. Screenplay by Mary Chase and Oscar Brodney, from the play by Chase. With Josephine Hull, Peggy Dow, Charles Drake, Cecil Kellaway, Victoria Horne, Jesse White, William Lynn, Wallace Ford. 104 minutes. b&w.*

41. *No Highway in the Sky* (20th Century–Fox). September 21, 1951. Produced by Louis D. Leighton. Directed by Henry Koster. Screenplay by R. C. Sherriff, Oscar Millard,

and Alec Coppel, from the novel *No Highway* by Nevil Shute. With Marlene Dietrich, Glynis Johns, Jack Hawkins, Janette Scott, Ronald Squire, Kenneth More, Elizabeth Allan. 98 minutes. b&w.

42. *The Greatest Show on Earth* (Paramount). January 10, 1952. Produced and directed by Cecil B. DeMille. Screenplay by Fredric M. Frank, Barre Lyndon, and Theodore St. John, from the screen story by Frank, St. John, and Frank Cavett. With Betty Hutton, Cornel Wilde, Charlton Heston, Dorothy Lamour, Gloria Grahame, Lyle Bettger. 153 minutes. color.*

43. *Bend of the River* (Universal). January 23, 1952 (Portland, Oreg.). Produced by Aaron Rosenberg. Directed by Anthony Mann. Screenplay by Borden Chase, from the novel *Bend of the Snake* by Bill Gulick. With Arthur Kennedy, Julie Adams, Rock Hudson, Lori Nelson, Jay C. Flippen, Chubby Johnson, Harry Morgan. 91 minutes. color.*

44. *Carbine Williams* (MGM). May 7, 1952. Produced by Armand Deutsch. Directed by Richard Thorpe. Screenplay by Art Cohn, from a magazine article by David Marshall Williams. With Jean Hagen, Wendell Corey, Carl Benton Reid, Paul Stewart, Otto Hulett, Rhys Williams, Herbert Heyes. 91 minutes. b&w.

45. *The Naked Spur* (MGM). March 25, 1953. Produced by William H. Wright. Directed by Anthony Mann. Screenplay by Sam Rolfe and Harold Jack Bloom. With Robert Ryan, Janet Leigh, Ralph Meeker, Millard Mitchell. 91 minutes. color.*

46. *Thunder Bay* (Universal). May 19, 1953. Produced by Aaron Rosenberg. Directed by Anthony Mann. Screenplay by Gil Doud and John Michael Hayes, from the screen story by Hayes, based on an idea by George W. George and George F. Slavin. With Joanne Dru, Gilbert Roland, Dan Duryea, Marcia Henderson, Jay C. Flippen, Antonio Moreno, Robert Monet, Harry Morgan. 102 minutes. color.*

47. *The Glenn Miller Story* (Universal). January 19, 1954 (Miami Beach, Fla.). Produced by Aaron Rosenberg. Directed by Anthony Mann. Screenplay by Valentine Davies and Oscar Brodney. With June Allyson, Harry Morgan, Charles Drake, George Tobias, Barton MacLane, Sig Ruman, Louis Armstrong, Gene Krupa, Ben Pollack, Frances Langford, the Modernaires. 116 minutes. color.*

48. *Rear Window* (Patron/Paramount). August 4, 1954. Produced and directed by Alfred Hitchcock. Screenplay by John Michael Hayes, from the short story by Cornell Woolrich. With Grace Kelly, Wendell Corey, Thelma Ritter, Raymond Burr. 112 minutes. color.*

49. *The Far Country* (Universal). February 1, 1955 (Miami Beach, Fla.). Produced by Aaron Rosenberg. Directed by Anthony Mann. Screenplay by Borden Chase. With Ruth Roman, Corinne Calvet, Walter Brennan, John McIntire, Jay C. Flippen, Harry Morgan, Steve Brodie. 97 minutes. color.*

50. *Strategic Air Command* (Paramount). May 20, 1955. Produced by Samuel J. Briskin. Directed by Anthony Mann. Screenplay by Valentine Davies and Beirne Lay Jr., from the screen story by Lay. With June Allyson, Frank Lovejoy, Barry Sullivan, Alex Nicol, James Millican, Jay C. Flippen, Harry Morgan. 114 minutes. color.*

51. *The Man From Laramie* (William Goetz Productions/Columbia). August 31, 1955. Produced by William Goetz. Directed by Anthony Mann. Screenplay by Philip Yordan and Frank Burt, from the novel by Thomas T. Flynn. With Arthur Kennedy, Donald Crisp, Cathy O'Donnell, Alex Nicol, Aline MacMahon, Wallace Ford, Jack Elam. 104 minutes. color.*

52. *The Man Who Knew Too Much* (Filwite/Paramount). May 1956. Produced and

directed by Alfred Hitchcock. Screenplay by John Michael Hayes and Angus McPhail, from the screen story by Charles Bennett and Dr. B. Wyndham-Lewis. With Doris Day, Brenda De Banzie, Bernard Miles, Ralph Truman, Daniel Gelin, Mogens Wieth, Alan Mowbray. 120 minutes. color.*

53. *The Spirit of St. Louis* (Warner Bros.). February 21, 1957. Produced by Leland Hayward. Directed by Billy Wilder. Screenplay by Wilder and Wendell Mayes, adaptation by Charles Lederer, from the book by Charles A. Lindbergh. With Murray Hamilton, Patricia Smith, Bartlett Robinson. 138 minutes. color.*

54. *Night Passage* (Universal). July 17, 1957 (Denver, Colo.). Produced by Aaron Rosenberg. Directed by James Neilson. Screenplay by Borden Chase, from the novel by Norman A. Fox. With Audie Murphy, Dan Duryea, Dianne Foster, Elaine Stewart, Brandon de Wilde, Jay C. Flippen, Hugh Beaumont, Jack Elam. 90 minutes. color.

55. *Vertigo* (Alfred J. Hitchcock Productions/Paramount). May 28, 1958. Produced and directed by Alfred Hitchcock. Screenplay by Alec Coppel and Samuel Taylor, from the novel *D'entre les Morts* by Pierre Boileau and Thomas Narcejac. With Kim Novak, Barbara Bel Geddes, Tom Helmore, Henry Jones. 128 minutes. color.*

56. *Bell, Book and Candle* (Phoenix/Columbia). December 25, 1958. Produced by Julian Blaustein. Directed by Richard Quine. Screenplay by Daniel Taradash, from the play by John Van Druten. With Kim Novak, Jack Lemmon, Ernie Kovacs, Hermione Gingold, Elsa Lanchester, Janice Rule. 103 minutes. color.*

57. Robert Traver. With Lee Remick, Ben Gazzara, Joseph N. Welch, Kathryn Grant, Arthur O'Connell, Eve Arden, George C. Scott, Brooks West, Orson Bean. 160 minutes. b&w.*

58. *The FBI Story* (Warner Bros.). September 24, 1959. Produced and directed by Mervyn LeRoy. Screenplay by Richard L. Breen and John Twist, from the book by Don Whitehead. With Vera Miles, Murray Hamilton, Larry Pennell, Nick Adams, Diane Jergens. 149 minutes. color.*

59. *The Mountain Road* (William Goetz Productions/Columbia). June 29, 1960. Produced by William Goetz. Directed by Daniel Mann. Screenplay by Alfred Hayes, from the novel by Theodore H. White. With Lisa Lu, Glenn Corbett, Harry Morgan, Frank Silvera, James Best, Rudy Bond, Mike Kellin. 102 minutes. b&w.

60. *Two Rode Together* (John Ford Productions/Shpetner Productions/Columbia). July 26, 1961. Produced by Stan Shpetner. Directed by John Ford. Screenplay by Frank Nugent, from the novel *Comanche Captives* by Will Cook. With Richard Widmark, Shirley Jones, Linda Cristal, Andy Devine, John McIntire. 109 minutes. color.*

61. *The Man Who Shot Liberty Valance* (John Ford Productions/Paramount). May 23, 1962. Produced by Willis Goldbeck. Directed by John Ford. Screenplay by Goldbeck and James Warner Bellah, from the short story by Dorothy M. Johnson. With John Wayne, Vera Miles, Lee Marvin, Edmond O'Brien, Andy Devine, Ken Murray, John Carradine, Jeanette Nolan, Woody Strode. 122 minutes. b&w.*

62. *Mr. Hobbs Takes a Vacation* (Jerry Wald Productions/20th Century–Fox). May 25, 1962 (Los Angeles, Calif.). Produced by Jerry Wald. Directed by Henry Koster. Screenplay by Nunnally Johnson, from the novel *Mr. Hobbs' Vacation* by Edward Streeter. With Maureen O'Hara, Fabian, Lauri Peters, Lili Gentle, John Saxon, John McGiver, Marie Wilson, Reginald Gardiner, Michael Burns. 116 minutes. color.*

63. *How the West Was Won* (MGM/Cinerama). November 1, 1962 (London, Eng.). Produced by Bernard Smith. Directed by Henry Hathaway (Stewart episode), George Marshall, John Ford. Screenplay by James R. Webb. With (Stewart episode) Carroll

Baker, Karl Malden, Walter Brennan, Debbie Reynolds, Agnes Moorehead. Also starring Lee J. Cobb, Henry Fonda, Carolyn Jones, Gregory Peck, George Peppard, Robert Preston, Eli Wallach, John Wayne, Richard Widmark. 162 minutes. color.*

64. *Take Her, She's Mine* (20th Century–Fox). November 13, 1963. Produced and directed by Henry Koster. Screenplay by Nunnally Johnson, from the play by Phoebe and Henry Ephron. With Sandra Dee, Audrey Meadows, Robert Morley, Philippe Forquet, John McGiver. 98 minutes. color.

65. *Cheyenne Autumn* (Ford-Smith Productions/Warner Bros.). October 1, 1964 (Cheyenne, Wyo.). Produced by Bernard Smith. Directed by John Ford. Screenplay by James R. Webb, from the book by Mari Sandoz. With (Stewart episode) Arthur Kennedy, Elizabeth Allen, John Carradine. Also starring Richard Widmark, Carroll Baker, Karl Malden, Sal Mineo, Dolores Del Rio, Ricardo Montalban, Gilbert Roland, Edward G. Robinson. 145 minutes (edited version). color.*

66. *Dear Brigitte* (20th Century–Fox). January 27, 1965. Produced and directed by Henry Koster. Screenplay by Hal Kanter, from the novel *Erasmus with Freckles* by John Haase. With Fabian, Glynis Johns, Cindy Carol, Billy Mumy, John Williams, Jack Kruschen, Ed Wynn, Jesse White, Brigitte Bardot. 100 minutes. color.*

67. *Shenandoah* (Universal). June 3, 1965 (Houston, Tex.). Produced by Robert Arthur. Directed by Andrew V. McLaglen. Screenplay by James Lee Barrett. With Doug McClure, Glenn Corbett, Patrick Wayne, Rosemary Forsyth, Philip Alford, Katharine Ross, Charles Robinson, James McMullan, Tim McIntire, Eugene Jackson Jr., George Kennedy, Strother Martin. 105 minutes. color.*

68. *The Flight of the Phoenix* (The Associates & Aldrich/20th Century–Fox). December 15, 1965. Produced and directed by Robert Aldrich. Screenplay by Lukas Heller, from the novel by Elleston Trevor. With Richard Attenborough, Peter Finch, Hardy Kruger, Ernest Borgnine, Ian Bannen, Ronald Fraser, Christian Marquand, Dan Duryea, George Kennedy. 147 minutes. color.*

69. *The Rare Breed* (Universal). February 2, 1966 (Fort Worth, Tex.). Produced by William Alland. Directed by Andrew V. McLaglen. Screenplay by Ric Hardman. With Maureen O'Hara, Brian Keith, Juliet Mills, Don Galloway, David Brian, Jack Elam. 97 minutes. color.*

70. *Firecreek* (Philip Leacock/John Mantley/Warner Bros.–Seven Arts). January 24, 1968 (El Paso, Tex.). Produced by Philip Leacock. Directed by Vincent McEveety. Screenplay by Calvin Clements. With Henry Fonda, Inger Stevens, Gary Lockwood, Dean Jagger, Ed Begley, Jay C. Flippen, Jack Elam, James Best, Barbara Luna, Jacqueline Scott. 104 minutes. color.*

71. *Bandolero!* (20th Century–Fox). June 18, 1968 (Dallas, Tex.). Produced by Robert L. Jacks. Directed by Andrew V. McLaglen. Screenplay by James Lee Barrett, from the screen story by Stanley L. Hough. With Dean Martin, Raquel Welch, George Kennedy, Andrew Prine, Will Geer. 106 minutes. color.*

72. *The Cheyenne Social Club* (National General). June 12, 1970 (Chicago, Ill.). Produced and directed by Gene Kelly. Screenplay by James Lee Barrett. With Henry Fonda, Shirley Jones, Sue Ann Langdon, Elaine Devry, Robert Middleton, Arch Johnson, Dabbs Greer. 103 minutes. color.*

73. *Fools' Parade* (Stanmore/Penbar/Columbia). August 18, 1971. Produced and directed by Andrew V. McLaglen. Screenplay by James Lee Barrett, from the novel by Davis Grubb. With George Kennedy, Anne Baxter, Strother Martin, Kurt Russell, William Windom, Mike Kellin, Kathy Cannon. 98 minutes. color.

74. *The Shootist* (Dino De Laurentiis/Paramount). August 11, 1976. Produced by M. J. Frankovich and William Self. Directed by Don Siegel. Screenplay by Miles Hood Swarthout and Scott Hale, from the novel by Glendon Swarthout. With John Wayne, Lauren Bacall, Ron Howard, Richard Boone, Hugh O'Brian, Bill McKinney, Harry Morgan, John Carradine, Sheree North, Rick Lenz, Scatman Crothers. 100 minutes. color.*

75. *Airport '77* (Universal). March 24, 1977 (Anchorage, Alaska). Produced by William Frye. Directed by Jerry Jameson. Screenplay by Michael Scheff and David Spector, from the screen story by H. A. L. Craig and Charles Kuenstle, inspired by the film *Airport* based on the novel by Arthur Hailey. With Jack Lemmon, Lee Grant, Brenda Vaccaro, Joseph Cotten, Olivia de Havilland, Darren McGavin, Christopher Lee, George Kennedy, Robert Foxworth, Robert Hooks, Monte Markham, Kathleen Quinlan, Gil Gerard, Pamela Bellwood. 114 minutes. color.

76. *The Big Sleep* (Winkast/ITC). March 15, 1978. Produced by Elliott Kastner and Michael Winner. Directed by Winner. Screenplay by Winner, from the novel by Raymond Chandler. With Robert Mitchum, Sarah Miles, Richard Boone, Candy Clark, Joan Collins, Edward Fox, John Mills, Oliver Reed, Harry Andrews, Colin Blakely. 99 minutes. color.*

77. *The Magic of Lassie* (Lassie Productions/International Picture Show). August 2, 1978. Produced by Bonita Granville Wrather and William Beaudine Jr. Directed by Don Chaffey. Screenplay by Jean Holloway, Richard M. Sherman, and Robert B. Sherman, from the screen story by the Shermans. With Mickey Rooney, Pernell Roberts, Stephanie Zimbalist, Michael Sharrett, Alice Faye, Gene Evans, Mike Mazurki. 99 minutes. color.*

78. *The Green Horizon (A Tale of Africa)* (Sanrio Communications). May 1981 (Japan). Produced by Terry Ogisu and Yoichi Matsue. Directed by Susumu Hani and Simon Trevor. Screenplay by Shintaro Tsuji from the screen story by Shuji Terayama. With Philip Sayer, Cathleen McOsker, Eleanora Vallone. 87 minutes. color.*

79. *An American Tail: Fievel Goes West* (Universal). November 22, 1991. Produced by Steven Spielberg and Robert Watts. Directed by Phil Nibbelink and Simon Wells. Screenplay by Flint Dille, from the screen story by Charles Swenson. Created by David Kirschner. Songs by James Horner and Will Jennings. With the voices of Philip Glasser, Erica Yohn, Cathy Cavadini, Nehemiah Persoff, Dom DeLuise, Amy Irving, John Cleese, Jon Lovitz. 74 minutes. color.*

Television (major acting appearances)

1. "The Windmill" (Revue Productions/*G.E. Theater*/CBS). April 26, 1955. Directed by James Neilson. Written by Bordon Chase. Hosted by Ronald Reagan. With Barbara Hale, Donald MacDonald, Cheryl Callaway, John McIntire, Walter Sande, James Millican, Edgar Buchanan. 30 min. b&w.

2. "The Town With a Past" (Revue Productions/*G.E. Theater*/CBS). February 10, 1957. Associate producer: William Frye. Directed by James Neilson. Written by Oscar Brodney and Frank Burt, from the radio script "Silver Annie" by Burt. Hosted by Ronald Reagan. With Beulah Bondi, Fredd Wayne, Walter Sande, Ted Mapes. 30 min. b&w.

3 "The Trail to Christmas" (Revue Productions/*G.E. Theater*/CBS). December 15, 1957. Produced by William Frye. Directed by Stewart. Written by Frank Burt, from the radio script "Britt Ponset's Christmas Carol" by Burt and from *A Christmas Carol*

by Charles Dickens. Hosted by Ronald Reagan. With Richard Eyer, John McIntire, Sam Edwards, Will Wright, Kevin Hagen, Sally Frazier, Mary Laurence, Dennis Holmes. 30 min. b&w.

4. "Cindy's Fella" (Revue Productions/*Lincoln-Mercury Startime*/NBC). December 15, 1959. Produced by William Frye. Directed by Gower Champion. Written by James Brewer from the story by Frank Burt. With Lois Smith, George Gobel, James Best, Mary Wickes, Kathie Browne, Alice Backes. 30 minutes. b&w.

5. "Flashing Spikes" (Avista/*Alcoa Premiere*/ABC). October 4, 1962. Produced by Frank Baur. Directed by John Ford. Written by Jameson Brewer, from the novel by Frank O'Rourke. With Patrick Wayne, Tige Andrews, Jack Warden, Carleton Young, Stephanie Hill, Don Drysdale, Edgar Buchanan, John Wayne. 60 minutes. b&w.

6. *The Jimmy Stewart Show* (Warner Bros./J. K. Ablidon Productions/NBC). September 19, 1971–September 3, 1972. Creator and executive producer: Hal Kanter. Principal director and chief writer: Kanter. With Julie Adams, Jonathan Daly, Ellen Geer, Kirby Furlong, Dennis Larson, John McGiver. 30 minutes. color.

7. *Harvey* (*Hallmark Hall of Fame*/NBC). March 22, 1972. Produced by David Susskind. Directed by Fielder Cook. Adaptation by Jacqueline Babbin and Audrey Gellen Maas from the play by Mary Chase. With Helen Hayes, Jesse White, Marian Hailey, John McGiver, Martin Gabel, Arlene Francis, Richard Mulligan, Madeline Kahn. 90 minutes. color.

8. "Hawkins on Murder" (pilot) (Arena/Leda/MGM—CBS). March 13, 1973. Executive producer: Norman Felton. Directed by Jud Taylor. Produced and written by David Karp. With Strother Martin, Bonnie Bedelia, Kate Reid, David Huddleston, Dana Elcar, Antoinette Bower, Charles McGraw, Robert Webber. (Subsequently retitled "Death and the Maiden" and aired as part of the *Hawkins* series.) 90 minutes. color.

9. *Hawkins* (Arena/Leda/MGM—CBS). October 2, 1973–September 3, 1974 (in rotation with *Shaft* and made-for-TV movies). Executive producer: Norman Felton. Directed by Jud Taylor (3 episodes), Paul Wendkos (3 episodes), Paul Scheerer (1 episode). Written by David Karp (4 episodes), Gene L. Coon (1 episode), Robert Hamner (2 episodes). With Strother Martin and guest actors. 90 minutes. color.

10. *Mr. Krueger's Christmas* (syndication). December 1980. Produced by Mike McLean. Directed by Keith Merrill. With the Mormon Tabernacle Choir. 30 minutes. color.

11. *Right of Way* (Schaefer/Karpf—HBO). November 21, 1983. Executive producer: Merrill H. Karpf. Directed by George Schaefer. Written by Richard Lees, from his play. With Bette Davis, Melinda Dillon, Priscilla Morrill, John Harkins. 106 minutes. color.*

12. *North and South, Book II* (ABC). May 4, 5, 6, 7, 11, 1986. Produced by David Wolper. Directed by Kevin Conner. Teleplay by Richard Fielder, Paul F. Edwards, Patricia Green, Bill Gordon, Douglas Hayes, B. W. Sandefur, and Guerdon S. Trueblood from the novel *Love and War* by John Jakes. With Patrick Swayze, James Read, Lesley-Anne Down, David Carradine, Terri Garber, Philip Casnoff, Kirstie Alley, Parker Stevenson, Lewis Smith, Genie Francis, Mary Crosby, Wayne Newton. (Stewart's appearance came on May 6.) 12 hours. color.*

Theater (Broadway and West End productions with Stewart in the original cast)

1. *Carry Nation.* October 29, 1932. Produced by Arthur J. Beckhard. Directed by Blanche Yurka. Written by Frank McGrath. With Esther Dale, Leslie Adams, plus a

large ensemble cast that included Joshua Logan, Mildred Natwick, and Myron McCormack. 31 performances.

2. *Goodbye Again.* December 28, 1932. Produced and directed by Arthur J. Beckhard. Written by Allan Scott and George Haight. With Osgood Perkins, Sally Bates, Katherine Squire, Hugh Rennie, Alfred Dalrymple, Leslie Adams, Dorthea Duckworth, Myron McCormick, Nell Burt, Jackie Kelk. 216 performances.

3. *Spring in Autumn.* October 24, 1933. Produced by Arthur J. Beckhard. Directed by Bretaigne Windust. Written by Nina Belmonte, from the Spanish play by Gregorio Martinez-Sierra. With Blanche Yurka, Richard Hale, Helen Walpole, Mildred Natwick, Esther Dale. 26 performances.

4. *All Good Americans.* December 5, 1933. Produced by Courtney Burr. Directed by Arthur Sircom. Written by Laura and S. J. Perelman. With Hope Williams, Fred Keating, Mary Philips, Eric Dressler, Coburn Goodwin. 39 performances.

5. *Yellow Jack.* March 6, 1934. Produced and directed by Guthrie McClintic. Written by Sidney Howard from the book *Microbe Hunters* by Paul de Kruif. With John Miltern, Robert Keith, Barton MacLane, Eduardo Ciannelli, Edward Acuff, Samuel Levene, Myron McCormick, Geoffrey Kane, Millard Mitchell, Robert Shayne, Katherine Wilson. 79 performances.

6. *Divided by Three.* October 2, 1934. Produced and directed by Guthrie McClintic. Written by Margaret Leech and Beatrice Kaufman. With Judith Anderson, Hunter Gardner, James Rennie, Hancey Castle. 24 performances.

7. *Page Miss Glory.* November 27, 1934. Produced by Laurence Schwab and Philip Dunning. Directed by George Abbott. Written by Joseph Schrank and Dunning. With Dorothy Hall, Charles D. Brown, Jane Seymour, J. Anthony Hughes, Bruce MacFarlane, Joe Vitale, Frederic Voight. 67 performances (estimate).

8. *Journey By Night.* April 16, 1935. Produced by the Shuberts. Directed by Robert Sinclair. Written by Arthur Goodrich, from the German play *A Journey By Night* by Leo Perutz. With Greta Maren, Albert Van Dekker, Eduardo Ciannelli, Jane Buchanan, Nicholas Joy, Jack Hartley. 5 performances.

9. *Harvey.* February 24, 1970. Produced by the American National Theater and Academy, Alfred de Ligre Jr., executive producer, Jean Dalrymple, executive director, the Phoenix production, T Edward Hambleton, managing director. Directed by Stephen Porter. Written by Mary Chase. With Helen Hayes, Jesse White, Marian Hailey, Joe Ponzecki, Henderson Forsythe. 80 performances.

10. *Harvey.* April 9, 1975. Produced by Bernard Delfont and Richard M. Mills (for Bernard Delfont Organization Ltd.) with Alexander H. Cohen. Directed by Anthony Quayle. With Mona Washbourne, Geoffrey Lumsden, Sarah Atkinson, Brian Coburn, Bob Sherman, Kathryn Leigh Scott. Seven months.

NOTES

Research for this book was taken from three principal sources: (1) interviews conducted by the author, principally between August 1995 and March 1996. Conversations that resulted in in-depth or significant information on a particular subject are cited at the outset of the notes for each chapter. Comments made in passing are attributed parenthetically in the body of the notes with the source's last name followed by "AI" (author interview); (2) books and periodicals. Reviews, announcements, and articles of no more than passing interest are cited below. Otherwise, information on the sources cited below can be found in the bibliography; and (3) primary source materials. Found in the Margaret Herrick Library of the Academy of Motion Picture Arts and Sciences are the Gloria Hall Collection (GHC), the Alfred Hitchcock Collection (AHC), the Hedda Hopper Collection (HHC), the George Stevens Collection (GSC), a bound transcript of *A Louis B. Mayer Foundation–American Film Institute Oral History of Pandro S. Berman*, Mike Steen, interviewer, completed 8/4/72, Hollywood, California (Steen), and an unidentified manuscript by Gloria Stewart dated 8/14/62 (GSM). The 20th Century–Fox Collection (TFC) is in the Department of Special Collections, University Research Library, University of California, Los Angeles. There, too, are the transcripts of two oral histories: *Recollections of George Cukor. An Oral History of the Motion Picture in America*, Stephen Farber, interviewer (Farber); and *Recollections of Nunnally Johnson. An Oral History of the Motion Picture in America*, Tom Stempel, interviewer (Stempel, 1969). In both cases the copyright is the Regents of the University of California, 1969, Sacramento, California. In the offices of the Directors Guild is a transcript of George Schaefer's *From Live Tape to Film: Sixty Years of Inconspicuous Directing*, the Directors Guild of America, 1994 (Schaefer), which supplemented my interview with Mr. Schaefer. At USC's Cinema-TV Library are the Universal Pictures Collection (UPC), the Jerry Wald Collection (JWC), the Jack L. Warner Collection (JLWC), and the Warner Bros. Collection (WBC). At the Louis B. Mayer Library of the American Film Institute is the Robert Aldrich Collection (RAC). Finally, author Brooke Hayward graciously provided me with the transcripts of interviews that she did with Stewart and with Johnny Swope as research for her book *Haywire* (Hayward/ms.). Those who helped me gather this information can be found in the acknowledgments.

Chapter One

Information for this chapter was drawn from interviews with Elinor Gordon Blair, Bill Moorhead, John and Elizabeth Simpson, Clarence Stephenson, and Peter Stewart (quotes attributed to them are derived from those interviews) and from local newspaper clippings in the collections of the Historical & Genealogical Society of Indiana County and of the Jimmy Stewart Museum. Other sources are: "man worth one" ("Recollections of J. M. Stewart" [manuscript], Historical & Genealogical Society of Indiana County); "He was a" (*Indiana Gazette*, n.d.); "genial, sunny, light-hearted" (local obituary, n.d.); "His life was" (unidentified publication); "He and his" (Stewart, 1964); "They went to" (Stewart, 2/18/61); "a square and" (Stewart, 1964); "one of Apollo's" (unidentified publication); "My earliest memories" (Stewart, 2/18/61); "full to the" (Stewart, 1964); "I threw them" (Universal press release, 1948); "They always had" (Stephenson); "During those sessions" (Stewart, 1964); "a lady of" (*Indiana Gazette*, n.d.); "She was so" (Stewart, 2/18/61); "the most tolerant" (ibid.); "You don't get" (McLaglen/AI); "In terms of" (Harcourt/AI); "He doesn't wear" (McLean/AI); "I came from" (Tom Lutz, *National Tattler*, 9/22/74); "She stopped Dad" (Amory); "In spite of" (McLean/AI); "they almost chloroformed" (Stewart, 1964); "My father loved" (Tim Hays, *Indiana Gazette*, c. 5/20/83); "They did their" (Stewart, 2/18/61); "I tried to" (Amory); "My father helped" (Stewart, 1948); "dad somehow convinced" (Stewart, 2/18/61); "bound together by" (Stewart, 1964); "Sometimes they'd hire" (Haber, 3/2/75); the story of Bounce (Stewart, 1992); "The three of" (Stewart, 1964); "Mr. Stewart is" (unidentified publication, 10/20/17); "We did a" (Stewart, 2/18/61); "Every man is" (Jimmy Stewart as told to Richard H. Schneider, *National Enquirer*, 1/26/82); the World War I–themed basement plays (Heggie); "I had spent" (James Stewart, "My Most Memorable Experience," unidentified publication); Stewart's ninth-grade grades (grade book, Special Collections Library, Indiana University of Pennsylvania); the kite story (Heggie); "a honey" (Wiles); Stewart's first airplane ride (Stewart, 2/18/61); "the first radio" (ibid.); "Later, when earphones" (ibid.); "It made a" (Stephenson); Jim's projectionist job (Sheilah Graham); "I concentrated on" (Amory); "We would go" (Stephenson); "Mercersburg was full" (Stewart, 2/18/61); "The things I've" (*People*, 6/6/83).

Chapter Two

Information for this chapter was drawn from interviews with Elinor Gordon Blair, John Fentress Gardner, Richard Peter Hoffman, Edward Hotschuh, Ted Lucas, Norris Houghton, Jay Quinn, and L. Owen Potts (quotes attributed to them are derived from those interviews) and from yearbooks, school newspapers, and related materials in the collections of Mercersburg Academy and Princeton University. Other sources are: Stewart's claim that he was an Academy hurdler and high jumper (Sheilah Graham); "a painted-up" (anonymous/AI); "He was very" (Fontaine/AI); Stewart's magic show engagements (*New York Sun*, 5/2/33); "It was like" (Stewart, 2/18/61); "Jimmy Stewart was" (Emory); "A big sophomore" (ibid.); "excellent. He swaggered" (*Mercersburg News*, 2/25/28); "I didn't shine" (Sheilah Graham); "right through the" (*Princeton Weekly Bulletin*, 3/5/90); "The draft was" (*Princetonian*, 2/24/47); "fighting a losing" (Stewart, 2/18/61); "Look here, old" (Heggie); "that got me" (Stewart, 2/18/61); "All sophomores with" (ibid.); "We plied our" (ibid.); Dr. Stuart's recollections (George H. Atkinson, *New Jersey Times Advertiser*, 2/8/70); "repeatedly called for" (*Princeton Bric a Brac* [yearbook], 1932); "You were thrown" (*Triangle Publication*, 5/80); "He walked away" (Logan, 1976); "Josh was a" (Delli Santi); "That show changed" (Kennedy); "So I didn't" (Stewart, 2/18/61); "Take a girl" (Sheilah Graham); "based on the" (*Princeton University Catalogue*, 1929–30); "Once I became" (Stewart, 2/18/61); "My father wanted" (unidentified publication); "Ties and jackets" (Selden); "its excellence easily" (*Time*, n.d.); "Stewart was gangling" (Logan, 1976); "She had this" (Hayward/ms); Stewart's first contact with Sullavan (Darnton); "Nobody gave us" (Stewart, 2/18/61); "smooth and coherent" (Donald A. Stauffer, *Daily Princetonian*, 4/29/31); critical response to *Nerissa* (*Daily Princetonian*, 4/26/32); "I took the" (Louis Berg); *Daily Princetonian*'s response to *Spanish Blades* (George H. Atkinson, *New Jersey Times Advertiser*, 2/8/70); "Princeton shows were" (Grady); the Max Arnow story (Stewart, 2/25/61); "getting my brain" (Stewart's Letter of Sponsorship for Princeton University Alumni trustee-at-large candidacy, 1959, archives, Princeton University Alumni Council).

Chapter Three

Information for this chapter was drawn from interviews with Norris Houghton and Peter
Fonda (unless otherwise indicated, quotes attributed to them are derived from those
interviews) and from Houghton's exhaustive and engaging book, *But Not Forgotten:
The Adventures of the University Players*. Other sources are: "It was a"
(Hayward/ms.); "The knowledge that" (Logan, 1976); "decided to abandon"
(Houghton); "a tremendous loss" (Logan, 1976); "The chance to" (Stewart, 2/18/61);
"Even people who" (Sullivan); "carefully selected so" (Stewart, 2/18/61); "Anyone
could try" (Logan, 1976); "The male lead" (Stewart, 2/18/61); "Previous to hitting"
(Houghton); "was a sort" (ibid.); "Before we knew" (Logan, 1976); "The tryout in"
(Yurka); Stewart's roles in *Carry Nation* (Stewart, 2/18/61); "We delivered a" (Logan,
1976); "groaning bore" (ibid.); "one of the" (Houghton); "Since I didn't" (Stewart,
2/18/61); "Quite suddenly I" (Reeve); "couldn't help thinking" (Stewart, 2/18/61);
"Like so many" (Yurka); "by all odds" (Stark Young, *New Republic*, 11/23/32); "more
of a" (John Chapman, *New York Daily News*, 10/31/32); "The Biltmore Theatre"
(*New York Evening Post*, 11/16/32); "alone in the" (Virginia Stewart); "We could not"
(Houghton); "with a confidence" (ibid.); the New York newspaper reviews of *Goodbye Again* are dated 12/29/32; "Mr. James Stewart's" (*New Yorker*, 1/7/33); "I saw a"
(Burgess Meredith); the *New York Sun* column on Stewart during the run of *Good-
bye Again* is dated 5/2/33; "The money wasn't" (Stewart, 2/25/61); "He was one"
(Bogdanovich); "Thank God it" (Christon); "a soot-colored bedroom" (Logan, 1976);
Stewart's appetite and the food budget (Brough); "We'd test it" (Fonda); "huge thick
slabs" (ibid.); "One night I" (Burgess Meredith); "When he came" (Darnton); "When
there was" (Reeve); "He was the" (Creelman); "When he lighted" (Stewart, 2/25/61);
"And he would" (Scott/AI); "a skill to" (Stewart, 2/25/61); "Milk shakes are" (ibid.);
"As a result" (ibid.).

Chapter Four

Information for this chapter was drawn from interviews with Norris Houghton and Peter
Fonda (unless otherwise indicated, quotes attributed to them are derived from those
interviews). Other sources are: "The electrician working" (Stewart, 2/25/61); "was
very loyal" (Yurka); the rewrites for *Spring in Autumn* (ibid.); the New York newspaper reviews for *Spring in Autumn* are dated 10/25/33; "in early East" (Fonda); the
New York newspaper reviews for *All Good Americans* are dated 12/6/33; "Then the
next" (Fonda); "Let's have a" (ibid.); "I wasn't exactly" (Stewart, 2/25/61); "It was a"
(ibid.); "The camouflage didn't" (ibid.); "He had had" (Logan, 1976); "When the
actor" (unidentified publication); "For the first" (Reagan); the New York newspaper
reviews of *Yellow Jack* are dated 3/7/34; "though I couldn't" (Grady); "The cast was"
(Stewart, 2/25/61); "I wasn't really" (Darnton); "But they're tryouts" (Robert Garland, *New York World-Telegram*, 7/28/34); "Somehow I got" (Stewart, 2/25/61); "it
still emerges" (John Whitney, *Newark Evening News*, n.d.); "It was the" (Darnton);
"If anything would" (Stewart, 2/25/61); "To carry all" (ibid.); "capacity audience of"
(*New York Times*, 7/24/34); "It was the" (Grady); "She was a" (Christon); the New
York newspaper reviews of *Divided by Three* are dated 10/3/34; "This man has"
(Grady); the statistics on Hollywood screen tests (Goodman); Stewart's screen tests
(Stewart, 2/25/61); "pre-eminent in the" (Percy Hammond, *New York Herald-Tri-
bune*, 11/28/34); "Additions and deletions" (*New York Herald-Tribune*, 12/2/34); the
New York newspaper reviews for *Page Miss Glory* are dated 11/28/34; Stewart,

Fonda, and the model airplane (Fonda); "If I'm not" (Stewart, 3/4/61); "I went to" (Ebert, 1985); "Every time I" (Stewart, 2/25/61); "wandered through the" (Ebert, 1985); the New York newspaper reviews for *Journey By Night* are dated 4/17/35; "lick my wounds" (Stewart, 2/25/61).

Chapter Five

Information for this chapter was drawn from interviews with Brooke Hayward and William Hayward (quotes attributed to them are derived from those interviews). Other sources are: "stood for 'production'" (Mordden); Stewart's version of his casting in *The Murder Man* (Stewart, 2/25/61); "Whelan and I" (Grady); "The only trouble" (Fonda); "Take it easy" (Dawes); "The kindness he" (Speck, 1992); "I told him" (Swindell, 1969); "didn't fit my" (Stewart, 1973); "It is the" (Thornton Delehanty, *New York Post*, 7/27/35); "wasted in a" (*New York Herald-Tribune*, 7/27/35, as cited in Molyneaux); "I was all" (Christon); "It's fun living" (Cheatham); "That guy—he" (Sharpe, 1937); "favorite meeting place" (Stewart, 3/4/61); "Now I ask" (Fonda); "It ain't true" (Sweeney); "might have happened" (Fonda); "If they take" (Virginia Stewart); "The reckless pace" (Sharpe, 1936); Stewart's three weeks on *Rose Marie* (Rich); Eddy's recollection of the scene with Stewart (ibid.); "Handsome, lavishly staged" (William Boehnel, *New York World-Telegram*, 2/1/36); "envisioned the film" (letter from Griffith to Hopper dated 10/31/63, HHC); the telegrams to Stewart regarding *Next Time We Love* (*New York Evening Post*, 1/25/36); "When you'd play" (Hayward/ms.); "It was Maggie" (Quirk, 1986); "That boy came" (ibid.); "He never fooled" (ibid.); "Peggy was Scarlett" (Fonda); "I'll never marry" (Edith Driscoll, *Movie Mirror*, n.d.); "We never discussed" (Karp/AI); "Oddly, her attitude" (Quirk, 1986); "Naturally I was" (Reeve); the New York newspaper reviews of *Next Time We Love* are dated 1/31/36; "She was just" (Stenn); "she took charge" (Stewart, 2/25/61); "a roly-poly little" (Darr Smith, *Los Angeles Daily News*, n.d.); "It was a" (McBride, 1977); "its own expensive" (Eileen Creelman, *New York Sun*, 2/24/36).

Chapter Six

Information for this chapter was drawn from interviews with Peter Fonda, Brooke Hayward, William Hayward, and Simone Simon (unless otherwise indicated, quotes attributed to them are derived from those interviews). Other sources are: "fell over themselves" (Logan, 1978); "It was perhaps" (ibid.); "Anybody that would" (ibid.); "I guess you" (Fonda); "a hilarious, wonderful" (ibid.); "There were no" (Rogers); "When I'm crazy" (Reeve); "Both Grady and" (Quirk, 1986); "He was always" (Whitney); "I'm having a" (Mook); the beet juice story (Fonda); "I think he" (Hayward/ms.); "Our house was" (Hayward); "enhanced her feelings" (Quirk, 1986); "There's no other" (Wixen); Stewart and Hayward's air race (Hayward/ms.); "a small but" (*Daily Variety*, 3/31/36); "excellent" (Richard Watts Jr., *New York Herald-Tribune*, 4/11/36); the New York newspaper reviews of *Speed* are dated 5/16/36; "one of the" (*New York Evening Post*, 1/25/36); "You may get" (D'Antonio); "The movie moguls" (Riordan); "In the studio" (Wapshott); "I must have" (*London Times*, 7/14/67); "He was a" (Burgess Meredith); Stewart's weight-gain efforts (Proctor); "There was no" (Stewart, 1969); "how to act" (ibid.); "a sense of" (*London Times*, 7/14/67); "But I got" (*Video Review*); "She was a" (Speck, 1992); the New York newspaper reviews for *The Gorgeous Hussy* are dated 9/5/36; "most interesting, if" (Eells, 1967); "He'd get up" (Pane); "And I have" (Small); "It was a" (*New York Post*, 9/23/88); "corking entertainment" (Bige., *Variety*,

12/9/36); "Girls, he dances" (Kate Cameron, *New York Daily News*, 12/5/36); "Two years after" (Eyles); "In Hollywood, they" (*Silver Screen*, 11/19/39); "There has never" (Sheilah Graham); "It seems this" (transcript of Stewart's interview with Hedda Hopper dated 10/26/55, HHC); "It was not" (Van Dyke); "To be honest" (Cohn); "He was very" (Kotsilibas-Davis and Loy); "The audience laughed" (Reed, 1979); "James Stewart is" (Flin., *Variety*, 12/30/36); the New York newspaper reviews of *After the Thin Man* are dated 12/26/36; MGM's earnings from the Stewart loanout for *Seventh Heaven* (UPC); the New York newspaper reviews for *Seventh Heaven* are dated 3/26/37, except Frank S. Nugent's *New York Times* review, which is dated 4/4/37; "As Chico, James" (*Newsweek*, 4/3/37).

Chapter Seven

Information for this chapter was drawn from interviews with Ed Bernds, Peter Fonda, Brooke Hayward, William Hayward, and Ann Miller (unless otherwise indicated, quotes attributed to them are derived from those interviews). Other sources are: "Money was the" (Robinson); "It was the" (Charles E. Davis); "James Stewart and" (Archer Winsten, *New York Post*, 12/10/37); "The return to" (MGM press book for *Of Human Hearts*); "What might have" (William Boehnel, *New York World-Telegram*, 2/18/38); the New York newspaper reviews for *Navy Blue and Gold* are dated 12/24/37; Stewart's 1937 illness (undated manuscript for an article in *Motion Picture* by Gloria Hall, GHC); "But he would" (interview with Stewart on 8/21/81 for *George Stevens: A Filmmaker's Journey*, interviewer Susan Winslow, GSC); "The fewer words" (filmed interview with Stewart on 6/14/82 for *George Stevens: A Filmmaker's Journey*, interviewer George Stevens Jr., GSC); "No-ow to overcome" (Bogdanovich); "the same ridiculous" (filmed interview with Ginger Rogers on 9/9/81 for *George Stevens: A Filmmaker's Journey*, interviewer George Stevens Jr., GSC); "Well, this was" (ibid.); "not only elegant" (Rose Pelswick, *New York Journal American*, 6/3/38); "They saw each" (Janis/AI); "Believing that in" (*New York Times*, 7/1/37); "Instead of the" (Hobe, *Variety*, 3/13/38); "It was so" (Quirk, 1986); "We were old" (Maltin, 1–2/73); "That's just what" (Brough); "Some of 'em" (manuscript for an article in *Modern Screen* by Gloria Hall dated 12/31/37, GHC); "In a moment" (Logan, 1976); "Jimmy gave Norma" (Rooney); "his badge as" (Logan, 1976); "There was a" (Stewart, 3/4/61); the New York newspaper reviews for *The Shopworn Angel* are dated 7/8/38; "Why, they're red-hot" (Quirk, 1986); "I wouldn't shell" (Capra); "Arnold had the" (ibid.); "I had seen" (ibid.); "I just had" (McBride, 1992); "He's the easiest" (ibid.); the New York newspaper reviews for *You Can't Take It With You* are dated 9/2/38; "much of the" (Char., *Variety*, 9/7/38); "If I had" (unidentified publication); "practically every stock" (J.H.D., *New York Sun*, 2/17/39); "I couldn't work" (Hopper, c. 1950); "She was truly" (Speck, 1989); "more sincere than" (Swindell, 1975); "it appears to" (Bland Johaneson, *New York Daily Mirror*, 2/17/39); "so brilliantly by" (William Boehnel, *New York World-Telegram*, 2/17/39); George Murphy's initial casting in *Ice Follies of 1939* (George Murphy); "When the producer" (Berges); "I adored working" (Crawford); "Crawford's singing is" (Considine); "hit the cutting-room" (Crawford); "an attractive package" (*Variety*, 3/7/39); "a pleasant and" (Kate Cameron, *New York Daily News*, 3/17/39); "I collected silver" (Charles Davis); "I'm certainly disappointed" (MGM press book for *It's a Wonderful World*); the New York newspaper reviews of *It's a Wonderful World* are dated 5/19/39.

Chapter Eight

Information for this chapter was drawn from an interview with Ed Bernds (quotes attributed to him are derived from that interview). Other sources are: "I then thought" (*Hollywood Citizen News*, 6/6/41); "Gary Cooper . . . had" (McBride, 1992); shooting Stewart at the Lincoln Memorial (Castos); "I don't want" (McBride, 1992); "used to get" (ibid.); "Stewart is almost" (McBride, 1992); "No, a doctor" (Speck, 1989); "outrageous, exactly the" (McBride, 1992); the New York newspaper reviews for *Mr. Smith Goes to Washington* are dated 10/20/39; "Everyone seemed so" (*ICN*, 8/29/44); "I found them" (ibid.); "We weren't allowed" (Abrams); "Let's do a" (Higham, 1977); "I called the" (ibid.); Dietrich's casting in *Destry* (Pasternak); Remarque's role in Dietrich's casting (Gilbert); "We are without" (M. F. Murphy, "Weekly Status Pictures in Production, Week Ending Friday, October 20th," 10/21/39, UPC); "The film is" (Riva); "So she did" (Higham, 1977); Stewart's relationship with Loretta Young (Lewis); "I liked taking" (Speck, 1992); "It was a" (Gilbert); "She never knew" (ibid.); "Maria told people" (Bach); "Obviously, his sense" (Dietrich); "If you've got" (Speck, 1989); "I rehearsed it" (*Galaxy*, 2/82); "a rousing comeback" (William Boehnel, *New York World-Telegram*, 11/30/39); "Here is a" (ibid.); "He is the" (Stack/AI); "He is the" (Smith/AI); "the audience would" (Silverman); "I suppose I" (*Hollywood Reporter*, 1955); "You loved his" (Hardman/AI); "He was one" (Saxon/AI); "He was just" (Alford/AI); "Jimmy's screen roles" (Burgess Meredith); "I couldn't mess" (*Fanfare*, 6/8/73); "overboard on the" (Rose Pelswick, *New York Journal American*, 2/28/41); "James Stewart plays" (Land., *Variety*, 4/9/41); "I take a" (Cohn).

Chapter Nine

Information for this chapter was drawn from interviews with Jackie Cooper, Julius Epstein, Ruth Hussey, Hedy Lamarr, and Robert Stack (unless otherwise indicated, quotes attributed to them are derived from those interviews). Other sources are: "the antithesis of" (Eyman); "little man, strongly" (*New York Herald-Tribune*, 1/28/40); "I have known" (ibid.); "Never did I" (Paul); "It was wonderful" (Stewart, 1970); "Lubitsch told me" (Quirk, 1986); "For some reason" (Hayward/ms.); "*The Shop Around*" (Lee Mortimer, *New York Daily Mirror*, 1/26/40); "Going about with" (Virginia Stewart); "Jimmy met me" (Christy); the La Salle story (Zolotow, 1974); "But he didn't" (O'Hara/AI); "Two hours after" (Fontaine); "I think his" (Pickard); "they would be" (manuscript dated 5/27/40 for an article by Gloria Hall in *Motion Picture*, GHC); "The new incidents" (Bottome); "a family's disintegration" (Coons); "Our picture won't" (ibid.); Higham's assertion regarding Sidney Franklin and Victor Saville (Higham, 1993); "I'd read the" (manuscript dated 5/27/40 for an article by Gloria Hall in *Motion Picture*, GHC); "taken care of" (Stack); "Wal, after the" (Davidson, 1971); how Stewart appeared to be skiing (Hayward/ms.); the New York newspaper reviews for *The Mortal Storm* are dated 6/21/40; "Funniest thing, I" (Creelman); the New York newspaper reviews for *No Time for Comedy* are dated 9/7/40; "Few actresses of" (Richard Watts Jr., *New York Herald-Tribune*, 3/29/39); "When I first" (Speck, 1992); "he also worked" (Levy); "I'm an interpretive" (Farber); "You couldn't take" (Lambert, 1972); "played it in" (*American Film*, 2/78); "once the picture" (*USA Today*, 3/6/87); "He's a helluva" (Quigg); "From the time" (Speck, 1989); "I'd decided I" (Wansell); "absolutely *fascinated* with" (Bogdanovich); "When you work" (Eyles); the New York newspaper and *Christian Science Monitor* reviews for *The Philadelphia Story* are dated 12/27/40; "Her only consolation" (Higham, 1984); "Everywhere they had" (Creelman); "I'd come on" (Stewart, n.d.); the New

York newspaper reviews for *Come Live With Me* are dated 2/28/41; "The only lottery" (Stewart, 3/4/61); the original stars for *Ziegfeld Girl* (Shipman); "deserved a much" (Steen); "Anyone can gulp" (Gilbert); "How did she" (Hopper, 1956); the New York newspaper reviews of *Pot o' Gold* are dated 4/4/41; "Stewart's lines and" (Land., *Variety*, 4/9/41); "another conventional musical" (T.S., *New York Times*, 4/25/41); "a thankless role" (*Newsweek*, 4/28/41); "I had to" (*Indiana Gazette*, n.d.); "The whole thing" (Louella Parsons, *Los Angeles Examiner*, n.d.); "Roz Russell kissed" (Stewart, 3/4/61); "I know it" (Pickard); "I want to" (ibid.); "What'd they give" (Haber, 1975); "I am glad" (Louella Parsons, *Los Angeles Examiner*, n.d.); "Man and boy" (Grady); "a crazy celebration" (Burgess Meredith).

Chapter Ten

Information for this chapter was drawn from interviews with Clarence Adams, Milton Arnold, Arthur S. Beavers, Jack Burton, Wilbur Clingan, Howard Kriedler, Andrew Low, and Ramsay Potts (unless otherwise indicated, quotes attributed to them are derived from those interviews) and from Rudolph J. Birsic's "The History of the 445th Bombardment Group," dated July 1947 (Birsic), *In Search of Peace* by Michael D. Benarcick (Benarcick), and *The Liberator Men of "Old Buc,"* Andrew Low, ed. (Low, ed.). Other sources are: "pigeon with a" (*Los Angeles Times*, 6/1/41); "I have only" (*Los Angeles News*, 5/2/41); "five of us" (Wixen); "The poor man" (Hayward/ms.); "We had a" (DeCarlo); "Suddenly I was" (Stewart, 3/4/61); "At the close" (unidentified publication); "I'll tell you" (Stewart, 1941); Arnold's assessment of *Winning Your Wings'* recruitment value (Bob Thomas, 1990); Stewart's appeal to Usher (Lay, 12/8/45); "In two months" (Stewart, 3/4/61); "He never scratched" (Lay, 12/8/45); "When I was" (Eyles); "It was a" (Stewart, 2/18/61); "There must be" (Lay, 12/8/45); "physically exhausting work" (Lay, 12/8/45); Stewart's role in Swope's wedding (Hayward/ms.); how Terrill recruited Stewart (Lay, 12/8/45); "We still did" (Birsic); "very self-conscious with" (Stewart, 1964); "Captain James Stewart" (*Los Angeles Examiner*, 11/29/43); "It was decidedly" (Birsic); "were always good" (ibid.); "So great was" (ibid.); "*Every*thing's different from" (Bogdanovich); "There were, oh" (Eyles); "I knew my" (ibid.); "workmanlike. He made" (Lay, 12/15/45); Lay's account of Stewart's return flight from Ludwigshafen (Lay, 12/15/45); "Brunswick was heavily" (Birsic); "In spite of" (Lay, 12/15/45); "mighty proud of" (MacGregor); "hardest decision" (Stewart, 3/4/61); Stewart's prank flight (Low and Stewart); "The more I" (ibid.); "As I look" (ibid.); "He just couldn't" (Blair/AI); "He was very" (McLean/AI); "I think it" (Sweeney).

Chapter Eleven

Information for this chapter was drawn from interviews with Peter Fonda and Lew Wasserman (unless otherwise indicated, quotes attributed to them are derived from those interviews) and from Rudolph J. Birsic's "The History of the 445th Bombardment Group," dated July 1947 (Birsic), *In Search of Peace* by Michael D. Benarcick (Benarcick), and *The Liberator Men of "Old Buc,"* Andrew Low, ed. (Low, ed.). Other sources are: "How he got" (Hayward/ms.); Stewart's mother's reaction to his appearance (Louella O. Parsons, *Los Angeles Examiner*, c. 1946–47); "It will take" (*Los Angeles Times*, 9/2/45); "I'm just another" (*Beverly Hills Citizen News*, 9/4/45); the *Life* magazine spread on Stewart (*Life*, 9/24/45); Stewart's return to Los Angeles (unidentified publication, 10/3/45); "To pass the" (Grady); "It got pretty" (*Los Angeles Examiner*, 10/3/45); "Well, hell! You" (Fonda); "I have this" (Dillon); "If Jimmy was" (Capra); "older, shyer, ill" (McBride, 1992); "Goddamn, Jim. I" (Capra); "Frank, if you" (McBride, 1992); Stewart and Fonda's concerns about returning to acting (Fonda); "never sat down" (Christon); "God knows who" (Fonda); "the most beautiful" (*Time*, 1/8/45); "eligible and often" (ibid.); "They are constantly" (unidentified publication); Colby's assertion that Stewart proposed marriage to her (*New York Times*, 8/11/70); "couldn't stand having" (Parsons, 1954); "When you get" (Susan Peters); "I don't want" (Heggie); "When I got" (Hayward); "You'd never have" (Hopper, 1946); "not in the" (unidentified publication); the number of independent production companies in Hollywood in the mid-1940s (*Time*, 12/23/46); "hand holding the" (Wechsburg); "a medium-priced machine" (Nord Riley, *TW*, 12/15/46).

Chapter Twelve

Information for this chapter was drawn from interviews with Joan Fontaine, Farley Granger, Jimmy Hawkins, Sheldon Leonard, and Jesse White (unless otherwise indicated, quotes attributed to them are derived from those interviews). Other sources are: "It was the" (Capra); "He wasn't the" (McBride, 1992); "had lost all" (Norton); "I just fell" (Leonard Maltin interview with Stewart, Basinger, 1986); "And we did" (ibid.); "Forget about being" (Silverman); "Well, leave it" (Leonard Maltin interview with Stewart, Basinger, 1986); "knew everything was" (McBride, 1992); the *New Yorker* and New York newspaper reviews of *It's a Wonderful Life* are dated 12/21/46; "It is truly" (John L. Scott, *Los Angeles Times*, 12/26/46); the year-end ranking and financial status of *It's a Wonderful Life* (David Germain, Associated Press, 12/21/89); "The country had" (Dillon); "Without any doubt" (Speck, 1992); "It bears out" (Kevin Thomas); "It stunk!" (McBride, 1992); the purchase price for the film rights to *Harvey* (UPC); "I did it" (Cohen); the New York newspaper reviews of Stewart's debut in *Harvey* on Broadway are dated 7/15/47; "A special detail" (20th Century–Fox press release dated 12/31/47); "was stampeded by" (Jane Corby, *Brooklyn Eagle*, 7/15/47); "Just to see" (O'Brian); "real hoot" (ibid.); "No. Too tough" (ibid.); "should be more" (memo by Zanuck dated 3/29/47, USC); "a slick piece" (Bosley Crowther, *New York Times*, n.d.); getting O'Hara for *A Miracle Can Happen* (interview with Stewart dated 8/21/81 for *George Stevens: A Filmmaker's Journey*, interviewer Susan Winslow, GSC); "We'd shot about" (ibid.); "kept everyone on" (filmed interview with Stewart dated 6/14/82 for *George Stevens: A Filmmaker's Journey*, interviewer George Stevens Jr., GSC); "pathetically unfunny" (*Cue*, 2/7/48); "most painful business" (Bosley Crowther, *New York Times*, 2/4/48); "sustain the mood" (Warner Bros. press release for *Rope*); "Those who can" (Brooks Atkinson, *New York Times*, 9/20/29); "a warped orchid" (Robert Littell, *New York World*, 9/20/29); "We must change" (Warner Bros. press release for *Rope*); "Jimmy, never do" (ibid.); "By the time" (ibid.); "a magnificent psychological" (*Cue*, 8/28/48); the New York newspaper reviews of *Rope* are dated 8/29/48; "nowhere to go" (Andrew Sarris, *Village Voice*, 12/23/83); "When I look" (George Turner); "So much of" (Eyles); "just didn't come" (*Variety*, 3/5/75); the location filming for *You Gotta Stay Happy* (production logs for the film, UPC); "Half an hour" (Fontaine); "There were times" (Parsons, 1948).

Chapter Thirteen

Information for this chapter was drawn from interviews with Joan Fontaine, Kelly Harcourt, Maria Cooper Janis, Michael McLean, Debra Paget, Robert Stack, and Lew Wasserman (unless otherwise indicated, quotes attributed to them are derived from those interviews). Other sources are: "the product of" (Reeve); "Nat King Cole" (Amory); "As I opened" (Burden); "I wanted to" (Waterbury); "But he didn't" (Amory); "I brought him" (Waterbury); "knocked himself out" (Mrs. James Stewart); "This is the" (*Time*, 11/22/48); "Shucks, a person'd" (Morrow); "How do you" (Zolotow, 1974); "He just kept" (Stratton); "When he'd throw" (ibid.); "All of a" (Frank Graham); "that rare achievement" (*Newsweek*, 5/23/49); the New York newspaper reviews of *The Stratton Story* are dated 5/13/49; "When and if" (*Los Angeles Times*, 2/4/49); "It was a" (Bill Davidson, 1990); "Every day we'd" (ibid.); "first-rate melodramatic" (*Cue*, 2/25/50); "intimate with a" (Elliott Arnold); Bosley Crowther's review of *Broken Arrow* (*New York Times*, 7/21/50); "a first-rate entertainment" (Robert Gessner, *Saturday Review*, 8/5/50); "an intelligent, literate" (*Cue*, 7/22/50); "I credit Gloria" (Hayes); Gloria's fears about Jim and her sons (Mrs. James Stewart); "I have never" (Louella Parsons, *Los Angeles Examiner*, n.d.); "So I asked" (Bacon, 1966); "I pretty much" (Rohter); "the real star" (Winters, 1980); "His knuckles were" (Pickard); "Strikingly photographed in" (*Time*, 6/19/50); "lean . . . concentrated" (Bron., *Variety*, 6/7/50); "drawls and fumbles" (Bosley Crowther, *New York Times*, 6/8/50); "I never detected" (Morgan/AI); "I never really" (Adams/AI); Marshall Green's opinion of the relationship between Stewart and Mann (Green/AI); Janet Leigh's opinion of the relationship between Stewart and Mann (Leigh/AI); "there wasn't one" (McLaglen/AI); Stewart's refusal to work with Donna Reed after *It's a Wonderful Life* (anonymous/AI); "It took us" (Pickard); "this beautiful sorrel" (Amory); "never got the" (Pickard); "You know, Jimmy" (Jones/AI); "Getting out on" (Universal press release, n.d.); "It is the" (Mary Murphy); "Gosh, *Winchester '73*" (McBride, 1976).

Chapter Fourteen

Information for this chapter was drawn from interviews with Julie Adams, Harold Jack Bloom, Fred De Cordova, Marshall Green, Barbara Hale, Kelly Harcourt, Charlton Heston, Janet Leigh, Michael McLean, Judy Merrill, Harry Morgan, Lew Wasserman, and Jesse White (unless otherwise indicated, quotes attributed to them are derived from those interviews). Other sources are: "*Harvey* is a" (Hopper, c. 1950); "I was truly" (Hull); other candidates for the role of Elwood (*Variety*, 4/22/48); "right up my" (Atkins); "implication is there" (*Los Angeles Evening Herald-Express*, 5/13/50); "When I'm talking" (Universal press release for *Harvey*); "Without that space" (Ebert, 1985); "We also had" (unidentified publication); Otis L. Guernsey's opinion of the film (Otis L. Guernsey Jr., *New York Herald-Tribune*, 12/22/50); "a movie that" (John McCarten, *New Yorker*, 12/23/50); "I acted in" (Mosby); "I played him" (Klemerud); "People will stop" (Speck, 1989); "just so many" (McNulty); "wasn't all laughs" (ibid.); "a rugged man" (Darr Smith, *Los Angeles Daily News*, 2/23/50); "one of the" (Darr Smith, *Los Angeles Daily News*, 11/9/50); "He had a" (Shute); "Well, that's what" (Peterson); "I used to" (ibid.); the story of Stewart and the camera store (Finletter); "There had been" (Hayne, ed.); Selznick's plans for the circus picture (*Los Angeles Times*, 4/15/48); "vignettes of life" (Hayne, ed.); "He heard that" (Martin, n.d.); "Wal, it's a" (unidentified publication); "I never got" (Tex McCrary and Jinx Falkenburg, unidentified publication); "He never shows" (Paramount press book for *The Greatest Show on Earth*); "Old DeMille was" (Kevin Thomas); "It was not" (North); Gloria Grahame's near miss with elephant (Pryor); "When I arrived" (Tex McCrary and Jinx Falkenburg, unidentified publication); "All of my" (ibid.); "As has come" (Herb., *Variety*, 1/2/52); "lavish, sentimental, eye-filling" (*Cue*, 1/12/52); "the most comfortable"

(Kirkley); "It was the" (Universal press book for *Bend of the River*); "This big, splashy" (*Cue*, 4/12/52); "Stewart is every" (Otis L. Guernsey Jr., *New York Herald-Tribune*, 4/10/52); "At that time" (unidentified publication); "factual than inspired" (*Time*, 5/12/52); "It was the" (Louis Black, program notes, Department of Radio/Television/Film, University of Texas at Austin, n.d.); "one of the" (Joe Pihodna, *New York Herald-Tribune*, 3/27/53); "This is not" (*Cue*, 3/28/53); Sidney Davis' ransom threat (*Hollywood Citizen News*, 8/21/52); "I work hard" (Scott); "I'll admit I" (manuscript for an article under Mann's byline, UPC); "tremendously impressive" (Brog., *Variety*, 5/6/53); Philip Scheuer's opinion of *Thunder Bay*'s wide-screen format (Philip K. Scheuer, *Los Angeles Times*, 7/30/53); "Sadly enough, *Thunder*" (Andrew Weiler, *New York Times*, 5/21/53); "Some of the" (Eyles); "Every studio in" (*Denver Post*, 7/13/53); Stewart was Helen Miller's choice to play her husband (ibid.); "He wasn't a" (Hopper, 1953); "The movie of" (Simon); "super-dependent upon" (ibid.); "sort of one" (McDougal); "By that time" (Universal press release for *The Glenn Miller Story*); "My music teacher" (Reed, 1979); "He blew out" (Universal press release for *The Glenn Miller Story*); "You're a good" (ibid.); "We buried her" (James Stewart, 1964); "We lost a" (telegram from Jack Diamond to Hopper dated 1/20/54, HHC); "Actor Stewart has" (*Time*, 3/2/54); "Not since *Yankee*" (Bosley Crowther, *New York Times*, 2/11/54).

Chapter Fifteen

Information for this chapter was drawn from interviews with Corinne Calvet, Doris Day (letter to author), Marshall Green, Barbara Hale, Kelly Harcourt, William Hayward, Michael McLean, Judy Merrill, Harry Morgan, Greg Paul, Lew Wasserman, and Billy Wilder (unless otherwise indicated, quotes attributed to them are derived from those interviews). Other sources are: "The cameras were" (Universal press release for *The Far Country*); "a very awesome" (script for radio interview to promote *The Far Country*, UPC); " 'Just thought I'd" (Kevin Thomas); the story of Pie and the stunt (Amory); "It's a mighty" (Jesse Zunser, *Cue*, 2/12/55); "a fairly standard" (Andrew Weiler, *New York Times*, 2/14/56); "the pattern of" (Basinger, 1979); "fast on the" (*Variety*, 9/23/53); "A lot of" (Spada, 1987); "In filming that" (Speck, 1992); "I was just" (*USA Today*, 3/6/87); "I think it's" (Spada, 1987); Spoto's case for Hitchcock's passion for Grace Kelly (Spoto); "First, Hitchcock would" (Ebert, 1968); lighting the *Rear Window* set (Atkinson); only one hundred feet of exposed *Rear Window* film went unused (Universal production notes, UPC); "The set and" (Spoto); "absorbing and entertaining" (Bosley Crowther, *New York Times*, 8/15/54); "a masterpiece" (*Newsweek*, 8/9/54); "an unusually good" (Brog., *Variety*, 7/14/54); "I don't think" (script of Stewart's appearance on Hopper's radio program dated 2/11/54, HHC); *Look*'s assertion that Stewart was the highest-paid actor in Hollywood (*Look*, 7/26/55); the earnings of Stewart's films by 1966 (Bacon, 1966); the sale of Stewart's California ranch (Suzy, *New York Daily News*, 2/27/75); "Sure, I like" (*Hollywood Reporter*, 1955); "the biggest single" (*Newsweek*, 5/9/55); "held within the" (Eyles); "papier-mâché" (ibid.); "far and away" (Bosley Crowther, *New York Times*, 5/21/55); "The story that" (*New Yorker*, 5/30/55); "the complexity of" (Basinger, 1979); "an easily recognizable" (Bosley Crowther, *New York Times*, 9/1/55); "Dad sure picked" (*Los Angeles Times*, 12/12/54); "drove along a" (Bob Thomas, 3/14/55); "a shot in" (Bob Thomas, 3/17/55); "a sort of" (Hyams); "James Stewart contributed" (*Variety*, 4/24/55); "I had never" (Hotchner); "Marrakech was one" (manuscript for a Hopper column dated 11/10/55, HHC); the *Life* spread on Stewart (*Life*, 9/5/55); "few rich" people" (Hotchner); "He didn't direct" (ibid.); "I continued to" (Paramount production notes for *The Man Who Knew Too Much*); "Doris thought he" (Hotchner); the shooting schedule for *The Man Who Knew Too Much* (production logs, AHC); "While the current" (*New Yorker*, 5/26/56); "the work of" (Paramount's production notes for *The Man Who Knew Too Much*); "a fast, lively" (Bosley Crowther, *New York Times*, 5/20/56); "invariably dismissed as" (David Denby, *New York*, 4/30/84); "a thrilling piece" (Andrew Sarris, *Village Voice*, 6/12/84); "got some terrific" (memo from Hayward to Steve Trilling dated 9/9/55, JLWC); Stewart's conflict with Wilder and Hayward in Paris (Hayward memos to Trilling dated 9/19/55 and 9/23/55, JLWC); "I've never seen" (Hayward memo to Trilling dated 9/23/55, JLWC); "I wanted to" (Harris); "I didn't know" (Hayward/ms.); "I hope I" (Harris); "I recall getting" (Speck, 1992); "wonderful fun to" (Hayward/ms.); "thrilling documentary drama" (*Cue*, 2/23/57); "as entertaining as" (*Newsweek*, 2/25/57); "remarkable" (John Beaufort, *Christian Science Monitor*, 2/26/57); "Class A picture-making" (Gene., *Variety*, 2/20/57); "disastrous failure. Every" (Pickard); "It was a" (Mosley, 1976); Basinger's assertion that Mann cast *Night Passage* (Basinger, 1979); "of such incoherence" (Eyles); "a prior commitment" (Universal press release for *Night Passage*); "solid rock gorges" (ibid.); "no better or" (William K. Zinsser, *New York Herald-Tribune*, 7/25/57).

Chapter Sixteen

Information for this chapter was drawn from interviews with Orson Bean, Ben Gazzara, Kelly Harcourt, Jack Lemmon, Michael McLean, Judy Merrill, Harry Morgan, Ramsay Potts, and Daniel Taradash (unless otherwise indicated, quotes attributed to them are derived from those interviews). Other sources are: "the morale of" (*Newsweek*, 9/2/57); "Stewart has made" (*Time*, 9/2/57); "That was more" (*Newsweek*, 7/27/59); "I didn't realize" (Spoto); "This film was" (ibid.); "If we'd had" (ibid.); "It was very" (Brown); "Kim, this is" (ibid.); "I was alarmed" (*London Times*, 7/14/67); "She was fun" (ibid.); "He was sexy" (Novak); "I still felt" (ibid.); "part thriller and" (Philip K. Scheuer, *Los Angeles Times*, 5/29/58); "far-fetched nonsense" (John McCarten, *New Yorker*, 6/7/58); the New York newspaper reviews of *Vertigo* are dated 5/29/58; "I had known" (Pickard); "masterful" (*Variety*, 12/17/57); "This is high" (William Hawkins, *New York World-Telegram*, 11/15/50); Hitchcock's discomfort over Stewart's interest in *North by Northwest* (Spoto); "a tall, handsome" (John L. Scott, *Los Angeles Times*, 9/29/58); "Somewhere between Broadway" (*Time*, 12/29/58); "on a dignified" (Hoover telegram to Jack Warner dated 5/21/58, WBC); "I have always" (Hoover letter to Jack Warner dated 11/14/57, WBC); "It was all" (LeRoy); "The actual filming" (ibid.); "It's a great" (ibid.); "As the author" (ibid.); "Obviously, this long" (Hollis Alpert, *Saturday Review*, 9/12/59); "remarkable job of" (Bosley Crowther, *New York Times*, 9/25/59); "Wherever the Stewarts" (LeRoy); "Oh, I'm not" (ibid.); "I spent a" (Stewart, 3/4/61); "The region is" (Stewart, 1959); "At night after" (Arden); "Lee Remick did" (ibid.); George C. Scott's respect for Stewart (Speck, 1992); "I'd like to" (Stewart, 1966); "something of a" (*Variety*, 7/1/59); "Not since *Witness*" (Powe., *Variety*, 7/1/59); "probably the best" (*Cue*, 7/4/59); "well nigh flawless" (Bosley Crowther, *New York Times*, 7/3/59); "one of the" (ibid.); "As the flashbulbs" (Heston); "the toughest location" (Fender); "Even with its" (Howard Thompson, *New York Times*, 6/30/60); "It reveals nothing" (Ron., *Variety*, 3/23/60); "tough, generally clear-eyed" (*Newsweek*, 5/30/60); "I voted it" (Erskine Johnson).

Chapter Seventeen

Information for this chapter was drawn from interviews with Elizabeth Allen, Harry Carey Jr., Linda Cristal, Sandra Dee, Gene Fowler Jr., Marjorie Fowler, Kelly Harcourt, Doris Johnson, Shirley Jones, Hal Kanter, Michael McLean, Audrey Meadows, Judy Merrill, Bill Mumy, Maureen O'Hara, Bernard Smith, and Richard Widmark (unless otherwise indicated, quotes attributed to them are derived from those interviews). Other sources are: "Does this SOB" (Stewart, 3/4/61); "On *Two Rode*" (Pickard); "probably John Ford's" (Philip K. Scheuer, *Los Angeles Times*, 8/17/61); *Time*'s review of *Two Rode Together* is dated 7/28/61; "Only rarely in" (Eugene Archer, *New York Times*, 7/27/61); the dropped segment of *How the West Was Won* (Howard Thompson, *New York Times*, 6/18/61); "Paducah was selected" (Baker); "After the hellos" (ibid.); "I know it" (ibid.); "Had the real" (*New Yorker*, 4/6/63); "probably the most" (Leo Mishkin, *New York Morning-Telegraph*, 3/28/63); "The thing about" (Alpert); "You don't want" (GSM); "You can't disrupt" (Reagan); Dan Ford's assertion that his grandfather lost interest in the making of *Liberty Valance* before filming began (Ford); "Now what pleases" (unidentified publication); "the top of" (Reagan); "Waall, s'a little" (Speck, 1992); "You thought you" (Pickard); "It was all" (Speck, 1992); "old-hat" (John L. Scott, *Los Angeles Times*, 4/20/62); "creaky" (Andrew H. Weiler, *New York Times*, 5/24/62); "a parody of" (Brendan Gill, *New Yorker*, 6/16/62); Wald, Stewart, and Koster's efforts to replace O'Hara in *Mr. Hobbs Takes a Vacation* (a variety of letters, memos, and transcribed telephone conversations from 6/61 to 9/61, JWC); "If any crisis" (Hopper, 1954); "winner" (Philip K. Scheuer, *Los Angeles Times*, 5/25/62); "an amiable comedy" (*Cue*, 6/16/62); "fun picture" (Tube., *Variety*, 5/16/62); "They're having enough" (Parsons, 1963); "very human study" (Robert Coleman, *New York Mirror*, 12/22/61); Zanuck's insistence on a Paris sequence in *Take Her, She's Mine* and Johnson's protest against it (Stempel, 1969); the New York newspaper reviews of *Take Her, She's Mine* are dated 11/14/63; the historic underpinnings of the Dodge City sequence in *Cheyenne Autumn* were recounted by Bernard Smith in a letter to attorney Martin Gang dated 9/16/63, JLWC); "It's just a" (Parsons, 1964); "John Ford rarely" (Eyles); "a beautiful and" (Bosley Crowther, *New York Times*, 12/24/64); "far and away" (*New Yorker*, 1/2/65); "Ford has apparently" (*Newsweek*, 1/11/65); "everything it takes" (*Time*, 1/8/65); "I hadn't wanted" (Stempel, 1969); "only kid actor" (Davidson, 1971); "I thought he" (Roberts); the New York newspaper reviews of *Dear Brigitte* are dated 1/28/65; "a vulgar little" (*Newsweek*, 2/15/65).

Chapter Eighteen

Information for this chapter was drawn from interviews with Philip Alford, Jack Elam, Rosemary Forsyth, Kelly Harcourt, Ric Hardman, Shirley Jones, Richard Kobritz, Howard Koch Jr., Hardy Kruger, Vincent McEveety, Andrew McLaglen, Michael McLean, Judy Merrill, Maureen O'Hara, Stephen Porter, Jacqueline Scott, Howard Stradling Jr., and Jesse White (unless otherwise indicated, quotes attributed to them are derived from those interviews). Other sources are: "*Shenandoah* is the" (Franklin); "perfectly cast" (Howard Thompson, *New York Times*, 7/29/65); "strength and simplicity" (*Newsweek*, 8/23/65); "James Stewart's movie" (P.M., *Christian Science Monitor*, 8/6/65); "as winning as" (Howard Thompson, *New York Times*, 4/14/66); "None of us" (Stewart, 1966); "In the thirty" (*Variety*, 7/21/65); Stewart's battle with Robert Aldrich over the African safari (memos from Aldrich to Richard Zanuck dated 7/21/65 and 7/29/65 and a letter from Zanuck to Aldrich dated 7/27/65,

TFC); the New York newspaper reviews of *Flight of the Phoenix* are dated 2/1/66; "No less important" (Arthur Knight, *Saturday Review*, 1/29/66); "I want to" (Russell); "Simply put, it's" (Hendrick); the origins of *Firecreek* (*Hollywood Reporter*, 3/20/66; Val Adams, *New York Times*, 4/15/67; *Variety*, 9/20/66); "a kind of" (Howard Thompson, *New York Times*, 2/22/68); "Not terribly original" (*Time*, 4/5/68); "I know I've" (unidentified publication); Stewart's regret at not undergoing plastic surgery (anonymous/AI); Bill Moorhead's belief that Stewart's hearing loss began with *It's a Wonderful Life* (Moorhead/AI); "Movies used to" (Kennedy); "sensational and sordid" (Stewart, 1963); "I think she'll" (Reed, 1979); "Debris from the" (*Variety*, 10/23/67); "As westerns go" (*Time*, 8/2/68); "It was the" (Arlen Peters); "The men in" (Scott); Stewart's being only the second Air Force Reserve officer to receive the Distinguished Service Medal (Associated Press, 6/21/68); "I've never seen" (*Los Angeles Times*, 6/12/69); "We simply think" (Martin, 1978); "The tragedy was" (ibid.); "I hate them" (Wixen); "Every time I" (Rohter); "Although the premise" (National General press book for *The Cheyenne Social Club*); "I don't see" (*Daily Variety*, 6/27/69); "Now, I did" (Fonda); "I knew what" (Hirschhorn); "I felt so" (Fonda); "That's when I" (ibid.); "You know, it's" (*The Star*, 5/24/83); "a wonderfully outdated" (*Time*, 6/29/70); "it's hard not" (A.K., *Newsweek*, 9/28/70); "I've always sort" (Haber, 1970); "I had almost" (Syse); "The performance went" (Hayes); "There is no" (Cohen); the New York newspaper reviews of *Harvey* are dated 2/25/70; John Bartholomew Tucker's review aired on WABC-TV on 2/24/70; "It was a" (Warga); "A frigid mist" (Stewart, 1989); "craggy-browed, towering and" (Grubb); the New York newspaper reviews of *Fools' Parade* are dated 8/19/71; "Stewart . . . stamps scene" (WW, *Cue*, 8/21/71); "one of the" (*Saturday Review*, 7/10/71); "suspenseful, surprising, entertaining" (Richard Schickel, *Life*, 6/11/71); "contrived" (Whit., *Variety*, 6/23/71).

Chapter Nineteen

Information for this chapter was drawn from interviews with Julie Adams, Norman Felton (letter to author), Jimmy Hawkins, Hal Kanter, David Karp, Michael McLean, Judy Merrill, Jud Taylor, and Paul Wendkos (unless otherwise indicated, quotes attributed to them are derived from those interviews). Other sources are: "After all, Jimmy's" (Bob Thomas, 7/70); "There are less" (Davidson, 1971); "We only wish" (Kay Gardella, *New York Daily News*, 9/20/71); "The typical situation" (ibid.); "I think I" (*Daily Variety*, 3/21/72); "It left us" (Polier); "There's no one" (Moss); the Los Angeles newspaper reviews of "Hawkins on Murder" are dated 3/13/73; "a pose the" (Bok., *Variety*, 3/21/73); "I wonder whatever" (Smith); "a corker" (ibid.); "the most impressively" (John J. O'Connor, *New York Times*, 10/2/73); "It just got" (Mary Murphy); "a piece of" (Michael Billington's review of *Harvey* quoted by the Associated Press, 4/10/75); "Things have changed" (*People*, 9/1/75); "I don't think" (McLaughlin); "I wasn't impressed" (ibid.); "It's going to" (Mary Murphy); "I didn't think" (Siegel); "The reason I'm" (Flatley); "The two veteran" (McBride, 1976); "It was very" (Siegel); "It was a" (McBride, 1976); "the welcome participation" (Jay Cocks, *Time*, 8/30/76); "The principal virtue" (Frank Rich, *New York Post*, 8/12/76).

Chapter Twenty

Information for this chapter was drawn from interviews with Pamela Bellwood, William Frye, Kelly Harcourt, Jerry Jameson, Jack Lemmon, Don Margulies, Michael McLean, Judy Merrill, Robert Mitchum, Ron Reagan Jr., Michael Sharrett, Michael Winner, and Stephanie Zimbalist (unless otherwise indicated, quotes attributed to them are derived from those interviews). Other sources are: "It's a disaster" (John Simon, *New York*, 4/11/77); "Well, you know" (Nyberg); "I don't believe" (Reed, 1977); the New York newspaper reviews of *The Big Sleep* are dated 3/15/78); "every scene in" (Andrew Sarris, *Village Voice*, 3/27/78); "*Big Sleep* Aptly" (*Los Angeles Times*, n.d.); "Marlowe, with his" (Molly Haskell, *New York*, 4/10/78); "There aren't too" (Summer); "I'm sixty-eight years" (*Newsweek*, 1/10/77); "It's very noisy" (Squire); "I knew I" (Bob Thomas, 1993); "I've had an" (Wixen); "Leaving the Palm" (*New York Daily News*, 7/30/78); *Variety*'s review of *The Magic of Lassie* (Step., *Variety*, 8/9/78); "syrupy" (Linda Gross, *Los Angeles Times*, 12/12/78); "To whom is" (Janet Maslin, *New York Times*, 8/3/78); the first-week earnings for *The Magic of Lassie* (Summer); "Never been s'nervous" (Champlin); "My heart is" (Reed, 1979); "After the laughs" (Schneider); "This may be" (Bail., *Variety*, 6/10/81).

Chapter Twenty-one

Information for this chapter was drawn from interviews with Elinor Gordon Blair, Fred De Cordova, Peter Fonda, William Hayward, David Heeley, Jean Kramer, Judy Merrill, Kevin O'Connor, Betty Prashker, and George Schaefer (unless otherwise indicated, quotes attributed to them are derived from those interviews). Other sources are: "a beautifully planned" (Hank Grant, *Hollywood Reporter*, 3/3/80); "one of the" (*Variety*, 4/4/80); "traces of the" (John Corry, *New York Times*, 12/24/85); "a fine opportunity" (Frank Torrez, *Los Angeles Herald-Examiner*, 12/19/80); "a complete recovery" (*Los Angeles Herald-Examiner*, 8/23/80); "I still think" (Speck, 1992); "sympathize with loneliness" (Mehren); "Bette said she" (ibid.); "I've never had" (Riese); "Bette is absolutely" (Reagan); "It was a" (Schaefer); Kay Gardella's review of *Right of Way* in the *New York Daily News* is dated 11/20/83; "even these two" (Fred Rothenberg, *New York Post*, 11/21/83); "something I'll never" (Spada, 1993); "At the heart" (Vincent Canby, *New York Times*, 10/9/83); "perhaps his most" (Peter Rainer, *Los Angeles Herald-Examiner*, 11/14/83); "*Vertigo* looks and" (Andrew Sarris, *Village Voice*, 1/3/84); "Mr. Stewart has" (John Corry, *New York Times*, 3/7/85); "I want to" (*Good Housekeeping*, 2/85); "I keep looking" (Riordan); "Adding a layer" (James Stewart, 1987); "That step in" (James Stewart, 1989); "And now he's" (ibid.); "I just hope" (Rothstein); "I'm not a" (Summer); "It sorta tickled" (Haun).

Chapter Twenty-two

Information for this chapter was drawn from interviews with Elinor Gordon Blair, Fred De Cordova, Kelly Harcourt, Michael McLean, Judy Merrill, and Bill Moorhead (unless otherwise indicated, quotes attributed to them are derived from those interviews). Other sources are: "It was charmless" (*New York Times*, 1/19/92); "It's over" (Christon); "I've been under" (Bob Thomas, 1993); "There's really nothing" (*New York Times*, 5/25/93); "She was a" (Myrna Oliver, *Los Angeles Times*, 2/18/94); "Naturally I feel" (Hinds); "America lost a" (Associated Press, 7/3/97); "the apple of" (*Entertainment Tonight*, Paramount Pictures, Inc., 7/3/97); "the true gift" (ibid.); "We would like" (ibid.); "filled with so" (Rothstein); "the most complete" (Sarris); "People call me" (Kennedy); "I'd like to" (*USA Today*, 3/6/87).

BIBLIOGRAPHY

Books

Allyson, June, with Frances Spatz Leighton. *June Allyson.* New York: G. P. Putnam's Sons, 1982.

Anderson, Christopher. *Citizen Jane: The Turbulent Life of Jane Fonda.* New York: Henry Holt and Co., 1990.

Arden, Eve. *Three Phases of Eve.* New York: St. Martin's Press, 1985.

Arnold, Edwin T., and Eugene L. Miller. *The Films and Career of Robert Aldrich.* Knoxville: University of Tennessee Press, 1986.

Arnold, Elliott. *Blood Brother.* New York: Duell, Sloan and Pearce, 1947.

Atkins, Irene Kahn, interviewer. *A Directors Guild of America Oral History: Henry Koster.* Metuchen, N.J.: Directors Guild of America and the Scarecrow Press, 1987.

Bach, Steven. *Marlene Dietrich: Life and Legend.* New York: William Morrow and Co., 1992.

Bacon, James. *Made in Hollywood.* New York: Contemporary Books, Inc., 1977.

Baker, Carroll. *Baby Doll.* New York: Arbor House, 1983.

Barrow, Kenneth. *Helen Hayes.* New York: Doubleday, 1985.

Basinger, Jeanine. *Anthony Mann.* Boston: Twayne Publishers, 1979.

———. *The It's a Wonderful Life Book.* New York: Alfred A. Knopf, 1986.

Benarcik, Michael D. *In Search of Peace.* Wilmington, Del.: Michael D. Benarcik Foundation, 1989.

Berg, A. Scott. *Goldwyn.* New York: Alfred A. Knopf, 1989.

Brady, Kathleen. *Lucille: The Life of Lucille Ball.* New York: Hyperion, 1994.

Brough, James. *The Fabulous Fondas.* New York: David McKay, 1973.

Brown, Peter Harry. *Kim Novak: Reluctant Goddess.* New York: St. Martin's Press, 1986.

Calvet, Corinne. *Has Corinne Been a Good Girl?* New York: St. Martin's Press, 1983.

Cannom, Robert C. *Van Dyke and the Mythical City of Hollywood.* Culver City, Calif.: Murray & Gee, 1948.

Capra, Frank. *The Name Above the Title: An Autobiography.* New York: Macmillan, 1971.

Collier, Peter. *The Fondas: A Hollywood Dynasty.* New York: G. P. Putnam's Sons, 1991.

Considine, Shaun. *Bette & Joan: The Divine Feud.* New York: E. P. Dutton, 1989.

Crawford, Joan, with Jane Kesner Ardmore. *A Portrait of Joan.* New York: Doubleday, 1962.

Crowther, Bosley. *Hollywood Rajah: The Life and Times of Louis B. Mayer.* New York: Henry Holt and Co., 1960.

Curtis, Tony, and Barry Paris. *Tony Curtis: The Autobiography.* New York: William Morrow and Co., 1993.

Davidson, Bill. *Spencer Tracy: Tragic Idol.* New York: Kensington Publishing Corp., 1990.

Davis, Ronald L. *John Ford: Hollywood's Old Master.* Norman: University of Oklahoma Press, 1995.

DeCarlo, Yvonne, with Doug Warren. *Yvonne.* New York: St. Martin's Press, 1987.

Dick, Bernard F. *Billy Wilder.* Boston: Twayne Publishers, 1980.

Dietrich, Marlene. Translated from the German by Salvator Attanasio. *Marlene.* New York: Grove Press, 1987.

Douglas, Kirk. *The Ragman's Son: An Autobiography.* New York: Simon & Schuster, 1988.

Dundy, Elaine. *Finch, Bloody Finch.* New York: Holt, Rinehart, Winston, 1980.

Dwiggins, Don. *Hollywood Pilot: The Biography of Paul Mantz.* New York: Doubleday, 1967.

Edwards, Anne. *A Remarkable Woman: A Biography of Katharine Hepburn.* New York: William Morrow and Company, Inc., 1985.

Eells, George. *The Life That Late He Led: A Biography of Cole Porter.* New York: G. P. Putnam's Sons, 1967.

————. *Robert Mitchum.* New York: Franklin Watts, 1984.

Emory, David. *One Hundred Years of Life: Mercersburg, 1893–1993.* Mercersburg, Pa.: Mercersburg Academy, 1993.

Eyles, Allen. *James Stewart.* New York: Stein and Day, 1984.

Eyman, Scott. *Ernst Lubitsch: Laughter in Paradise.* New York: Simon & Schuster, 1993.

Faulkner, Trader. *Peter Finch: A Biography.* New York: Taplinger Publishing Co., 1979.

Fein, Irving A. *Jack Benny: An Intimate Biography.* New York: G. P. Putnam's Sons, 1976.

Fonda, Henry, as told to Howard Teichmann. *Fonda: My Life.* New York: New American Library, Inc., 1981.

Fontaine, Joan. *No Bed of Roses.* New York: William Morrow, 1978.

Ford, Dan. *Pappy: The Life of John Ford.* Englewood Cliffs, N.J.: Prentice-Hall, Inc., 1979.

Frank, Gerold. *Judy.* New York: Harper & Row Publishers, 1975.

Gallagher, Tag. *John Ford: The Man and His Films.* Berkeley: University of California Press, 1986.

Geist, Kenneth L. *Pictures Will Talk: The Life and Films of Joseph L. Mankiewicz.* New York: Charles Scribner's Sons, 1978.

Gilbert, Julie. *Opposite Attraction: The Lives of Erich Maria Remarque and Paulette Goddard.* New York: Pantheon Books, 1995.

Gingold, Hermione. *How to Grow Old Gracefully.* New York: St. Martin's Press, 1988.

Goldstein, Malcolm. *George S. Kaufman: His Life, His Theater.* Oxford: Oxford University Press, 1979.

Goodman, Ezra. *The Fifty-Year Decline and Fall of Hollywood.* New York: Simon & Schuster, 1961.

Grady, Billy. *The Irish Peacock: The Confessions of a Legendary Talent Agent.* New Rochelle, N.Y.: Arlington House, 1972.

Graham, Don. *No Name on the Bullet: A Biography of Audie Murphy.* New York: Viking Penguin, 1989.

Grubb, Davis. *Fools' Parade.* Cleveland, Ohio: World Publishing Company, 1969.

Hayes, Helen, with Katherine Hatch. *My Life in Three Acts.* San Diego: Harcourt Brace Jovanovich, 1990.

Hayne, Donald, ed. *The Autobiography of Cecil B. DeMille.* Englewood Cliffs, N.J.: Prentice-Hall, Inc., 1959.

Hayward, Brooke. *Haywire.* New York: Alfred A. Knopf, 1977.

Hepburn, Katharine. *Me: Stories of My Life.* New York: Alfred A. Knopf, 1991.

Heston, Charlton. *In the Arena.* New York: Simon & Schuster, 1995.

Higham, Charles. *Cecil B. DeMille.* New York: Charles Scribner's Sons, 1973.

————. *Kate: The Life of Katharine Hepburn.* New York: W. W. Norton and Co., 1975.

————. *Marlene: The Life of Marlene Dietrich.* New York: W. W. Norton & Co., 1977.

————. *Merchant of Dreams: Louis B. Mayer, M.G.M. and the Secret Hollywood.* New York: Donald I. Fine, Inc., 1993.

————. *Sisters: The Story of Olivia de Havilland and Joan Fontaine.* New York: Coward-McCann, Inc., 1984.

Higham, Charles, and Roy Moseley. *Cary Grant: The Lonely Heart.* San Diego: Harcourt Brace Jovanovich, 1989.

Hirschhorn, Clive. *Gene Kelly.* Chicago: Henry Regnery Co., 1974.

Hotchner, A. E. *Doris Day: Her Own Story.* New York: William Morrow and Co., 1976.

Houghton, Norris. *But Not Forgotten: The Adventures of the University Players.* New York: William Sloan Associates, 1951.

Hudson, Rock, and Sarah Davidson. *Rock Hudson: His Story.* New York: William Morrow and Co., 1986.

Hunter, Allan. *Walter Matthau.* New York: St. Martin's Press, 1984.

Johnson, Dorris, and Ellen Leventhal, eds. *The Letters of Nunnally Johnson.* New York: Alfred A. Knopf, 1981.

Johnson, Nora. *Flashback: Nora Johnson on Nunnally Johnson.* New York: Doubleday, 1979.

Josefsberg, Milt. *The Jack Benny Show.* New Rochelle, N.Y.: Arlington House, 1977.

Kelley, Kitty. *Nancy Reagan: The Unauthorized Biography.* New York: Simon & Schuster, 1991.

Kotsilibas-Davis, James, and Myrna Loy. *Myrna Loy: Being and Becoming.* New York: Alfred A. Knopf, 1988.

Lacey, Robert. *Grace.* New York: G. P. Putnam's Sons, 1994.

Lambert, Gavin. *Norma Shearer.* New York: Alfred A. Knopf, 1990.

———. *On Cukor.* New York: G. P. Putnam's Sons, 1972.

Leaming, Barbara. *Katharine Hepburn.* New York: Crown Publishers, Inc., 1995.

LeRoy, Mervin, as told to Dick Kleiner. *Mervin LeRoy: Take One.* New York: Hawthorn Books, Inc., 1974.

Levy, Emanuel. *George Cukor, Master of Elegance: Hollywood's Legendary Director and His Stars.* New York: William Morrow and Company, Inc., 1994.

Lewis, Judy. *Uncommon Knowledge.* New York: Pocket Books, 1994.

Logan, Joshua. *Josh: My Up and Down, In and Out Life.* New York: Delacorte Press, 1976.

———. *Movie Stars, Real People, and Me.* New York: Delacorte Press, 1978.

MacAdams, William. *Ben Hecht: The Man Behind the Legend.* New York: Charles Scribner's Sons, 1990.

Madsen, Axel. *Billy Wilder.* London: Secker & Warburg, 1968.

———. *Stanwyck.* New York: HarperCollins Publishers, 1994.

Maland, Charles J. *Frank Capra.* Boston: Twayne Publishers, 1980.

McBride, Joseph. *Frank Capra: The Catastrophe of Success.* New York: Simon & Schuster, 1992.

McGilligan, Patrick. *George Cukor: A Double Life.* New York: St. Martin's Press, 1991.

Meredith, Burgess. *So Far, So Good: A Memoir.* Boston: Little, Brown and Company, 1994.

Meredith, Scott. *George S. Kaufman and His Friends.* New York: Doubleday, 1974.

Miller, Ann, with Norma Lee Browning. *Miller's High Life.* New York: Doubleday, 1972.

Molyneaux, Gerard. *James Stewart: A Bio-Bibliography.* New York: Greenwood Press, 1992.

Mordden, Ethan. *The Hollywood Studios: House Style in the Golden Age of the Movies.* New York: Alfred A. Knopf, 1988.

Morella, Joe, and Edward Z. Epstein. *Paulette: The Adventurous Life of Paulette Goddard.* New York: St. Martin's Press, 1985.

Mosley, Leonard. *Lindbergh.* New York: Doubleday & Co., 1976.

————. *Zanuck: The Rise and Fall of Hollywood's Last Tycoon.* Boston: Little, Brown and Co., 1984.

Murphy, George. *Say . . . Didn't You Used to Be George Murphy?* New York: Bartholomew House Ltd., 1970.

North, Henry Ringling, and Alden Hatch. *The Circus Kings.* New York: Doubleday, 1960.

Parrish, James Robert. *The Jeanette MacDonald Story.* New York: Mason/Charter, 1976.

Pasternak, Joe, as told to David Chandler. *Easy the Hard Way.* New York: G. P. Putnam's Sons, 1956.

Paul, William. *Ernst Lubitsch's American Comedy.* New York: Columbia University Press, 1983.

Peters, Margot. *The House of Barrymore.* New York: Alfred A. Knopf, 1990.

Pickard, Roy. *Jimmy Stewart: A Life in Film.* New York: St. Martin's Press, 1992.

Poague, Leland A. *The Cinema of Ernst Lubitsch.* South Brunswick, N.J.: A. S. Barnes, 1978.

Preminger, Otto. *Preminger: An Autobiography.* New York: Doubleday & Co., Inc., 1977.

Quirk, Lawrence J. *Fasten Your Seat Belts: The Passionate Life of Bette Davis.* New York: William Morrow and Co., 1990.

————. *Margaret Sullavan: Child of Fate.* New York: St. Martin's Press, 1986.

Reed, Rex. *Travolta to Keaton.* New York: William Morrow and Co., 1979.

Rich, Sharon. *Sweethearts: The Timeless Love Affair—On-Screen and Off—Between Jeanette MacDonald and Nelson Eddy.* New York: Donald I. Fine, Inc., 1994.

Rico, Diana. *Kovacsland.* San Diego: Harcourt Brace Jovanovich, 1990.

Riese, Randall. *All About Bette: Her Life from A to Z.* Chicago: Contemporary Books, 1993.

Riva, Maria. *Marlene Dietrich.* New York: Alfred A. Knopf, 1993.

Roberts, Glenys. *Bardot.* New York: St. Martin's Press, 1984.

Roberts, Randy, and James S. Olson. *John Wayne: American.* New York: Free Press, 1995.

Robinson, Edward G., with Leonard Spigelgass. *All My Yesterdays: An Autobiography.* New York: Hawthorn Books, Inc., 1973.

Rogers, Ginger. *Ginger: My Story.* New York: HarperCollins Publishers, 1991.

Rooney, Mickey. *Life Is Too Short.* New York: Villard Books, 1991.

Russell, Rosalind, and Chris Chase. *Life Is a Banquet.* New York: Random House, 1977.

Schatz, Thomas. *The Genius of the System: Hollywood Filmmaking in the Studio Era.* New York: Pantheon Books, 1988.

Selden, William K. *Club Life at Princeton: An Historical Account of the Eating Clubs at Princeton University.* Princeton, N.J.: Princeton Prospect Foundation, 1994.

Sennett, Ted. *Hollywood's Golden Year, 1939: A Fiftieth Anniversary Celebration.* New York: St. Martin's Press, 1989.

Shepherd, Donald, and Robert Slazer, with Dave Grayson. *Duke: The Life and Times of John Wayne.* New York: Doubleday and Co., 1985.

Shipman, David. *Judy Garland: The Secret Life of an American Legend.* New York: Hyperion, 1993.

Shute, Nevil. *No Highway.* London: William Heinemann Ltd., 1948.

Siegel, Don. *A Siegel Film: An Autobiography.* London: Faber and Faber, 1993.

Simon, George T. *Glenn Miller and His Orchestra.* New York: Thomas Y. Crowell Co., 1974.

Sinclair, Andrew. *John Ford.* New York: Dial Press/James Wade, 1979.

Spada, James. *Grace: The Secret Lives of a Princess.* New York: Doubleday & Co., 1987.

————. *More Than a Woman: An Intimate Biography of Bette Davis.* New York: Bantam Books, 1993.

Speck, Gregory. *Hollywood Royalty*. New York: Carol Publishing, 1992.

Spoto, Donald. *The Dark Side of Genius: The Life of Alfred Hitchcock*. Boston: Little, Brown and Co., 1983.

Stack, Robert, with Mark Evans. *Straight Shooting*. New York: Macmillan Publishing Co., 1980.

Stempel, Tom. *Screenwriter: The Life and Times of Nunnally Johnson*. San Diego: A. S. Barnes & Co., 1980.

Stenn, David. *Bombshell: The Life and Death of Jean Harlow*. New York: Doubleday, 1993.

Stewart, James. *Jimmy Stewart and His Poems*. New York: Crown Publishers, 1989.

Stine, Whitney. *"I'd Love to Kiss You": Conversations with Bette Davis*. New York: Pocket Books, 1990.

Swindell, Larry. *The Last Hero: A Biography of Gary Cooper*. New York: Doubleday & Co., Inc., 1980.

———. *Screwball: The Life of Carole Lombard*. New York: William Morrow and Co., 1975.

———. *Spencer Tracy*. New York: New American Library, Inc., 1969.

Taylor, John Russell. *Hitch: The Life and Times of Alfred Hitchcock*. New York: Pantheon Books, 1978.

Teichmann, Howard. *George S. Kaufman: An Intimate Portrait*. New York: Atheneum, 1972.

Thomas, Bob. *Clown Prince of Hollywood: The Antic Life and Times of Jack L. Warner*. New York: McGraw-Hill Publishing Co., 1990.

———. *Joan Crawford*. New York: Simon & Schuster, 1978.

———. *King Cohn: The Life and Times of Harry Cohn*. New York: G. P. Putnam's Sons, 1967.

———. *Selznick*. New York: Doubleday, 1970.

Thompson, David. *Showman: The Life of David O. Selznick*. New York: Alfred A. Knopf, 1992.

Thompson, Frank T. *William A. Wellman*. Metuchen, N.J.: The Scarecrow Press, 1983.

Tosches, Nick. *Dino: Living High in the Dirty Business of Dreams*. New York: Doubleday, 1992.

Turner, Lana. *Lana: The Lady, the Legend, the Truth*. New York: E. P. Dutton, Inc., 1982.

Wansell, Geoffrey. *Haunted Idol: The Story of the Real Cary Grant*. New York: William Morrow and Co., 1984.

Westmore, Frank, and Muriel Davidson. *The Westmores of Hollywood*. Philadelphia: J. B. Lippincott, 1976.

Widener, Don. *Lemmon: A Biography*. New York: Macmillan, 1975.

Winters, Shelley. *Shelley, Also Known as Shirley*. New York: William Morrow and Co., 1980.

———. *Shelley II: The Middle of My Century*. New York: Simon & Schuster, 1989.

Yurka, Blanche. *Bohemian Girl: Blanche Yurka's Theatrical Life*. Athens: Ohio University Press, 1970.

Zolotow, Maurice. *Billy Wilder in Hollywood*. New York: G. P. Putnam's Sons, 1977.

Magazine Articles

Abrams, Norma. *New York Daily News*, August 28, 1939.

Alpert, Don. *Los Angeles Times*, c. 1962–63.

American Film, February 1978.

Amory, Cleveland. *Parade Magazine*, October 21, 1984.

Atkinson, David. *American Cinematographer*, January 1990.

Bacon, James. *Los Angeles Mirror-News*, July 12, 1966.

Berg, Louis. *This Week,* March 30, 1952.

Berges, Marshall. *Los Angeles Times Home Magazine,* February 2, 1975.

Bogdanovich, Peter. "The Respawnsibility of bein' J . . . Jimmy Stewart. Gosh!" *Esquire,* July 1966.

Bottome, Phyllis. *New York Times,* June 16, 1940.

Burden, Martin. *New York Post,* September 23, 1988.

Castos, Gregory J. M. *Filmfax,* 1991.

Champlin, Charles. *Los Angeles Times,* December 7, 1978.

Cheatham, Maude. *Silver Screen,* October 1936.

Christon, Lawrence. *Los Angeles Times,* May 10, 1992.

Christy, George. *Hollywood Reporter,* January 3, 1980.

Cohen, Nathan. *Toronto Daily Star,* February 7, 1970.

Cohn, Al. *Newsday,* November 20, 1963.

Coons, Robin. *Richmond News Dealer,* March 18, 1940.

Creelman, Eileen. *New York Sun,* October 21, 1940.

D'Antonio, Dennis. *National Enquirer,* March 14, 1978.

Darnton, Charles. *New York Herald-Tribune,* May 21, 1939.

Davidson, Bill. *TV Guide,* October 2, 1971.

Davis, Charles E., Jr. *Los Angeles Times,* September 29, 1963.

Dawes, Amy. *Daily Variety,* May 23, 1989.

Delli Santi, Angela. *Princeton Living,* December 1993.

Denver Post, July 13, 1953.

Dillon, Nancy. *Modern Maturity,* December 1989–January 1990.

Ebert, Roger. *Chicago Sun-Times,* March 17, 1968.

———. *Chicago Sun-Times,* June 2, 1985.

Fender, Robert. *New York Times,* July 26, 1959.

Finletter, Alice. *Modern Screen,* c. 1954–55.

Flatley, Guy. *New York Times,* July 16, 1976.

Franklin, Stephen. *Weekend Magazine,* June 19, 1965.

Graham, Frank. *New York Journal,* April 21, 1955.

Graham, Sheilah. *Cleveland Plain Dealer,* July 11, 1937.

Haber, Joyce. *Los Angeles Times Calendar,* March 15, 1970.

———. *Los Angeles Times,* March 2, 1975.

Harris, Eleanor. *American Weekly,* January 1, 1956.

Haun, Harry. *New York Daily News,* October 9, 1989.

Heggie, Barbara. *Woman's Home Companion,* April 1947.

Hendrick, Kimmis. *Christian Science Monitor,* March 31, 1967.

Hinds, Michael deCourcy. *New York Times,* January 31, 1994.

Hollywood Reporter, 25th anniversary issue, November 14, 1955.

Hopper, Hedda. *Los Angeles Times,* May 21, 1946.

———. *Los Angeles Times,* c. 1950.

———. *Los Angeles Times,* December 13, 1953.

———. *Chicago Tribune Magazine,* April 18, 1954.

———. *Los Angeles Times,* January 22, 1956.

Hull, Josephine. *New York Times,* November 26, 1950.

Hyams, Joe. *TV Radio Magazine, New York Herald-Tribune,* December 13, 1959.

Johnson, Erskine. *Los Angeles Mirror,* October 31, 1960.

Kennedy, Ward. *Pageant,* January 1992.

Kirkley, Donald. *Baltimore Sun,* February 23, 1952.

Klemerud, Judy. *New York Times,* February 22, 1970.

Lay, Col. Beirne, Jr. "Jimmy Stewart's Finest Performance." *Saturday Evening Post.* Part 1, December 8, 1945; part 2, December 15, 1945.

Life, September 24, 1945.

Life, September 5, 1955.

Low, Andrew, and James Stewart. *Second Air Division Association Journal,* June 1984.

MacGregor, Leslie. *Photoplay,* October 1945.

Maltin, Leonard. *Action,* January–February 1973.

Martin, Pete. "The Shyest Guy in Hollywood." *Saturday Evening Post,* n.d.

———. *Saturday Evening Post,* March 1978.

McBride, Joseph. *American Film,* June 1976.

———. *Daily Variety,* July 18, 1977.

McDougal, Dennis. *Los Angeles Times,* November 27, 1986.

McLaughlin, Donald J. *National Enquirer,* c. 1975.

McNulty, John. *New York Herald-Tribune,* November 19, 1950.

Mehren, Elizabeth. *Emmy Magazine,* March–April 1983.

Mook, S. R. *Screenland,* August 1936.

Morrow, Douglas. *Los Angeles Times This Week Magazine,* c. 1949–50.

Mosby, Aline. *Beverly Hills Newslife,* May 19, 1954.

Moss, Morton. *TV Weekly, Los Angeles Herald-Examiner,* March 11, 1973.

Murphy, Mary. *Los Angeles Times,* December 20, 1975.

New York Sun, May 2, 1933.

Norton, Elliot. *Boston Post,* January 28, 1947.

Novak, Kim. *TV Guide,* March 7, 1987.

Nyberg, Tobi. *W,* April 29–May 6, 1977.

O'Brian, Jack. *Los Angeles Times,* c. July 1947.

Pane, Jim. *Indiana Gazette,* c. May 1983.

Parsons, Louella O. *Los Angeles Examiner,* October 10, 1948.

———. *Cosmopolitan,* February 1954.

———. *Los Angeles Herald-Examiner,* March 3, 1963.

———. *New York Journal-American,* November 29, 1964.

Peters, Arlen. *National Tattler,* September 14, 1974.

Peters, Susan. *Photoplay,* c. 1947–48.

Peterson, Marcia. *Modern Screen,* c. 1952–53.

Polier, Rex. *TV Time, Philadelphia Sunday Bulletin,* September 30, 1973.

Proctor, Kay. *Photoplay,* November 1938.

Pryor, Thomas M. *New York Times,* May 27, 1951.

Quigg, Philip W. *The Daily Princetonian,* March 6, 1942.

Rau, Neil. *Los Angeles Examiner,* September 6, 1959.

Reagan, Ron, Jr. *The Movies,* July 1983.

Reed, Rex. *New York Daily News,* October 23, 1977.

Reeve, Warren. "Introducing James Stewart," *Photoplay,* August 1936.

Riordan, Kevin. *South Jersey Courier-Post,* n.d.

Rohter, Larry. *New York Times,* April 23, 1990.

Rothstein, Mervin. *New York Times,* September 2, 1989.

Sarris, Andrew. *Film Comment,* March–April 1990.

Schneider, Wolf. *Hollywood Reporter Magazine,* December 1987.

Scott, Vernon. *New York World-Telegram,* August 13, 1959.

Sharpe, Howard. *Photoplay,* December 1936.

————. *Photoplay,* January 1937.

Silverman, Jeff. *Los Angeles Herald-Examiner,* May 25, 1986.

Small, Frank. *Photoplay,* March 1937.

Smith, Cecil. *TV Times, Los Angeles Times,* September 30–October 6, 1973.

Speck, Gregory. *Cable Guide,* February 1989.

Squire, Susan. *Los Angeles Herald-Examiner,* July 22, 1976.

Stephenson, Clarence. *Indiana Tribune-Review,* May 22, 1983.

Stewart, James. *Los Angeles Times,* July 13, 1941.

————. *Coronet,* September 1948.

————. *New York Journal,* June 24, 1959.

————. *Hollywood Reporter,* November 19, 1963.

————. *Films and Filming,* April 1966.

————. *Hollywood Citizen-News,* May 13, 1969.

————. *Cue,* March 21, 1970.

————. "My Superstition," *National Enquirer,* July 22, 1973.

————. *Screen Actor,* fall 1987.

Stewart, James, as told to Pete Martin. "James Stewart," a five-part series. *Saturday Evening Post,* February 11–March 4, 1961.

Stewart, James, as told to Floyd Miller. "This Was My Father." *McCall's,* May 1964.

Stewart, James, as told to James Reid. *Movie Story,* n.d.

Stewart, James, as told to Richard H. Schneider. *National Enquirer,* January 26, 1982.

Stewart, James, as told to Dick Schneider. "The Dog Next Door." *Guideposts,* June 1992.

Stewart, Mrs. James. *Photoplay,* c. 1950–51.

Stewart, Virginia. "My Brother Becomes a Star." *Coronet,* February 1940.

Stratton, Monty. *Screen Guide,* c. 1949–50.

Sullivan, Ed. *Beverly Hills Citizen,* January 9, 1940.

Summer, Anita. *Family Weekly,* October 22, 1978.

Sweeney, Louise. *Christian Science Monitor,* February 19, 1980.

Syse, Glenna. *Chicago Sun-Times,* March 31, 1970.

Thomas, Bob. *New York World-Telegram,* March 14, 1955.

————. *Hollywood Citizen-News,* March 17, 1955.

————. Associated Press story, July 21, 1970.

————. *New York Post,* May 20, 1993.

Thomas, Kevin. *Los Angeles Times,* October 15, 1967.

Turner, George E. *American Cinematographer,* February 1985.

Van Dyke, W. S. *Stage,* n.d.

Video Review, June 1986.

Wapshott, Nicholas. *London Observer,* June 23, 1985.

Warga, Wayne. *Los Angeles Times,* July 7, 1970.

Waterbury, Ruth. *Coronet,* July 1970.

Wechsburg, Joseph. *Collier's,* April 5, 1947.

Whitney, Dwight. *TV Guide,* May 16, 1970.

Wiles, Otis. *Screen Book Magazine,* n.d.

Wixen, Joan. *Modern Maturity,* December 1976–January 1977.

Zolotow, Maurice. *TV Guide,* March 2, 1974.

Index

Abbott, George, 69, 70, 77
Abend, Sheldon, 361
Actors Studio, 133, 274
Adams, Clarence, 162, 172
Adams, Julie, 214, 229, 230, 329, 330
Adams, Leslie, 55
After the Thin Man, 99–101, 185
Air Force One, 363
Airport '77, 339–43, 345, 354, 364
Albert, Eddie, 201
Alcoa Premiere, 291
Aldrich, Robert, 306, 307, 308–9
Alexander, Malcolm, 360
Alford, Philip, 133, 302–3
Allan, Ted, 98
Alland, William, 305
Allen, Elizabeth, 295, 297
All Good Americans (Perelman and Perelman), 62–63, 64
All Paris Knows (Savoir), 67
Allwyn, Astrid, 127
Allyson, June, 205, 237, 239–40, 247, 249, 250, 363
Alpert, Hollis, 270
Altman, Al, 69
American Tale: Fievel Goes West, An, 368
Anatomy of a Murder, 271–76, 330, 331
Anderson, Judith, 68, 77
Anderson, Maxwell, 123*n*, 264
Archer, Eugene, 283
Arden, Eve, 273–74
Arnold, Edward, 114, 117, 124, 126, 159
Arnold, Elliott, 208, 209
Arnold, Henry (Hap), 160
Arnold, Milton, 169, 171–72
Arnold, Pop, 161, 162
Arnow, Max, 48
Arthur, Jean, 114, 116, 117, 123, 125, 186
Arthur, Robert, 303
Art Trouble, 65–66, 78, 93, 309
Ashley, Elizabeth, 292
Astaire, Fred, 88, 90, 106, 231, 334, 362
Atkinson, Brooks, 62, 65, 70, 72, 197
Attenborough, Richard, 307
Auer, Mischa, 148
Ayres, Lew, 119

Bacall, Lauren, 337, 338, 342
Bach, Steven, 130
Bacon, James, 247–48
Baker, Carroll, 284, 285, 295
Ball, Lucille, 88, 290
Bancroft, Anne, 232

Bandolero!, 314–15, 324
Bannen, Ian, 307
Bardot, Brigitte, 297, 299
Barnes, Howard, 93, 116–17, 126, 141, 143, 188, 200, 206
Barrett, James Lee, 301, 304, 314, 315, 317–18, 319, 322, 323, 324
Barrie, Wendy, 92, 99
Barry, Philip, 143–44
Barrymore, Lionel, 76, 94, 95, 114, 117, 126, 186, 187, 190, 207
Basinger, Jeanine, 243, 251, 260
Baxter, Anne, 322
Bean, Orson, 273, 274
Beaufort, John, 259
Beavers, Arthur S., 158
Beckhard, Arthur, 52–56, 61, 62
Beckley, Paul V., 265
Bedelia, Bonnie, 331
Beery, Wallace, 76, 95, 108
Behrman, S. N., 141, 143
Bel Geddes, Barbara, 266
Bell, Book and Candle, 266–68
Bellah, James Warner, 287
Bellwood, Pamela, 340
Benaderet, Bea, 236
Bend of the River, 214, 224, 229–31, 233, 241–42, 248, 260, 295, 303, 329
Bergen, Edgar, 159
Berman, Pandro, 150, 231
Bernds, Ed, 115, 116
Bernstein, Sidney, 197
Best, James, 278, 311
Best Years of Our Lives, The, 189*n*
Big Sleep, The, 342–44, 345, 354
Billington, Michael, 335
Biroc, Joseph, 187*n*
Birsic, Rudolph J., 162, 164, 167
Black, Louis, 232
Blair, Elinor Gordon, 25, 27, 30, 31, 32, 38, 172, 360
Blair, Hall, 25, 26, 31, 32, 360
Blankfort, Michael, 208*n*
Blaustein, Julian, 208, 209, 267
Blondell, Joan, 181
Bloom, Harold Jack, 232, 233
Boehnel, William, 82, 102, 105, 106, 112, 116, 119, 132
Bogart, Humphrey, 52, 87, 133, 142, 203, 247, 256, 278, 342
Bogdanovich, Peter, 107, 147, 336
Boileau, Pierre, 263

Bolton, Jack, 207, 210, 282
Bolton, Peggy, 207
Bond, Ward, 190, 281
Bondi, Beulah, 104–5, 107, 190, 262, 354
Borgnine, Ernest, 307
Born to Dance, 96–99, 116, 121, 122, 151*n*, 335, 362
Borzage, Frank, 101, 139–40, 141
Bottome, Phyllis, 139
Bradley, Omar, 348, 355
Brand, Max, 128
Brando, Marlon, 69, 245, 247, 277, 278
Breen, Richard L., 269
Brennan, Walter, 241
Breslow, Lou, 195–96
Briskin, Sam, 176, 250
Brisson, Frederick, 309–10
Brodney, Oscar, 219, 237
Broken Arrow, 208–10, 213, 216, 223, 311
Brown, Clarence, 86, 96, 104, 105, 148–49
Brown, Stephens Porter, 41, 42
Brown, Tom, 105
Bruce, Virginia, 97
Buchman, Sidney, 123, 127, 185
Bundsmann, Anton, 66
Burks, Robert, 246
Burnett, Carol, 348, 362–63
Burns, Michael, 290
Burr, Courtney, 63
Burt, Frank, 244, 266
Burton, Jack, 161–62
Byrnes, Jimmy, 126

Cagney, James, 94–95, 132, 153, 191, 240, 278, 354*n*, 356, 362
Call Northside 777, 194–95, 196, 201, 204, 223
Calvet, Corinne, 241, 242, 243
Cameron, Kate, 93, 98, 101, 106, 112, 120, 126, 200, 309
Campbell's Home Cookin' soup, 367
Canby, Vincent, 361
Capra, Frank, 113–17, 123–26, 145, 151, 176, 180, 185–91, 215, 300, 353, 354, 355, 365
Carbine Williams, 231–32
Carey, Harry, 124, 127
Carey, Harry, Jr., 281, 288, 297
Carmichael, Hoagy, 225
Carradine, John, 104, 337
Carry Nation (McGrath), 53–56, 57, 61
Carson, Johnny, 353, 355, 364
Carson, Robert, 201
Cass, Carl, 39
Cattleman, Harris, 331
Cavett, Frank, 226
CBS, 120, 310, 332, 333
Chaffey, Don, 345
Chandler, Jeff, 208, 209
Chandler, Raymond, 342, 343
Chapman, John, 55, 193
Chase, Barrie, 309

Chase, Borden, 213, 241, 260
Chase, Mary, 192, 219, 220, 221, 319, 335
Cheyenne Autumn, 132, 294–97
Cheyenne Social Club, 151*n*, 215, 216, 317–19
Cinerama, 278, 284, 285
Citron, Herman, 308
Clark, Mark, 165
Clements, Calvin, 310
Clingan, Wilbur, 161, 165–66, 170
Clothier, William, 296, 315, 318
Cobb, Lee J., 69, 194, 284
Coburn, Charles, 107, 118
Cocks, Jay, 337–38
Cohen, Nathan, 320
Cohn, Art, 231
Cohn, Harry, 113, 114, 115, 123, 126, 176, 187*n*, 192*n*, 250, 264, 267, 278
Colbert, Claudette, 121, 122, 224, 310
Colby, Anita, 178–79
Coleman, Robert, 267, 292
Collier, Shirley, 185
Columbia Pictures, 113, 115, 117, 124, 142, 250, 280, 322
Come Live with Me, 134, 148–49, 243
Cook, Willis, 276
Cooper, Gary, 99, 108, 109, 115, 123–24, 125, 132, 144, 158, 180, 203–5, 210, 232, 245, 247, 260, 278, 283, 306
Cooper, Rocky, 203, 204, 210
Copland, Aaron, 339
Coppel, Alec, 264
Corby, Jane, 193
Cornell, Katharine, 58, 64, 141–42
Corry, John, 355, 363
Coward, Noël, 146, 267
Cowl, Jane, 61
Craig, H.A.L., 340
Cravath, Paul D., 67
Crawford, Joan, 76, 94, 96, 109, 119–20, 144, 150, 152, 306
Creelman, Eileen, 85, 86, 102, 116, 122, 141
Crewe, Regina, 85
Crisp, Donald, 251
Crist, Judith, 299–300, 343
Cristal, Linda, 281, 282
Cromwell, John, 117, 118
Cronyn, Hume, 198
Crosby, Bing, 147*n*, 250, 284*n*, 327
Crowther, Bosley, 68, 143, 147, 188, 195, 196, 200, 210, 214, 240, 247, 250, 251, 255, 265, 270, 275, 294, 297, 299, 309
Cukor, George, 144, 145, 146, 153, 300
Cullinan, Frank, 64
Cummings, Jack, 98
Cummings, John M., 126
Curtis, Tony, 213, 329

Dailey, Dan, 140
Dale, Esther, 53–54, 55
Daly, Jonathan, 329

Daniels, William, 75, 220, 236, 261
Daves, Delmer, 209
Davidson, Bill, 298
Davies, Marion, 70, 111, 112, 178
Davies, Valentine, 237, 249
Davis, Bette, 94–95, 142, 306, 354n, 356, 357, 358, 360
Davis, Sidney C., 233–34
Day, Doris, 253, 254–55, 264, 298
Dean Martin Show, The, 327, 353
Dear Brigitte, 222, 297–300, 327
De Bona, Joe, 210, 260
DeCarlo, Yvonne, 158
de Cordova, Fred, 236, 354, 370
Dee, Sandra, 292, 293–94
de Havilland, Olivia, 107, 137–39, 142, 148, 180, 186, 290, 340
Deknatel, Jane, 357–58
Delehanty, Thornton, 78, 85
Del Rio, Dolores, 295
Demarest, William, 195, 196
DeMille, Cecil B., 225, 226–29
Denby, David, 255
Des Lierres, Irene, 248
Destry Rides Again, 125, 128–32, 133, 135, 142, 148, 151, 180–81, 208, 214, 216, 304
Devine, Andy, 288
Dickey, Bill, 206
Dietrich, Marlene, 129–31, 132, 143, 223
Dillon, Melinda, 358, 359, 360
Divided by Three (Leech and Kaufman), 68–69, 70
Donat, Robert, 127
Dooley, Daisy, 112, 180
Doolittle, James, 167–68
Douglas, Kirk, 204–5, 260, 310, 319
Douglas, Melvyn, 94
Dow, Peggy, 219
Draddy, Gregg, 210
Draddy, Ruth, 210
Drake, Charles, 219
Dreyfuss, Richard, 364, 365
Driscoll, Edith, 84
Dru, Joanne, 234, 291
Drysdale, Don, 291
Duff, Frances Robinson, 71
Duryea, Dan, 213, 214, 234, 303, 307

Earp, Wyatt, 281, 295
Eastwood, Clint, 134, 317, 337, 364
Ebsen, Buddy, 96, 97
Eddy, Nelson, 80, 81, 82
Edens, Martha, 90
Edens, Roger, 90, 98, 110
Eisenhower, Dwight D., 262, 263
Elam, Jack, 241, 305–6, 311
Elizabeth II, Queen of England, 224
Ellington, Duke, 273
Ellis, Anderson, 139
Ephron, Henry, 222, 292

Ephron, Phoebe, 222, 292
Epstein, Julius, 142, 143
Epstein, Philip, 142

Fabian, 291, 292, 298, 299
Far Country, The, 241–43, 244, 251, 260, 305, 346–47
Fay, Frank, 193, 201, 219, 221
FBI Story, The, 268–72, 274, 276, 330
Felton, Norman, 331, 333
Fenton, Frank, 207
Fenton, Lesley, 196
Ferguson, Perry, 198
Ferrer, Jose, 221
Finch, Peter, 307
Firecreek, 59, 310–12, 314
First Love, 121
Fitzgerald, F. Scott, 42
Flatley, Guy, 337
Flight of the Phoenix, The, 306–9, 370
Flippen, Jay C., 213, 229, 230, 234, 241
Fonda, Frances, 90, 175
Fonda, Henry, 69, 84, 347, 349, 362
    children of, 111, 158
    in films, 72, 127, 151n, 153, 180, 195–96, 260, 264, 281, 283, 284, 310–11, 312, 317–18, 319, 336, 354n, 356, 357, 359
    JS's friendship with, 57–58, 62, 63, 70, 76–79, 83, 87–90, 108, 111, 148, 153, 154, 175, 176–78, 311, 316, 317, 318–19, 335, 347, 348, 354, 356–57
    on stage, 50, 51, 56, 63n, 70, 72, 335
Fonda, Jane, 111, 294
Fonda, Peter, 57, 89–90, 111, 175, 177–78, 319, 356, 357
Fontaine, Joan, 37, 137, 201–2, 203, 204
Fools' Parade, 322–24, 331, 345
Ford, Dan, 287–88
Ford, Gerald, 339, 348
Ford, John, 25, 153, 186, 281–91, 294–97, 301, 302, 306, 349, 354n
Ford, Wallace, 251
Ford Startime, 278
Forsyth, Rosemary, 302
Forsythe, Henderson, 320
Fossey, Dian, 286, 341, 365
Foster, Lewis R., 123, 127
Fowler, Marjorie, 290
Fox, Norman A., 260
Frank, Fredric M., 226
Franklin, Sidney, 140
Frankovich, M. J., 336, 337
Fremont, Lisa, 244
Froeschel, George, 139
Frye, William, 310, 340, 341
Fuchs, Michael, 359
Furlong, Kirby, 329

Gable, Clark, 76, 85, 86, 95, 99, 121–22, 132, 144, 164, 179, 232, 245, 247, 278

Gabriel, Gilbert W., 68
Gadbois, Guy, 248
Gallo, Sam, 32
Galloway, Don, 305
Garbo, Greta, 76, 79, 86, 90, 95–96, 120, 135,
    154, 367
Gardella, Kay, 329, 359
Gardiner, Reginald, 98
Gardner, John Fentress, 35, 40
Garfield, John, 69
Garland, Judy, 88, 95, 119, 137n, 150, 152, 353
Garland, Robert, 62, 65, 66, 70
Gaynor, Janet, 91, 101, 102
Gazzara, Ben, 272, 274
Geer, Ellen, 329
Gessner, Robert, 210
G.E. Theater, 252, 260, 262, 266
Gibbons, Cedric, 75, 104
Gilbert, John, 97
Gilbert, Julie, 129
Gill, Brendan, 288
Glassberg, Irving, 230
Gleason, Frank, 276
Glenn Miller Story, The, 173, 236–40, 243, 247,
    248, 249, 363
Gobel, George, 278
Goddard, Paulette, 129, 150, 151, 195
Goetz, William, 212, 220–21, 250, 310
Goldbeck, Willis, 287
Goldwater, Barry, 347
Goldwyn, Samuel, 123, 144, 227
Goodbye Again (Scott and Haight), 52–53,
    57–60, 68, 69, 142
Good Earth, The, 99
Goodman, Benny, 58–59
Goodman, Ezra, 69
Goodrich, Frances, 100, 185
Gordon, Angus, 39–40
Gordon, Mildred, 193
Gorgeous Hussy, The, 94, 96, 105, 109, 119
Grace, Princess of Monaco, 147n, 244–45, 247,
    264, 267, 354, 361
Grady, Billy, 48, 65, 67–68, 69, 72, 76, 83, 89,
    153–54, 175, 204, 210
Graham, Sheilah, 99, 108
Grahame, Gloria, 226, 228
Granger, Farley, 198, 200
Grant, Cary, 133, 134, 144, 145, 147, 159, 198,
    219, 232, 267, 310, 327, 356
Grant, Hank, 354
Grant, Kathryn, 275
Granville, Bonita, 344
Greatest Show on Earth, The, 224, 225–29
Great Performances, 363–64
Green, Marshall, 214, 234, 238–39, 261
Green Horizon, The, 349–50
Greenspun, Robert, 323
Gribbon, Harry, 65, 66
Griffith, Andy, 131n, 331
Griffith, Edward, 82–83

Grofe, Fred, Jr., 339
Gross, Cheryl, 366
Gross, Linda, 348
Guernsey, Otis L., Jr., 221, 231

Haase, John, 297, 298
Hackett, Albert, 100, 185
Hailey, Marian, 320
Hale, Barbara, 222, 252
Hale, Wanda, 151
Hall, Dorothy, 69–70
Hall, Gloria, 106, 111, 138–39
Hallmark Hall of Fame, 321
Hamilton, Patrick, 197
Hammond, Percy, 68, 70, 72
Hani, Susumu, 349, 350
Harcourt, Alexander, 286n, 341–42
Harcourt, Kelly Stewart, 25, 203, 224, 225, 248,
    249, 286, 309, 313, 341–42, 348, 349, 365,
    369, 370, 371
Harding, Warren G., 28, 31, 371
Hardman, Ric, 132–33, 305
Harlow, Jean, 76, 85–86, 99
Harris, Sam, 113
Harrison, Rex, 268
Hart, Moss, 113, 114
Hartman, David, 356
Harvey (Chase), 192–94, 201, 319–21, 327, 335,
    347, 372
Harvey (film), 192, 211–12, 219–21, 222, 223,
    239, 248, 275, 300
Haskell, Molly, 343–44
Hathaway, Harry, 194–95, 284, 285
Haun, Harry, 344
Hawkins, 84, 330–34
Hawkins, Jimmy, 188
Hawkins, William, 266–67
Haycox, Ernest, 241
Hayes, Alfred, 276
Hayes, Helen, 58, 211, 319–21, 335, 362
Hayes, John Michael, 244, 253, 254
Hayward, Bridget, 110, 111
Hayward, Brooke, 83, 84, 90, 91, 110, 111, 141,
    158, 174, 179, 257
Hayward, Leland, 90, 91, 110, 137, 157, 160,
    162, 174, 179, 204, 244, 256–58, 303, 310,
    349, 364
Hayward, William, 110, 157, 364
Haywire (Hayward), 90
Healy, Ted, 93
Hearst, William Randolph, 111, 178
Hecht, Ben, 122
Heeley, David, 363–64
Heidt, Horace, 150
Heller, Lukas, 306, 307
Henderson, Marcia, 234
Hepburn, Katharine, 143, 144–47, 151n, 153,
    159, 207, 359, 364, 367
Herrmann, Bernard, 254
Heston, Charlton, 226, 275, 315, 340, 355

Higham, Charles, 140, 148
Hitchcock, Alfred, 147, 178, 196–200, 244–47,
    253–56, 263–67, 269, 354*n*, 361
Hively, Jack, 201
Hoffman, Dustin, 133, 354
Hoffman, Richard, 35–36, 40
Hollywood Ten, 208*n*
Holm, Norma, 201
Hoover, J. Edgar, 268, 269–70, 271
Hopper, Hedda, 68, 118, 120, 146, 151, 179–80,
    237, 247, 253, 264, 291
Horne, Van, 305
Horne, Victoria, 219
Hotschuh, Edward, 35
Houghton, Norris, 47, 51–57, 61
Howard, Ron, 337, 338
Howard, Shemp, 65, 66
Howard, Sidney, 64, 65
How the West Was Won, 132, 283–86, 301, 304,
    332
Hudson, Rock, 213, 230, 329, 333*n*
Hughes, Howard, 144, 146
Hull, Josephine, 193–94, 219, 221
Hussey, Ruth, 145, 146, 152, 153, 159, 291
Huston, John, 148, 196
Huston, Walter, 104, 159
Hutton, Betty, 226, 228

Ice Follies of 1939, The, 119–20
Important News, 92, 309
Irvine, William Mann, 34, 35, 37, 39, 40, 75, 94
It's a Wonderful Life, 105, 176, 180, 181,
    185–91, 205, 211, 215, 221, 262, 312, 323,
    335, 353, 354, 362, 365
It's a Wonderful World, 121–22, 224

Jack Benny Show, The, 236, 268, 291, 314, 328,
    353
Jackpot, The, 221–22, 223, 252
Jackson, Felix, 128, 129
Jackson, Samuel, 9, 23, 24
Jameson, Jerry, 341
Janis, Maria, 108, 204
Jimmy Stewart Museum, 370–71
Jimmy Stewart Show, The, 105, 327–30, 334
Johaneson, Bland, 85, 102, 112, 118, 122, 126
John Paul II, Pope, 356
Johns, Glynis, 223, 300
Johnson, Bess, 259–60, 272, 286, 366
Johnson, Doris, 289–90
Johnson, Dorothy M., 287
Johnson, Fran, 259–60, 272, 286, 365–66
Johnson, Nunnally, 215, 289, 290, 292, 297,
    298, 300, 301, 327
Johnson, Van, 137*n*, 177, 206, 207
Johnstone, Jack, 244
Jones, Shirley, 216, 280, 282, 291, 317, 318, 348
Journey by Night (Goodrich), 71–72, 110

Kanter, Hal, 298, 327–30, 333–34
Karp, David, 84, 330–31, 332, 333–34
Kastner, Elliott, 343
Katz, Sam, 96
Kaufman, Beatrice, 68
Kaufman, George S., 68, 113, 114
Kaye, Danny, 219, 250
Kazan, Elia, 254, 262
Keeler, Leonard, 195
Keighley, William, 143, 181
Keith, Brian, 305
Kellaway, Cecil, 219
Kells, Clarence H., 174
Kelly, Gene, 316, 318, 334, 356, 362
Kelly, Grace, 147*n*, 244–45, 247, 264, 267, 354,
    361
Kelly, James, 9, 20, 21
Kennedy, Arthur, 229–30, 251, 295–96, 303
Kennedy, George, 307, 314, 322, 329, 340
Kennedy, John F., 289
Kennedy, Joseph P., 68, 126
Kerr, John, 257
King, Henry, 101, 102, 213
Knight, Arthur, 309
Knopf, Eddie, 90
Kobritz, Richard, 318
Koch, Howard, Jr., 322, 323
Koerner, Charles, 185
Koster, Henry, 219, 223, 226, 289, 290, 292,
    293, 297, 298, 299, 300, 301
Kovacs, Ernie, 268
Kramer, Jean, 363–64
Kriedler, Howard, 163, 164, 165
Kruger, Hardy, 307–8, 309
Krumgold, Joseph, 191
Kuenstle, Charles, 340

Laemmle, Carl, 82
Lamarr, Hedy, 148, 149, 150
Lamour, Dorothy, 195, 196
Lancaster, Burt, 204–5, 260, 277, 306, 319, 340,
    362, 364
Landi, Elissa, 100
Lang, Charles, 251
Lang, Fritz, 213
Lang, Jennings, 340, 341
Lang, Walter, 222
Langford, Frances, 97, 237
Lasky, Jesse, 227
Last Gangster, The, 103–4, 121, 194
Laszlo, Nikolaus, 135, 136
Laurel, Stan, 76, 112
Laurents, Arthur, 198
Lay, Beirne, Jr., 160, 161, 166, 167, 249
Leacock, Philip, 310
Leatherbee, Charles Crane, 49–50, 51, 53
Leavett, Sam, 275
Leech, Margaret, 68
Lees, Richard, 357, 358, 359

Leigh, Janet, 214, 232–33, 268
LeMay, Curtis E., 234
Lemmon, Jack, 268, 275, 319, 327, 340
Leonard, Robert Z., 150
Leonard, Sheldon, 187–88
LeRoy, Mervyn, 269–70, 271
Levien, Sonya, 150
Levy, Emanuel, 145
Lewis, William C., Jr., 262
Liberty Films, 176, 180, 188–91
Lindbergh, Charles A., 38–39, 256–58, 363
Lindsay, John V., 321
Littell, Robert, 198
Little, Rich, 348
Lockridge, Richard, 70
Loeffler, Louis M., 275
Loew, Marcus, 75
Logan, Joshua, 42–44, 46–58, 64, 83, 87, 89–90,
     111–12, 137, 236, 244, 310, 365
Logan, Nedda, 310
Lombard, Carole, 88, 117, 118
Lost Horizon, 113, 114, 123
Low, Andrew, 168, 169–71, 234, 303
Loy, Myrna, 76, 85, 100, 356
Lu, Lisa, 277
Lubitsch, Ernst, 135–36, 137, 140
Lucas, Ted, 35, 45
Lux Radio Theatre, 121, 159, 180–81
Lyndon, Barre, 226

MacArthur, Charles, 211
McBride, Joseph, 115, 125, 185, 337
McCarten, John, 188, 221, 265
McCarthy, Joseph, 272
McClintic, Guthrie, 64, 68, 77, 252
McClure, Doug, 304
McCormick, Myron, 47, 50, 57–58, 60, 64, 84
MacDonald, Frank, 44
MacDonald, Jeanette, 80, 81, 120
McEveety, Vincent, 310–11
McGiver, John, 289, 293, 329
McGrath, Frank, 53, 54, 55
MacGregor, Chummy, 237–38
McGuire, Dorothy, 162, 210
McIntire, John, 213, 241, 243
Mackendrick, Alexander, 267
McLaglen, Andrew, 215, 301–2, 303, 304–6,
     310, 312, 314, 322–23, 324
McLean, Barbara Thompson, 316, 332, 370
McLean, Benjamin, 332
McLean, Edward Beale, II, 203–4
McLean, James, 339
McLean, Michael (JS's stepson), 25, 26, 173,
     204, 210n, 211, 248, 271, 308, 309, 313,
     316, 317, 332, 355, 370
McLean, Mike (producer), 355
McLean, Ronald, 204, 210n, 211, 248, 271, 309,
     310, 316–17
MacMurray, Fred, 195, 196, 348

McMurtry, Larry, 336
McNally, Stephen, 213
McNaughton, Kenneth, 160
McNulty, John, 222
Made for Each Other, 117–19, 120, 126, 272
Magic of Lassie, The, 151n, 344–46, 347–48,
     354
Magic Town, 191–92, 211
Malaya, 207, 208, 231, 234
Malden, Karl, 284
Maltz, Albert, 208
Man from Laramie, The, 250–51, 260, 295, 305
Mankiewicz, Herman, 90, 122
Mankiewicz, Joseph L., 94, 96, 109, 145
Mann, Anthony, 213, 214–16, 219, 229, 230,
     232–36, 241, 242, 243, 249, 250, 251, 260,
     261, 277, 281, 294, 306
Mann, Daniel, 276
Mannix, Eddie, 89
Mantle, Burns, 68, 72
Man Who Knew Too Much, The, 253–56, 257,
     263, 266, 361
Man Who Shot Liberty Valance, The, 287–89,
     307, 318
March, Fredric, 189n
Maren, Greta, 67–68, 71
Margulies, Don, 344
Marin, Edwin L., 92
Marquand, Christian, 307
Marshall, George, 129, 151, 284
Martin, Dean, 247, 310, 314, 315, 327, 340, 347
Martin, Pete, 366
Martin, Strother, 322, 331
Marvin, Lee, 287, 288
Marx Brothers, 76, 178
Maslin, Janet, 348
Massey, Raymond, 153, 284
Mathieu, James T., 316
Matsue, Yoichi, 350
Matthau, Walter, 169, 318, 319, 354
Mayer, Louis B., 75, 76, 99, 112–13, 117, 135,
     140, 144, 180, 205–6, 212, 231, 278, 301
Mayes, Wendell, 258, 271–72, 275
MCA (Music Corporation of America), 174,
     232, 278, 280, 301n
Meadows, Audrey, 292, 300
Meeker, Ralph, 232
Mehren, Elizabeth, 358
Melcher, Marty, 253
Mellor, Joe, 233
Melziner, Jo, 64
Mercer, Frances, 107
Mercersburg Academy, 33, 34–37, 39–40, 42,
     45, 75, 309
Meredith, Burgess, 56, 58, 95, 133, 152, 153,
     154, 158, 175, 195
Merkel, Una, 97, 132
Merrill, David, 349
Merrill, John, 349

Merrill, Judy Stewart, 225, 335, 248, 270, 286,
   309, 313, 314, 348–49, 366, 369–70, 371
Merrill, Keith, 355
Merrill, Steven, 348, 349
MGM, 69, 75–76, 95, 113, 115, 144, 180, 205–6,
   231, 284, 331, 332
Miles, Vera, 264, 269, 270, 287
Miller, Ann, 115, 116
Miller, (Alton) Glenn, 236–38
Miller, Helen, 237, 238
Miller, John L., 363
Miller, Joseph A., 168
Mills, Juliet, 305
Milner, Victor, 187n
Milton, Ernest, 197, 198
Mineo, Sal, 295
Miracle Can Happen, A, 195–96
Mishkin, Leo, 200, 286, 294
Misty Mountain, 121
Mitchell, Cameron, 334
Mitchell, Millard, 70n, 213, 232
Mitchell, Thomas, 124, 127, 186
Mitchum, Robert, 204–5, 306, 342, 343
Montalban, Ricardo, 295
Montgomery, Robert, 66, 288
Moore, Irving, 276
Moore, Victor, 195
Moorehead, Agnes, 205, 284
Moorhead, Bill, 26, 312, 370
Moorhead, Fergus, 9, 20, 21, 26
Mordden, Ethan, 75
Morgan, Frank, 137, 140, 150, 210
Morgan, Harry, 214, 229, 234, 237, 241, 277,
   337
Morrow, Douglas, 205
Morse, Terry, 305
Mortal Storm, The, 139–41, 344
Mortimer, Lee, 137
Moss, Morton, 332–33
Mountain Road, The, 173, 276–78
Mr. Hobbs Takes a Vacation, 215, 222, 269,
   289–93, 297–98, 299, 305, 329
Mr. Krueger's Christmas, 355
Mr. Smith Goes to Washington, 105, 122–27,
   132, 133, 142, 144, 153, 185, 186, 250, 262,
   340, 362
Mumy, Billy, 298–99, 300
Murder Man, The, 76, 78, 81, 94, 97, 103, 119,
   194, 207
Murphy, Audie, 131n, 260, 261
Murphy, George, 119, 150
Murphy, Mary, 334
Music Corporation of America (MCA), 278,
   280, 301n
Myers, Stevie, 215

Naked Spur, The, 214, 232–33, 242, 251, 260,
   281
Narcejac, Thomas, 263

Natwick, Mildred, 50
Navy Blue and Gold, 104, 105–6, 115, 126, 205
NBC, 327–28
Needham, Hal, 305
Neff, Bill, 38
Neilson, James, 252, 260, 261, 262
Next Time We Love, 82–85, 86, 91, 99, 101, 121,
   194
Night Passage, 151n, 260–62, 277, 301, 305, 370
Niven, David, 80, 210, 219
No Highway in the Sky, 223–26, 323
North, Henry Ringling, 228
North, Sheree, 334, 337
North and South, Book II, 363
No Time for Comedy, 139, 141–43, 181
Novak, Kim, 264–65, 266, 267–68
Nugent, Frank S., 102

O'Brian, Jack, 194
O'Brien, Edmond, 288
O'Connell, Arthur, 275
O'Connor, John J., 334
O'Connor, Sandra Day, 362
Odets, Clifford, 59, 69, 185
O'Donnell, Cathy, 251
O'Donnell, Emmett, 263
Of Human Hearts, 104–5
Ogisu, Terry, 350
O'Hara, John, 196
O'Hara, Maureen, 138, 290, 291, 300, 302, 305
Okey, Jack, 186
Olivier, Laurence, 142, 153, 323
O'Rourke, Frank, 291
Orr, William T., 140

Page Miss Glory (Schrank and Dunning),
   69–70, 213
Paget, Debra, 209
Palmer, Lilli, 267
Paramount, 226, 228, 244, 250, 252
Parker, Dorothy, 185
Parsons, Herb, 213
Parsons, Louella, 152, 153, 179, 202, 211, 292,
   295
Pasternak, Joe, 128, 129, 130
Paul, Greg, 248
Peck, Gregory, 177, 206, 213, 284, 316
Pelswick, Rose, 93, 107–8, 134
Pemberton, Brock, 192
Peppard, George, 284
Perkins, Osgood, 59, 60, 68, 77, 78
Perry, Antoinette, 193
Perry, Mary Wilson Stewart (Doddie), 24, 25,
   42, 43, 137, 349
Perry, Robert, 42, 43, 45, 371
Peters, Lauri, 289
Peters, Susan, 179
Philadelphia Story, The, 143–47, 148, 151n,
   152–53, 159, 194, 367

Pidgeon, Walter, 90, 109, 150, 349
Pihodna, Joe, 233
Pollack, Ben, 237
Ponzecki, Joe, 320
Porter, Cole, 96–97, 98, 147*n*
Porter, Stephen, 320
Pot o' Gold, 134, 150–51, 152, 231
Potter, H. C., 109, 110, 153, 201, 202
Potts, L. Owen, 35, 36, 37, 39
Potts, Ramsay, 162, 167, 168, 169, 170, 173,
  234, 262, 263
Powell, Eleanor, 96, 97, 99, 150
Powell, William, 76, 100
Power, Tyrone, 101, 102, 148
Prashker, Betty, 365, 366–67
Preminger, Otto, 272, 273, 274, 275
Preston, Jim, 124
Preston, Robert, 284
Princeton University, 23, 33, 34, 41–49, 192,
  278, 368
Prine, Andrew, 314
Pryor, Thomas M., 206–7, 228

Quayle, Anthony, 335
Quine, Richard, 267–68
Quinn, Jay, 34, 35, 37, 40
Quirk, Lawrence, 83, 84, 89

Rabin, Mark, 225
Rainer, Peter, 361
Rains, Claude, 124, 127
Rapf, Harry, 76, 119
Raphaelson, Samson, 135, 136
Rare Breed, The, 132, 304–6, 309
Reagan, Ron, Jr., 286, 339, 369
Reagan, Ronald, 204, 252, 339, 353, 355–56,
  362, 363
Rear Window, 190*n*, 244–47, 249, 252, 254,
  255, 263, 265 66, 304, 323, 361–62
Reed, Donna, 186, 187, 190, 215
Reed, Rex, 314, 343
Reeve, Warren, 88
Remarque, Erich Maria, 129, 130
Remick, Lee, 272, 273, 291
Rettig, Tommy, 222
Reynolds, Debbie, 284, 335
Rice, Florence, 105
Rich, Frank, 338
Rich, Sharon, 81
Richards, Robert, 212, 213
Right of Way, 357–60
Riskin, Robert, 114, 123, 185, 191
Ritter, Thelma, 244
Riva, Maria, 129, 130
RKO, 185, 186, 188, 191, 278
Roberts, Marguerite, 150
Robinson, Edward G., 103, 159, 209, 295
Rogers, Ginger, 88, 106, 107, 153, 186, 290, 356
Roland, Gilbert, 234, 295

Rolfe, Sam, 232, 233
Roman, Ruth, 241
Romero, Cesar, 97, 316
Rooney, Mickey, 76, 95, 112, 119, 347
Roosevelt, Franklin, 149, 150
Roosevelt, James, 150
Rope, 196–201, 204, 244, 246, 254, 263, 267,
  335, 361
Rose Marie, 80–82, 85, 86, 96, 100, 185
Rosenberg, Aaron, 229, 234, 235, 237, 241, 261
Rothenberg, Fred, 359–60
Rubin, Jay, 371
Russell, Kurt, 322
Russell, Rosalind, 120–21, 142, 143, 152, 290,
  291, 309–10, 316
Ryan, Robert, 232

St. John, Theodore, 226
Sales, Chic, 92
Salisbury, Leah, 90
Sandoz, Mari, 294
Sarris, Andrew, 200, 255–56, 343, 361, 372
Saville, Victor, 140
Saxon, John, 133
Schaefer, George, 357, 358–59
Schary, Dore, 231
Scheff, Michael, 340
Scheuer, Philip, 235, 265, 283, 291
Schickel, Richard, 323–24
Schildkraut, Joseph, 136
Scott, George C., 272, 274, 275
Scott, Jacqueline, 59, 311
Scott, John L., 188, 288
Scott, Vernon, 234
Selden, William K., 45
Self, William, 336
Selznick, David O., 117, 118, 119, 137, 142,
  197, 208, 225–26
Selznick, Irene Mayer, 137
Selznick, Myron, 118
Sentimental Journey, 339
Seventh Heaven, 99, 101–2, 136, 140
Sharrett, Michael, 344–45, 346
Shearer, Norma, 76, 111–12, 144, 152, 178
Sheehan, William, 306
Shenandoah, 133, 215, 301–4, 305, 308, 309,
  315, 323, 324
Shootist, The, 336–39
Shop Around the Corner, The, 135–37, 304
Shopworn Angel, The, 108–10, 111, 112–13,
  122, 126, 145, 201, 231, 285
Shpetner, Stan, 280
Shute, Nevil, 223
Siegel, Don, 337
Silver, Dave, 330
Silverman, Fred, 333
Silvers, Sid, 97
Silver Theatre, 120–21
Simon, George T., 237–38

Simon, John, 341
Simon, Simone, 101–2
Simpson, John, 25
Sinatra, Frank, 309–10, 334
Sistrom, Joe, 123
Six Shooter, The, 243–44, 262, 266
Small, Frank, 97
Small Town Girl, 91–92, 93, 191
Smith, Bernard, 132, 284, 294, 295, 296–97
Smith, Cecil, 332, 334
Smith, Darr, 222
Smith, Kent, 50, 51, 56, 79, 83
Smith, Lois, 278
Smith, Margaret Chase, 262, 263
Sothern, Ann, 204, 210, 316
Speck, Gregory, 357
Spector, David, 340
Speed, 92–93, 97, 142
Spielberg, Steven, 368
Spirit of St. Louis, The, 256–59, 268, 275, 303, 308
Spoto, Donald, 245–46, 263–64
Spring in Autumn (Belmonte), 61–62
Stack, Robert, 132, 140–41, 203
Stackpole, Peter, 174
Stallings, Laurence, 195–96
Stanwyck, Barbara, 89, 315
Stauffer, Donald A., 47
Stern, Philip Van Doren, 185, 186, 190*n*
Stevens, George, 106–7, 109, 196, 213, 300, 301
Stevens, Inger, 311
Stewart, Alexander M., 9, 15, 19, 22–29, 31, 33, 34, 41, 51, 57, 75, 153, 158–59, 163, 239, 251–52, 291
Stewart, Donald Ogden, 153
Stewart, Elizabeth Ruth Jackson (Bessie), 9, 19, 23–26, 29, 163, 174, 239
Stewart, Ernest, 22, 23, 24
Stewart, Gloria Hatrick McLean:
    background of, 203–4, 299
    charitable work of, 284, 347, 356, 369
    death of, 369–70
    health of, 225, 228
    homes of, 224, 248, 335, 371
    JS's career and, 236, 239, 291, 306, 319, 328, 330
    marriage of, 207, 208, 210–11, 349
    as mother, 203–4, 211, 223, 224, 225, 309, 316, 332, 341–42
    television appearances of, 236, 291, 328, 330
    travels of, 211, 252, 254, 259–60, 262, 266, 270–71, 272, 286–87, 308, 315–16, 321, 347, 349, 356, 360, 365–66
Stewart, James Maitland (JS's grandfather), 9, 21–23, 25, 27, 239
Stewart, Jimmy:
    actors admired by, 59, 68, 77–78, 84, 86, 146, 193–94, 202, 245, 358, 360
    aviation and, 31, 36, 38–39, 70, 76–77, 90–91, 102, 146–47, 177, 180, 210, 346

career progress of, 15, 54, 60, 64, 69, 70–71, 76, 77, 79, 83, 91–95, 98, 105, 113, 117, 127, 134, 177, 180, 188–89, 192, 207, 221, 247, 279, 300, 304, 312–13, 324, 336, 364, 368
childhood of, 19, 24–40
comedic abilities of, 52, 122, 153, 222, 328, 330
early film appearances of, 65–66, 77–78, 81–82, 83–85, 147
education of, 15, 30, 33–45, 48, 54
family background of, 9, 15, 19–24, 57
as father, 15, 26, 211, 223–25, 279, 309, 316–17, 341–42, 348–49
as grandfather, 332, 339, 349
hearing loss of, 312, 343, 345, 346, 357, 358–59, 364, 370
homes of, 179–80, 224, 225, 248
honors received by, 127, 152–53, 167–68, 170, 270, 315, 335, 347, 348, 354, 356, 360, 362–65, 368, 370–71
ill health of, 24, 38, 106, 148–49, 172, 223, 256–57, 309, 312, 323, 333, 335, 343, 345, 346, 355, 357, 358–59, 364, 368–69, 370
income of, 51, 57, 154, 192, 211, 212, 226, 239, 247–48
leading ladies of, 82, 83, 85, 86, 97, 99, 101–2, 105, 106, 107, 109, 112–13, 116–22, 125, 129–31, 136, 139, 142–43, 145–46, 187, 191, 201–2, 215, 222, 223, 232, 234, 237, 240–42, 244–45, 249, 253, 265–66, 269, 276, 284, 285, 287, 290–92, 300, 305, 311, 317, 319, 320, 328–30, 335, 358
male costars of, 105, 119, 147, 186, 207–8, 219, 229–30, 237–38, 260, 261, 280, 282, 283, 287, 288, 295–96, 305, 307, 310–11, 312, 317, 319, 322, 331, 336–38
marriage of, 15, 88–89, 170, 179, 203, 207, 208, 210, 221, 236, 245, 279, 349, 358, 369–70
in military service, 149–54, 157–75, 179, 234, 249, 259, 262–63, 279, 283, 303, 309, 313–15, 330, 334, 360
personality of, 15, 22, 25, 33, 35, 57, 108, 131, 133, 176, 179, 275, 302–3, 308, 330, 345–46, 372
philanthropic involvements of, 284, 315, 347, 356, 371
physical appearance of, 16, 24, 63–64, 78, 94, 98–99, 102, 103, 133, 136, 174, 215, 223, 225, 257, 279, 289, 322, 332
poetry written by, 321, 353, 365–66
political views of, 57, 249, 313–14, 316, 317, 334, 339, 355–56
popularity of, 132–33, 137, 193, 211, 221, 242–43, 247, 279, 320–21, 341, 347, 354, 360
professionalism of, 59, 83, 102, 109–10, 116, 187–88, 195, 199, 206, 238, 272–74,

293–94, 302, 303, 311, 318, 330, 332, 333, 343, 345–46, 358
on radio, 120–21, 159, 180–81, 243–44
religious beliefs developed by, 27, 29, 40, 161, 163, 166
reviews of, 40, 47, 48, 56–57, 65, 68–69, 70, 72, 78, 85, 91–92, 98, 101, 102, 103, 108, 112, 119, 122, 132, 143, 149, 151, 152, 188, 204, 206–7, 221, 231, 233, 240, 259, 265, 268, 275, 277, 283, 304, 309, 321, 323, 333, 338, 344, 355, 359, 361, 372
romantic involvements of, 37, 47, 83, 84, 88–90, 94, 107, 109, 110–11, 130–31, 178–79, 203, 204, 207, 214, 245
in school plays, 39–40, 42–44, 46–48, 137–39, 148, 158
screen persona of, 16, 81, 93, 97, 98–99, 106, 122, 126–27, 132–34, 188, 204–5, 221, 222, 232, 237, 256, 264–65, 267, 279, 300, 304, 306, 333, 340, 347, 353–54, 372
sense of humor of, 35, 81, 107, 146, 169, 294, 308, 353–54
social life of, 32, 44, 58–59, 79, 87–90, 108, 110, 170, 177–78, 195, 259–60, 309–10, 370
stage career of, 48–57, 59–72, 77, 78, 92–94, 201, 319–21, 335
on television, 15, 236, 252, 262, 266, 278, 279, 291, 300, 314, 315, 327–34, 346–47, 353–60, 363–64, 367
travels of, 43, 127–28, 148, 181, 211, 252, 253–54, 259–60, 262, 266, 270–73, 286–87, 315–16, 321, 347, 349–50, 356, 360, 365–66
vocal qualities of, 85, 93, 99, 133, 136, 195, 214, 221, 223
in westerns, 128–32, 208–16, 229–33, 241–43, 250–51, 260–61, 266, 278, 280–89, 294–97, 304–6, 310–12, 314–15, 317–19, 336–38, 364
Stewart, John, 97
Stewart, Judy, *see* Merrill, Judy Stewart
Stewart, Kelly, *see* Harcourt, Kelly Stewart
Stewart, Mary Wilson (Doddie), 24, 25, 42, 43, 137, 349
Stewart, Virginia Kelly (Jennie) (JS's grand-mother), 9, 21, 22, 24, 225
Stewart, Virginia Kelly (JS's sister), 24, 25, 26, 55, 72, 79, 137, 349
Stewart, William, 9, 20
Stout, Gene, 157
Stradling, Harry, Jr., 323
Stradner, Rose, 103
Strategic Air Command, 173, 244, 249–50, 251, 259, 301
Stratton, Monty, 205, 206, 231, 249
Stratton Story, The, 205–7, 211, 237
Strauss, John, 371
Streeter, Edward, 289
Strode, Woody, 288

Stuart, Donald Clive, 42–43
Sullavan, Margaret, 58, 83–84, 85, 89, 90, 99, 157, 158, 364
  film roles of, 82, 83, 109, 110, 112–13, 135, 136, 139, 140, 141, 150
  stage appearances of, 46–47, 50, 51, 56
Sullivan, Ed, 52, 236, 252
Swarthout, Glendon, 336
Swarthout, Miles, 336
Swerling, Jo, 117, 185
Swope, John, 50, 79, 87, 89–90, 110–11, 152, 162, 178, 210, 349

Take Her, She's Mine, 222, 292–94, 297–98, 299, 300, 329
Taradash, Daniel, 267, 268
Taylor, Jud, 331, 332, 333
Taylor, Robert, 91, 92, 94, 98, 99
Taylor, Samuel, 264, 266
Teichmann, Howard, 63*n*, 79
Terayama, Shuji, 349
Terrill, Robert, 162, 166, 167, 168, 169
That's Entertainment!, 334–35, 338
Thier, Irene, 112
Thomas, Bob, 252, 327
Thompson, Howard, 277, 304, 306, 312
Thorpe, Richard, 231
Thunder Bay, 234–36, 244, 248, 251
Timberlake, Edward, 163–64, 166, 169, 171
Tomlin, Lily, 98
Tone, Franchot, 94, 96, 153
Tonight Show, The, 353–54, 366
Torrez, Frank, 355
Tracy, Helen, 98
Tracy, Spencer, 76, 77–78, 94–95, 99, 122, 131, 144, 153, 207–8, 210, 283, 284, 289, 295
Transatlantic Pictures, 197, 199, 244
Traver, Robert (John D. Voelker), 271, 273
Travers, Henry, 113, 186
Trevor, Simon, 349
Trilling, Steve, 256, 257
Trumbo, Dalton, 185
Tsuji, Shintaro, 349, 350
Tucker, John Bartholomew, 321
Turner, Lana, 150, 151, 152, 272
20th Century-Fox, 194–95, 278, 292
Twist, John, 66, 269
Two Rode Together, 280–83, 287, 295, 314, 318

Udall, Stuart, 296
Universal Pictures, 128, 129, 142, 192, 211–12, 235, 278, 301, 361, 364
University Players, 48–56, 57, 79, 365
Up from Darkness, 120–21
Usher, George L., 160

Van Druten, John, 67, 266–67, 268
Van Dyke, W. S. (Woody), 80–81, 100, 122
Vertigo, 263–66, 269, 275, 361
Vetluguin, Voldemar, 178

Vidor, King, 196
Vietnam War, 313–14, 315–17, 328
VistaVision, 250, 278
Vivacious Lady, 104, 105, 106–8, 112, 116, 118, 119, 121, 196
Voelker, John D. (Robert Traver), 271, 273

Wade, Alfred, 43
Wagner, Robert, 356
Wald, Jerry, 289, 290, 298
Walker, Joseph, 187, 365
Wallis, Hal, 142
Wanger, Walter, 87
Warga, Wayne, 321
Warner, Jack, 142, 256, 257, 259, 269, 278, 294, 362
Warner Bros., 65, 142, 144, 180, 256, 268, 278, 310, 312, 328
Wasserman, Lew, 174, 175, 176, 180, 192, 198, 207, 208–9, 211, 212, 214, 224, 239, 244, 258, 301n
Watt, Douglas, 321
Watts, Richard, Jr., 92, 144, 193, 321
Wayne, John, 133, 134, 186, 247, 280, 282, 284, 287, 288, 291, 294, 302, 307, 310, 314, 336–38, 339, 343, 347–49
Weatherwax, Rex, 344
Webb, James R., 283–84, 295, 296
Wechsburg, Joseph, 181
We Die Exquisitely (Twist and Henry), 66–67
Weiler, Andrew, 235, 243, 288
Weissmuller, Johnny, 122
Welch, Joseph, 272
Welch, Raquel, 314
Wellman, William, 91, 191–92
Wendkos, Paul, 333
West, Claudine, 139
Westmore, Wally, 227
Whelan, Tim, 76
White, Jesse, 194, 219, 298, 320, 321
White, Theodore H., 276
Whitehead, Don, 268–69, 270, 271
Whitney, John, 66–67
Widmark, Richard, 280–84, 295, 297
Wife v. Secretary, 85–86, 99, 148
Wilde, Cornel, 226
Wilder, Billy, 256–59, 303

Wile, Frederic William, 126
Williams, David Marshall, 231
Williams, John, 298
Williams, Lee, 244
Wilson, Marie, 289
Wilson, Michael, 185
Wilson, Woodrow, 29
Winchester '73, 70n, 211–16, 221, 222, 224, 229–33, 241, 248, 260, 303
Windust, Bretaigne (Windy), 49–50, 51, 53, 62
Winner, Michael, 342, 343
Winning Your Wings, 160
Winsten, Archer, 103, 106, 116–17, 141, 143, 309, 324
Winters, Shelley, 131n, 213
Wolper, David, 363
Wood, Natalie, 222
Wood, Sam, 105, 205, 206
Woodward, Clyde, 174
Woolrich, Cornell, 244, 361–62
Wright, Bill, 90
Wright, Greta, 90
Wyler, William, 84, 144, 176, 189, 354
Wyman, Jane, 191, 211
Wynn, Ed, 298, 299

Yellow Jack (Howard), 64–65, 66, 68, 71, 78, 121, 252, 371
You Can't Take It With You, 113–17, 118, 122, 125, 126, 148, 185, 186, 192n
You Gotta Stay Happy, 201–3, 204, 205
Young, Loretta, 130, 219, 290
Young, Robert, 105, 140
Young, Stark, 55
Yukl, Joe, 238
Yukon Passage, 346–47
Yurka, Blanche, 53, 54, 61, 62, 77

Zanuck, Darryl F., 101, 144, 194, 223, 278, 286, 292, 293
Zanuck, Richard, 308
Ziegfeld Girl, 149–50, 151, 152
Zimbalist, Stephanie, 344–46
Zinnemann, Fred, 213, 312
Zinsser, William K., 261
Zunser, Jesse, 243